Penguin
Management Handbook

Edited by Thomas Kempner
FOURTH EDITION

Penguin Books

PENGUIN BOOKS

Published by the Penguin Group
Penguin Books Ltd, 27 Wrights Lane, London W8 5TZ, England
Penguin Books USA Inc., 375 Hudson Street, New York, New York 10014, USA
Penguin Books Australia Ltd, Ringwood, Victoria, Australia
Penguin Books Canada Ltd, 2801 John Street, Markham, Ontario, Canada L3R 1B4
Penguin Books (NZ) Ltd, 182–190 Wairau Road, Auckland 10, New Zealand

Penguin Books Ltd, Registered Offices: Harmondsworth, Middlesex, England

First published by Weidenfeld & Nicolson 1971
Revised edition published by Penguin Books 1976
Third edition 1980
Fourth edition 1987
10 9 8 7 6 5 4 3

Copyright © Thomas Kempner, 1971, 1976, 1980, 1987
All rights reserved

Printed in England by Clays Ltd, St Ives plc
Set in Monotype Times

PENGUIN MANAGEMENT HANDBOOK

Thomas Kempner was Principal of Henley, The Management College (formerly the Administrative Staff College), and Professor and Director of Business Studies at Brunel University from 1972 until his retirement in 1990. He is Emeritus Professor at Henley and Honorary Professor at Brunel University. He graduated in Economics from University College, London, and subsequently worked at the Administrative Staff College, Henley, and at the University of Sheffield. In 1963 he started the Management Centre at the University of Bradford and became Professor of Management Studies as well as the Centre's first director. Professor Kempner is the author of numerous articles and several books on management topics. He is a business consultant, and also the director of several companies. Among his publications are *A Guide to the Study of Management* (1969), *Management Thinkers* (co-edited, 1978), *Business and Society* (with K. Macmillan and K. Hawkins, 1974) and *Models for Participation* (1976).

Introduction

This book has been written to provide a handy work of reference on the main concepts and ideas which underpin the work of management. The authors hope that it will provide useful information on a complex subject for both managers and students – indeed the two are often the same. Our main purpose was to help managers survive in an increasingly complex and jargon-obsessed society.

The subjects of management studies are many and varied; there are few topics that can be regarded as completely useless to managers. Nevertheless certain boundaries have become established – at least for the time being. This handbook contains the topics and subjects generally regarded as essential. These include:

(1) The relevant parts of the social sciences applicable to management: economics, sociology and psychology. They describe the underlying or background situations that all managers face, that is, the behaviour of individuals and groups at work and in society as a whole, their reactions to monetary and other stimuli and the process of social, political, economic and technological change.

(2) The quantitative aspects of management – the process of measurement analysis and comparison of the available data.

(3) The functional areas such as marketing, production, personnel, finance, purchasing.

(4) The integration of management activities through the subject of 'business policy', which includes strategy formulation and planning. It is under this heading that specific attention is given to the future prospects of all parts of the organization.

All the authors have tried to take a concise and synoptic view of the topics comprising their subject areas, giving as much coverage as possible and yet without producing a book of impossible length.

How to use this book

This handbook divides the subject matter of management into eleven main headings, each of which is covered by an entry giving a brief overview of that subject. The eleven headings are:

1. *Business Policy and Corporate Planning*

2.   *Industrial Relations, Trade Unions and Collective Bargaining*
3.   *Industrial and Occupational Psychology and Ergonomics*
4.   *Industrial and Commercial Law*
5.   *Management Accounting and Financial Management*
6.   *Industrial Sociology (including Organization and Structure)*
7.   *Quantitative Aspects of Management (including Statistics, Operational Research and Computer Applications)*
8.   *Economics, Econometrics and Managerial Economics*
9.   *Personnel Management*
10.   *Marketing (including Purchasing and Public Relations)*
11.   *Production Management*

To obtain an overview of the whole field of management the reader can simply look up the eleven main headings. To obtain a more detailed view of the subjects covered by a main heading, the reader should refer to the synoptic index (pages ix–xxxi). Here, under each of the eleven main headings, the whole range of topics that fall within them is given, together with cross-references (◊ see; ◊◊ see also) to the major links between topics.

Throughout the handbook cross-references are included in most entries. These should be read to obtain a fuller grasp of the topic concerned.

Most entries also contain reading references to the leading books on the topic, which will help readers to build up their own library on the fields which concern them.

List of Contributors

with their initials and subjects

A.J.A.A.	A. J. A. Argenti Management Consultant	Business Policy
E.E.	Professor E. Edwards lately University of Aston in Birmingham	Industrial and Occupational Psychology and Ergonomics
D.H.F.	Professor D. H. Farmer Henley – The Management College	Purchasing and Materials Management
P.J.A.H.	P. J. A. Herbert Henley – The Management College (previous entries by E. A. Lowe and C. J. Jones)	Financial Management
C.M.H.H	C. M. H. Hutchinson	The Managerial Grid
E.L.	E. A. Life Henley – The Management College (previous entries by L. Stephens)	Personnel Management
J.C.E.M.	Janice C. Elliott Montague Senior Lecturer in Law Coventry (Lanchester) Polytechnic (previous entries by the late Dr W. F. Frank and D. V. E. Royall)	Commercial Law
J.V.P.	J. V. Pearson Henley – The Management College (previous entries by E. A. Lowe and C. J. Jones)	Management Accounting
M.J.F.P.	Dr M. J. F. Poole University of Wales Institute of Science & Technology (previous entries by Dr N. H. Cuthbert)	Industrial Relations and Trade Unions
D.J.S.	Dr D. J. Silk Henley – The Management College	Information Management

L.T.S.	Dr L. T. Simister	Economics,
	Principal Lecturer in Economics	Econometrics and
	Dept of Business Studies	Management
	The Polytechnic, Huddersfield	Economics
R.S.S.	Dr R. S. Stainton	Quantitative
	Henley – The Management College	Aspects of
	(previous entries by Dr J. C. Martin)	Management
M.W.	Professor M. Warner	Industrial
	Henley – The Management College	Sociology and
	and Brunel University	Behavioural
	(previous entries by P. Bowen and	Studies
	I. C. McGivering)	
R.W.	Professor R. Wild	Production
	Henley – The Management College	Management
	and Brunel University	
K.M.W.	K. M. Williams	Industrial Law
	Senior Lecturer in Law	
	Coventry (Lanchester) Polytechnic	
	(previous entries by the late Dr W. F.	
	Frank and D. V. E. Royall)	
G.S.C.W.	Professor G. S. C. Wills	Marketing
	MCB University Press	

Synoptic Index

3. *Industrial and Occupational Psychology and Ergonomics*

4. *Industrial and Commercial Law*

Decentralization ⟡ Delegation
Delegation ⟡ Authority
Department
Discipline ⟡ Authority; Norm; Social Control
Division of Labour ⟡ Specialization
Dysfunctional ⟡ Functional (2)
Fayol, Henri ⟡ Classical Organization Theory
Follett, Mary Parker ⟡ Authority
Formal Organization ⟡ Bureaucracy; Organization Theory; Social
  System
Functional (1) ⟡ Authority; Line and Staff (1)
Functional (2)
Group ⟡ Conflict; Socio-technical System
Group Methods of Training
Hawthorne Investigations ⟡ Human Relations; Organization Theory
Human Relations ⟡ Hawthorne Investigations; Morale; Organization
  Theory
Ideology ⟡ Values
Industrial Sociology ⟡ Social Sciences
Industrialization
Informal Organization ⟡ Formal Organization
Institution ⟡ Culture; Norm; Role; Values
Jaques, Elliot ⟡ Time-span of Discretion
Laboratory Training ⟡ Group Methods of Training
Leadership ⟡ Authority; Power; Status
Line and Staff (1)
Line and Staff (2) ⟡ Authority; Chain of Command; Functional (1)
McGregor, Douglas ⟡ Line and Staff (2)
Managerial Grid ⟡ Group Relations Training
Mayo, Elton ⟡ Hawthorne Investigations
Mechanistic and Organic Management ⟡ Formal Organization;
  Bureaucracy
Morale ⟡ Alienation; Conflict
Motivation (of Individuals and Groups) ⟡ Morale; Business Motivation
Norm ⟡ Informal Organization; Social Control; Values
Organization ⟡ Authority; Bureaucracy
Organization Development
Organization Theory ⟡ Human Relations; Scientific Management
Participation ⟡ Alienation; Authority; Job Enlargement; Joint Consul-
  tation
Power ⟡ Authority; Status; Charisma
Prestige ⟡ Status

7. *Quantitative Aspects of Management* (*including Statistics, Operational Research and Computer Applications*)

8. *Economics, Econometrics and Managerial Economics*

Automated Warehouse ⟡ Automatic Guided Vehicle
Automatic Guided Vehicle (AGV) ⟡ Materials Handling
Batch Production ⟡ Batch Sizes
Batch Sizes (Lot Size; Economic Lot Size)
Bill of Materials
Branch and Bound Technique ⟡ Decision Theory; Decision Trees
Buffer Stocks (in Flow Lines)
Cell Production
Coding and Classification ⟡ Group Technology
Computer-aided Design (CAD)
Computer-aided Engineering (CAE)
Computer-aided Manufacture (CAM)
Computer-aided Production Management (CAPM)
Computer-integrated Manufacture (CIM)
Computer Numerical Control (CNC) ⟡ Numerical Control
Control Charts ⟡ Quality Control
Cyclegraph/Chronocyclegraph ⟡ Method Study
Economic Lot Sizes ⟡ Batch Sizes
Estimating ⟡ Work Measurement; Synthetic Timing; Costing Systems
Family of Parts ⟡ Group Technology; Flexible Manufacturing System
Flexible Manufacturing System (FMS)
Flow Lines ⟡ Assembly Lines
Flow Process Charts ⟡ Process Charts
Gantt, H. L. ⟡ Gantt Charts
Gantt Charts ⟡ Production Planning and Control
Group Technology
Group Working
Industrial Engineering
Inspection ⟡ Quality Control
Interference (Machines) ⟡ Machine Assignment and Interference
Inventories or Stocks
Jobbing Production ⟡ Production Planning and Control; Sequencing;
  Plant Layout
'Just in Time' Production
Kanban
Lot Sizes ⟡ Batch Sizes
Machine Assignment and Interference
Maintenance ⟡ Preventive Maintenance
Man–machine Chart ⟡ Multiple-activity Chart
Manufacturing Policy
Mass Production
Materials Administration ⟡ Materials Management

A

Absenteeism Time away from work due to sickness or other cause. A distinction is made between voluntary and involuntary absenteeism. Absence is described as voluntary when there is no acceptable reason for it and it could have been avoided; it is described as involuntary when it is the result of sickness, an accident, breakdown of transport or other cause that is largely outside the control of an employee. Rates of absenteeism are calculated as a percentage of hours lost in relation to normal working hours, so that comparisons can be made between individuals, departments, factories and classes of worker (e.g. married and single women, works and office staffs, etc.). However, it has become increasingly difficult to establish the number of hours actually lost because of widespread variations in terms and conditions of employment.

In the year beginning June 1982 just over 375 million days were covered by claims for social-security sickness and invalidity benefits paid out by the Department of Health and Social Security and supported by doctors' statements. The main causes of sickness were diseases of the circulatory and respiratory systems, and of muscles and joints, with the greatest proportion of 'lost days' attributable to men and women between the ages of fifty and fifty-nine, a doctor's certificate being given after three days' incapacity. However, under the Statutory Sick Pay Scheme introduced in 1983 a doctor's certificate only became available to employers after seven days' incapacity, so that statistics on briefer absences were less comprehensive thereafter.

The General Household Survey for 1982, based on a sample of 11,970 households, found that 8 per cent of both male and female workers (employees and self-employed) had been absent from work in the week before they were interviewed, a rate similar to that found in previous years. The main reason was the worker's own illness or injury, 5 per cent of all workers having been off sick in the week before the interview. In manual and non-manual jobs women were more liable than men to be off sick. On an annual basis male employees were found to be off sick for an average of 8·3 days and female employees for 8·8 days in 1982. Absences tended to be highest in the groups of industries involving coal-mining, the manufacture of metals, minerals and chemicals, and transport and communications.

When the facts about absenteeism are known an investigation on the causes may reveal variations in the effectiveness of supervision, particular pressures of work, the effect of different levels of earning or methods of payment, conflicts between responsibilities at home and at work, the state of the labour market for particular kinds of worker, and so on. In many cases a thorough diagnosis of the facts and causes of absenteeism will lead to remedial action by changes in personnel policy. If absences through sickness or accident are analysed separately, they may bring to light defects in medical services, in sickness pay schemes or in methods of ⟡ Accident Prevention. L.S., amended by E.L.

J. Matthewman, *Controlling Absenteeism* (Junction Books, 1983); W. Gardner, *How to Prevent Absenteeism* (Applecross Books, 1983); Central Statistical Office, *Annual Abstract of Statistics 1985* (HMSO, 1985); Office of Population Censuses, *General Household Survey 1982* (HMSO, 1984).

Absorption Costing ⟡ Overheads

ACAS ⟡ Advisory, Conciliation and Arbitration Service

Acceptance Sampling ⟡ Quality Control

Accident, Industrial Under the Notification of Accidents and Dangerous Occurrences Regulations 1980 (NADOR) an accident causing death or major injury to an employee, a self-employed person or to a member of the public had to be reported by the responsible person to the appropriate enforcing authority. Normally the responsible person would be the employer or the person controlling the premises in connection with which the incident occurred, such as a mine manager or quarry owner. Similarly the enforcing authority would normally be either the appropriate inspectorate of the Health and Safety Executive (e.g. Factory, Mines, Nuclear, etc.) or the relevant local authority.

Under the regulations major injuries included: the loss of sight of an eye; fracture of the skull, spine or pelvis; amputation of hand or foot; or any injury that put the person concerned into hospital as an in-patient, other than for observation, for more than twenty-four hours. Other injuries to employees were notifiable if they resulted in more than three days' absence from normal work, when the local DHSS office would ask the employer to complete a form relating to a claim for Industrial Injury Benefit for the employee. The regulations also required the responsible person to report a variety of specified dangerous occurrences, such as an explosion or the collapse of a crane.

Changes in the Statutory Sick Pay scheme in 1983 had the effect that a doctor's certificate for an injured person's incapacity for work only became available to employers after seven days' incapacity (Industrial Injury Benefit being abolished), and the number of reported accidents of a less serious nature declined. Faced by an 80 per cent reduction in the flow of information about accidents, in 1983 the Health and Safety Executive put out a consultative document proposing new reporting arrangements to replace N A D O R. These wove together into one system lost-time accidents, fatalities and major injuries, dangerous occurrences, and illness known to be associated with work – the latter being the only entirely new category compared with N A D O R. The proposed system would have the advantage of using a single report-form, which would facilitate computer storage, retrieval and analysis of information.

Accidents are classified according to their severity and the industry within which they occur. Incidence rates for accidents are calculated per 100,000 employees in each industry, based on the average numbers reported in the 1981 Census of Employment. Provisional figures for 1983 covering employees in all manufacturing industries showed 109 fatal and 4,089 major injuries, with an incidence rate of 76·9, compared with 126 deaths and 4,048 major injuries for 1982. Incidence rates vary considerably between industries, the rate for metal manufacture in 1983 being 180·2, for timber and furniture 162·7, and for the construction industry 227·1. If accidents to self-employed and non-employed persons resulting from work activities are also taken into account over the period 1981–3, the total number of major injuries reported to H M Factory Inspectorate fluctuated around 15,000 per year, resulting in the loss of 16 million working days. E.L.

Department of Employment, *Employment Gazette* (November 1984); Health and Safety Commission, *Proposals for Revised Arrangements for Reporting Accidents, Ill Health and Dangerous Occurrences at Work* (H M S O, 1983)

Accident Prevention The steps that are taken to increase the safety of employees with a view to reducing both the total number of accidents and the number of serious accidents. The process starts with a detailed record of accidents, which is analysed to show what kinds of accident occur, where they occur and to which categories of employee. Widely used measures of standards of safety are the frequency rate, which shows the number of accidents that have happened in a given period in relation to the man-hours worked, and the severity rate, which indicates the number of hours lost through accidents in relation to the man-hours worked. A policy of accident prevention aims: (1) to make the conditions of work as safe as possible by good 'housekeeping', proper maintenance and the enclosure of dangerous machinery and processes (incorporated when possible in the original design of the machine or plant); (2) to provide protection for the employee when certain dangers are unavoidable, e.g. by safety devices, protective clothing and eye shields, etc.; (3) by organization, supervision and training to encourage employers to adopt safe working methods, e.g. by the appointment of a Safety Officer, establishment of a Safety Committee and safety training of young employees. Codes of practice and regulations are issued by the ⟡ Health and Safety Commission. As a large majority of industrial accidents do not occur on machinery but result from handling goods, falls and the use of handtools, etc., training and supervision are as important to the prevention of accidents as the enclosure or guarding of dangerous parts of machinery. It is common knowledge that some people have more accidents than others, but research shows that factors such as the nature of the job, the amount of exposure to risk, the climate of work (e.g. the strength or weakness of supervision) and individual fatigue play a bigger part in causing accidents than 'accident-proneness'. Nevertheless research has been undertaken and tests have been devised to discover the human traits that are the basis for 'accident-proneness' and to use this information in selecting people for jobs of varying risk. ⟡ Ergonomics; Critical Incidents Technique in Accidents. L.S.

A. W. Stevenson, *Planned Safety Management* (A. Osborne, 1980); D. Holliman, *Croner's Health and Safety at Work* (Croner Publications, 1982).

Accountability ⟡ Responsibility

Accountancy The practical art of the accountant. The term also refers to the generally accepted rules and conventions of practising accountants (⟡ Accountancy Conventions). Sometimes these rules of accountancy practice are referred to variously as 'postulates', 'principles' or 'standards', but in view of the arbitrariness and lack of scientific criteria in much of accountancy, which may well be unavoidable, such terms seem presumptuous. As one eminent writer observed, 'The work of the accountant and the writings on accounting, until very recently, proceeded by a sort of patchwork and tinkering' (J. B. Canning, 1929).[1] 'Much has changed since . . . Yet, the fundamentals of our discipline have not yet found a formulation that is general and rigorous enough' (R. Mattessich, 1964,

1. *The Economics of Accountancy* (Ronald Press, 1929).

referring to Canning's dictum).[2] ⟡ Accounting; Accounting Standards; Bookkeeping. E.A.L.

Accountancy Conventions The generally accepted practices of accountants (⟡ Accountancy). Some of the principal conventions and assumptions are as follows:

(1) *The accounting entity.* By convention an entity is defined as the unit or organization that is treated as the separate whole for the purposes of accounting control. The entity is not necessarily coextensive with a legal entity. For example the various branches or departments of a firm may be treated as separate entities. A 'group of companies' will generally be treated as an entity for purposes of publication of financial accounts (⟡ Consolidated Accounts).

(2) *The going-concern assumption.* In preparing financial accounts an assumption is made, where nothing is specifically known to the contrary, that a firm has an indefinitely long existence and will continue in its present kind of business indefinitely. Accordingly valuations are made on the basis that assets will continue to be used for their present purposes and therefore may not reflect market values (⟡ Valuation of Assets).

(3) *Money values.* In preparing accounts accountants have traditionally used historical monetary values, despite their recognition of the fact that 'real' economic values may well be changing and will differ. The impact of inflation has, however, resulted in demands for changes in the measurement process, which, if applied, would alter the application of this convention (⟡ Changing Price Levels, Accounting for).

(4) *Conservatism.* As a general rule accountants tend to select the basis for measurement that gives the most unfavourable interpretation of events. This convention gives rise to particular precepts, such as: 'Do not anticipate gains but provide for all foreseeable losses;' 'Write off any asset's value if it is doubtful;' 'Asset values should generally not be written up;' 'Value stock-in-trade at the lower of cost or net-realizable value;' 'Understatement of asset values is commendable.' It can be argued that such rules may tend to bring accounting into disrepute as a science of measurement.

(5) *Objectivity.* In order to serve as a basis for accounting

2. *Accounting and Analytical Methods* (Irwin, 1964).

measurement, evidence must be easily and clearly verifiable, hence the emphasis by accountants on original costs or certifications by 'experts'. Clearly such objectivity may result in the sacrifice of relevance in accounting statements.

(6) *Stewardship*. The separation of ownership from management results in the delegation of authority and control over resources by owners. Management act as stewards of the financial resources entrusted to them and are accountable to owners for their actions. Accounting reports, such as the profit-and-loss statement and balance sheet, are a means of ensuring accountability, by providing a check on management honesty (e.g. safeguarding of assets) and efficiency (e.g. use of assets to earn profits). The concept of stewardship leads to the term stewardship accounting.

Other conventions of note relate to the matching of costs and revenues in profit calculations, consistency, materiality, time intervals for accounting periods, etc.

In accounting usage such terms as 'accounting principles', 'practices', 'rules', 'conventions', 'methods' or 'procedures' are often treated as interchangeable; however, in this context accounting conventions may be regarded as broad fundamental assumptions that underpin the preparation of financial statements. E.A.L., amended by J.V.P.

> Statement of Standard Accounting Practice No. 2, *Disclosure of Accounting Policies* (Accounting Standards Committee, 1971).

Accounting An analytical method perhaps best defined as a technique (and in this sense a statistical technique) for collecting, analysing, summarizing and presenting financial data relating to a particular entity or organization, so as to describe its financial position and the changes therein. As such it should be distinguished from ⟨⟩ Accountancy, which is the practical art of professional accountants.

The entity in question is most likely to be a business firm but similar accounting principles may be applied also to the affairs of a nation (the National Income 'Blue Book' is an example) and its agencies (e.g. statutory bodies like the BBC and the various nationalized industries); non-profit making bodies, as they are conventionally called (e.g. churches, clubs, hospitals, etc.); a household; private individuals. The use of this analytical method will enable an entity to run its affairs in a more systematic administrative manner and also give useful information about the efficiency with which it is carrying out its task. The concept of financial efficiency, or effectiveness of expenditure, is just as applicable to a church as to an ordinary business.

Accounting method is based upon the essentially simple notion that any asset or resource has two important aspects: (1) its money value and (2) the corresponding money claim on that asset accruing to the party who has a legal claim arising from it (whether as owner or as a creditor). The accounting system of any business is a collection of accounts in which an up-to-date record is constantly maintained of the assets belonging to the entity as they change their form and value through business transactions and market forces, and of the corresponding claims arising from these events (⟨⟩ Valuation of Assets).

In the language of the bookkeeper this duality of accounting method is termed 'debit' and 'credit'. Other descriptions of this fundamental duality may be given in terms of inputs and outputs, costs and revenues, assets and claims. Since the asset and claim aspects of any transaction, expressed in monetary values, must be identical, it is clear that any properly kept set of books of account must 'balance'.

The primary impetus to the development of accounting lies in the usefulness of an accounting system to an organization. At the everyday level of importance it is the means by which vast numbers of contractual obligations are recognized in terms of their monetary implications. Within organizations it is the accounting system that keeps track of all the flows of resources (goods, capital equipment, persons employed, etc.) between the various managers and factories that are responsible and accountable for their proper use. Further, the system also controls the use of such resources by means of the application of efficiency criteria concerning the outputs to be expected from them.

At a higher level of economic control the use of basic accounting statements enables interested parties in any arm to watch over their particular interests effectively. Perhaps even more crucially, it enables the management to assess its present financial and economic status and to examine the consequences of past important decisions and therefore to plan better for the future. E.A.L.

> M. W. E. Glautier and B. Underdown, *Accounting Theory and Practice* (Pitman, 2nd ed., 1982).

Accounting Standards Published financial statements are prepared within the framework of generally accepted ⟨⟩ Accountancy Conventions. Within this framework, however, the accounting treatment of particular items allows considerable flexibility, e.g. how to value stocks, methods of accounting for depreciation, goodwill, etc. This element of flexibility can lead to identical transactions being treated in markedly dissimilar ways in the accounts of different companies. It may be argued that it is impossible and indeed undesirable to attempt to impose rigid rules regulating how particular items should be treated in financial accounts. On the other hand complete flexibility as to accounting practices may result in misleading comparisons between companies by users of the information such as shareholders and investors.

The six major UK accounting bodies take the view that it is desirable to narrow areas of difference in accounting practice and establish objective standards of financial reporting. The Accounting Standards Committee exists to investigate, on behalf of these bodies, areas for which it may be desirable to formulate accounting standards. The Committee publishes discussion papers, exposure drafts, statements of recommended practice and statements of standard accounting practice. An accounting standard, once formally adopted by an accounting body, imposes on a member the obligation to observe the standard in the preparation of financial reports. Only if good reasons exist, e.g. that the application of a standard in a given situation would result in misleading financial statements, is the member freed from compliance. Non-compliance with a standard should be disclosed. Statements of recommended practice, on the other hand, are not mandatory. They are, however, of a quality and status to encourage respect and compliance. Where companies do not follow statements of recommended practice there is no requirement to disclose the fact in their financial statements. An International Accounting Standards Committee has also been established, which imposes similar obligations on members. The UK committee can serve as a useful focus for the discussion of accounting problems and act as a spur for research. An example of this relates to the publication by the Accountancy Standards Committee in 1975 of the *Corporate Report*, which reviewed the users, purposes and methods of modern financial reporting. C.J.J., amended by J.V.P.

Accounting Standards Steering Committee, *Corporate Report* (Institute of Chartered Accountants in England and Wales, 1975).

Accounting System The accounting system of an organization consists of all those policies, procedures, records and reports of a financial nature that assist in managerial administration, planning and control.

The figure opposite gives a description of an accounting system. It is important to note that the system not only consists of the double-entry bookkeeping system but also of the source documents reflecting the basic observation of business transactions and events, and of the policies, procedures and definitions formulated at top-management level concerning accounting information.

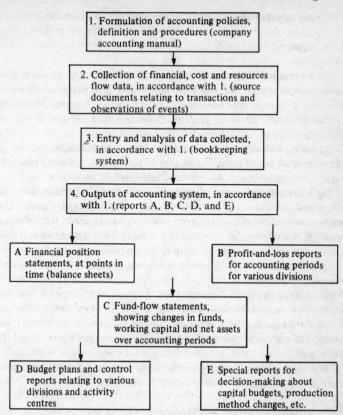

1. Formulation of accounting policies, definition and procedures (company accounting manual)

2. Collection of financial, cost and resources flow data, in accordance with 1. (source documents relating to transactions and observations of events)

3. Entry and analysis of data collected, in accordance with 1. (bookkeeping system)

4. Outputs of accounting system, in accordance with 1. (reports A, B, C, D, and E)

A Financial position statements, at points in time (balance sheets)

B Profit-and-loss reports for accounting periods for various divisions

C Fund-flow statements, showing changes in funds, working capital and net assets over accounting periods

D Budget plans and control reports relating to various divisions and activity centres

E Special reports for decision-making about capital budgets, production method changes, etc.

The design of efficient accounting systems is a difficult task, since on the one hand it is essential that the system should, from a planning viewpoint, be flexible, that is, capable of giving multipurpose information quickly; on the other hand, from a control viewpoint, it should give uniform and consistent standards of performance so that valid comparisons can be made. ⟡ Management Accounting; Costing Systems. E.A.L.

R. N. Anthony, J. Dearden and N. M. Bedford, *Management Control Systems* (Irwin, 5th ed., 1984).

Accrual Accounting The process of accounting that recognizes the incidence of income and expenditure, irrespective of the timing of associated cash flows. Non-accrual accounting systems are called 'receipts and payments' or just 'cash' accounting. ⟡ Cash Flow. J.V.P.

Activity Sampling ◊ Work Sampling

Acuity ◊ Hearing; Vision

Adaptation If a sensory input is maintained at a constant level over a period of time, the subjective impression of its magnitude tends to decrease. This process of adaptation probably has biological significance, in that it directs attention away from the constant features of the environment and highlights the dynamic ones.

Odour provides the most dramatic example of adaptation; the apparent disappearance of odours after a period of exposure is well known. In other sensory modalities the effect is less marked.

The mechanisms involved fall into two categories: they may be either peripheral or central. In the case of audition, for example, neural discharge in response to a constant stimulus falls off to about half its initial rate, but this phenomenon takes place in much less than one second. The longer-term effect whereby we learn to ignore continued sounds is central in origin: the neural signals continue to reach the brain but fail to affect conscious awareness.

Dark adaptation is something of a misnomer, since it involves an increase in sensory sensitivity. The range of adaptation of the eye is quite enormous, the sensitivity varying by a ratio of 5,000:1 between the dark-adapted eye and the eye perceiving bright light (◊ Threshold).

More generally, adaptation refers to the human capability of adjustment to environmental variability (◊ Homeostasis). E.E.

Adaptive Control Classical control theory is largely concerned with the problems of minimizing the difference between an actual output value of a system and a fixed reference value (◊ Feedback). Adaptive control involves the additional sophistication of having the reference value itself also subject to regulatory control in order to improve the performance of the system in a changing environment.

A hypothetical example may best illustrate the significance of adaptive control. The governor of a steam engine is perhaps the best known, and historically the earliest, example of automatic regulation using feedback. The control characteristics of such a device are, however, fixed at the time of its design and manufacture. An adaptive governor would be one with variable characteristics that would, in turn, be controlled by the output of other systems. Thus if the object of an adaptive governor were to minimize the cost of operating a vehicle, the adjustment of the governor would vary in relation to such economic factors as the cost of fuel, the hourly pay of the crew and the rates of depreciation of the machinery at various operating speeds. Thus an adaptive control system of this type would be utilizing a versatile form of self-regulation appropriate to a changing environment. ⟡ Cybernetics. E.E.

Adaptivizing ⟡ Optimization

Added Value 'The wealth the reporting entity has been able to create by its own and its employees' efforts.'[1] It may be viewed as sales revenues less materials and services purchased. It has been suggested that added-value statements should be published in the annual financial report to show how the wealth generated by the enterprise is shared between the providers of capital, the employees, the Government and reinvestment. It is argued that such statements would assist users in the evaluation of the performances of the enterprise and would help to put profit into perspective as only a part of added value. The *Corporate Report* suggested that such statements should contain the following minimum information: turnover; bought-in materials and services; employees' wages and benefits; dividends and interest payable; tax payable; amount retained for reinvestment. C.J.J.

Advertising The process of persuasively communicating information concerning a product or service to its market. It employs the printed and spoken word as well as visual material. It is undoubtedly on a par with personal salesmanship (⟡ Selling) as a vitally important element in marketing communications (⟡ Marketing Communications Mix). The effective creation of advertising involves the use of ⟡ Marketing Research, the formulation of a creative brief, the visualization of the context of illustrative material, the writing of the copy or words involved, the preparation of art work, the purchase of space in the relevant medium and the supervision of production. The task of purchasing media space involves the use of sophisticated methods of measuring penetration and effectiveness (⟡ Audience Measurement) to minimize the cost of reaching defined audiences. G.S.C.W.

B. B. Elliott, *A History of English Advertising* (Business Publications, 1962).

Advisory, Conciliation and Arbitration Service (ACAS) This independent body was established under the Employment Protection Act 1974 to help employers, workers and their representatives resolve trade disputes and improve industrial relations. It seeks to discharge these responsibilities through the voluntary co-operation of the parties

1. *Corporate Report* (Institute of Chartered Accountants in England and Wales, 1975).

concerned. Its approach is impartial and confidential and its services are free.

The main functions of ACAS are: the provision of conciliation and arbitration in collective disputes; individual conciliation in cases where claims are or may be made to industrial tribunals; and the provision of advisory services. A series of free advisory booklets on basic industrial-relations subjects has been published. There are also three *Codes of Practice*, obtainable from HMSO.

The Service is staffed by about 600 people, has a head office in London, offices in Scotland, Wales and seven English regions, and is publicly funded. The service is directed by a council comprising a full-time chairman (since 1981, Sir Patrick Lowry) and nine part-time members, appointed by the Secretary of State for Employment. Three members are appointed after consultation with the CBI; three after consultation with the TUC and three are independent.

The provision of conciliation, mediation and arbitration in collective disputes is the most publicized aspect of ACAS's work. Conciliation is a voluntary process and agreements are the responsibility of the parties concerned. There is a settlement or progress towards a settlement in approximately 80 per cent of cases. Failure to reach a settlement may lead, by agreement, to arbitration or mediation. Arbitrators and mediators are appointed by ACAS from panels of specialists in industrial relations.

About half of the staff resources are devoted to providing individual conciliation in the some 40,000 complaints about alleged infringements of individual employment rights registered each year, about 90 per cent of which are unfair-dismissal claims. Over two thirds of these do not go forward to tribunals, being either settled or withdrawn. About one third of staff resources are devoted to advisory work, on the premise that prevention is better than cure, and this is the Service's chief means of promoting an improvement in industrial relations. The independence of ACAS makes it acceptable to both employers and trade unions as a source of impartial advice and allows it to develop the joint approach as a way of resolving problems and developing initiatives. The assistance provided includes information given over the telephone, some 300,000 enquiries per annum being dealt with by regional enquiry points, and some 10,000 short visits a year by advisors to discuss industrial relations and personnel matters and employment legislation. Senior staff also offer in-depth advisory work to employers and trade unions to resolve more deeply seated industrial-relations problems. A specialist unit within ACAS, the Work Research Unit (WRU), gives advice on and assistance with 'quality of working life' initiatives. ACAS also arranges and participates in conferences and seminars. ⇨ Arbitration, Industrial; Conciliation. M.J.F.P.

Ageing At no time in life is the human organism in a completely stable state. The processes of growth and development continue through infancy, childhood and adolescence, culminating in a peak period of adulthood between about twenty and twenty-five years of age. Thereafter, in the case of most physical and mental functions, the ageing process begins. This is characterized by a slow but steady decline, which continues its course until death.

Some decrements in sensory sensitivity, short-term memory and speed of movement are likely to be measurable by the time individuals reach their early thirties. It is unusual for such decrements to amount to an occupational or everyday handicap, particularly as their effect is masked by the acquisition of experience. After the passage of a further decade, however, persons engaged upon work involving speed, stress, unfavourable environmental conditions, high energy outputs or severe irregularities in working conditions are likely to find their work-load intolerable.

A good deal can be done by the application of human-engineering principles to relieve the stresses placed upon the ageing worker. In particular, older workers should not be required to cope with tasks involving a high degree of novelty, tight tolerances, machine pacing of work, high levels of energy expenditure or severe environments. That is to say, all the factors that make work onerous to the younger person are likely to have more marked effects upon older work people. E.E.

D. B. Bromley, *The Psychology of Human Ageing* (Penguin, 2nd ed., 1974).

Agency An agent, in law, is a person who has authority to enter into a contract on behalf of another party, known as their principal. The agent's authority may either have been conferred on them expressly by their principal or its existence may be implied by law. Thus, where someone leads others to believe by words or conduct that a certain person is their agent, they will be responsible for any contractual commitments entered into by this apparent agent, even if the agent acted without any express authority.

Where the agent has their principal's express authority, they may, but need not, be acting under a contract with the principal. Where such a contract exists, the agent is under an obligation to the principal to perform the agency transaction and is entitled to claim from the principal the agreed remuneration for their services. In the absence of such a contract the agent may refrain from acting on the principal's behalf; if the agent does act for the principal, they are not entitled to remuneration.

Apart from general agents there also exist certain classes of special agent whose authority is generally determined by commercial custom or by statute. These include mercantile agents (factors), estate agents and brokers. W.F.F.

G. H. L. Fridman, *The Law of Agency* (Butterworths, 5th ed., 1983).

Alienation A negative emotional state. Alienation may be manifest in apathetic withdrawal, blind unthinking obedience or aggressive, destructive acts. The term was first introduced into sociology by Karl Marx (1818–83) (K. Marx, *Economic and Philosophical Manuscripts*, 1844). In the Marxist view workers were deprived of any opportunity for personal involvement in their work by the system of property ownership typical of the capitalist system. The modern sociologist accepts the fact of alienation but not the Marxist explanation of it, preferring to attribute alienation to the size of the industrial organization, the impersonality of the system, the elaborate techniques of control and the minute sub-tasks in which the individual is required to specialize. In a recent study of alienation in four different industries Robert Blauner identified four types that were commonly experienced by industrial workers. These were *powerlessness*, experienced when individuals are subjected to controls that they are unable to influence; *meaninglessness*, which occurs when individuals are unable to perceive the basic purpose of their own work either in relation to their own personal needs or to the purposes of the organization as a whole; *isolation*, which arises from the absence of meaningful social identifications; and *self-estrangement*, which they experience when work becomes simply a means to an end, a temporary activity undertaken solely because of the need to earn a living.

These various forms of alienation are not uniformly experienced by all industrial workers but the incidence of alienation is sufficiently widespread to cause concern. The more enlightened industrial managements, therefore, are inclined to welcome the existence of a trade union organization as a partial antidote to powerlessness and to seek ways of making work more meaningful. ⟡ Anomie; Authority; Job Enlargement; Morale; Participation; Specialization. I.C.McG.

Robert Blauner, *Alienation and Freedom* (University of Chicago Press, 1964); P. Thompson, *The Meaning of Work* (Macmillan, 1983).

Allocation Problems A company may manufacture a number of different products and there may be a 'best' way of making each. However, the company may have insufficient resources available to make each product in the 'best' way and will therefore have to decide which allocation of resources provides the 'best' way of making all the products taken together. A number of operational research techniques have been developed to solve this problem (⟡ Mathematical Programming), giving an answer that is better than that given by common sense.

As well as in production planning, allocation problems also occur when deciding: (1) where to build a new plant; (2) how to allocate workers to jobs; (3) how to plan the distribution of finished products from factories to customers so as to minimize transport costs. M.J.C.M.

P. G. Moore, *Basic Operational Research* (Pitman, 1976).

Allowances In ⟡ Work Measurement the standard time for a job must include an allowance to compensate for necessary rest and relaxation, delays and interruptions in the normal job cycle.

An allowance is added to the basic time for the job (i.e. the time required assuming continuous working at the standard rate) to produce the standard time (i.e. the time required assuming continuous working at the standard rate and permitting necessary relaxation, interruptions, delays, etc.).

Allowances, normally given as a percentage of basic time, usually include:

(1)   Relaxation allowance. (a) Fatigue allowance to give the worker opportunity to recover from the physiological and psychological effort required by the job. This allowance depends on the job, the worker and the environment, e.g. energy required; types of movement; visual movements; comfort; atmospheric and thermal conditions, etc. (b) Personal needs.

(2)   Contingency allowances, to compensate for the time required to perform necessary additional activities, which, because of their intermittent and irregular nature, were not included in the basic time, e.g. consulting drawings, etc.

(3)   Tool allowance, to compensate for the adjustment and sharpening of tools.

(4)   Reject allowance, necessary where a worker must necessarily produce a proportion of defective items.

(5)   Excess work allowance, to compensate for extra work necessary because of a temporary change in the standard conditions.

(6)   Interference allowance, to compensate for time necessarily lost because of the synchronization of stoppages on two or more

machines attended by one worker. ⟪⟫ Machine Assignment and Interference. R.W.

Analysis of Variance It is sometimes helpful to know if there might be a relationship between several sets of data. One way of determining a relationship would be to see if the mean (⟪⟫ Measures of Location) of each set were sufficiently close for it to be said that they were equal. It is possible to test such a hypothesis (⟪⟫ Hypothesis Testing) by examining the variances (⟪⟫ Measures of Dispersion) of the sets of data and the variance of the set as a whole. The 'F' test, after R. A. Fisher who developed it, is used for problems of this kind (⟪⟫ Statistical Tests). Fisher was concerned with comparing the effects of treatments applied to plant growth. The analysis of variance procedure (known as ANOVA) can be applied one way (e.g. each row of plants treated in different ways) or two ways (e.g. rows treated with different fertilizers with columns of different soil types) or in three dimensions (e.g. trays of plants stacked vertically with different soils in each tray. In the two vertical planes different fertilizers are applied cross-sectionally in one plane and the seeds are planted at different depths cross-sectionally in the other plane.) ANOVA examines whether these treatments produce different results by seeking to reject the hypothesis that the effects are uniform (i.e. for plants, that the growth is the same irrespective of treatment in any direction). Replication in each cell (tray cross-section in the example) can also be accommodated.

It may not be convenient to design an experiment in three dimensions, but ANOVA can be applied to a Latin square, thus.

A	B	C	D	E
E	A	B	C	D
D	E	A	B	C
C	D	E	A	B
B	C	D	E	A

Different treatments may be applied to diagonal as well as horizontal and vertical rows, as indicated by the letters. No letter appears more than once in any row or column. R.S.S.

Stephen P. Shao, *Statistics for Business and Economics* (Merrill, 1976).

Annual Report and Accounts The annual published report of an organization, containing both a narrative and a financial description of the operation of the organization during the year. The minimum contents of an annual report and accounts for a limited company is prescribed in the Companies Act 1985 and by various professional standards. ⟨⟩ Accounting Standards. J.V.P.

Anomie A social condition characterized by the absence of a clear and consistent normative structure.

A highly integrated community develops norms which regulate personal behaviour and interpersonal relationships and define the limits of individual aspiration. Within such a community individuals know what is expected of them and their conformity is rewarded with the approval and support of their fellows. The system provides security and emotional support for its members and is conducive to the maintenance of their mental health. Conversely the absence of clear norms leads to individual doubts and anxieties and the loss of supportive social relationships.

The term anomie was first introduced in sociology by Emile Durkheim at the end of the nineteenth century. In a classic study (*Suicide*, 1897) he showed, *inter alia*, a positive relationship between suicide rates and anomie. More recently the concept has been shown to be related to the incidence of various forms of social deviation and individual stress.

In the industrial organization some degree of anomie may be manifest in the absence of closely knit social groups or their break-up by technological requirements. Consequently the persons so affected may be deprived of meaningful social relationships and, if lacking compensatory job commitment, become alienated. Blauner's 'isolation' category of alienation is closely related to anomie. ⟨⟩ Alienation; Institution; Morale; Norm; Role Conflict; Socio-technical System. I.C.MCG.

R. K. Merton, *Social Theory and Social Structure* (Free Press, 1968), pp. 131–60; S. Fenton, *Durkheim and Modern Sociology* (CUP, 1984).

Anthropometry The study of the size and shape of the body. In its applications in industry it is concerned with the sizing of clothing, equipment and buildings to ensure compatibility with human measurements. Three particular observations are worthy of note:

(1) Anthropometry is concerned with the variability in human measurements and not merely with the 'average' person. Thus hardware must be constructed to suit as large a proportion of individuals as possible, with an appropriate range of adjustments provided where practicable (⟨⟩ Percentiles).

(2) It is important in any particular application to obtain data from

the relevant population. There are anthropometric differences between the sexes, races, different age groups and different occupational groups.

(3)   It is important to study human movements and not merely static sizes. More headroom is required, for example, for a person descending a staircase than for the same person ascending.

Numerous compilations of anthropometric measurements for a variety of population groups are available. E.E.

NASA, *Anthropometric Source Book* (NASA, 1978).

Appraisal ◇ Performance Appraisal

Apprentice Training ◇ Industrial Training

Apprenticeship, Contract of A contract of apprenticeship does not today differ significantly from other ◇ Contracts of Employment. Apprentices are merely a special type of employee differing from other employees in that the consideration for their services is represented by the employer's duty to teach them the basic skills of the trade or profession concerned. Although many apprentices are infants (under eighteen years of age), an adult could equally well be apprenticed. The apprenticeship agreement, unlike other contracts of employment, must be made in writing and is often made in the formal manner as a deed. Although it may be desirable to make an infant apprentice's parent or guardian a party to the contract, it is not essential that they should be associated with it. Since, however, in earlier days the employer occupied a quasi-parental position *vis-à-vis* the apprentice, even today it is not possible for an employer to sue the apprentice for breach of contract, but if the apprentice's parent or guardian were a party to the contract the employer could sue them. Although apprentices are treated as employees by the employment-protection legislation, apprentices who are not kept on as qualified employees at the end of their apprenticeship will not be entitled to a redundancy payment nor (ordinarily) to compensation for unfair dismissal. Young persons engaged on work experience and youth training programmes sponsored by the Manpower Services Commission are not normally regarded as either apprentices or as employees and so are outside the scope of the employment-protection legislation, though not of the health and safety legislation. ◇ Dismissal of Employees (Law). W.F.F. amended by K.W.

F. R. Batt, *The Law of Master and Servant* (Pitman, 5th ed. by G. Webber, 1967), ch. 15.

Aptitude Tests For purposes of selecting personnel for courses of training, it is desirable to have available a predictive index of potential ability. Thus aptitude tests (as opposed to tests of existing achievement or proficiency) have been developed.

The method of construction of these tests begins with a careful analysis of the demands of a particular job and the formulation of a large number of trial test items, each of which relates to some aspect of that job. Scores obtained by persons already known to possess job proficiency are obtained and in this way the validity of the proposed test items may be empirically examined (⟡ Intelligence).

Large numbers of aptitude tests have been designed and developed for such purposes as aircrew selection and for measuring artistic, clerical, mechanical and musical aptitudes.

Batteries of aptitude tests, along with intelligence and achievement tests, personality measures and schedules of attitudes and interests, are in frequent use for purposes of ⟡ Vocational Guidance. ⟡ Psychology. E.E.

Arbitration, Commercial A method of settling commercial disputes by referring them for adjudication to a nominated person or group of persons who will decide the issue by means of an arbitration award after having given both sides an opportunity to present their respective cases. Referral of a dispute to arbitration has generally to be made in writing and is governed in the UK by the provisions of the Arbitration Acts 1950–79. Valid arbitration awards are enforceable in much the same way as judgments of a court of law.

Commercial arbitration is often preferred to judicial proceedings in a court of law for the following reasons:

(1)   The arbitrator or arbitrators may be selected by the parties to the dispute from among persons who combine knowledge of the law with knowledge of the particular commercial or technical problems that are involved in the dispute. Arbitrators, unlike judges, may use their practical experience of commerce in reaching their award.

(2)   Arbitration proceedings may be conducted privately and not necessarily in open court. This is particularly useful where some confidential information is likely to be disclosed in the course of the proceedings.

(3)   Arbitration proceedings may be held where and when the parties wish and some of the delays of the law may thus be avoided. Previously much of the time saved could be lost when the award was subsequently challenged in the courts, but the Arbitration Act 1979 severely restricted the right to apply for judicial review of

arbitration awards. In some cases the parties may exclude this altogether and the award will be final.

(4)   It is doubtful whether arbitration is much less costly than court proceedings, but some economies may be made in the number of expert witnesses who have to be called.

The Arbitration Act 1975 enables arbitration agreements with an international element to be recognized and enforced in the United Kingdom. W.F.F., amended by D.V.E.R. and J.C.E.M.

> Russell, Walton *et al.*, *The Law of Arbitration* (Stevens & Sons, 20th ed., 1982).

Arbitration, Industrial The settlement of a trade dispute, i.e. one concerning wages and other conditions of employment, by the award of an independent third party, who may be either an individual or an arbitration board or tribunal. Industrial arbitration must not be confused with ◇ Commercial Arbitration. While the latter is governed by the Arbitration Acts 1950–79, these Acts do not apply to industrial-arbitration proceedings.

The awards of an industrial arbitrator are normally today only legally enforceable if adopted by the parties and embodied in individual contracts of employment. However, the statutory ◇ Central Arbitration Committee (known as the Industrial Arbitration Board before 1976, and before 1971 as the Industrial Court) can in certain circumstances make an award that becomes binding by being incorporated in the employment contracts concerned, e.g. where a recognized union complains of an employer's failure to supply information to its bargaining representatives under the Employment Protection Act 1975 (◇ Disclosure of Information).

The 1975 Act also provides that where a trade dispute exists or is apprehended, the ◇ Advisory, Conciliation and Arbitration Service may refer the dispute, if all parties to the dispute so agree and, generally speaking, agreed disputes procedures have been exhausted, to an arbitrator or to the Central Arbitration Committee ◇ Collective Bargaining; Lockout; Strike. W.F.F., amended by K.W.

> K. W. Wedderburn and P. L. Davies, *Employment Grievances and Disputes in Britain* (California University Press, 1969); R. Kidner, *Trade Union Law*, Ch. 15. (Stevens & Sons, 2nd ed., 1983).

Arithmetic Unit ◇ Computer

Artificial Intelligence ◇ Information System

Assembly-line Balancing One requirement for the efficient operation of assembly- or flow-line production is that each station on the line requires an equal amount of time to perform their respective operations. The work content for the complete assembly line must therefore be allocated in, as near as possible, equal amounts to each station, otherwise inefficiences will be introduced, as operators at stations with less work either wait for the arrival of work from the previous station on the line, or work more slowly to compensate ($\diamondsuit$ Assembly Lines).

The assembly-line balancing procedure takes no account of 'human' characteristics, since the object of the exercise is normally to balance the standard times (determined by $\diamondsuit$ Work Measurement) for each station. This assumes that a given constant time will be required by the operator at each station, whereas in fact an operator's cycle time will vary because of variations in work method, mistakes, faulty materials, etc. ($\diamondsuit$ System Loss). Assembly-line balancing considers the situation to be deterministic and constant, like a transfer line consisting entirely of machines.

Given the required line output (P), the cycle time (C) can be calculated. For example, if P = 60 per hour

$$C = \frac{1}{P} = 1 \text{ min}$$

The work to be performed on the line can be broken down into a set of minimum rational work units, i.e. the smallest logical units of work. The problem is then to allocate these units of work to work stations to satisfy the following constraints and requirements: (1) precedence constraints, i.e. certain units must appear in a certain order, for example holes must be drilled before being tapped; (2) zoning constraints, i.e. it may be necessary for (a) certain units to occur at the same work station, for example because they both require the same piece of expensive equipment; (b) certain units *not* to occur at the same work station, for example because they involve work on opposite sides of the job; (3) Equal work content (t_1) at each station; (4) Station work contents, or maximum station work content (t_1 max) equal to the required cycle time(C);

Requirements (3) and (4) together ensure that total balancing loss is minimized and spread evenly over all stations.

$$\text{Balancing loss} = \text{Total allowed time} - \text{Total work content}$$
$$= n(C) - \Sigma_1^n \, t_1$$
$$\text{or} = n(t_1 \text{ max}) - \Sigma_1^n t_1$$

Numerous methods have been developed for solving the assembly-line balancing problem; however, because of its complexity no rigorous method is available to obtain an optimal solution for the general practical case. One of several heuristic procedures is normally used, to obtain a near optimal solution, perhaps the best known being the ranked-positional-weight technique. ⟨⟩ Heuristic Programming. R.W.

R. Wild, *Mass Production Management* (J. Wiley, 1972).

Assembly Lines (Flow or Production Lines) Assembly and flow lines are the chief methods of production used for high-quantity standardized items. The operations necessary for completion of the job are located at successive stations on the lines, an approximately equal amount of work being undertaken at each station.

This method of production has the following characteristics: (1) minimum distance moved by product, hence minimum handling and minimum space are required; (2) job specialization, hence little training is necessary and a high level of performance is possible; (3) minimum work in progress, hence minimum production time; (4) inflexibility, hence dependence upon continued, stable, quantity demand for a standardized product; (5) maximum resource utilization.

Even with complete line balancing, i.e. equal standard times at each station, underutilization of resources may occur because of the variability of operation times resulting from human error, faulty material, etc. (system loss). Too rigorous pacing of work may also result in the production of defective or incomplete work. ⟨⟩ Assembly-line Balancing; System Loss; Pacing.

Production planning for this type of production is comparatively complex because of its inflexibility. A continuous supply of raw material and subassemblies is essential and the output rate is effectively fixed:

$$\text{Output rate/hr} = \frac{1}{\text{Cycle time (hrs)}}$$

However, production control is comparatively simple.

Job simplification has been a continuing trend since the beginning of industrial engineering, and assembly-line work incorporates many of the traditional concepts of work design. Recently, however, there has been a counter trend, i.e. ⟨⟩ Job Enlargement, based on the theory that oversimplification of work affects the needs of the individual and leads to diminishing economic returns.

Perhaps the two principles of assembly-line work that are most questionable are the principles of work simplification and ⟨⟩ Pacing. Assembly lines differ a great deal in the extent to which these principles are adopted. Cycle times vary from a few seconds to several hours, and similarly situations where work is rigorously paced often exist alongside assembly lines incorporating large buffer stocks.

Assembly-line manufacture is normally in anticipation of demand, i.e. for stock, unlike jobbing manufacture, which is in response to demand, i.e. direct to customer order.

Two basic types of assembly or flow line exist: 'non-mechanical lines' and 'moving-belt lines'. In the latter, items, either removable from or fixed to the line, are carried past stations by a mechanical-transfer device. On such lines the mechanical pacing effects may be high and incomplete items may be produced. Mechanical pacing is absent on non-mechanical lines, since items are passed from station to station on completion; however, for effective operation, such lines must normally operate with ⟨⟩ Buffer Stocks of work-in-progress between stations. R.W.

R. Wild, *Mass Production Management* (J. Wiley, 1972).

Assets An asset may be broadly defined as a valuable possession or, alternatively, as any economic resource that is expected to yield future benefits to its owner. ⟨⟩ Valuation of Assets.

Legally an asset is an enforceable right or relation between persons. For example in the case of a business asset, such as a machine, the law recognizes and will enforce a right of the owner to 'quiet possession' as against other parties. In the case of a debt, which is an intangible right, the law recognizes the debtor–creditor relation by enforcing payment, once the debt has been proven.

In balance sheets assets are classified into two main categories, namely 'current assets' and 'fixed assets'. Current assets consist of: (1) cash; (2) items that are held with a view to conversion into cash in the ordinary course of business, e.g. trade debtors, stocks of finished output, investments held as near cash; (3) assets that will be used up shortly in the ordinary course of business or production, e.g. payments in advance for rent, rates, insurances, etc., work-in-progress, raw materials, stocks. Assets that are intended to be held for the longer term (more than one year) for use in ordinary business and manufacturing operations are classed as fixed assets, e.g. plant, fixtures, transport vehicles, factory premises.

Thus it is clear that it is the *intention* of the owner that is paramount in this classification of assets. A motor vehicle is a fixed asset when used as transport but to a motor-vehicle manufacturer, it is stock-in-trade, a current asset.

It is often the practice to divide up the category of fixed assets into the three categories of 'intangible', 'tangible' and 'investments', where appropriate. Intangible assets are those fixed assets that are not represented by material possessions (other than investments), e.g. patents, trademarks, ⟷ Goodwill. Investments – the remaining non-material asset category – consists of those investments held not for quick conversion into cash but for purposes of economic integration or of control of other companies, as in the case of groups of companies. Tangible assets include such items as land, buildings, plant, etc. ⟷ Claims; Consolidated Accounts. E.A.L., amended by J.V.P.

Assignment Method ⟷ Mathematical Programming

Attitude Scales Individual responses, evoked by particular stimuli, tend to fall into relatively stable and consistent patterns, which may conveniently be described as attitudes. Thus a person's reaction to one particular policeman on one occasion will be, to some extent, predictable from a knowledge of his or her semi-permanent attitude towards the police. Sets of such attitudes, integrated into a total complex behavioural system, comprise the individuality characteristic of each human being. ⟷ Personality.

Attitude scales, derived usually from questionnaire data, set out to evaluate the direction of a person's attitude, the magnitude of its deviation from a central value, the tenacity with which it is maintained, and its relative importance within the total personality organization.

For purposes of industrial management, attitudes are relevant in such areas as job placement, studies of job satisfaction and the identification of occupational difficulties, in addition, of course, to applications within the field of consumer research. E.E.

Attitude Survey The systematic collection of attitudinal data, usually for the purpose of predicting behaviour, testing reactions to specific phenomena, or ascertaining the relationship between attitudes and other variables.

The data may be collected in a variety of ways but the most common are probably interviews, questionnaires, ⟷ Attitude Scales, and, for the more sophisticated, the use of projective techniques. As techniques of attitude scaling and measurement have developed, so the use of attitude surveys has increased, and opinion polling is now an established profession. Attitude surveys are a valuable research tool in the hands of the trained psychologist or sociologist, but despite an apparent simplicity, the design and conduct of such a survey contain many pitfalls. It is necessary to be absolutely clear what data are needed and how they can best be collected; what population is to be studied and what kind and size of sample is to be drawn; how the questions should be phrased and by whom, and where the questioning should be carried out; what statistical analysis is appropriate and what inferences may properly be drawn. Additionally it must be borne in mind that attitudes are often ephemeral and subject to considerable influence from perhaps temporary circumstances. I.C.MCG.

A. N. Oppenheim, *Questionnaire Design and Attitude Measurement* (Heinemann, 1966); Peter H. Mann, *Methods of Sociological Enquiry* (Blackwell, 1968); O. Hellevik, *Introduction to Causal Analysis* (Allen & Unwin, 1984).

Audience Measurement Definition and quantification of the readers/viewers/listeners reached by a medium, to determine the impact achieved by advertisements placed within the particular medium. Individual press media publish details of their own readership, predominantly in the form of the *Media Data Form*, which is registered with and authenticated by the I P A. Major controversy concerns the value of such data as a guide to the effectiveness of any advertisement (◇ Advertising) and also the relevant way in which the measurement of readership should be made. An affirmative reply to the question whether a given medium, e.g. a newspaper, has been seen is frequently supplemented by questions to ascertain the level of reading and noting of particular elements. An additional measure of page traffic, the propensity to read particular positions within papers as well as particular pages, is also frequently employed. Readership should be clearly differentiated from circulation, which is a measure of the number of copies distributed. The methodological problems of readership research are particularly well treated in W. Belson, *Studies in Readership* (Business Publications, 1963). For TV the equivalent audience measurement is again syndicated under the control of the advertising profession. Similar methodological problems exist regarding the extent to which viewing can be adequately defined; ratings are obtained by metered measurement of the time a TV set is switched on in a sample of homes. Cinema audience measurement is normally made in terms of box-office units receipts, poster and outdoor sites by a measure of passers-by, and radio listening by sample-survey methods. G.S.C.W.

Auditing The principal function of an auditor (when appointed for the purpose of the audit of a limited company) is to certify that a company's annual accounts show a 'true and fair view' of the company's affairs. The auditor is also required to certify that proper books of account have been kept and that the annual accounts are in accord with the books. The meaning of the terms 'true and fair' and 'proper books' is not obvious but accountants acting as auditors have generally interpreted these terms to mean that the books and accounts are in accordance with currently accepted principles of accountancy (⟡ Accountancy Conventions). However, auditing practice does not consist only of the application of accounting principles. At least as important is the comparison of the books and accounts with independent evidence to verify the transactions entered into by the company and its present financial status in terms of the values of assets and liabilities. The verification process consists mainly of the examination of documents such as invoices, receipts, contracts, documents of title, etc., as well as an investigation of the company's administrative system in order to determine whether it is such as to encourage fraud, embezzlement or defalcations. Owing to the size of the task, it is generally accepted practice that auditors should carry out intelligent test checks of the company's system of accounting and administration and original documents rather than carry out an exhaustive check. The use of statistical methods of sampling for this purpose is growing. An internal audit, by employees of the organization, is frequently used to complement the work of the external auditor.

Auditing may be seen as being concerned not just with the honesty of employees and the accuracy of financial records and accounting measurements, but also with managerial efficiency. Appropriate methods of investigation may therefore be used in a management audit aimed at measuring and improving managerial performance. In a wider sense concern with the relationship between business and society has led to calls for the practice of social auditing, as a means of ensuring greater accountability between an enterprise and the community at large (⟡ Social Accounting). Limited companies and nationalized industries are audited by auditors in private practice; many public bodies are audited by either the National Audit Office or the Audit Commission for Local Authorities. The accounts of public bodies are often required to present the affairs of the organization 'fairly', rather than give a 'true and fair view'. E.A.L., amended by J.V.P.

> *Auditing and Reporting 1983/4* (Institute of Chartered Accountants in England and Wales, 1983).

Authority The right to use ⟡ Power. In the formal organization this right is usually defined and the definition promulgated so that all members of the organization understand the extent of the authority vested in their own positions and in the positions held by others. It is axiomatic that such authority should be just sufficient to enable the proper discharge of the duties assigned to the position and that the incumbent should be held accountable for its proper use.

Authority is not power itself and it is quite possible to have one without the other. For example the ineffective supervisor may have authority but little power and there are many situations in which individuals have power without authority. Incidentally, in so far as there exists a *right* to strike, those participating in an official strike are exercising not only power but authority. Authority is more likely to be acceptable to subordinates when superiors are respected personally and technically, and when their manner of exercising authority is in accordance with the subordinates' expectations and values.

Organizations differ in the extent to which they rely on authority as a means of achieving control or motivation. An authoritarian organization is one that relies on authority and in such organizations there is usually a heightened status consciousness and an emphasis on ⬧ Social Distance. Authoritarianism tends to reduce upward communication, to discourage subordinates from using initiative and to minimize their personal involvement in the tasks that are allocated to them. Current thinking favours a superior–subordinate relationship in which the exercise of authority is replaced by personal influence through ⬧ Leadership: a concept of teamwork in which the superior perceives his or her role as one involving working with, rather than being placed over, subordinates. This concept was first introduced into the management literature by Mary Parker Follett (1868–1933) with her distinction between 'power with' and 'power over'. ⬧ Discipline; Responsibility; Status. I.C.MCG.

Arnold S. Tannenbaum *et al.*, *Hierarchy in Organizations* (Jossey-Baas Ltd, 1974); H. G. Metcalf and L. F. Urwick, *Dynamic Administration: The Collected Papers of Mary Parker Follett* (Pitman, 1941); J. Child, *Organizations: A Guide to Problems and Practices* (Harper & Row, 1984).

Autocorrelation ⬦ Correlation and Regression

Automated Warehouse A storage facility that provides for the automatic placing of items into stock and automatic retrieval by means of automatic, computer-controlled fork-lift devices, running on rails between 'banks' of storage racks where items are stored on pallets. Used extensively in large warehouses, and in factories for materials, parts and component stores, such warehouses will often be linked to automatic transport devices such as automatic guided vehicles (AGVs). ⬧ Automatic Guided Vehicle. R.W.

Automatic Guided Vehicle (AGV) Load-carrying vehicle (e.g.

truck, pallet) that is self-propelled and capable of following a pre-determined or selected path, e.g. by following wires buried in the ground, wires or lines on the ground, or by means of remote control. Such vehicles are used in automated factories to transport parts from and to storage areas or production machines. ⟳ Materials Handling. R.W.

Automatic Vending A method of ⟳ Retailing where a vending machine automatically provides merchandise and thereby completes a sales transaction on the insertion of coins or notes. This method of retailing has significant potential, for although it is currently not a low-cost method of selling, it has inherent cost advantages over more labour-intensive methods. Labour constitutes one of the greatest cost pressures in retailing. There are four major types of vending machines; (1) package vendors for wrapped items, e.g. nylons, biscuits, bars of chocolate; (2) bulk vendors, e.g. hair cream, petrol; (3) bottle vendors, e.g. cold drinks; (4) cup vendors, e.g. hot drinks. Vendors in category (3) are rapidly being replaced by (4) style machines because of problems of acceptance and disposal of waste. This method of distribution has had substantial growth over the last thirty years but has an extensive history in that 'slot machines', which fall into category 1, were traditionally used on railway stations.

One of the most significant recent additions to automatic vending is in the world of banking and financial services. Here automatic teller machines trading with a variety of brand names offer immediate access by personal customers to cash funds. This development presages major changes in the coming decades for the entire pattern of funds transfer. G.S.C.W.

Automation In mechanized systems the primary source of power and some simple, repetitive control operations are typically provided by machinery. In such systems the main load of detecting, measuring, calculating, communicating, inspecting, controlling and decision-making is undertaken by the human operator. When a substantial amount of these information-handling functions is carried out by machine, the system may be said to be automated. Obviously automation is a matter of degree, and its level is defined by the extent to which 'intelligent' (i.e. information-handling) behaviour may proceed without human inter-vention.

The word 'automation', which was coined in Detroit in the mid-fifties, has caused a good deal of misunderstanding and misapprehension in industry. It remains, none the less, a useful word to describe the present trend towards the carrying out by machine of a variety of functions that have traditionally been regarded as a uniquely human capability. These functions stand in contrast to the energy-generating tasks that were taken over by machine during the first industrial revolution.

Sir Leon Bagrit, in the 1964 Reith Lectures, described the elements of automation as 'the three Cs', i.e. communication, computation and control. Each of these has been the subject of very considerable development during the course of this century.

Just after the turn of the century Marconi's successful experiments in long-distance communication heralded the beginning of the revolution in information-transmission technology. Since this time developments have been made in several directions leading to such systems as colour television, aircraft communications and satellite links (◊ Information Theory).

The history of computers can be traced back to the mechanical inventions of Pascal and Leibnitz in the seventeenth century, through the nineteenth-century contributions of Babbage and Hollerith to the emergence of the electronic analog and digital machines of today. The electronic computer has revolutionized scientific, technical and business computations and has made possible the rational solution of problems that in a previous era were left unsolved.

Automatic control (◊ Feedback), as typified in a simple form by the governor, has made possible the elimination of the need for human intervention in the regulation of systems. The advantages of automatic control elements may include speed, reliability, accuracy and cost.

The development of small, cheap, digital devices combined with advances in communication technology has led to something of a revolution in the processing and transmission of information (◊ Information System).

Inevitably there have been economic, political, educational, managerial and social consequences of automation, not all of which are favourable either to the individuals concerned or to society at large. A good deal of research in the social sciences needs to be done and implemented if the full benefits of the technological innovations are to be reaped. E.E.

L. Bagrit, *The Age of Automation* (Penguin, 1966).

Average ◊ Measures of Location

B

Balance of Payments The purpose of a balance of payments statement is to show what a country pays and receives in the course of its international transactions. As an example, the U K balance of payments for 1983 is given below.

United Kingdom summary balance of payments 1983

	£m
Current account	
Visible balance	− 500
Invisible balance	+ 2,549
Current balance	+ 2,049
Investment and other capital flows	− 2,044
Balancing item	− 821
Balance for official financing	− 816
Official financing	
Net transactions with the I M F	− 36
Net transactions with overseas monetary authorities plus foreign borrowing by H M Government and public sector	+ 249
Official reserves (drawings on + /additions to −)	+ 603
Total official financing	+ 816

Source: *Economic Trends*, H M S O, March 1984.

The visible balance measures the difference between a country's exports and imports of manufactured and semi-manufactured goods, raw materials, fuel and foodstuffs. As is evident from the above account and others for previous years, there is normally a debit balance on visible trade for the U K. However, there were surpluses in 1980, 1981 and 1982, in part due to the severe recession.

The invisible account is concerned with the payments and receipts derived from the provision of services. It includes payments and receipts derived from shipping, air freight, tourism and insurance; income earned and paid on overseas investment and foreign-owned home investment; current government expenditure abroad on the maintenance of the armed forces and the provision of grant aid to underdeveloped countries.

Taken together, these two give the current balance, which could be broadly said to represent the profit or loss in day-to-day dealings. Normally the UK has had a considerable credit balance from the invisibles account to buttress frequent visible trade deficits. In recent years, with the advent of North Sea oil, our surplus on the oil account has increased and this has helped to offset the declining surpluses in manufactured goods, which finally turned into a deficit (the first since the industrial revolution) in 1983.

If the country's current account transactions were our only dealings with the world then the balance of payments accounts would be quite simple. For example a surplus on current account would allow us to build up our reserves or repay debts. However, there are other transactions, which are reflected in the item 'investment and other capital flows'. These transactions include overseas investment in the UK public and private sector, UK private investment overseas, overseas currency borrowing and lending by UK banks, changes in the exchange reserves of overseas central monetary institutions and changes in trade credit. When the total effect of all these capital transactions is added to the current balance, the total never adds up exactly to the amount of foreign currency the country has in fact gained or lost, which is known by the Bank of England. Hence a 'balancing item' is introduced.

The combination of current and capital account transactions gave a deficit for official financing in 1983 of £816 m. This can be covered either by reducing the official external assets or increasing the official external liabilities of the UK. Both methods were used in 1983. L.T.S.

Balance Sheet A statement in money terms of the assets, liabilities and capital relating to a business or other organization. However, one might be tempted to infer from such a definition that its construction represents an attempt to value that entity. Conventional balance sheets are not drawn up with this purpose in mind, however. A reading of the recommendations of the Institute of Chartered Accountants in England and Wales, for instance, will make this clear. Fixed assets are generally stated at cost less 'reasonable' depreciation, and current assets at the lower of the cost or market value, in some cases, and realizable value in others, therefore a conventional balance sheet is usually not a statement of the net worth of an entity. ⟡ Assets; Claims; Capital; Valuation of Assets; Changing Price Levels, Accounting for.

The general format of company balance sheets is laid down in the Companies Act 1985 and has been much influenced by the EEC fourth directive on company accounts. For the general form of a balance sheet ⟡ Claims. E.A.L., amended by J.V.P.

> G. Holmes and A. Sugden, *Interpreting Company Reports and Accounts* (Woodhead Faulkner, 2nd ed., 1982).

Bankers' Commercial Credits Of considerable importance in international trade. An exporter who has agreed to supply goods to a foreign customer will wish to have some guarantee of being paid when the goods are delivered. The exporter may insist, therefore, as part of the deal that a reputable British bank should undertake to pay for the goods. The buyer will then have to approach his own bank to arrange the opening of such credit for him. The importer's bank, if satisfied as to the customer's credit rating, will then contact its agents or correspondent bank in Britain, asking that they should open an irrevocable documentary credit in the exporter's favour, accepting responsibility for reimbursing the British bank in due course. The exporter will then be informed by the British bank of their willingness to honour drafts (⟡ Negotiable Instruments), up to a stated maximum amount, provided that these drafts are accompanied by the appropriate shipping documents. Unless these documents are produced in the exact form stipulated in the bank's letter of confirmation to the exporter, the bank will not be obliged to accept the draft. The documents will then be forwarded by the bank to the instructing bank in the importer's country, who will reimburse them and hold the documents until the importer has paid the amount involved and the charges incurred. The documents in question are those that are needed to claim the goods from the carrier who has been conveying them to the importer's country. W.F.F.

> C. M. Schmitthoff, *Export Trade: Law and Practice of International Trade* (Stevens & Sons, 7th ed., 1980).

Bankruptcy The name given to legal proceedings, the purpose of which is to secure the assets of a person who is unable to pay their debts, with a view to realizing these assets and using the proceeds to satisfy, in part or in full, the claims of their creditors. In this way the interests of all parties can be safeguarded: the creditors are treated equitably and the debtor, once discharged from bankruptcy, will be able to start again in business without the burden of the old debts. Only individuals can be made bankrupt; a joint stock company that is unable to pay its debts will be wound up (liquidated) compulsorily.

Any creditor or group of creditors, or indeed the debtor, may present to the court a bankruptcy petition (provided the debts owing to them exceed £200), which must indicate that the debtor has committed an 'act of bankruptcy'. If the court is satisfied that an act of bankruptcy has been committed, i.e. the debtor has done something indicating their inability to pay their debts, a receiving order will be made against them allowing the official receiver to take charge of the debtor's assets. The creditors will then meet and will decide whether to ask the court to declare the debtor bankrupt. If this is done, a trustee in bankruptcy will be appointed who has to take over the bankrupt's assets, realize them and distribute the proceeds among the creditors, acting throughout under the supervision of the court. The bankrupt will be examined as to the whereabouts of their assets and the reasons for their inability to pay their debts. If their conduct has been blameless, they may in due course apply to be discharged from bankruptcy, which means that they will no longer be liable on the unpaid balance of their debts. Discharge of a bankrupt is automatic after the lapse of (at most) ten years from their bankruptcy adjudication.

The law relating to bankruptcy is mainly found in the Bankruptcy Act, 1914 and Insolvency Act, 1976.

At the time of writing, new legislation is passing through Parliament that may become law as the Insolvency Act 1985, which will probably change the position of bankrupts. W.F.F., amended by J.C.E.M.

Schmitthoff and Sarre, *Charlesworth's Mercantile Law* (Stevens & Sons, 14th ed., 1984).

Batch Production Falls between jobbing production and mass (assembly-line) production, in that products are produced neither as single, unique units nor continuously as standardized items. Either a standard range of products is available and sufficient orders exist to facilitate batch manufacture even though there are individual orders for only small quantities; and/or individual orders are received for fairly large quantities of special products.

The nature of the product and demand will determine whether the production layout approaches that of mass production, i.e. layout by product, or that of the jobbing shop, i.e. layout by process. Furthermore the nature of the product and demand will determine whether products are made in anticipation of demand for stock, or are made to customer order.

Normally there is a compromise situation. Either sufficient standard products exist or products contain sufficient common or similar parts to justify large batch manufacture on a group of facilities reserved or designed for this purpose. Additionally general-purpose equipment is normally available for production in small quantities to customer order.

Production planning and control in batch production therefore consists of elements of the processes adopted in assembly-line and jobbing-shop procedures, plus procedures to deal with the problems unique to this type of production, e.g. economic ◇ Batch Sizes. R.W.

Batch Sizes (Lot Size; Economic Lot Size) Careful determination of the size and frequency of the production or purchase of batches or lots of items is an important method by which total costs can be reduced (◇ Batch Production; Inventory Problems).

For example in production the total annual cost of setting up and preparing machinery for the manufacture of a certain part will clearly depend upon the number of occasions such set-ups are necessary, and hence, for a given demand, will reduce with increasing batch size. A similar situation exists in purchasing, since total ordering costs will reduce as order quantity increases.

Conversely the total costs of carrying stock will increase as the stock, and hence either manufactured or purchased batch size, increases.

When production or purchasing in batches is necessary, the economic batch size may be determined, often accurately and analytically, as in the following example. Take the simple situation where (1) demand is known and constant, (2) production or purchased parts move into stock together, (3) no shortages occur.

$$\text{Economic batch size} = \sqrt{\frac{2RS}{I}}$$

where R = Annual demand
S = Set-up or order cost
I = stock-keeping cost/part/year

Analytical solutions are also available in more complex and realistic situations, e.g. where shortages, quantity discounts, variable stock-keeping costs, probabilistic demand, etc., are allowed. R.W.

R. Wild, *Techniques of Production Management* (Holt, Rinehart & Winston, 1971); R. Wild, *Production and Operations Management* (Holt, Rinehart & Winston, 3rd ed., 1984).

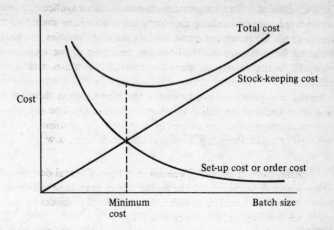

Bayes Formula ⟡ Subjective Probability

Beta ⟡ Risk Premium

Bill of Materials (Bill of Requirements) A list of the component parts of a product, usually arranged in a 'structured' manner so that different 'levels' are identified, e.g. the final product level, below which there are the major subassemblies, then the component level, and so on. Bills of material are used in inventory control, production scheduling, and in purchasing. ⟡ Materials Requirement Planning. R.W.

Bills of Exchange ⟡ Negotiable Instruments

Bills of Lading A person who wishes to send a consignment of goods by sea will enter into a contract of affreightment with a carrier by sea. This contract is evidenced by a document known as a bill of lading. A bill of lading differs from a ⟡ Charter Party, which represents a contract for the hire of an entire ship. A bill of lading not only contains the terms of the contract of affreightment but it also acts as a receipt for the goods shipped and by mercantile custom it has come to represent a document of title to the goods, to the extent that a transfer of the bill of lading is taken to mean that the property in the goods represented by the bill is being transferred. In this way the property in goods that are still afloat may be transferred to a buyer who will pay for them on receipt of the bill

of lading. Bills of lading are generally issued by the shipowner or charterer of a ship in sets of three, one being retained by the master of the ship on which the goods are carried, while the other two are handed to the consignor of the goods. The consignor will then dispatch one copy by airmail to the consignee, the other copy being sent separately by surface mail. The recipient of the bill of lading may endorse it to a third party, who would then on production of the bill be entitled to claim the goods from the master of the ship. W.F.F.

Payne and Ivamy, *Carriage of Goods by Sea* (Butterworth, 12th ed., 1985).

Binary Scale This is used to represent numbers in a computer rather than the familiar decimal scale. The latter, a 'ten-state' scale, uses the arabic digits 0–9 inclusive, and is based on powers of 10 (that is, 1, 10, 100, etc.). The conventional method of writing a decimal number is really a shorthand notation for expressing the coefficients and successive powers of 10.

For example the decimal number 329 is really

$$3 \times 10^2 + 2 \times 10^1 + 9 \times 10^0$$

The choice of a basis of 10 is arbitrary and was probably originally determined by the number of digits on two hands, which would provide a convenient basis for counting. Other scales are in common use, for example, a duo-decimal scale (12) to convert inches to feet, and a tertiary scale (3) to convert feet to yards. The binary scale is used to convert pints into quarts.

Electronic circuits represents digits, and hence numbers, in a computer by adopting alternative configurations or states for each digit. It is much more convenient to design 'two-state' rather than 'ten-state' circuits, so in a computer the binary rather than the conventional decimal scale is used to represent numbers. Further, a computer makes decisions that require alternatives to be formulated logically. These formulations must be expressed electronically and a two-valued, or binary, logic is preferable to a ten-valued or decimal one.

The binary scale uses the two digits 0 and 1 and is based on powers of 2. By analogy with decimal numbers, binary numbers are expressed as the coefficients of successive powers of 2. For example the binary number 1101 is really

$$1 \times 2^3 + 1 \times 2^2 + 0 \times 2^1 + 1 \times 2^0$$

Its decimal representation is

8 + 4 + 0 + 1 = 13

The decimal number 329 can be written in binary as 101001001, that is

$1 \times 2^8 + 0 \times 2^7 + 1 \times 2^6 + 0 \times 2^5 + 0 \times 2^4 + 1 \times 2^3 + 0 \times 2^2 + 0 \times 2^1 + 1 \times 2^0$

That is

$1 \times 256 + 0 \times 128 + 1 \times 64 + 0 \times 32 + 0 \times 16 + 1 \times 8 + 0 \times 2 + 1 \times 1 = 329$

Binary arithmetic is analogous to decimal arithmetic and is illustrated by two simple sums expressed in binary and decimal arithmetic:

110101	53	11010	26
10001	17 +	10001	17 −
1000110	70	1001	9

Similar analogies hold for multiplication and division and are described in the specialist textbooks on computers. Binary code, i.e. the number system of the radix 2, is of especial significance as it is the natural language of many two-state physical components used within a digital system. (Switches, for example, are either open or closed; relays are either energized or de-energized.) Hence the allocation of 0 and 1 to the alternative states of such components provides a convenient way of performing arithmetic operations. Furthermore, since 1 and 0 may conveniently represent respectively 'true' and 'false', there are useful analogies between binary arithmetic and two-state symbolic logic.
M.J.C.M.

John C. Cluley, *Electronic Computer* (Oliver & Boyd, 1967), pp. 65–72.

Binomial Distribution ⟡ Frequency Distributions

Blackleg A blackleg or 'scab' is a member of a work group, usually also a trade unionist, who breaks the cohesion of the work group in an ⟡ Industrial Dispute with an employer by taking independent action. Thus any workers who refuse to take part in a strike, regardless of whether or not they are trade unionists, are blacklegs. Blacklegging is a more serious offence in the trade union calendar than mere non-unionism.

Some union rule books carry the ultimate sanction of expulsion for blacklegging but the moral stigma alone is so great that the incidence of this offence is relatively rare. The fear of being 'sent to Coventry' and other forms of ostracism by workmates both at work and elsewhere is usually sufficient to ensure conformity.

Blacklegs especially recruited for the purpose have sometimes been used by employers as strike-breakers. Historically troops have been used as blacklegs and on other occasions have been called in to protect blacklegs. N.H.C.

> H. A. Clegg, *The Changing System of Industrial Relations in Great Britain* (Blackwell, 1979).

Bookkeeping The recording of financial transactions in the 'books' of an organization. The system of bookkeeping records two aspects to every transaction. These are known as 'debits and credits', on the basis that an increase in one record, or 'account', must be offset by a decrease in another. Bookkeeping systems have been developed over many centuries and have proved well suited to computerization. Bookkeeping relies upon the strict application of rules and is mechanistic, whereas ⟡ Accountancy is the art of presenting, interpreting and manipulating the bookkeeping records. ⟡ Accounting. J.V.P.

Branch and Bound Technique Many decision problems can be usefully represented in the form of a tree. For example the determination of the optimum order in which to execute three tasks can be represented as follows:

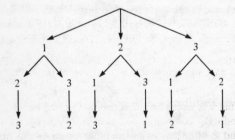

Two decision levels are evident. Firstly, deciding whether to place 1, 2, or 3 first, and, secondly, which of the remaining two to place second. This is a simple example, but in a complex case the number of branches to the tree may be considerable and consequently some method of arriving at an optimal solution without evaluating all possible alternatives is desirable.

The branch and bound algorithm was developed as a method of

solving precisely this type of problem and relies on an intelligent search of the decision tree. Two concepts are involved and are described with reference to the above three-task example.

Branch. When a task is committed to the sequence a node is produced, and further branching from that node commits the remaining jobs to the sequence, i.e. if task 1 appears at the first node, further branching produces the nodes at which 2 or 3 are committed to the sequence.

Bound. The 'lower bound' is calculated for each node and represents the merit of the solution from that point, e.g. in the above example our objective is to minimize the time required to complete all three tasks. The lower bound will give the minimum processing time for the solutions emanating from that node.

The use of the lower bounds enables us to concentrate on the most promising sequences, and provisionally to neglect the unpromising ones, i.e. we branch from the nodes with the lowest lower bounds. By this procedure we are able to make an intelligent branch rather than a random one.

The branch and bound method was developed in 1963 for the solution of the 'travelling salesman' problem, which involves the routing of a salesman from a base once through several locations and back to base, in minimum distance or time. More recent applications have included (1) the special case of the sequencing problem where jobs have to be processed in the same order on each machine; (2) plant location problems; (3) electrical circuit design. ⬦ Decision Theory; Decision Trees. R.W.

F. S. Hillier and G. J. Lieberman, *Introduction to Operations Research* (Holden-Day Inc., 1967).

Branding The ascription to a product or service of a name other than the producing company's full name, in order to identify it more effectively and to differentiate it from other similar goods or services. At its most successful it may become the generic term for describing the category to which it belongs, as Hoover did for vacuum cleaners. Such a high level of awareness can create an insistence by customers which can force distribution in consumer markets. The phenomenon of branding is less common in industrial markets and in the sale of technical products. The efficacy of branding lies in its ability to coalesce the constellation of ideas and concepts surrounding a product or service and thereby facilitate the communication process; this is generally termed the brand image and reflects at any point in time the overall status of users' perceptions of a company's offering. Where a company makes a range of products it may do so under a house brand name, e.g. the Dulux range of painting and decorating products. Common branding across a product range offers economies in promotion, but calls for sustained and consistent planning and presentation of constituent products. Major new developments, out of tune with an overall image for a brand name, are frequently launched under a different brand name. It is also becoming familiar for large distributors to adopt house branding; the pioneer of this in Britain has been Marks and Spencer, with its St Michael brand. An organization's own corporate identity is susceptible to similar analysis, but where the brand names adopted differ from the company name any corporate image is normally less apparent. Growth of distributor or retailer brand names and the dominance of many channels of distribution, particularly in groceries, by a limited number of organizations has, to some extent, diminished the power of branding by the manufacturer. In this respect their retailer or distributor name and any brand that might be associated with it has become an alternative guarantee of assurance to customers. The use of even the heaviest advertising programmes to enhance customer awareness cannot necessarily force the relevant retail outlet with a sufficiently high-quality reputation to stock such brands. G.S.C.W.

Breakaway Union A new trade union formed by a group of dissident members who have withdrawn from an existing trade union.

Secession from a trade union and the formation of a breakaway occurs when a section, having lost confidence in the union and developed different goals, becomes large enough and active enough to form an independent body.

While the rights of workers to join unions of their own choice need to be respected, the right to break away and form a new union has always been condemned as likely to undermine the strength of the parent union, to encourage discontented members to seek a solution outside the union rather than internally through the democratic process, and to weaken the unity of the trade-union movement. The formation of a breakaway union is the most serious crime in the trade-union calendar.

The larger, more complex, more centralized unions with a heterogeneous membership can better withstand external stresses because of their numerical strength, but are more vulnerable to internal stress than the smaller, more homogeneous and less centralized unions. Thus the Transport and General Workers' Union has suffered breakaways in the form of the National Amalgamated Stevedores' and Dockers' Union and in the National Passenger Workers' Union; and the Aeronautical Engineers' Association is a breakaway from the fomer Amalgamated Engineering Union. Breakaway unionism may come about through the enhanced status of a membership group, now acquiring a feeling of exclusiveness. For example, for their now high-status workers the National Association of Signalmen aims to provide an organization similar to the footplatemen's and salaried staffs' unions, and separate from the National Union of Railwaymen, which is formally responsible for the organization of signalmen.

The official policy of the ◇ T U C is to refuse to affiliate a new union if there is already one in existence organizing the type of worker concerned. Employers are reluctant to incur the ire of powerful, established unions by dealing with breakaways; indeed an employer may not bargain with a breakaway even if it represents a majority of those employed by the firm.

Public policy has tended to discriminate against breakaway unions and their formation in the civil service has compelled the government, as an employer, to define its policy towards them. Following the report of the Terrington Committee (Cmd. 8470) the government will not recognize for bargaining purposes any new union unless it can prove that existing associations have failed and were unable to look after the interests of those concerned. In practice this is extremely difficult.

It can be argued that more inter-union competition would stimulate the trade-union movement, but liberal and sensible union policies can only be developed in conditions of reasonable security. Nevertheless the right of trade-union members to vote with their feet is the ultimate right in the face of poor or unrepresentative leadership. Successful breakaway unions are few in Britain, and win recognition only by their own unrelenting efforts. Moreover amalgamation has been far more of a characteristic of British unions, even though fresh attempts at breakaway unions are recorded in most years (the vote by the Nottinghamshire miners to form an association independent from the National Union of Mineworkers being an obvious case in point). ◇ Trade Union – Amalgamations N.H.C. amended by M.J.F.P.

S. W. Lerner, *Breakaway Unions and the Small Trade Union* (Allen & Unwin, 1961); R. Undy and R. Martin, *Ballots and Trade Union Democracy* (Blackwell, 1984).

Break-even Analysis The study of how costs and profits vary with the volume of production, using accounting methods of analysis. The technique can be illustrated by the figure below.

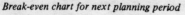

Break-even chart for next planning period

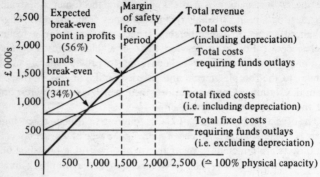

Sales volume (£ 000s)
Expected volume for planning period = 80%

In this traditional form total cost in relation to volume is shown as a straight-line relationship, extending from zero production to a point indicating 100 per cent of production capacity. Since sales generally represent a mixture of many products, production capacity is usually measured in terms of sales volume rather than physical units. The chart is an oversimplification because it is generally thought by accountants that the straight-line relation is only valid around 'the relevant range of volume', i.e. in the capacity range in which the firm expects to operate, say from about 60 per cent to 100 per cent. The projection back to the cost axis is only made in order to give a general explanation concerning the nature of fixed costs. The sales revenue line will generally be at a 45° angle to both axes, since output is in terms of sales volume. Consequently sales price changes will affect the slope of the cost line, not the total revenue line, in this particular representation.

The name generally given to this kind of analysis is somewhat misleading since its uses are meant to be wider than the ascertainment of the break-even point. This point cannot be looked upon as a guide to managerial decisions generally.

Probably the most important aspect of this simple budgeting model is that it turns a profit target into a general operation plan: a given profit target on the chart gives a production manager an output target and the sales manager a sales target. But unless this chart is used very carefully it can, in view of its limitations (particularly its validity within only limited ranges) and the assumptions made, be badly misinterpreted (e.g. in terms of constant prices, product mix, cost relationships).

The wider uses of a break-even analysis approach are often referred to

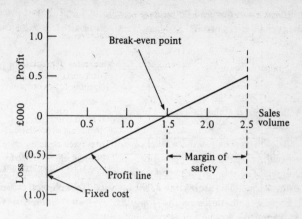

Profit–volume chart (1)

by various names, such as marginal or direct costing, contribution accounting, incremental profit analysis. The data contained in a break-even chart can be redrawn as a 'profit–volume' chart. At any level of sales the expected profit can be determined from the profit line.

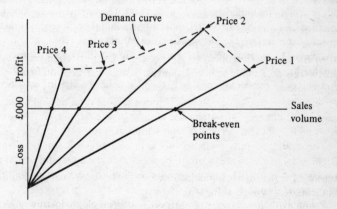

Profit–volume chart (2)

The profit–volume chart is often considered to be of use to management for decision-making. For example take a company with, say, four alternative price possibilities; the profit–volume chart can be used to display both expected demand at each price and break-even points for each alternative. In chart (2) above, the indication is that there is very little difference in demand between prices 3 and 4 and that at price 2 the company maximizes profits. ⋄⟩ Marginal Costing; Costs. E.A.L., amended by J.V.P.

J. Sizer, *Perspectives in Management Accounting* (Heinemann/ICMA, 1981).

Bridlington Rules ⟡ Trade Union – Jurisdiction

Brightness The intensity level of both a physical stimulus and the corresponding subjective sensation is sometimes referred to as 'brightness'. The relation between these objective and subjective levels is not a simple one. The ambiguity in meaning is removed by the use of the term *luminance* to describe the stimulus level and *luminosity* for the subjective level.

The amount of light radiated by a source is termed *luminous flux*. The unit in which this is measured is the *lumen*. (Approximately 1,200 lumens are radiated by a 100-watt tungsten bulb.) Luminous intensity in a given direction is measured in candelas, which express the luminous flux divided by the solid angle of radiation. The *illumination* of a surface is defined by the luminous flux per unit area falling upon it. Thus units of illumination are lumens/m^2 (also called lux). The luminance emitted by a surface is a function of both the incident light and the reflecting characteristics of the surface, and is measured in candelas/m^2.

Brightness contrast provides a measure of the difference between the luminance of a viewed object (e.g. a letter on a road sign) and the luminance of the background (e.g. the field area of a sign). The contrast is expressed as

$$\frac{B_1 - B_2}{B_1} \times 100$$

where B_1 is the higher luminance and B_2 the lower. Visual performance is facilitated by high values of contrast.

Luminosity, or apparent brightness, depends not only upon luminance but also upon such factors as colour, contrast and state of adaptation of the eye. ⋄⟩ Colour; Illumination; Vision. E.E.

P. R. Royce, 'Vision, Light and Colour', in W. T. Singleton (ed.), *The Body at Work* (CUP, 1982).

Brown, Wilfred ⟡ Functional (1); Line and Staff (2)

Budgeting, Short-term An accounting budget is a short-term (annual) plan of action made in terms of physical resources and their monetary equivalents. If it is to be a business plan, a budget must necessarily begin with a financial objective, e.g. a specified rate of return on capital or the maximization of sales revenue given a minimum specified rate of return on capital invested. The complete plan of action is then prepared in terms of subsidiary operation budgets for sales, production, selling and distribution, administration and finance, so as to arrive at a budgeted manufacturing, trading and profit-and-loss account, showing how the historical accounts should turn out if all matters go according to plan. The implications for cash flows, changes in stocks, debtors and creditors are then calculated and given a separately determined figure for additions to fixed assets (⟡ Capital Budgeting). A budgeted ⟡ Balance Sheet can also be prepared, showing the expected financial position at the end of the budgeting period.

Theoretically the budgeting process should consist of the formulation of various alternative plans of action, from which the 'best' in terms of achievement of objectives is selected. However, in practice, such is the present state of the methods of budgeting, the only budget that is fully written down is usually the one that is to be accepted. In the future mathematical programming methods may help to improve this aspect of budgeting.

It is important to stress the control functions of the short-term budget, as well as those of planning. Provided that the budget plan is fully worked out in substantive and physical terms as well as financial terms, a budget provides a specification of activities and targets for all levels of management and therefore also acts as a management control device. ⟡ Control. E.A.L.

W. J. Chandler, J. Pearson *et al.*, 'Planning Budgets and Forecasting', in *Finance for Managers*, vol. 1 (Gee/ICAEN/BIM, 1984).

Buffer Stocks (in Flow Lines) All stocks in manufacturing systems act as a form of buffer between, or means of disconnecting, supply and demand (⟡ Inventories or Stocks). Such a function is vital in certain types of flow-line production systems (⟡ Assembly Lines), where, without interstation buffer stocks, considerable under-utilization of resources would occur. Non-mechanical type flow lines generally operate with capacity for buffer stocks between stations. The larger such stocks, the lower the amount of idle time or delay at stations, and the lower the operator pacing effect (⟡ Pacing). R.W.

R. Wild, *Mass Production Management* (J. Wiley, 1972).

Bullock Report ◊ Industrial Democracy

Burden A term in common use in US organizations meaning overhead cost (◊ Overheads). J.V.P.

Bureaucracy An organizational form possessing to a high degree the characteristics enumerated below. The use of the term in sociology can be attributed to the German scholar Max Weber (1864–1924) (M. Weber, *The Theory of Social and Economic Organisation*). It is important to recognize (1) that the term is used by the sociologist in a non-pejorative sense and (2) that bureaucratization is a matter of degree – *all* organizations exhibit some characteristics of bureaucracy even if only slightly. These characteristics were described by Weber as follows: (1) the duties and responsibilities of all members of the organization are clearly defined; (2) the various positions in the organization are arranged hierarchically, with each official responsible to a superior and responsible for subordinates (with the exception, of course, of the extreme top and bottom of the pyramid); (3) an elaborate system of rules governs the manner in which each official carries out his duties and decisions are recorded and preserved so as to constitute precedents to guide future decisions; (4) each official holds office on the basis of merit formally attested, and is subject to systematic selection and training (seniority and merit were considered to be synonymous); (5) each official carries out his duties without regard to any personal or family commitment, impartially and without emotion. His authority is confined to the discharge of his official duties and he is motivated both by a sense of duty and by the promise of a career.

Weber recognized that no bureaucracy existed in absolute form but he believed that the more closely an organization approximated to the 'ideal type', the greater would be its efficiency. To some extent his belief has been justified by the development of bureaucratic traits in industrial organizations over the last generation or so. There has been an increasing emphasis on specialization within the ranks of management and formal qualifications have become increasingly important; the greater size and complexity of organizations have necessitated the development of more elaborate administrative procedures; and the need for co-ordination and control has brought a corresponding need for accurate specifications of duties and relationships. On the other hand, experience supplemented by formal research suggests that certain dysfunctions seem to be inherent in the bureaucratic form; there is a tendency for rules and procedures to become ends in themselves and for the hierarchical principles to result in too great a reliance on the use of authority, with its concomitant discouragement of personal initiative. Weber's seminal work, however, has helped to stimulate the research interest of the sociologist in problems of organizational behaviour. ⟡ Classical Organization Theory; Formal Organization. I.C.McG.

M. Crozier, *The Bureaucratic Phenomenon* (Tavistock, 1965); E. Jaques, *A General Theory of Bureaucracy* (Heinemann, 1976); D. S. Pugh, D. J. Hickson and C. R. Hinings, *Writers on Organizations* (Penguin, new ed., 1983).

Business Motivation An integral part of any analysis of the firm is a definition of the goal(s) of the firm. Whilst information on demand and cost functions and market structures may be available, goals need to be defined so that the information may be effectively used. It is also true that adequate definition of the goals may conceivably alter the information required to achieve them.

Traditionally economists have approached the firm from an optimizing standpoint and, at its simplest, the goal of the firm has been taken as the maximizing of profits. It should be stressed, however, that for a long time the firm was not really the centre of interest for economists, but was merely a convenient building block in an elaborate theoretical structure that determined prices and hence allocated resources.

With the growth of oligopoly as a market structure and the division between ownership and control in the modern large corporation, the traditional theory has come under increasing criticism. This has been reinforced by various surveys that have questioned businessmen about their goals. One critic has argued that the nature of the modern corporation is such that the maximization of sales receipts is a much more plausible goal. This is partly because the professional managers are concerned with the competitive position of the company, and partly because they are naturally concerned with their own rewards. Both of these, it is argued, are more closely geared to absolute sales receipts than profits. Of course, the shareholders are not entirely neglected and so this goal is subject to a minimum profit constraint to provide satisfactory dividends and funds for capital investment. Another critic has argued that the main goal is the growth of gross assets. Management is again free to pursue this goal because of the demise of shareholder power and the growing significance of undistributed business profits. However, again a constraint is introduced by the wish to avoid loss of employment, that is, the need to avoid being taken over by a predator who sees undervalued assets.

Both these approaches are developed from an optimizing standpoint.

Over against these are goals that have been developed from a 'satisficing' standpoint. Their roots are in psychology rather than classical economic theory, and in particular in the view that the motive to act stems from drives, and action terminates when the drives are satisfied. The term 'satisficing' means being satisfied with some standard of achievement below the maximum possible. Hence the goals that would follow from this approach are achieving a particular level of profit, market share, or sales.

Latterly, work in this field has concentrated even more closely upon the managers and postulates that they are utility maximizers. Their utility is said to depend upon such things as the size of salaries, the number of staff they control, managerial perks and the freedom they have to invest discretionary profits, which are those above the necessary minimum to keep shareholders happy and finance essential capital investment. This freedom on the part of managers to pursue their own goals again stems partly from the divorce of ownership and control. However, it is also argued that it can thrive because of the diminished power of the market to force large firms to operate with maximum efficiency.

Another recent view is that organizational change may curb managerial discretion. As firms have moved from a unitary (U-form) basis to a multi-divisional (M-form) basis, it has been argued that this change, by eliminating interfunctional dispute and co-ordination failure, favours goal pursuit and least-cost behaviour along profit maximizing lines. ⟨⟩ Motivation. L.T.S.

W. Stewart Howe, *Industrial Economics* (Macmillan, 1978).

Business Policy A general rule or set of rules laid down to guide executives in making their decisions. They are therefore statements of the type, 'When faced with a situation of the type X, always choose course of action A, rather than B or C.'

Policy statements are usually broad and far-reaching in their effect on the company and it may require only a comparatively few such statements to define the character of a company completely. To achieve this complete delineation, policy statements must be made covering three aspects of a company: its objectives, the means by which it intends to achieve these, and the constraints upon it (see p. 49). Policy decisions are more often made as a result of moral, political, aesthetic or personal considerations than as the result of logical or scientific analysis, and are usually made by the owners or the directors of a company rather than by executives at the lower or middle levels.

The subject of business policy had received little systematic thought until recent years when management techniques for use in this area began to be devised (⇨ Corporate Planning; Decision Theory; Company Models). Of these the first is probably the only technique that attempts to systematize all areas of policy, while the latter two tend to be more useful in the area known as strategy (⇨ Strategy; Tactics). There is in fact considerable confusion as to the distinction between policy and strategy but it may be said that policy decisions refer more often to the character or nature that the company wishes to adopt, while strategy refers to the means to be employed in bringing about these desired characteristics.

The three areas of the company in which policy decisions are required are considered under ⇨ Objectives; Means; Constraints, but the following is relevant here. The nature or character of a company – and indeed of every organization of every type – is made up of two elements: the purpose of the organization and how it chooses to go about the task of fulfilling it; this in turn can logically be split into two elements: those actions that it will take to achieve its objectives (i.e. means) and those that it will not take even though they may have helped it to achieve its objectives (i.e. constraints).

The decision as to its objectives must be the first to be taken, for unless these are known, no appropriate strategy can be selected to achieve them. Normally the founders of the company state explicitly or implicitly what the purpose of the company is (and the pursuit of profit must be the main or perhaps the sole purpose of any company), and this decision is unlikely ever to be changed radically, for any major change made to the fundamental objectives of a company may so alter its character that it ceases to be a company as such and becomes instead a charity or a nationalized organization or some other type of organization not having the pursuit of profit as one of its fundamental objectives. It may be possible for changes to be made in some of the less fundamental objectives of a company, but there must be some doubt as to whether an objective that can be altered frequently is an objective at all. In general, the more precisely the objectives are defined, the more accurately can strategy be devised to achieve them, and the more precisely can the progress of a company towards its objectives be judged.

Once the objectives are known, it is then necessary to decide what strategy is to be adopted to achieve them. However, strategic decisions are usually circumscribed by the policy decisions of the owners or directors who may state in broad terms both what may and may not be done: whether, for example, the company is to remain in private hands or seek a public quotation, whether it is to remain independent or to merge, to remain only in the present area of business or to diversify

($\diamond$ Diversification; Patterns of Growth), and if so into what areas of business.

Thus many of these strategic decisions can be, and are, taken at the instigation of the owners or directors on the basis of their own personal inclinations, but such decisions can also be taken as a result of cold analytical calculation in view of all the relevant facts; the extent to which personal as opposed to analytical considerations enter into these decisions depends upon how far the owners or directors feel that the decision is liable to affect the nature or character of the company, and how far the decision can be said to be of purely practical importance. Many decisions, especially those concerned with constraints, can only be regarded as policy – the attitude of the company towards its employees or government officials, for example.

In general, policy decisions are the broad, far-reaching guide-lines laid down by owners or directors to shape the company so as to reflect their personal beliefs as to what sort of a company they wish to run and how it should behave. Strategic decisions, on the other hand, are mainly concerned with the long-term actions necessary to put the policy decisions into effect, and these are usually taken by senior executives after considerable study and rational analysis of the alternatives. A.J.A.A.

John Argenti, *Practical Corporate Planning* (Allen & Unwin, 1980); George A. Steiner, *Strategic Planning: What Every Manager Must Know* (Collier Macmillan, 1979).

Business Risk $\diamond$ Risk and Uncertainty

Business Unionism Trade unionism viewed as a business, with the leader's job to sell his members' labour at the highest obtainable price.

Business unionism is a concept that originated in the USA where trade unionism is concerned almost exclusively with larger wage packets, shorter working hours, better fringe benefits, etc., i.e. with the protection and improvement of the economic position of members rather than with political and social reform. In Britain there has been a mixture of both; throughout the twentieth century many trade unions have supported the Labour Party, financially and otherwise. At the same time, British unions have moved nearer to the business union form.

In so far as it may be said to operate in Britain, business unionism is associated with the changing structure of the trade union movement. New techniques, services and skills have changed the workforce, with increasing emphasis on white-collar and female employment. $\diamond$ White-collar Unions are a twentieth-century phenomenon, and, reflecting the changing political attitudes of their members, are on the whole more interested in business unionism than political commitment to the Labour Party (◊ Trade Union – Politics).

The growth in size of British unions since 1918 is also significant. The larger the membership, the more a union may veer towards business unionism. Increasing size means more professional officials and the danger of lower membership participation, with still greater reliance on full-time officials. In some large unions senior officials may virtually appoint their own successors, a situation quite alien to the theory of British trade-union democracy. If officials get results in terms of larger pay packets, however, the members may well be satisfied. Even the bargaining activities of part-time officers at the level of the workplace (◊ Shop Stewards) clearly evidence an interest in economic rather than political goals, although in the USA much of this would be conducted by full-time union 'business managers'. ◊ Trade Union – Membership; Trade Union – Officers. N.H.C.

D. Q. Mills, *Labor–Management Relations* (McGraw-Hill, 1982).

C

Call Option ◇ Options

Capital (in Accounting and Economics**)** In contrast to income, capital may generally be defined as a stock of wealth, income being a flow of goods and services over a period of time. Capital comprises all material objects and other 'real' assets that form the means of production of goods and services. The conceptual basis of the valuation of economic capital is in terms of the present value of the future services and satisfactions or incomes to be derived from it. ◇ Valuation of Assets.

Accountants use the term capital in somewhat different ways, for instance when referring to:

(1) *Owners' capital.* This is the money amount attributed to the total claim of the owners of the business. This total claim will be equal to the difference between the stated values of assets and liabilities, including debt finance, in a balance sheet. ◇ Claims.

(2) *Classification of expenditure.* Capital expenditure refers to the acquisition of an asset for purposes of increasing the earning power of the business when the earnings benefit is likely to extend over a number of years. Such an expenditure is usually termed a fixed asset and will be subject to depreciation charges. It follows that revenue expenditure is all expenditure other than capital expenditure.

(3) *Asset definition.* For example, fixed capital is used to denote fixed assets and working capital to denote the difference between current assets and current liabilities. This usage is somewhat misleading and reference should be made to assets not capital.

(4) *Capital gains.* These are profits not arising in the 'ordinary course of business'. E.A.L., amended by P.J.A.H.

E. O. Edwards and P. H. Bell, *Theory and Measurement of Business Income* (University of California Press, 1961); I. Fisher, *The Nature of Capital and Income* (Macmillan, 1906; new impression, Kelley, 1970); T. A. Lee, *Income and Value Measurement: Theory and Practice* (Van Nostrand Reinhold, 1982).

Capital Asset Pricing Model (CAPM) This model is central to contemporary thinking in finance since it states that in an efficient capital market the return to be expected from an investment (i.e. the origin of an investment's work) is directly proportional to the degree of ⟨⟩ Systematic Risk (the beta) attaching to it. The CAPM may be expressed as follows:

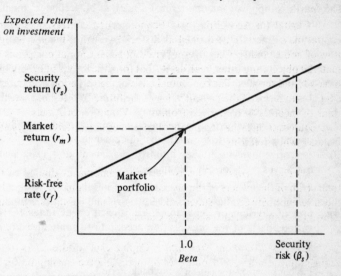

It can be seen that the ⟨⟩ Risk Premium expected on a given security (or other asset) is a product of its beta (β_s) and the market risk premium ($r_m - r_f$), i.e.

expected risk provision for security =
                    security beta × market risk provision
or, algebraically

$$r_s - r_f = \beta(r_m - r_f)$$

Much research has been undertaken into the practical validity of the CAPM and although the results are inconclusive, there is little doubt that the notion of the beta, particularly, is commanding increasing attention by investment analysts and corporate-finance policy-makers.
P.J.A.H.

54   *Capital Budgeting*

Capital Budgeting The investment decision-making procedures of firms. These procedures consist of four principal components: (1) the search for necessary and desirable projects respectively; (2) the evaluation of feasible projects and the specific projects to be implemented; (3) the agreement of the amount to be invested in each accounting period; (4) the economic and financial 'auditing' of past investment decisions so as to improve future decisions.

Satisfactory criteria for evaluating the desirability of investment projects should deal with all of the first three aspects mentioned above. The fourth component may be termed a method of 'feedback' for improving the workings of the criteria.

A number of criteria of varying degrees of sophistication are used in practice, the principal ones being the following:

Qualitative methods (i.e. those that do not use a framework of economic measurement).

(1) Degree of necessity, i.e. investment in the renewal of those capital items that have ceased to function.
(2) 'Squeaky wheel' principle, i.e. investment in the renewal of those items that appear (or sound) most dilapidated.
(3) Executive judgement, i.e. intuitive judgement and experience; executives meet (or otherwise decide) to agree upon a list of projects to be implemented.

Quantitative methods

(4) Size of division or department, i.e. allocation of funds to the various parts of the organization according to some measure of relative size.
(5) Rate of return measure ⟡ Rate of Return.
(6) Payback period measure ⟡ Payback Period.
(7) Discounted cash-flow methods: (a) ⟡ Internal Rate of Return, (b) ⟡ Net Present Value criterion.

The above methods are given in order of increasing sophistication. Methods (1)–(4) do not allow in any scientific way for the important factors affecting the profitability of an investment. The rate of return and payback period measures have defects, and of the two discounted cash-flow methods the present value criterion is generally to be preferred to the internal rate of return approach. E.A.L., amended by P.J.A.H.

H. Bierman and S. Smidt, *The Capital Budgeting Decision* (Collier Macmillan, 1975); A. J. Merrett and A. Sykes, *The Finance and Analysis of Capital Projects* (Longman, 2nd ed., 1973).

Capital, Cost of The cost of capital is the minimum rate of return which an investment project must be expected to earn if it is to be worth while (⟨⟩ Capital Budgeting). This criterion of worthwhileness can only be arrived at in the light of some objective for the investing organization, e.g. maximizing the present value of shareholders' interests in the company; achieving a certain rate of expected dividend to shareholders, etc.

'What is the cost of capital?' This problem causes much controversy amongst academics and financial managers. Basically there are two schools of thought: the traditional school looks upon the cost of capital as the weighted average of the various kinds of equity and debt capital of the firm. It follows from this line of thought that there is an optimal capital structure for a firm. The other school of thought, led by Modigliani and Miller, contends that apart from the taxation aspects of the problem there is no optimal capital structure for a firm and that the cost of capital is equal to the expected rate of return on investment for firms subject to the same degree of risk.

The approaches outlined above are clearly very different from traditional accounting thinking on the cost of capital. Conventionally the accountant has seen this cost as the out-of-pocket interest expense recorded in the profit-and-loss account. According to this view the funds derived from shareholders are viewed as costless, or if dividends are recognized as a cost then retained earnings are costless. A more realistic approach suggests that funds can only be costless if they have no alternative investment opportunities. The cost of capital is then that rate of return on the alternative investment opportunity yielding the highest return. ⟨⟩ Opportunity Cost. However, the presence of financial risk and uncertainty makes measurement of comparable alternatives immensely difficult. ⟨⟩ Risk and Uncertainty. E.A.L.

R. A. Brealey and S. C. Myers, *Principles of Corporate Finance* (McGraw-Hill, 1981).

Capital Market The capital market, through which companies raise the long-term finance necessary for additional investment in plant, factories, working capital, etc., consists of all those institutions concerned with the issue of shares and securities to investors. The principal institutions directly involved are issuing houses, underwriters and stockbrokers. The general function of an issuing house is to act as an intermediary for its client, the company raising capital, whom it sponsors. The issuing house advises the company on all aspects of the issue, in particular on the type of share, debenture or loan stock to issue, the method of issue and the price and other terms of offer. Usually it acts as the main

underwriter to the issue, subsequently sub-underwriting the majority of its risk with institutional investors, e.g. insurance companies and pension funds. The most usual methods of issue are:
(1)   A public issue, by which the company offers its shares or other securities directly to the public.
(2)   An offer for sale, by which the company's shares are sold to an issuing house, which then sells them on its own behalf to the public.
(3)   A placing, whereby the issue advisers 'place', or sell direct, the issued securities to selected clients.
(4)   An offer to existing shareholders, i.e. a 'rights' issue.

   The part of the market that consists of institutions whose role is to provide finance for companies is generally referred to as the primary or new-issue market. The so-called secondary market is simply concerned with trading in corporate securities that have already been issued and that are quoted on the Stock Exchange – either on the main board or the unlisted securities market. Recently a tertiary market has begun to emerge, namely the traded-options market (⟨⟩ Options). This market exists for investors to deal in the value of an option to buy or to sell, for future delivery, certain underlying shares quoted on the secondary market.
E.A.L., amended by P.J.A.H.

> J. Rutterford, *Introduction to Stock Exchange Investment* (Macmillan, 1983); *Money for Business* (Bank of England and City Communications Centre, 1985).

Capital Structure The capital structure of a business can be measured by the ratios of the various kinds of permanent loan and equity capital to total capital. The term 'gearing' is used to refer to the proportion of loan to equity (or alternatively total) capital. 'Financial leverage' is another term used to express the same kind of idea but is sometimes used to measure capital structure in a slightly different way: by the ratio of debt (both short- and long-term) to total ⟨⟩ Assets or alternatively by the ratio of long-term debt to total assets. Whilst both measures of leverage are useful, it can be argued that the first is preferable in that it more clearly measures the risk connected with trading on debt, since current liabilities, as a class of claims, may be regarded also as a permanent part of capital. Clearly the use of leverage carries with it the possibility of higher gains for ordinary shareholders. When the rate of return on total assets exceeds the cost of debt, ordinary shareholders obtain increased returns through leverage but when it is less their returns are reduced by leverage. What is the 'right' amount of leverage must depend heavily on the riskiness and other characteristics of the industry, whether interest charges on loan finance are at fixed or variable rates and, in the case of loans denominated in a foreign currency, the risk of deterioration in the exchange rate of the domestic currency with respect to the foreign currency.

The concepts of leverage and gearing and the idea of financial risk connected with them can be used to formulate alternative theories of the cost of capital and valuation of equities. E.A.L., amended by P.J.A.H.

E. Schwartz, 'Theory of the Capital Structure of the Firm', *Journal of Finance* (14 March 1959).

Capitalism An individual system characterized by the private ownership of resources by individuals or public companies, competition in pursuit of financial profit and minimal regulation of activities by the government.

The term has connotations more emotional than scientific and it is probably reasonable to suggest that it be more properly classified as a political than as an economic concept. Its supporters claim that a capitalist system maximizes production, stimulates enterprise and invention, distributes resources in the most socially advantageous way and results in a high degree of individual freedom. Its critics deny that production for financial profit necessarily results in the most socially desirable utilization of resources, argue that freedom in a capitalist system is heavily dependent on the possession of personal wealth and that the system results in steadily increasing social inequality that is not only unjust but also politically explosive.

This is not the place to attempt an evaluation of the capitalist system but it is relevant to note the tendency for the governments of 'capitalist' countries increasingly to undertake a general direction of the economy, to regulate the activities of private businesses and to make direct provision of social services, particularly in the fields of education, health, housing and welfare. Conversely, 'socialist' countries appear to be tending to permit, even to encourage, a measure of competition amongst production units and to permit market demand a measure of influence on productive resources. I.C.MCG.

J. K. Galbraith, *The Affluent Society* (Houghton Mifflin, 1958); Gordon C. Bjork, *Private Enterprise and Public Interest: The Development of American Capitalism* (Prentice-Hall, 1969); J. K. Galbraith, *The Age of Uncertainty* (BBC/André Deutsch, 1977).

Capitalization Rate ⟡ Price–earnings Ratio

Cash Flow Net cash flow is the difference between the receipts and payments of an organization for a given period of time. ✿ Funds Flow Analysis.

It has been suggested that statements of historic cash flows combined with forecasts of future cash flows should either replace or be published as supplementary information to traditional financial reports. The main arguments in support of this contention relate to the overriding importance of cash to the survival of the company, and the role of cash in the form of expected future dividend payments in the valuation of shareholders' equity (✿ Dividend Policy). It is further suggested that there can be no 'correct' measure of profit, due to the problems of valuation (✿ Valuation of Assets). Net cash flows, in contrast, at least historically, are capable of direct measurement and verification. An argument against cash-flow reporting relates to existing legal requirements in relation to the publication of a profit-and-loss account and balance sheet. However, the main argument relates to the supposed need for a measure of profit, both as an aid to the determination of dividend policy and to assist in judging the efficiency of the organization and management. The timing difference between spending money and obtaining a return combined with annual or biannual reporting periods gives rise to the need to match costs with revenues. Whilst there may be strong arguments against the substitution of statements of cash flow for existing financial reports, there remains considerable merit in arguments for their publication as additional financial information. C.J.J.

R. J. Briston and R. A. Fawthrop, 'Accounting Principles and Investor Protection', *Journal of Business Finance* (Summer 1971); T. A. Lee, 'A Case for Cash Flow Reporting', *Journal of Business Finance* (Summer 1972).

Cell Production The 'cell' system of work organization may be employed in batch production when ✿ Group Technology is adopted. A cell consists of a group of workers and machine tools whose task is the manufacture of one or more groups or families of components. Such cells are often arranged in a manner which facilitates item flow (✿ Mass Production) and because of the difficulty in balancing resources in these cells, workers are generally required to exhibit some flexibility, i.e. to operate more than one machine. If coupled with the delegation of some responsibility for work scheduling, etc., to the workers in the cell, this flexibility may give rise to a form of semi-autonomous work group of the type often advocated in mass production. ✿ Group Working; Group Technology; Flexible Manufacturing System. R.W.

Central Arbitration Committee (CAC) Established under the Employment Protection Act 1975 to deal with breakdowns in negotiations between employers and trade unions. ⇨ Advisory, Conciliation and Arbitration Service. M.J.F.P.

Central Processor ⇨ Computer

Centralization ⇨ Delegation

Certification Officer The post of certification officer was established under section 7 of the Employment Protection Act 1975. The functions of the post involve several responsibilities defined by various pieces of legislation. These include ensuring the observance of political funds, the amalgamation of trade unions, and the review ballots for political expenditure of trade unions under the ⇨ Trade Union Act 1984. M.J.F.P.

Annual Report of the Certification Officer (Certification Office for Trade Unions and Employers' Associations, 1984).

Chain of Command The vertical arrangement of direct authority relationships, also called the 'scaler-chain' or the 'line'. The length of the chain is the number of persons who constitute the superior/subordinate continuum. It is widely considered to be desirable to keep the chain of command as short as possible, otherwise problems of remoteness and rigidity are likely to be experienced. ⇨ Authority; Delegation; Line and Staff (2). I.C.MCG.

Changing Price Levels, Accounting for It has long been recognized that the conventional basis of accounting in terms of historical cost (i.e. in terms of the purchasing power of the pound at the date when an asset was acquired or revalued, a liability was incurred or capital was raised) produces results that may differ significantly from those that take the effects of inflation into account. In recent years the increasing rate of inflation has caused considerable attention to be paid to this problem, the main objective being to put users of financial statements, particularly managements and shareholders, in a better position to appreciate the effects of inflation on costs, profits, depreciation, return on capital, distribution policies (including dividend covers), borrowing powers and future cash requirements.

There are two main methods of taking inflation into account. One method, known as replacement-cost accounting, charges the replacement cost of items wholly or partly used up in the profit-and-loss account. For example if raw materials have risen in value since bought, the amount charged in the profit-and-loss account would be the current cost of buying an equivalent quantity of the same raw materials (whether these were in fact bought or not); as fixed assets would cost more to replace than their original cost, the annual depreciation charge would be increased to cover the replacement cost.

The second method adjusts values for changes in general purchasing power and is frequently referred to as current purchasing power (CPP) accounting. This approach aims to translate historical cost values representing different original purchasing powers into figures of current general purchasing power. The approach is therefore a modification of traditional historic cost accounting. In 1974 the major accounting bodies recommended that a profit-and-loss account and balance sheet, based upon CPP accounting, should be provided as supplementary information in company annual reports.[1] Movements in the retail price index (RPI) were to be taken as the basis for value adjustments. In the preparation of such statements it is important to distinguish between monetary and non-monetary assets and liabilities. Monetary assets and liabilities such as cash, debtors, creditors, debentures, etc., have the same monetary values at a given date irrespective of the valuation base adopted for accounting purposes. Therefore at the balance sheet date the values shown for such assets and liabilities, whether under historic cost accounting or CPP accounting, are the same. It is argued, however, that holding monetary assets and liabilities gives rise to losses and gains in purchasing power over time. Such losses and gains from holding monetary assets or liabilities then represent an adjustment to the profit-and-loss account. Non-monetary items would be revalued for balance sheet purposes according to the movement in the RPI. In the profit-and-loss account, adjustments would be made to sales and cost items also on the basis of RPI changes.

The proposals for CPP accounting led to considerable public debate and were followed by the establishment of a Committee of Inquiry by the then government in 1974. The committee, under the chairmanship of F. E. P. Sandilands, rejected the concept of CPP accounting, stating, '. . . during a period of inflation, historic-cost accounts may have significant deficiencies. However, in the long-term, the CPP method does not remedy these deficiencies and introduces a new set of problems by ex-

---

1. *E.D.8* (1973) and *P S S A P7* (1974) (The Institute of Chartered Accountants in England and Wales).

pressing company accounts in terms of a new unit of measurement.'[1]

The Sandilands report recommended that a new concept of value, namely 'value to the business', be introduced as the basis for accounting (⟡ Valuation of Assets). It concluded that, in the majority of cases, value to the business would be replacement cost, and accordingly recommended that companies adopt an accounting system to be known as current cost accounting. Under this system, non-monetary assets would be valued in accordance with the value to the business concept. Monetary assets and liabilities would be disclosed at their monetary value at the balance sheet date. Sandilands rejected the notion that gains or losses in purchasing power should be calculated, stating,

> Because we are recommending that accounts should continue to be drawn up in terms of monetary units (pounds) it follows that no gains or losses in terms of money can arise solely through holding monetary items when prices are changing. The question as to whether such gains should be classed as profit does not therefore arise as it does when accounts are drawn up in terms of current purchasing power units.[2]

Sandilands further recommended that a figure of operating profit be shown in the profit-and-loss account, which would be calculated after charging the 'value to the business' of assets consumed during the period. Gains from holding assets (holding gains), e.g. from land and buildings, were to be disclosed separately from operating profit, as were any extraordinary gains. The intention was to enable users to distinguish between current-cost profit relating to normal trading activities, and other gains or losses.

The Sandilands proposals were broadly accepted by the major accountancy bodies, who established a committee to prepare a draft accounting standard. The draft standard, *E.D. 18 Current Cost Accounting*, was published in November 1976.

The Accounting Standards Committee issued an accounting standard, *SSAP*.16[3], in March 1980, the purpose of which was to make it mandatory for most companies to publish both historical and current-cost profit-and-loss accounts and balance sheets. This standard has never been fully accepted, and a further exposure draft, *ED*.35[4], was issued in 1984, which attempted to simplify matters. However, in 1985, the

1. *Inflation Accounting: Report of the Inflation Accounting Committee*, Cmnd. 6225 (HMSO, 1975), p. 135.

2. *Inflation Accounting*, p. 163.

3. *SSAP.16, Current Cost Accounting* (Accounting Standards Committee, March 1980).

4. *E.D.35, Accounting for the Effects of Changing Prices*, (Accounting Standards Committee, July 1984).

requirement for companies to comply with *SSAP.16* was suspended and, at the time of writing, a generally accepted solution to the extremely complex problem of accounting for changing price levels has not yet been found. E.A.L., amended by J.V.P.

> W. T. Baxter, *Accounting Values and Inflation* (McGraw-Hill, 1975); *Inflation Accounting: Report of the Inflation Accounting Committee*, Cmnd. 6225 (HMSO, 1975).

Charisma An endowment of outstanding leadership qualities or powers of personality. The term has been taken by sociology from ecclesiastical history, where it meant 'the gift of divine grace'. Some writers, following the sociologist Max Weber, regard charisma as a source of authority. It is suggested, however, that confusion is less likely if charisma be regarded not as a source of authority but as a source of power, as we have defined these terms. In this sense a person with authority will have that authority enhanced if he also possesses charisma, whilst a person lacking authority may yet wield considerable influence over others through the possession of charismatic qualities. The precise qualities which would constitute charisma are likely to vary from one situation to another and, indeed, from one individual to another, and for that reason cannot usefully be enumerated. ⟡ Authority; Power; Leadership. I.C.MCG.

Charter Party A contract between a shipowner and a person wishing to hire the ship, whereby the latter, the charterer, hires or charters the ship for a particular period of time or a specified voyage. The term is derived from the Latin *carta partita* (a split document), which refers to the medieval practice of writing the terms of the contract on a piece of parchment which was then split down the middle, with each party retaining one half of the document.

In an ordinary charter the shipowner retains control over the ship and its crew but has to place the ship at the disposal of the charterer for the purpose and the time stated in the charter party. If the charterer is unable to fill the available capacity of the ship with his own cargo, he may decide to carry the cargoes of other people and for this purpose issue ⟡ Bills of Lading to them. W.F.F.

> *Carver on Carriage by Sea* (Sweet and Maxwell, 1971).

Check-off An arrangement whereby employers deduct trade union contributions from the wages or salaries of members in their employment and pay them over to the union(s) concerned.

Check-off is an American term and others are often employed in Britain, for example 'payroll deductions', 'contribution deduction schemes'. Currently nearly half of all establishments employing manual workers have a check-off system. In nationalized industries and public corporations the practice is nearly universal.

Union attitudes towards the practice have changed in recent years. The collection of contributions either at the branch or by workshop representatives, often ⟡ Shop Stewards, was formerly regarded as a guarantee of union independence and an essential point of contact between members and their union. It has now been realized that this traditional method produces arrears of contributions, accounting and human problems, and a significant loss of revenue. Failure to collect contributions encourages lapsing of membership and problems of qualifications for benefits. The check-off helps to solve such problems and in practice does not on the whole seem to harm union independence or to damage contacts between the union and its members. There is doubt in some cases about its impact on attendances at branch meetings.

Employers are coming to see the check-off as a concession that can be used in ⟡ Collective Bargaining; as an inexpensive gesture of goodwill to trade unions; or as a means of encouraging union financial stability and thus responsible trade unionism.

The check-off appears to have had little effect on the growth or containment of the ⟡ Closed Shop, and it is possible to operate it in a way that safeguards the position of those union members who wish to contract out of the political levy. ⟡ Trade Union – Politics. N.H.C., amended by M.J.F.P.

Royal Commission on Trade Unions and Employers' Associations, Research Papers 8, *Three Studies in Collective Bargaining* (HMSO, 1968); W. W. Daniel and M. Millward, *Workplace Industrial Relations in Britain* (Heinemann, 1983).

CIF Contracts Cost, insurance, freight contracts are contracts for the sale of goods and consist of the seller handing to the buyer the documents that represent the goods. These are the documents that entitle the buyer to claim the goods from the carrier and they include ⟡ Negotiable Instruments, the insurance policy in respect of the goods, the invoice and the necessary consular certificates which prove the origin of the goods. On delivery of the documents by the seller, the buyer has to pay for the goods and he may not delay payment until he has actually taken physical possession of the goods. All expenses at the receiving end, including the cost of unloading and landing the goods and customs duties, have to be borne by the buyer. While the goods are in transit they are at the buyer's risk and he will have to accept the documents and pay for them

even though the goods have been lost, being of course protected by the insurance policy taken out on his behalf by the consignor of the goods. The price of the goods includes all insurance and freight charges, but does not include the above-mentioned expenses to be borne by the buyer.
W.F.F.

D. Sassoon, *C.I.F. and F.O.B. Contracts* (Sweet & Maxwell, 3rd ed., 1984).

Claims (or Equities) Valuable possessions owned by a business are generally called assets. Each asset owned gives rise to a corresponding claim (or equity) which accrues to the person(s) who contributed the funds that enabled the firm to acquire the asset. Claims are classified in a balance sheet either as liabilities or capital. Liabilities arise where the claimant has a non-ownership interest in the organization, that is to say is legally entitled to no more than satisfaction of the debt arising from the asset contributed. Liabilities are usually subdivided into current liabilities – those that are normally payable within one year, e.g. trade and expense creditors – and longer-term liabilities, e.g. debentures and other long-term loans. In financial discussions debentures are often referred to quite realistically as long-term capital, since they typically carry a maturity period of twenty to twenty-five years. Long-term loans will sometimes include convertible loan stock, which is an intermediate form of finance beginning its life as a liability and ending it as capital.

Capital, the other principal claim, is a residual, being generally the excess of the stated value of assets over all liabilities. Clearly capital could also be negative. As defined for balance sheet purposes, it is also referred to as 'the equity' or 'net worth' of the business, and in the case of a limited company is usually classified under the following main categories:

(1) *Issued shares*, representing the claims arising from the capital contributed in the form of cash or other assets by shareholders. Shareholders are classified as ordinary or equity shareholders (common stockholders in the U S) and preference shareholders. Whereas the former are legally entitled to no more than a vote at shareholder meetings, the latter typically enjoy preferred rights to both dividends and capital repayment.

(2) *Capital reserves*, representing claims arising from shareholder contributions, e.g. a share premium account; from profits or a surplus not arising in the 'ordinary course of business', e.g. profits on fixed assets, fixed assets revaluations; or from profits set aside specifically as being available for dividends.

(3) *Retained profits*, representing the balance of profits after all appropriations in respect of dividends, taxes and transfers to reserves have been made.

The principal claim categories are illustrated in the sample below:

Balance sheet at 31 December 1985

	£ 000s	£ 000s
Fixed assets		
Intangible Assets	320	
Tangible Assets	8,640	
Investments	380	9,340
Current Assets		
Stocks	3,855	
Debtors	4,250	
Investments	60	
Cash at bank and in hand	1,150	
Prepayments	150	
	9,465	
Creditors: amounts falling due within one year	3,450	
Net current assets		6,015
Total assets less current liabilities		£15,355
Creditors: amounts falling due after more than one year		
Debenture loans	2,300	
Bank loans, etc.	200	2,500
Capital and reserves		
Share capital	5,000	
Capital reserves	5,480	
Retained profits	2,375	12,855
		£15,355

The format of the balance sheet is prescribed in the Companies Act 1985. E.A.L., amended by J.V.P. and P.J.A.H.

Classical Organization Theory The approach to the development of organizational theory that is exemplified by the writings of, most notably, Henri Fayol, Luther Gulick, L. F. Urwick, J. D. Mooney and A. C. Reiley. The approach is characterized by an attempt to identify the important elements in the process of administration and the features common to administrative structures so that a set of principles that would serve as a guide to good practice can be developed. Recognizing the considerable advantages accruing from the division of labour, the classical theorists sought to ascertain the basis or bases on which such a division should take place and the most effective means of ensuring the co-ordination and unified direction of the organizational sections thus created. Considerable emphasis is placed on the precise definition of tasks and of the relationships between tasks. Control is achieved through a reliance on a system of checks and the use of authority.

The writings of the classical theorists have fallen into some disfavour. The principles that they advanced proved to be of less value than was hoped; they were not always consistent one with another and some were little more than exhortations. There was too much concern with what ought to be and this tended to inhibit the more rigorous investigation of actual behaviour and its causes and consequences. Without such investigation the attempt to formulate principles of universal application was premature. It may be suggested that the main contribution of the classical writers was threefold: (1) they pioneered the idea that management was a suitable subject for intellectual analysis; (2) they developed a set of concepts and a terminology that have provided a foundation on which subsequent theorists have built; (3) criticism of their work has stimulated the recent rapid growth in the number of empirical studies of organizational behaviour. ⟫ Henri Fayol; Organization Theory; Scientific Management. I.C.MCG.

E. Dale, *Management: Theory and Practice*, Pt. 3 (McGraw-Hill, 1965); O. S. Pugh, D. J. Hickson and C. R. Hinings, *Writers on Organizations* (Penguin, new ed., 1983).

Closed Shop A workplace in which a job is only to be obtained and retained if employees become and remain members of a particular trade union, or of one of a specified number of trade unions.

The closed shop affects about 5·2 million workers, approximately 23 per cent of all employees. The practice increased in the late 1960s and early–mid 1970s but by 1980 compulsory unionism had come to exist in most areas where conditions were conducive to it.

The closed shop is prevalent among craftsmen, traditionally groups wishing to protect their skill monopoly; casual workers, where there is little or no job security, for example, seamen, dockers, wholesale market workers and film and television technicians; trades with a high labour turnover and/or problems of contact, for example, building workers, engineering workers, road haulage workers and miners; process workers in iron and steel manufacture where historically there were union re-cognition problems; musicians and other artists in the entertainment industry where there are wide fluctuations in the demand for labour, little job security and frequent unemployment; employees of co-operative societies and some local authorities that have employer-initiated closed shops.

In the 1970s the closed shop spread to new industries in the manu-facturing sector (which accounted for 30 per cent of net growth); food, drink and tobacco, clothing and footwear, chemical and allied industries, and coal and petroleum products were the industries most affected. It also increasingly penetrated the nationalized industries (a quarter of all closed shops are in these industries, with three-quarters of all employees being covered by closed-shop arrangements). There are currently at least 1·1 million non-manual workers in closed shops, compared with 300,000 in the early 1960s.

The two main forms are the 'pre-entry closed shop' (USA – 'closed shop'), where workers have to join the union or be accepted by it before they can be engaged by the employer; and the 'post-entry closed shop' (USA – 'union shop'), where the employer is free to engage non-unionists so long as they agree to join the union immediately or shortly after engagement. The pre-entry closed shop (16 per cent of all cases) is associated with job-entry control by a trade union and can affect all grades of worker from the skilled to the relatively unskilled. In the case of skilled work where accredited apprenticeship is a necessary qualifi-cation for the job, the union may limit entry to its membership to qualified apprentices and then seek to limit the number of apprentices trained, bargaining with employers to get a fixed proportion of appren-tices to trained craftsmen. This form is known as the 'craft-qualification shop'. The case of relatively unskilled work is known as the 'labour-supply closed shop'. Sometimes the ⚌ Check-off is a substitute for the closed shop, but in practice they often complement each other.

Variations in the manner of enforcement of the closed shop range from the formally recognized closed shop, which is the subject of a written agreement between union and employer; the informally recog-nized variety with no agreement but a possible screening by management for union membership of applicants for jobs; to the union-enforced closed shop, where the employer is not prepared to agree to the practice and union members refuse to work with non-members. In some cases managements have forced the closed shop on their employees.

Application of the closed shop varies widely in scope. Sometimes the most that is involved in refusing to belong to a union is the loss of a particular job in a particular location; by agreeing to be moved to a similar job within the same works the employee can evade the effects of the closed shop. Where an entire plant is affected there may be variations in the prevalence of the closed shop from one plant to another within the same town or region. There are relatively few occupations comprehensively closed to the non-unionist throughout the UK; printing is one of them.

When participating in job regulation, unions have three objectives: to maximize membership, to discipline membership in relation to union workplace rules, and to control entry to the job. Thus the closed shop cannot be explained simply by reference to its relative disadvantages to employers, or in terms of union solidarity. It should be seen as a device that unions want to assist in dealing with particular problems concerned with organizing, controlling, or excluding specific categories of worker. This explains why some groups with a high density of union organization do not insist on the closed shop; it also provides a reason for its complexity of type. It is designed to solve pressing and immediate problems and it cannot guarantee that no future organizational problems arise. Unions with a closed-shop tradition may be helped, hindered, or even destroyed by changes in technology, markets or leadership.

While from the trade union point of view it may be functionally necessary, operation of the closed shop sometimes results in the restriction of individual liberty and it may have disadvantageous economic effects. In its pre-entry form it is sometimes used to deny whole classes of worker the right to compete for particular jobs. American experience indicates that the practice cannot be eliminated by legal enactment.

Like any other union demand, the closed shop can be the subject of ⟨⟩ Collective Bargaining. Management may demand, for example, a limitation of the right to strike in exchange for recognition, and in several industries formal recognition has been accompanied by an arbitration agreement containing a no-strike clause. It is also sometimes encouraged by management as a useful component in the reform of ⟨⟩ Workplace Bargaining, the success of which depends on the shop floor conforming to formal agreements and practices. Strikes to impose or maintain the closed shop are a fraction of all strikes but are a rough indication of demands for the practice and employer resistance to it (⟨⟩ Strike – Statistics). The practice is not a historical relic, but an increasingly common contemporary phenomenon.

Some members of the professions, such as teachers, are also trade union members and their position in relation to the closed shop is similar to that of other trade unionists. The majority of professional workers are not members of a trade union, but some professions operate practices analogous to the closed shop. In the case of barristers and veterinary surgeons, for example, membership of their respective associations is a condition of employment. In the case of registered professions, monopoly resides in those on the state-held register. Even without legal monopoly, institutional monopolistic advantages accrue to associations that can make membership a hallmark of qualification. All unregistered professions are prone to the closed shop. ⟨⟩ Profession.

The legal status of closed shops has changed substantially over the years. The ⟨⟩ Industrial Relations Act 1971, repealed in 1974, made void all pre-entry closed-shop arrangements and agreements. By contrast the ⟨⟩ Trade Union and Labour Relations Acts 1974 and 1976 reinforced the closed-shop situations by their support for the concept of the 'union-membership agreement or arrangement'. The situation changed again under the ⟨⟩ Employment Act 1980. Any person employed or seeking employment in a job where it is the practice to require membership of a trade union is now given the right not to have an application for membership unreasonably refused and the right not to be unreasonably expelled from the union. Complaints before industrial tribunals are judged on the grounds of equity and the merits of the case, and not merely on the basis of being consistent with procedures laid down in union rule books.

This statutory protection is further strengthened by the ⟨⟩ Employment Act 1982. This stipulates that the dismissal of an employee for non-union membership under a closed shop is unfair where the employee concerned has obtained a declaration from the courts of either unreasonable expulsion or of expulsion from the union under the 1980 Act, or where he or she has an application for such a declaration pending. This provision increases the chances of an individual retaining or regaining his or her job. Moreover, in their judgments, tribunals now have to take into consideration the *Code of Practice on Closed Shop Agreements and Arrangements* and are able to award higher levels of compensation than were allowed for under the 1980 Act. N.H.C., amended by M.J.F.P.

S. Dunn and J. Gennard, *The Closed Shop in British Industry* (Macmillan, 1984).

Coding and Classification ⟨⟩ Group Technology

Collective Agreements in Law The question whether English law *should* treat collective agreements as binding contracts has been a recurrent theme in the debate on industrial-relations reform for more than twenty years. In 1969 the High Court held that collective agreements were not normally legally binding because neither side *intended* them to be enforceable by legal sanction. Subsequently the position changed when the Industrial Relations Act 1971 introduced a statutory presumption that collective agreements made in writing after the Act *were* intended to be enforced in the courts, except where the collective agreement itself specifically provided otherwise. In fact most agreements made during the life of the Act did so provide, with the result that the 1971 Act brought no significant practical change. The 1971 Act was repealed in 1974 by the Trade Union and Labour Relations Act, which currently provides that no collective agreement, or part of one, shall be enforceable unless it is in writing and contains a clause that expressly declares that the parties intend it to be treated as a legally binding contract.

A number of agreements made in recent years between some British unions and a number of 'high-tech' (usually foreign-owned) companies contain what appear to be legally binding promises. In return for 'no-strike' and 'binding-arbitration' clauses, such agreements usually concede sole bargaining rights to the union in question, as well as containing commitments on job security and staff status for all workers. Whether such deals herald a general change of attitude towards legal enforceability is an open question. Further statutory change may force the pace in this area. The House of Commons Select Committee on Employment recommended in 1981 that the introduction by law of binding disputes procedures should be treated as a matter of legislative priority.

Even though most current collective agreements are not directly enforceable as contracts between employer and union, many of them may, none the less, acquire a certain legal force by being expressly or implicitly incorporated into contracts of employment – in this event the employer and each individual employee acquire legal rights and duties. ◊〉 Collective Bargaining. K.W.

Sir Otto Kahn-Freund, *Labour and the Law* (Stevens & Sons, 3rd ed. by P. Davies and M. Freedland, 1983), ch. 6.

Collective Bargaining Group, as opposed to individual, bargaining about wages and salaries and/or conditions of work in the widest sense. The parties are, on the one hand, trade unions, groups within them or federations of them, and an employer, the employer's representatives, or an employers' association or federation on the other. ◊〉 Employers' Association; Federation; Trade Union.

In the private sector three quarters of employees have their pay determined by some sort of arrangement between employers and trade unions, and the bulk of the public sector's workforce is covered by collective bargaining agreements. However, there is considerable variation in the extent of collective bargaining by occupational level in the two sectors. Whereas over 90 per cent of managers, professionals, and non-manual workers in the public sector have their pay and conditions affected by collective bargaining, only a minority of their colleagues in the private sector are covered by such arrangements. It is also likely that those employees not covered by collective bargaining have their wages and salaries greatly influenced by the level of remuneration of comparable workers who are covered. ⟨⟩ Wage; Wage Systems.

Collective bargaining takes place at a number of levels: at the level of the workplace, between ⟨⟩ Shop Stewards and plant management (often called ⟨⟩ 'Workplace Bargaining' or 'plant bargaining'); at the level of the company or other establishment, between union(s) and management ('company bargaining'); and at the level of the industry, between a union or federation of unions and an employers' association or federation of employers' associations. International bargaining, as between an international trade union federation and a multinational company, exists in embryonic form.

Historically collective bargaining in Britain has evolved from bargaining at the level of the workplace and small firm in the eighteenth and early nineteenth centuries, to district bargaining later in the nineteenth century, so-called 'national' bargaining for the whole industry between the two world wars, and a mix of industry-wide, company and workplace bargaining since 1945, with the last two types reasserting themselves strongly. Company and workplace bargaining are most typical of industries that operate substantially on piece rates and financial incentives of various kinds. They may be characterized by 'effort bargaining', where the amount of work to be done for a given wage becomes as negotiable as the wage itself, and, irrespective of the wage system involved, they may include ⟨⟩ Productivity Bargaining. ⟨⟩ Motivation.

The Royal Commission on Trade Unions and Employers' Associations, 1968, indicated the declining effectiveness of industry-wide bargaining in determining actual pay levels and the significance of company and workplace bargaining.

The wide autonomy of managers in individual companies and work situations and the power of work groups comprise an informal industrial-relations system in some industries substantially in conflict with the formal system of industry-wide organizations that assume capability of imposing their decisions on members. Often informal bargaining in the factory is of equal or greater importance than the matters in industry agreements. The latter tend to cover a narrow range of issues, such as basic wage rates and basic conditions of work, whereas the range in the informal system is much wider, including financial incentives, discipline, work practices, recruitment and redundancy. The informal system consists largely of tacit arrangements and understandings, in custom and practice, although written plant and company ⟨⟩ Procedural Agreements have tended to grow in number. The formal system assumes that collective bargaining is a matter of reaching written agreements. ⟨⟩ Group; Recruitment; Redundancy; Restrictive Labour Practices; Shop Steward; Wage Drift.

Industry-wide collective bargaining, then, comprises a formal set of relationships and institutions. In many industries the collective bargaining committee composed of employer and trade union representatives, by whatever name it is known, has been developed on a voluntary basis and often by a process of collective bargaining. There is a statutory obligation laid on each of the nationalized industries to set up a collective bargaining system. In some industries the parties come together *ad hoc* to bargain, while in others there are standing arrangements. This last is true for those industries which adopt the ⟨⟩ Joint Industrial Council model.

For industries that the state has judged in need of support in the field of collective bargaining, ⟨⟩ Wages Councils or similar bodies, e.g. Agricultural Wages Boards, have been established by law as minimum wage-fixing bodies. These have some of the characteristics of voluntary collective bargaining in that they involve negotiations between representatives of managements and of unions in the industries concerned with a view to reaching agreement. The main differences are that statutory bodies also contain independent members whose votes can settle an issue in the event of a disagreement between the main parties, and their awards are legally binding and are enforced by an inspectorate on the staff of the ⟨⟩ Department of Employment.

In recent years there have been appreciable changes in the levels at which collective bargaining is conducted. The 1970s witnessed a dramatic increase in bargaining at establishment or plant level (in over half of British firms this became the most important bargaining level for manual workers' pay). However, in the 1980s there was a decline in establishment-level bargaining and an increase in 'no bargaining'. Above all, there was an interesting growth in company-level bargaining *above* plant level (in over a quarter of British firms this is the most significant level of bargaining for the pay of manual workers). In the public sector, however, centrally negotiated agreements have remained the dominant bargaining arrangements.

Sometimes collective bargaining results in deadlock. The parties may then avail themselves of ⟨⟩ Conciliation or arbitration. Conciliation (or 'mediation' as it should more properly be called) is the process of bringing the parties in a dispute together and of inducing them to bargain. An industry may provide conciliation services for itself on an *ad hoc* basis, but more usually an employers' association, a union or a company traditionally called on the services of the Department of Employment. This role has now been taken over by the ⟨⟩ Advisory, Conciliation and Arbitration Service. Conciliation officers from A C A S attend to thousands of cases at company level each year. Arbitration is a means of making an independent decision on the merits of the case put by both parties. An industry may set up its own arbitration system to provide for those cases where collective bargaining results in deadlock and this provision may be built into the national agreement. Alternatively the parties might avail themselves of the state provision of a hearing by a single arbitrator, by a Board of Arbitration, or by the ⟨⟩ Central Arbitration Committee, formerly the Industrial Court. Disputes and other problems that do not lend themselves to treatment by conciliation or arbitration may be of sufficient public importance to merit an inquiry. The D E's role in these matters and the officers and institutions concerned were all transferred to A C A S in 1974.

The objective of all these devices ancillary to the original voluntary system of collective bargaining is to support the voluntary system and to make it work. The law, however, intervenes in the voluntary collective bargaining system. Under the ⟨⟩ Employment Protection Act of 1975, a claim could be made to A C A S where it appeared that an employer was not observing terms or conditions of employment established for the industry, but this is now void following the abolition of schedule 11. An award by A C A S requires the employer to observe the recognized terms or conditions of the industry and such award becomes an implied term of the employment contracts of the workers concerned.

The British system of collective bargaining developed in a piecemeal and haphazard fashion but nevertheless came to contain certain principles:

(1) It took priority over other methods of external job regulation, for example tripartite regulation, as in wages councils and state regulation.

(2) It has not been made the subject of much legal regulation compared with similar systems, for example in the U S A.

(3) It has accorded priority to voluntary principles and keeping third party intervention to a minimum.

74   *Colour*

(4)   The parties to collective bargaining have generally preferred to
       build their relations on procedural rules (i.e. the 'machinery' for
       joint negotiation, its constitution and its procedure) rather than
       on substantive rules about systematic structures for wages, rights
       and obligations attached to jobs.

Preference for procedural rules is exemplified by 'open-ended'
agreements, which are revised only under pressure from one of the parties
and by a wide range of accepted but uncodified practices.

British collective bargaining is dissimilar to that of most European
countries in not distinguishing between 'conflicts of interest' (disputes
over changes in the existing provisions of agreements), and 'conflicts of
right' (concerning the application, interpretation or observance of these
provisions). N.H.C., amended by M.J.F.P.

Advisory, Conciliation and Arbitration Service, *Collective Bargaining in
Britain* (ACAS, 1983); E. Batstone, *Working Order* (Blackwell, 1984); W.
Brown (ed.), *The Changing Contours of British Industrial Relations*
(Blackwell, 1981); W. W. Daniel and N. Millward, *Workplace Industrial
Relations in Britain* (Heinemann, 1983).

Colour The retina of the eye is made up of two types of receptors,
rods and cones. The former, of which there are about 130 million, respond to light in the spectral range 400–650 millimicrons, but yield no
sensation of colour. The cones, of which there are only about 7 million,
require higher brightness intensities before they are activated but are
sensitive to a wider portion of the spectrum, i.e. 400–750 millimicrons.
They provide colour sensation. ⟐ Threshold.

Colour is described in terms of three dimensions: hue is the subjective
correlate of the predominant wavelength; brightness corresponds to the
intensity of stimulation; saturation determines the degree of difference
between a particular colour and a grey of the same level of brightness – a
well saturated colour is far removed from grey.

Green, red and blue are the three primary colours. They may be added
together to form others. If, for example, a red and a green patch are
projected simultaneously on the same area, the result is yellow. If blue is
added, the result is white. This notion of mixing *colours* should be distinguished from that of mixing *pigments*. The latter process, which is essentially a subtractive rather than an additive one, produces quite different
effects.

Considerations of colour are relevant both to visual performance and
comfort, in addition to having certain special applications.

The luminance emitted by a surface is a function of the reflecting characteristics of that surface as well as of the illumination ⇨ Brightness. Thus the darker the colour of objects, the more incident light is required for detail to be clearly perceived. Contrast between figure and ground also facilitates visibility, and judicious use of colour can be put to good effect.

The general pleasantness of the visual environment depends a good deal upon the use of suitable colours. Hot work may be relieved by the use of 'cool' colours. Conversely in a cold environment the 'warm' colours produce a pleasing effect.

For purposes of certain types of sorting, matching and inspection processes, appropriate lighting may be of vital importance.

Colour is widely used for coding signal lights, pipes and cables. ⇨ Colour Blindness; Vision. E.E.

Colour Blindness Total colour blindness, in the sense that only brightness is present in the sensation of light, is extremely rare. This monochromatism may be due either to a congenital nonfunctioning of the retinal cones, or due to an acquired abnormality in the eye or optic nerve. In the latter case, reactions to brightness are fairly normal, whereas in the former case the patient can only tolerate lights of low brightness.

Far more common are the various forms of dichromatic vision. In both protanopia and deuteranopia there is confusion of red and green. In tritanopia and tetratanopia the confusion is between blue and yellow.

The figure below compares the spectral colours seen by the normal person with those seen by the various types of dichromatics.

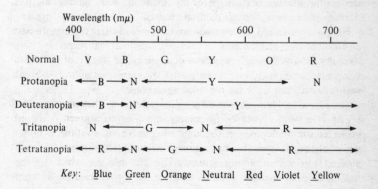

Key: Blue   Green   Orange   Neutral   Red   Violet   Yellow

The figure shows, in simplified form, the differences between normal colour sensation and anomalous colour vision. In addition to differences in perceived hue, there may also be brightness differences as a function of wavelength.

Numerous tests of colour vision are available, the best known being the Ishihara isochromatic plates.

There is a tendency for persons with anomalous colour vision to be reluctant to admit the defect. This reluctance seems absent in persons who have other visual defects such as long-sightedness. E.E.

Commercial Law Also called mercantile law, this does not form a distinct part of English law, being an artificial combination of all those parts of English law that have relevance for commercial transactions. It has its foundations in the general law of contract and then branches out into those particular contracts that have special commercial significance, i.e. ⟡ Sale of Goods; Agency; Partnership; Insurance Law; Transportation Method; Negotiable Instruments. ⟡ Bankruptcy Law and ⟡ Company Law are also sometimes included under this umbrella.

Historically commercial law originated in the customs of the foreign traders who in medieval days provided the trade links between England and the outside world. These traders, who came mainly from the eastern shores of the Mediterranean, brought their commercial customs with them and were allowed to operate these in their own courts in the so-called staple towns, where they had established their English head-quarters. Some of the customs were followed also by home traders who took them round the country while attending local fairs. Here again, special courts, known as *pie powder* courts, were available to administer instant justice in commercial disputes.

Lord Mansfield, Lord Chief Justice of the King's Bench Court in the late eighteenth century, is generally credited with having merged commercial customs into the common law of England, mainly by using special juries of merchants to settle the customs so that their nature had not to be proved in each case.

Similar developments have taken place in other countries and there exist probably fewer differences between the commercial laws of different legal systems than there do for any other branch of law. The original customs have been supplemented by international treaties on particular aspects of commercial law (e.g. air transport, protection of industrial property) and where these treaties have been received into the national laws of countries there exists a large measure of identity of law, which is so necessary for healthy international trade. The next step will be for the customs of international trade to be given legal force within the legal systems of the main trading nations and agreement on this may not be far away.

Commercial law is sometimes distinguished from business law, which, while dealing with the same topics as commercial law, is more concerned with the practical application of legal principles, studied against their economic and social background. More recently still, the term 'economic law' has been applied to those legal rules concerned with state intervention in the processes of commerce and industry, e.g. the control of monopolies and consumer protection. W.F.F., amended by J.C.E.M.

Schmitthoff and Sarre (eds.), *Charlesworth's Mercantile Law* (Stevens & Sons, 14th ed., 1984).

Common Stock ⟡ Claims

Communication The process of transmitting or exchanging abstractions such as ideas or beliefs through the use of symbols – usually, but not necessarily, language.

Communication is an essential element in any co-operative activity and is of supreme importance in the large industrial organization for the motivation and co-ordination of those involved in its highly specialized and interdependent divisions and subdivisions. Furthermore in the formal organization the need for good communications is particularly enhanced by the fact that those first perceiving the need for action are seldom those with the authority to initiate the action. Despite the fact that systems of communication may be carefully and elaborately prescribed, there must be very few large organizations in which communications are generally considered to be satisfactory. This is hardly surprising, as the barriers to effective communication are formidable. They include the problems of selectivity and timing to ensure the transmission of an unambiguous message at the most appropriate moment, the possibility of distortion during transmission and the psycho-social context within which the communication takes place and which so influences the interpretation of the message.

Upward communication in an authority hierarchy and communication between persons of widely dissimilar status are both particularly liable to distortion. Recognition of the need to strengthen the channels of upward communication has led to the establishment of techniques such as suggestion schemes and joint consultative and negotiating bodies using a representative system. ⟡ Authority; Communication Networks; Co-ordination; Information Theory; Social Distance; Status. I.C.MCG.

P. M. Blau and W. R. Scott, *Formal Organisations* (Routledge & Kegan Paul, 1963), ch. 5; Michael Lillico, *Managerial Communication* (Pergamon, 1972); C. B. Handy, *Understanding Organizations* (Penguin, 1981).

Communication Networks Patterns or channels of communication.

Communication networks have been the subject of a number of experiments designed to test the effectiveness of different networks in a variety of problem-solving situations. Typically the experimental group consists of five persons confronted with a devised task, the successful completion of which requires communication amongst all five members. Various patterns of two-way communication are established (or, in some experiments, one-way communication) and it has been found that the pattern of communication employed by the group affects both the group's ability to perform its task and the morale of its members. Some examples of two-way communication networks are:

Circle   Chain   Wheel

Given a fairly simple task, the 'wheel' was consistently quicker and more accurate than either of the others. The person situated at position A, the hub of the communication system, almost invariably emerged as the leader. The 'circle', on the other hand, was slower and more erratic. No one position could be identified as providing a leader. The 'chain' was slowest and, on the whole, least effective. The person at position C, the most central, consistently emerged as leader. However, in terms of the satisfaction and interest of the group members, the 'circle' was much more effective than either of the other two patterns. Furthermore, when the groups were faced with more complicated tasks involving the transmission of ambiguous information, the 'circle' network enabled its group to adapt more readily so that they quickly achieved their previous level of performance. The 'wheel', with its pattern of centralized control, inhibited the adaptation of the group to its changed situation.

The different characteristics of the 'wheel' and 'circle' networks have been compared to the mechanistic and organic system of management. ⟡ Mechanistic and Organic Management. I.C.MCG.

H. J. Leavitt, *Managerial Psychology*, (University of Chicago Press, 1967), ch. 15; J. A. Litterer, *The Analysis of Organizations*, ch. 14 (J. Wiley, 1965); R. Klauss and B. M. Bass, *Interpersonal Communication in Organizations* (Academic Press, 1982).

Communication System/Network ⟡ Telecommunications

Communication Theory ⟡ Information Theory

Communism and Trade Unions ⟡ Trade Union – Communism

Company Bargaining ⟡ Collective Bargaining; Workplace Bargaining

Company Law A company is in law a type of corporation, i.e. a collection of persons who have combined for some common purpose and who are treated by law as a person with rights and duties distinct from those of its individual members. Thus, a company differs from a ⟡ Partnership in that the company is a legal person enjoying perpetual succession so that it does not come to an end through the death of any of its members.

Companies may be either chartered (established by royal charter), or statutory (created by Act of Parliament) or registered (formed under the Companies Act 1985 or earlier Acts). Registered companies are by far the most important numerically. They are further subdivided into public and private companies. Since 1980, to bring English law into line with EEC directives, the criterion for establishing whether a company is a public company or a private company has been that a public company must state that it is such in its memorandum, end its name with 'public limited company' or PLC (or the Welsh equivalent) and have a minimum share capital, currently £50,000. A private company is any company that is not a public company and there is no longer any restriction on the maximum number of its members. Both private and public companies need a minimum of two members.

Registered companies are also divided into limited and unlimited companies. In an unlimited company, which is very rare, members have unlimited liability for the debts of the company, while in a limited company the liability of members is limited either by shares or by guarantee. In the former the members' liability is restricted to the amount, if any, unpaid on the shares they each hold, while in the latter members have to contribute towards the assets of the company only when it is being wound up and only to the extent of the guarantee that they have accepted at the time of the company's formation.

A registered company is formed by its name being included on the register of companies kept by the Registrar of Companies. In order to secure registration, the promoters of the company have to submit to the Registrar certain documents, the most important of which are the Memorandum and the Articles of Association. The Memorandum outlines the name, objects and capital of the company, while the Articles

describe the proposed internal government of the company and the
relationship between the company and its members.

A public company must deposit further documents, and the company
cannot begin trading until it has received a certificate from the Registrar
of Companies to the effect that it has satisfied the new capital requirements of public companies and that it has received at least one
quarter of the nominal value of each issued share, plus the whole of any
premium payable.

Small and medium-sized private companies do not have to prepare
and disclose accounts to the extent required of public companies, insurance, banking and shipping companies,which have extensive duties
in this respect.

The Companies Act 1985 was a long-awaited consolidation of legislation that had been greatly amended in recent years in the light of EEC
requirements. It deals, *inter alia*, with the formation of a company and
the issuing, increase and reduction of capital; accounts and audit requirements; distribution of profits and assets; directors' duties and
restrictions on them in matters such as share dealing; company administration and procedure, including maintenance of the register of
members and the conduct of meetings; the outside investigation of a
company's activities; appointment of receivers, liquidators and the
winding up of the company's affairs. However, further EEC directives
remain to be implemented and two additional Acts deal with related
topics, i.e., The Company Securities (Insider Dealing) Act 1985 and the
Business Names Act 1985. W.F.F., amended by J.C.E.M.

Palmer's Company Law (Stevens & Sons, 23rd ed. by C. M. Schmitthof,
1983).

Company Models A wide variety of very sophisticated computer
models may now be purchased off-the-shelf from software companies.
The availability of spreadsheet programs also allows executives with
adequate knowledge to devise their own models on a personal computer.
Such models may range from financial models of a company, or of a
group of companies, to a model of the market – showing market shares,
price elasticities, imports, etc. – or of product life-cycles and so forth.
Most computer programs provide goal-seeking, 'What if?' questioning
and other useful facilities. A.J.A.A.

Thomas H. Naylor and Michele H. Mann, *Computer-Based Planning
Systems* (Planning Executives Institute, Ohio, 1982).

Company Union A company (or house) union is an organization of employees instituted or supported by their employer, who thereby effectively controls the membership, representation, business and consequently the power of the organization. It is not a bona fide trade union.

Company unions violate the provisions of International Labour Convention No. 98 (⟡ International Labour Organization), which has been ratified by the U K.

In Britain company unions were set up on a fairly large scale after the General Strike in 1926, often in the form of non-union works committees. There is also a strong link with the ⟡ Joint Consultation stream of industrial relations, which has in the past been used by some firms as a means of preventing the development of independent trade unions. Company unions are now chiefly to be found in white-collar employments (⟡ Trade Union Types – White-collar Union). N.H.C., amended by M.J.F.P.

Competition The idea of competition and the nature of an economy in which it is prevalent has exercised a powerful hold over economic and political theorists for many years. It finds its earliest expression in the writings of Adam Smith: 'Every individual endeavours to employ his capital so that its produce may be of greatest value. He generally neither intends to promote the public interest, nor knows how much he is promoting it. He intends only his own security, only his own gain. And he is in this led by an INVISIBLE HAND to promote an end which was no part of his intention. By pursuing his own interest he frequently promotes that of society more effectively than when he really intends to promote it.' Adam Smith, *Wealth of Nations*, 1776.

Later economists developed the thoughts of Adam Smith into the model of perfect competition (⟡ Market Models), whilst many politicians have craved for a society in which the good of society was promoted through the active pursuit of self-interest by its members. The competitive economy is usually seen as one in which there are few great concentrations of economic power, either in firms or trade unions, and in which the consumer is 'king'. Thus we find the following passage in the writings of the late Senator Estes Kefauver: 'At least up to now no better system has been devised to protect the public than the competitive system. . . . The distinct advantage of the market as the instrument of control is that, in its way, it constitutes a form of representative government. It allows the massive aggregate of the country's consumers to vote their preferences by extending or withholding their custom. And where there is a multitude of independent producers each vying for business, there need be no cause for concern.' Estes Kefauver, *In a Few Hands* (Penguin Books, 1966).

Within such an economy there may appear to be little room for the trade union, the large firm or massive advertising. The practical benefits of such an economy are not so apparent, however, if we consider those industries in most countries that reproduce most closely the competitive conditions. Thus agriculture frequently needs government assistance and the same is true of the cotton industry and sections of the coal industry. Nor must we ignore the fact that resources are not fully mobile, that economies of large-scale production are available in many industries, and that trade unions give individual workers power *vis-à-vis* their employer. All this is merely to suggest that we must not hold too rigid a conception of a competitive economy, for it is perfectly possible for there to be more effective competition in an industry of four producers than in one of forty. Equally well, of course, there could be less. Thus both the UK and the US can be called competitive economies, for in both the dominant spirit is that of competition. Some industries have a large number of firms, whilst some have only a handful; some industries are state-owned monopolies, whilst others are heavily subsidized. In both countries the Government, through its anti-monopoly and anti-restrictive practices legislation (⟡ Monopoly Policy; Restrictive Practices) tries to ensure that competition is not stifled and that large blocs of economic power are not allowed to be run in ways contrary to the national interest. Both Governments also try to ensure that the pursuit of self-gain is moderated when it threatens the welfare of groups in society or geographical areas in the country (⟡ Location of Industry; Regional Problems). These features will be found to be common to most competitive economies. L.T.S.

Competitive Problems Since the UK's economy is based on the ideal of private enterprise, it is platitudinous to note that in many business situations the outcome of a decision taken by a given company may be affected by a decision taken by its competitors. Examples of competitive situations are the bidding for a specific contract and the pricing and advertising of one's products in the open market. Game theory has been developed to provide a useful conceptual framework for considering these problems but, unfortunately, its development has been too limited to solve any real-life problems. An extension of this theory, known as statistical ⟡ Decision Theory, has been of greater value.

A technique that has been of value both in the military and the business context is known as operational gaming. This is a variant on the simulation technique (⟡ Simulation) and the nineteenth-century German *Krieg Spiel* (war game). Two or more teams play each other in a game. The structure of the competitive situation or rules of the game is built into a computer program. The interactions between the players (that is,

strategies pursued by the teams) are evaluated by the computer and reported back to the teams. As the game develops, using the experience built up, the teams try to improve their strategies in an effort to reach a winning position. Although the games lack psychological realism (e.g. managers playing a game would know that a serious mistake will not really bankrupt their 'firm'), it is believed that they can be of value in determining the possible outcome in novel competitive situations. For example this technique has been used to try to predict the introduction of a new product into a market. Two teams were formed, one representing the sponsors of the product and the other representing the competitors. The sponsors tried to pursue strategies that maximized the market share of the product and their competitors tried to prevent this.
M.J.C.M.

P. G. Moore, *Basic Operational Research* (Pitman, 1976).

Computer In a managerial context this term usually refers to an electronic digital stored-program computer. Its characteristics are:
(1)   It performs arithmetic operations (adds, subtracts, multiplies and divides) and a limited number of logical operations on a set of numerical (digital) data – that is, it performs computations and is hence known as a computer.
(2)   It is ordered to perform these operations by a sequence of instructions, or Program, which is stored in the 'memory' of the computer.
(3)   The operations are performed and the data and instructions stored by varying the electrical and magnetic configurations of a large aggregate of electronic circuits.
   The computer is a very powerful management tool because, having an electronic structure, it can: (1) perform operations very quickly (for example, it can add two numbers together in less than a millionth of a second); (2) store data compactly and thus handle very large quantities of it. These two properties mean that it can perform very effectively both the routine large-scale data-processing tasks (for example, wages and salary calculations, customers' invoicing and billing, etc.) and the sophisticated mathematical tasks (for example determining a production plan using linear programming) that arise in modern industry.
   Data and instructions (the computer program) are fed in through an input unit to be stored. Instructions are then fed sequentially to the control unit, which then 'orders' the arithmetic unit to perform these instructions on the data. The results are fed out through the output unit. The control unit, arithmetic unit and any core storage (◊ Storage Media) are also known collectively as the central processor unit (CPU). The

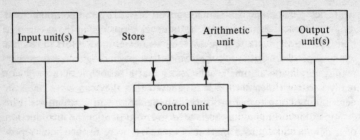

remaining pieces of equipment – input/output units, backing store, remote access units, etc. – are known as peripherals. Further details of the structure and method of operation of computers are given in entries elsewhere. ⟨⟩ Binary Scale; Computer Program; Hardware; Input/Output; Off-line/On-line; Storage Media; Time Sharing.

Apart from their many scientific and engineering uses, computers have been used significantly in managerial applications. These applications can be crudely grouped into three types, although there is an appreciable overlap between them:

(1) Automation of clerical and routine administrative tasks. Typically the calculation of wages and salaries, of sales invoices and billing, customer accounts (particularly in banking), and monitoring of stock-holding, etc., are examples of the earliest business applications of computers. The tasks are relatively unsophisticated in concept and require a computer to take no decisions normally taken by managers.

(2) Rapid access to information. This type of application is represented by the airline or hotel reservation system. An airline has a central computer-file that gives details of the seats available and all its flights for a given future period. Remote-access equipment in all the airline booking offices can interrogate and amend this file, so that a customer's reservation may be made within a matter of seconds without fear of 'double booking'. Easier booking encourages customers to use airlines and so increases seat utilization – factors that critically affect profitability. Another application is in the provision of information to stock-market investors. It is possible to rent a remote-access console connected to a computer installation that is continuously evaluating stocks, shares and market movement. It can provide immediate financial information to stockbrokers, banks and other large investors. ⟨⟩ Information Retrieval.

(3) Production and process control. Installations are now exercising 'on-line' (⟨⟩ Off-line/On-line) control of production processing.

They can range from the numerical control of a single machine, to a particular installation in the steel industry that consists of a three-tier hierarchy of computers. At the bottom tier on-line control ensures, among other activities, that orders are satisfied with the minimum of steel-scrap loss. At the middle tier, computers control the overall flow of material to ensure evenly balanced production lines. Finally, the top tier has a computer that performs production planning for the whole works. Sophisticated applications making important decisions also occur in the chemical and oil industries. An important element in the economic benefits of on-line process control is that, because a computer can respond quickly to unpredictable changes in process variables, the plant controls can be re-set quickly by computer to maintain optimum process performance under varying conditions. ⟡ Data Protection. M.J.C.M.

John C. Cluley, *Electronic Computer* (Oliver & Boyd, 1967), pp. 54–83, 148–70.

Computer-aided Design (CAD) The designer working with a (CAD) system operates from a design terminal or workstation, typically comprising a VDU screen, keyboard, graphics tablet, light pen and printer. Here the designer interacts with the computer system to develop a detailed product design, monitoring his or her work constantly on the VDU display. By issuing commands to the computer system the designer creates a design, manipulating, modifying and refining it, all without putting pen to paper. To facilitate this design process, the computer can manipulate the designer's 'drawing' by enlarging, rotating or sectioning any part of it. The software can be used for design calculations, to insert dimensions and to work out tolerances. All such information can then be retained in the computer file and printed out as a drawing of the detailed product design.

A computer can file this design using an appropriate coding/classification system. It can be accessed by other designers at a later stage so that parts can be used for other designs and to ensure adequate product standardization. The CAD system considerably facilitates the design process and greatly increases design productivity. The use of such a facility also enables a comprehensive design database to be generated. The sophistication of such a database and the ease of access to it encourage product standardization and provide an interface with a system of ⟡ Computer-aided Manufacture (CAM). R.W.

M. P. Grooves and E. W. Zimmers, *CAD/CAM* (Prentice-Hall, 1984).

Computer-aided Engineering (CAE) An alternative term for activities that are largely described as ⟡ Computer-aided Design (CAD) and ⟡ Computer-aided Manufacture (CAM). R.W.

Computer-aided Manufacture (CAM) The design specification of a product largely comprises details of dimensions and shape and a materials specification. Traditionally such information was used by production engineers to produce manufacturing-process instructions comprising operations lists, lists of tools and machinery requirements, operations routeing details, details of jigs, fixtures, etc. Now this information can be added to the computer database for each product. Indeed the determination of some of these details, e.g. process routeing, can be undertaken automatically. Further, a CAM system can produce information for computer-controlled manufacturing processes; for example, to produce an item to dimensional specifications, a computer-controlled machining centre will require data to enable it to make the necessary cuts in the material. The sequence of operations can be produced from the database as a magnetic tape for transfer to the machining centre, or can be 'downloaded' directly to the machining centre through the CAD/CAM system. In addition, tooling requirements, tool-change requirements for machines, and production schedules can be produced from the CAD/CAM database, given information on available capacity, delivery requirements and so on.

An adequate design/manufacturing database is thus a prerequisite for the effective use of CAD/CAM and for computer-controlled integrated manufacture. The existence of an adequate database, computer-controlled manufacturing facilities and the adoption of particular design principles also provide other advantages. For example, in batch production, similar items can be identified to facilitate machine set-up. ⟡ Computer-aided Design. R.W.

Computer-aided Production Management (CAPM) The use of computers in inventory management, production planning and scheduling, maintenance management, production control, performance monitoring, quality assurance and control, and in the simulation of production systems. In particular CAPM involves the interlinking of such computer-based systems and their interfacing with procurement, sales, distribution and financial systems within the company. ⟡ Production Management. R.W.

Computer-integrated Manufacturing (CIM) The planning and control of manufacture in a plant by computers and data-driven automation. The approach, developed in engineering manufacture and in some process industries, seeks to achieve the fully integrated control of manufacture, from design to the delivery of finished goods. Thus hitherto separate areas of responsibility, such as design, process planning, production planning and scheduling, inventory management, production control, materials handling, quality assurance and control and performance monitoring, in addition to the actual manufacturing processes, are each substantially computer-controlled and are interlinked. A database approach is employed, with hierarchies of computers and direct data-transmission between functions. ⟡ Computer-aided Design; Computer-aided Manufacture; Computer-aided Production Management. R.W.

Computer Numerical Control (CNC) ⟡ Numerical Control

Computer Program [1] A ⟡ Computer performs calculations on a set of data. These calculations must be broken down into a sequence of arithmetic and logical operations, which the computer is instructed to perform. This sequence is known as a computer program and is fed into the computer on one of the standard input media (⟡ Input/Output Media). Before a program is written a flow chart that represents schematically the logic of the program is drawn up. Programs must be written in a language that the computer understands. Programming languages can be divided into two classes:

(1)   Machine codes, or languages, which are directly meaningful to the computer, but which require specialist knowledge on the part of the programmer to write, being unintelligible to a non-specialist reader.

(2)   Autocodes, which are not directly meaningful to the computer, but can be written by individuals after a relatively short training period (typically three days) and are usually understandable to a non-specialist reader. Programs in autocode are fed into the computer and then translated into the equivalent program in machine code by the computer itself. This operation is performed by a translation program known as a compiler.

The advantage of machine code over autocode is that it is more efficient, that is, a calculation will be performed quicker if programmed in the former rather than the latter. The advantage of autocode over machine code is that it is easier to write, thus allowing individuals who

1.   The American spelling is normally adopted, although some books still use the traditional 'programme'.

only use computers infrequently (e.g. engineers, scientists and managers) to write their own programs without excessive difficulty.

Each computer has its own unique machine code but there are a relatively small number of autocodes that can be used, with slight alteration, on a range of computers. These autocodes can be divided into two groups:

(1)   Scientific autocodes, which are designed to be used for scientific and engineering calculations. A commonly used scientific autocode is Fortran.

(2)   Commercial autocodes, which are designed to be used for commercial and business data-processing applications. A commonly used commercial autocode is Cobol.

An example of a program written in machine code and Fortran for an IBM 1620 computer is shown below. Its purpose is to read two numbers, add them together and punch out the sum. The flow chart is:

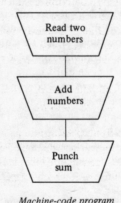

Machine-code program

Operation code	P address	Q address
36	04096	00400
32	04096	00000
32	04106	00000
21	04100	04110
26	04180	04100
33	04176	00000
38	04176	00400
48	00000	00000

This program is unintelligible to a reader who does not know the machine code, whereas the Fortran program below is much easier to follow:

Fortran program

```
READ 1, I, J        1 FORMAT (15, I10)
NUMB = I + J        2 FORMAT (I10)
PUNCH 2, NUMB  STOP
```

The operations performed by the computer on receiving each of the above instructions are as follows:

READ 1, I, J   This tells the computer to READ the numbers I and J and that this input layout or 'format' is described in the statement labelled 1.

NUMB = I + J   This instruction means set the value of NUMB equal to the sum of the numbers I and J.

PUNCH 2, N U M B   Similar to the READ instruction. It tells the computer to PUNCH a card with the value of NUMB, in the output layout or 'format' described in the statement labelled 2.

1 FORMAT (15,I10)   A descriptive statement used in this program to describe the READ instruction, where the two actual numbers represented by the symbols I and J are to be found on an input card.

2 FORMAT (I10)   As above. It is used in this program to describe the PUNCH instruction, where the value of NUMB is to be punched on an output card.

STOP   This tells the computer to stop processing. M.J.C.M.

John C. Cluley, *Electronic Computer* (Oliver & Boyd, 1967), pp. 120–47.

Conciliation Differs from ⟨⟩ Arbitration in that an arbitrator's task is to resolve a dispute for the parties who have been unable or unwilling to do so themselves, while a conciliator's aim is the more modest one of bringing the parties together with a view to persuading them to settle their differences themselves.

The ⟨⟩ Advisory, Conciliation and Arbitration Service's conciliation officers are under statutory duties to promote settlements of complaints made to ⟨⟩ Industrial Tribunals in respect of, among other matters, ⟨⟩ Unfair Dismissal and ⟨⟩ Discrimination on grounds of sex, marital status or race. ACAS may also assist with conciliation where a trade dispute exists or is apprehended. D.V.E.R.

Conciliation Officer Specially trained conciliation officers are made available at all regional offices of the ⟨⟩ Advisory, Conciliation and Arbitration Service. Since conciliation is voluntary, conciliation officers only intervene when asked by the parties concerned to give advice or to conciliate, as for example in a situation where an employer and a trade union cannot reach agreement by the normal process of ⟨⟩ Collective Bargaining.

The procedure is slightly different when individuals are concerned. Employees who allege that their rights have not been observed can make complaints to industrial tribunals and a copy of each complaint is passed to ACAS. It is then the task of a conciliation officer to try to settle the complaint, without reference to the tribunal, by conciliation between the individual and the employer. The conciliation officer seeks to clarify the situation on both sides, transmits the views of each party to the other and acquaints the parties with their rights under the law. The conciliation officer tries to help them to reach an agreement, but does not act as an arbitrator or recommend a particular settlement. In 1984 industrial conciliation engaged the majority of the operational staff of ACAS, 90 per cent of the claims involving allegations of unfair dismissal. Of these, 69 per cent were resolved voluntarily without recourse to a tribunal. E.L.

Confederation of British Industry (CBI) An organization comprising British companies and associations founded in 1965 as a result of the fusion of the National Association of British Manufacturers, the Federation of British Industries, the British Employers' Confederation and the Industrial Association of Wales and Monmouthshire.

The CBI was granted a royal charter in which its principal objects are laid down: to provide for British industry the means of formulating, making known, and influencing general policy in regard to industrial, economic, fiscal, commercial, labour, social, legal and technical questions; to develop the contribution of British industry to the national economy; to encourage the efficiency and competitive power of British industry and provide services to that end. Financed from the subscriptions of members, it is an independent body and has no party-political affiliations. To promote its aims, the CBI maintains a close relationship with the ministries and agencies of government and with the ⟨⟩ Trades Union Congress.

Membership of the CBI at present embraces approximately 12,500 individual manufacturing and service-supplying companies; 220 trade associations and employers' organizations, including the National Farmers' Union; most of the nationalized industries; the major banking institutions; and twenty commercial associations.

The governing body of the CBI is the council, with 430 members representing all sections of the membership. It has some thirty standing committees, dealing with economic affairs, taxation, wages and conditions, overseas policy, fuel and energy, education and training, transport, etc. There are also thirteen regional councils with offices, and representatives and correspondents in more than 100 business centres overseas, together with a permanent staff of 350 employees. At the head of the CBI are the President and the Director General, whose pronouncements are of major influence in projecting the policy of the CBI. N.H.C., amended by M.J.F.P.

Confidence Level ⟡ Hypothesis Testing

Conflict Any perceived divergence of interests between groups or individuals, or lack of adjustment between an individual or group and the requirements of the job or the circumstances in which it is to be performed.

Many types of behaviour may indicate the existence of conflict, the most obvious being strike action. However, the emphasis placed on strikes, both official and unofficial, as the most dramatic manifestation of conflict, should not cause other manifestations to be overlooked: demarcation disputes, differing departmental viewpoints, inter-shift rivalries, absenteeism, sabotage, incompatible personalities, autocratic supervision, high labour turnover, poor timekeeping, etc. A certain level of conflict in an organization is not only inevitable but desirable, for conflict is both a cause and an effect of change. When conflict, or the possibility of conflict, exists, it is usually advantageous to secure its free expression so that conflicting viewpoints may be fully explored and resolved or compromised, with a consequent improvement in the subsequent administrative decision and a greater degree of commitment to it. Accordingly modern management practice emphasizes the encouragement of open communications, particularly between superiors and subordinates, and of habits of continuing consultation and negotiation.

However, different groups may differ in their ability to express conflict and a useful distinction may be made between 'organized' and 'unorganized' conflict. Organized conflict is normally expressed by positive action on a personal or group basis through recognized procedures or practices, whilst unorganized conflict tends to be haphazard and personal, being expressed through negative action such as vague grumbles and dissatisfactions, poor timekeeping and indiscipline or withdrawals from the situation by apathy, absenteeism or labour turnover. It seems reasonable to suppose that unorganized conflict is associated with low morale and, as has been suggested elsewhere (⟡ Morale), organized conflict may well be related to high morale. ⟡ Authority; Group. I.C.McG.

Stephen P. Robbins, *Managing Organisational Conflict* (Prentice-Hall, 1974); Alan Fox, *Industrial Sociology and Industrial Relations,* Royal Commission on Trade Unions and Employers' Associations Research Papers, No. 3 (HMSO, 1966); R. Hyman, *Strikes* (Fontana, new ed., 1984).

Conglomerates ⬦ Diversification

Consolidated Accounts Company law in England since 1948 has provided for financial statements that relate to the business entity as opposed to the legal entity (⬦ Accounting Conventions) and this is why the publication of consolidated accounts relating to a group of companies under common control is necessary.

In the absence of special circumstances, as defined by the Companies Acts, consolidated accounts are required that reflect the underlying fact that the activities of the various companies are under a common control and represent the operations and interests of a central financial controlling interest. The controlling party is usually either the board of directors of the parent company or the shareholder with a controlling interest in the parent company.

In the preparation of group accounts, therefore, account balances of one company that are reciprocal account balances in the books of another company within the group are eliminated as contra accounts when preparing the consolidated balance sheet and profit-and-loss account of the group of companies. Examples of such accounts are inter-company loans, sales and purchases within the group, the investment asset account in the parent company and the corresponding share capital, reserves and profit balance of the subsidiary companies. Another important part of group accounting is the inclusion within the consolidated balance sheet of an account representing the aggregate interests of shareholdings other than those of the controlling interest, usually referred to as 'minority shareholders' accounts'. E.A.L.

G. A. Lee, *Modern Financial Accounting* (Nelson, 3rd ed., 1981).

Constraint A constraint is any action that a company's executives have decided they will not take even though they believe that it might help them to achieve an objective.

Two versions of this word are found: executives may feel constrained from taking an action either (1) because it is not prudent or (2) because it is contrary to their personal convictions. In the first case the decision not to take action of some sort is likely to have been made because it would conflict with some other objective; thus it might be possible to improve profits in the short term (the first objective) by taking some action that might, however, also reduce profits in the longer term (the second objective) and hence executives might feel constrained from taking it.

In the second case the executives may know that an action would certainly help to achieve the objective and that it would have no adverse effects on any other objective. Even so they may not take this action if they believe it to be contrary to their own, or the company's, moral code. These are sometimes known as moral constraints.

All companies have their own moral code, which is either developed by case-history and tradition or, more rarely, is laid down as a conscious act of policy. Typical examples of moral constraints might be: 'This company will manufacture and sell only products of the highest quality, even though it might be possible to make a larger profit by selling shoddy goods,' or, 'This company will treat its employees with humanity, even if this results in a lower profit than enforcing strict discipline.'

To define a company's moral code completely requires statements of its attitude to its shareholders, employees, customers, suppliers, the government and its officials, and to the local community. ⟨⟩ Business Policy. A.J.A.A.

> J. Melrose-Woodman and I. Kverndal, *Towards Social Responsibility: Company Codes of Ethics and Practice* (British Institute of Management, 1979).

Consumer Credit The law relating to consumer credit transactions has undergone a major overhaul in the Consumer Credit Act 1974. The 1974 Act covers a wide range of activities associated with the provision of credit and the hiring of goods to individuals, who for the purpose of the Act include partnerships and sole traders. It was necessary to bring the Act into force in stages by means of statutory instruments and it only became fully operative in May 1985.

One of the cornerstones of the Act is the *regulated* agreement, of which there are two types. The first, the 'consumer credit agreement', is an agreement between an individual (the debtor) and another person (the creditor) by which the creditor provides the debtor with credit not exceeding £15,000. The term 'credit' includes a cash loan and any other form of financial accommodation. Examples of this type of agreement include hire-purchase, conditional sale, credit sale, money loans and credit cards. In most cases these agreements are regulated by the Act, although some have been exempted, e.g. building-society and local-authority mortgages. Furthermore some consumer credit agreements, though regulated by the Act, are exempt from certain of its provisions.

The second type of regulated agreement is the 'consumer hire agreement', which is an agreement made with an individual (the hirer) for the hiring of goods. The agreement must be capable of subsisting for more than three months and must not require the hirer to make payments exceeding £15,000. Again, certain consumer hire agreements have been exempted, in whole or in part, from the Act's provisions.

The credit provided by the creditor under a consumer credit agreement may fall into one of two categories: fixed sum or running account. The latter, which includes bank overdrafts and credit cards, relates to those transactions where the credit provided is being constantly reduced and topped up by the debtor's withdrawals, purchases and repayments. In addition, the credit may be 'restricted use' or 'unrestricted use', the difference between the two being dependent on the degree of control exercised by the creditor over the use of the credit provided.

A further classification made by the Act is the 'debtor–creditor–supplier agreement' and the 'debtor–creditor agreement'. The distinction between the two rests on the presence or absence of some business connection between the creditor and the person supplying the debtor with the goods or services obtained with the credit. Examples of a debtor–creditor–supplier agreement include hire-purchase, conditional sale and credit card agreements; a debtor–creditor agreement includes bank overdrafts and personal loans.

Provision is also made in the Act for those transactions that are linked to the consumer credit agreement, e.g. a contract of insurance taken out on goods subject to a hire-purchase agreement.

Broadly the aims of the 1974 Act were to bring all credit transactions under one statutory umbrella, to clear up a number of anomalies and to afford greater protection to the debtor and hirer. As regards this last objective, the following provisions of the statute may be noted.

(1) *Licensing*. Subject to certain exceptions, all persons and organizations carrying on a consumer credit or consumer hire business require a licence. The licence is issued by the Director General of Fair Trading and may take the form of a standard licence, that is, a licence issued in the name of the applicant, or a group licence, which covers such persons as are described in the licence. Licences are required not only by those who offer credit or hire out goods but also by credit brokers, debt adjusters and counsellors, debt collectors and credit reference agencies.

(2) *Seeking business*. The advertising of credit and hire facilities is controlled, in that advertisements have to comply with regulations relating to their form and content. The canvassing of regulated agreements off trade premises is also strictly controlled.

(3) *Disclosure of information*. Creditors must provide written

quotations on request, including therein certain specified information such as the APR (the annual or true rate of interest) in the prescribed form. The agreement itself must also comply with regulations made in 1985 as to their form and content. Certain information must also be made available during and after the currency of the agreement and copies supplied. Failure to comply with aspects of these rules may result in the agreement being unenforceable, or in some circumstances only enforceable by court order.

(4) *Provision of copies of the agreement*. The debtor or hirer must be supplied with copies of the agreement. Failure to comply with this requirement renders the agreement unenforceable without a court order.

(5) *Cancellation*. Some agreements ('cancellable agreements') can be cancelled by the debtor or hirer within a prescribed time period, sometimes called the 'cooling-off period'. Such agreements are, broadly, those signed off the creditor's business premises. Notice of this right must be given to the debtor or hirer. Moneys paid by debtors or hirers are recoverable, as are any goods supplied by them, e.g. goods given in part-exchange, where they have exercised their right of cancellation. Provision is also made for the recovery of money or goods by the creditor or owner.

(6) *Liability of creditor*. In some circumstances the creditor may incur liability to the debtor for any misrepresentation or breach of contract by the supplier of goods or services.

(7) *Breach by debtor or hirer*. The creditor or owner wishing to, say, terminate the agreement because of a breach by the debtor or hirer must comply with the procedure laid down in the Act.

(8) *Recovery of goods*. Restrictions are placed on the recovery of goods subject to a regulated hire-purchase or conditional-sale agreement and in particular those goods ('protected goods') on which one third or more of the total price has been paid by the debtor. Such goods cannot be recovered by the creditor except by order of the court.

(9) *Judicial control*. The Act empowers the court to make a number of orders depending on the circumstances of the case. These orders can provide for the enforcement of the repayment period, protection of property, repayment of sums to the hirer, return of the goods to the creditor and re-opening of extortionate credit bargains.

(10) *Credit reference agencies*. The Act imposes a duty on creditors and owners to disclose, on request, to the debtor or hirer the name and address of any credit reference agency consulted. The agency is under a duty to give consumers, on request, a copy of the file relating to them and may also have to correct any wrong information contained in that file. An alternative procedure is laid down for business consumers. D.V.E.R., amended by J.C.E.M.

Encyclopedia of Consumer Credit Law (Sweet & Maxwell, 1975).

Consumer Panel A representative group of consumers who agree to provide data on a continuous basis about a particular product or service. It is in the continuous nature of the respondent's participation that the panel differs from the consumer-survey method of data collection (⟡ Market Survey). A diary is normally left with the household or other participating unit, and is completed and returned on a weekly basis. The particular value of this method lies in the elimination of the need for respondents to think back to past behaviour; purchases are recorded as and when made, giving much greater accuracy. Data collected in this way are the major source for the analysis of brand loyalties and switching behaviour amongst consumers. By making the act of recording information such a conscious effort, however, it is often suggested that respondents are biased in their purchasing; to meet this problem many panels are self-renewing over a reasonably long period of time, e.g. every two years. This is a service that any market-research organization can provide. Although primarily used in consumer marketing, the panel method can be used amongst any group of users, and is occasionally used in research involving distributors and manufacturers. The advent of electronics at the point of sale in many retail outlets offers great scope for considerably enhanced information about purchasing, which, if cross-referenced with demographic characteristics of customers, would be available to managers at extremely short notice. This will prove invaluable in the context of test markets and also for studying patterns of repeat-buying behaviour. G.S.C.W.

Consumer-protection Movement The general name given to a series of consumer organizations that emerged in strength during the 1950s. Their pressures led in 1959 to the establishment of the Moloney Committee, which reported in 1962. The *Final Report of the Committee on Consumer Protection*, HMSO, recommended the establishment of the Consumer Council. This body was set up in 1963 to integrate consumer-protection activities, but was abolished in 1970. In 1973 a much more powerful agency, the Office of Fair Trading, was established with powers to keep watch on trading matters in the United Kingdom and to protect consumers against unfair practices.

The Director General of Fair Trading looks after consumers' interests directly, for example by encouraging the adoption of Codes of Practice by trade associations, or by obtaining assurances from traders who have persistently broken the law that they will mend their ways. The Director General also has a duty to encourage competition amongst traders and businesses, to keep a watch on monopolies and mergers, and to initiate action to curb trade practices that may be anti-competitive.

In 1971 the Crowther Committee reported on consumer credit and this led to the Consumer Credit Act 1974, one of the most important pieces of consumer-protection legislation. Responsibility for issuing licences under the Act rests with the Office of Fair Trading, which also administers the Estate Agents Act 1979.

In 1957 the Consumers' Association was founded by private enthusiasts and began publishing *Which?* magazine. Although readership of consumer publications is more substantial than the registered level of sales, research surveys have indicated that only a relatively small proportion of shoppers act directly on the findings. Businessmen whose products and services are examined, however, generally act quickly to meet any defects found in the tests, since the reports are frequently newsworthy and receive wide press coverage. Other major bodies involved in consumer protection are the National Consumer Council, the National Federation of Consumer Groups and the National Association of Citizens Advice Bureaux.

The movement's major targets for action have included safety, labelling, honesty in advertising, consumer credit, guarantees, quality standards and protection of consumers' prepayments. G.S.C.W.

Consumption Function The general name given by economists to the relationship between consumers' expenditure and income. The concept lies at the heart of Keynes's theoretical system and many would say it is at the centre of modern macro-economic theory. This is because of the importance of consumers' expenditure for the gross national product (◊ National Income Accounts); any adequate explanation of the size of the gross national product of a country must grapple with the determination of expenditures by the consumers of that country.

Figure 1 shows the simplest type of consumption function, the line C_0B, which can be contrasted with the line OD, the locus of all points for which consumption exactly equals income. Hence the slope of OD is unity.

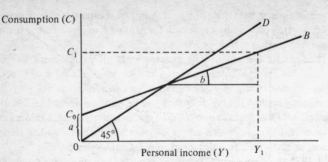

Figure 1

The functional form of the relationship would be

$$C = a + bY$$

where a and b are parameters (or constants) of the equation, as opposed
to the variables C and Y.

This function indicates that if income is equal to OY_1 then consumers'
expenditure will be OC_1. If income falls to zero then consumers' expenditure will be OC_0, indicating that consumers will dis-save rather
than consume nothing. Two important concepts can also be shown from
this diagram. The slope of the consumption function, b, is less than 1
and this means that only a proportion of any increase in income will be
consumed. This proportion will be constant, irrespective of the income
level from which the change is measured, and is known as the *marginal
propensity to consume*. The other concept is the *average propensity to
consume*, which measures the proportion of total income that is
consumed at any income level. This clearly falls as one proceeds along
the function from a zero income level; at the point of the intersection of
the two lines it is unity. Thus, in the above equation, if b were equal to
0·6, any increase in income would mean that consumers would spend 60
per cent and would save 40 per cent. This means that if we knew the
precise form of the function, a prediction of future income levels would
enable us also to predict future consumption levels.

As befits its importance, a great deal of empirical research work has
been undertaken into the most appropriate form of the consumption
function. The variables that enter into it have been refined, cross-section
and time-series data have been examined, and a division drawn between
the short-period and the long-period consumption function.

The variables most frequently used are consumers' real expenditure
(i.e. at constant prices) and real personal disposable income (i.e. after

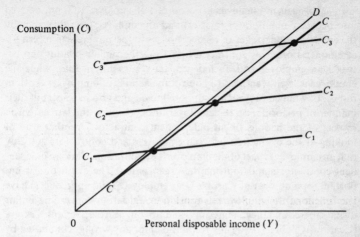

Figure 2

taxes). The general evidence for short-period data of up to ten years points towards a value of between 0·5 and 0·7 for the marginal propensity to consume. However, long-period studies extending over fifty to 100 years and based upon data over ten-year averages (to iron out cycles) often give substantially higher values for the marginal propensity. Various explanations of this difference have been provided, which can be visually interpreted from figure 2. C_1C_1, etc. are short-period consumption functions, whilst CC is the estimated long-period relationship. The slope of CC, the long-period marginal propensity, is greater than the slope of any of the functions C_1C_1, etc. Since it goes through the origin, the average and marginal propensity have the same value which is around 0·9, given that the slope of CC is somewhat less than OD, which has a slope of unity.

Some writers have suggested that these results occur because the fundamental relationship resembles C_1C_1 but the curve gradually shifts upwards because of changes in income distribution, changes in the real level of assets held by consumers and the introduction of new products. Others have suggested that, on the contrary, the fundamental relationship is like CC but that behaviour deviates from this as consumers' current income departs from their idea of permanent income or falls relative to their previous peak-level of income. L.T.S.

E. Shapiro, *Macroeconomic Theory* (Harcourt Brace Jovanovich, 5th rev. ed., 1982).

Contracts of Employment A contract of employment is one entered into between an employer (master) and an employee (servant) whereby the employee undertakes to render services to the employer in return for a remuneration. This contract differs from the similar relationship between an employer and an independent contractor in that, while the employer is legally entitled to control the actions of employees, both in respect of what employees are supposed to do and also in respect of their manner of performance, the employer does not enjoy the latter right in respect of the actions of an independent contractor. Another way of looking at the distinction between employees and contractors is to say that an employee is part of the employer's organization, while an independent contractor stands outside the organization. The distinction is important for a number of reasons. Only employees (and apprentices) have the benefit of the employment-protection legislation concerning unfair dismissal, redundancy, maternity and so on. Further, employers are 'vicariously liable' (i.e. legally responsible) for any wrongs committed by their employees while they are acting in the course of their employment. Employers also owe a greater duty of care, as regards health and safety, to employees than to independent contractors and others who provide them with services. Despite its importance, however, the distinction is unfortunately not always easy to draw in practice. Doubts remain, for example, whether certain categories of casual and home workers are truly employees as a matter of law. Nowadays the courts tend to favour an approach that looks at all the features of a particular relationship rather than treating any single criterion, such as 'control', as determinative of the parties' legal status. None the less, it seems that a contract of employment must, as a minimum, oblige the employer to offer some work and correspondingly commit the employee to doing that work personally.

Contracts of employment need not be made in any particular form, e.g. in writing, but under the Employment Protection (Consolidation) Act 1978 an employer must give written particulars of the terms of a contract of employment (unless the contract itself was made in writing) to all employees within thirteen weeks of the commencement of their employment. These particulars must include an identification of the parties to the contract, the date of commencement of the employment, the rate of remuneration and the method of calculating it, the intervals at which remuneration is payable, terms and conditions relating to hours of work, entitlement to holidays and holiday pay, provisions regarding sick pay and pension rights, if any, the length of notice that the employee has to give and the notice to which he or she is entitled. The statement must also identify a person to whom any grievances regarding the employment are to be submitted, the manner in which such application should be made and the nature of the subsequent grievance procedure. ⟡ Dismissal of Employees (Law); Vicarious Liability. w.f.f., amended by k.w.

D. K. Dix, *Contracts of Employment* (Butterworths, 6th ed. by D. W. Crump, 1980, supplement 1983); T. Aldridge, *Service Agreements* (Oyez Longman, 4th ed., 1982); M. Freedland, *The Contract of Employment* (Clarendon Press, 1976).

Contribution Account ⟡ Break-even Analysis

Contribution Deduction Schemes ⟡ Check-off

Contribution Margin ⟡ Cost (in Accounting Systems)

Control ⟡ Automation; Machine Controls

Control (Accounting) The means by which a business organization attempts to ensure that its operations are in accordance with the plans formulated for achieving its objectives. Accounting systems provide part of the basis for control of a business in two ways: firstly by methods of custodial control and secondly by methods of efficiency control. Custodial control is facilitated mainly by means of financial accounting procedures (⟡ Accountancy Conventions – Stewardship), which are directed towards checking on the actual quantities of assets for which company officials are responsible (or accountable), and by means of the auditing procedures verifying the existence and ownership of assets (⟡ Auditing).

The control of management efficiency is facilitated by budgeting, costing and managerial accounting procedures (⟡ Budgeting; Costing Systems; Management Accounting) pertaining to the construction of budgets and analysis of cost data relating to the various divisions, departments, cost centres, manufacturing processes, contracts, capital projects, etc. The accountant assists the control of efficiency by isolating the differences between budgeted figures and actual costs (⟡ Management by Exception). These differences (or variances) give management a point of departure in attempting to analyse the causes of deviations from plans. It is important to appreciate that most accounting-control procedures assist control and are not complete controlling devices in the sense of, for instance, a system that incorporates formal adaptive control by means of feedback mechanisms. Neither do they pinpoint causes of variances. E.A.L.

R. N. Anthony and J. Dearden, *Management Control Systems* (Irwin, 4th ed., 1980).

Control Charts A method of examining, and hence controlling, the variation in, say, the weight, dimensions or composition of an item, or the number of defective items produced either as a result of chance variation or assignable causes such as variation in material, wear on tools, etc.

A manufacturing process is said to be under control if the variables or attributes of the product conform to certain standards, i.e. are within certain predefined limits. Control charts are used in quality control to define such limits of acceptance and to indicate when items fall beyond such limits.

Control charts for variance in the mean (i.e. average value of a variable from a sample) or range (i.e. the variability about the mean) and the percentage of defective items are common. ⟡ Quality Control.

The figure on p. 103 shows control charts for the mean and range for a certain item. Two types of limit are used: warning limits, to obtain advance warning of possible changes in mean or range, and action limits, beyond which the items are unacceptable. Warning limits are normally set such that, assuming a normal probability distribution, only 5 per cent of items will by chance fall beyond them, and the action limits such that only 0·2 per cent will fall beyond them. The process is under control if both mean and range are under control. R.W.

Convertible ⟡ Claims

Co-operative Movement A group of democratic trading organizations, in which any profits available for disposal are allotted to members in proportion to the value of their purchases. Founded in 1844 in Rochdale, it is now a world-wide movement, and in Britain accounts for approximately 5 per cent of all retail trade, with over 8·5 million members. Its trade grew continuously until after the Second World War, when it was overtaken by the growth of powerful multiple selling – in particular by supermarkets entering the food trade, where co-operatives had formerly been strongest (⟡ Retailing).

The movement is made up of around 100 retail societies. In the nineteenth century retail societies established wholesale societies in England and Scotland (which merged in 1973), which set up a wide range of manufacturing units.

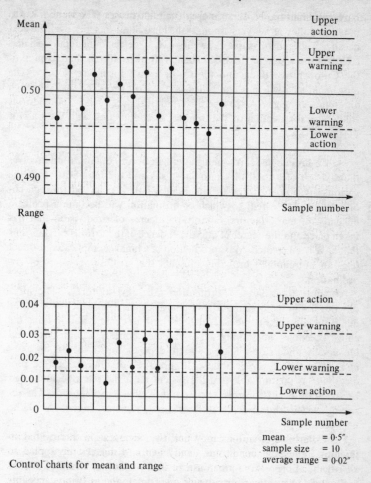

Control charts for mean and range

mean = 0·5"
sample size = 10
average range = 0·02"

The democratic structure, the independence of retail societies and the general dearth of good managerial ability are said to have created considerable difficulties for co-operatives since the mid-1950s. However, in 1966 the board of the Co-operative Wholesale Society was reorganized into product divisions, in line with contemporary marketing ideas, and a professional chief executive employed from outside the movement. Two further major decisions were taken by the new management, which affected the future shape of the Co-operative Movement. The first was to rationalize brand names under the Co-op label; previously the movement had traded under more than 2,000 names. The second was to pursue a policy of mergers amongst the local retail societies over the next decade. The end objective is twenty-five large regional retail societies covering the whole of the UK. The CWS owns all the share capital of the Co-operative Bank and the Co-operative Insurance Society. The movement as a whole is controlled by the Co-operative Union through an annual congress. A Co-operative political party exists and endorses candidates for election to Westminster in conjunction with the Labour Party. G.S.C.W.

Co-ordination Harmonious interaction. Any organization involves the division of a total task into sub-tasks and the reunification of the various divisions to form an integrated whole is achieved through co-ordination. The extent to which co-ordination will become a problem depends on many factors, notably the degree of subdivision that has taken place and the degree of interdependence of the various subdivisions that have been created. Mass production of a highly complicated product (e.g. an automobile) probably presents the greatest problems of co-ordination.

Attempts to achieve co-ordination take several forms. The most obvious lies in the design of the organization itself, in which each of the manifold sub-tasks is precisely defined both in content and in time, the entire schedule constituting a programme centrally administered and universally understood. Such a system depends for its success on, *inter alia*, near-perfect predictability. In practice, of course, perfect predictability is unattainable and the system must therefore be supported by the addition of controls, checks and feedback mechanisms. The resulting system, however carefully devised, remains vulnerable to the unexpected.

Particularly in situations in which the organization is required to function in unstable conditions – and to varying degrees this applies to all organizations – recourse must be had to the voluntary efforts of individuals to use their initiative to co-ordinate themselves as the situation of the moment may seem to require. Thus, increasingly, organizational provision is being made for horizontal communication at all levels through the use of co-ordinating committees, the encouragement of free interaction amongst peers and, as far as possible, the close social and geographical positioning of work groups whose activities are particularly interdependent. ⟡ Communication; Organization; Socio-technical System. I.C.MCG.

Copy ⟡ Advertising

Copyright The sole right to produce or reproduce any particular literary, artistic or musical work or any substantial part thereof in any material form whatsoever. A copyright protects only the work itself and not the ideas behind it. Thus, the author of a book has a copyright in the words that they have chosen to present their ideas but not in the ideas expressed as such.

Unlike ⋗ Patents and ⋗ Trade Marks, copyright does not require registration for its protection. Authors of literary works enjoy copyright in them for their lifetime and their estate owns the copyright for fifty years after their death. Copyright in photographs, films and records exists for fifty years from the end of the year of their making.

Copyright may be assigned in writing by the author to another party and the assignee will then enjoy all the author's rights for the remainder of the copyright period. w.f.f., amended by j.c.e.m.

W. A. Copinger and E. P. S. James, *Copyright* (Sweet & Maxwell, 12th ed., 1980).

Corporate Image ⋗ Branding; Public Relations

Corporate Planner The official of a company responsible for introducing or maintaining a corporate planning system.

Two schools of thought exist as to the precise role of corporate planners. In the first they take over all the company's long-range planning themselves, leaning on other executives for advice and only handing these plans over to them for action when they have been approved by the board or a planning committee. This view is criticized on the grounds that it leads to excessively large planning departments, may result in 'ivory tower' plans that are impractical, and does not encourage enthusiastic participation by the executives who have to carry out the plans.

The second school, which has been in the majority since the late 1960s, suggests that corporate planners should limit their activities to ensuring that long-range plans are drawn up by the line executives themselves, helping them to do this and ensuring that their plans are adequate to achieve the objectives and are in line with the company's policy.

Whichever school is correct, corporate planners must be responsible to the Chief Executive and must have a broad and forward-looking attitude towards their company and its environment. ⋗ Corporate Planning; Business Policy. a.j.a.a.

Corporate Planning An activity that probably started in the USA in the mid-fifties, corporate planning is the systematic study of long-term company objectives and the strategy required to achieve them.

It should be stressed that many companies do study these two problems but only those that do so systematically and methodically can be said to be using corporate planning.

This approach lays particular emphasis upon treating a company as a corporate whole rather than as a collection of departments, upon the long term rather than the short, upon a careful study of the company within its environment, past, present and future, and upon the precise definition of its objectives. It is probably the only 'management technique' that has yet been devised to study systematically the entire company (as opposed to parts of it) at the policy as well as the strategic level. ⇕ Objectives; Business Policy; Strategy. A.J.A.A.

Corporate Report ⇕ Annual Report and Accounts

Correlation and Regression Very often statisticians wish to consider if and how variables are related. Correlation and regression techniques are used to estimate the relationship between one variable and one or more others. For example statisticians may wish to know if daily ice-cream sales are related to the number of hours of sunshine on that day. Intuitively they may believe that ice-cream sales are larger on sunny days than on dull days. To test this they may compare the daily ice-cream sales with daily sunshine hours by correlation analysis. If the two sets of data are strongly correlated the hypothesis is vindicated. The degree of correlation is measured on a numerical scale between 0 and 1. Two variables that are strongly correlated will have a correlation coefficient of 0·8–1, whilst that of two weakly correlated variables will be 0–0·2. The sign (+ or −) of the correlation coefficient will be dependent on the direction of variation between the variables. For example if daily ice-cream sales increase with sunshine hours, the correlation coefficient will be positive. Conversely if we examined the correlation between daily sales of raincoats and sunshine hours, we should expect the former to decrease as the latter increased. If this were so, the correlation coefficient would be negative.

An expression that is being increasingly used in terms of forecasting is autocorrelation. This means that there may be a relationship between data at one time period and data of the same kind at an earlier fixed time period. For example tests may be made to see whether there is a correlation betweeen sales on each day and sales one week before.

If, however, the variables daily sales and sunshine are correlated, we may then wish to determine the exact form of the relationship between them, that is we may want to identify an algebraic equation that describes their relationship. This may be done by regression analysis. Positive and negative regression is defined similarly to correlation. A regression analysis performed on sales related to time will provide a means of forecasting future sales.

In performing correlation and regression analysis statisticians must be wary of attaching too much weight to a high degree of correlation between two variables that, on other grounds, might not be considered to be associated in any way. A high degree of correlation does not necessarily imply a causal connection between the variables. Thus, there is a high degree of correlation between the increase in life expectancy of individuals in England and the increase in the annual numbers of register-office marriages in successive years since 1900.[1] However, no one supposes that a register-office marriage will lengthen their life. It so happens that during this century there have been continual advances in medical science and improvements in living standards both increasing life expectancy and, at the same time, an unconnected secularization of our society. A more dramatic example of spurious correlation is that which is claimed between the numbers of storks nesting in spring in Central Europe and the human birth rate later in the year! M.J.C.M., amended by R.S.S.

Stephen P. Shao, *Statistics for Business and Economics* (Merrill, 1976).

Cost (in Accounting Systems) An accountant usually measures the resources acquired by a business in terms of their acquisition cost. Thus an accounting system will generally be a record in terms of historical costs of resources and the costings of outputs and finished goods will generally be fully-allocated unit costs. In addition to the recording of acquisition costs, many accounting systems incorporate predetermined standard costs as a basis of measurement (⇳ Standard Costing).

There are, however, a number of different cost concepts, and for decision-making purposes it is vital to adopt the appropriate approach. An over-reliance upon conventionally based acquisition or standard costs may mislead management, resulting in poor decision-making. A useful concept for analytical purposes is that of relevant costs. The relevant-cost approach is concerned with identifying changes in future total costs if alternative courses of action are taken. This is also sometimes referred to as an incremental- or differential-cost approach. Two useful cost concepts derived from economics relate to ⇳ Marginal Costing and

1. Given in C. Mack, *Essentials of Statistics for Scientists and Technologists* (Heinemann, 1966).

⟨⟩ Opportunity Cost. Marginal cost is the incremental cost of one additional unit of output. This leads to the use of marginal costing, i.e. an approach to cost analysis based upon isolating those costs and revenues that will change as the result of a given decision. In many cases cost changes will occur in variable costs only. The approach that separates variable product costs, such as materials, from general organization fixed costs, such as rent and rates, is frequently referred to as variable or direct costing. The difference between income from sales and direct or variable costs is known as the contribution margin. Contribution-margin analysis is a major analytical tool for the accountant (⟨⟩ Break-even Analysis; Overheads). Opportunity cost represents sacrifice. It is the maximum amount forgone by taking a particular action. By their very nature, opportunity costs may be difficult to measure directly from the accounting system but may be of great importance for decision-makers. It is unlikely to be possible for all cost concepts to be incorporated within the accounting measurement system as a matter of routine. The accounting system, however, is likely to be the primary source of base data for analytical purposes. Where necessary, these data must be modified to meet the informational needs of the decision-maker. ⟨⟩ Costs; Pricing (Accounting Information for); Management Accounting; Cost Functions. C.J.J.

Mangement Accounting – Official Terminology (ICMA, 1982).

Cost-benefit Analysis 'A practical way of assessing the desirability of projects, where it is important to take a long view (in the sense of looking at repercussions in the further, as well as the nearer, future) and a wide view (in the sense of allowing for side-effects of many kinds on many persons, industries, regions, etc.), i.e. it implies the enumeration and evaluation of all the relevant costs and benefits.'[1]

Many cost-benefit studies are carried out by teams composed of a variety of specialists. It is clear from the definition that the value of cost-benefit analysis depends very largely on how completely the side-effects can be traced and the future repercussions forecast. Equally important is the extent to which the costs and benefits can be expressed in comparable terms.

The fact that we are dealing with future benefits and costs means that we have to use discounted cash-flow techniques (⟨⟩ Discounted Present Value), to take account of the incidence of the cash flows over the length of life of the project. This raises the problem of the appropriate rate of

1. A. R. Prest and R. Turvey, 'Cost-benefit Analysis: A Survey', *Economic Journal*, vol. 75 (December 1965), p. 683.

discount to use. Another problem is that in many cases the social costs and benefits have no prices attached to them and hence considerable judgement and ingenuity are called for in deciding upon the monetary values to use.

In recent years cost-benefit analyses have been carried out in fields as diverse as water-supply, education, and research and development, and considerable stimulus has come from government agencies, as the share of the Government in national investment-expenditure has increased. L.T.S.

D. W. Pearce, *Cost-benefit Analysis* (Macmillan, 2nd ed., 1983).

Cost Functions A mathematical expression of the relationship between costs and output. The purpose of obtaining cost functions is to test the hypotheses regarding short-run and long-run cost behaviour that are mentioned in the ⟨⟩ Costs entry.

The sort of function that would give rise to the U-shaped average cost curves of traditional short-run theory is as follows:

$$Y = a + bX - cX^2 + dX^3 \tag{1}$$

where Y = total costs

X = *output*

a, b, c, d = parameters (or constants) of the equation

Then $\dfrac{Y}{X}$ = average total cost = $\dfrac{a}{X} + b - cX + dX^2 \tag{2}$

$$\dfrac{dY}{dX} = \text{marginal cost} = b - 2cX + 3dX^2 \tag{3}$$

Thus one test of the short-run hypothesis would be to fit an equation of the form in equation (1) to data on costs and output. If the estimates of the parameters are significant, this will add weight to the hypothesis. If they are not then another form, such as a quadratic or a straight line, can be tried.

The following points should be borne in mind in conducting such an investigation.

(1)   The time-period chosen for the observations should be one during which the level of output was achieved by constant rather than variable production rates.

(2)   Cost and output data should relate to each other.

(3)   The period should be one of sufficient length to allow a wide variation in output and yet not too long to allow changes in capital stock to take place.

(4)   The only variation in costs should be because of output changes. Thus changes in factor prices and changes in the fixed factors should not be allowed to contaminate the data.

As a general rule an approximation to such conditions is found in individual firms. The general findings are that quadratics or straight lines fit the data better than the cubic functions of equation (1). In the case of the straight-line total-cost function this would mean that the average variable-cost curve and the marginal-cost curve were the same, whilst average total cost falls as output increases (figure 1). In the case of the quadratic cost function, by contrast, the average variable-cost curve and the marginal-cost curve would be upward sloping straight lines, whilst the average total-cost curve would be U-shaped (figure 2).

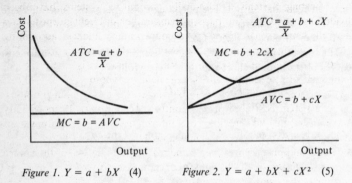

Figure 1. $Y = a + bX$ (4)   Figure 2. $Y = a + bX + cX^2$ (5)

The examination of long-run cost behaviour also requires some care in the sample data. The following points should be borne in mind in addition to those mentioned in connection with short-run cost functions: (1) the need for a wide range of output observations is even more important because there is no capacity restriction; (2) the state of technical knowledge must be assumed to be constant.

In this case it would appear that the best source of information would be a cross-section of firms in a particular industry, preferably one subject to show technological change. Ideally, although the firms should be of different sizes, they should all have been open to the same state of technical knowledge. However, this is not always possible and ways must be found to cope with this feature of the sample data.

In general, investigations have shown that average total costs fall from left to right, giving rise to the so-called L-shaped cost curve. Only occasionally is there evidence of an up-turn and hence of diseconomies of scale.

The evidence on short- and long-run cost curves conflicts with traditional economic theory. This is because the analysis of production has been too superficial. The evidence suggests that capital equipment is often not only adaptable to varying quantities of labour and raw materials but is divisible also. It also suggests that the managerial constraint on long-run costs is of little importance over most output ranges so far encountered. L.T.S.

E. F. Brigham and J. L. Pappas, *Managerial Economics* (Holt, Rinehart & Winston, 4th rev. ed. by M. Hirschey, 1983).

Cost of Living ◊ Index Numbers

Costing Systems Traditionally accounting systems have been divided into two separate parts, serving rather different purposes and generally kept in separate books of account, namely financial accounting (for external reporting) and cost accounting (for internal reporting). The attempt to integrate these two systems has been assisted by the development of a concept of ◊ Management Accounting.

A cost-accounting system may be said to have two main purposes: (1) to assist in cost control (◊ Control (Accounting); Responsibility Accounting); (2) to provide cost information for the purposes of making specific decisions and long-run plans.

The second purpose is served principally by an analysis of the nature of cost in terms of the various important concepts of cost (e.g. opportunity, marginal (or incremental), fixed, variable, full, joint, sunk, historical, etc.) combined with an appreciation of how this cost analysis relates to various kinds of short-term and long-term decisions. ◊ Costs; Accounting System. L.T.S.

J. C. Drury, *Management and Cost Accounting* (Van Nostrand Reinhold (UK), 1985).

Costs In order to make a profit a business must be able to sell its output at a price greater than the total cost of production. The margin between these two may be large or small and it may well vary with the size of output. Thus, if we assume that profits are to be as large as possible (◊ Business Motivation), then in planning the output to achieve this goal a knowledge of cost/output variation is essential.

In the past economists have been interested in costs and their variation with output because they represent one step along the road towards the theory of price formation and resource allocation. Hypotheses based upon *a priori* reasoning have been put forward enabling one to produce the U-shaped cost curves shown in most elementary economics textbooks.

A distinction is drawn between variable costs and fixed costs, always with respect to some period of time, be it a week or a month. The distinction is based, in general, upon the possibility of variation in the utilization of the factors of production during the given period of time. Labour, raw materials and fuel are usually classified as variable costs, whilst rent, rates, depreciation, interest charges and supervisory management salaries are classified as fixed costs. However, it must be recognized that difficulties of classification occur. For example, depreciation contains both a wear and tear element and an obsolescence element. The former belongs properly to the variable side, the latter to the fixed side. In addition, a variation in the basic time-period can also cause a classification change.

The variation of costs with output can be considered from two viewpoints: firstly, some factors are considered fixed in allocation to the firm, and secondly all the factors are considered variable and hence the firm can combine them in optimum proportions.

The basic hypothesis relating to the short-period is embodied in the so-called law of diminishing returns or variable proportions. The law states that as more and more of a variable factor is used in conjunction with a fixed factor, ultimately the increments to total production will fall off. The law gives rise to the familiar figure below, relating various cost concepts to output. It is important to note the fundamental assumption that the fixed factor is in use all the time.

As will be seen, average total costs decline until output OA is reached, at which point unit costs are a minimum and the fixed and variable factors are combined together most efficiently, for this level of fixed factors. Thereafter unit costs begin to rise as output increases.

There is no equivalent hypothesis relating to the long period when all factors become variable, but merely a collection of cases. The manager can now consider the cost/output variation without any restrictions, and this means that for any output the most appropriate combination of all factors can be chosen.

As the scale of operation changes, costs per unit of output can either rise, fall or remain constant. If we gradually increase output, initially unit costs might fall because of increased use of specialized machinery, increased opportunity for labour to specialize and because of administrative and managerial economies. The rise in unit costs is generally assumed to occur because ultimately managerial efficiency declines. In effect this means management itself is still a fixed factor in the long-

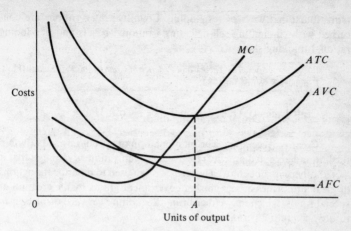

ATC = Average total cost per unit of output
AVC = Average variable cost per unit of output
AFC = Average fixed cost per unit of output
MC = Marginal cost = Increment to total cost as output changes by one
       unit

period. ⇨ Cost (in Accounting Systems); Cost Functions; Opportunity Cost. L.T.S.

R. G. Lipsey, *Introduction to Positive Economics* (Weidenfeld & Nicolson, 6th ed., 1983).

Counselling Counselling ranges in application from routine career discussions with school-leavers (⇨ Vocational Guidance) to clinical interviews with disturbed clients. The aim of counselling is to assist people to manage their own lives effectively. It is concerned with helping a client to make decisions, to solve problems or to learn to cope with stress, anxiety, or lack of assertiveness.

Perhaps the most important dimension on which counsellors differ is the extent to which they are directive in relation to the client. Those who follow the psychotherapist Carl Rogers emphasize the importance of personal growth and are non-directive. By contrast, cognitive and behavioural approaches are concerned with actively teaching the client ways of thinking and behaving more effectively.

One behavioural method to reduce anxiety is progressive muscular relaxation, in which clients are taught to tense and relax the main muscle groups (⇨ Stress). Behaviour rehearsal (role playing) is effective in modifying unassertive behaviour and facilitating the development of more functional ways of responding. Cognitive interventions are concerned with eliminating self-defeating irrational beliefs and developing rational thinking skills. E.E.

R. Nelson-Jones, *The Theory and Practice of Counselling Psychology* (Holt, Rinehart & Winston, 1982).

Craft Union ⋄ Trade Union Types – Craft Union

Creative Accounting The manipulation of accounting data (within the law and accepted practice) to give an organization advantages that it would otherwise not enjoy. The term is often used to describe the actions of local authorities in maximizing government grants by the creation of special funds, which may either bring expenditure forward or place it in future accounting periods. J.V.P.

Critical Incidents Technique One method of evaluating the safety of equipment and workplaces is to seek, by means of interviews or questionnaires, lists of errors, difficulties, near misses or other incidents experienced by operators. This method of elucidating information has the advantage, compared with accident investigations, that many more instances are likely to be available for classification and study. In addition to its application to the evaluation of hardware, the technique may also be used to obtain an index of job proficiency. ⋗ Accident Prevention. E.E.

Critical Path Method (CPM) ⋄ Network Analysis

Culture The sum total of the beliefs, knowledge, attitudes of mind and customs to which people are exposed during their social conditioning. Through contact with a particular culture individuals learn a language, acquire values and learn habits of behaviour and thought. The culture of their society will define objects and situations for individuals, whereas other societies with other cultures may define the same objects or situations differently. For example in some societies the tomato is regarded as a delicacy, whilst in others it is believed to be poisonous; and some societies regard self-advancement in competition with one's fellows as meritorious, whereas in others it is shameful.

Members of the same society will have a common culture to a considerable extent, but as societies become more complex, subgroups may be identified with distinctive subcultures, which, although having much in common, will differ from each other in significant ways. In Britain, for example, there are marked cultural differences between Merseyside, Tyneside, South Wales, the Scottish highlands and London, to mention only a few areas, and anyone familiar with the culture of one will face problems of adjustment when moving to another. Similarly, there are marked cultural differences between different social classes.

Organizations, too, have distinctive cultures and newcomers must make the necessary adaptation before they can become fully effective: behaviour in one organizational context may be quite inappropriate in another. Culture may become modified over time and a number of industrial case-studies show this process. ⟡ Ideology; Institution; Norm; Role; Social System; Status; Values. I.C.MCG.

A. W. Gouldner, *Patterns of Industrial Bureaucracy* (Free Press, 1964); J. E. T. Eldridge and A. D. Crombie, *A Sociology of Organizations*, Ch. 5 (Allen & Unwin, 1974); T. E. Deal and A. A. Kennedy, *Corporate Cultures* (Addison-Wesley, 1982).

Current-cost Accounting ⟡ Changing Price Levels, Accounting for

Cybernetics The term *cybernetique* was first coined in 1834 by A. M. Ampère to describe that area of the social sciences concerned with the art of government. About a century later Norbert Wiener first used the anglicized form to describe the study of 'control and communication in the animal and the machine'.

Many people in the 1940s, converging from a variety of different starting-points, developed the view that a general theory of communication and control might well be equally applicable to a wide range of systems. That is to say, there is much in common between the brain and the computer; between problems of radar detection and inferential statistics; between diplomatic cyphers and the mechanisms of genetic transmission. In general, cybernetics is concerned with the theory of information flow in control systems. ⟡ Automation; Information Theory.

There has been a good deal of controversy over the formal definition of cybernetics, and a considerable degree of variety in the type of work carried out under its banner. Much of the work has been concerned with the mathematical basis of control theory; other studies have been directed more towards the theoretical foundations of telecommunications. Indeed cybernetics might be described as the theoretical basis of automation's three Cs – communication, computation and control. While cybernetics itself remains a formal rather than a practical subject, its results find application in such areas as automatic language translation, teaching machines, digital computation, machine-tool control and perhaps even politics. E.E.

N. Wiener, *Cybernetics* (MIT Press and J. Wiley, 2nd ed., 1961).

Cyclegraph/Chronocylegraph Records of the paths of movement obtained by attaching light sources to moving objects and exposing them to a photographic plate.

A cyclegraph uses continuous light sources to give continuous traces on the photograph. Alternatively, by pulsing the light sources, a chrono-cyclegraph is obtained showing the path of movement as a broken line, the spacing of the pear-shaped spots of light giving the speed of movement and the shape of the direction of movement.

The lights are normally attached to a worker's wrists, etc., to obtain a detailed record of the movement of limbs at the workplace, and hence facilitate detailed method study. ⇔ Method Study. R.W.

A. G. Shaw, *The Purpose and Practice of Motion Study* (Columbine Press, 2nd ed., 1960).

D

Data Network ⟡ Telecommunications

Data Processing (in Accounting) The continuous process of accumulation, classification and analysis of large quantities of facts and evidence in order to produce information reports. Hence data processing is basically concerned with the conversation of evidence and facts into information that, by reducing uncertainty, has value for decision-making purposes.

Data processing has become more and more closely associated with the computer, since the latter has the necessary capacity for classifying, adding, subtracting, storing and reporting a very large number of pieces of datum quickly. Accounting systems, being already precisely defined and operated, were from this viewpoint ideal for the earliest applications of the computer in matters such as order-processing, invoicing, sales and purchases ledger compilation, purchasing routines, sales analysis, stores control, wages accounting and financial statement construction. E.A.L., amended by J.V.P.

Data Processing (Automatic/Electronic/Integrated) In an organization data must be gathered, processed, stored and reported for various reasons (e.g. to provide cost estimates, customer bills, wages and salaries, etc.). Any arrangement for doing this can be described as a data-processing system. Such systems have evolved historically as follows:

(1)   Purely manual systems, based on pen-and-paper records of transactions.

(2)   Mechanical and electro-mechanical systems, in which the data are partially processed by punched-card systems, calculating machines, accounting machines, etc.

(3)   Electronic systems, in which the data are partially processed by electronic digital computers.

Systems (2) and (3) that incorporate some automatic elements are called automatic data-processing (ADP) systems. Type (3) systems that incorporate one or more electronic digital computing elements are called electronic data-processing (EDP) systems.

Systems being developed to handle the data entirely by machine (from collection of the source data to the production of the final output data) are called integrated data-processing (IDP) systems. ⟡ Computer. M.J.C.M.

Data Protection Legislation has been introduced to comply with the terms of the Council of Europe Convention for the Protection of Individuals with Regard to the Automatic Processing of Personal Data. The Data Protection Act 1984 provides for the introduction of a Data Protection Registrar to maintain a register of data-users and of persons who run computer bureaux concerned with personal data in both the public and private sectors. The provisions apply to automatically processed information, mainly that stored in computers, and do not cover records stored in manual files.

The Act introduces a series of criminal sanctions for failing to register etc., and gives the Registrar enforcement powers to ensure compliance with the eight 'data-protection principles' set out in schedule 1 of the Act, which broadly correspond to the convention's requirements. These are:

(1)   The information to be contained in personal data shall be obtained, and personal data shall be processed, fairly and lawfully.

(2)   Personal data shall be held only for one or more specified and lawful purposes.

(3)   Personal data held for any purpose or purposes shall not be used or disclosed in any manner incompatible with that purpose or those purposes.

(4)   Personal data held for any purpose or purposes shall be adequate, relevant and not excessive in relation to that purpose or those purposes.

(5)   Personal data shall be accurate and, where necessary, kept up to date.

(6)   Personal data held for any purpose or purposes shall not be kept for longer than is necessary for that purpose or those purposes.

(7)   An individual shall be entitled, (*a*) at reasonable intervals and without undue delay or expense, (i) to be informed by any data-user whether they hold personal data of which that individual is the subject; and (ii) to have access to any such data held by a data-user; and (*b*) where appropriate, to have such data corrected or erased.

(8)   Appropriate security measures shall be taken against unauthorized access to, or alteration, disclosure or destruction of, personal data and against accidental loss or destruction of personal data.

The Act also provides civil remedies for data-subjects. These include a right of access to personal data, compensation for loss occasioned by inaccurate data and an order that the data be rectified or erased. Certain exemptions apply to information such as tax and criminal records.

The Data Protection Tribunal will hear appeals from data-users and computer bureaux against refusal of registration and enforcement orders.

There are transitional provisions to allow for the implementation of the act in stages, beginning with the appointment of the Registrar in 1984, and there will be a two-year period after registration has begun, in November 1985, before data-subjects acquire their right of access.
J.C.E.M.

B. Niblett, *Data Protection Act 1984* (Oyez Longman, 1984).

Debentures ⟡ Claims

Debt Capital ⟡ Claims

Decentralization ⟡ Delegation

Decision Support System ⟡ Information System

Decision Theory Management is concerned with decision-making, so in an effort to help managers, statisticians and operations research scientists have developed a theoretical approach to decision-making known as statistical decision theory. This consists of constructing a pay-off matrix or table in which: (1) the rows list the alternative decisions that may be made; (2) the columns list the alternative environments or 'states of nature' that may occur; (3) the 'cells' at the intersection of a given pair of rows and columns represent the outcome of the given combination of decision and environment.

As a simple example, suppose that a manager who has a £100 unit to invest in the stock market has a choice of three alternative investments: (1) gilt-edged stocks, which will yield 5 per cent regardless of the state of the market; (2) highly speculative stocks, which will give a 20 per cent yield if the market booms, 2 per cent if it remains steady and − 10 per cent if there is a slump (i.e. the stocks will depreciate in value); (3) unit trusts, which will give a 10 per cent yield if the market booms, 5 per cent if it remains steady and 0 per cent if there is a slump.

A pay-off matrix incorporating this information may be constructed thus:

	Boom	Steady	Slump
Gilt-edged stocks	5	5	5
Speculative stocks	20	0	−10
Unit trusts	10	5	0

A statistician may then determine the best stock to buy, on the basis of the probabilities of the market behaving in any one of the alternative ways and the criteria the manager wishes to use as the basis of his decision. A more general problem of this kind might involve a manager constructing a decision tree (◊ Decision Trees) and resorting to subjective probabilities (◊ Subjective Probability). To consider utilities and equivalent monetary values (◊ Utility), decision analysis can be conducted.

A similar pay-off matrix may be constructed when the outcome of the manager's decision is dependent on the decision made by a competitor. This approach is known as game theory. M.J.C.M.

P. G. Moore, *Basic Operational Research* (Pitman, 1976).

Decision Trees A conceptual approach to making 'one off' decisions is offered under ◊ Decision Theory. However, very often a manager has to make a sequence of decisions in which, at any one decision-taking stage, the alternative decisions open are dependent on those taken earlier and their outcomes. This situation may be viewed conceptually using decision trees.

For example, consider a manufacturer who is asked by a chain-store owner to produce a product under a private label for sale in the latter's stores.[1] The manufacturer has the choice of agreeing to the request, ignoring it or offering a price reduction on the same product sold under his own brand label. If the manufacturer does not agree to the request, the store's owner can then make one of a set of alternative decisions, which in turn may lead to a further decision by the manufacturer. The sequence of alternative decisions may be represented by the decision tree shown on p. 121.

Once the decision tree has been constructed, from a knowledge of the probabilities of alternative decisions being made and the costs or profits associated with them, it may be possible to determine the best decision for the manufacturer to take. M.J.C.M.

1. This example is given by A. Mercer, *Operational Research Quarterly 17*, September 1966.

J. F. Magee, 'Decision Trees for Decision Making', *Harvard Business Review*, July–August 1964, p. 126.

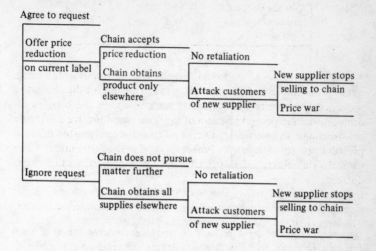

Degrees of Freedom ⟡ Statistical Tests

Delegation The act by which a person or group of persons possessing authority transfers part of that authority to a subordinate person or group. In all organizations there must be some delegation of authority, although organizations differ in the extent to which delegation takes place. The terms 'centralization' and 'decentralization' refer to the extent to which authority is concentrated at high levels or is diffused throughout the organization. The present climate of organizational thinking encourages the belief that centralization should be avoided in favour of the maximum degree of delegation compatible with efficient decision-making. By this means, the organization achieves greater flexibility, subordinates develop decision-making skills and, it is believed, organization members become more committed to the decisions that are taken.

To delegate effectively, managers must define the limits of the authority delegated to their subordinates, satisfy themselves that the subordinates are competent to exercise that authority and then discipline themselves to permit the subordinates the full use of that authority without constant checks and interference. There is a paradox, however, in that although managers may delegate authority to subordinates, they remain responsible for the subordinates' use of that authority – a state of affairs which does not encourage delegation. In practice, the effect of the

122   *Demand, Theory of*

Price

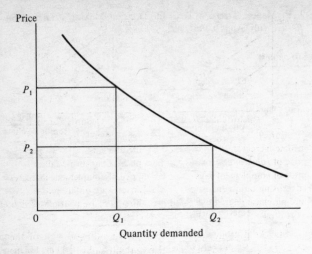

P_1

P_2

0   Q_1 Q_2

Quantity demanded

paradox is reduced by a realistically indulgent interpretation of such responsibility and by subordinates learning the requirements and prejudices of their supervisors beyond the limits of formal directives and job descriptions. ⟡ Authority. I.C.McG.

H. D. Koontz and C. J. O'Donnell, *Essentials of Management* (McGraw-Hill, 1972); J. Child, *Organization: A Guide to Problems and Practice*, Ch. 3 (Harper & Row, 1984).

Demand, Theory of In the theory of competitive markets demand is one of the two factors that determine market price; supply is the other. Manufacturers, however, are most frequently price-setters rather than price-takers and hence are interested in the various quantities of their products that will be demanded, given certain prices and certain other factors. Introspection and observation then play a part in isolating the factors that appear to have an influence on the demand for a particular product. Theories of consumer behaviour may be able to go further in providing a logical foundation for treating some factors as more important than others, but it is fair to say that they do not add much to the overall appreciation by manufacturers of the demand situation facing their products.

The most familiar relationship is that between the quantity demanded for a product and its price, and this is shown above. Because economists have usually been more interested in price determination, the price variable appears on the *y* axis, even though we treat it here as an independ-

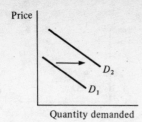

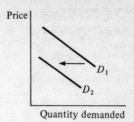

Figure 1
income increases
price of substitute increases
price of complement falls
advertising outlay increases
hire-purchase restrictions eased

Figure 2
income falls
price of substitute falls
price of complement increases
advertising outlay falls
hire-purchase restrictions tightened

ent variable. As it stands, this demand curve indicates that if the price were set at OP_1 then the quantity demanded would be OQ_1. If the price falls to OP_2 then quantity demanded will increase to OQ_2. Hence the demand curve gives a hypothetical schedule of prices and quantities, and it is drawn on the assumption that any other factors that might influence quantity demanded are held constant.

What are these other factors and what will happen if they do change? Factors that may be important include consumers' income, prices of other products, tastes, advertising outlays, hire-purchase restrictions. When such factors are set down it is evident that changes in these factors are probably much more important to manufacturers than changes in their prices in determining their sales. The figures above illustrate the likely relationships, using the basic concept of the demand curve.

In figure 1 we say that demand has increased because the curve has shifted outwards. In figure 2 demand has fallen because the curve has shifted inwards. Such moves are to be distinguished from movements along the demand curve, which are solely brought about by price changes. ⟨⟩ Prices, Theory of; Pricing (Market Pricing); Demand Functions; Elasticity. L.T.S.

R. G. Lipsey, *Introduction to Positive Economics* (Weidenfeld & Nicolson, 6th ed., 1983).

Demand Functions A demand function shows mathematically the relationship between quantity demanded and the factors that influence consumers' spending decisions. With this information one can measure the effect of price changes upon quantity demanded and also the effect of such factors as income and prices of competitive products.

Demand functions

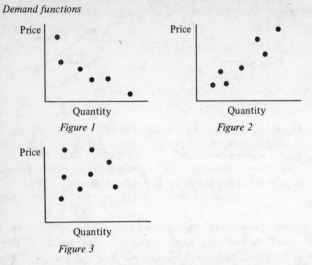

Figure 1

Figure 2

Figure 3

The first task in any demand investigation is to examine the mechanism that has generated the data available. The simplest example of this is the data on quantities exchanged and prices that are yielded through the workings of a competitive market. The figures above illustrate the way in which the three sets of data have been produced.

In figure 1 the data trace out the shape of the demand curve and in this market the supply curve is much more variable than the demand curve. In figure 2 it is the supply curve that is traced out because of the greater variability of the demand curve. In figure 3, on the basis of the evidence so far, neither relationship is traced out. The problem illustrated here is generally referred to as the *identification problem*.

Although we may be fortunate in finding that our data will enable us to identify either the demand curve or the supply curve, there is a second difficulty: how do we estimate the parameters of the demand or supply curve? Since the market involves two simultaneous relationships simple regression analysis (◊ Correlation and Regression) is not appropriate because the parameter estimates are biased. Other estimation methods have been developed to overcome this problem such as limited-information and two-stage least squares and details can be found in *Introductory Econometrics*, Ch. 4.

In addition to the problem of which estimation method to use, the researcher must choose an appropriate mathematical form for the relationship to be estimated. The simplest of these is obviously a linear form and thus we might estimate the following relationship:

$$q_t^d = a + \beta p_t + \gamma y_t + u_t$$

where

q_t^d = Quantity demanded at time t

p_t = Price at time t

y_t = Income at time t

a, β, γ = Parameters (or constants) of the equation

u_t = Random variable or disturbance term at time t

If, however, the data exhibit some degree of curvature then the following transformation may be more appropriate for estimation purposes:

$$\log q_t^d = a + b \log p + c \log y_t + v_t$$

where

a, b, c = parameters

v_t = random variable

logs to base e

The great advantage of the second relationship is that the price and income elasticities of demand are constants, irrespective of price, income and quantity levels. They are, in fact, equal to the estimates of b and c respectively.

Although least squares is often inappropriate there are some models for which it is appropriate. The simplest example is the model underlying the so-called cobweb theorem of elementary economic theory.

$$p_t^s = a + \beta q_t^d + u_t \tag{1}$$

$$q_t^s = \gamma + \delta p_{t-1} + u_t \tag{2}$$

$$q_t^d = q_t^s + w_t \tag{3}$$

In this model, in which the usual definitions apply, equation (1) is our demand relationship and we notice that the direction of causality is from quantity to price. Similarly, in our supply relationship, equation (2), we see that the direction of causality is from price of the previous period to current quantity. Hence the relationships are not simultaneous and least squares is quite appropriate.

Work in this field began in the USA in the 1920s and was particularly concentrated on the demand for agricultural produce. In recent years, however, the work has widened to include the study of consumer durables such as cars, televisions and washing machines. ⟨⟩ Prices, Theory of; Demand, Theory of; Elasticity. L.T.S.

R. L. Thomas, *Introductory Econometrics* (Longman, 1985).

Demarcation ◇ Trade Union – Demarcation

Department A subdivision of an organization, commonly, although not necessarily, under the authority of a manager. The term is general and there is no agreement as to its precise usage. Such subdivision is necessitated by the problem of the span of control – the inability of an executive to direct the activities of more than a limited number of subordinates. The basis on which departments are formed varies but in the industrial organization the most common criteria are function, product, customer, process and geographical location. Each has its attendant advantages and disadvantages and the designers of an organizational structure must evaluate each basis or mixture of bases in terms of the needs of the particular organization concerned. I.C.McG.

J. Woodward, *Industrial Organization: Theory and Practice* (OUP, 1965); H. D. Koontz and C. J. O'Donnell, *Principles of Management*, Ch. 13 (McGraw-Hill, 1964); C. B. Handy, *Understanding Organizations* (Penguin, 1985).

Department of Employment This large government department has wide-ranging responsibilities, its chief task being to promote the efficient use of manpower in a socially responsible way.

The title Department of Employment was adopted in 1970, following an alteration in the functions of the earlier Department of Employment and Productivity curtailing its responsibilities for government policy on productivity, prices and incomes (◇ Prices and Incomes Policy). Its earliest origins can be traced to 1909, when, as a result of the first Trade Board Act, the Board of Trade set up sixty-two Labour Exchanges with the purpose of bringing together employers and unemployed workers. Other developments which have affected DE activities include the establishment of the Ministry of Labour in 1917 and of the Ministry of National Insurance in 1945. In 1974 there was a major reorganization that split the DE from the ◇ Manpower Services Commission (MSC) and the independent ◇ Advisory, Conciliation and Arbitration Services (ACAS).

The Secretary of State for Employment is responsible for manpower policy, for the manpower aspects of regional policy and regional economic planning, and has senior representatives in each regional centre. Other responsibilities include promoting the policy of equal employment opportunity for workers, regardless of race, colour, origin or sex, and redundancy payments policy.

The Secretary of State also has powers to provide temporary employment for unemployed people and to finance schemes such as Community Industry, under which socially useful tasks are carried out by unemployed young people. These powers can be delegated to the MSC. The payment of unemployment benefit and supplementary benefit to people is carried out by the DE as the agent of the Department of Health and Social Security. The Secretary of State for Employment is also responsible for the Government's dealings with the MSC, ACAS and HSC and answers to Parliament for their work.

The Department consists of a London headquarters and a number of regional offices, each headed by a controller responsible for the execution of DE policy in that area through employment exchanges, sub-offices, branch employment offices and local agencies. Regional offices ensure compliance with orders made under the Wages Councils Acts. There are also several Factory Inspectorate divisions.

The Department's manpower policy is based on the maintenance of a high and stable level of employment and its basic objective is to make the best use of the labour and skills in the economy. It publishes statistical and other information in its monthly journal, the *Employment Gazette*, and sponsors research. A National Joint Advisory Council consisting of representatives of the ⟨⟩ Confederation of British Industry and the ⟨⟩ Trades Union Congress meets periodically to advise the Secretary to the DE on broad policy questions. Present policy emphasizes the need to increase labour mobility.

The employment services of the Department include employment exchanges, transfer schemes, and a youth employment service. The employment exchanges provide a free employment service for employers seeking labour and for employees, whether employed or not, seeking jobs. Vacancies that cannot be filled locally are circulated to exchanges over a wide area and, if necessary, over the whole country. Special services at many of the exchanges exist for ex-regular members of HM forces; those seeking professional, managerial, executive or trainee posts; nurses and midwives; disabled and blind persons.

The training function of the DE is dominated by its role laid down in the ⟨⟩ Industrial Training Act 1964, which empowered the Secretary to the Department to establish ⟨⟩ Industrial Training Boards, each responsible for training in a particular industry.

On ⟨⟩ Safety, health and ⟨⟩ Welfare at work, the DE is responsible, via its Factory Inspectorate, for the administration and enforcement of the Factories Act, 1961 and associated legislation (⟨⟩ Factory Inspector).

The industrial-relations function of the DE has a long history, but this function passed to the ⟨⟩ Advisory, Conciliation and Arbitration Service on its foundation in 1974. ⟨⟩ Industrial Relations – Reform in Great Britain. N.H.C., amended by M.J.F.P.

Department of Employment, *A Guide to the DE Group* (DE, 1978).

Depreciation 'The measure of the wearing out, consumption or other permanent loss of value of a fixed asset, whether arising from use, effluxion of time or obsolescence through technological or market changes.'[1] ⬦ Assets.

In accountancy practice the object of depreciation policy is to reduce the historical or revalued cost of fixed assets, at which figure they are entered in the books of account, to scrap or realizable value by the end of their expected lives. To this end an amount for depreciation, estimated according to some formula, is entered in the annual profit-and-loss account and deducted from the book value of the fixed assets. By this procedure the accountant maintains what he considers to be the most reasonable stated value for each fixed asset.

It is important to appreciate that this bookkeeping procedure cannot, as is often supposed, result in the saving up of a fund of money with which to replace fixed assets. A mere entry in a book of account could hardly achieve this. What such an entry does ensure, however, is that recognition is given to the using up of assets when calculating the net profits of a business. Hence in so far as owners or directors are guided in making drawings or dividend decisions by their accounting net profits, the depreciation entry prevents them from drawing more than they otherwise might.

Accountants use certain formulas for calculating depreciation deductions; the most usual are:

(1)   The straight-line method, by which the asset value (less estimated scrap value) is written off by equal instalments over its estimated life.

(2)   The reducing-balance method, by which depreciation for any year is a certain fixed percentage of the balance at the beginning of that year. Thus the depreciation charge per period gradually diminishes throughout the asset's life.

Straight-line depreciation is generally considered to be better practice amongst accountants, yet it may well be that the latter more nearly reflects the actual loss in value of many industrial assets, since obsolescence is often heavy during the first few years where a significant rate of technological change is present. However, some people are unhappy about present depreciation practice, especially those, including many accountants, who are concerned to use depreciation accounting as a means of maintaining the earning power of assets in tact. ⬦ Changing Price Levels, Accounting for. E.A.L., amended by J.V.P.

W. T. Baxter, *Depreciation* (Sweet & Maxwell, 1971).

1. *SSAP.12: Accounting for Depreciation* (Accounting Standards Committee, 1977).

Deprival Value ⟡ Valuation of Assets.

Depth Interview ⟡ Motivation Research.

Design The act of deciding into what form materials should be manipulated in order to have value added; hence design is not something which can be done at will by a manufacturing organization. In building, design is termed architecture, in machinery, engineering. The requirements of a product that the designer normally takes into account are: function, ⟡ Ergonomics, mechanism, structure, production, economics, brand presentation, aesthetics and motivation. Having isolated the relevant requirements for any particular product, their integration in an end-product becomes a problem-solving situation. The design of services, e.g. advertisements, print, letter-headings, is susceptible to the same analysis. A powerful school of thought contends that this integration of requirements in a design is a totally creative act, which cannot be reached by methodological analysis. An important influence in recent years has been the development of a new technique called 'value analysis'. This entails the systematic evaluation of products, component by component, with the object of minimizing cost without impairing their specifically functional performance. However, an overall design methodology has also emerged along the lines of formal problem-solving/optimization procedures. In addition, of course, the computer has been harnessed to the effective exploration of a full range of design possibilities and options under the generic name ⟡ Computer-aided Design. G.S.C.W.

L. B. Archer, *Systematic Method for Designers* (Council of Industrial Design, 1965).

Desk Research (in Marketing) The collation of relevant data, already collected for a different purpose, and its evaluation in terms of a given marketing situation. This form of research in relation to markets is most frequently conducted where extensive published data is available, and/or where the use of sample surveys (⟡ Market Survey) is not practicable for reasons of cost, urgency, or a lack of co-operation from the potential informants. Such collation of extant data is also entirely appropriate as a preliminary to any new investigation that is contemplated. Quite frequently some data is only available on an informal basis, such as a comment over the telephone. The resulting report will often be fragmented and incomplete in certain details, particularly where commercial secrecy hinders data collection (⟡ Industrial Espionage).

The computer is increasingly offering databases that can provide rapid access to the relevant statistical information available in industrial and, to a lesser extent, consumer markets. Such services, e.g. Prestel, are available on a subscription basis. G.S.C.W.

M. Adler, 'The Use of the Telephone in Industrial Market Research', in *Marketing and Market Research* (Crosby Lockwood, 1967); G. Wills, *Sources of UK Information* (Benn Brothers, 1974).

Dials ⟡ Displays

Dilution The relaxation of standards in the use of labour, in particular the relaxation of existing customs on the employment of skilled workers. This includes the introduction of alternative classes of labour, or 'dilutees', on jobs previously regarded as skilled; the use of semi-skilled or unskilled labour to assist skilled workers; and the employment of women on work hitherto performed by men. Alternatively, work itself may be diluted by increased mechanization or by the breaking up of jobs into smaller operations, some of which can be performed by semi-skilled or unskilled operatives.

Resistance to the dilution of labour is largely a function of trade-union strength and policy. It is strongest where craft traditions are strongest. It can militate against the employment of workers who have taken courses at government training centres. Nevertheless dilution occurred on a large scale during both world wars to alleviate labour shortages. In the First World War dilution caused much labour unrest but in the Second World War there were a number of Relaxation Agreements between unions and employers or their federations (⟡ Employers' Associations). These were designed to last the duration of the war, but many have by common consent been continued into peacetime use. Apart from those occurring under formal procedures, many cases of dilution take place by informal agreement at the workplace. Dilution may take place as a result of ⟡ Productivity Bargaining. A modern equivalent is de-skilling of work accompanying technological change.

Under some industry agreements, e.g. engineering, dilutees must be registered. N.H.C. amended by M.J.F.P.

K. Hall and I. Miller, 'Industrial Attitudes to Skills Dilution', *British Journal of Industrial Relations*, vol. 9, no. 1 (March 1971), pp. 1–20; J. Hinton, *The First Shop-stewards Movement* (Allen & Unwin, 1973); C. Goodrich, *The Frontier of Control* (Pluto Press, 1975).

Direct Mail ⟡ Advertising

Disabled Persons' Employment The Disabled Persons (Employment) Act 1944 provides that every employer of twenty or more persons must employ a quota of registered disabled persons. The size of the quota, expressed in percentage terms, is laid down by the Secretary for Employment. The Minister may, in addition, designate certain employments as being reserved entirely for disabled persons.

Employers have to maintain records showing the total number of their employees and the number and names of registered disabled persons. Failure to employ the requisite quota of disabled persons is an offence. For the purposes of the Act a disabled person is one who, on account of injury, disease or congenital deformity, is substantially handicapped in obtaining or keeping employment or in undertaking work on his or her own account of a kind which, apart from that injury, disease or deformity, would be suited to his age, experience and qualifications.
W.F.F.

Discipline Control over behaviour. Any successful group activity requires each member of the group to understand what behaviour is expected of him and to be able and willing to produce that behaviour. It may be argued, therefore, that a necessary basis for a sound disciplinary policy is that all employees should understand the requirements of their own job, should possess the requisite skill and knowledge and should be convinced of the usefulness of their activities in relation to neighbouring activities and to the purposes of the organization as a whole. When company rules are clearly seen to arise out of necessity they are likely to command respect and disciplinary problems will be few. Where, however, there is no general confidence in the ability, reasonableness or integrity of management, good discipline will be exceedingly difficult to obtain.

Whenever possible rules should be positive rather than prohibitive, clear and well publicized. It is desirable that rules be formulated in collaboration with employee representatives. Penalties should be known in advance and applied without favouritism, although with due regard to particular circumstances. An impartial procedure for the investigation of the more serious infringements should be instituted, together with an appeals procedure. Disciplinary action against an employee should be recorded in his or her personal file, although it may be suggested that there should be a time limit after which the record of the offence be expunged. Finally one may add that members of supervision and management must be scrupulous in their own observation of rules. ⬦ Authority; Norm; Social Control. I.C.MCG.

P. Pigors and C. A. Myers, *Personnel Administration* (McGraw-Hill, 6th ed., 1973), Ch. 19.

Disclosure of Information The antecedents are early ⟐ Profit-sharing schemes and formal ⟐ Joint Consultation within works councils. The ⟐ Industrial Relations Act 1971 provided that employers 'of more than 350 persons' should make an annual written statement to all employees, and placed upon them a duty 'to disclose to representatives of recognized registered unions all information within their possession relating to their undertakings', in order not to impede trade unions in carrying out collective bargaining and in accordance with good industrial-relations practice. Following the repeal of this act, a number of the disclosure clauses were reintroduced and extended in subsequent legislation. In particular the ⟐ Employment Protection Act 1975 included some significant changes regarding enforcement (allowing trade unions, for example, to make complaints to the Central Arbitration Committee), while the ⟐ Industry Act of the same year made a number of provisions for information-sharing within planning agreements. There is now no legal obligation on employers to make annual statements to employees on disclosure (although there is to make a statement of participation), but none the less the practice has continued to flourish. Indeed, despite a falling off in the number of companies newly adopting employee reporting at the end of the 1970s, 42 per cent of firms report this practice (80 per cent of those with more than 1,000 employees). There are discrepancies in managers' and trade unionists' accounts of the information actually given (consistently on pay and conditions of service, manpower requirements and the financial position of the company, managements were found to take the more favourable view of what had actually been provided). Moreover, there is little doubt that codes on disclosure of information have had only a circumscribed impact upon actual practice. But disclosure of information is an important element in the changing policies of managements in the 1970s and it is clear that supportive legislation significantly encouraged its general expansion. Again, in the 1980s disclosure of information received a further impetus as a consequence of the rise of the new technologies and the emergent problems which managements face in ensuring that they are successfully implemented. M.J.F.P.

W. W. Daniel and N. Millward, *Workplace Industrial Relations in Britain* (Heinemann, 1983); R. Hussey and A. Marsh, *Disclosure of Information and Employee Reporting* (Gower, 1983).

Discounted Cash Flow (DCF) A generic term applying to the ⟐ Net Present Value and ⟐ Internal Rate of Return approaches to investment appraisal. The process of 'discounting' involves the valuation of cash flows (inflows and outflows) expected to occur in the future in terms of their worth today (present value). The present value of a future cash flow is therefore a function of the income per unit time to be forgone by receiving that cash flow in the future rather than at the present, and the interval between the present and the future occurrence of the cash flow, i.e. there exists a 'time-value of money'.

The concept of discounting may be seen as similar to the principle of 'compound interest'; £100 invested for two years at 10 per cent per annum compound will, at the end of the period, yield a receipt of £121. Thus, given the opportunity to invest at 10 per cent per annum compound, the present value of £121 to be received in two years' time is £100. This relationship may be generalized in the form:

$$Po = \frac{Yn}{(1 + i)} n$$

where Po = Present value

Yn = Undiscounted value of cash flow occurring at the end of the nth time period, e.g. one year

i = Interest rate (expressed as a decimal)

n = Number of time periods between the present and the occurrence of Yn

The present value of a future income stream may be compared with the investment sum required to generate it – the difference between them being called the ⟨⟩ Net Present Value – in order to assess the attractiveness of the investment opportunity. ⟨⟩ Capital Budgeting. P.J.A.H.

R. A. Brealey and S. C. Myers, *Principles of Corporate Finance* (McGraw-Hill, 1981); H. Bierman and S. Smidt, *The Capital Budgeting Decision*, (Collier Macmillan, 1975).

Discretionary Income The proportion of the income of an individual or household that is not committed to regular, basic expenditure to maintain a prevailing style of living. As such, it is a continually changing concept both within and between social groups. The prevailing perception of an appropriate standard of living is basic to the classification of goods and services that such discretionary income can be expected to purchase at any given time. In a developing society many products and services can be expected as time passes to move from being an object of discretionary expenditure to becoming a basic requirement, both socially and psychologically, e.g. the motorcar, holidays. Within

Discrimination

any particular society, however, there will be differing perceptions of these classifications (⬦ Market Segmentation), particularly between different income groups. Most new products or services are introduced into markets where their purchase must make a call on discretionary income. Hence the understanding of the determinants of such disbursements is vitally important to marketing management. Until such time as a product becomes a basic need, however, competition is not just between similar brands of a single product but also between one discretionary product group and all other product groups within a customer's current discretionary environment. ⬦ Consumption Function. G.S.C.W.

Discrimination The lengthy Sex Discrimination Act 1975 and Race Relations Act 1976 prohibit discrimination on grounds of sex, marital status, colour, race, nationality, ethnic or national origin. For example it is generally unlawful to discriminate on any of the above grounds in advertising for, taking on, promoting, training or dismissing employees. Broadly, the legislation requires individuals to be treated on their merits and aims to make less favourable treatment based simply on grounds of sex or race unlawful. This is so whether such treatment is obvious, like sexual harassment or racial abuse, or indirect and unintentional. Thus it has been held unlawful to adopt a policy of not employing those with young children, even if it could be shown that this policy was applied equally to men and women, since in practice it would disproportionately disqualify mothers. The legislation, however, goes no further than seeking to ensure the fair treatment of individuals. A strategy that attempted to redress historical imbalances in the labour market, whether between the sexes or between persons of differing racial backgrounds, would itself be unlawful in this country. Consequently, so-called 'positive' or 'reverse' discrimination, which purports to give preferential treatment to traditionally disadvantaged minorities identified by reference to sex or race, is not permissible, except in limited circumstances in the context of vocational training.

Individuals may take complaints of discrimination to an ⬦ Industrial Tribunal, or, in non-employment matters, to the County Court. The tribunal or court may then make an order declaring the rights of the parties, award compensation in cases of intentional discrimination and recommend measures to obviate or reduce the discriminatory practice.

The Equal Opportunities Commission and the Commission for Racial Equality established by the legislation, have a strategic role in identifying and combating widespread patterns of inequality. Each commission has issued a Code of Practice, which gives guidance on the scope of the law and practical advice about the promotion of fair and non-discriminatory employment practices. The provisions of the codes are admissible in evidence in any proceedings and must be taken into account by the tribunal or court. The commissions are empowered to investigate and eliminate unequal practices by, for example, the service of non-discrimination notices which, if breached, can be enforced by injunctions. They may also assist individual complainants, and may institute proceedings themselves in respect of discriminatory advertisements or instructions.

Neither of the two Acts purports to affect other statutory provisions, such as the Factories Act 1961, which regulate the employment of women or which provide special rules relating to, for example, retirement or maternity. However, our membership of the Common Market has meant that UK domestic legislation can no longer be read in isolation. EEC law has priority and the Community has adopted various 'equal rights' provisions that are more extensive than the protections guaranteed by the British anti-discrimination legislation. The EEC rules are likely to prove increasingly important in the future, particularly in the area of ⬦ Equal Pay. ⬦ EEC Law. KW.

M. Malone, *A Practical Guide to Discrimination Law* (Grant McIntyre, 1980).

Dismissal of Employees (Law) Dismissal law is complex, partly because the common-law rules (i.e. those made by judges) and a variety of statutory provisions overlap. A dismissal may be wrongful or unfair or for redundancy; occasionally it may be all of these, sometimes none of them.

At common law, all employees who are dismissed without the proper notice to which they are entitled (or in breach of an agreed procedure that is contractually binding on their employer) may sue for *wrongful dismissal*. This action for damages will be heard in the ordinary courts. It is the absence of due notice that renders a dismissal *wrongful* and accordingly employees cannot sue at common law where they have been dismissed on full notice, even if the employer has no good reason for giving them notice. Nor can employees complain where they are sacked summarily (i.e. without notice) if they are themselves guilty of serious contractual misconduct, such as theft or wilful refusal to obey a lawful and reasonable order. The usual remedy for wrongful dismissal is damages, limited to the sum the employees would have earned net during the period of notice that they should have been given. The fact that this amount may not adequately compensate an employee for any period of unemployment following dismissal will not increase the damages. Employees cannot ordinarily prevent their employer from dismissing them wrongfully, nor can they obtain reinstatement once the dismissal has been affected.

The right to terminate employment by giving proper notice is one that the courts will ordinarily imply into a contract of employment unless, for example, the contract is for a fixed term. What amounts to proper notice is primarily a matter to be settled by the parties themselves at the outset of the contract. In default of this, the common law requires 'reasonable' notice (which may be fixed by reference to what is customary in the trade or occupation), subject to the minimum periods of notice prescribed by s. 49 of the Employment Protection (Consolidation) Act 1978. The Act provides that where an employee has been continuously employed for between four weeks and two years, one week's notice is the minimum. Thereafter he or she is entitled to an additional week's notice for every year of service up to a maximum of twelve weeks' notice after twelve or more years. These periods are minima and so may be increased, but not reduced, by agreement between the parties.

Employees, however, may agree to accept wages in lieu of the appropriate notice. As indicated earlier, they forfeit their right to notice or to accept wages in lieu where they are guilty of serious misconduct.

Because of the inadequacies of the common-law action for wrongful dismissal, a quite separate right to complain to an Industrial Tribunal of *unfair dismissal* has been in existence since 1972. An employee must have been employed for two years prior to dismissal in order to claim the dismissal was unfair. A dismissal that is wrongful is not necessarily also unfair, nor vice versa. ⟨⟩ Unfair Dismissal.

Where an employee's job disappears, and the employee is dismissed in consequence, he or she may be entitled to a statutory redundancy payment in addition to any right to sue for wrongful dismissal where the employment was terminated without due notice having been given. Again, there is a minimum qualifying period of two years' service. Ordinarily, a genuine redundancy dismissal will not be unfair unless, for example, the selection procedure was inadequate. As a matter of law redundancy occurs where job losses result from the employer ceasing to trade or moving location, or because a business's requirements for employees to do work of the particular kind in question have ceased or diminished (whether as a result of the introduction of new technology, reorganization or a decline in demand for the firm's products). ⟨⟩ Redundancy. K.W.

R. Fox, *Payments on the Termination of Employment* (Oyez Longman,

1981); B. Titman and P. Camp, *Dismissal and Taxation of Employees* (Butterworths, 1982).

Dismissal Procedure An arrangement whereby an employer terminates his contract of employment with an employee, whether on grounds of incompetence, misconduct or ⟡ Redundancy. The dismissal procedure of a company defines the method of deciding that a person shall be dismissed, with whom the authority for dismissals rests, and what form an appeal against dismissal should take. L.S., amended by E.L.

Advisory, Conciliation and Arbitration Service, *Disciplinary Practice and Procedure in Employment* (HMSO, 1977).

Displays Any part of a machine that provides information to the controller is termed a 'display'. By far the most important displays for the purpose of controlling most machines are, of course, visual ones.

There are two complementary aspects to the design of good displays. The first is concerned with the basic form in which information is to be presented (e.g. should it be pictorial or symbolic; continuous or intermittent?) and clearly it is necessary to relate these basic design features to the control decisions and actions that follow. The second aspect is concerned with the detail of design once the overall form has been established.

Displays may be used in many ways: they may provide precise quantitative values such as those obtained from odometers; they may provide approximate value indications such as those obtained from many motor vehicle thermometers; they may provide indications of current trend or signals of warning. On the basis of the information received, the human operator is required to make a decision and to act. Thus display design decisions should be based upon the operator's input requirements in relation to his consequent actions.

A good deal of published research describes detailed design recommendations concerning dials and other forms of visual display, and includes guidance concerning the size and shape of the whole display, pointers, graduation marks and numerals. ⟡ Machine Controls. E.E.

E. J. McCormick and M. S. Sanders, *Human Factors in Engineering and Design* (McGraw-Hill, 5th ed., 1983).

Dispute ⟡ Industrial Dispute

Distribution Mix The particular combination of channels or in-

Direct	Mail order	Retailing	Wholesaling
Manufacturer	Manufacturer	Manufacturer	Manufacturer
↓	↓	↓	↓
Customer	Post Office	Retailer	Wholesaler
	↓	↓	↓
	Customer	Customer	Retailer
			↓
			Customer

stitutions through which a manufacturer distributes his product at any time. The more common are indicated in the figure above.

It is normal for a manufacturer to use one sequence predominantly, although at times a combination may well be used, where one does not exclude another. Extensive direct distribution and/or mail order (⟡Selling; Mail Order) often generates resistance in other less direct channels. Marketing channels, once adopted, tend to become traditional; effective management requires their continual revaluation. The effective sharing of management and sales development within a marketing channel requires a high level of management skill. A different balance of contributions from various members will depend on their skills under particular competitive circumstances at each stage. The more effective approach to such activities essentially sees each level in a marketing channel marketing to the next one along and sometimes goes under the name of trade marketing (⟡ Retail Audit). The value of distribution secured in retail outlets and a wholesaler's agreement to handle a product is an item of goodwill that can be very expensive to obtain, particularly in competitive markets. The particular channels chosen to distribute any product or service must take into account the other elements in the total ⟡ Marketing Mix, and in particular the image that it is desired to project (⟡ Branding). For example it is unlikely that *all* retail outlets will be permitted to offer a particular product or service. The appropriate outlets must be selected, with the convenience of the eventual customer in mind. G.S.C.W.

B. Mallen, *The Marketing Channel* (J. Wiley, 1967).

Diversification A company is said to diversify when it extends its activities outside its existing field of business. This it can do in a number of ways; diversify, integrate, merge or acquire (take over).

Briefly considering the last two, a company may acquire (or take over) or merge with another company, which may or may not be in the same line of business as itself; a takeover is generally of advantage to the company making the bid but not necessarily of advantage to the one being taken over, while a merger is a union that both companies see as being to their mutual advantage.

Integration can be 'forward' or 'backward'. A forward integration implies that the company is extending its activities down the natural route that is taken by its produce as it passes from the company to its eventual consumption – in other words the company goes into competition with some of its customers. A backward integration implies that the company is extending its activities up the product route into the raw materials or components from which it is made – in other words the company goes into competition with some of its suppliers. Thus a company making sulphuric acid could integrate forward into, for example, making fertilizers or could integrate backwards into mining or transporting raw sulphur.

Diversification, as well as having the meanings above, also implies extending beyond the existing field of business in three ways:

(1)   Introducing new products into the same market (for example a company selling soft drinks through public houses might start selling potato crisps through the same route).

(2)   Introducing existing products into new markets (for example a company selling soft drinks through public houses might start selling through cafés).

(3)   Introducing new products into new markets (for example a company selling soft drinks through public houses might start selling potato crisps through cafés.

As a general rule it is said that successful diversifications are those that involve a close relationship with the company's existing markets, as in (1) above, or its existing technology, as in (2) above. However, some successful examples of type (3), sometimes known as conglomerates, do exist. Conglomerates are companies with a wide range of products, not necessarily related to each other in any way, selling to a wide range of unrelated markets.

In the context of diversification it is worth noting 'divestment'. This means selling off a part of a company that is no longer considered appropriate; it is thus the opposite of diversification and is a disinvestment ⟡ Patterns of Growth. A.J.A.A.

E. Ralph Biggadike, *Corporate Diversification: Entry, Strategy and Performance* (Harvard University Press, 1979).

Divestment ⟡ Diversification

Dividend Policy Dividend policy is concerned with the division of net profits after taxes between payments to shareholders and retentions for reinvestment ostensibly on behalf of the shareholders.

From the legal viewpoint, dividends may generally be paid out of the balance of the past profits. It is not essential that profits should have been made in the company's accounting year to which the dividend relates.

Clearly there are a great number of factors which influence dividend policy, including the immediate cash position, the timing of capital repayments for redeemable debentures and preference shares, the financing requirements for growth of assets, profit expectations, future plans for capital raising and therefore the degree of need to please existing and potential investors.

A different, more analytical approach to the question of dividend policy is that of exploring the impact of dividend policy on shareholders' wealth in order to arrive at some optimal rate of dividend payment. The importance to the company of a consideration of this approach is evident, since a high retention rate, although providing a source of financial merit, adversely affects the price of its shares and therefore its attractiveness for the investor. E.A.L.

> J. C. Van Horne, *Financial Management and Policy*, (Prentice-Hall, 3rd ed., 1974), chs. 11 and 12.

Division of Labour ◇ Specialization

Double-entry ◇ Accounting

Dynamic Programming (DP) A method of solving decision problems that can be broken down into a sequence of smaller ones, each of which has an optimization objective associated with it. It is based on Bellman's 'principle of optimality', which states that an optimal policy has the property that, whatever the initial state and initial decisions are, the remaining decisions must constitute an optimal policy with regard to the state resulting from the first decision. Examples of areas of application are: (1) the appointment of effort between competing projects to maximize expected gain; (2) the replacement of individual vehicles in a company's fleet of vehicles (◇ Replacement Problems); (3) the determination of the shortest (or least-cost) route between two locations. R.S.S.

> Harvey M. Wagner, *Principles of Operational Research* (Prentice-Hall, 1975).

Dysfunctional ◇ Functional (2)

E

Earnings Yield ⟡ Price–earnings Ratio

Econometrics Suppose one were interested in explaining the demand for motorcars in the U K over the last decade, perhaps because one wanted to forecast likely demand over the next decade. To do this one would need to isolate those factors, such as income and prices, etc., that have been important in explaining car demand in the past. The subject that deals with this sort of problem is called econometrics.

The subject matter of econometrics is the measurement of economic relationships that are produced from *a priori* reasoning. Such knowledge is useful for the testing of *a priori* reasoning and also for the opportunity that it gives of studying the implications of alternative courses of action. To take the example above, economic theory postulates a relationship between quantity demanded, price and income, one form of which is given below:

$$q_t^d = a + b\,p_t + c\,y_t + u_t$$

where q_t^d = quantity demanded at time t

p_t = relative price at time t

y_t = real income at time t

u_t = disturbance term at time t

a, b, c = parameters (or constants) whose values are unknown

In this case the problem is to obtain estimates of a, b and c, given knowledge q_t^d, p_t and y_t.

According to economic theory the sign of the parameter attached to the price variable should be negative, whilst that attached to the income variable should be positive. An econometric analysis of such a relationship for a particular product will throw light on the theory and will also allow one to examine the consequences of alterations in the price and income variables. In particular, a forecast of future real income and prices will enable one to forecast car demand.

Econometrics as a subject in its own right builds upon several other disciplines. The relationships to be measured are derived from economic theory and expressed in the language of mathematics. Before measurement can occur, data on the variables is needed and this is obtained from the field of economic statistics. Finally mathematical statistics provides the tools for measuring and testing the estimates for reliability.

The relationships to be measured may refer to a sector of the economy or the whole economy. Thus much early work was concentrated upon the measurement of demand functions, particularly in agriculture. However, in recent years, with the development of the high-speed computer, a great deal of effort has been devoted to building models of the whole economy, particularly in the USA, Holland and the UK.

Any relationship involves parameters and variables and one must have data on the variables before one can obtain estimates of the parameters. This data may be available from government or trade sources but this is not always the case. Econometricians may have to compile their own data from primary sources. They may also have to adjust official data so that it refers to the same variables as the theoretical relationship.

Finally, the data used by econometricians constitutes only a sample of human experience, whereas economic theories are formed quite generally. It is at this point, therefore, that statistical inference becomes necessary in order to ensure that the estimates of the parameters derived from a particular sample have a wider significance. ◊ Forecasting (Medium-term). L.T.S.

R. L. Thomas, *Introductory Econometrics* (Longman, 1985)

Economic Lot Sizes ◊ Batch Sizes

Economic Order Quantity ◊ Inventory or Stock-control Problems

Economics Academic literature abounds with definitions of economics. Rather than attempting another one we can say that 'Economics is what economists do'. In the main economists have been concerned with three areas: the problem of resource allocation; the problems of unemployment and over-full employment; and the problem of growth of output per head.

A still-useful division is that between *economic theory* and *applied economics*. The role of economic theory is to explain the workings of the economic system, or parts of it, in a simplified manner, whilst that of applied economics is to apply the theory to selected topics, e.g. the study of inflation or the control of monopoly. Clearly the development of economics as a body of knowledge depends heavily upon the interaction of these two branches of the subject, for theories are modified as they fail to explain reality and new theories are often called forth by a growing awareness of new facts that older theories cannot explain. ⇨ Model (in Economic Analysis).

A division often found in the literature is that between *micro-economics*, or the economics of small units, and *macro-economics*, or the economics of aggregates. ⇨ Macro-economic Models.

Micro-economists study the way that resources in a country are allocated through the market system and this involves them in detailed studies of firms, industries and the relationships of government and industry. ⇨ Business Motivation; Costs; Cost Functions; Demand, Theory of; Demand Functions; Elasticity; Forecasting, Medium-term; Growth of the Firm; Input/Output; Location of Industry; Market Models; Monopoly Policy; Patterns of Growth; Prices, Theory of; Production Theory; Profits; Restrictive Practices.

Macro-economists look at the economic system in a different way, asking themselves the question, 'Why is the level of gross national product what it is?' This means that they have to measure the production of the economic system (⇨ National Income Accounts) and then search for explanations of its level in terms of the decisions of consumers, businessmen and the government. ⇨ Balance of Payments; Consumption Function; Employment; Forecasting for the Economy; Fiscal Policy; Inflation; Investment in the Economy; Monetary Policy; The Multiplier; Planning (in the Economy).

The growth specialist is asking the question, 'What makes the rate of growth in output per head of a country increase (or decrease)?' This means once again that one has to decide what is meant by growth before one can search for explanations of why it occurs (or fails to occur). ⇨ Growth in the Economy (Determinants); Growth (Measurement).

As economics has developed we find that some areas of study have been transferred to other specialists whilst new areas of study have arisen. *Demography* is an example of the former whilst *growth* and *cost-benefit analysis* are examples of the latter. The development of one subject, *econometrics*, deserves special mention, however.

The nature of economic theory is such that it can be translated into the language of mathematics, thus yielding significant benefits in terms of clarity and ease of argument. Side by side with this development came the urge to measure economic relationships and so subject the *a priori* theories to rigorous tests. Thus from early work in the field of agricultural supply-and-demand functions the subject of econometrics developed, fusing together economics, mathematics and statistics. ⇨ Econometrics; Index Numbers.

One last development is worth noting. As management education has progressed so economics has appeared as one of the background subjects of study. This has caused economists engaged in the field to look closely at the subject through the eyes of the entrepreneur and has to some extent paved the way for the development of a new subject, ⟨⟩⟩ Managerial Economics.

The methods used in economics have changed over time, making it more akin to the physical sciences. As greater stress has been laid on the testing of hypotheses, measurements and predictions, so the use of mathematics and statistics has increased at the expense of more literary and qualitative methods. The quest for scientific detachment and rigour is perhaps most clearly seen in the work of academic economists. The influence of political and social values and the exercise of qualitative methods, on the other hand, are most clearly seen in economic analysis when one considers the public pronouncements of economists.

All this has meant that students of economics cover a different range of subjects than did their predecessors of thirty years ago. The course is likely to contain mathematics, statistics and accountancy to a considerable degree and there is likely to be less emphasis upon economic history and the historical development of economic analysis. L.T.S.

A. J. Culyer, *Economics* (Blackwell, 1985).

EEC Law When the UK became a member of the EEC on 1 January 1973, by virtue of the European Communities Act 1972 it became subject to the Treaty of Rome 1957, which established the Community, and to all laws made before and since by the legislative body, the Council of Ministers. Laws made in Brussels are in the form of either Regulations or Directives, the former being automatically effective in all member states and the latter requiring implementation by the member states' legislature. In this country this is done by means of Statutory Instrument, the provisions having been adapted to our own system. Directives have been used to try to bring about the harmonization of member states' laws.

The European Court of Justice interprets EEC law and can hear appeals against decisions of the Commission and between member states, but most provisions are directly applicable and can be relied on in cases heard in member states' domestic courts. The European Court may give a preliminary ruling on the meaning of a provision of EEC law, but the case will be returned to the domestic courts for the ruling to be applied.

Where there is a conflict between national and EEC law, EEC law prevails and new members are required to bring their law in line. The 1972 Act itself introduced some changes into company law, and other major changes in structure and practice are now consolidated in the Companies Act 1985 (◊ Company Law). Other areas where E E C law has had a major influence are those of employment (◊ Equal Pay), ◊ Product Liability and competition law. Articles 85 and 86 of the Treaty of Rome forbid cartel arrangements (◊ Restrictive Practices), which interfere with competition, and abuse of a dominant position within the Common Market. Fines of up to 10 per cent of the previous year's turnover can be imposed for breach of these provisions. J.C.E.M.

P. Mathijsen, *A Guide to European Community Law* (Sweet & Maxwell, 4th ed., 1985)

Efficient-market Hypothesis (EMH) The theory of efficient markets appears to have its origin in work by the Frenchman Bachelier in 1900. Focusing its attention on the question 'Do stock prices behave randomly?' the theory gained considerable impetus in 1953 when work by Kendall suggested that prices did indeed behave randomly. This was a seminal proposition (embodied in the so-called random-walk hypothesis) because it implied that non-random patterns of price behaviour could arise only from imperfections in the pricing mechanism of the market.

According to the EMH, correct prices, i.e. those having 'true' values, will only arise when the market place is sufficiently competitive and participants are working with all of the relevant information available. Changes from equilibrium prices will only occur when new information becomes available. Thus, three levels of efficiency are now judged to be appropriate in the consideration of stock-market pricing, namely, weak, semi-strong and strong. The weak form states that current prices reflect all information contained in earlier prices; the semi-strong form requires prices to capture all other published information, e.g. dividend announcements, as well as past prices; the strong form places further requirements on the quality, quantity and interpretation of *all* information considered relevant to the price-formulating process. P.J.A.H.

S. M. Keane, *Stock Market Efficiency – Theory, Evidence, Implications* (Philip Allan, 1983).

Effort Bargaining ◊ Collective Bargaining

Elasticity As a general concept the elasticity between two variables, X and Y, measures the response in one variable to a 1 per cent change in the other. The two most common measures are the price elasticity of demand, measuring the response of quantity demanded to a change in price, and the income elasticity of demand, measuring the response of quantity demanded to an income change. Algebraically the concept can be written as follows:

$$\frac{E}{XY} = \frac{\Delta Y}{\Delta X} \cdot \frac{X}{Y}$$

where $\dfrac{E}{XY}$ = elasticity of Y with respect to X

$\Delta Y, \Delta X$ = change in Y and X

Y, X = values of Y and X

Because different values for the elasticity can occur depending upon the values of Y and X from which the changes are measured, some writers prefer to use the arc elasticity concept. Algebraically we have:

$$\frac{E}{XY} = \frac{\Delta Y}{\Delta X} \cdot \frac{X_1 + X_2}{Y_1 + Y_2}$$

where Y_1, X_1 = initial values of Y and X

Y_2, X_2 = value of Y and X after changes have occurred

The elasticity for the data given below would be calculated as follows:

Variable	Y_1	X_1	Y_2	X_2	ΔY	ΔX
Value	100	10	150	8	+ 50	− 2

$$\frac{E}{XY} = \frac{50}{-2} \cdot \frac{18}{250} = -1 \cdot 8$$

Elasticity can be either positive or negative, depending upon the fundamental relationship existing between the variables. Price elasticity of demand is always negative because price changes lead to changes of quantity demanded in the opposite direction ($\Leftrightarrow$ Demand), whilst income elasticity of demand is usually positive.

Many estimates have been obtained of the price elasticity of demand of goods, both durable and non-durable. Knowledge of this concept is extremely valuable to businessmen, since it indicates the effect of a price change on their total receipts. Specifically, if the price elasticity is greater than unity, total receipts will increase as price is reduced, whilst if elasticity is less than unity, total receipts will fall. Some typical values of the price elasticity of demand taken from recent studies for the United Kingdom are: potatoes $-0\cdot3$, cigarettes $-0\cdot5$, consumer durables $-0\cdot8$, electricity $-1\cdot3$, automobiles $-2\cdot1$. Thus a 1 per cent fall in the price of automobiles would lead to a $2\cdot1$ per cent increase in the quantity demanded.

The income elasticity concept has also been extensively studied, data often being provided as a by-product of the construction of the retail price index. It is particularly useful in indicating to a manufacturer the effect of future income changes upon his sales. Some typical values of the income elasticity of demand for the United Kingdom are: all food 0·2, beef 0·5, cream 1·7, consumer durables 1·8. Thus a 1 per cent increase in income would lead to a 1·7 per cent increase in the demand for cream.

In general, examination of a wider set of data reveals that for price elasticity, the more broadly the good is defined, the lower the value, because there are fewer close substitutes. For income elasticity, the more basic, or staple, a commodity, the lower its income elasticity. ⟨⟩ Prices, Theory of; Demand, Theory of; Demand Functions. L.T.S.

A. J. Culyer, *Economics* (Blackwell, 1985).

Electrophysiological Techniques Neural transmission within the body takes place by means of the conduction of electrical pulses along nerve fibres. By the suitable placing of electrodes and the use of high-gain amplifiers and recorders, it is possible to study this neural transmission at various places in the body. Numerous applications have been made of these electrophysiological recordings.

Electrocardiogram (ECG or EKG). Analysis of the wave shape is used in the diagnosis of cardiac dysfunction. The electrical impulses also provide a useful input into automatic pulse-rate counters, which may be used in assessments of physical work load or mental stress (⟨⟩ Muscular Work; Pulse Rate).

Electroencephalogram (EEG). Electrodes placed upon the skull detect the activity in the brain. Under normal resting conditions, the predominant rhythm is a regular 10/sec. one. This is disturbed by the appearance of sensory stimulation, or by emotional arousal. Various patterns of activity are known to be characteristic of sleep or of neurological disorders. Electrocorticogram recordings, made directly from the brain surface, can obviously be made only under rather special circumstances.

Electromyogram (EMG). Muscle tension can be detected using either needle or surface electrodes. Applications of EMG include studies of posture, physical work load and emotional tension (⟨⟩ Posture).

Electroretinogram (ERG). By placing one electrode on the cornea and one on the back of the eyeball it is possible to detect signals resulting from momentary stimulation of the retina. This technique makes possible studies of the sensitivity of the retina. E.E.

Employee Services ⟡ Welfare

Employers' Association An organization of employers that seeks to assist, influence or control the industrial-relations decisions of member-firms and/or that engages in trade activities on behalf of members.

Employers thus associate for two basic purposes: labour matters and trade matters. In some industries there are two associations, one dealing with labour matters and the other a 'trade association', which deals with technical matters, supplies, relations with government, public authorities, professional bodies and customers, and possibly co-operative research. Before anti-monopoly legislation, price-fixing was a key activity of many trade associations. In other industries both sets of activities are carried on in one association. In yet other cases a complex of associations has been simplified on the labour side by the formation of an overall federal body to deal with labour matters, whereas each section of the industry has its own 'trade association'.

Amongst employers the distinction between 'association' and 'federation' is relatively unimportant, but it is common to find the term 'association' used for local organizations and 'federation' for national organizations. A firm outside membership of the appropriate association or federation is generally known as 'non-federated'; a firm inside the organization as 'federated'. Non-federated firms tend to be either very small ones or large ones that wish to manage their affairs independently. In some industries firms have abandoned membership of their association in order to take an independent line, for example on ⟡ Productivity Bargaining.

Varieties of organization of employers' bodies include local organizations affiliated to national federations; national associations with regional branches and single organizations with a national coverage.

Employers' organizations are usually organized by industry for labour matters, but not necessarily for trade matters. They are thus 'industrial unions' on the employers' side. ⟡ Trade Union Types – Industrial Unions; Collective Bargaining.

Eligibility for membership is commonly based on three main factors; participation in the appropriate industry; agreement to abide by policy decisions of the association; and satisfaction of the other members that the applicant has a 'reputable' business. Discipline over members may be effected by using sanctions, which can include stigma in the society in which the employer moves, loss of the member's share in the accumulated strike fund, loss of sundry services (usually the most important loss) and expulsion from membership.

The range of services provided by employers' associations is very wide and the amount and kind of service varies according to the attitudes of the association. This in turn is a function of the prevailing view of member firms as to the role the association should play. Some see the body as a forum where views and experiences may be exchanged; others as a means of attaining joint action to solve common problems in the industry. Where labour relations in an industry are good, the employers' association may run joint ventures with the trade union(s) concerned – the Shoe Industry Research Centre is one example.

The industrial-relations activities of employers' organizations fall into two categories: the representation of employers' interests in dealing with trade unions, including the negotiations of wages and conditions of employment, and the handling of disputes between employers and workers (◊ Collective Bargaining); and assistance to members in dealing with their own management–labour problems. All associations concerned with industrial relations negotiate a national wage agreement, some as a means of establishing a pay structure for the whole industry, others negotiating basic rates, which may be supplemented by company and factory plus rates and bonuses of various kinds. ◊ Wage; Wage Drift; Wage Systems.

Other than industrial-relations matters, the main activities of employers' organizations include representation of employers' interests to government and other bodies; the provision of information services, including statistics; assistance in manpower matters including its efficient use, labour supply and demand, recruitment and selection, education and training, health, safety and welfare; and assistance in trade and commercial matters.

Although they are not mass organizations like trade unions, employers' associations with industrial-relations functions have many organizational similarities to their counterparts on the employees' side. The final authority of a small national association or of a local association can be a meeting of all the members, whereas in larger organizations some method of representation is adopted. Where local associations are grouped into regions, divisions or areas, election of representatives is normally through these bodies.

In 1983 there were 153 listed and 184 unlisted employers' associations recorded by the Certification Officer. Their gross income amounted to £84 million, with funds of £44·1 million and gross assets of £78 million.

Like trade unions, employers' associations as a whole would benefit from structural reform. Similarly they employ too few full-time officers, many of whom have even less formal training for their tasks than do trade union officials. Local employers' association officials may be unpaid, or their function may be carried out part-time by a solicitor or accountant in private practice. N.H.C., amended by M.J.F.P.

H. A. Clegg, *The System of Industrial Relations in Great Britain* (Blackwell, 1970); J. P. Windmuller and A. Gladstone (eds.), *Employers' Associations and Industrial Relations* (OUP, 1984).

Employers' Federation ⟡ Employers' Association; Federation

Employers' Liability Employers have a legal duty to take all reasonable steps to protect the safety of the persons employed by them. This includes providing employees with reasonably safe premises to work in, reasonably safe tools, materials and appliances to work with and a reasonably safe system of work. If an employer should be in breach of this duty and this breach were to lead to an employee sustaining injuries, the employer will be liable in damages to the employee concerned. The duty is not, however, absolute: employers are not responsible for all accidents but only for those that they should reasonably have anticipated and prevented by taking appropriate measures. However, an employer's breach of some of the older ⟡ Health and Safety Legislation (e.g. the duty to fence dangerous machinery under section 14 of the Factories Act 1961) may involve absolute liability in damages. The Employers' Liability (Compulsory Insurance) Act 1969 requires employers (other than nationalized industries, the police and local authorities) to take out insurance against this potential liability to pay damages. It is a criminal offence to fail to effect such insurance and to fail to display the certificate of insurance at the place of work.

Employees also have a duty to take reasonable precautions for their own safety and if they should fail to do so, the employer, who has also been in breach of his duties, may offer the defence of contributory negligence. If contributory negligence by the employee is proved, the court will divide the loss suffered between the employee/plaintiff and the employer/defendant in proportion to their respective degrees of negligence. W.F.F., amended by K.W.

J. Munkman, *Employer's Liability at Common Law* (Butterworths, 10th ed., 1985).

Employment One of the central problems of macro-economics is the determination of the level of output in the economy and hence the level of employment. The prevailing climate of opinion before the publication of Lord Keynes's *The General Theory of Employment, Interest and Money* in 1936 was that there would be a tendency towards full

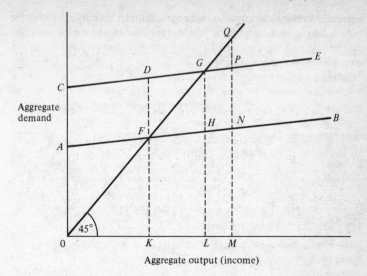

Aggregate output (income)

employment in an economy because of wage–price flexibility. This was manifestly untrue in the 1930s and Keynes's book changed the approach of economists so that full employment was seen as a possible outcome for the economy, but not the only outcome.

The essence of the Keynesian approach is a blending together of consumption demand and investment demand as determinants of the aggregate level of output, and hence employment. Consumption demand depends mainly upon the level of income, whilst investment demand depends upon profit expectations, the rate of interest and the rate of change of output (⟡ Consumption Function; Investment in the Economy). Thus the equilibrium level of output, and hence employment, will occur when the demands upon the economic system balance the supply of goods from the system. This need not occur at the level of output corresponding to full employment.

The diagram above illustrates the point for a simple economy having only a consumer sector and a business sector. The aggregate demand schedule, CE, consists of a consumption schedule, AB, which shows how consumption varies with income, and an investment demand, which is constant for all levels of income. At output OK aggregate demand will exceed aggregate output, $KD > KF (= OK)$, and hence aggregate output will rise. Conversely, at output OM aggregate demand will be lower than aggregate output, $MP < MQ (= OM)$, and hence aggregate output will fall. Only at output level OL is it the case that aggregate demand is equal to aggregate supply, $LG = LG \ (= OL)$.

In a simple economy this is how output and hence employment are determined and the essence of the argument remains unchanged if we introduce more sectors, such as the government and foreign trade sectors. There is no guarantee, of course, that OL will correspond to the full-employment output level; if it does not, aggregate demand may be boosted by either fiscal or monetary policy in order to raise employment.

In recent years this view of how the macro-economy works has been challenged because of its failure to explain the concurrent high rates of unemployment and inflation in the sixties and seventies. Policies using demand-management techniques were criticized by monetarists and by those who favoured more attention to the supply side of the economy. ⟡ Consumption Function; Investment in the Economy; Monetarism; The Multiplier; Supply-side Economics. L.T.S.

E. Shapiro, *Macroeconomic Theory* (Harcourt Brace Jovanovich, 5th ed., 1982).

Employment Act 1980 This was the first of the main pieces of industrial-relations legislation introduced by the Conservative Government after winning the general election in 1979. It covered trade union ballots, codes of practice, exclusion from trade union membership (⟡ Closed Shop), unfair dismissal, maternity rights, action short of dismissal relating to trade union membership, ⟡ Picketing, secondary industrial action and coercive recruitment tactics.

Section 1 empowers the Secretary of State to make, by regulations, a scheme to be administered by the Certification Officer providing for payment towards expenditure incurred by independent trade unions in conducting secret ballots. Section 2 places an obligation on employers with more than twenty workers to comply with a request from a trade union recognized by them to provide a place on their premises where members of the trade union may vote in a secret ballot. Section 3 enables the Secretary of State to issue codes of practice containing practical guidance for promoting the improvement of industrial relations. Such codes are admissable as evidence in industrial-tribunal or court proceedings and may be taken into account by tribunals or courts in determining questions to which they are relevant. They do not, in themselves, render anyone liable to proceedings. Section 4 gives a person who is, or seeks to be, in employment where there is a union membership agreement (a ⟡ Closed Shop) the right not to be unreasonably excluded or expelled from a trade union. This new right is additional to present common-law rights. Complaints of infringement of the right are heard by industrial tribunals, which are required to consider the matter on its merits and not just on the particular union rules that apply. Section 5 enables a person whose complaint of unreasonable exclusion or expulsion is declared to be well-founded, and who is admitted or re-admitted to membership of the union, to apply to the industrial tribunal for compensation for any loss sustained. Section 6 provides that, in deciding whether or not an employer has carried out a dismissal fairly, an industrial tribunal should take into account the size and administrative resources of that employer. Section 7 enlarges the grounds upon which dismissal for non-membership of a trade union is to be regarded as unfair where there is a union membership agreement (closed shop). The enlarged grounds are:

(1)   Where the employee genuinely objects to membership of any union or a particular union on grounds of conscience or other deeply held personal conviction.

(2)   Where the employee has belonged to the class of employee covered by the closed-shop agreement since before it took effect and has not subsequently been a member of a union specified in the agreement.

(3)   (In the case of agreements coming into effect after section 7 is brought into operation) where the agreement is not approved in a secret ballot in which at least 80 per cent of those covered support it.

Section 11 makes changes to the procedure laid down in the Employment Protection (Consolidation) Act 1978 by which a woman may claim the right to return to work after having a baby. Section 15 provides a general right (qualified where a closed shop operates) for employees not to have action short of dismissal taken against them by their employer to compel them to join a union. Where a closed shop operates, those categories of employees who are protected by section 7 from unfair dismissal for not being a member of a trade union as specified in the closed-shop agreement will also have the right not to have action short of dismissal taken against them by their employer to compel them to belong to a union. Section 16 limits lawful picketing to:

(1)   A person picketing at or near his or her own place of work.

(2)   A trade union official accompanying a member of that union who is picketing at or near his or her own place of work and whom the official represents.

Section 17 is primarily concerned with other forms of secondary action such as blacking and sympathetic strikes. It provides that there shall be immunity for the organization of secondary action only where the principal purpose of that action is to interfere with the supply of goods or services during the dispute between the employer in dispute and a first supplier or customer whose employees are taking the action, *and* where it is reasonably likely to achieve that purpose. M.J.F.P.

> Department of Employment, *Employment Gazette* (August 1980), pp. 876–7.

Employment Act 1982 This Act gives new rights to employees and employers, coupled with new responsibilities for trade unions. It covers the areas of employee involvement, compensation for closed-shop dismissals, dismissals in connection with a strike, union 'labour only' requirements and trade union immunities.

Section 1 amends section 16 of the Companies Act 1967 so as to require the reports by directors of larger companies to contain a statement describing what action has been taken during the year to introduce, maintain or develop arrangements aimed at furthering employee involvement. Section 2 and Schedule 1 enable the Secretary of State to pay compensation to some people who were dismissed for not being a union member in a closed shop between 1974 and 1980. The people concerned are employees whose dismissal would have been 'unfair' had the main closed-shop provisions of the Employment Act 1980 been in force at the time when they were dismissed.

Section 3 enlarges the circumstances in which dismissal for non-membership of a trade union in a closed shop is to be regarded as unfair. The additional circumstances are:

(1)   Where in the five years preceding the dismissal a closed-shop agreement has not been supported in a secret ballot by 80 per cent of the employees covered by it or by 85 per cent of those voting.

(2)   Where the employee has obtained or is seeking a declaration from an industrial tribunal of unreasonable exclusion or expulsion from the trade union to which he or she belonged under the closed-shop agreement.

(3)   Where the employee is bound because of his or her qualifications to observe a written code of conduct and has left or been expelled from a union, or refused to join a union, because of a conflict between that code of conduct and a requirement to take industrial action.

Section 4 introduces a minimum basic award of compensation of £2,000 (subject to annual revision) for people who are unfairly dismissed because of their non-membership of a union or because of their trade union membership or activities. This minimum may, however, be reduced on account of matters such as the employee's conduct before dismissal. Section 5 creates a new 'special award' of compensation which will be payable to some people who are unfairly dismissed because of their non-membership of a trade union or because of their trade union membership or activities. Section 8 enables people who claim they have been unfairly dismissed for non-membership of a trade union to apply to a tribunal for an order of 'interim relief' (which is an order that their contract of employment should continue until their complaint of unfair dismissal is decided).

Section 9 provides that an employee who is dismissed while participating in a strike or other industrial action cannot claim unfair dismissal if his or her employer (1) has dismissed all who were taking part in the action at the same establishment as the complainant at the date of his or her dismissal; and (2) has not offered re-engagement to any of them within three months of their date of dismissal without making the complainant a similar offer. Section 10 adds to the circumstances set out in section 3 the right of employees not to have action short of dismissal taken against them by their employer to compel them to be a trade union member in a closed shop. Section 11 introduces changes in respect of 'joinder' in cases of action short of dismissal taken to compel membership of a trade union, which are parallel to the changes introduced by section 7 in relation to joinder in unfair-dismissal cases.

Section 12 makes void any term in a commercial contract that requires a person to use only union labour (or only non-union labour) in fulfilling a contract. It also makes it unlawful to exclude someone from a tender list or to fail to award a contract to them or to terminate a contract with them on the grounds that anyone employed or likely to be employed on work connected with the contract is, or is not, a union member. Section 13 makes void any term in a commercial contract that requires the contractor to recognize, negotiate or consult with trade unions or trade union officials. It also makes it unlawful to exclude someone from a tender list, or to fail to award them a contract or to terminate a contract with them on the grounds that they do not recognize, negotiate or consult with trade unions or trade union officials. Section 14 removes immunity from trade unions and other persons who organize industrial action to put pressure on an employer to act contrary to sections 12 or 13. It also removes immunity from those who organize or threaten industrial action that interferes with the supply of goods or services on the grounds that:

(1)   Work done in connection with the supply of goods or services has been or is likely to be done by non-union (or union) members.

(2)   The supplier of the goods or services in question does not

recognize, negotiate or consult with trade unions or trade union officials.

Section 15 repeals section 14 of the Trade Union and Labour Relations Act 1974. It thus abolishes the special and wider immunities for trade unions and brings them into line with those given to other persons, such as individual union officials. As a result, those who suffer loss because of unlawful action (e.g. action that is not in contemplation or furtherance of a trade dispute; unlawful secondary action; secondary picketing) that is authorized by a union will be able to sue that union in its own name for injunctions and seek damages from the union's funds. It will also become possible, for the first time, to sue a trade union if it is responsible for other unlawful acts, whether or not connected with industrial action, such as libel, defamation, negligence, nuisance and breach of duty. Section 15 also sets out when a trade union is to be regarded as liable for unlawful industrial action organized by its officials. The union is to be held automatically and irrevocably liable for unlawful action authorized or endorsed by its Executive Committee, its President, its General Secretary or any of its officials with authority to call industrial action under the union's own rules. It is also to be held liable for unlawful action authorized or endorsed by its *employed* officials or any committees to which they report, except where the authorization is overruled by the Executive Committee, President or General Secretary or where the union rules prohibit the official concerned from calling industrial action.

Section 16 sets upper limits on the damages that may be awarded against a trade union in any single set of legal proceedings. The limits, which will apply in all cases except the particular ones involving personal injury or the use of property for which unions may already face awards of damages without any upper limit, are set by reference to the numbers of members in the union concerned. They are:

fewer than	5,000 members	£10,000
	5,000–24,999	£50,000
	25,000–99,999	£125,000
	100,000 or more	£250,000

M.J.F.P.

Department of Employment, *Employment Gazette* (November 1982), pp. 459–60, 473–6.

Employment Appeal Tribunal ◊ Industrial Tribunals

Employment Medical Advisory Service, The (EMAS) As the

operational arm of the Medical Division of the Health and Safety Executive this provides national advice on the medical aspects of employment problems to employers, employees, trade unions, doctors and others. Workers in hazardous occupations are examined medically and surveys are made of employment hazards. Doctors in the E M A S co-operate with school medical officers and careers officers in helping to solve the employment problems of handicapped school-leavers. E.L.

Employment Protection Act 1975 The Labour Government of the day introduced a new legal framework for British industrial relations with its repeal of the ⟡ Industrial Relations Act 1971. the provisions of the ⟡ Trade Union and Labour Relations Act 1974 and the passage of the Employment Protection Act. The emphasis of legal regulation changed from that of the 1971 Act, but the principle of legal regulation remained. It was accepted that the law could be a force for greater order in industrial relations. The new provisions restricted the use of bargaining power by trade unions much less, and other aspects of industrial relations became more closely regulated than before. N.H.C., amended by M.J.F.P.

Employment Protection Act, 1975 (H M S O), ch. 71; H. A. Clegg, *The Changing Systems of Industrial Relations in Great Britain* (Blackwell, 1979).

Entropy ⟡ Information Theory

Environment An organism's environment comprises all those features of the surrounding world that are in some way detectable and that affect the organism's behaviour. The term 'internal environment' is used to describe a number of physiological states but is something of a misnomer (⟡ Homeostasis).

It is usual to distinguish between the physical environment and the social environment. The former includes such aspects as temperature, humidity, air pressure, vibration, gravitational loading, air pollution, noise, radiation and lighting, all of which affect human performance in a variety of ways (⟡ Heat; Illumination; Noise; Vibration). Of complementary importance in their effect on human behaviour are aspects of the social environment (⟡ Incentives; Personnel Management).

In considering the effects of the environment upon behaviour it is essential to note that the effect of the total environmental pattern is not necessarily predictable from the separate effects of single variables. In many instances interaction effects are such that decrements resulting from simultaneous environmental stresses are a good deal in excess of the sum of the incremental values. It seems likely that many accidents and breakdowns are attributable to these large cumulative effects. E.E.

Equal Pay While the main aim of the Sex Discrimination Act 1975 is to see that women (and men) are treated fairly so far as appointment, training and promotion are concerned, the Equal Pay Act 1970 is designed to ensure equality in the terms and conditions of employment they enjoy. 'Pay' for this purpose includes not just wages or salary but other benefits, whether in cash or in kind, such as holidays, bonuses and subsidized travel or home loans, etc. Article 119 of the Common Market's Treaty of Rome also guarantees 'equal pay for equal work' and its provisions override any inconsistency or restriction contained in the domestic legislation of member states, including, of course, the British Equal Pay Act. The supremacy of EEC law in this context has been established by litigation on several occasions.

Under the 1970 Act (which came into effect at the end of 1975) a woman is entitled to the same pay and conditions as a man in the same employment, provided either that their work is 'like work' (i.e. 'the same or broadly similar') or that their jobs, though different, have been 'rated as equivalent' in a ◊ Job Evaluation study. In either case the woman's contract is deemed to contain an 'equality clause', which is enforceable before an industrial tribunal, which can award damages or arrears of pay backdated for up to two years. Any collective agreement or employer's pay structure that contains provisions that apply separately to men and women can be referred to the Central Arbitration Committee, which shall declare what amendments are necessary to ensure that it is no longer discriminatory.

In 1982 the European Court of Justice found British legislation to be inadequate to the extent that it did not also guarantee equal pay for work of equal value, as required by the 1975 Equal Pay Directive made under Article 119 of the Treaty of Rome. The 1970 Act was defective because women workers had no right to insist that their employer undertake a job-evaluation exercise. Accordingly, the 1970 Act was amended in 1984 by detailed regulations, that now permit a claim to be made to an industrial tribunal even though there is neither 'like work' nor 'work rated as equivalent'. Under a complex procedure an 'independent expert', appointed by the tribunal, will compile a report on whether the woman's work and that of her male comparators employed at the same establishment are of equal value, having regard to the demands the jobs make when judged against various criteria such as skill, effort, decision-making content, etc. In the first case to be heard, a tribunal in 1984 accepted the conclusions of the independent expert that the work of a female canteen cook employed at a shipyard was equal in value to the work of male painters, joiners and thermal-insulation engineers.

Whether this reform will, in the longer term, significantly narrow the gap between male and female earnings must be open to doubt, however, not least because of the potential breadth of the 'material difference' defence, which is available to employers to explain a difference in pay by reference to, for example, the operation of market forces. ⟡ Discrimination; Job Evaluation; EEC Law. K.W.

T. Gill and L. Whitty, *Women's Rights in the Workplace* (Penguin, 1983); M. Rubenstein, *Equal Pay for Work of Equal Value* (Macmillan, 1985).

Equitable Payment ⟡ Time-span of Discretion; Job Analysis

Equity (in Accounting) ⟡ Claims

Equivalent Monetary Value ⟡ Utility

Ergonomics The branch of technology concerned with the problems of the mutual adjustment between people and their work. Drawing upon the sciences of psychology, anatomy and physiology, ergonomics sets out to optimize the design of equipment, the environment and working procedures in respect of both the well-being of personnel and the effectiveness of the working unit.

Historically ergonomics derives from several relatively independent sources. Industrial medicine contributes some of the aspects of protection of the worker from the hazards of extreme environmental severities, such as the effects of heat or of toxic substances. The concept of protection may be broadened to encompass such items as the long-term effects of exposure to noise or of bad posture during lifting or even during prolonged periods of sitting. The complementary aspects of effectiveness owe much to pioneering studies in the rationalization of work methods (⟡ Taylor) and the introduction of the techniques of experimental psychology (⟡ Gilbreth).

Although the word 'ergonomics' was not coined until 1950, it is during the Second World War, in the face of a host of problems regarding human work, that the birth of ergonomics may best be located. Two features distinguish ergonomics from its antecedent disciplines. Firstly, it is based upon the scientific study of the capabilities and limitations of human performance. Secondly, it embraces all the facets of the study of people at work.

Human performance in industry may be classified under two broad

Level	Control	Energy
Pre-mechanization	Operator	Operator
Mechanization	Operator	Machine
Automation	Operator and machine	Machine

categories: information and control, and physical energy. The relative importance of these two performance categories varies with the level of technological development achieved. The table illustrates the trend of change in task allocation between operators and machines consequent upon technological progress ($\diamondsuit$ Automation).

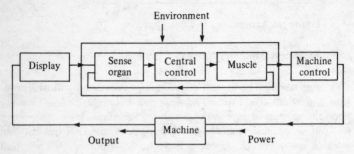

The human operator within an information loop in a mechanized man–machine system

At the most primitive level an operator provides both control and power, as in a task demanding, for example, the use of hand tools. Typical ergonomics problems here would include the study of the expenditure of energy, the forces necessary to manipulate the tools, the shape of the handles in relation to the anthropometry of the hand and the layout of the workplace. $\diamondsuit$ Anthropometry; Muscular Work; Posture.

It is probably at the level of mechanization that the contribution of ergonomics is best known. A schematic representation of the information flow in a man–machine system appears in the figure above. The task of the human operator in such a system is to accept information from the displays, to interpret and process this information and convey the appropriate command signals by way of the machine control. This response generates a further signal from the machine and information passes in this way around the loop. The ergonomist is concerned to optimize the performance of the man–machine system by attending to the design characteristics of the $\diamondsuit$ Displays, the controls ($\diamondsuit$ Machine

Controls), and of the machine's dynamics (⟡ Machine Dynamics; Tracking). The operator's performance is, in addition, affected by the properties of the physical ⟡ Environment in which he or she is working (⟡ Glare; Heat; Illumination; Noise; Vibration) and by the prevailing social and motivational conditions. ⟡ Socio-technical System; Organization Theory.

At a more sophisticated level of development, a different approach to the problems of the human factor is required. In recent years, the role of the human operator in complex computer-supported systems has been studied and has generated new problems for the ergonomist concerned in the design of such systems. At an early stage in the design process decisions have to be made regarding the allocation of function between operator and machine. Clearly such decisions demand the contribution of several experts, including the ergonomist. Thereafter, at later stages in the development of the system, the ergonomist will be called upon to advise on matters of interface design, job analysis, operating procedures, training and system performance. Part of the change in emphasis in the ergonomics of automated systems is the shift of attention from hardware to software (⟡ Language). Swift and efficient communication-media are essential ingredients of an effective man–machine dialogue.

Ergonomics has now become a fairly well-established discipline in most parts of the world. Several universities offer degree courses in ergonomics, and there exist professional societies and scientific journals. Numerous industrial and governmental organizations support units devoted to research and developmental work. E.E.

W. T. Singleton (ed.), *The Body at Work* (CUP, 1982); R. W. Bailey, *Human Performance Engineering* (Prentice-Hall, 1982); D. Meister, *Behavioural Foundations of System Development* (J. Wiley, 1976).

Errors (Types I and II) ⟡ Hypothesis Testing

Estimating

(1) *Analytical estimating* (in work measurement). A method used to determine basic times for jobs for which it has not been possible to compile sufficient data to obtain a synthetic timing (⟡ Work Measurement; Synthetic Timing). It is the most inaccurate and inconsistent work-measurement technique, relying almost entirely on the ability, experience and knowledge of the estimator.

Once the job method has been established and agreed, basic times at standard rating are given to each job element. The same principles are used for breaking the job into elements as in direct ⟨⟩ Time Study but normally larger elements are used.

The estimator will use available, perhaps incomplete, synthetic data where possible, and working conditions will be considered in arriving at the estimated basic times. Allowances are added to produce standard times.

The method is frequently used in maintenance work and other one-off jobs.

(2) *Cost estimating*. This is necessary to predict the cost of manufacture of a product or component, in order to establish a sales price prior to manufacture, tendering, etc.

Using information from component drawings, material lists, specifications of materials, quality and performance, production quantities and rates, an estimate in sufficient detail is constructed, or is obtained by adjusting estimates or actual costs for previous similar jobs. ⟨⟩ Costing Systems. R.W.

> H. B. Maynard (ed.), *Industrial Engineering Handbook* (McGraw-Hill, 2nd ed., 1963).

Exclusion clauses Clauses in contracts designed to exclude or limit rights that would otherwise accrue to the other party. In the past such clauses have been used to deprive a weaker contracting party of rights such as those implied by the terms of the Sale of Goods Act 1979; provided that such clauses were correctly incorporated into the contract they were very effective. Exclusion clauses are now subject to the Unfair Contract Terms Act 1977. In addition to dealing with the implied terms (⟨⟩ Sale of Goods), this Act provides that all notices or contract terms that exclude liability for death or personal injury are void, although no penalty attaches to their continued use. All clauses excluding liability for other loss or damage are subject to the 'reasonableness test'. When businesses use a standard form contract or enter into a contract with a consumer (i.e. someone dealing other than in the course of a business), any attempt to exclude or limit liability for breach of contract or to claim to be entitled to perform the contract substantially differently, or not at all, is also subject to the test.

The requirement of reasonableness is satisfied if the term is a fair and reasonable one to be included, having regard to the circumstances known or contemplated by the parties at the time the contract was made. Such factors as the relative bargaining strength of the parties and the frequency of use of such clauses will be important in determining this question, but it is for the person seeking to rely on the clause to show reasonableness. Relatively few cases establishing the exact scope of the test have been heard.

Exclusion of liability is only regulated if it is liability occasioned during the course of a business, but contracts of insurance and certain other categories of contract are not subject to the Act. J.C.E.M.

D. Yates, *Exclusion Clauses in Contracts* (Sweet & Maxwell, 2nd ed., 1982)

Executive Development ◊ Management Development

Expected Value ◊ Measures of Location

Expert System ◊ Information System

Exponential Smoothing ◊ Forecasting Techniques, Short-term

Exporting Problems ◊ International Marketing

Exports ◊ Balance of Payments

F

Factor Analysis This important and powerful statistical technique provides a method of examining a set of data in order to establish the underlying pattern of organization that brings about certain relations between groups of measurements.

An example is provided in the context of intelligence testing. Scores may be obtained on a battery of tests administered to a group of subjects. Inter-correlation coefficients (◊ Correlation and Regression) indicate the degree of association between all pairs of tests in the total battery. Further analysis yields factor loadings, i.e. measures of the extent to which the observed degrees of association might be due to the existence of a fairly small number of causative factors.

This statistical technique has proved invaluable in the testing of hypotheses concerning the nature of human ◊ Personality. E.E.

Factories Act, 1961 ◊ Employers' Liability; Factory Inspectors; Health and Safety Legislation

Factoring The provision of a range of services to an organization, including an optional financial facility. At its most highly developed, it embraces the subcontracting by a company of its sales ledger department to the factor who will carry out all transactions from raising an invoice to control and collection. Such an agreement brings with it a range of financial advice and economies of scale, which would not normally be available to an organization. This pattern of activity was developed in Britain during the early 1960s but has a history in the USA dating from the nineteenth century. It is an operation particularly suited to the needs of small and medium-sized businesses in manufacturing and wholesaling. G.S.C.W.

Factory Inspector HM Inspectors of Factories were first appointed in 1833 and now work in the Executive of the ◊ Health and Safety Commission. Their principal duty is to see that the provisions of the ◊ Health and Safety Legislation are carried out. To achieve this, inspectors have wide powers, including the right of entry to examine and investigate industrial premises. They can issue notices to order the improvement of hazardous health and safety conditions within a limited period of time, and to prohibit work where they consider there is imminent danger of serious injury or disease. An appeal against the issue of an Improvement or a Prohibition Notice can be made to an industrial tribunal. Authorized inspectors may also institute a prosecution alleging a specific breach of the law.

Inspectors are supported by groups of specialists whose primary function is to provide rapid technical advice, and who are concerned to help employers adopt the best-known practices for the health, ◇ Safety and ◇ Welfare of employees. E.L.

Fair Wages Clause In 1891, when sweated labour was a major social evil, the House of Commons determined by a resolution that at least one class of employers, namely government contractors, should observe terms and conditions no less favourable than those established in the relevant industry by the process of collective bargaining. Such contractors were also required to recognize the (now statutory) right of employees to join independent trade unions. The resolution was given practical effect by government departments refusing to accept tenders other than from 'approved' contractors and by inserting 'fair wages clauses' into any contract awarded. Many local authorities and nationalized industries voluntarily adopted a similar policy. The resolution was reaffirmed in 1946, the British Government having also subscribed to the International Labour Organization Convention 94, which similarly binds signatory states to insert such clauses into public contracts.

Subsequently, schedule 11 of the Employment Protection Act 1975 created an analogous, if broader, obligation, potentially binding all employers, not just those engaged on government contracts, to observe recognized terms and conditions as fixed by collective bargaining or arbitration awards. This provision was considered to be inflationary and was repealed in 1980. The Conservative Government, pursuing a policy of free-market economics and the promotion of non-unionism, then 'denounced' its commitment to ILO Convention 94 and in 1982 the House of Commons was asked to set aside the Fair Wages Resolution itself. This was done with effect from September 1983. ◇ Collective Bargaining; International Labour Organization; Freedom of Association. K.W.

B. Bercusson, *Fair Wages Resolutions* (Mansell, 1978).

Family of Parts ◇ Group Technology; Flexible Manufacturing System

Fatigue Used to describe an observable decrement in performance resulting from a repetition of behavioural activity, fatigue serves as a useful label to group together a wide variety of well-known phenomena. Its use as a causal explanation of these decrements is, however, questionable. It is unlikely that a single causative factor brings about the numerous observable effects that are probably due to a wide variety of mechanisms including loss of sleep, the accumulation of metabolic waste products, boredom, neural inhibition, and loss of sensory acuity (♢ Adaptation).

Concepts of fatigue include reference to subjective feelings of tiredness and to certain physiological states in addition to performance decrements. Experimental studies have usually failed to establish any clear relationship between these three aspects. Subjective feelings of tiredness are difficult to separate from those of boredom; a professional man may well describe himself as 'very tired' at the end of a working day but is then able to indulge in quite strenuous recreational pastimes. None of the numerous physiological indices proposed as an index of fatigue has yet shown itself to be closely related to the individual's work achievement, or to serve as a reliable predictor of work potential.

Various attempts have been made to establish the ideal length of a work period between rest pauses. Only a very limited amount of success has resulted, as a good deal depends not only upon the particular tasks but also upon the individual. For certain types of task where a high standard of attention is required from the worker, half-hour periods interspersed with short rest pauses appear to be suitable.

There is no doubt that a very significant practical problem exists in attempting to consider the problems of fatigue in relation to working periods and conditions, particularly where safety is involved. Examples such as the working hours of bus drivers and aircraft pilots are obvious. Unfortunately, there is very little scientific evidence available at the moment to assist in the provision of guiding rules. E.E.

Fayol, Henri (1841–1925) One of the pioneers of management thought and ♢ Classical Organization Theory.

Born in France in 1841, Fayol became a mining engineer and eventually managing director of a metallurgical and coal combine. From his experience as a chief executive, he developed a framework for a unifying doctrine of administration, which he believed would hold good for business, public service and wherever the art of management had to be exercised. He believed there were basic principles of management that could and should be taught.

In attempting to set up efficient business procedures, Fayol produced a theoretical model that appears mechanistic, but he noted that personal qualities could be of enormous significance and seems to have been aware of an informal structure existing alongside the formal ones (✧ Formal Organization). He compared the ✧ Organization to the animal, using the expression *corps social* (or body corporate) to mean all those engaged in any given corporate activity. This mode of thinking in biological terms continues and forms one of the sources of the modern study of ✧ Cybernetics.

Fayol declared that in conducting an undertaking towards an objective, technical activities needed to be supplemented by managerial activity, and 'to manage is to forecast and plan, to organize, to command, to co-ordinate and to control'. Here he clearly influenced Lyndall F. Urwick in Britain.

'Gouverner c'est prévoir' ('to govern is to foresee'): in giving prominence to foresight as the first characteristic of sound administration, Fayol laid stress on the judgement and intelligent anticipation that are prerequisite to the success of the whole management process. Observing that long-term planning and development studies were often neglected by the busy executive, Fayol proposed a staff of specialized assistants to senior management.

Fayol's central theme in his discussion of organization is the *hiérarchie*. This was translated into English as 'scalar chain', an expression that has taken root in management writings. To indicate that a formal plan could and should be constructed, Fayol emphasized his concept of the organization chart, suggesting that each position on the chart be accompanied by a job description (✧ Job Analysis) and that lists be prepared showing the 'value' of each employee. Here lay the foundation for his scheme of ✧ Management Development. Fayol indicated that each superior should normally have a 'span of control' comprising no more than four or five immediate subordinates, a concept that has sometimes been attributed to his compatriot, Graicunas.

Managers, he alleged, should develop initiative by allowing subordinates 'the maximum share of activity consistent with their position and capability, even at the cost of some mistakes . . .' Freedom to use initiative was a source of job satisfaction. General control could be maintained by a periodic 'management audit'. In dealing with subordinates Fayol emphasized the need to be fair and equitable. Union agreements must be clear and as fair as possible. He deprecated national bargaining and frequent state intervention in industrial relations and favoured plant agreements. ✧ Collective Bargaining.

Preparation was necessary for those posts requiring managerial ability.

Specialized expertise in engineering or accounting was inadequate preparation and might even be a hindrance. Though there was a dearth of management theory, managerial ability could be developed in the same way as technical ability, first in educational institutions, later in the workshop or other appropriate place.

Fayol's work in France, a country with a long tradition of administration, was complementary to that of ⟡ Taylor in the USA, where the notion of 'coming up the hard way' has always been revered. Taylor worked primarily on the operative level, from the bottom of the hierarchy upwards, while Fayol concentrated on the senior manager and worked downwards. While Fayol was less clear than Max Weber, his principles of management are akin to the characteristics of the formal organization, or ⟡ Bureaucracy, laid down by the latter, although it is extremely unlikely that Weber's work was known to him. N.H.C.

H. Fayol, trans. C. Storrs, *General and Industrial Management* (Pitman, 1949); N. H. Cuthbert, 'Fayol and the Principles of Organization', in A. Tillett, T. Kempner and G. Wills (eds.), *Management Thinkers* (Penguin, 1970); D. S Pugh, D. J. Hickson and C. R. Hinings, *Writers on Organizations* (Penguin, rev. ed., 1984).

Federation The banding together of organizations to form a unity for some common object while remaining independent in internal affairs.

Federated groupings are typical of employers and of trade unions in Britain. Employers' federations may be associations of employers in an industry formed either to manage ⟡ Collective Bargaining with trade unions or to deal with trade matters on behalf of members. Alternatively, they may be multi-functional. ⟡ Employers' Associations. The major federation formed to represent British employers as a whole is the ⟡ Confederation of British Industry.

Among trade unions, federations are one device for achieving inter-union decision-making; others include the Bridlington Rules (⟡ Trade Union – Jurisdiction), agreements on 'closer working', and amalgamation (⟡ Trade Union – Structure).

The Webbs, in *Industrial Democracy*, envisaged the development of a complex of trade union federations within each of which it would be difficult to decide where sovereignty lay. In practice the retention of sovereignty by member unions of a federation has been marked, with few exceptions. Normally there are difficulties in communication with affiliated memberships, particularly when joint negotiations run into difficulties. There are other difficulties in connection with policy-formulation, finance and administration. The largest union federation is the Confederation of Shipbuilding and Engineering Unions; other important federations exist in carpets and textiles, the Civil Service, entertainment and broadcasting, furniture, insurance and banking, metal manufacture, the Post Office and sea transport.

Particularly when the collective-bargaining unit is an industrial one, trade unions pursue varying degrees of co-ordinated action in their external relations and the borderline between regular meetings of union representatives who sit together on national negotiating bodies and more formal federations is an uncertain one. A very large number of ⟨⟩ Joint Industrial Councils have multiple union representation. The federal principle has also been at work on the internal structure of unions where the basis for arriving at amalgamation has involved a degree of internal autonomy and continued identity to the original unions, or where the union is so large that separate 'trade groups' are established, as in the Transport and General Workers' Union.

The major federal organization representing British trade unions is the ⟨⟩ Trades Union Congress, but there is a small body of a somewhat similar kind, the General Federation of Trade Unions, formed in 1899 because of dissatisfaction with TUC policy. The original intention was to create an organization that would draw all unions together for joint industrial action and to build up a central strike fund. Its originators wanted the General Federation to have authority lacking in the TUC. In the event only a number of smaller unions joined the new body, which retains its support from those that feel lost among the big battalions.

There are a number of international federations of trade unions, each of which has come together to exchange information and ideas on common problems within an industry. Some of these are developing policies for dealing with the multinational company. N.H.C., amended by M.J.F.P.

Trades Union Congress, *Directory* (1985).

Feedback A controllable system may be regulated (i.e. its output may be brought to any desired value) by the provision of an adjustment to the input. In figure 1 (p. 170), an input I_1 produces a corresponding output O_1. This output may differ from the required output O_R by an amount of error e, where

$$e = O_R - O_1$$

A human observer might note this error and adjust the input value in such a way that the system output corresponds to the required value.

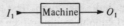

Figure 1. The open loop system

The system illustrated in figure 1 is termed 'open loop', since the input is not directly affected by the output. The addition of the human operator 'closes the loop' by providing at the input some information about the output. The closed loop is illustrated in figure 2.

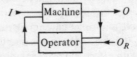

Figure 2. Closing the control loop by means of the human operator

In many cases this human function may be automated. The error is measured by a comparator, which provides a feedback signal that is combined with the input to the system. In this way the output of the system will be adjusted automatically so that it remains at O_R in spite of input fluctuations. Figure 3 illustrates the system with automatic feedback.

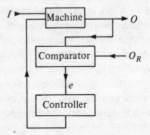

Figure 3. The basis of automatic control

The governor used in James Watt's steam engine provides an early example of the provision of automatic control by means of feedback. If, as a result of a down gradient on the track, the speed of the engine increases, the centrifugal force on the weights in the governor causes the weights to rise. A mechanical linkage then causes the regulator to adopt a lower setting, which in turn causes the speed to fall. Thus an automatic feedback loop consisting of the essential steps – detect, compare, communicate, adjust – keeps the locomotive running at a constant speed.

Ideally a feedback loop will satisfy completely the required output conditions. In practice, however, there are two classes of constraint. Firstly, there will be certain limits within which the input may vary and a satisfactory output be achieved; beyond these limits, the feedback loop will fail to cope. For example, there will be limits on the range of gradients upon which the locomotive governor may bring about constant running speeds. Secondly, there may be time lags between the detection of an error and the corresponding adjustment of the input value. If the independent input is itself varying at a fast rate, the system may fail to respond with sufficient speed. The extent to which a system is capable of keeping pace with change in input values is termed its 'frequency response'. Associated both with feedback magnitude and frequency response is the notion of stability. A system is said to be stable when input disturbances are met with effective corrective tendencies, such that the output values from the system will remain within definable limits. ⟡ Automation; Cybernetics. E.E.

Finance Lease ⟡ Leasing

Financial Institutions ⟡ Capital Market

Financial Management The practical tasks of financial management are those of capital raising; determining the mixture of debt and ordinary capital for a business; deciding upon alternative investment opportunities; valuing shares and businesses as going concerns; considering the financial basis for amalgamations; calculating the basis for reconstructions or takeover bids; recommending the basis of dividend policy, etc.

As a subject of study, financial management is concerned with achieving a given financial objective for a business by solving three interdependent problems: what total volume of assets a business should acquire and maintain; what its composition should be in terms of kinds of assets; how the total funds required for this purpose should be financed (⟡ Capital Budgeting).

The financial-management objective that most accords with legal and economic principles is that of maximizing the present value of existing shareholders' financial interests. However, the pursuit of this objective involves formidable theoretical and practical difficulties, notably the need to find an efficient method of search for profitable and feasible business projects and to reconcile the differing circumstances and individual values of any given body of shareholders.

The management of a business may therefore adopt other objectives, both financial and non-financial, especially where management is wholly or partially divorced from the ownership of a business. For instance, a more operational objective might be that of maintaining the minimum return to shareholders judged to be essential for an adequate flow of capital from the stock market to the particular business. In taking account of shareholder interests when setting financial objectives, dividends and the price of a firm's shares must be assumed to be the focal points of interest for corporate management.

Once the relevance of shareholder objectives to financial management has been established, the scope of its subject matter is accordingly increased to include empirical studies of the capital market and other financial institutions as well as theories of investor behaviour. The answers to questions such as, 'How should the maximum return from a portfolio of investments be obtained for a given degree of risk (i.e. variability of expected future investment income)?' and, 'How do individuals make share-investment decisions?' become as important as answers to company-policy questions such as, 'What, if any, is the optimal capital structure of a firm?' and, 'What is the cost of capital to the company?'

The consensus of opinion concerning the kinds of methods necessary for a 'proper' financial-management function within an enterprise has broadened in its outlook during the last two decades or so. A discussion of these methods may be divided into three main parts: (1) antecedents to financial analysis; (2) components of an analytic approach; (3) financial environment.

(1) *Antecedents*. Financial analysis has its roots in accounting. Consequently an appreciation of accounting methods is a first necessity in order to understand the basic concepts of financial analysis, including the valuation of assets and liabilities, the definition of income and the measurement of cash flow (¢⟩ Accounting System).

Some understanding of both macro- and micro-economic theory is also a prerequisite for a study of financial management. National-income analysis is used extensively by business economists to forecast the level of business activity and thus gives a basis for the construction of enterprise budgets, both short- and long-term. An understanding of the theory of money and interest rates as well as the general body of the economist's theory of the firm is equally important in order to construct plans for an enterprise. Capital theory is also of central importance as the basis for realistic capital-budgeting rules (¢⟩ Capital Budgeting; Capital, Cost of).

(2) *Components*. A brief consideration of the analytic approach to financial management should consider financial objectives and long-term and short-term financing and investment decisions.

The analytic models of finance tend, like most models of economic theory, to be prescriptive (what 'ought' to be done) rather than descriptive. Such models remain important as opportunity-cost approaches to the evaluation of alternative policies. A growing body of empirically based work is beginning to make models such as the ⟡ Capital Asset Pricing Model more relevant to practical financial management. The reader should refer particularly to the *Journal of Finance* (USA) and the *Journal of Business Finance and Accounting* (UK) for a view of contemporary work in this field.

In relation to the shorter term the financial manager needs to specify the cash requirements for the firm's operations over, say, one year and hence needs to be able to understand the accounting and budgeting procedures that can identify fairly precisely the needs for liquid resources in the shorter term.

(3) *Financial environment.* In order to carry out their function properly financial managers must also have an understanding and working knowledge of the relevant financial institutions and the legal framework of finance. Indeed the descriptive and analytical approaches must be viewed as complementary; neither can do without the other. ⟡ Capital Market. E.A.L., amended by P.J.A.H.

R. A. Brealey and S. C. Myers, *Principles of Corporate Finance* (McGraw-Hill, 1981); D. Hodson (ed.), *Corporate Finance and Treasury Management* (Gee & Co., 1984).

Financial Risk ⟡ Risk and Uncertainty; Capital Structure

Fiscal Policy The fiscal policy of a government is the name given to the taxation and expenditure policies by which it seeks to influence the workings of the economy. Such a policy can obviously affect all the main components of expenditure and income in the country (⟡ National Income Accounts). The objectives of fiscal policy may be many. Initially fiscal policy was largely determined by the Government's budget, the aim being to ensure that sufficient income was raised to meet expenditure in the same financial year. However, in the modern economy there are additional objectives such as the desire to preserve a balance between demand and utilization of resources, the desire for a reasonable rate of growth and the desire to improve the balance of payments. Fiscal policy can play a part in the realization of all these objectives. ⟡ Forecasting for the Economy, Short-term; Growth in the Economy (Determinants).

The main sectors of the economy are the personal sector, business sector, government sector and foreign sector (⟡ National Income Accounts). Dealing firstly with the personal sector, the various fiscal measures available are changes in income-tax rates and allowances, changes in value added tax and customs-and-excise duties, and lastly, changes in social-security contributions and payments. In the UK value added tax can be varied by up to 25 per cent of its existing level between budgets and customs-and-excise duties by up to 10 per cent. In both cases this is subject to parliamentary approval.

The business sector of the economy is affected by investment incentives and also changes in corporation tax and allowances. With regard to investment incentives, country-wide taxation allowances are available on capital expenditure, and in the Development Areas this is supplemented by cash grants of 15 per cent on new plant and buildings.

If fiscal policy is the responsibility of the Government, what can the Government do about its own income and expenditure plans? The key areas on the income side have already been mentioned, but on the expenditure side we find that capital-investment programmes are often an item to be considered. In the past a cut in the investment programmes of the nationalized industries was a favourite way of controlling the economy, but in recent years the emphasis has moved towards the control of government expenditure in such areas as health, education and housing. This is to help the Government's avowed aim of lowering the proportion of public expenditure to gross domestic product.

The foreign sector of the economy is affected directly by changes in tariffs, taxes and subsidies and also, indirectly, by many of the measures that have been mentioned previously. For example, as fiscal policy dampens down the growth of the home economy, so the growth of imports may slow down and exports rise.

In recent years much greater stress has also been placed upon the monetary implications of government expenditures and revenues. In particular a serious attempt has been made to lower the Public Sector Borrowing Requirement (PSBR), both in absolute terms and as a percentage of the gross domestic product. The PSBR is the amount by which the revenue of public sector organizations (central and local government and nationalized industries) falls short of expenditure. This must be financed by sales of government stock to the non-bank private sector, increases in currency, borrowing from overseas or bank lending to the public sector. The effects of such financing are likely to be inflationary if new currency comes into circulation, and increased sales of government stocks may drive up interest rates, causing difficulties for company investment. It has been argued by some economists that the size of the PSBR may drain resources, both financial and physical, from the private sector.

In the 1985 Budget the following projections were produced for the PSBR: 1984/5 estimate, £10·5 billion (3·25 per cent of GDP); 1985/6 forecast, £7 billion (2 per cent of GDP). ⟡ Forecasting for the Economy, Short-term; Monetary Policy. L.T.S.

A. R. Prest and D. J. Coppock, *The UK Economy: A Manual of Applied Economics* (Weidenfeld & Nicolson, 10th ed., 1984).

Flexible Manufacturing System (FMS) Traditionally in batch production, each time a particular item is manufactured a batch is produced in order to build up an output stock that will satisfy demand until that item is manufactured again. The appropriate, i.e. most economic, batch size is a function of the cost of setting up facilities for the manufacture of an item and the cost of holding completed items in stock. As the setting-up cost increases, for a given stock-holding cost the economic batch size will increase. As the setting-up cost reduces, for a given stock-holding cost the economic batch size will fall. In general, the more similar the items to be made, the smaller the facilities set-up cost. Further, the more flexible the facilities to be used, i.e. the more easily adaptable they are to the manufacture of different items, the smaller the facilities set-up cost. Thus, if items can be grouped in families, and if inherently flexible manufacturing facilities can be used, a particularly efficient method of 'batch' production can be employed, in which batch sizes are small, throughput time is reduced, and output stock levels are minimized.

The concept of family or group production has been employed for some time. However, the recent availability of inherently flexible manufacturing facilities has begun to transform traditional batch production. In the engineering industry, for example, the use of computer-controlled machine tools with automatic tool-changing facilities, together with the automatic transport of items between machines and automatic loading using robotic devices, all under computer control, have resulted in the development of flexible manufacturing systems (FMS). The use of an FMS in the manufacture of 'family-grouped', i.e. similar, items gives rise to a particularly efficient form of manufacture in comparison with the traditional batch working method through a function or process-type layout.

Efficient computer-controlled flexible manufacture is increasingly important in other manufacturing industries, e.g. foodstuffs, pharmaceuticals and clothing, where there is a need for the manufacture of a range of possibly similar products and, for economic reasons, work-in-progress and throughput times must be reduced, delivery times must be reduced and output stocks must be kept to a minimum. ◊ Group Technology; ◊◊ Computer-aided Manufacture. R.W.

P. Ranky, *The Design and Operation of Flexible Manufacturing Systems* (*IFS Publications, 1983*).

Flow Lines ◊ Assembly Lines

Flow Process Charts ◊ Process Charts

FOB Contracts The free-on-board contract for the sale of goods differs from a CIF contract in that the agreed price covers, in addition to the cost of the goods only, the cost of having them placed on board ship. The remaining costs, including freight and insurance charges, will have to be borne by the buyer. The goods are treated as having been delivered to the buyer as soon as they are placed on board ship and the buyer has been informed. It is then the buyer's responsibility to arrange insurance cover, since the goods will be at the buyer's risk once they are on board. If the seller has, however, failed to inform the buyer of the goods being shipped, the risk of loss or damage will remain with the seller. ◊ CIF Contracts. W.F.F.

C. M. Schmitthoff, *The Export Trade* (Stevens & Sons, 7th ed., 1980).

Follett, Mary Parker (1868–1933) ◊ Authority

Forecasting for the Economy, Short-term Since the Second World War the British Government, in common with many others, has accepted considerable responsibility for the running and performance of the economy. This stems from a desire to avoid the waste of resources and potential output and the misery of the 1930s. This responsibility means that the modern Government must ascertain the direction in which the economy is moving and take appropriate action if it appears that difficulties might arise. Thus it is necessary for the Government to know if demand is likely to outstrip production overall or in certain sectors, for appropriate action can then be taken before price rises begin or wage demands are made. Similarly corrective action can be taken if it appears that resources will be under-utilized. The purpose of short-term forecasting procedures is to ensure that this knowledge is available so that corrective action may be introduced through fiscal or monetary measures.

Forecasting exercises have been carried out in Whitehall for the last forty-five years and present practice in the Treasury is to use both formal methods (including econometric models) and informal ones (including business surveys and intuition). Since the passing of the 1975 Industry Act, these forecasts must be published at least twice a year; they are now published with each Budget and again later in the year. The forecasts extend about fifteen months ahead and contain, in addition to the table of constant price GDP and its components, forecasts of retail prices, public-sector borrowing and the balance of payments on current account, all assuming a continuation of existing policies.

Formal methods involve the use of the Treasury model, which consists of some 700 economic relationships determining the main economic variables, many of which interact with each other. However, this does not preclude the use of judgement where formal and informal methods differ.

Forecasting of categories of aggregate demand, such as consumers' expenditure and public expenditure (both current and capital), can be either functional or autonomous. For example, consumers' expenditure is functionally derived from a knowledge of its previous relationship with personal disposable income and other variables, whilst public expenditure is autonomous, because it is deduced from the plans and programmes laid down by the Government. The various approaches for the other categories of aggregrate demand are as follows. Exports are closely dependent upon world production and relative prices. Fixed investment by business is derived from anticipations data, interest rates and modified accelerator relationships (⟡ Investment in the Economy). House-building data is obtained from data on housing starts and permits or licences, the average time taken to build and Building Society advances. Investment in stocks, in principle, is determined by the concept of a normal relationship between stocks and total sales. If each of these categories is forecast for the next period (be it a quarter or year), then we will almost have total final demand. However, since consumers' expenditure is closely related to personal disposable income (⟡ Consumption Function), this cannot be known until total demand is known.

One way of proceeding at this point is to take a plausible figure for consumption, thus obtaining total final demand, and then deduct the forecasts for imports and indirect taxes to give a forecast for gross domestic product (⟡ National Income Accounts). From this we must now work out the implications of the future level of GDP for employment, given the general expectations about labour productivity. When this is combined with a forecast of average earnings, transfers, salaries and dividends and taxation, we have arrived at our required figure of personal disposable income, which will yield a figure for consumers' expenditure. If this fails to agree with our initial plausible assumption, then the process is repeated until consistency is achieved.

Besides publishing the forecasts, the Treasury is required by the Industry Act to analyse from time to time the errors in the forecasts. The reference article below contains a report of an analysis of the early forecasts. The general conclusion is that errors increase the further ahead the forecast looks, and that whilst there is no clear evidence of bias, there is some tendency to overstate the growth of exports, understate the growth in consumers' expenditure and, when forecasting twelve months or more ahead, to underestimate the rise in prices. ⟳ Fiscal Policy; Monetary Policy. L.T.S.

> *Economic Progress Report* (Treasury, June 1981); D. Morris (ed.) *The Economic System in the UK* (OUP, 3rd ed., 1985).

Forecasting, Medium-term The environment of modern business is characterized by uncertainty. This being so, it is hardly surprising that managers have sought to forecast future demand for their product(s) as an aid to better decision-making now. Such forecasts are necessary for the correct planning of capital expenditure, otherwise demand may have to remain unsatisfied because capacity is unavailable, or capacity may be underutilized because demand has been overestimated. Although uncertainty characterizes our world, the forecaster believes that there are regular patterns of behaviour and that knowledge of them will be helpful in looking into the future. Even the simplest forecast based upon previous patterns of behaviour can be instructive and aid the learning process, whereas a forecast based upon 'judgement' is almost immune from constructive criticism. A useful framework for forecasting for the individual firm was suggested in an article in the *Journal of Industrial Economics*, November 1965, by C. Robinson. This envisages a three-stage procedure for the forecasting of future demand for a firm's product(s). Firstly, one should forecast future movements of the economy; secondly, future movements of the industry and product group; and thirdly, future market shares and demand for the individual product(s).

A considerable amount of work has been undertaken by government statisticians and economists and also by private organizations such as the National Institute of Economic and Social Research into forecasting the future of the economy. Whilst it is true that forecasting is both an art and a science, nevertheless such forecasts are based upon quantitative relationships and are, therefore, open to modification as they are compared with actual events.

The second stage of forecasting future demand for the industry or product group depends upon the existence of stable relationships between, for example, industry demand and personal disposable income. Such relationships can be estimated (⟡ Econometrics) from past data and then projected into the future, given a forecast of personal disposable income from the first stage of the procedure. Two industries that have been exhaustively studied along these lines are the car industry and the steel industry.

The final stage is to forecast the market share of the individual firm and this is probably the most difficult stage of the procedure, as one enters the realm of interdependent decision-making. It is a crucial stage, however, for on it depend future capital and labour requirements.

Although forecasting has been treated here exclusively in terms of demand for a product, interest is growing in the application of forecasting techniques in other areas of business. The whole area is known as corporate or long-range planning and it encompasses not only demand forecasting but also manpower planning and forecasting and the forecasting of changes in technology. The linking factor in these diverse fields is the growing utilization of models expressed mathematically and estimated statistically. ⟡ Decision Theory; Plans: Corporate Planning; Demand Functions; Econometrics. L.T.S.

M. Barron and D. Targett, *Practical Business Forecasting* (Blackwell, 1985).

Forecasting Techniques, Short-term Short-term forecasting, that is for periods up to six months, is needed throughout industry and commerce, especially within the context of sales forecasting and production planning/stock control. This entry discusses some statistical techniques, but it should be remembered that forecasts produced by these techniques should always be complemented by management judgement.

If we consider the monthly demand for a product, the general level or mean may be analysed in terms of the following: (1) a trend, which may be up, down or zero, depending on whether demand is expanding, contracting or stationary; (2) a seasonal variation, which reflects varying demand throughout the year (e.g. ice-cream or heating fuel); (3) a residual random variation.

Techniques consist of analysing past data to identify (1) and (2) to provide as accurate a forecast as possible (⟡ Correlation and Regression). The most common ones used are:

(1) *Moving average*. This is one of the simplest techniques and takes the average of the last 'n' months as the forecast for the next month. For example, with $n = 5$ and the following past demands:

January	February	March	April	May
11	9	10	8	12

the forecast for June is:

$$\frac{11 + 9 + 10 + 8 + 12}{5} = 10$$

(2) *Weighted moving average*. If the above individual demands had occurred in a different sequence (say 8, 9, 10, 11, 12), the moving average forecast of '10' would have been obtained and an opposite trend would have been ignored. This follows because the demand five months ago carries equal weight compared with the demand last month. To overcome this, weighting factors can be attached to monthly figures to give increased weight to the most recent demands:

Month	Weighting (%)	Demand	Weighted demand
January	10	11	1·1
February	15	9	1·4
March	20	10	2·0
April	25	8	2·0
May	30	12	3·6
June forecast	100		10·1

(3) *Exponentially weighted moving average, or Exponential smoothing*. The above technique is cumbersome and it is better to attach a constant weighting factor (less than one) to each successive month, working backwards. Thus in the above example the forecast would be:

$$0·2 \, [12 + 8 \, (0·8) + 10 \, (0·8)^2 + 9 \, (0·8)^3 + 11 \, (0·8)^4 + \ldots]^1$$

This technique too looks cumbersome, but it may be shown algebraically that if $1 - a$ is the weighting factor (in the above case $a = 0·2$):

---

1. The factor of 0·2, or $1 - 0·8$, outside the bracket is required to ensure that a true weighted average is obtained.

(4) *Seasonality*. If demand for a product is seasonal it is relatively easy to calculate a seasonality factor that can be incorporated into the forecast. M.J.C.M.

Stephen P. Shao, *Statistics for Business and Economics* (Merrill, 1976); R. Fildes and D. Wood, *Forecasting for Business* (Longman, 1976).

Formal Organization 'The patterns of human interrelations, as defined by the systems, rules, policies and regulations of the company' (F. J. Roethlisberger and W. J. Dickson, *Management and the Worker*, Harvard University Press, 1939). The formal organization is deliberately and rationally designed to achieve the objectives of the enterprise both directly and indirectly. It is manifest in organization charts, rule books, manuals, rules of procedure, negotiating machinery, etc., and is implicit in a general understanding of officially expected behaviour.

The classical theorists focused exclusively on the formal aspects of organization but after the publication of the report on the ⟨⟩ Hawthorne Investigations attention was directed to the tendency of employees to form small social groups with their own status systems, behavioural patterns, beliefs and objectives, which are different from, and often opposed to, the requirements and expectations of the formal organization. These social groups and their associated behaviour have been called the informal organization, presumably in order to emphasize the contrast with formal organization.

Much research work has centred on the informal group and on the relationship between it and the industrial supervisor. The findings suggest that membership of such groups provides satisfactions that the formal organization cannot or does not supply. For example, the impersonality of the formal system may be counterbalanced by the opportunities for personal friendships and personality expression that the informal group provides; necessary information may be communicated more effectively via informal contacts; and the security of the group provides its members with psychological support and enables the members to protect or to further their collective interests. The ability of the group to take action is dependent, *inter alia*, on its solidarity and to this end the group will tend to exert some measure of control over its members' attitudes and behaviour. The term informal organization, however, is no longer applied exclusively to social groups but refers to all relationships in the organization that are not officially prescribed or expected. Such relations may further the personal interests of the people concerned or, perhaps more frequently, may be highly relevant to the achievement of organizational objectives, for such informal practices often develop to counter bureaucratic tendencies and other deficiencies in the formal structure. Modern organizational theorists are not concerned exclusively with either formal or informal elements of organization but recognize that neither can usefully be considered in isolation. Their concern is, therefore, with both formal and informal aspects of organizational structure and behaviour and with the interaction between the two. ⟡ Bureaucracy; Classical Organization Theory; Hawthorne Investigations; Human Relations; Organization Theory; Social System. I.C.MCG.

M. Albrow, *Bureaucracy* (Macmillan, 1970); T. Watson, *Sociology, Work and Industry* (Routledge & Kegan Paul, 1980).

Freedom of Association In its 1968 report the Donovan Commission noted the absence of positive action by the state to encourage workers to join trade unions or to protect them from retaliatory action by hostile employers should they do so. Yet the freedom to form, join and take part in the activities of trade unions is regarded as a fundamental civil liberty by bodies such as the Universal and European Human Rights Conventions. Without effective trade unions there could be no real collective bargaining. British law now seeks to protect this freedom of association, sometimes also called 'the right to organize', in a number of ways.

Trade unions themselves are no longer viewed as illegal organizations, as they were for much of the nineteenth century. Nowadays they possess a number of important rights and indeed the law attempts to protect their position from unfair competition by sham unions. ⟡ Company Unions. It does so by reserving the benefits of modern legislation to 'independent' unions, which have been certified as being free of employer dominance, control or interference. Thus only independent trade unions are entitled to negotiate closed-shop agreements, to require the disclosure of bargaining information by employers, or to be consulted in advance of proposed redundancies being implemented.

To some extent the law also guarantees employees the right to join the union of their choice against the wishes of their employer. Thus, while it is lawful for an employer to refuse to hire workers for anti-union reasons, it is automatically unfair to dismiss employees (or to take discriminatory action short of dismissal against them) because of their actual or proposed membership of an independent trade union, or because of their participation, at an appropriate time, in its activities. No minimum qualifying period of service is necessary for the presentation of a complaint of unfair dismissal on these grounds to an industrial tribunal. More recently, the Employment Act 1982 has substantially equated the right to join and not to join, in effect creating a parallel 'freedom to disassociate'. Once in employment every person is protected against dismissal (and action short of dismissal) where the reason for it is his non-membership of a trade union, except where there is an approved closed shop in operation. Even here, however, individuals may be entitled to refuse to take a union card if, for example, they were non-union employees when the closed shop was introduced or if they have a conscientious or other deeply held personal objection to being members of a (particular) trade union.

Once an independent trade union has been recognized for bargaining purposes, employees who are members are entitled to a reasonable amount of time off, without pay, to participate in its activities – for example voting in a union ballot. Employees who are also officials of the union, such as shop stewards, are entitled to *paid* time off to carry out their industrial-relations duties and to attend necessary training courses approved by their union or the TUC. An ACAS Code of Practice gives guidance on the exercise of these rights. ⟡ Collective Bargaining; Company Union; Trade Union – at Law. K.W.

P. Davies and M. Freedland, *Labour Law: Text and Materials.* (Weidenfeld & Nicolson, 2nd ed., 1984), ch. 2.

Frequency Distributions The concept of frequency-distribution curves is fundamental to ⟡ Statistics. The shape of such curves, that is, the pattern of variability they display, can vary widely, but some distributions occur very often. Three commonly occurring distributions are:

(1) *Normal distribution.* Many present-day goods are manufactured by mass-production methods on machines that repetitively produce almost identical items. However, owing to uncontrollable variations in the quality of the processed materials and the settings of the processing machines, no two units are exactly identical. Thus, if we operate a manufacturing process that produces one-inch-diameter ball bearings, we cannot expect every bearing to have a diameter of exactly one inch. Rather, we can expect to produce quantities of the bearings with a mean (⟡ Measures of Location) diameter of one inch, but although some individual bearings will have one-inch diameters, others will have diameters slightly below or above this value. If we plot a histogram (with sufficiently small class intervals) of the diameters of the bearings, we shall generate a distribution curve of diameters with mean values of one inch and the variation about this mean. Such a curve would be a normal distribution.

Hence a normal distribution curve is produced when we plot measures that are subject to variation, for a variety of causes, about some mean value. Another example is the distribution curve for the heights of Cup Final spectators discussed under ⟨⟩ Statistics, since men's heights are determined by numerous factors in their heredity and environment.

(2) *Binomial distribution.* Suppose that instead of manufacturing ball bearings we are making transistors. Our manufacturing process is a very inefficient one and each transistor has a 30 per cent chance of being defective and therefore a 'reject'. Suppose that the transistors are made in batches of ten, so that on average three in each batch are rejects. However, just as the diameters of ball bearings discussed above varied about an average diameter of one inch, similarly the number of rejects in successive batches of transistors will vary about an average of three. This follows because each transistor has a 30 per cent chance of being defective, so, purely by chance, some batches will contain anything from none to ten rejects. Using the laws of probability, we can calculate the probability of obtaining 0, 1, 2, etc. rejects in a batch. These probabilities are shown as follows:

Number of rejects in a batch	0	1	2	3	4	5	6	7	8	9	10
Probability (per cent)		2·82	12·11	23·35	26·68	20·01	10·29	3·68	0·90	0·14	0·01	0·00

These probabilities could be plotted as a histogram with unit class intervals, which would represent the pattern of variation of the number of rejects per batch.

Suppose that, instead of making transistors in batches of ten, we make them in batches of 10,000. Then the average number of rejects per batch would be 3,000 and, again using the laws of probability, we could calculate the probabilities of a batch containing from 0 to 10,000 rejects. These probabilities could be plotted as a distribution curve, which again would represent the pattern of variation of the number of rejects per batch. Because the underlying probability theory is based on a mathematical theorem known as the binomial theorem, such a curve is known as a binomial distribution.

(3) *Poisson distribution.* In the above example the manufacture of a defective transistor occurred quite frequently (30 per cent of the time). Managers are often concerned with the pattern of variations of events that occur quite rarely – for example, the pattern of variation of the occurrence of industrial accidents in a company. Such patterns often form a distribution known as a Poisson distribution.

For example, in the nineteenth century, Bortkewitch performed an analysis of the pattern of variation of deaths from horse kicks of cavalry men in the Prussian army. He analysed the records of ten cavalry corps over twenty years, thus obtaining 200 corps-years of observations. From these records he was able to construct a table showing the number of corps-years in which 0, 1, 2, etc. deaths occurred. The total number of deaths was 122, so the average number of deaths was 122/200, or 0·61 per corps-year. However, as the table below shows, this average is spread over sets of years in which 0, 1, 2, etc. deaths occur because of all the chance influences that are present. Since there were a large number of men in a cavalry corps and on average only 0·61 men were killed per year, the probability of a fatality per man at risk was small. Therefore, Bortkewitch predicted the pattern number of years in which 0, 1, 2, 3 and 4 deaths would occur using a Poisson distribution. These predicted values are compared with the observed values in the table below:

Number of deaths/year/corps	0	1	2	3	4
Actual number of corps-years	109	65	22	3	1
Predicted number of corps-years	109	66·3	20·2	4·1	0.6

It can be seen that the agreement between prediction based on the Poisson distribution and the observed values is very good.

Data that is subjected to variability following a Poisson distribution occurs quite often in organizations. M.J.C.M.

Stephen P. Shao, *Statistics for Business and Economics* (Merrill, 1976).

Fringe Benefits The supplements to wages and salaries that are part of total labour costs but do not constitute a direct reward geared to the output, effort and merit of an employee.

Strictly speaking a labour cost is a fringe benefit only when it is an avoidable factor, i.e. when it could be replaced by money wages without detriment to productive efficiency, but in practice the borderline between avoidable and unavoidable labour costs cannot be drawn with any precision. Consequently the size and scope of fringe benefits may vary quite substantially from one firm to another and from one industry to another. A survey of 350 companies in 1960 showed that there were wide variations in fringe benefits paid to manual workers. Two thirds of the companies spent between 7·5 per cent and 15 per cent of the payroll on fringe benefits and one fifth spent between 15 per cent and 25 per cent.

Fringe benefits for salaried employees tended to be higher than those for wage-earners.

Normally, however, fringe benefits include most of the following items: (1) pay for time not worked, such as sickness, accidents and holidays; (2) awards for special status, such as long service; (3) social-security payments by employers, such as statutory and voluntary social insurance arrangements like unemployment, sickness and pensions; (4) the cost of services provided for the benefit of employees, often by means of subsidies or loans, such as canteen and sports facilities, employee discounts and mortgages; (5) other payments not directly related to work done, such as profit sharing, severance pay over and above payments necessary under the Redundancy Payments Act (⟡ Redundancy) and payments made for attendance on training courses.

Fringe benefits, therefore, exert an equalizing tendency in so far as they are conferred on the diligent and the indolent alike. Critics regard the piecemeal extension of these benefits as inimical to increased effort and higher productivity in so far as they appear to be moulding the factory environment into a comfortable welfare state in miniature. However, in the absence of any conclusive evidence one way or the other it can be argued with equal plausibility that fringe benefits contribute directly to the creation of a working environment conducive to good human relations and indirectly therefore to higher productivity.

In recent years the rigours of ⟡ Prices and Incomes Policy have compelled some trade unionists to look upon fringe benefits as at least a partial alternative to conventional wage increases. This awakened interest on the part of the unions has met with a favourable response from those employers who regard the concession of more fringe benefits as the least expensive way of obtaining increased productivity from their workforce. For this reason fringe benefits have played a prominent part in the negotiation of a number of productivity bargains (⟡ Productivity Bargaining) in recent years, most notably in the electricity supply industry, and their future role in ⟡ Collective Bargaining seems assured. It would certainly appear that many British firms have a good deal of ground to make up compared with their West European competitors in the size and scope of the fringe benefits they provide. N.H.C.

G. L. Reid and D. J. Robertson (eds.), *Fringe Benefits, Labour Costs and Social Security* (Allen & Unwin, 1968).

Functional (1) Specialized in terms of a general purpose. Thus functional organization is that which is based on administrative units each representing a specialist activity: for example, a multi-product company may have as its basic divisions production, marketing, accounting, purchasing and personnel, with further subdivision following the lines of these basic divisions. Functional organization has certain advantages: it enables the maximum attainment of the advantages accruing from specialization; it facilitates centralized direction and control; special equipment can be economically utilized; professional expertise is more readily built up. On the other hand, an overenthusiastic adherence to functional principles has its attendant disadvantages: decentralization of decision-making is more difficult to achieve; there is a tendency for subunits to develop too narrow a specialist viewpoint and to perceive their own activities as ends in themselves with consequent problems of communication and co-ordination; and, particularly at the lowest levels in the organization, too much specialization may result in monotonous, repetitive work with reduced job satisfaction and motivation.

Organization along functional lines raises problems of authority relationships and concomitant responsibility. F. W. Taylor (*Shop Management*, 1911) was the first writer to draw attention to the need for specialists to exercise authority within the area of their specialist expertise in order for the organization to make best use of specialist knowledge and skills and to achieve a consistent application of company policy. Such authority is called functional authority and occurs wherever a manager is empowered to prescribe processes, methods, policies or actions for personnel who are not his own subordinates. Functional authority violates the principle of unity of command and makes it difficult to equate authority with responsibility. ⪧ Authority; Department; Responsibility; Specialization; Line and Staff (1); Unity of Command. L.C.McG.

W. Brown, *Exploration in Management* (Penguin Books, 1965); C. B. Handy, *Understanding Organizations* (Penguin, 1981).

Functional (2) The extent to which a social phenomenon facilitates the achievement of a given objective. The phenomenon is *dysfunctional* to the extent that it militates against the achievement of the objective. The terms, commonly encountered in sociological writings, should not be used unless the objective in respect of which the phenomenon is functional or dysfunctional is clearly stated or understood. It is frequently the case that a phenomenon may be functional in regard to one objective, whilst at the same time it is dysfunctional in regard to another. L.C.McG.

Funds-flow Analysis The term 'funds' has several meanings. In its widest accounting meaning it refers to purchasing power, and the flow of funds refers to the flow of purchasing power into and out of a business or other organization. The chief sources of such funds flows are:

(1) *Funds flows into the firm.* Gross revenues from product; sales of fixed assets; sales of investments; issues of debentures, loans and shares.

(2) *Funds flows out of the firm.* Outlay costs, i.e. costs incurred in earning revenues from product requiring payments to creditors (depreciation costs are therefore excluded); purchases of fixed assets and investments for credit or cash; repayment of capital or long-term debt; payment, or the recognition as owing, of dividends and taxes on profits.

The most widely used method of showing funds-flow movements is to consider the effect of changes in working capital. All transactions that result in an increase in working capital are shown as sources of funds, e.g. gross revenues are sources since they result in an increase in debtors or cash. All transactions that result in a decrease in working capital are applications (or dispositions), e.g. incurring the outlay cost of production, which involves purchases of materials for cash or credit. Thus the objective of this form of analysis is to show the net change in working capital for a particular period.[1] Although funds flows are sometimes defined merely as cash flows, this is not a reasonable definition. ⟡ Cash Flow.

The accounting status of the funds-flow statement has gradually increased and it is now widely recognized as being as important a document as the balance sheet or profit-and-loss account. E.A.L.

R. K. Jaedicke and R. T. Sprouse, *Accounting Flows: Income, Funds and Cash* (Prentice-Hall, 1965); *SSAP.10, Statements of source and application of funds* (Accounting Standards Committee, 1975).

Further Education That part of the national system of education which is concerned with the full-time and part-time education of those who have left secondary school but have not yet moved into higher education at the universities. In the 1980s a government policy of reducing public expenditure, widespread youth unemployment and the effects of an earlier decline in the birth rate all stimulated major changes in the financing and content of further education in Britain.

Advanced further education, more commonly described as public

1. However, since current asset valuations are affected by profit calculations this definition of funds is a less objective one than other possible definitions.

sector higher education (PSHE) took place in some thirty polytechnics and seventy or so colleges and institutes of further education, concentrating on academic qualifications beyond GCE 'A' level, such as a degree, or upon vocational qualifications like those of the accountancy and banking professions, or the higher certificates and diplomas of the Business and Technician Education Council (BTEC). Because of the high cost of advanced courses, the cost of PSHE was pooled amongst all the local authorities, each authority being assessed for a contribution to the 'pool' on the basis of its school population and non-domestic rateable value by central government. In recent years these institutions have provided an increasing number of part-time courses leading to degrees.

Non-advanced further education (NAFE) was provided by local education authorities and funded by the Rate Support Grant from central government and from local rates. It took place mostly in colleges of further education. These tended to offer: (1) traditional vocational courses leading to BTEC certificates and diplomas for the qualifications of the City and Guilds of London Institute; (2) 'academic' courses leading to GCE 'O' and 'A' level qualifications; (3) an increasing number of pre-vocational courses in response to initiatives from the Manpower Services Commission, which introduced the Youth Training Scheme (YTS) in 1983. This offered a one-year full-time programme of work experience, linked with further education and a certificate of training. In 1984 the Government allocated the MSC considerable funds to enable it to purchase more work-related NAFE for school-leavers, provided by local education authorities, complicating yet again the funding process of further education.

The MSC was also closely involved in the establishment of the Open Tech, initially in association with the Technician Education Council (TEC, which later became BTEC). The Open Tech programme was set up to extend opportunities for adult training and retraining using a 'distance' (or 'open') learning approach, the emphasis at first being upon the knowledge and skills required by technicians. The production of suitable material to meet the needs of such students was funded by the MSC, which created an Open Tech Unit for this purpose. TEC and the Business Education Centre (BEC) had already entered the field, TEC running distance learning schemes and BEC directing private study and correspondence courses. Other institutions, such as Henley – The Management College, operated variants of the distance learning model where students studied mostly at home, but were supported by a network of tutors available for consultation or by a series of short residential courses.

The further education sector has traditionally provided a wide range of recreational and cultural courses through adult education centres and institutes, these courses being held mainly in the evenings. Other courses, usually of a cultural nature, are offered to adults by institutions outside the further education sector, such as the extra-mural departments of universities and the Workers' Educational Association. E.L.

L. M. Cantor and I. F. Roberts, *Further Education Today* (Routledge & Kegan Paul, 1983).

Fuzzy Sets One of the major strengths of mathematics is its pre-ciseness. Yet in the real world, it is often difficult, if not impossible, to specify exactly what value a parameter might take. To a limited extent this may be overcome by expressing a range of values for each parameter, together with measures of their likely occurrence. These so-called 'fuzzy' values make up fuzzy sets. A branch of mathematics has been developed to deal with fuzzy sets and it has found application in the development of ⇨ Expert Systems. R.S.S.

G

Games, Operational and Business ◇ Competitive Problems; Simulation; Decision Theory

Gantt Charts The Gantt chart, developed by Henry L. Gantt *c.* 1900, is a graphical method of depicting work schedules or work loads. Each job or activity is represented as a block or bar drawn on a time-scale, e.g.

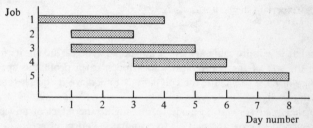

Such charts are used extensively in production planning and control and also appear as multiple activity charts in method study. ◇◇ Production Planning and Control; Multiple-activity Charts. R.W.

Gantt, H. L. ◇ Gantt Charts

Gap Analysis The mathematical calculation made to investigate the difference between two curves.

A typical example is the difference between a profit target curve and a profit forecast curve: a company may have decided that a suitable target to aim for is a 10 per cent growth in profits each year starting at the current year's profit of £100,000. The target will appear as illustrated in figure 1 on p. 192.

The company may also calculate that, if it continues to trade in the existing manner, its profits will probably turn out as illustrated in figure 2.

By superimposing one graph on the other it is possible to observe the widening gap between what the company wishes to achieve (its target)

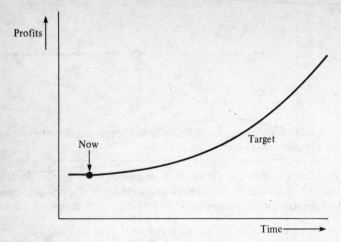

Figure 1

and what it will probably achieve if no special action is taken (its forecast): the size of the gap indicates how much extra profit this special action will have to yield if the company is to achieve its target rate of growth (see figure 3).

Further analyses can be made to investigate the effect of any proposed action to close the gap, or to examine the effect of errors in the forecast.

In general, gap analysis is used to investigate the difference between any target and any forecast. ⇦⇨ Forecasting Techniques; Target. A.J.A.A.

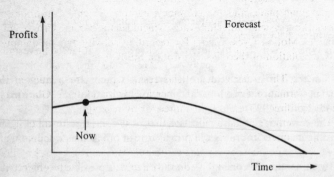

Figure 2

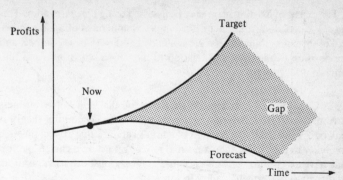

Figure 3

Gearing ◊ Capital Structure

General Union ◊ Trade Union Types – General Union

Gilbreth, Frank B. and Lillian M. The combination of engineer and psychologist in this famous pioneering team seemed ideal for tackling the numerous problems associated with the description, measurement and improvement of manual work.

Frank B. Gilbreth's earliest studies were carried out in the building industry, where he was able, by means of careful observation and ingenious invention, to bring about enormous improvements in the work output of bricklayers. The Gilbreths' approach, involving the development of numerous techniques of motion study, was later brought to bear upon problems in a wide variety of industrial settings. In 1912 the Gilbreths described the technique of micro-motion study, using movie film and an accurate clock. Other photographic techniques included the cyclegraph, in which movement patterns are recorded on a photographic plate, and the chronocyclegraph, which incorporates a time marking system. Other innovations included the ◊ Simo Chart (Simultaneous Motion Cycle Chart) for recording activity and the famous analytic notation of therbligs. ◊ Motion Study. E.E.

Glare Three deleterious effects result from glare: reduction in visual performance, discomfort and increase in visual fatigue. Glare may be induced directly from a light source, or by reflection.

Several methods of glare reduction are available: (1) removal of light source from direct line of sight; (2) reduction of brightness of source, e.g. by using large numbers of low-intensity sources instead of fewer, brighter ones; (3) use of screens and visors; (4) avoidance of highly reflective surfaces e.g. high-gloss paint, polished metal.

The extent of existing glare may be assessed using the glare index. This may be calculated from data describing the luminances of a light source and of the background, the angle subtended at the eye by the source, and the position of the source in relation to the viewer. ⟡ Brightness; Illumination; Vision. E.E.

Goodwill (in Accounting) That part of the value of a business attributable to its reputation and connections. In accounting theory it may be considered to be that part of a firm's capital value arising through an ability to earn more than a normal rate of return on its assets. A firm may have exceptional earnings because of monopolistic market position, quality of management, ability to innovate, etc.

Conceptually goodwill can be measured by reference to an assessment of the present value of expected future earnings (⟡ Present Value). Hence goodwill is the difference between that figure of present value and the aggregate total of the individual economic values of the tangible assets less liabilities. However, the measurement difficulties are quite formidable since they include the forecasting of expected total earnings and the basis for a 'normal' rate of return on businesses of a similar kind. For these kinds of reasons it is accountancy convention to record goodwill in books of account only when it has been paid for as, for example, on the purchase of a business. It is then normally recorded as the difference between the market or realizable values of tangible assets less liabilities and the total purchase price. It is considered not necessary, although 'prudent', to write goodwill off, but essential not to write it up. ⟡ Capital (Cost of). E.A.L.

J. C. Bonbright, *Valuation of Property* (McGraw-Hill, 1937); T. A. Lee, 'Goodwill – An Example of Will-o'-the-Wisp Accounting,' *Accounting and Business Research* (Autumn 1971).

Goodwill (in Law) Goodwill has been defined as 'the benefit arising from connection or reputation' of an existing business. While it clearly has a monetary value it is not at all easy to quantify this. Lawyers have distinguished between 'cat goodwill' and 'dog goodwill'. The former is goodwill attached to premises that occupy a convenient and valuable site for particular business purposes, while the latter is goodwill that is based on the special knowledge or skill of the people running a business. The difference is important when it comes to disposing of the goodwill. Cat goodwill can only be sold with the premises, while dog goodwill is either not saleable at all or, if saleable, implies that some know-how or other information is being sold with the tangible assets of a business.

A new partner admitted to a ⟡ Partnership will be required to make a payment to the existing partners for a share in the goodwill. When a partnership is dissolved and the assets of the firm are sold, goodwill is generally disposed of as one of the assets and the purchaser of it will have a sole right to it. If, however, no provision is made for the sale of the goodwill, any of the former partners could use the goodwill of the firm's business (e.g. to the extent of using the former firm's name), provided always that in doing so they do not imply that their former co-partners are associated with them in their new enterprise. W.F.F.

C. D. Drake, *Law of Partnership* (Stevens & Sons, 3rd ed., 1983).

Grievance Procedure The arrangements for settling disputes arising on the shop floor between trade union members and management.

In most other industrial countries these arrangements tend to be formal, written agreements, often enforceable at law. Under the continental and American systems of ⟡ Collective Bargaining most substantive agreements, i.e. those dealing with terms and conditions of employment, tend to carry their own negotiating procedures for the settlement of disputes. In Britain, however, there has traditionally been a clear distinction between substantive and procedural agreements, and, in both cases, much less emphasis on formality and enforceability. Almost all industries have some kind of dispute procedure, including arbitration (⟡ Arbitration, Industrial), though there are considerable differences in terms of complexity, speed and general effectiveness. Historically most industry-wide procedures have developed piecemeal, often as a result of ⟡ Strike action, and may therefore still reflect an anachronistic balance of bargaining power between management and trade unions.

In the engineering industry the provisions for avoiding disputes required any worker concerned to first raise any question in person with their foreman. If the worker was not satisfied they went with the ⟡ Shop Steward to the departmental manager. Subsequent stages might take the form of a works committee (if one existed), or a works conference with official representatives of the appropriate ⟡ Trade Union and ⟡ Employers' Association, and then a local conference at which a panel of employers not directly involved in the question at issue met to hear the two sides of the case from the union and the firm concerned. If no agreement was reached the final stage was a central conference at which a panel of national representatives of the Engineering Employers' Federation formed 'courts' to hear the case of the firm and of the workers. Only when this procedure was exhausted and no agreement reached did strike action become constitutional.

Not surprisingly the engineering procedure and several other industry-wide arrangements were attacked on the grounds that they were cumbersome, outdated, biased in favour of delay rather than settlement, and totally at variance with the current trend towards decentralized collective bargaining. By and large both managements and trade unions prefer to settle a dispute within the confines of the establishment in which it originated and for this reason, and in the absence of any effective reform of industry-wide procedures, more and more companies are paying attention to their own domestic conciliation (⟡ Industrial Conciliation) machinery. Evidence for this is that in 1984 the staff of the ⟡ Advisory, Conciliation and Arbitration Service made more advisory visits to discuss grievance, dispute and disciplinary procedures than any other subject. The Royal Commission urged that boards of directors should take a long look at their own procedural arrangements with a view to clarifying and formalizing them, thereby making a resort to national procedures less necessary (⟡ Industrial Relations – Reform in Great Britain). One school of thought sees procedural reform as the *sine qua non* of a better system of industrial relations, believing that most grievances can be redressed to the satisfaction of both parties if only they use the right methods. However, a grievance procedure, no matter how enlightened and efficient it may appear on paper, is only effective if both parties operate it in good faith. It is perhaps rather naïve to expect 'model' procedures to smooth over all or even most of the real conflicts of interest that do arise from time to time in many industrial situations. ⟡ Industrial Relations Code of Practice. N.H.C. and E.L.

A. W. J. Thomson and V. V. Murray, *Grievance Procedures* (Saxon House, 1976); Advisory Conciliation and Arbitration Service, *Annual Report 1984* (ACAS, 1985).

Gross Domestic Product (GDP) ⟡ National Income Accounts

Gross National Product (GNP) ⟡ National Income Accounts

Group A number of persons viewed as a collectivity. Primary groups are commonly distinguished from secondary groups. Primary groups are sufficiently small to enable the members to interact on an informal face-to-face basis, as, for example, in the family or a small friendship clique. Secondary groups are those too large to be classed as primary and therefore require a formal structure; a trade union or a factory community is an example. In practice it is often impossible to draw precise boundaries round groups or to designate them firmly as primary or secondary. In another usage of the term, 'group' is applied to any aggregate of persons who share a given characteristic such as the same income (income group), the same age (age group), the same occupation (occupational group), etc.

The type of group most relevant to an understanding of organizational behaviour is probably the interest group, composed of those persons who consider themselves to have socio-economic interests in common. These interests are usually believed to be different from, and in varying degrees to be in conflict with, the interests of other groups. There are many possible bases for interest groups but in the industrial organization the most important are probably common occupation, similarity of function, and face-to-face or primary group membership. Recognition that they possess interests in common will frequently lead the members of the group to develop practices designed to defend or to promote their interests or to establish formal organizations for that purpose. ⟡ Conflict; Formal Organization; Hawthorne Investigations; Socio-technical System. L.C.McG.

S. Hill, 'Norms, Groups and Power: The Sociology of Workplace Industrial Relations', *British Journal of Industrial Relations*, vol. 12, no. 2 (July 1974); T. Lupton, *Management and the Social Sciences* (Penguin new ed., 1983), pp. 71–5.

Group Discussion/Interview ⟡ Motivation Research

Group Incentives ⟡ Wage; Wage Systems; Motivation

Group Methods of Training In the training process groups can be used to satisfy a variety of learning goals. When the objective is to enable specialists from different backgrounds to learn to work together or to combine forces to attack a problem, a group can be formed and put to work on appropriate tasks. The group thus becomes a source of knowledge and information available to its members. It may also serve as a vehicle through which its members learn about groups and about each other's behaviour from observation and discussion whilst engaged upon a common task. In this process the members of a group can obviously become important influences on each other, sometimes with lasting effect upon an individual's behaviour. Learning about inter-group behaviour may be similarly fostered by involving several groups in a common task that requires interaction between them. In all of these instances a member of the training staff is present, primarily to assist group members to learn from what is happening to them.

In pursuit of the first objective – helping experts to learn to work together – the British Army has used carefully structured groups in courses for senior officers at its Staff College for more than sixty years. The method was later adapted for the training of managers in industry and administrators in the public service by the Management College at Henley; variants of the method are now widely applied in Britain, the Commonwealth and Scandinavia.

The use of small groups as vehicles for learning about behaviour from personal experience has taken subtly different forms in the USA and Britain. In the USA Kurt Lewin and his followers developed basic skill-training groups, whose objectives were to help participants to diagnose group problems and to improve their skills in dealing with interpersonal relations and leadership. Later, the goals of these 'T-groups' changed more towards self-awareness, so the process became known as 'sensitivity training'. In Britain, as a result of work by W. R. Bion at the Tavistock Institute, the emphasis was initially more upon group than individual behaviour. Consequently training in small groups along the Tavistock model became a method of gaining insight into the unconscious forces influencing group behaviour and attitudes towards authority.

A common ingredient in these small-group methods was a tension-creating phase resulting from a deliberate refusal by the staff to give structure to the proceedings. Lewin believed that individuals were stimulated by uncertainty to experiment with their behaviour, whilst Bion, as a 'group consultant', took a role rather like that of a psychoanalyst with a patient. In a typical T-group the trainer may begin by stating the purpose of the group and then lapsing into silence, leaving an apparent power vacuum. This gives scope to the group members to create a social system that will satisfy their own goals and needs but that poses problems of power, influence and the degree of intimacy demanded. The trainer's contribution may then be to express personal feelings, thereby legitimating members to do so and to show that he or she cares about the members. The trainer also tries to help their understanding of what is going on by occasional comments, in addition to managing time and deciding the sequence of events.

During the 1960s there were pressures for a return to the original concern of sensitivity training with increasing the competence of individuals and their personal skills ⟨⟩ Interpersonal Skill Development. Blake and Mouton introduced structured task training as a part of their ⟨⟩ Managerial Grid approach to organization development, during which individuals in phase one receive face-to-face feedback on their management styles from members of six-strong problem-solving groups ⟨⟩ Teams. The managerial-grid approach postulates an ideal management style that all managers should try to adopt, so feedback from the group becomes important as a means of shaping behaviour in a prescribed direction. In Britain a similar use of feedback associated with relatively simple group problem-solving tasks has characterized a management training approach used by Ralph Coverdale and a number of other trainers in industry.

Group decision-making exercises have also been an integral part of the business 'games' that became popular in the late 1950s. In these, participants work in small groups, each of which may represent the board of a competing manufacturing company, or a representative of an organization in its external environment, such as a trade union or clearing bank. Together the groups form part of a highly interactive complex system, which makes the consequences of their decisions difficult to predict unless they understand the system and can discover its sensitivities to change. Small decision-making groups of this kind have also been used effectively in management training in association with a computer model of a national economy as a means of learning about economics and the dilemmas facing those in government. In all of these instances the groups tend to be formed of members from different professional disciplines and management functions who possess valuable expertise but often differ markedly in their ordering of priorities, so that agreement on objectives becomes a prerequisite for sound decision-making in these circumstances.

The rich potential of group situations for generating emotion, as well as learning, attracted attention outside the fields of training and therapy in the 1960s, especially in the USA. This led to a proliferation of offers of group experience, including some that employed methods considered dubious or dangerous by professional trainers and clinicians, and these damaged the reputation of some group methods for a time. However, in 1972, J. W. Pfeiffer initiated a valuable series of Annual Handbooks, which supply theoretical and practical suggestions from experienced practitioners about small-group methods, together with the necessary directions for applying them. The same era also saw an increase in the number of organizations, staffed by experienced professionals, prepared to offer training to individuals with the right attributes who wished to run T-groups. E.L.

M. L. and P. J. Berger (eds.), *Group Training Techniques* (Gower, 1972); A. Blumberg and R. T. Golembiewski, *Learning and Change in Groups* (Penguin, 1976); J. W. Pfeiffer and L. D. Goodstein, *The 1983 Annual for Facilitators, Trainers and Consultants* (University Associates, 1983).

Group Selection Methods ◊ Selection

Group Technology A production method involving the manufacture of parts in 'families' or groups of related parts, rather than in small numbers, hence achieving the improved resource utilization inherent in quantity production.

The basis of a group-technology production system is the definition and description of groups of families of parts. Similarity of shape (design classification) and/or similarity of manufacturing requirement (production classification) may exist. Although the two classifications are usually related, only a detailed investigation within a company will indicate whether this relationship exists and whether there are sufficient suitable parts to merit this type of production.

Several proprietary systems exist (e.g. the Opitz and Brisch systems), their main difference being the method of classification and coding. Two techniques – production-flow analysis and component-flow analysis – take account of the sequence of operations required in the manufacture of items, whilst the formation of production 'cells' is a common consequence of the adoption of group technology in batch production. ◊ Cell Production; Flexible Manufacturing System. R.W.

J. L. Burbidge, *The Introduction of Group Technology* (Heinemann, 1975).

Group Working Prompted largely by the behavioural problems commonly thought to be associated with repetitive assembly-line work, efforts have recently been made to redesign production systems in order to provide more satisfying jobs. One approach concentrates upon the design of the individual's job (◊ Job Restructuring), whilst an alternative approach, which often leads to job restructuring, concentrates on the organization of workers in the production group. This approach aims to increase the degree of autonomy and responsibility exercised by the worker through the delegation of certain responsibilities to the work group. Thus group working involves the creation of formal functional work groups able to exercise some degree of self-organization and possessing delegated autonomy and responsibility beyond the area of the immediate task. Group working is often mistakenly seen as an alternative to assembly- or flow-line working, i.e. as an alternative production system. However, this type of semi-autonomous and responsible functional work group can be created within the constraints imposed by the production system and thus this form of work organization is appropriate in mass, jobbing and batch production. ◊ Cell Production. R.W.

R. Wild, *Work Organization* (J. Wiley, 1975).

Growth in the Economy (Determinants) What are the factors that determine the rate of growth in a country's productive potential? This question is invited by tables that show Britain's poor rate of growth compared to many of her competitors. Two sets of arguments have been advanced, one from the supply side and one from the demand side. From the supply side some or all of the following factors have been blamed: poor management, restrictive trade unions, rigid educational structure, social attitude to competition, laziness, insufficient investment, too much government interference and crippling taxes. On the demand side it has been suggested that stop-go policies have created such an unsettled climate that businessmen have been reluctant to plan too far ahead and have been reluctant to invest, thus reducing the growth of productive potential. It is interesting in this context to consider some of the many findings of Edward Denison relating to the sources of economic growth in the United States. During the period 1929–76 the annual average growth rate of total output was 2·98 per cent. Of this, the change in quantity of labour input was 1·36 per cent, that of capital 0·46 per cent, and the increase in output per unit of input 1·16 per cent (of which advances in knowledge was 0·73 per cent). Whilst one must stress the tentative and approximate nature of this work, what is noteworthy is the importance given to the labour input, amounting to nearly 50 per cent.

Table 1. International comparison of growth rates 1970–9 (annual percentages)

Country	Gross domestic product	Gross domestic product per capita
Belgium	3·3	3·0
Denmark	2·5	2·1
France	3·9	3·3
Germany	2·9	2·8
Italy	3·0	2·4
Japan	4·9	3·6
Netherlands	3·1	2·3
Sweden	2·1	1·8
United Kingdom	2·2	2·2
Canada	4·5	3·2
United States	3·4	2·3

Source: A. R. Prest and D. J. Coppock (eds.) *The UK Economy: A Manual of Applied Economics* (Weidenfeld & Nicolson, 10th ed., 1984), p. 53.

Other figures for the above countries, not here quoted, do suggest some positive association between growth in output and the percentage of GDP devoted to investment, although the link is tenuous. For the UK table 2 shows the effect of increases in labour force and capital stock on the rate of growth.

Table 2. Economic growth in the UK 1900–79

	GDP	GDP per capita	Employed labour force	Capital stock (excluding dwelling)
1900–13	1·5	0·6	0·9	1·7
1922–38	2·3	1·2	1·1	1·7
1950–60	2·6	2·2	0·4	2·8
1960–70	2·9	2·6	0·3	4·3
1970–79	2·1	1·9	0·2	3·2

Source: Prest and Coppock, *The UK Economy*, p. 51

Table 2 illustrates the point that as the rate of growth of the capital stock has increased so has the rate of growth of GDP and GDP per capita. Also illustrated is the fact that, at least in terms of the past, the growth performance of the UK economy in the post-war period has been reasonably impressive until the last decade. However, the omens for the future are not encouraging since of late the share of annual production that is devoted to gross investment has been declining (from 20 per cent in 1972 to 16 per cent in 1983) and the rate of growth of the employed labour force has tailed off. The quantity of investment is not enough, however, and it is vitally important that the investment is of the right quality and that it is undertaken in the right industries. Equally, in view of the importance ascribed to them by Denison, advances in knowledge must be encouraged, and labour must be encouraged to be more mobile with regard to skills and industry to reflect the changing economic structure. L.T.S.

E. F. Denison, *Accounting for Slower Economic Growth: United States in the 1970s* (Brookings Institution, 1980); D. Morris (ed.), *The Economic System in the UK* (OUP, 3rd ed., 1985).

Growth (Measurement) International league tables of rates of growth have become a common index. Generally they show the poor progress of the UK compared with her major competitors. A growing economy as opposed to a static economy is clearly desirable if living standards are to be improved and commitments abroad maintained. But what exactly is growth and how do we measure it?

Growth is most conveniently measured by the rate of change in the real gross domestic product (GDP) at factor cost ⟐ National Income Accounts. This gives us the total value of the goods and services produced as a result of economic activity in the UK, before providing for capital consumption. However, a glance at the year-to-year changes since 1960 shows that the highest change was around +5 per cent in 1964 and the lowest was −1 per cent in 1975. Changes such as these occur very largely because of the year-to-year changes in the pressure of demand upon resources. This factor can clearly affect our calculations, for the resources of the country may well have increased but the increase have failed to be utilized because of a shortfall in demand. What we therefore measure, or want to measure, is the growth in the nation's capacity to produce, that is the growth of its productive potential. This is best measured by comparing years in which the pressures on resources of labour and capital are broadly similar, for then the change in GDP will be a real reflection of the change in capacity to produce. The rate of growth in productive potential is then calculated as the compound growth rate, which will make the two GDPs equal. Table 2 in ⟐ Growth of the Economy (Determinants) shows the growth in the productive potential of the UK economy for selected periods since 1900. These periods, with the exception of the last one, have been selected so that they begin and end with years of similar unemployment. It is suggested that if the level of unemployment in 1979 had been as low as in 1970 0·3 might have been added to the growth rate. L.T.S.

Growth of the Firm The reasons for the growth of a firm can be divided into two categories: impersonal and personal.

It has been customary to play down the role of business leadership, or entrepreneurial ability, in contributing to the growth of firms. This accords with the approach to history that deals with political and economic forces rather than with great statesmen and monarchs. However, students of the past growth of firms detect at least some qualities or skills that must be present for growth to take place, although their presence does not guarantee it. Sheer physical strength appears necessary and this must be coupled with an ability to work hard and concentrate entirely upon the business if needs be. Since uncertainty is part of the framework of life there must be present a willingness, almost a desire, to take risks. To this must be coupled a determination that can amount to ruthlessness, if necessary. Finally, in the past successful entrepreneurs have not always had technical or commercial training. However, the growth of knowledge in the field of management plus the general raising of educational standards means that this will be much less true in the

204   *Guarantee Pay*

future and we would expect successful entrepreneurs to have a training in science, engineering, accountancy or perhaps one of the newer areas such as marketing or corporate planning.

The impersonal forces that create the conditions for growth can range from the possibility of government financial aid to the threat of competition in established markets. The existence of unexploited technical economies of scale will obviously favour growth, as will the possibility of marketing or managerial economies. Finally one should not neglect the internal pressures from research and product improvement departments.

To classify the growth patterns that emerge from a combination of these two sets of forces, economists have talked about three types of integration: horizontal, vertical and lateral (⟡ Patterns of Growth). One should note, however, that although integration tends to imply takeover or amalgamation, expansion may also come purely from within the firm itself.

The parameters used to determine the growth of a company are varied. Turnover is often used, as are the value of assets, number of employees, profits or share of the market. More recently a further criterion has been used, namely net present value to shareholders and this may well be the most all-embracing criterion of growth for a company. ⟡ Present Value; Financial Management; Patterns of Growth. L.T.S.

> P. J. Devine *et al.*, *An Introduction to Industrial Economics* (Allen & Unwin, 3rd ed., 1985); W. Goldsmith and D. Clutterbuck, *The Winning Streak* (Penguin, 1984).

Guarantee Pay There is no general right to withhold wages merely because no work is available, although employers can reserve this right by inserting a suitable clause into their contracts of employment. Even where this has been done, however, legislation guarantees earnings up to a maximum of five workless days in any rolling three-month period. In 1985 the maximum per day was £10.50. The statutory guarantee does not operate where the temporary lack of work is due to industrial action involving any employee of the employer or of an associated employer. To qualify, an employee must have been employed for at least one month, be available for work, and be prepared to accept any temporary alternative work that is suitable if the employer offers it.

Partly because the statutory maximum is fairly modest, it is not uncommon to find that trade unions have negotiated more generous 'guaranteed week' agreements with many employers in manufacturing industry. K.W.

Guarantees A guarantee is a collateral promise by a person to be answerable for the debt or wrongful act of another party. A collateral promise means that there must exist a primary liability by another person and that the guarantor has merely indicated an undertaking to be liable if the main debtor should be unable or unwilling to discharge their obligation. Where a person promises to be responsible for the debt of another party and it is not made clear that this promise is merely a collateral one, in the sense of depending on the existence and validity of the main debt, this would constitute an indemnity and not a guarantee. The difference between them is important, since a guarantee is not legally enforceable against the guarantor unless there exists written evidence of it, while an indemnity could be proved by any form of evidence. However, if the primary agreement is a regulated agreement for the purposes of the Consumer Credit Act (◇ Consumer Credit) then the form and content of the security instrument must comply with regulations made under the Act and copies of all relevant documents must be supplied to sureties. Failure to do so renders the security unenforceable without a court order.

The creditor to whom the guarantee has been given is legally bound to inform the guarantor of any change in the circumstances affecting the transaction or the person of the debtor, so as to enable the guarantor to reconsider his position if there has been a serious change in circumstances. If the guarantor is obliged to honour their guarantee, they, rather than the creditor, are entitled to be handed all securities supplied by the debtor, and generally speaking the guarantor steps into the creditor's shoes, taking over all legal rights that the creditor enjoyed against the debtor whose debt the guarantor has now discharged. W.F.F., amended by J.C.E.M.

R. M. Goode, *Legal Problems of Credit and Security* (Sweet & Maxwell, 1982).

H

Hardware/Liveware/Software These are slang terms used to describe the three parts of a computer installation:

(1) *Hardware*. The electronic and mechanical equipment (central processor and peripheral equipment) that constitutes the physical installation.

(2) *Liveware*. The specialist staff (programmers, systems analysts, data-preparation clerks, etc.) who are responsible for operating the installation.

(3) *Software*. The library and general support services that are available for use on the computer. Library describes the collection of standard programs that are available for use on a computer. Since it is expensive to develop programs, the range of programs, or library, that a manufacturer can offer with a computer can be an important selling point.

It is important to note that the costs of developing adequate software and providing sufficient liveware often exceed the capital cost of the hardware. ⟡ Computer. M.J.C.M.

Hawthorne Investigations A programme of research conducted at the Hawthorne plant (Chicago) of the Western Electric Co. into various aspects of individual and group behaviour. The main research took place during the period 1927–32 and must be the best known and most widely quoted investigation in the history of social research.

In November 1924 the Western Electric Co. commenced a series of short experiments to determine the relationship between different intensities of illumination and productive efficiency. The experiments were inconclusive and prompted the consideration that relevant variables of a psychological nature had been inadequately controlled. Accordingly advice was sought from academics, notably Professor Elton Mayo of the Industrial Research Department, Harvard Graduate School of Business Administration, and in April 1927 six female workers were isolated in a room where output could be measured whilst various conditions relating to rest pauses and hours of work could be varied, and the effects noted by an observer. This stage of the investigation, the Relay Assembly Test

Room, lasted for approximately five years. The experimenters were surprised to discover that, although output increased fairly steadily throughout the first two years of the Test Room, the variables with which they were primarily concerned apparently had little effect on production. Instead, what seemed of particular importance was the change in social climate created by the experimental conditions, including the development of personal friendships amongst the girls and their freedom from supervisory pressures. This change in the social environment was associated with a marked change in the girls' attitudes towards their work.

Subsequent stages in the investigations overlapped with, and arose out of, the first. The apparent importance of employee attitudes to work and to supervision suggested the advisability of discovering more about the attitudes of employees generally. In September 1928, therefore, a programme of formal interviews was started, first in the Inspection Branch and later in other branches, so that by the end of 1930 well over 20,000 employees had been given the opportunity to talk confidentially with a member of the interviewing team. The data from the interviews revealed, *inter alia*, that there might be a connection between worker attitudes and productivity and that worker attitudes were considerably influenced by the other members of the work group to which the worker belonged: in other words, attitudes were less personal than social phenomena.

The final stage in the research was the systematic observation of such a work group. It consisted of fourteen men engaged in wiring, soldering and inspecting a 'bank' of telephone terminals. The Bank Wiring Observation Room was set up in November 1931 and continued until May 1932, when it was abandoned because of the economic depression. The investigators discovered that the operators adhered to a more or less fixed standard of output regardless of the existence of individual and group incentive payments and that they maintained output at that level consistently, this being achieved partly by exaggerating in the records the amount of work actually done and by claiming 'allowances' for work stoppages which, in fact, had not occurred. These breaches of company regulations were condoned by the men's immediate superior. The investigators noted the difficulty of the supervisor's position as he tried to satisfy the demands of his superiors without losing the essential goodwill of his workforce. This stage of the investigation, with its emphasis on workgroup and supervisory behaviour, was particularly important for its theoretical implications.

The value of the Hawthorne studies is inestimable. Industrial psychology was transformed as an academic discipline. Prior to the investigations the individual was viewed and treated as an isolated unit; after the investigations this view was no longer tenable. For the next thirty years research workers utilized the theoretical concepts generated by the investigations and directed their research along lines suggested by the Hawthorne findings. As a seminal work it is virtually without equal. Unfortunately the work contained too much that was new for it to be readily assimilated, even by its authors, and a grossly oversimplified interpretation of its contents helped to give rise to the ◇ Human Relations school; Organization Theory. I.C.MCG.

F. J. Roethlisberger and W. J. Dickson, *Management and the Worker* (Harvard University Press, 1939); H. A. Landsberger, *Hawthorne Revisited* (Cornell University Press, 1958); M. Rose, *Industrial Behaviour* (Penguin, 1979), pp. 103–74.

Health and Safety Commission, The This is responsible to appropriate ministers for the administration of the Health and Safety at Work etc. Act 1974. Members of the Commission are appointed by the Secretary of State for Employment after consultation with the T U C, C B I and local authorities. It reviews health and safety legislation and submits proposals for new or revised regulations. Its operational arm is the ◇ Health and Safety Executive. The Commission also has responsibility for the health and safety of all persons (including divers) engaged in the offshore oil and gas industry. E.L.

Health and Safety Executive, The The Health and Safety Executive (H S E) consists of three persons: the Director General is appointed by the ◇ Health and Safety Commission with the approval of the Secretary of State and consulted over the appointment by the same procedure of a deputy and one other member. The H S E is responsible for enforcing the relevant statutory provisions of the Health and Safety at Work etc. Act 1974 and a number of earlier Acts, and operates through a management board reporting to the Director General.

Six chief inspectors – for agriculture, mines and quarries, factories (◇ Factory Inspector), explosives, industrial air pollution and nuclear installations – are responsible for enforcing the statutes through their staff located in nineteen areas. To this end, the six inspectorates are supported by knowledge and advice from scientific and technical directorates covering Medical Services (◇ Employment and Medical Advisory Services), Hazardous Substances, and Research and Laboratory Services. In addition, each major manufacturing industry in Britain, such as steel or engineering, is served by a National Industry Group of

HSE staff, who are strategically located in an area where the industry is dominant and provide expertise appropriate to it.

In recent years, increasing attention has been paid to installations that might be potentially hazardous if an accident occurred. Under sections of the Nuclear Installations Act 1965, the HSE is the authority that grants nuclear site licences for commercial nuclear installations. The factory inspectorate, the mines-and-quarries inspectorate and local authorities also jointly enforce the provisions of the Offices, Shop and Railway Premises Act 1963. E.L.

Health and Safety Legislation Every year about 1,000 employees are killed, and half a million injured at work through industrial injuries and diseases. The first Act to deal with health and safety at work was passed in 1802, and by 1974 no fewer than thirty-one Acts dealt with the subject. In 1972 a committee, under the chairmanship of Lord Robens, on Safety and Health at Work (Cmnd. 5034), made a number of criticisms of the old system: there was too much apathy at work about safety and health, too many haphazard and intricate rules and regulations, and the administration of the system was too fragmented. The far-reaching provisions of the Health and Safety at Work, etc. Act 1974 are based on the recommendations of the Robens Report.

The 1974 Act seeks to provide a comprehensive and integrated system of law to: (1) secure workers' health, safety and welfare; (2) protect other persons against health or safety risks arising out of or in connection with the activities of persons at work; (3) control the keeping and use of explosives or highly flammable or dangerous substances, and generally prevent the unlawful acquisition, possession and use of such substances; and (4) control the emission into the atmosphere of noxious or offensive substances from certain premises.

The Act establishes a ⟨⟩ Health and Safety Commission and ⟨⟩ Health and Safety Executive to be generally responsible for administering the Act and regulations made thereunder, together with the older legislation (such as the Factories Act 1961), which the 1974 Act and regulations will progressively replace. Sections 2–9 of the Act impose a number of very extensive duties on various persons, contravention of which may lead to criminal proceedings. Thus section 2 requires every employer to ensure, so far as is reasonably practicable, employees' health, safety and welfare. Employers must also prepare and bring to employees' notice a written statement of their general safety policy and arrangements for implementing it. The Act also provides for the making of regulations requiring the appointment of safety representatives by a recognized trade union. Section 3 of the Act makes it the duty of every employer and self-employed person so to conduct their undertakings as to ensure, so far as is reasonably practicable, that they and others not in their employment who may be affected are not thereby exposed to health or safety risks.

Section 6 requires persons who design, manufacture, import or supply articles for use at work to ensure, so far as is reasonably practicable, that the articles are so designed and constructed as to be safe and without health risks when properly used. Section 7 requires all employees while at work: (1) to take reasonable care for the health and safety of themselves and others who may be affected by their acts or omissions at work; and (2) as regards any statutory duty on their employer or other person, to co-operate with them to enable that duty to be complied with.

Section 8 forbids the intentional or reckless interference with, or misuse of, anything provided in the interests of health, safety or welfare; section 9 forbids employees being charged for anything done or provided in pursuance of the legislation.

The Health and Safety Commission is empowered to issue codes of practice to provide guidance with respect to the sections 2–7 duties or regulations made by the Secretary of State for Employment under the Act. The Commission may also hold inquiries into accidents etc.

The 1974 Act is policed by inspectors with wide powers to enter premises, test materials and conduct investigations, etc. Where a person contravenes the legislation, an inspector may serve on them an 'improvement notice' requiring them to remedy the contravention. If an inspector believes that a particular activity occasions risk of serious personal injury, they may issue a 'prohibition notice' specifying remedial measures to be taken and fixing a time after which the activity will be prohibited until such measures are taken. The inspector can put the notice into immediate effect where they consider that the risk is imminent. Appeals against improvement and prohibition notices may be made to ⟡ Industrial Tribunals. ⟡ Employers' Liability. D.V.E.R., amended by K.W.

C. Drake and F. Wright, *Law of Health and Safety at Work: The New Approach* (Sweet & Maxwell, 1983); N. Selwyn, *Law of Health and Safety at Work* (Butterworths, 1982).

Hearing Sound is produced by vibration and transmitted, usually through the air, by means of pressure waves. A 'pure' tone is produced by a sinusoidal pressure wave, the amplitude of which determines the loudness of the sound, and the frequency of which determines the pitch. Differences in timbre or quality of sounds are brought about by differences in complexity of waves, which can be regarded as consisting of a number of individual sinusoidal components.

The speed of sound in air is approximately 750 mph; in liquids and solids it is considerably increased.

In the human ear the tympanic membrane vibrates in response to pressure waves. The vibration is transmitted via the three bony ossicles of the middle ear into the cochlea, the spiral tube of the inner ear, wherein the mechanical vibrations are converted into hydraulic form and ultimately transduced into nerve impulses.

The frequency range of human audition extends from about 20 Hz to 20 kHz, there being considerable differences between individuals. Subjective loudness of sounds depends upon frequency as well as amplitude, the maximum sensitivity occurring between 4 and 5 kHz. In this frequency range perception of sound occurs at a sound pressure of about 0·0002 dynes/sq. cm. Sound intensity levels are usually measured in decibels above this basal value (◊◊ Threshold). The overall intensity level of normal speech, for example, is about 66 decibels (◊◊ Speech).

Hearing is generally dichotic, that is, each ear gets a slightly different signal. Localization in the horizontal plane is brought about by the interpretation of differences in phase and intensity of signals arriving at each ear. It is necessary, however, for the listener to move his head in order to identify the elevation of the source.

Loss of hearing ability occurs as part of the normal ageing process and takes the form of a steady decline from the age of twenty onwards. High-frequency sounds are subject to greater loss with age than low-frequency ones (◊◊ Ageing). E.E.

D. R. Davies and D. M. Jones, 'Hearing and Noise' in W. T. Singleton (ed.), *The Body at Work* (CUP, 1982).

Heat Various automatic physiological mechanisms, notably rate of blood flow and sweat rate, contribute to the maintenance of body temperature at a constant value near to 37° C. Only small increases (about 4° C) can be survived, although cooling to temperatures below 20° C is sometimes possible. In order to achieve thermal equilibrium, the following equation involving metabolism (M), evaporation (E), conduction and convection (C) and radiation (R) must be satisfied:

$$M - E \pm C \pm R = 0$$

Sensations of thermal comfort are affected by air temperature, humidity, rate of air movement and amount of radiant heat. Numerous attempts have been made to derive a single index to combine these atmospheric variables. The corrected effective temperature is probably the most useful of these indices and is derived from radiant temperature, wet-bulb temperature and rate of air flow. It is defined as the numerical value of the temperature of still saturated air that would induce an identical sensation. Comfort zones have been established empirically.

Decrements in both physical and mental work output result from high temperatures. Most work tasks become almost impossible to perform at corrected effective temperatures in excess of about 34° C. Temperature differences of only about 5° C at constant relative humidity separate 'impossible' from 'relatively easy' performance. A similar difference in judgements results from changes in relative humidity of about 15 per cent at constant temperature.

Several studies have demonstrated decrements in physical work performance at low temperatures. There is no evidence of corresponding mental work deterioration. E.E.

D. McK. Kerslake, 'Effects of Climate' in W. T. Singleton (ed.), *The Body at Work* (CUP, 1982).

Heuristic Programming Operational research scientists sometimes use ◊ Simulation to tackle problems on which a rigorous mathematical analysis is not feasible. Simulation is a particularly useful approach to representing the behaviour in time of complex systems incorporating a large degree of uncertainty. Other problems may be complex because there are a large number of factors and constraints involved, which may be combined in an astronomical number of ways to produce feasible solutions. These problems are often not amenable to rigorous analysis or are particularly suited to simulation; heuristic programming provides an alternative non-rigorous approach, which has proved most useful. Such problems are typically managerial. Managers need to be able to distinguish the relatively few good approaches to a problem from the many feasible alternatives available. They may do this by developing 'rules of thumb' by which they try to account either consciously or subconsciously (that is, by 'hunch') for all the factors or constraints involved. Owing to the limitations on the human brain's ability consciously to store and manipulate information and/or managers' lack of time, they may not be able to evaluate all promising alternatives, so 'solutions' better than those adopted may escape their attention. Typically, the person responsible for production scheduling in a large jobbing shop faces this situation.

A computer, on the other hand, can store and manipulate large amounts of information quickly and, if it can be programmed to use similar 'rules of thumb' to the manager, it is likely to produce better solutions. The term 'heuristic' means a procedure or 'rule of thumb' used to solve a particular problem and so heuristic programs have been written for computers to solve the problem by this method.

Heuristic programming is proving very useful and has been used with success on problems of assembly-line balancing and job-shop scheduling, plant layout, warehouse location, stock control, resource allocation to large projects and portfolio selection. M.J.C.M.

R. S. Stainton and D. B. Papolias, 'Heuristics – The Relationed Approach', *European Journal of Operational Research*, vol. 17, no. 1 (1984).

Hire Purchase Law ◊ Consumer Credit

Histogram ◊ Statistics

Historic Cost ◊ Accountancy Conventions; Cost (in Accounting Systems); Changing Price Levels, Accounting for; Profit (in Accounting)

Homeostasis The significance of a number of physiological control mechanisms in maintaining constancy of the internal bodily variables was first recognized by W. B. Cannon, who coined the term homeostasis to designate these states of equilibrium. In respect of many bodily variables it is necessary to control values within quite narrow tolerances in order to avoid severe damage or death. Examples of variables that are maintained by automatic physiological control systems include body temperature, blood-sugar level and blood pH. The concept of homeostasis may be enlarged beyond such autonomic activities and may include gross somatic activity including, for example, the hungry animal's search for food.

Numerous symptoms of disease involve the breakdown of the usual homeostatic mechanisms, so that the individual is unable to make the usual effective adjustments to cope with environmental stresses. The ageing process is characterized by a slow decline in the efficiency of homeostatic mechanisms. ◊◊ Ageing; Environment. E.E.

Horizontal Integration ◊ Patterns of Growth

House Union ◊ Company Union

Human Engineering ◊ Ergonomics; Psychology

Human Factors In the USA the term human factors (or sometimes human engineering) is used in place of the European 'ergonomics'.

Broadly, the discipline covers the same area although there have been differences in emphasis between the activities on opposite sides of the Atlantic. ⟡ Ergonomics. E.E.

Human Relations An approach to organization theory that places heavy emphasis on the importance of morale and informal social relationships as determinants of organizational effectiveness.

The human-relations approach drew much of its inspiration from the ⟡ Hawthorne Investigations and subsequent research work and had an immediate appeal for those welfare workers and others who deplored the dehumanization of the workplace implicit in the scientific management approach, or who were disturbed by the phenomena of industrial conflict. That both approaches had something valid to offer was immediately apparent to the classical theorists who found little difficulty in synthesizing them. The proponents of the two approaches, however, regarded the others with hostility, each claiming that the other ignored the most important variables. Whilst much in the human-relations approach remains valid, several of its basic assumptions have been challenged. In particular, its critics claim that there was a tendency to make generalizations about social relationships *in vacuo*, without regard to their cultural, economic and technological environments; that the beneficial effects of sympathetic, supportive supervision were not universal but depended on a complex of factors; that harmony in relationships and job satisfaction were too readily equated with productive efficiency; and that explanations for the various phenomena of conflict were too facile. The criticisms were well founded, and the number of empirical studies of organizational behaviour has increased the body of knowledge available, so that the human-relations school, preoccupied with too narrow a range of variables, has been superseded by the social-systems approach. ⟡ Hawthorne Investigations; Morale; Organization Theory. I.C.MCG.

S. Parker *et al.*, *The Sociology of Industry*, ch. 8 (Allen & Unwin, 3rd ed., 1977).

Human-resource Accounting With the exception of accounting for expenditure on such items as recruitment advertising, training, personnel management etc., accountancy has not in general attempted to value employees as a resource. It has been suggested that the failure to value the human resource in the balance sheet deprives shareholders and other interested parties of potentially important economic information. R. Likert has further suggested that the failure to account for human resources internally, results in management taking short-run decisions at the expense of the long-run economic benefit.[1] Indeed, Likert suggests that accounting systems encourage the misuse of human resources. Human-resource accounting has been defined as 'the process of identifying, measuring and communicating information about human resources to decision-makers'.[2] It is considered to incorporate the measurement and treatment of costs incurred in recruiting, training and using employees, as well as the measurement of economic value. The aim of human-resource accounting is primarily economic. The intention is to provide better information for decision-makers, which will result in better economic decisions. Whilst the 'art' of human-resource accounting is in its infancy, it has the potential to develop as an area of major importance. c.j.j.

E. Flamholtz, *Human Resource Accounting* (Dickenson, 1973).

Hypothesis Testing Many investigations are performed by statisticians to determine whether a certain belief is true or false. A frequently used procedure is to set up the null hypothesis that the belief is false and then perform experiments to see if the observed results agree with the proposed hypothesis. Details of the types of experiment or tests that may be performed are described elsewhere (⟨⟩ Statistical Tests).

For example, a statistician may suspect that a penny is biased towards heads and may wish to determine whether this belief is true. The null hypothesis is that the coin is unbiased, that is, that there is an equal chance (or 50 per cent probability) of obtaining a head or tail each time it is tossed. The statistician then performs the 'experiment' of tossing the coin ten times and recording the number of heads occurring. Using the laws of probability, it is possible to calculate the chances of obtaining 0, 1, 2, etc., heads in the experiment. If the coin is unbiased, these chances are given below:

Number of heads	0	1	2	3	4	5	6	7	8	9	10
Probability (per cent)	0·10	0·98	4·39	11·72	20·51	23·73	20·51	11·72	4·39	0·98	0·10

The observed number of heads can be compared with these figures to test the null hypothesis.

Suppose seven heads are observed. The chance of seven or more heads occurring with an unbiased coin is 17·2 per cent. This is reasonably high,

1. R. Likert, *The Human Organization, its Management and Value* (McGraw-Hill, 1967).
2. American Accounting Association, *Report of the Committee on Human Resource Accounting* (Accounting Review Supplement to vol. 48, 1973).

so the evidence cannot be said to suggest that the coin is biased. Therefore the results are 'not significant' and the null hypothesis is not rejected. Suppose eight heads are observed. The chance of eight or more occurring with an unbiased coin is 5·5 per cent. This result is less likely to occur by chance and the results are therefore 'probably significant'; unless very convincing evidence is required, the null hypothesis will be rejected. Similarly the chances of nine or ten heads occurring with an unbiased coin are 1·1 per cent and 0·1 per cent, or 1 in 100 or 1 in 1,000, respectively. Clearly these results are very unlikely to occur by chance and they are said to be significant and highly significant respectively. If either of these results occurs the null hypothesis will be rejected.

The level of truth required for accepting or rejecting a hypothesis is sometimes known as the significance or confidence level. A statistician who needs to be reasonably convinced will set the significance level at 5 per cent: if the hypothesis is true, there is less than a 1 in 20 chance of the observed results occurring and the hypothesis will therefore be rejected. If more convincing evidence is required, the significance level will be set at 1 per cent, such that if the hypothesis is true, there is less than a 1 in 100 chance of the observed results occurring and the hypothesis will therefore be rejected. A level of 0·1 per cent represents very convincing evidence: if the hypothesis is true, there is less than a 1 in 1,000 chance of the observed results occurring.

When accepting or rejecting a hypothesis, statisticians usually state the significance level used. Thus in the coin-tossing example, if the 5 per cent significance level were being used and nine heads were observed, they would state that the null hypothesis that the coin is unbiased is rejected at the 5 per cent level. Conversely, if the 1 per cent significance level were adopted, they would state that the null hypothesis that the coin is unbiased cannot be rejected at the 1 per cent level.

In performing tests of significance statisticians are comparing two sets of data, say the means in a 't' test, to see if they are different. Because of the nature of variability, there is a small probability that although the test indicates a significant difference, the two sets of data do come from populations with the same mean. This is known as a Type I Error.

Conversely, the test may indicate no significant difference although there is a difference in the population means. This is known as a Type II Error. M.J.C.M.

Stephen P. Shao, *Statistics for Business and Economics* (Merrill, 1976).

I

Ideology A system of beliefs that provides for the members of a group a moral justification for their individual and collective behaviour and that offers satisfying, although often grossly oversimplified, explanations of various social phenomena. All social groups develop ideologies, although it is seldom that any ideology is capable of precise definition or that all members of the group subscribe equally to all elements of it. An ideology will reflect the ⟨⟩ Values of the group members and serves to unite the group. The adherents of a given ideology have an emotional commitment to it and will tend to select supportive facts and to ignore or deny contradictory facts. The racist, for example, whose ideology stresses the inherent superiority of one racial group over another, will be strongly inclined to repudiate genetic evidence to the contrary. Where an ideology is patently demonstrated to be inadequate, its adherents may have recourse to the identification of scapegoats whose malevolent activities may then be claimed to have prevented the manifestation of phenomena consistent with the ideology: the ideology can thus be vindicated. For example, a manager whose ideology embraces the concept of the essential unity of interests of management and labour, may attribute recurrent industrial disputes to the activities of agitators.
I.C.MCG.

R. Bendix, *Work and Authority in Industry* (University of California Press, 1974); H. Beynon, *Working for Ford* (Penguin, 2nd ed., 1983).

Illumination Good lighting serves to promote safety, working efficiency and comfort. Recommendations for appropriate levels of illumination have been prepared from studies of performance and user preferences. Some typical recommended levels of illumination are indicated below.

Location	Lumens/m^2
Halls, lifts, stairways	150
Offices and laboratories	500
Hand-tailoring workshop	1,000
Inspection bench for minute objects	3,000

In addition to levels applying to task areas, recommendations are available for surrounding areas and general backgrounds. In general, it is desirable that areas surrounding objects being viewed should not vary substantially in luminance from that of the viewed object. The difference in luminance levels is measured by the brightness contrast (⟡ Brightness).

Lighting installations should take account of the avoidance of glare, the control of flicker effects and the proper rendering of colour (⟡ Colour; Glare).

If daylight is to be used, careful attention should be paid to the fenestration of buildings to achieve satisfactory levels of illumination and to avoid poor distribution of light. If large windows are used, excessive penetration of sunlight may be troublesome. It is important to ensure that the glazing is regularly cleaned, and the windows are kept clear of large obstructions.

Artificial light fittings vary in terms of their characteristics and their initial and maintenance costs. Tungsten filament lamps have a life expectancy of about 1,000 hours and an average light output of about 15 lumens/watt. Fluorescent tubes involve increased capital cost but lower maintenance charges, since their life expectancy is about five times greater and their output twice as efficient. Regular cleaning of light fittings is of the utmost importance.

When a combination of artificial lighting and daylight is to be employed, it is usually necessary for the artificially lit sections of an area to have about 1,000 lumens/m² to avoid apparent gloominess on bright days. It is important too that the bluer light fittings are used to produce satisfactory colour blending. E.E.

Chartered Institution of Building Services (formerly Illuminating Engineering Society), *IES Code for Interior Lighting* (CIBS, 1977).

Imports ⟡ Balance of Payments

Incentives ⟡ Motivation

Income ⟡ Profit, in Accounting

Incomes Policy ⟡ Prices and Incomes Policy

Index Number of Industrial Production ⟡ Index Numbers

Index Number of Retail Prices ⟡ Index Numbers

Index Numbers A convenient way of comparing the level of a set of data at a particular time with its level at some base period. It is useful to know, for example, that the level of retail prices in a certain period is 10 per cent greater than it was in some base period. Similar useful statements can be made about the level of production and the level of import and export prices, to take the more obvious examples.

Suppose we want to calculate an index number of retail prices. The easiest way is to regard such an index number as a weighted average of price relatives. This follows because to measure the level of prices requires that we link together the changes in prices of a diverse selection of goods whose importance in consumers' budgets varies considerably. The weights used reflect the importance in consumers' budgets of the product concerned.

The following example illustrates the algebraic construction of a simple price index number involving only two products. Because the weights used refer to the base period it is called a Laspeyres price index number.

Let p_1^1, p_1^2 be the price of products 1 and 2 in period 1

p_2^1, p_2^2 be the price of products 1 and 2 in period 2

q_1^1, q_1^2 be the quantity produced of products 1 and 2 in period 1

q_2^1, q_2^2 be the quantity purchased of products 1 and 2 in period 2

Σ indicates summation over all products

$I_{2,1}$ is the Laspeyres index number for period 2 compared to period 1

Then

$$I_{2,1}^{LA} = \frac{p_1^1 q_1^1 \left(\frac{p_2^1}{p_1^1}\right) + p_1^2 q_1^2 \left(\frac{p_2^2}{p_1^2}\right)}{p_1^1 q_1^1 + p_1^2 q_1^2} \times 100$$

$$= \frac{\Sigma p_2 q_1}{\Sigma p_1 q_1} \times 100$$

Using the same symbols we can form another index number, known as a Paasche price index number. In this case the weights used refer to the current time-period.

$$I_{2,1}^{PA} = \frac{p_2^1 q_2^1 + p_2^2 q_2^2}{p_2^1 q_2^1 \left(\frac{p_1^1}{p_2^1}\right) + p_2^2 q_2^2 \left(\frac{p_1^2}{p_2^2}\right)} \times 100$$

$$= \frac{\Sigma p_2 q_2}{\Sigma p_1 q_2} \times 100$$

In theory, in comparing any two periods one has the choice of using either form. Since the answers for the same set of data will usually differ, Fisher's ideal index number is sometimes used. This is obtained by taking the geometric mean of the two index numbers above.

$$FI_{2,1} = \sqrt{\frac{LA}{I_{2,1}} \times \frac{PA}{I_{2,1}}}$$

However, in practice base-period weighting is nearly always chosen for regularly published indices because the weights of the current period are usually unavailable and the Laspeyres index is easier to calculate.

If a production index had been required rather than a price index, the same procedure would be followed but in the above formulas the terms in brackets would be replaced by quantities. Also the weights used would represent the importance of the products in national output.

Perhaps the two most frequently quoted index numbers are those measuring the changes in retail prices and industrial production.

The present index of retail prices is best described as a modified Laspeyres index and it can be thought of as measuring the change in cost from month to month of a very large and representative 'basket' of goods. The composition of this basket – that is, the relative importance, or 'weight', attached to the various goods and services it contains – is revised each year using the latest results from the Family Expenditure Survey. The weights for the current index were obtained using 1984 data. The index is published each month in the *Employment Gazette*, details being given for the 'All items' index and also for eleven major groups. For example, at 14 May 1985, the 'All items' index stood at 375·6 compared with January 1974 = 100. In addition, indices are produced for pensioner households.

The index number of output of the production industries is again of the Laspeyres form and is intended to provide a general measure of monthly changes in their volume of output. To combine the 329 separate indicators, each of which describes the activity of a small sector of industry, weights are used that are proportional to the value added in 1980, derived from the 1980 Annual Census of Production. The index numbers in effect compare the average weekly rates of production in the different months with average production in 1980. In addition, seasonally adjusted figures are produced that take account of regular holiday periods in different industries and other normal seasonal influences. The index is produced each month in *British Business*, details being given for Total Production Industries (energy plus manufacturing) and eight major groups. For example, the April 1985 index for Total Production Industries was provisionally estimated at 107·4 (seasonally adjusted) compared to 1980 = 100. In addition an index number is produced for construction. L.T.S.

'The unstatistical reader's guide to the Retail Price Index', *Employment Gazette* (HMSO, October 1975); 'The rebased estimates of the index of the output of the production industries', *Economic Trends* (HMSO, Oct 1983); J. E. Freund and F. J. Williams, *Elementary Business Statistics* (Prentice-Hall, 4th ed., 1982).

Induction The introduction of new members to the objectives, policies and practices of an enterprise and to their place and tasks as workers in it. The aim of induction is to make clear the relationship that should exist between a person and their work, i.e. their job, workmates and firm. Induction is a matter of telling and showing: explaining about the works rules, the products, the organization; showing the welfare facilities, the processes, the workplace, the safety devices. In many firms induction includes a tour of the works, films about the products and talks by senior managers. It may last for two or three days for school-leavers, or half a day or a day for adult employees. A second induction course is sometimes held after six months, when new employees have settled in and are ready for further knowledge and information. Induction on the job or in the workplace may include a period in a training department but will be largely the responsibility of the foreman under whom the new employee is to work. It starts at the engagement interview and ends when the employee has settled down to his or her job and has achieved a normal output. I.S.

'Induction', *Industrial Society* (1973).

Industrial Arbitration Board ◊ Arbitration, Industrial

Industrial Democracy A term used to describe a number of theories about the government of industry and a number of schemes for reorganizing industrial management. Schemes for industrial democracy involve some degree of exercise of power by workers or their representatives over decisions within their places of employment, coupled with a modification in the locus and distribution of authority within the workplace.

There are very many different types of industrial democracy. *Workers' self-management* (as in Yugoslavia) occurs in decentralized market socialist countries and is usually based on workers' councils (made up of representatives of the workforce). *Producer co-operatives* involve workers' ownership and participation in enterprise management; Mondragon (in the Basque province of Spain) is a key example.

Co-determination involves the right of workers' representatives to joint decision-making on enterprise boards, with West Germany being a proto-typical case. *Works councils* are boards composed of workers' representatives, which meet with management on a regular basis (again West Germany is a principal example). Trade union action is also a form of industrial democracy that operates either through *collective bargaining* (as in the USA or in Britain, where it is the most significant form of employee participation in managerial decision-making) or through integrative channels (as in the USSR). Finally there are a number of shop-floor programmes involving the workforce as a whole, such as the autonomous working groups or quality of working-life programmes of Scandinavia or the USA.

Early approaches to industrial democracy advocated workers' control of industry and were developed from the controversy between Marx and Bakunin in the second half of the nineteenth century about the means to socialism. There followed a syndicalist movement in French trade unions, the rise of the Industrial Workers of the World in opposition to the American Federation of Labour and the First World War shop stewards' movement in Britain. These movements were casualties of postwar depression.

A link between the early revolutionaries, who wished to replace existing industrial management, and later reformist theorists was provided in Britain by the Guild Socialists, who kept workers' control of industry as their objective but recognized industry's need for technical skills and managerial ability. The guilds that would control industry were to include workers both by hand and by brain. The Guild Socialists also recognized the roles of the consumer and of the state and their suggestion for gradually encroaching workers' control was parallel to that of the Fabians' gradual extension of public ownership.

Reformists after the First World War took the view that under capitalism the role of the employer should be taken into account. The Whitley Committee, appointed in 1916 to consider the future shape of industrial relations, suggested not only model national ⟨⟩ Joint Industrial Councils to allow representatives of employers and employees in an industry to settle wages and basic conditions of work, but also Works Committees and District Councils. Whitley (Joint Industrial) Councils were set up in a number of industries, but interwar depression emasculated the movement.

During the Second World War there developed a movement intended to harness the energies and ideas of employees to increase output through Joint Production Consultative and Advisory Committees; that is, workplace committees jointly staffed by representatives of management and of workers. These were set up to deal with any matters that affected production, other than wages and basic conditions of work. ⟡ Joint Consultation systems were set up in the newly nationalized industries and, furthermore, trade union officials were appointed to the boards of these industries. Both here and in the private sector of the economy, however, joint consultation has often failed. Prominent among the many reasons has been the refusal of workers' representatives, especially ⟡ Shop Stewards, to interest themselves in joint committees where no ⟡ Collective Bargaining could take place. Significantly, successful ⟡ Productivity Bargaining and other plant-level negotiations often ensure that joint consultation and collective bargaining become fused into one activity.

Theories of industrial democracy vary appreciably but the union debates centre on the diverse approaches of the *evolutionary* school, which sees a continuous process of advance towards greater participation, and the *cyclical* school, which envisages a disjunctive pattern of advance and retrenchment.

The recent history of industrial democracy is dominated by the demise of the proposals of the Bullock Report and the growth in ⟡ Joint Consultation; Disclosure of Information; Profit Sharing; Producer Co-operatives.

The task of the Committee of Inquiry on Industrial Democracy chaired by Lord Bullock was to consider how the establishment of worker directors on company boards could best be achieved and the effects of such representation on the efficient management of companies and on company law. The 'need for a radical extension of industrial democracy in the control of companies by means of representation on boards of directors' and 'the essential role of trade union organizations in this process' were to be taken as given. Needless to say these terms of reference were criticized as being too narrow for a full investigation of the possibilities for the development in Britain of industrial democracy or employee participation in managerial decision-making.

In the event the committee produced two reports. The first (the Majority Report) was signed by three trade unionists, three academics and a solicitor, Mr N. S. Wilson. To this Majority Report Mr Wilson added a significant 'Note of Dissent'. The second (the Minority Report) was signed by three industrialists.

The Majority Report held that employee representation in parity with shareholder representatives at board level was self-evidently necessary and desirable – a recognition that industry is a joint venture between capital and labour. They saw no contradiction between unitary board-level representation and collective bargaining as both had the same objective: employee participation in decision-making.

In his Note of Dissent Mr Wilson asserted that the majority had erroneously held that the number of employee representatives should necessarily equal the number of shareholder representatives. Shareholders should be able to appoint a majority of board members, a course of action that would have the advantage of a reduced risk of polarization of attitudes, less alteration to the size and composition of boards, no need for co-opted directors, and that would give rise to less concern on the part of unrepresented employees at home and abroad. Mr Wilson also noted that there are limits to the rate at which legislation could successfully achieve social engineering in advance of public opinion.

The Minority Report proposed the establishment of Supervisory Boards, to include large holding companies but excluding financial institutions and UK subsidiaries of foreign-based companies. Further, belief in the West German insistence on effective works councils as one of the key factors in the success of German participation led the minority to recommend the setting up of participation substructures below board level, tailor-made in each case to suit the plant and company concerned. Such arrangements could lead to the creation of a Company Council. Where such a council operated satisfactorily for three years, this could result in the establishment of a Supervisory Board. ⟡ Participation. N.H.C., amended by M.J.F.P.

M. J. F. Poole, 'Theories of Industrial Democracy', *Sociological Review*, vol. 30 (1982) pp. 181–207; M. J. F. Poole, *Workers' Participation in Industry* (Routledge & Kegan Paul, 1978); P. Brannen, *Authority and Participation in Industry* (Batsford, 1983); *Report of the Committee of Inquiry on Industrial Democracy*, Cmnd. 6706 (HMSO, 1977).

Industrial Disease A disease that is caused by exposure to harmful or poisonous substances or rays at work. The diseases range from toxic conditions such as poisoning by lead or mercury to fibrosis of the lungs caused by silica or asbestos, skin ailments such as dermatitis and ulceration caused by chromic acid, pitch or tar. The more serious diseases have to be notified to the factory inspectorate under the ⟡ Health and Safety Legislation, and numerous regulations require employers to take certain steps to reduce the risks, and employees to use protective devices, wear protective clothing and submit to medical examination. Under the Health and Safety at Work etc. Act 1974, employees are required to take reasonable care to safeguard the health of themselves and of other persons who may be affected by their acts or omissions at work. ⟡ Industrial Injuries. E.L.

J. M. Harrington and F. S. Gill, *Occupational Health Pocket Consultant*

(Blackwell, 1983); Department of Health and Social Security, *Notes on the Diagnosis of Occupational Diseases* (HMSO, 1979).

Industrial Dispute Under the ⟨⟩ Industrial Relations Act 1971, repealed 1974, an industrial dispute was defined as a dispute between one or more employers or organizations of employers and one or more workers or organizations of workers, where the dispute relates wholly or mainly to any one or more of the following; (1) terms and conditions of employment or the physical conditions in which any workers are required to work; (2) engagement or non-engagement, or termination or suspension of employment, of one or more workers; (3) allocation of work as between workers or groups of workers; (4) a procedural agreement, or any matter to which a ⟨⟩ Procedural Agreement can relate.

The Industrial Relations Act repealed the Trades Disputes Act, 1906, which defined a 'trade dispute' as any dispute between employers and workmen, or between workmen and workmen, that is connected with the employment or non-employment, or the terms of the employment, or the conditions of labour of any person. The Industrial Relations Act was thus more restrictive of definition, excluding disputes between 'workmen and workmen' except where an employer was a party concerned.

The ⟨⟩ Trade Union and Labour Relations Act 1974 restored the pre-1971 protection against legal action that was given to people involved in strikes and reverted to the original term 'trade dispute'. ⟨⟩ Trade Dispute. N.H.C.

Industrial Engineering The American Institute of Industrial Engineers defines industrial engineering as being 'concerned with the design, improvement and installation of integrated systems of men, materials and equipment. It draws upon specialized knowledge and skill in the mathematical, physical and social sciences together with the principles and methods of engineering analysis and design, to specify, predict and evaluate the results to be obtained from such systems.'

A common misapprehension in the UK, where the term industrial engineering is not in general use, is that it is a function equivalent to work study. The emphasis, however, is on the total production system and there is a continuing trend to draw upon and use all relevant branches of science, e.g. operational research, industrial psychology, etc.

The emphasis on the production system suggests the equivalence of industrial engineering to what is normally called production management in the UK. Notice, however, that like the components of production management, e.g. work study, inventory control, facilities layout, etc., industrial engineering is not restricted to the manufacturing industries, and is widely practised in government, public services, etc. R.W.

H. B. Maynard (ed.), *Handbook of Industrial Engineering* (McGraw-Hill, 3rd ed., 1971).

Industrial Espionage Espionage undertaken with the object of obtaining information that will be of economic or political advantage. Its major rewards will tend to be in terms of personal and/or corporate profit and political subversion. There is little indication of the extent of industrial espionage in Britain, and it is not a criminal offence to steal trade secrets. In *McPherson* v. *Downey*, 1965, the defendant received a three-month prison sentence for stealing £3 worth of paper from his employers on which company secrets were recorded. Had he merely made a photocopy, presumably no theft would have been involved and no sentence at all incurred. The use of espionage for political subversion, for example to foster unofficial strikes when grievances are detected, is again unmeasured but thought to be present. Counter-espionage is most effectively achieved by maintaining the secret that there is a secret, by concentrating the risk, and by ensuring that a maximum of complicity is required to break security. It has become increasingly apparent during the last decade that not only have individuals and organizations used methods of industrial espionage but entire country trading strategies have been based on such a practice. The electronics industry in the USA has been particularly prone to this and countless examples involving countries from South-east Asia have been reported. G.S.C.W.

P. Hamilton, *Espionage and Subversion in an Industrial Society* (Hutchinson, 1967).

Industrial Injuries Employees who are injured in the course of their employment may claim damages from their employer if they can prove negligence or breach of statutory duty (⟡ Employers' Liability).

In addition, and regardless of whether they can prove legal liability, injured employees who lose time off work will be entitled to *statutory sick pay*. This is payable by their employer at one of three flat rates, depending on earnings, for up to eight weeks' absence in any tax year. No payment is due for the first three days of incapacity. Where any incapacity for work lasts for more than eight weeks (so exhausting entitlement to statutory sick pay) the individual is then entitled to state *sickness benefit*, which is payable weekly for up to a further twenty weeks. After a total of twenty-eight weeks' incapacity, *invalidity benefit* takes over. Like sickness benefit, it is paid by the DHSS, though at a higher rate. It is payable for so long as the invalidity lasts, up to retirement if necessary.

Where an injury has some lasting effect, an employee becomes eligible after ninety days' disability (disregarding Sundays) for *disablement benefit*. This is not a fixed sum but depends upon the extent of the 'loss of mental or physical faculty' sustained. The degree of injury is expressed as a percentage as given in a table or scale of assessments. Where disablement is assessed at less than 20 per cent a lump sum is paid and a weekly pension awarded for more serious disablement. The pension can be supplemented in certain circumstances by, for example, a special hardship allowance.

In order to maintain a claim for any of the state benefits individuals must be employed earners under the Social Security Act 1975, although they need have no minimum number of national insurance contributions provided their injuries were caused by an 'accident arising out of and in the course of employment'. Disability caused by certain industrial diseases is also covered by the national insurance scheme so long as detailed regulations have prescribed the disease as creating a special occupational hazard in one or more specific industrial operations. ⟨⟩ Sick Pay. K.W.

Industrial Law In Britain the term industrial law is used for that branch of law which deals with ⟨⟩ Contracts of Employment, the special provisions concerning particular aspects of employment (e.g. ⟨⟩ Health and Safety Legislation) and the law dealing with collective labour relations, such as ⟨⟩ Trade Union Law and ⟨⟩ Collective Bargaining. In some other countries and increasingly in Britain this branch of the law is referred to as labour law.

British industrial law has come into existence by accident rather than by design. Part of it is represented by the common-law rules dealing with the master–servant relationship as modified over the centuries by statute as and when Parliament found it necessary to deal with particular abuses. Trade unions in Britain have by and large preferred to deal with their problems by direct negotiation with employers rather than by invoking legal sanctions, since they have had little confidence in the impartiality of the law when faced with industrial problems. Academically, the subject has been somewhat neglected in the past, although most law degrees offer it nowdays, at least as an optional subject. There is an Industrial Law Society.

At one time British writers on industrial law could be divided into those who felt the scope of the subject should not be enlarged and those who saw the law as potentially a key regulator of the employment

228 *Industrial Marketing*

relationship and of industrial relations generally. The volume of legislation over the last twenty years and the case law it has spawned make it increasingly difficult to continue to characterize the role of the law as largely 'abstentionist'. W.F.F., amended by K.W.

Sir Otto Kahn-Freund, *Labour and the Law* (Stevens & Sons, 3rd ed. by P. Davies and M. Freedland, 1983); R. Rideout, *Principles of Labour Law* (Sweet & Maxwell, 4th ed., 1983).

Industrial Marketing ⬦ Marketing

Industrial Relations Also known as labour relations or employee relations. These concern the complex of relationships between employees, managements and government, together with their respective organizations, trade unions, employers' associations and governmental agencies.

Strictly the term 'industrial relations' is a misnomer. Not all the relationships associated with the organization of industry are relevant; for example the term does not include relationships between firms as to their price policy or market share, or between firms and their customers. At the same time the expression 'industrial' is conceived in the broadest possible terms. It includes all environments where paid work is carried out, for example shops, banks, hospitals, etc., as well as manufacturing industry. The study of industrial relations is the study of job regulation.

The term is used in two different senses: the all-inclusive sense may be defined as all the relationships between management and employees in the community and thus covers relations between individuals at work, such as the individual employer and employee, relationships within and between work groups, sometimes known as ⬦ Human Relations, and also interaction between organized groups such as trade unions and employers' associations. The term covers formal relations, as embodied in collective agreements and written works rules, and informal relations, as characterized by informal agreements on the allocation of overtime, discipline and the distribution of work loads and by the ⬦ Norms imposed by work groups on their own performance.

In the restricted sense industrial relations denotes only collective relations between trade unions, or sections of them, and employers.

In either event, relationships are constrained by the interests of, and rules set up by, the agencies of government, for example the ⬦ Department of Employment.

Industrial-relations problems may arise at the level of the plant or workplace, as in the case of disputes over piece-rates or discipline; at the level of the firm, as in the case of trade union recognition; at the level of the industry, as in the case of 'national' wage rates in dispute between unions and an employer (or employers' association); and at the level of the economy, as where a government attempts to implement some form of incomes policy.

Industrial-relations discussion may centre on human efficiency at the workplace; on employee–management co-operation, as (supposedly) in ✍ Joint Consultation; or on employee–management ✍ Conflict, as in ✍ Collective Bargaining. Studies may concentrate on the industrial-relations system of the workplace, the plant, the firm, the industry, or the economy; or on institutions operating at one or more of these levels, for example the trade union or the employers' association.

Initially much investigation in the industrial-relations field took the form of historical and descriptive studies of institutions, particularly of trade unions, their battles, leadership and growth. Many of these studies were made by practitioners or historians. They were soon followed by economists, whose approach was initially descriptive of institutions but latterly analytical, examining the economic environment in which industrial relations operate and also labour markets, collective bargaining, wage levels (✍ Wage), productivity (✍ Productivity Bargaining), and incomes policies (✍ Prices and Incomes Policy). Lawyers have examined the legal environment and surveyed ✍ Industrial Law, ✍ Trade Union Law and strikes (✍ Strike and the Law). The contribution of political science has lain in studies of the political climate in which industrial relations operate, with detailed work on trade union organization and government. ✍ Trade Union – Government and Administration. Behavioural scientists and statisticians have come most recently to study the industrial-relations scene. Industrial sociology has contributed work on ideological differences between management and employees (✍ Ideology), on complementary and competitive goals in the work situation and on conflict and its resolution; psychologists have discussed motivation, incentives (✍ Motivation; Wage Systems) and adaptation to work; group formation, attitudes, functions, formal and informal group structures and behaviour have been investigated by social psychologists (✍ Formal Organization; Group). Statisticians have, *inter alia*, analysed ✍ Strikes and ✍ Wage Drift.

Only recently have there been attempts to offer an integrated view of the whole complex of activity in this field, to produce theories of industrial relations, set up industrial-relations models and explain industrial relations in a company, an industry, or a country in terms of systems. John T. Dunlop has made such an attempt, explaining industrial relations as a system involving three groups of actors: workers and their organizations, managers and their organizations, and governmental agencies concerned with the work environment. They create and operate a system of rules of many kinds within an environment comprised of three interrelated contexts: technology, market or budgetary constraints, and the power relations and statuses of all the actors, bound together by understandings shared by the actors.

It remains true, however, that there is as yet no generally accepted overall theory of industrial relations. Indeed, the systems approach has been traditionally opposed by pluralists of the so-called Oxford school, who have placed far more emphasis on the consequences for industrial relations of the structure of collective bargaining than on wider environmental influences. Radical scholars, too, have argued that industrial relations is concerned with processes of control over work relations rather than with job regulation. Modern attempts at synthesis have endeavoured to combine the strengths of each position and to include environmental and institutional variables and the distribution of power in broad, analytical frameworks.

Institutional studies, particularly of trade unions, still tend to dominate the literature of industrial relations. However, there has been an appreciable increase of interest in ⟡ Industrial Relations Management in recent years. Union studies, too, are becoming less descriptive and more analytical. There are so far few studies of employers' associations and even fewer of government agencies. There are many studies of the industrial-relations systems of industries and of countries, but the growth areas seem to be the micro-study of workplaces, plants and firms; the macro-study of the development of the national industrial-relations system in relation to governmental policy; comparative industrial relations; and, again, the study of managerial roles in industrial relations.

Many of the key features of the British industrial-relations system are cross-referenced above. For others, ⟡ Business Unionism; Check-off; Closed Shop; Confederation of British Industry; Demarcation; Dilution; Federation; Industrial Democracy; Industrial Relations – Reform in Great Britain; Lock-out; Manpower Adviser; Restrictive Labour Practices; Shop Steward; Strike (sundry references); Trade Union (sundry references); Trade Union Types (sundry references); Trades Council; Trades Union Congress; Wage (sundry references); Workplace Bargaining. N.H.C., amended by M.J.F.P.

G. S. Bain (ed.), *Industrial Relations in Britain* (Blackwell, 1983); H. A. Clegg, *The Changing System of Industrial Relations in Great Britain* (Blackwell, 1979); J. T. Dunlop, *Industrial Relations Systems* (Holt, 1958); A. Flanders, *Management and Unions* (Faber & Faber, 1970); R. Hyman,

Industrial Relations (Macmillan, 1975); M. Poole, *Theories of Trade Unionism* (Routledge & Kegan Paul, 1984); M. Poole, W. Brown, J. Rubery, K. Sisson, R. Tarling and F. Wilkinson, *Industrial Relations in the Future* (Routledge & Kegan Paul, 1984).

Industrial Relations – Reform in Great Britain The Royal Commission on Trade Unions and Employers' Associations emphasized the dual system of British industrial relations: one is formal and embodied in official institutions, the other informal and produced by the behaviour at the workplace of managers, ⟨⟩ Shop Stewards and workers, with the resulting competitive sectional wage adjustments, chaotic pay structures, ⟨⟩ Wage Drift, unofficial ⟨⟩ Strikes and other forms of workshop pressure.

The Royal Commission's suggested remedy was the development of positive company industrial-relations policies, specifically to incude such matters as the setting up of formal company collective bargaining systems, disciplinary and ⟨⟩ Grievance Procedures, rules regulating the position of shop stewards, ⟨⟩ Redundancy agreements, and ⟨⟩ Joint Consultation on safety. Deliberate attempts by companies to control incentive schemes, to regulate working hours and to introduce rational ⟨⟩ Wage Systems, including those based on ⟨⟩ Job Evaluation, were also suggested. Further, the Commission recommended that ⟨⟩ Wages Councils would be better replaced by a national minimum ⟨⟩ Wage.

Since it was not confident that voluntary action alone would be speedy enough, the Commission proposed an Industrial Relations Act, which would require companies – initially those with more than 5,000 employees – to register their collective agreements with the ⟨⟩ Department of Employment; and an Industrial Relations Commission, which would in effect monitor company industrial-relations systems for smooth working (⟨⟩ Commission on Industrial Relations).

A majority of the Commission rejected the making of all agreements into legally enforceable contracts (⟨⟩ Collective Agreements in Law) as a remedy for strikes, although Mr Andrew Shonfield dissented and pressed also for a Restrictive Practices Office for control of work practices (⟨⟩ Restrictive Labour Practices). The Conservative Party policy pamphlet, *Fair Deal at Work*, went further, urging that sympathetic strikes, secondary boycotts and inter-union strikes be made illegal (⟨⟩ Strike – Forms).

One of the Commission's most far-reaching proposals was to recommend transformation of the present industrial tribunals (⟨⟩ Redundancy Payments Act) into labour tribunals, to cover all disputes between employer and employee arising out of ⟨⟩ Contracts of Employment or from statutory claims they might have on each other as employer and employee. Labour tribunals would thus deal with allegations of unfair dismissal, including dismissal as a result of the introduction of a ⟨$⟩ Closed Shop (the Commission did not, however, advocate the abolition of the closed shop). Complaints of unfair expulsion from a union and of union electoral malpractice could also be dealt with by labour tribunals.

The Commission rejected industrial unionism (⟨$⟩ Trade Union Types – Industrial Union) as a solution to multi-unionism, recommending more union mergers and 'one union for one grade of work within one factory' (⟨$⟩ Trade Union – Structure). It also advocated properly organized shop stewards' committees; a revision of union rules on shop stewards to define their role, authority and functions; more full-time officers (⟨$⟩ Trade Union – Officers) and better salaries for them; and further extension of the ⟨$⟩ Check-off. The Commission recommended compulsory registration for unions with a new Registrar of Trade Unions and Employers' Associations, which would have close supervision over union rules.

Despite dissentients, the proposal of the ⟨$⟩ TUC for worker-directors was rejected by a majority of the Commission, although this principle was applied in the renationalized steel industry.

The Royal Commission concentrated on suggestions for making the voluntary system of ⟨$⟩ Collective Bargaining work by persuasion and publicity rather than by radical changes in the law and took the view that the unions needed strengthening if they were to be more 'responsible'. Some members of the Commission doubted the efficacy of any attempted reform that did not constrain the freedom of trade unionists to break agreements, and in this they were nearer the harder line suggested in the Conservative Party's statement, *Fair Deal at Work*, which proposed a legal framework for industrial relations somewhat similar to that in the USA.

The Labour Government's White Paper, *In Place of Strife*, endorsed many of the Commission's suggestions in its proposals for an Industrial Relations Act, including the establishment of the Industrial Relations Commission. It also introduced notions of government financial aid for rational trade-union development, including the costs of training; of a cooling-off period ('conciliation pause') for unconstitutional strikes and strikes where inadequate joint discussions have taken place; and of an industrial board to deal with conflicts of recognition between rival unions (⟨$⟩ Trade Union – Jurisdiction). It was also suggested that employers might be ordered to recognize a particular trade union and might be required to bargain in good faith against financial penalties. This White Paper provided much of the foundation for the Labour Government's abortive Industrial Relations Bill.

The eventual legislation enacted by the subsequent Conservative Government, the ◊ Industrial Relations Act 1971, now repealed, was based on the Conservative Party's policy statement, *Fair Deal at Work*, and the Inns of Court Conservative and Unionist Society's study, *A Giant's Strength*.

The decision of most unions to de-register and to oppose the Act's provisions resulted in its repeal and replacement by the much slighter ◊ Trade Union and Labour Relations Act in 1974. The voluntary nature of UK industrial relations then became subject to the development of a new legal framework with the passage of the ◊ Health and Safety at Work etc. Act 1974, the ◊ Employment Protection Act 1975; the Industry Act 1975 and the Trade Union and Labour Relations (Amendment) Act 1976. Additionally the debate on employee participation in managerial decision-making and its significance for industrial relations was given a stimulus by the publication of the Bullock Report in 1976 (◊ Industrial Democracy).

There was a further substantial change in emphasis in the reform of Britain's industrial relations following the election of the Conservative Party to office in 1979. This was reflected in the ◊ Employment Acts of 1980 and 1982 and the ◊ Trade Union Act of 1984. Unlike the ◊ Industrial Relations Act, the new legislation did not establish a comprehensive framework administered by new institutions but endeavoured to achieve a 'step by step' amendment of earlier structures and case law. ◊ The Employment Act 1980 changed the existing law on ◊ Picketing and restricted lawful picketing to a person's own place of work. It also attempted to reduce the extent of the ◊ Closed Shop by reinforcing the right of individuals not to join a trade union. The 1982 Act removed a series of trade-union immunities (notably for unlawful acts that are not 'in contemplation or furtherance of a trade dispute' and for action that is unlawful for individuals by virtue of the limitations to section B of the 1974 Act made by the Employment Act 1980 in the area of secondary picketing). Moreover the same measures were designed to amend the statutory definition of a trade dispute, to legislate against selective dismissals in a strike, to reinforce the provisions of the 1980 Act on the closed shop and to proceed against union 'labour-only' contracts. The purposes of the Trade Union Act 1984 were to provide for the members of trade-union governing bodies to be directly elected by individual secret ballots of the main members (◊ Trade Union – Ballots), to make trade unions' immunity for organizing industrial action conditional on the holding of secretly and properly conducted strike ballots, and to enable workers in trade unions with political funds to vote at regular intervals on whether their union should continue to spend money on party political matters (◊ Trade Union – Politics).

It is too early to judge just how successful this legislation will prove to be and its content is dependent upon the political fortunes of the respective parties. What is clear, however, is that all the main political parties are concerned with the reform of industrial relations in Great Britain and that the tradition of voluntarism (which implied a low-key legislative role) has been substantially eroded since the late 1960s. N.H.C., amended by M.J.F.P.

Industrial Relations Act The objective of the Industrial Relations Act 1971, abrogated 1974, was to provide a legal framework for the conduct of industrial relations in contrast to the pre-existing voluntarist system.

The Act contained four broad categories of provision: (1) the rights of employees; (2) the registration and conduct of trade unions and employee associations; (3) strikes and lockouts; (4) the reform of collective bargaining.

Unions affiliated to the ⟡ TUC opposed this legislation before and after its enactment and adopted a policy of non-cooperation in the implementation of the Act. In particular, they refused to register and to co-operate with the institutions established under the Act, except in self-defence. Any affiliated unions not complying were expelled from the TUC. The TUC unions were particularly incensed by the making of their former legal immunities conditional on registration; by the constraint on the powers of trade-union officers; by the outlawing of the traditional pre-entry closed shop; by the new right of employees not to join a trade union or other workers' organization; by the provision for making collective agreements legally binding unless specifically provided otherwise by the parties; and by the arrangements for the use of the National Industrial Relations Court and the Commission on Industrial Relations to determine disputed bargaining rights.

In practice the Act was particularly effective in two areas: unfair dismissal and procedures. The unfair dismissal provisions continue as amended by the ⟡ Employment Acts 1980 and 1982. With respect to procedures, many companies have been stimulated to improve their industrial-relations systems with the aid of the Industrial Relations Code of Practice, which remained in force when the Act was repealed and replaced by the ⟡ Trade Union and Labour Relations Act 1974. N.H.C., amended by M.J.F.P.

Industrial Relations Act 1971 (HMSO) ch. 73; W. E. K. McCarthy and N. D. Ellis, *Management by Agreement* (Hutchinson, 1973); B. Weekes, *et al.*, *Industrial Relations and the Limits of Law* (Blackwell, 1975).

Industrial Relations Adviser Specially trained industrial relations advisers are made available by ⟨⟩ the Advisory, Conciliation and Arbitration Service (ACAS) to provide assistance and advice on the whole field of industrial relations and personnel management, including alleged infringements of individual rights. Advisers may make short advisory visits to discuss specific problems or a series of visits over a period of time to give technical advice to management and employee representatives as they work towards a particular objective (such as a job evaluation scheme). Industrial relations advisers may also be involved as a small team making a survey of a situation with the object of making a rapid diagnosis of what is wrong and suggesting a course of action; this may involve interviewing a cross-section of all the people concerned. E.L.

Industrial Relations Code of Practice Sometimes said to be the industrial relations equivalent of the Highway Code, the Industrial Relations Code of Practice was set up under the provisions of sections 2–4 of the ⟨⟩ Industrial Relations Act 1971. Its objects were to provide industrial relations standards for companies and other employing organizations, which, though not legally enforceable, would be admissible in evidence before an ⟨⟩ Industrial Tribunal or other legal bodies required to handle labour disputes. The Code remains in force despite the repeal of the Act in 1974.

The Code provides standards for the responsibilities of managements, trade unions, (⟨⟩ Trade Union – at Law), ⟨⟩ Employers' Associations, and the individual employee; for employment policies (⟨⟩ Industrial Training; Manpower Planning; Recruitment; Redundancy; Selection; Wage Systems); for ⟨⟩ Communication and ⟨⟩ Joint Consultation; for ⟨⟩ Collective Bargaining; for employee representation (⟨⟩ Shop Steward); and for grievances, disputes, and disciplinary procedures (⟨⟩ Discipline; Grievance Procedure).

Additionally to the basic Industrial Relations Code of Practice, the ⟨⟩ Employment Protection Act 1975 lays down that ACAS may issue further codes and that, in particular, it should issue codes of practice on ⟨⟩ Disclosure of Information and on time off from work in respect of trade-union officials and trade-union members in certain circumstances.

However, the effectiveness of these codes of practice is probably limited. N.H.C., amended by M.J.F.P.

Industrial Relations Code of Practice (HMSO, 1972); W. W. Daniel and N. Millward, *Workplace Industrial Relations in Britain* (Heinemann, 1983); P. Willman and H. Gospel, 'The Role of Codes in Labour Relations: The Case of Disclosure', *Industrial Relations Journal*, 14, 1983, pp. 76–82.

Industrial Relations Management In recent years interest in the role of managers in industrial relations has grown appreciably. Within the firm industrial-relations management may form only a part of the total responsibility of ⟡ Personnel Management, irrespective of the size and influence of the personnel department; or it may be so significant for the enterprise that the industrial-relations manager has a seat on the board of directors whilst the personnel manager does not, although this is so far relatively rare in Britain. In practice there are dangers that differing industrial-relations policies are carried out by operational managers, personnel managers, and other service managers, e.g. industrial engineers. Increasingly, however, British management is moving towards more coherent, more rational and more positive industrial-relations policies.

The analysis of industrial-relations management has centred on the notions of *strategy*, *style* and *frame of reference*. Industrial-relations *strategies* are long-term policies that are developed by the management of an organization in order to preserve or change the procedures, practice or results of industrial-relations activities over time. They may be designed to curtail or, alternatively, to enhance trade unionism. They may be centralist or decentralist (i.e. they may involve pushing all industrial-relations decisions down to enterprise level). They may or may not involve employers' associations. Also they can take a paternalist or human-relations approach or be coercive. Almost certainly they change over time according to economic circumstances and the power of unions.

A managerial industrial-relations *style* refers to the approach of managers to labour issues. The four pure types are *directive* (or authoritarian), *paternalist* (or welfare oriented), *constitutional* (i.e. accepting a 'web of rules' formed in negotiations with organized labour and governments) and *participative* (involving the workforce and their representatives in decision-making processes). In practice, however, actual industrial-relations styles are more complex. In Britain they include *sophisticated paternalism*, characterized by a deliberate attempt to avoid collective bargaining and often a refusal to recognize trade unions, *constitutionalism*, which is still typical where unions are strong and *consultative management* (very common, involving information-sharing and employee involvement but not full participation). The much publicized directive style of the so-called 'macho' managers is not typical of most British firms.

A managerial *frame of reference* refers to the overall conception of decision-making in the organization and whether this is viewed in *unitary* or *pluralist* terms. A unitary frame of reference emphasizes that the enterprise has one locus of power and authority and is hence linked with authoritarian or paternalist managerial styles. A pluralist approach accepts that there are a number of centres of power and influence and considers the organization to be comprised of groups with diverse interests. It is associated with constitutional and participative managerial industrial-relations styles.

In Britain in the 1970s, despite a preference for a unitary frame of reference, managers in many companies in practice adopted a pluralist position and encouraged the growth of ⟡ Shop Stewards (including full-time convenors and other senior stewards), while providing a number of facilities for lay officers to carry out their union duties. In the 1980s unitary perspectives have been reasserted far more and are evident in the growth of consultative practices and procedures and a number of direct appeals to the workforce.

The different strategies of management have also been identifiable in the shifts in preference for different collective bargaining levels in the 1970s and 1980s. In the earlier period managers helped to change the locus of bargaining by encouraging enterprise-level agreements with the workforce. Later, however, there was a preference to move to the head office at company level (i.e. above the establishment), where policies could be formulated that were applied consistently throughout the constituent work units and where managements were free to develop their ideas without recourse to either union or government. Nevertheless, practice still varies in Britain amongst different sectors and firms. Moreover, there are distinctive styles of management associated with Japanese concerns (paternalism and a pronounced unitary frame of reference) and with various national cultures. ⟡ Trade Union Types; Managerial Unionism. M.J.F.P.

M. Poole *et al.*, *Industrial Relations in the Future* (Routledge & Kegan Paul, 1984); M. Poole and R. Mansfield (eds.), *Managerial Roles in Industrial Relations* (Gower, 1980); J. Purcell and K. Sisson, 'Strategies and Practice in the Management of Industrial Relations', in G. S. Bain (ed.), *Industrial Relations in Britain* (Blackwell, 1983); K. Thurley and S. Wood, *Industrial Relations and Management Strategy* (C U P, 1983).

Industrial Sociology ⟡ Social Sciences

Industrial Training That part of ⟡ Personnel Management which is directed to helping people acquire the knowledge, skills and capacities necessary to do their work well, to prepare them for transfer to other jobs and for promotion, and to help them to fit into the working group, department and enterprise in which they work. The Youth Training

Scheme provides some knowledge and skill before work starts; industry builds on this by more specialized training. Industrial training is relevant to all levels of employment, from the 'unskilled worker' who needs skill to lift, carry, move and assemble with ease and efficiency, to the senior manager who may need to understand the use of computers and of operational research as well as those aspects of human behaviour that affect performance at work and relations between groups. Training starts with ⟡ Induction, i.e. introductory courses and on-the-job instruction for new employees. It includes intensive training for unskilled and semi-skilled workers, who by means of tailor-made, works-based courses may be able to achieve a normal output in half the time required if operators are left to pick up a job by watching others. Training in craft skills, traditionally associated with systems of apprenticeship, is increasingly started with a year's general training off the job. It is as important that the content of outside courses for training foremen and supervisors should be related to the actual work they will be doing as it is for operators, process workers and apprentices. For training professional and technical staff, there is a large variety of courses many of them provided by colleges of further education. They also provide a growing volume of courses in business and management studies, which at higher levels are available at a number of universities and at independent establishments such as the Management College at Henley and the Management College at Ashridge. 'Training' is often considered to be narrowly vocational, in contrast to 'education', which is liberal and concerned with the whole person. This may be broadly true, but employers are interested in the responsibility, capacity for leadership and foresight of their managers and supervisors, so that experiences such as training courses, which demand initiative, test stamina or broaden people's understanding of social and economic processes, are as important at some stages and at certain levels as those that increase technical knowledge or improve manual skills. Furthermore young employees bring the whole of themselves to their training, and awareness of this makes teachers, however technical their subject, more 'liberal' in their approach.

   Training policies, to be effective, have to be related both to ⟡ Manpower Planning, which indicates the future requirements of different categories of employee, and to ⟡ Job Analysis, which gives a clear and accurate description of the job that people do and for which they need training. It is necessary to keep these job descriptions up to date to allow for changes in technology and organization. With these guides it is possible to estimate the numbers and types of trained personnel required and to decide which parts of the training are best given on the job, in a training department or on outside courses. Specialist advice on such matters is available in some industries from the appropriate ⟨⟩ Industrial Training Boards. ⟨⟩ Further Education; Group Methods of Training; Management Development; Training within Industry (TWI). L.S., amended by E L.

A. D. Pepper, *Managing the Training and Development Function* (Gower, 1984).

Industrial Training Act 1964 Designed to ensure that all employers would contribute to the cost of training employees within a particular industry, the Act provided for the setting up of ⟨⟩ Industrial Training Boards for the major British industries. Each board could approve suitable training courses for persons employed in its industry and make recommendations about suitable training programmes for them. The cost of these boards was to be met from a levy imposed on the firms in each industry by the Secretary of State for Employment. Boards then made grants to firms providing approved training for their employees. The provisions of the Act were subsequently amended by the Employment and Training Acts of 1973 and 1981. The 1981 Act was followed by the abolition of a number of boards by the Secretary of State and their replacement by non-statutory training organizations, of which there were 162 in 1983. E.L.

Industrial Training Boards Originally established by the Secretary of State for Employment under the ⟨⟩ Industrial Training Act 1964 to ensure that the provision of training (⟨⟩ Industrial Training) is adequate to meet the needs of the industries for which they are instituted. In 1978 there were twenty-six training boards, if one included the Foundry Industry Training Committee (technically a committee of the Engineering Industry Training Board), the Local Government Training Board (which was set up voluntarily) and the Agricultural Training Board (which had a different method of funding from the others).

Boards were initially appointed by the Minister of Labour and had to consist of a chairman with industrial or commercial experience; an equal number of persons appointed from the two sides of industry after consultation with the appropriate employers' association and trade unions; and people with educational or training experience appointed after consultation with the Minister of Education. A board has two main duties: to ensure that sufficient training is provided in its industry, and to publish information on such matters as the nature, content and length of training for different occupations. A board's authority extends to all forms of training and to any further education that should be associated with the training. It can approve training facilities and courses, lay down standards, impose tests, inspect and advise, and undertake research.

When first constituted under the Industrial Training Act, each board had the duty of imposing upon employers in its industry a financial levy and of making grants to employers in accordance with its assessment of the quantity and quality of the training provided. Following the introduction of the Employment and Training Act 1973, the Industrial Training Boards no longer had the duty to raise a levy, but had power to do so provided that the levy did not exceed 1 per cent of the total wages and salary bill of an employer. The Employment and Training Act 1981 amended the Industrial Training Act 1964 and allowed the Secretary of State for Employment to abolish or change the scope of an industrial training board after consulting the ⟨⟩ Manpower Services Commission. Under the 1981 Act, a board can still finance its operating expenses from a levy, but requires the support of the majority of employer members before a levy can be imposed.

In November 1981 the Secretary of State announced the abolition of sixteen training boards, the statutory system of training in the sectors of industry concerned being replaced by a voluntary system, to be based upon trade associations. This has left seven industrial training boards under the statutory system covering the construction, engineering, hotel and catering, clothing and allied products, offshore petroleum, plastics processing and road transport industries. E.L.

Industrial Tribunals Industrial tribunals were originally set up in 1964 to hear a limited range of disputes relating to industrial training. Their functions have since been widely extended. They deal now also with disputes concerning, among other things, redundancy pay, unfair dismissal, sex discrimination and guarantee payments. Each tribunal consists of a legally qualified chairman together with two lay members. Parties appearing before a tribunal may be represented by a solicitor or counsel, a representative of a trade union or an employers' association or by any other person of their choice. Despite the often complex legal issues that arise in employment disputes, legal aid is not available for industrial tribunals, which effectively constitute a system of specialist labour courts. Appeals against the decisions of an industrial tribunal are heard by the Employment Appeal Tribunal, which consists of a presiding high court judge and appointed members with special knowledge or experience of industrial relations. W.F.E., amended by K.W.

J. Angel, *Tolley's Industrial Tribunals* (Tolley Publishing, 1984).

Industrial Union ◊ Trade Union Types – Industrial Union

Industrialization The process of change in a society from a predominantly agrarian economy to one based on manufacturing techniques involving modern technology, mass production, standardization and a pronounced division of labour.

Whilst the purpose of industrialization is ostensibly to improve the standard of living of the general population of the society, its introduction leads inevitably to far-reaching social changes, many of which are unforeseen (although often foreseeable). The changes are too complex to be discussed fully here and the details will vary from one society to another. In general terms, however, changes are likely in the power structure and hence, perhaps, in the political system; previously traditional economic activity that often involved ritual will become rational and purposive; there will be an increase in the importance of science and technology at the expense of religion and magic; there will be a rapid growth in the size of towns and an increase in geographical and social mobility; there will occur a need for widespread educational opportunity, particularly at the secondary level; there will be a reduction in the power and influence of the wider kinship system in favour of the nuclear family and a need for the development of social services to replace the supportive functions previously undertaken by the extended family or trial unit.

These substantial changes in social organization and traditional habits, customs and beliefs create strains and tensions both social and personal. Indeed, even after the transitional period, industrialization imposes social change at an apparently ever-increasing rate with its concomitant problems of adaptation. I.C.MCG.

Wilbert E. Moore, *The Impact of Industry* (Prentice-Hall, 1965); W. Form, 'Comparative Industrial Sociology and the Convergence Thesis', *Annual Review of Sociology*, 5 (1979), pp. 1–25.

Inflation A situation in which prices are rising, usually measured by annual changes in the retail price index (◊ Index Numbers). Inflation in the UK only became serious in the 1970s; a price increase of 24 per cent was recorded in 1975 and the average annual increase for the decade was 13 per cent. Previously average annual increases during the post-war period were of the order of 2–3 per cent. Since 1980 inflation has fallen dramatically from 18 per cent and is currently running at around 6–7 per cent per annum (May 1985).

The word inflation is to some extent an emotive one, the general feeling being that inflation is a bad thing because of the ill effects it forces upon people unable to protect themselves, e.g. people on fixed incomes and creditors. However, price increases are only the symptom of inflation and we must now look at the process of inflation itself. It is customary to argue that an inflationary process can be either demand-induced or cost-induced. Such a dichotomy is useful as a starting point although it is doubtful if the distinction can be held in advanced analysis.

The usual phrase of 'too much money chasing too few goods' aptly describes demand-induced inflation. Such a statement implies that money demand in the economy runs ahead of physical supplies, thus leading to price rises, which, to some extent, choke off the demand. However, prices of products in the economic system do not appear to be as flexible as this approach suggests; in addition, one should remember that interconnections appear on the macro scene that are absent on the micro scene and thus if prices increase this will feed back to increased incomes. Most industrial prices are 'administered' prices that respond only slowly to changes in demand conditions. On the other hand they do seem to respond to general changes in cost conditions. This means, therefore, that whilst a rise in money demand may not lead to price increases because firms are afraid of spoiling the market and inviting retaliation, prices may well rise when all the firms are experiencing cost increases due to changes in raw material or labour prices. This situation may then develop as price rises are reflected in the retail index and hence lead to renewed wage demands. Whilst excess demand appears to have little direct effect on prices of products it does appear to have an indirect effect on the labour market. Excess demand for products can easily lead to bidding among manufacturers for scarce labour, which consequently gives an upward twist to wage-rates and earnings and, later, prices.

What explanations have been offered for the acceleration of inflation in the UK (also a world-wide phenomenon)? The general consensus of opinion is that until the 1970s much of our inflation was demand-induced, several studies having established links between the pressure of demand and wage/price inflation. However, the acceleration was ascribed by some economists to the power of unions pushing up wages independently of market forces – so-called wage-push inflation. Various explanations have been put forward for this behaviour, including frustration with the slow growth of real incomes, a defensive response to the rapid rise in import (and hence retail) prices and a desire to anticipate expected future price rises. Others have laid most of the blame on the inflationary impulses generated by the huge rises in oil and commodity prices.

An alternative explanation of the rapid inflation of the 1970s is given by the monetarists, whose leading exponent is Professor Milton Friedman. They argue that the main causal factor is too rapid a growth of the money supply and that for prices to be stable, the money supply should grow at a rate in line with the growth in productive potential. They also stress the long time-lags between changes in monetary policy and their effect on the economy and hence are particularly critical of the short-term demand-management policies followed by many governments in the post-war period. Monetarists would explain the fall in inflation in the 1980s as being due to the close control (and deceleration) of the rate of growth of the money supply. Others, however, would point to the extremely high levels of unemployment as being the major restraining influence on wage and price increases. ⟐ Index Numbers; Monetary Policy. L.T.S.

D. Morris (ed.), *The Economic System in the UK* (OUP, 3rd ed., 1985).

Inflation Accounting ⟐ Changing Price Levels, Accounting for

Informal Organization ⟐ Formal Organization

Information Management Information management is the application of ⟐ Information Technology (IT) to achieve that flow of information which will best enable an enterprise to achieve its goals. The relationship between IT and the management of the enterprise can be represented thus:

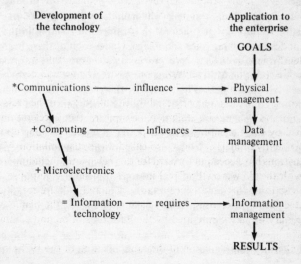

The availability of communications influences the physical management of the enterprise. Without communications it must operate from a single site, building, or even room; with good communications it can operate from many sites in many countries. The technology of computing similarly influences the management of data in an enterprise, for example by focusing on a large mainframe computer. Today, IT offers new opportunities for the collection, storage, processing and communication of information. The key change is that technology is no longer a limitation but can (at a price) do anything managers could reasonably want it to do.

This throws a new responsibility on to managers. They must assess what the technology can do, and invest in the types that are appropriate to their needs. There are three aspects to this: an awareness of the potential and limitations of modern IT; an awareness of the current systems and the legal or regulatory environment within which they operate (⟺Information System; Telecommunications); and a practical procedure for the development and implementation of information systems to meet the needs of the particular enterprise (suggested below).

Information that does not contribute to the success of the enterprise is unnecessary and wasteful. The first step, therefore, is to look at the strategic goals of the enterprise. When the information necessary for the enterprise has been deduced from its business strategy, a strategy must then be formulated to define how people will handle that information. Finally, it must be decided how the technology can assist the people.

The total information system will include people, procedures and supporting technology. It is helpful to consider information in the four main modes: text, data, voice and image. Under each of these headings, consider the need to collect, store, process and communicate information (see the Information Matrix). When this has been done, it is right to ask how technology can help. First, consider the various types of management information systems (MIS) (⟺ Information System). Next, consider the need for people or machines to communicate within or between the various sites from which the enterprise operates, and to interface with external systems. Under each heading the information system needs can be identified at one or more of three levels: transmission, switching, and value-adding. The result of such an analysis can be the common point of contact between the user (who knows and understands the enterprise) and the IT expert (who knows the technology and will design and implement the systems required).

In a disciplined way such as this, an information strategy should be defined for the enterprise. There are some policy factors that the

Information mode

INFORMATION-SYSTEM REQUIREMENTS	TEXT	DATA	VOICE	IMAGE
Collect				
Store				
Process				
Communicate				
MIS: TPS				
MIS: IPS				
MIS: DSS				
MIS: PDS				
MIS: Expert System				
MIS: Database				
Organization: Intra-site				
Organization: Inter-site				
Organization: External				
Communications: Transmission				
Communications: Switching				
Communications: VAN				
Communications: VAS				

Information-system matrix

enterprise may wish to include in its information strategy, such as a commitment to a particular supplier or to a particular set of technical standards. The information strategy should take a five-year view; this is a balance between the time it realistically takes to implement the strategy, and the time in which rapid advances in technology could render it obsolete. A five-year strategy, reviewed every eighteen months or two years, will suit most enterprises. It is the starting-point for the next two stages: system design and implementation. For these, there is much case-history and comment available. Most commentators emphasize the importance of preparing a clear and comprehensive statement of the user's requirement. The information-system matrix is a good approach to this. It is then necessary to conduct a feasibility study, leading to a report (including a business case) and a refined statement of user requirement, which can be submitted to senior management for approval. Given the active support of senior management, it is then necessary to set up project management and review procedures that will monitor the implementation. At the same time there needs to be a programme of training and human preparation. Finally, the introduction to use must be planned, managed and the results appraised.

The information strategy may have wider implications than initially thought. It may have quite a radical impact on the way the enterprise does business. Consider two extremes: the office, and the organization structure. Most managers work in offices where information is handled in all four basic forms. 'Office automation' is a term that reflects the combining of separate functions using IT. The traditional devices associated with text, data, voice and image are, respectively, the typewriter, the computer, the telephone and the television set. IT has very successfully brought together the telephone and the TV to form viewdata systems; the function can then be added to a Personal Computer (PC) and finally all information functions can be combined into a single 'workstation'. Such workstations can form the basis of 'electronic-office' technology within an organization. The main problem is interfacing with a world that is still largely paper-based. The 'paperless office' is a remote prospect at present.

At the level of organization structure, new information systems can open channels of communication and interaction between people that the traditional arrangements did not encourage or did not allow. This particularly applies to informal interactions such as electronic mail. The result may be that the enterprise would benefit from a looser style of organization, or at least one with fewer levels in its hierarchy. Such changes should flow from the practical experience of information systems, but it is a factor to be conscious of in the design phase. ⟡ Information System. D.J.S.

Tom Forester, *The Information Technology Revolution* (Blackwell, 1985); Malcolm Peltu, *The Electronic Office* (BBC, 1984); L. E. Long, *Managers Guide to Computers and Information Systems* (Prentice-Hall, 1983).

Information Retrieval This term is often used in the context of a computer-based management information system. Such a system would incorporate a data bank held on appropriate ⟡ Storage Media (Computer), consisting of files of company data that are being continually up-dated. Information retrieval is a term used to describe the organization of the storage of data in the files and the procedures for the selection and extraction of any particular item from the files, so that relevant data is easily accessible when required. For example in the airline reservation system referred to elsewhere (⟨⟩ Computer), it must be possible for a booking clerk to check for vacant seats on flights quickly.

The term is also used to describe document retrieval, in the context of manual or computer-based library or abstracting services.

Information retrieval in an airline reservation system is comparatively straightforward, but more sophisticated applications are difficult to design. The design of a retrieval system can pose complex logical and semantic problems and considerable effort is being put into solving these problems. Indeed, what data to store and how to store and retrieve it is the basic problem in the design of computer-based management information systems. M.J.C.M.

Information System Modern information technology (IT) makes new information systems possible. Such systems can integrate all four basic methods of handling information: text, data, voice and image. They can operate over a Local Area Network (LAN, serving access points on a single site) or over a Wide Area Network (WAN, serving access points on several different sites). The diagram on p. 248 reviews the types of information system that are currently available. There are two levels of communication services: transmission and switched networks. Transmission is the simpler of the two, involving the transfer of information, without change, from one point to another. Switching involves many users or access points and gives the ability to transfer information from one point in a network to any other selected point. The diagram then shows the communication networks that have evolved to support these services, and the trends for the future. Next it shows the 'value-added networks' (VANs) that provide storage, messaging or processing in addition to simple communication. Finally it gives examples of the 'value-added services' (VASs) that are supported by VANs and that suppliers are currently offering in many countries. VANs and VASs were traditionally built up as private systems, and for many enterprises this will still be right. However, they are becoming widely available in the open market, directed at users in particular industries. The terminology has not yet settled: the term value-added network service (VANS) is also used to embrace both VANs and VASs.

There is one type of VAS that deserves fuller comment here: management information systems (MIS). MIS are designed to help managers do their job. The functions of management can be divided into three categories: operational control (concerned with the day-to-day operation of the enterprise); management control (concerned with short-term

Examples of information systems

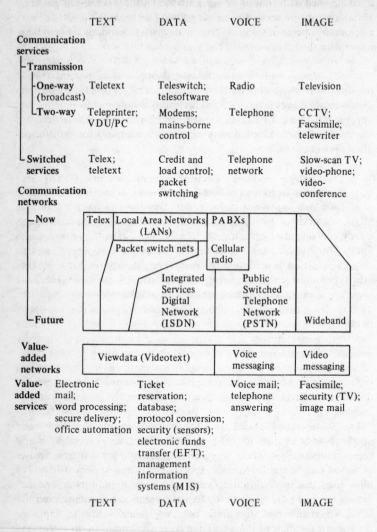

	TEXT	DATA	VOICE	IMAGE
Communication services				
├ **Transmission**				
├ **One-way** (broadcast)	Teletext	Teleswitch; telesoftware	Radio	Television
└ **Two-way**	Teleprinter; VDU/PC	Modems; mains-borne control	Telephone	CCTV; Facsimile; telewriter
└ **Switched services**	Telex; teletext	Credit and load control; packet switching	Telephone network	Slow-scan TV; video-phone; video-conference

Communication networks

Now	Telex	Local Area Networks (LANs)	PABXs	
		Packet switch nets	Cellular radio	
		Integrated Services Digital Network (ISDN)	Public Switched Telephone Network (PSTN)	
Future				Wideband

Value-added networks	Viewdata (Videotext)		Voice messaging	Video messaging

Value-added services	Electronic mail; word processing; secure delivery; office automation	Ticket reservation; database; protocol conversion; security (sensors); electronic funds transfer (EFT); management information systems (MIS)	Voice mail; telephone answering	Facsimile; security (TV); image mail

	TEXT	DATA	VOICE	IMAGE

planning); and strategic planning (concerned with long-term strategy). Where the management task is fairly well structured, a corresponding type of MIS is available:

(1) *Operational control.* Transaction processing systems (TPS) are concerned with routine administration of such functions as payroll, stock control, invoicing and mailing lists. They deal with well-defined mechanical operations and do not in themselves produce information relevant to the other categories of management.

(2) *Management control.* Information provision systems (IPS) provide either routine or *ad hoc* summaries and reports based on the detailed data handled by a TPS. The IPS function may in practice be integrated with the TPS function, abstracting data from it. The reports from an IPS, such as sales-trend analysis, are valuable for short-term management control.

(3) *Strategic planning.* Decision support systems (DSS) are designed for managers to ask 'what if' questions, to predict the results of possible courses of action. The results help them to reach a rational decision. DSS will contain a model of the system being considered; it may be a financial model, a market forecasting model or a mathematical model of a physical system, for example. DSS therefore contain implicit or explicit assumptions about the real world; they may also work on probabilities rather than on certainties. For both reasons managers must be aware of the scope and limitations of their DSS. However, they can quickly give managers a feel for the implication of options that are open to them.

A further development is the programmed decision system (PDS), in which a well-understood and trusted DSS is programmed to initiate action as a result of 'decisions' it takes based on criteria specified by the user. The control of chemical plant is an example, where control-decisions are too complex or are required too quickly for a human being to make.

The above types of MIS are available using conventional IT. The next level of MIS is an Expert System. This is based on quite different computer techniques, where 'knowledge' is given to the system in terms of 'rules' formulated by human experts. The expert system will apply those rules, and indeed formulate new ones in the light of its experience (which has to be fed back to it). Expert systems are normally used to advise a human expert, and in this role they should be able to 'explain' the reasons for their recommendation when challenged to do so by the human user. Simple expert systems have already been successfully applied to management. Because of their apparent ability to learn and improve upon individual human performance, they are associated with the term 'artificial intelligence'.

When MIS first became available it was popularly thought that all the functions appropriate to the various levels of management could be supported from a single comprehensive system. This view has declined. The information needed for any particular purpose should be considered in terms of the accuracy, timeliness and update-interval that are necessary for that purpose. These criteria apply more stringently to information required for operational control than to that required for strategic planning. In general IPS need to abstract from TPS and DSS need to abstract from IPS. Separate systems with the ability to transfer abstracted data may therefore be a better solution. Indeed the trend is towards having the 'database' as the common resource, with individual processing systems interacting with it. An elementary principle is that raw data should only be entered once into the information system and thereafter handled entirely electrically. ⟷ Information Technology; Information Management; Telecommunications. D.J.S.

L. E. Long, *Managers Guide to Computers and Information* (Prentice-Hall, 1983); D. Michie and R. Johnston *The Creative Computer* (Viking, 1984).

Information Technology Information is essential to achieve concerted action by an individual or by an enterprise. Some working definitions are useful to clarify the technology of handling information:

Data. Numbers representing an observable object or event.
Information. Human significance associated with an observable object or event.
Knowledge. Theoretical or practical understanding of a subject.
Wisdom. Experience and knowledge judiciously applied.

These terms form a hierarchy; each item is built upon the previous one but adds to it in terms of human significance. Computers and information systems actually handle data, but present the result to the human user so that it looks like information, or even knowledge. So far, they make a poor job of appearing wise.

'Information technology' (IT) is a modern term. It was coined to mark the convergence of two technologies that had traditionally been separate: computing and communications. This convergence was made possible by microelectronics. A major advance came with the invention of the transistor in 1948, then in the early 1960s came integrated circuits (ICs), in which many transistors and other components could be fabricated on to a single 'chip', or crystal of semiconductor such as silicon. The capacity of these ICs developed at a remarkable pace, consistently doubling every year. By the early 1970s it was possible to fabricate more than 10,000 components on a single chip; this was termed very large scale integration (VLSI).

It turned out that the new technology was best suited to processing data that is in digital rather than analogue form. In an analogue representation, some continuously varying physical quantity (such as the variation in air pressure caused by the human voice) is represented by a continuously varying electrical signal. The signal is then an 'analogue' of the physical quantity, but it is not easy to process signals in this form accurately. In a digital representation, the physical quantity is described numerically. The numbers might, for example, represent a graph of sound-pressure as a function of time. The numbers are usually handled in 'binary' form, comprising only the digits 0 and 1; this is because it is technically easiest to handle numbers using devices that have only two physical states.

The emergence of IT has produced human problems as well as technical ones. People trained in one discipline find it difficult to understand the problems and rationale of another discipline, where the traditions, in particular of co-operation and standardization, may be very different. Some of these problems have had effects of which the general manager needs to be aware, because it limits what the technology is able to offer in practice. The interface between operator and machine is also receiving increased attention. ⟡ Information System; Man–machine Interface. D.J.S.

Garry Marshall, *Beginners Guide to Information Technology* (Newnes Technical Books, 1984); Peter Zorkoczy, *Information Technology – An Introduction* (Pitman, 2nd ed., 1985).

Information Theory The mathematical theory of information sets out to provide a measure of the amount of information that exists in a message, and to provide a formal basis for the study of information flow in systems of communication and control.

The amount of information (referred to as 'entropy' or 'uncertainty') associated with a source of signals is related to the unexpectedness of the signals. Thus a signal with a high prior probability has a low information value, and a rare or unexpected signal has a high value.

It is a requirement of such a system of measurement that all possible signals must be definable in advance, and that their respective prior probabilities must be known. Messages (i.e. sequences of signals) may form an infinite set. In the case, for example, of a teleprinter communication system, the number of possible signal elements may number only twenty-seven (i.e. capital letters and spaces) and the relative frequency of occurrence of each element may be known for a given class of messages (e.g. those in the English language). Thus the average rate of information transmission through such a system may be calculated, although there is no upper limit to the number of possible transmittable messages.

The unit of such selective information is the 'bit', which is the amount of uncertainty associated with the choice between two equally likely outcomes. Probabilities of occurrence of signal elements usually depend not only upon relative frequencies, but also upon the sequential relationships between elements, which exist within most language structures.
E.E.

E. Edwards, *Information Transmission* (Chapman & Hall, 1964).

Input/Output Analysis Input/output analysis is an attempt to reveal the structural interdependence of the economic system. An input/output table shows the purchases by a particular sector from all the other sectors, and sales by the sector to the other sectors. Table 1 is an example of a simple hypothetical input/output table.

Table 1

	Purchases			Final demand	Total output (£)
	X	Y	Z		
Sales					
X	—	60	40	100	200
Y	40	—	100	260	400
Z	50	100	—	50	200
Labour	110	240	60	—	410
Total input	200	400	200	410	1,210

If we consider the output of industry X, £200, we find that £60 was purchased by industry, Y, £40 by industry Z and £100 by final consumers. Similarly, to produce this output, industry X purchased £40 of output from industry Y, £50 from industry Z and £110 of labour services.

From Table 1 we can easily obtain the table of input coefficients given opposite.

Table 2

	User of output		
	X	Y	Z
Producer of input			
X	—	0·15	0·2
Y	0·2	—	0·5
Z	0·25	0·25	—
Labour	0·55	0·6	0·3

Table 2 shows the amount of input that needs to be purchased from the various sectors to produce one unit of output for a particular sector. Thus the first column shows that to obtain £1 of output from industry X requires purchases of £0·2 of input from Y, £0·25 from Z and £0·55 of labour services.

Provided some simplifying assumptions are made, the uses of this type of analysis are considerable, although argument remains as to whether or not the simplifying assumptions are too restrictive. For example, we may wish to know what the effect would be of an increase in final demand for the product of industry X to £120, other final demands remaining constant. Thus an assumption is made about consumer demand. We also assume that prices remain unchanged and that the input coefficients remain unchanged. This latter assumption is a special case of constant returns to scale, the important point being that factor substitution due to either changes in the relative prices of inputs or changes in technology is ruled out.

The answers to our question can be obtained by solution of the three simultaneous equations given below, where x, y, z, are the outputs in pounds from industries X, Y, and Z. Clearly all three outputs will change because of structural interdependence.

$$x = 0·15y + 0·2z + 120 \qquad (1)$$
$$y = 0·2x + 0·5z + 260 \qquad (2)$$
$$z = 0·25x + 0·25y + 50 \qquad (3)$$

Equation (1), for example, tells us the demands that are made upon the output of industry X by industries Y, Z and final consumers. The solution to the equations are:

$$x = £222 \qquad y = £408 \qquad z = £208$$

This indicates the amount of new output required to satisfy intermediate and final demand.

A final step would be to work out the new demand for labour services to see if this is feasible in view of known resources.

Input/output tables can only be produced from a census of production data. The latest in the United Kingdom were published in 1983 and relate to 1979. They distinguish over 100 industry and commodity groups.

Such tables add an extra dimension to the national accounts as normally compiled and presented (⟡ National Income Accounts). The latter are concerned with the composition and value of goods and services entering into final demand, and the factor-incomes generated in the economic process, but not with the transactions between industries that form part of the process of supplying final demand. Input/output tables present these intermediate transactions, together with the flows of goods and services to final demand and the incomes generated, within a framework that records all transactions among the industries or commodity groups distinguished in the tables. As a result, input/output tables show the detailed input structures of each industry, whereas the mainstream national accounts show only the value added or factor-incomes generated in the industry. L.T.S.

'Input–output Tables for the United Kingdom 1968', *Studies in Official Statistics,* no. 22 (HMSO, 1973); 'Input–output Tables for the United Kingdom 1979', *Business Monitor,* PA 1004 (HMSO, 1983).

Input/Output Devices and Media For a computer to communicate with the outside world input/output facilities are required.

The data given to the computer are manipulated within it by electrical pulses. Initially they are hand- or typewritten on paper, so input facilities are required to convert them into electrical forms. Since computers operate very quickly, input facilities must be designed to operate as fast as possible. Similar considerations apply to output facilities.

There are several types of input facilities available and the type most suitable is dependent upon the particular application. Computer installations usually have two or more alternatives present to provide flexibility.

(1) *Punch cards.* These are basically the punched cards used in data processing since 1890. Information is coded by punching holes in alternative positions (usually twelve) in a vertical column. Cards are usually 'eighty column' or 'forty column' in size. The cards are 'read',

that is the positions of the holes are 'sensed' by a card reader. Sensing is performed in a number of ways: (a) electrically – by passing the card between an electrically energized roller and a set of wire brushes. Where holes are present electric circuits are completed: (b) mechanically – a set of steel pins, each coincident with a punching position, is pushed down on the card face. Where a hole is present, the pin passes through, activating a mechanism: (c) photoelectrically – light is focused on the card, which is supported over a set of photoelectric cells, each coincident with a punching position. The presence of a hole activates the appropriate cell.

Card readers performing this operation can 'read' at 1,000 or more cards a minute.

(2) *Punched paper tape*. This consists of a continuous strip of paper or plastic tape $\frac{3}{4}$–1 in. wide. Data are recorded by punching holes laterally across the tape. There are between five and eight punching positions, giving 5–8 track tape. Data from the tape are read serially by a tape reader operating photoelectrically. Tape readers can read at 1,000 or more characters per second.

(3) *Magnetic tape*. This is analogous to the material used in domestic tape recorders and consists of a magnetically sensitive deposit on a plastic tape substrate $\frac{1}{4}$–1 in. wide. The spots of sensitive material can be magnetized in either of two directions, corresponding to a 'hole' or 'no hole'. Magnetization is performed by small electromagnets (writing heads) and similar electromagnets recognize the polarity of the magnetic spots (reading heads). Data from magnetic tape can be read serially twenty or more times faster than from paper tape, but magnetic tape is more expensive and is difficult to edit and correct. It is more commonly used for transferring data from one unit to another and for backing storage ($\Diamond$ Storage Media).

Handwritten data are usually transferred to punched or paper tape by manual keyboard operators. To produce paper tape, operators 'copy type' the data using a typewriter-style keyboard that automatically translates and punches the data. Some units automatically produce typescript copies of the data. Similar equipment exists for producing punched cards and magnetic tape.

Similar data can be used for output as for input. The computer records output directly on to cards or paper tape by card or paper-tape punches. Output punches are slower than card and paper-tape readers. Magnetic tape input/output may also be recorded directly on to magnetic tape. Card or tape output is converted to a conventional typescript by appropriate type printers.

The output can be printed directly using a line printer connected directly to the computer. This produces a typed script a line at a time (hence the name), whereas a conventional typewriter produces each character serially. This mode of printing is adopted to obtain maximum data output speed. Speeds of over 1,000 lines per minute are obtained.
M.J.C.M.

Insolvency Strictly, there are two forms of insolvency. *Legal* insolvency occurs when a business is unable to obtain the necessary cash to pay its debts; that is, the demands of all creditors of the business could not be satisfied despite realization for cash of all of its assets. *Technical* insolvency occurs when the business is unable to meet its debts at a particular time, despite the fact that it is not legally insolvent, and is therefore a particular result of mismanaging the timing of cash flows.
P.J.A.H.

Inspection Every firm is concerned with the quality of its output, and that its products meet certain minimum standards. This involves two aspects: the quality of past production, i.e., the inspection of articles already produced; and the quality of future production, i.e. action, usually resulting from inspection, taken to ensure that future production is acceptable, such as a change in material, machine settings, etc. Inspection, therefore, is one aspect of ⬦ Quality Control.

Inspection is not restricted to the end product, but is also applied to purchased material, components, etc., and at intermediate stages of manufacture. Intermediate inspection should be located to provide maximum economic benefit:

i.e. Cost of inspection < Expected saving < Number of new rejects produced at stage × Subsequent production costs

A 100 per cent inspection of items is rarely possible or economically practical; for example the time required may be excessive or inspection may be of a destructive nature. This gives rise to the practice of ⬦ Acceptance Sampling, whereby the overall quality of production is measured from a random sample. This method of inspection reduces costs and handling.

Eternal vigilance is the key to efficient inspection. Wartime studies of watch-keeping on radar and other apparatus laid the foundation of our knowledge of the characteristics of human performance in inspection tasks. The variables that affect inspection efficiency include the number of possible faults, their frequency of occurrence, the length of the work and period, the action required following upon fault detection, and, of course, the numerous aspects of the worker's environment. R.W. & E.E.

Institution A more or less permanent complex of related behavioural expectations that have a positive social value. A social institution is thus an aspect of culture that relates to the satisfaction of specific basic human needs. The family, for example, is a social institution in that there exist generally held expectations about the behaviour required of the family members and the nature of the relationships amongst them. The expectations in question may be formally prescribed in legal enactments, in constitutions, rule books, etc., or may simply be generally understood. Social institutions both reflect and determine the values of the society; they determine the roles that people act and comprise the norms to which they should conform. ⟡ Culture; Norm; Role; Values. I.C. MCG.

Insurance Law A contract of insurance is one whereby the insurer (generally an insurance company) undertakes in return for a premium to indemnify the insured against the financial consequences of the contingency insured against, up to the maximum amount stated in the insurance policy. The term 'assurance' is sometimes used for those contracts where the contingency (e.g. death) is one that is bound to occur at some time.

Contracts of insurance have three general features:

(1)   They are contracts of utmost good faith. This means that the insured must volunteer to the insurer all information about the risk that might influence the insurer's decision whether, and if so at what premium, to insure. Failure to do so would entitle the insurer to disclaim his liability under the contract.

(2)   The insured must have an 'insurable interest' in the subject matter of the policy. This means that the insured faces a financial loss in the event of the contingency materializing. If the insured lacks an insurable interest, the transaction would be treated as void, being in the nature of a gamble.

(3)   All contracts of insurance, except for life and accident insurance, are treated as contracts of indemnity and the insured may, irrespective of the amount of the policy, recover no more than the loss that they have actually suffered. If this loss exceeds the amount of the policy, no more than the sum insured for could be claimed. W.F.F.

R. P. Colinvaux, *Law of Insurance* (Sweet & Maxwell, 5th ed., 1984).

Integration (Vertical and Horizontal) ▷ Diversification; Patterns of Growth.

Intelligence Sometimes defined as overall mental ability, a safer but somewhat uninformative definition is the operational one: 'that which intelligence tests measure'. Interest in the differences between individual human abilities led J. McKern Cattell to construct batteries of tests at the end of the nineteenth century. Later work carried out on French schoolchildren by Alfred Binet led to the construction of the first set of standardized test items.

Early thinking was centred around the concept of mental age, which is defined as the mean chronological age of children with comparable ability. The ratio of mental age to chronological yields the mental quotient which, if multiplied by 100, produces the familiar intelligence quotient:

$$IQ = \frac{MA}{CA} \times 100$$

If, for example, a child of eight years of age produces test scores comparable with those of the average child of nine years, we have

$$IQ = \frac{9}{8} \times 100 = 112 \cdot 5$$

More recently, the concept of mental age has been abandoned and intelligence is measured in terms of percentile ranks for persons within a given age range (▷ Percentiles).

Factor studies (▷ Factor Analysis) indicate the existence of such aspects of test ability as Numerical Ability, Spatial Relations, Verbal Fluency and Abstract Reasoning. Test scores are known to be dependent upon age, sex, racial and national origin, geographical background, and socio-economic level.

The chief application of the technology of intelligence testing lies in the prediction of scholastic and occupational success (▷ Personality; Psychology). E.E.

Interference (Machines) ▷ Machine Assignment and Interference

Internal Rate of Return (Marginal Efficiency of Capital) This measure of the profitability of an investment project was made prominent by the economist J. M. Keynes, who called it the marginal efficiency of capital.

It may be defined as that rate of discount (interest or return) which would make the initial investment outlay exactly equal to the discounted present value of the expected net flows of funds (or cash) from that project. More concisely it is the value for r in the following equation:

$$I_0 = \frac{Y_1}{(1 + r)} + \frac{Y_2}{(1 + r)_2} + \ldots + \frac{Y_n}{(1 + r)^n},$$

where I_0 = the initial investment outlay, made now

Y_j = the net cash flow in year j (j = 1, 2, 3 ... n)

n = the number of periods over which the cash flows are expected to continue

r = the internal rate of return (I R R)

Given that expected values can be placed on I_0 and Y_1, Y_2 ... Y_n, the expression can be solved for the value of r. The I R R can be interpreted as the rate of profit implicit in the project's expected cash flows, that is to say it is the rate of profit earned on the capital initially invested after providing for the depreciation of that capital. However, it should be noted that in some cases there may be more than one value for r (✧ Present Value versus ✧ Internal Rate of Return).

Thus according to this criterion of capital investment, projects are ranked in descending order of profitability according to the value of r – the higher the value of r, the greater the profitability. In principle, all projects should be accepted that have a higher value for r than the company's cost of capital.

In principle and sometimes in practice, this method will not give the 'correct' ranking of projects and is generally inferior to the present value method when capital is 'rationed'. ✧ Present Value; Capital Budgeting. E.A.L.

A. A. Alchian, 'The Rate of Interest, Fisher's Rate of Return over Cost, and Keynes' Internal Rate of Return', *American Economic Review*, vol. 45 (December 1955), pp. 938–43.

International Labour Organization Set up in 1919 under the Treaty of Versailles, the basic aim of the International Labour Organization was the promotion of social justice by ensuring minimum standards of employment in all member states. The two main organs of the organization are the International Labour Conference and the International Labour Office.

The conference is the policy-making body. Each member state is represented by four persons, two of whom represent the government, one the employers and one the employees. The conference makes its policy decisions in three forms, namely *resolutions*, *recommendations* and *conventions*. Resolutions may be passed by a simple majority of the delegates and represent some statement of collective opinion not calling for any particular action by member states. Recommendations and conventions have to be passed by a two-thirds majority of votes and must then be submitted by the governments of member states to their respective parliaments. The difference between them is that a convention, if ratified by a member state, becomes directly binding on it and the national law will have to be altered accordingly. A recommendation calls for certain changes in national laws without (as with conventions) laying down the exact terms of the proposed change.

The International Labour Office, situated in Geneva, is the fact-finding, research and administrative section of the organization. W.F.F.

G. Johnston, *The International Labour Organization* (Europa, 1970).

International Marketing The marketing of goods and services across national boundaries gives rise to all or some of the following additional obstacles in the marketing process: language, tariffs, foreign-exchange arrangements, international credit, political disturbances and cultural disturbances. The term is synonymous with export marketing. Although it has been traditional in most British companies to institutionalize international marketing within a separate organizational framework, the development of product-oriented structures, frequently based on segmentation analysis (⟡ Market Segmentation) has also led to an integration with domestic marketing. The two common patterns of organization are currently geographical areas and products. Although language and trading aspects have always received detailed attention, the contribution of anthropology and sociology in different nations to the development of international marketing is of growing significance. The indigenous population is generally employed in order to avoid localized cultural and social factors being overlooked, and to avoid the cost of expatriates acquiring knowledge of such things as local distribution and media facilities. G.S.C.W.

Keegan, *Multinational Marketing Management* (Prentice-Hall, 1985).

Interpersonal Skill Development Interpersonal skills come to the fore when two persons interact socially. When Albert communicates his intentions to Barbara, verbally or non-verbally, he has to make assumptions, for example, about her knowledge, feelings, attitudes, abilities and level of interest. And when Barbara responds, he in turn must listen with care or interpret accurately non-verbal signals or gestures, in order to assess whether or not she has understood his message.

Sending understandable messages, listening, anticipating others' reactions to one's behaviour and interpreting their responses are all examples of interpersonal skills, which can be developed by training. ⟡ Group Methods of Training, for example, enable an individual to behave in front of others, to receive information about the effect of that behaviour on their feelings and attitudes, and to plan modifications if necessary. If people respond negatively to Albert because he continually interrupts them, the elimination of such interruptions can then become an appropriate learning objective for him.

The development of sophisticated interpersonal skills, like interviewing or negotiation techniques, may initially require instruction in the complexities of the process, illustrated by demonstrations of good practice, such as the skilful use of questions. Practice interviews or role-played negotiations can then be organized, observed (preferably with the aid of videotape) and discussed with the participants to discover what went well and what behavioural modifications would lead to a more skilled performance next time. Similar feedback of a constructive nature from colleagues can be encouraged in the working environment when the skills are being used in earnest. ⟡ Performance Appraisal.

In a training design suggested by Harrison and Berger for programmes concerned with interpersonal skill development, during the first one and a half hours participants consider the feedback they have already received within their organizations, complete a self-assessment questionnaire, and perform a variety of tasks with others. This phase enables participants to assess their own strengths and weaknesses and to diagnose their own training needs, which are then discussed with the training staff. Improvements are most commonly sought in the areas of communication, leadership and influence, decision-making and problem-solving. The next two and a half days are spent helping the participants to develop the skills they need. To this end, task situations are designed to meet individual requirements, taking into account the person's situation within their enterprise. A final day is then devoted to the practical problems likely to be encountered within the enterprise when the individual applies his or her newly learned skills. E.L.

P. Honey, *Face to Face: A Practical Guide to Interactive Skills* (IPM, 1976); K. Harrison and M. Berger, 'A New Approach to Interpersonal Skills Development', in C. L. Cooper (ed.), *Developing Social Skills in Managers* (Macmillan, 1976).

Interviewing The interview is the most widely used technique for assessing human ability. Its popularity derives from the ease with which it can be carried out, its flexibility and enormous face validity.

There is no doubt that the interview is also the most widely misused technique. Interviewers are frequently untrained, inexperienced, stereotyped in their approach and unaware of the lack of validity in their conclusions.

Good interviewing demands skill, patience, careful planning and preparation and, above all, an appreciation of the limitations of the method. Interviewers should be quite clear about the data they are attempting to elicit; they should have a flexible, yet systematic plan of procedure; should make the most of the opportunity to observe all aspects of the subject's behaviour; and must have the ability to establish swiftly the type of personal relationship appropriate to the particular situation.

The evidence on the validity of interviewing as a means of assessment and selection is far from encouraging. Several studies suggest that interviewing is of no value, or is even detrimental to judgements that may depend, in part, on more objective evidence. In spite of the evidence, most interviewers feel that they themselves are able to make successful use of the method. This important fact is, in itself, a cause of further problems. E.E.

S. A. Richardson *et al.*, *Interviewing: Its Forms and Functions* (Basic Books, 1965).

Inventories or Stocks The three basic types of inventory or stock in manufacturing systems and their main purposes are as follows:

(1) *Stocks of finished items.* (a) Act as a buffer against fluctuations in demand for a product. Even if such fluctuations in demand could be predicted, it is often undesirable or inconvenient to accommodate them by corresponding fluctuations in the level of production. Consequently stocks of finished items are often maintained in order to permit a reasonably level production rate in the face of fluctuating demand. (b) Provide quick service to the customer. (c) Reduce the risk associated with stoppages or reductions in production caused by breakdowns, strikes, shortages of materials, etc.

(2) *Work-in-progress.* Disconnects or decouples the various stages of production thus facilitating production planning and enabling fluctuation in output at successive stages to occur without immediately affecting other stages. This decoupling process might also enable the

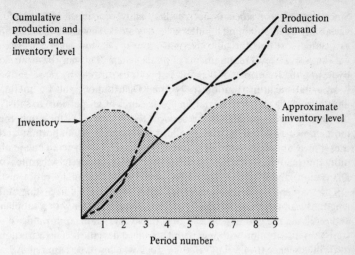

Period number

production rates at successive stages to be stabilized (⟡ Buffer stocks). The use of inventory to permit level production rate in the face of fluctuating demand.

(3) *Raw materials and purchased items.* (a) Enable advantages to be taken of bulk or other favourable purchasing terms. (b) Reduce the risk associated with delays in deliveries for other reasons (⟡ Inventory or Stock-control Problems). R.W.

R. Wild, *Management and Production* (Penguin, 1980).

Inventory or Stock-control Problems In this context inventory is defined as idle resources. The company usually needs to maintain some of its resources, e.g. raw materials or finished good stocks, men or money, in reserve and therefore idle stock. The function of inventory control is to determine the best level for these reserves. Taking raw material stock as an example, we may say that some costs increase and some decrease as the level of stock is increased: (a) Tied-up capital, storage space, taxes and insurance costs, together with risks of obsolescence and spoilage all increase as stockholding increases. (b) Shortage, ordering and purchasing costs generally all decrease as stockholding increases.

An inventory control system must be able to answer two questions: how much to order and how frequently. The order quantity is determined so that it achieves an appropriate balance between the opposing costs above, and is sometimes known as the economic order quantity (EOC).

Since demand for stock is not regular, allowance must be made for variability by maintaining a buffer or safety stock; this stock also has an associated cost and the objective is to keep it at a low level consistent with the service level requirements of management. This may be achieved by noting the frequency of demand in previous periods, by representing it on a statistical distribution (◊ Normal Distribution) and by holding multiples of the standard deviation (◊Measures of Dispersion) to satisfy the service level: the higher the service, the greater the stock and the more the cost. Although the standard deviation is an important and useful measure of statistics, it is sometimes inconvenient to calculate. A more practical calculation is the mean absolute deviation (◊ Measures of Dispersion) and is more commonly applied in stock-control problems.

The frequency of ordering depends upon accuracy of forecasting and length of lead time, i.e. the time between placing an order with a supplier and receiving the goods. The lead time may vary, again conforming to a statistical distribution with mean and standard deviation. This variation too will influence the level of safety in stock which will be required. R.S.S.

P. G. Moore, *Basic Operational Research* (Pitman, 1976).

Investment Appraisal ◊ Capital Budgeting

Investment in the Economy The proportion of the Gross National Product (◊ National Income Accounts) devoted to investment is an

Table 1. Comparison of gross investment and consumer expenditure (1980 prices with year-on-year percentage changes in parentheses)

Year	Consumer expenditure (£m)		Gross domestic fixed capital formation (£m)	
1972	121,204		40,594	
1973	127,436	(5·1)	43,535	(7·2)
1974	125,630	(−1·4)	41,734	(−4·1)
1975	124,748	(−0·7)	41,808	(0·2)
1976	125,175	(0·3)	42,434	(1·5)
1977	124,564	(−0·5)	41,323	(−2·6)
1978	131,373	(5·5)	42,938	(3·9)
1979	137,256	(4·5)	43,925	(2·3)
1980	136,789	(−0·3)	41,628	(−5·2)
1981	136,714	(—)	38,075	(−8·5)
1982	138,135	(1·0)	40,645	(6·7)
1983	144,008	(4·3)	42,348	(4·2)

Source: United Kingdom National Accounts (HMSO, 1984).

important determinant of a country's rate of growth of productive potential. The level of investment demand is also important in determining how much of the country's productive potential is being utilized (⟨⟩ Multiplier). It is, therefore, of some importance to investigate the factors that determine investment demand.

Table 1 gives some indication of the course of gross investment since 1972 in the UK; in particular we note that it is more variable than consumer expenditure.

One of the most famous explanations of investment demand is known as the acceleration principle. Although it has deficiencies as an explanation of such a diverse concept as gross investment it does provide a useful starting point. The example given in Table 2 is for an individual firm and for our purposes we assume that behaviour for the whole economy is an aggregation of individual behaviour patterns.

Table 2. Acceleration principle (£ 000s)

Time period (years)	Output per period	Capital required	Replacement	Net investment	Gross investment
1	50	100	10	0	10
2	50	100	10	0	10
3	60	120	10	20	30
4	70	140	10	20	30
5	85	170	10	· 30	40
6	85	170	10	0	10

In this example we assume that the optimum capital–output ratio is 2:1, which means that two units of capital are necessary to produce one unit of output without involving either strain or under-utilization of capacity. Hence an output rate of £50,000 per year would require £100,000 of capital and we assume £10,000 of this would require replacing each year. From period 3, however, the output rate moves as shown. As output increases new capital is required and the effect is that whilst output increases by 20 per cent between periods 2 and 3, gross investment demand increases by 200 per cent. Similarly between periods 5 and 6, there is no increase in output, whilst gross investment demand falls by 75 per cent. The term 'acceleration principle' is used because net investment depends upon the acceleration or deceleration of output. Clearly when aggregation takes place over all firms this would lead to severe fluctuations in investment demand, certainly far more severe than appears to happen in practice. Why is this? The fundamental answer is that the acceleration principle, whilst beautiful in its simplicity, cannot

stand by itself as an explanation of investment demand. It needs qualifications and we must also introduce other factors. To take the qualifications first, it is unlikely that a rigid capital–output ratio is adhered to as
output expands or contracts. Much depends upon the existence of unused
capacity and businessmen's estimates of the likely permanence of increases and decreases in demand. We must also take account of businessmen's expectations about the future, and the time scale on which
investment projects are planned, and capacity in the capital goods industries.

As far as other factors are concerned, accounts must be taken of
present and future profits, since they are a source of funds for investment
and the reason why it takes place. Another factor often stressed is the
rate of interest, which was introduced by Keynes through his concept of
the marginal efficiency of capital (⟡Internal Rate of Return). There is
much debate amongst economists and businessmen regarding the sensitivity of investment decisions to changes in the rate of interest. ⟡ Growth;
The Multiplier. L.T.S.

D. Morris (ed.), *The Economic System in the UK* (OUP, 3rd ed., 1985).

J

Jaques, Elliot ◊ Time-span of Discretion

Job Analysis The method or technique of obtaining all the facts about a job in such a way that they can be used for various purposes in ◊ Personnel Management. The process starts with a detailed study and description of the tasks that make up a job; this is then analysed under headings such as job requirements (skill, knowledge, physical and mental effort), responsibility (for people, materials, to customers), and working conditions (physical environment and hazards). The job analysis forms the basis of a job specification, which is a description of the individual qualifications and disqualifications (age, sex, education history, experience, etc.) required of a person who is to do the job. A job analysis can be used for the ◊ Selection, placement, ◊ Industrial Training and promotion of employees. It can also be used for job evaluation, i.e. the rating of jobs against each other on the basis of comparative skills, responsibilities, etc. Job evaluation is used to determine wage and salary differentials. It may be described as a rational method of doing this, but it is not scientific, as it is not possible to quantify accurately the relative importance in a job of such different aspects as, for example, skill and effort. In practice, the basis of most systems of job evaluation involves a reference to traditional views of grading jobs; nevertheless it is a technique that brings to light inconsistencies and is more objective than the alternatives. ◊ Job Evaluation. L.S.

S. Gael, *Job Analysis: A Guide to Assessing Work Activities* (Jossey-Bass, 1983).

Job Description ◊ Job Analysis; Job Evaluation

Job Enlargement To build up the content of jobs so as to increase the skill, interest, initiative and responsibility required of employees. It aims to reduce the frustration and monotony associated with much routine factory and office work and it challenges the view that higher productivity is inevitably associated with an extension of the division of labour. If, it is argued, more use is made of human capacities, stronger ⟡ Motivation can lead to levels of labour productivity that are higher than those associated with a narrow specialization of tasks. An example occurred in a factory making typewriters. Workers had only been responsible for fitting parts of typewriters to a frame on an assembly belt. They were given the additional tasks of aligning the parts, of inspecting the completed task and of some maintenance work. Job enlargement meant increased scope for initiative and skill; it up-graded the job and increased both the earnings of the workers and the productivity of the process. Job enlargement is an aspect of policies for the improved use of manpower (⟡ Manpower Planning) and is closely associated with selection and training. ⟡ Selection; Industrial Training; Job Restructuring. L.S.

L. E. Davis and J. C. Taylor (eds.), *Design of Jobs* (Penguin, 1972); J. Child, *Organization: A Guide to Problems and Practice* (Harper & Row, 1984), ch. 2.

Job Enrichment ⟡ Job Restructuring

Job Evaluation The comparison of jobs through formal and systematic procedures in order to determine the position of one job relative to another in a wage or salary hierarchy.

Job evaluation is essentially concerned with relationships and not absolutes. It provides data for developing basic pay structures but cannot determine what the pay levels should be. It is the job that is evaluated, not the job's current occupant. Job evaluation methods do, however, depend to some extent on a series of subjective judgements made in the light of concepts like logic, justice and equity, and the progressive refinement of job evaluation techniques is in large measure an attempt to minimize the subjective personal element.

Before embarking on job evaluation it is advisable to undertake ⟡ Job Analysis in order to gain detailed knowledge of the requirements and specifications of the jobs under review. Once this has been done it will then be possible to decide which particular job evaluation scheme is most suitable. The size and complexity of the graded job hierarchy that emerges, and ultimately of the revised pay structure (⟡ Wage Systems) that is the end-product of the whole exercise, depend upon the type of job evaluation adopted.

There are four main types of job evaluation in common use:

(1) *Ranking*. This method is simple and non-quantitative. It aims to determine the importance of a job by descriptive comparison with

another. Under this approach a few 'key' jobs tend to determine the rank of all the others. The advantages are that it is easily understood and administered but, on the other hand, it has no defined standards of judgement, it becomes increasingly difficult to apply as the range of jobs widens (i.e. as the firm grows) and leaves the assessors more open to influence by the current occupants of the jobs under review.

(2) *Grading.* Basically the same as (1) except that with ranking the number of grades and their pay levels are determined *after* the jobs have been evaluated and ranked, whereas under the grading system the order is reversed.

(3) *Factor comparison.* Examines jobs in terms of selected factors such as mental, physical and skill requirements, responsibility and working conditions. 'Key' jobs are examined factor by factor and a rank order produced for each factor used. An attempt is then made to establish how much of the current wage rate of each key job is being paid for each factor. The total rate for all the other jobs is similarly determined by the sum of the individual factor values. The criteria employed under this method are more objective but it is complex, difficult to explain to those affected, and is arbitrary in the way in which existing wage rates are ascribed to different factors.

(4) *Points rating.* Also analyses jobs in terms of a number of components but here the results are expressed in numerical rather than monetary rank-order. This method utilizes a wider and more flexible range of factors, each of which is allocated a set of points. A total points' score then determines the position of each job in a hierarchy, at the same time indicating numerically the relationship between one job and another. One big advantage here is that the processes of money wage fixing and job evaluation are clearly separated, since the translation of points into money values is a distinct process.

Analytical methods like (3) and (4) obviously allow a finer distinction to be drawn between jobs and so provide a more acceptable basis for showing whether jobs that have changed in content should also change in pay. Control over the wage structure is thus made easier. One of the basic causes of wage inflation (⟡ Wage Drift) is that ⟡ Workplace Bargaining so often takes place on a piecemeal, fragmented basis, giving rise to anomalies and compensatory counter-claims from individual work groups. Job evaluation means the comparison of jobs, not people by systematic analysis, to determine their place in a hierarchy and thus offers a basis for a structure of pay that can at least be presented as rational. Job evaluation, therefore, forces on management the same disciplined approach to personnel problems as is required in other spheres. Conversely, for the employee, job evaluation means that increase in skills and responsibility can be rewarded and recognized.

From the evidence gathered by the Ministry of Labour in a survey (June 1967) it is clear that job evaluation is used predominantly by large firms. Some 23 per cent of the 6,431,100 employees covered had their pay grade determined by job evaluation, but these were employed in only 9 per cent of all establishments. Only 6·4 per cent of firms with less than 500 employees used job evaluation, compared with 32·2 per cent for firms with over 500. Industries like timber, construction, printing, shipbuilding and leather goods, where job relationships seem deeply rooted in tradition and craftsmen are numerous, are those that are least affected by job evaluation. The NBPI *Report No. 83* found that job evaluation is applied most widely to the 'managerial' occupational group (30 per cent of the workers covered in the survey) followed by staff (27 per cent) and non-craft workers (26 per cent). The smallest coverage was of craftsmen (11 per cent). Coal-mining, a single-employer industry, and tobacco manufacture, an industry dominated by a few large companies, are the two industries in which job evaluation is most widespread. N.H.C.

NBPI *Report No. 83*, and Statistical Supplement, *Job Evaluation*, Cmnd. 3772 (HMSO, 1968).

Job Restructuring Job restructuring is concerned with job and work changes, i.e. the modification of the tasks and involvement of individuals. Restructuring that leads to the addition of further similar tasks is often referred to as job enlargement and can be seen as a horizontal change. Vertical changes involve increased individual involvement, perhaps through the addition of different tasks and duties. Such changes are generally referred to as job enrichment.

Job restructuring, i.e. individual work and job changes, should be distinguished from organizational changes that generally concentrate on groups of workers (⟡ Group Working) or aim to provide increased job variety for individuals without the modification of jobs, e.g. job rotation. Such organizational changes will often give rise to some form of job restructuring – indeed, in many cases job restructuring is possible only as a consequence of organizational changes. R.W.

R. Wild, *Work Organization* (J. Wiley, 1975).

Job Rotation ⟡ Job Restructuring

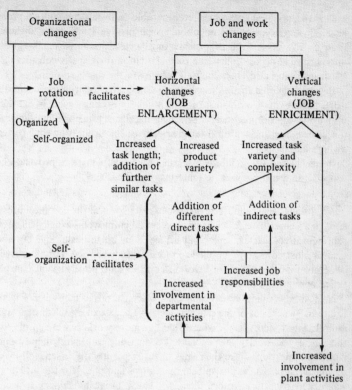

Types of job restructuring

Job Specification ⇨ Job Analysis

Jobbing Production Jobbing type production is concerned with the simultaneous manufacture of a series of different products in very small or unit batch sizes to customer orders.

Because of the differing and often unique nature of the products, a jobbing shop is normally characterized by the following:

(1) General-purpose production equipment.
(2) Equipment arranged according to the type of work performed (layout by process).
(3) Differing sequence of operations for each product.
(4) Large range of operation times for different operations and jobs and inaccurate prediction of individual operation times.

Items (3) and (4) give rise to considerable planning and control problems. Production control in jobbing type production is more difficult than in any other type of production. Accurate scheduling is almost impossible, and the sequencing or dispatching problem is considerable (⟡ Sequencing and Dispatching Problems).

Because of the difficulty in planning and control a situation normally exists where high work-in-progress stock is accompanied by under-utilization of equipment, and products require a total production time (i.e. processing and waiting) far greater than the processing time (often as high as 10:1).

Items (1) and (2) facilitate ⟡ Plant Layout, supervision, provision of services, etc., but complicate materials handling. R.W.

Joint Consultation The process of discussion of the common problems of an enterprise between employers and employees, usually through representatives. It takes place at all levels of an undertaking, but the term is most commonly applied to meetings between the representatives of senior managment and of workers on the shop floor in joint consultative committees or works councils.

In a survey made in Britain in 1980, consultative committees were found in 37 per cent of the establishments. The size of establishment was an influential factor, since where 1,000 or more workers were employed the figure was nearly 80 per cent. Production, employment, pay and working conditions were the issues most frequently discussed, followed by welfare services, health and safety matters and plans for the future. It was about four times more likely for consultative machinery to exist alongside ⟡ Collective Bargaining than on its own, and there was often some overlap in the issues dealt with by the two systems.

Joint consultation became more widespread in the early 1980s. A Confederation of British Industry survey in 1981 found that 17 per cent of existing councils or joint consultative committees had been introduced during the previous three years. It has been suggested that the economic recession made joint consultation more important to companies that needed to make radical changes in order to survive, and to employees worried about their future and desirous of influencing the policies adopted to cope with change. E.L.

W. W. Daniel and N. Millward, *Workplace Industrial Relations in Britain* (Heinemann Educational, 1983); *Current Employee Involvement Practice* (CBI, 1981); R. C. Adains, *Participation Today* (IPA, 1984). P. Brannen, *Authority and Participation in Industry* (Batsford, 1983).

Joint Consultative Committee ⟡ Joint Consultation

Joint Industrial Council A collective bargaining and/or consultative committee for an industry or public service with a constitution based on the model laid down by the Whitley Committee, which was set up by the government in 1916. Hence some Joint Industrial Councils are known as Whitley Councils (⟡ Collective Bargaining; Joint Consultation).

During the First World War the government became concerned about industrial unrest, much of which seemed to stem from the unofficial shop stewards' movement (⟡ Industrial Democracy; Trade Union Types – Industrial Union; Shop Steward). It therefore set up the Whitley Committee to make suggestions for improving relations between employers and employees. The Committee proposed the formation of Joint Industrial Councils at industry level and Works Committees at the workplace, both representative of managements and employees; the extension of statutory wage regulation in industries badly organized in terms of trade unions and employers' associations (⟡ Wages Councils); the setting up of a permanent court of arbitration; and the authorization of governmental inquiry into disputes (⟡ Industrial Dispute). The policy suggested was adopted, although Joint Industrial Councils were not set up in industries where adequate collective bargaining arrangements existed. There are today some 200 Joint Industrial Councils or bodies of a similar character.

Although largely based on a model constitution, Joint Industrial Councils present considerable variety in structure, in their degree of authority in the industry, and in the nature and extent of their activities. While a few councils deal only with the negotiation of wages and conditions, most have at some time dealt with other matters. Conversely, there are examples of councils that do not negotiate wages. Among the matters dealt with are research, welfare, health and safety, and training, including apprenticeship. In some Joint Industrial Council industries there are District Councils, which may have a limited amount of local autonomy.

Joint Industrial Councils with District Councils have been established for local authorities in England and Wales, one each for white-collar and manual workers. There is a National Whitley Council together with Departmental Councils for the administrative and legal department of the Civil Service and, for government industrial employees, a council for each of the main employing departments. Food manufacture provides a private sector example. Sometimes there is a failure to agree on Joint Industrial Councils. The Food Manufacturing JIC, the Bacon Curing JIC, the Slaughtering Industry JIC, and the Cocoa, Chocolate and

Confectionery JIC all failed to agree, for example, in 1980. In those cases, there may be intervention by ACAS. N.H.C., amended by M.J.F.P.

Industrial Relations Handbook (HMSO, rev. ed., 1965); W. Brown and K. Sisson, 'Current Trends and Future Possibilities', in M. Poole *et al.*, *Industrial Relations in the Future* (Routledge & Kegan Paul, 1984).

Joint Stock Company ◊ Company Law

'Just in Time' Production A scheduling procedure used in production to ensure that each item is made only when it is required, thus reducing all stock levels. For example, if purchased materials can be scheduled to arrive when required for production, then input stocks need not be held. If items are made only when required for a subsequent process, work-in-progress stocks can be reduced. If goods are made when required for delivery, output stocks can be eliminated. This manufacturing policy requires accurate scheduling and strict adherence to schedules, since little 'buffer' exists in the system. The benefits are reduced inventories, costs and throughput times. Frequently the implementation of this approach necessitates the reduction of production batch sizes, the use of mixed-model production and the employment of flexible manufacturing systems. The approach was pioneered in Japan and is now being pursued in many discrete-parts manufacturing industries throughout the world. ◊◊ Flexible Manufacturing System. R.W.

K

Kanban A production scheduling and inventory control system, developed and widely used in Japan (for example by Toyota). Based upon a simple card system, the Kanban procedure, especially when used with ⟡ 'Just in Time' Production, helps minimize work-in-progress and throughput times. R.W.

C. Lorenz, 'Learning from the Japanese' *Financial Times* (1981); J. W. Rice and T. Yoshikawa, in *Production and Inventory Management* (first quarter, 1982).

L

Laboratory Training A method of training in interpersonal and intergroup relationships that consists of a temporary (and often residential) community of persons who undergo a series of planned experiences in a social atmosphere that supports personal experiment and learning. A frequent feature of laboratory training is the T-group ⟡⟩ Group Methods of Training, but other more structured activities may also be used. I.C.MCG.

Labour Relations ⟡ **Industrial Relations**

Labour Stability ⟡ **Labour Turnover**

Labour Turnover An index of the number of people who leave an enterprise in a given period as a percentage of the average number of people employed during that period. The standard formula for calculating labour turnover is:

$$\frac{\text{Number of separations during the period}}{\text{Average number employed during period}} \times \frac{100}{1} \times \frac{12}{x}$$

In certain circumstances labour turnover may be an index of the effectiveness of company policy in personnel matters. If there is a high *overall* figure in an establishment, with all departments and categories of workers affected to a similar degree, then some fundamental defects in pay, recruitment, training and promotion are highly likely. But this situation is almost hypothetical and it is far more common for a particular department or a particular class of employee within a firm to display a significantly higher rate of turnover than others, and here the nature of the work undertaken is the key factor.

In the vast majority of firms unskilled workers have an annual rate of turnover that is markedly higher than their skilled colleagues, female workers have a higher rate than male, and young workers a higher rate than their seniors. Departments like the foundry and the canteen may always, by their very nature, be unable to retain more than a relatively low percentage of their workforce for any length of time. In these circumstances personnel policies can have little more than a purely marginal effect on labour turnover. Because of social and family pre-occupations female labour is notoriously unstable, so that industries employing relatively large proportions of women, such as textiles and the distributive trades, tend to have relatively high average rates of turn-over irrespective of the quality of individual personnel management. This high turnover tends to keep wages down and often prevents trade unions from achieving a sufficient level of organization in an establish-ment to achieve much in the way of improved conditions, all of which in turn promotes labour instability. In the four weeks ending 15 September 1984, for example, the following labour turnover figures were recorded:

Industry	Number of engagements per 100 employed at beginning of period			Number of discharges per 100 employed at beginning of period		
	Males	Females	Total	Males	Females	Total
Food, drink, tobacco	1·8	3·4	2·4	2·5	3·4	2·9
Chemical	1·2	2·3	1·5	1·2	2·7	1·7
Metal manufacture	1·5	1·8	1·5	1·4	1·9	1·5
Electrical engineering	1·7	2·3	1·9	1·4	2·2	1·7
Vehicles and parts	1·0	1·9	1·1	1·0	2·2	1·2
Textiles	1·7	2·7	2·2	1·9	2·5	2·2
Clothing/footwear	1·7	2·5	2·3	2·0	2·4	2·3
Paper/printing	1·0	2·3	1·4	1·0	2·2	1·4

Source: Employment Gazette, November 1984, Table 1.6.

High labour turnover and low stability indices bring to light the number and kind of replacements that a company is having to make. Replacement, which means finding, selecting and training new em-ployees, is expensive and adds appreciably to labour costs. Thus in order to discover the causes of wastage many firms have systematic interviews with all leavers. An analysis of the results provides evidence that may lead to changes in personnel policy. In other words, more and more personnel managers are approaching the problem of labour turnover with the object in mind of maximizing retention rates. The one sure way to reduce high rates of turnover is to strengthen the incentives for em-ployees to keep their current jobs.

High turnover can have a bad effect on the morale of the remainder of the workforce, especially that of supervisory staff. It is important, there-fore, to distinguish between the loss of newly hired workers and of long-serving employees. The key index is the proportion of workers who stay with the firm for an appreciable time.

One of the most common reasons for high turnover is the division of responsibility between those who engage labour and those who manage it. Foremen and supervisors, for example, frequently complain that they are sent unsuitable people. One way of tackling turnover in the larger firms, therefore, would appear to be the appointment of a manager with specific responsibilities for the 'nursing' of new labour. N.H.C. and E.L.

Central Information Service, *The Analysis and Control of Labour Turnover* (1972); M. Pilch, *Labour Turnover: What It Costs and How to Do Something About It* (Noble Lowndes, 1973).

Language Efficient communication depends largely upon the existence and use of an appropriate language, whether the communication is between human beings or between operators and machines. Languages for human communication exhibit an enormous complexity: their vocabularies are large and the rules by which words can be assembled into meaningful utterances are many. Over and above the questions of literal meaning are the further complications associated with the emotive overtones of statements, and the aesthetic value of certain word juxtapositions.

Apart from the natural languages, extensive use is made of other information sources during person–person communication, such as the interpretation of posture and gesture. Other indirect means of communication between people involve special-purpose symbol systems such as those used in mathematics, musical notation, maps and engineering drawings. Very little research has yet been done in an attempt to study the efficiency of such language systems or to produce superior ones.

The study of language in the context of operator–machine communication is still in its infancy, but will certainly occupy an ever-increasing role in human-factors studies as technological innovation proceeds. Obvious examples of areas where some progress has already been made include telephone dialling codes, aircraft instrumentation and computer autocodes.

The existence of an appropriate language facilitates not only efficient person–person or operator–machine communication but also contributes a good deal to the way in which an individual can handle problems. Mathematics provides a ready example. It is a simple matter to evaluate the sum $134 + 69$ using the familar Arabic notation, but extremely difficult to solve the same problem translated into Roman notation, CXXXIV + LXIX. E.E.

Lateral Integration ◊ Patterns of Growth

Lead Time ◇ Inventory or Stock-control Problems

Leadership J. M. Burns has defined the process of leadership as 'leaders inducing followers to act for certain goals that represent the values and the motivations – the wants and needs, the aspirations and expectations – of both leaders and followers'.

Leadership is important for the success of any group activity, although the nature or style of the leadership needed in one situation may differ substantially from that required in another. Traditionally leadership has tended to be equated with autocratic command and there are still many who see leadership mainly in terms of the issuing of orders which are eagerly obeyed by followers whose loyalty is largely determined by the ◇ Charisma of the leader. An earlier generation of social psychologists devoted much time to endeavouring to indentify those specific traits of character or personality that distinguished leaders from followers. The attempt was unsuccessful and attention has since been directed towards the conception of leadership as a process rather than as a particular pattern of personality traits.

To understand a leader's behaviour, and to judge its effectiveness, one has to take into account the leader's traits and skills, the situation in which leadership is being exercised, and the goals being pursued. The situation may be influenced by economic or political factors external to the business, or internally by such factors as the technology, the organizational culture or the aspirations of subordinates. These in turn can modify the impact of the leader's behaviour by affecting the leader's power, the efforts made by subordinates and the way in which work is organized.

It is now recognized that an effective leader needs to possess a variety of skills that can be learned and applied to technical, political, cultural and human problems affecting the enterprise (◇ Interpersonal Skill Development; Group Methods of Training). Leaders can also enhance their own effectiveness by choosing groups of subordinates whose attributes complement their own traits and skills, enabling them to work well together as a team whilst performing a variety of necessary roles. Several cases have now been documented of an effective leader, supported by a carefully selected team, being able to transform an organization by setting new goals and making major changes in its internal political system, its human resources and its culture. ◇ Teams. E.L.

J. M. Burns, *Leadership* (Harper & Row, 1978); G. A. Yuki, *Leadership in Organizations* (Prentice-Hall, 1981); W. Bennis and B. Nanus, *Leaders* (Harper & Row, 1985).

Learning and Training In view of the variety of different occupational skills that personnel are called upon to acquire, it is impossible to lay down a set of simple and comprehensive rules by which training programmes should be devised. None the less there are some general principles of human learning that must be observed in the development of any training programme.

Little or no improvement will result from unmotivated trainees. Appropriate incentives, such as cash rewards, promotion prospects or the attainment of status and reputation, may serve as methods for producing an adequate motivational level.

Generally speaking, learning will be facilitated by short periods of instruction followed by rest or at least a relief from novelty. As skill is acquired, the length of the training session may be increased.

It is essential that trainees should be provided with information about their achievement. This should be accurate and comprehensive and should be given as soon as possible after each trial. One of the advantages of using automatic machines as trainers is the speed and precision with which they may display results of trials.

In many cases it is advisable to present the trainee with an overall view of the total task before detailed instruction about the individual task elements is provided. In this way, the trainee is able to build up a correct view of the whole skill and bring about an appropriate synthesis of the elements when these have been learned. In certain types of skilled activity this synthesis (perhaps involving elements of timing) is the essence of successful performance.

Habit interference occurs when practice at one activity brings about a decrement in another. This may be minimized by making as different as possible both inputs and ouputs which might be confused. Consistency in training procedures similarly minimizes interference. Thus meticulous standardization is required when, for example, several different instructors contribute to a training programme.

There is a good deal of evidence to contradict the widely held misconception that older people cannot benefit from training. It is, however, usually the case that more time is required by an older person to acquire new knowledge and skills. ⟡ Industrial Training. E.E.

R. B. Stammers and J. Patrick, *The Psychology of Training* (Methuen, 1975).

Leasing A lease contract is one where a lessor agrees to hire an asset to a lessee for a sum of money – a rent. The lessor retains ownership but conveys the right to use the asset to the lessee.

A 'finance lease' is one that substantially transfers all the risks and rewards of ownership of an asset to the lessee. The economic substance of a finance lease has led the Accounting Standards Committee to issue an accounting standard (*SSAP.21*) requiring lessee companies to treat leased assets as 'owned' and to record both the value of such assets and the liability for future lease payments in the balance sheet. Prior to the issue of this accounting standard it was common practice for lessees to treat finance leases as 'off balance sheet' items.

Leases other than finance leases are known as 'operating leases'. J.V.P.

> Accounting Standards Committee, *SSAP.21 Accounting for Leases and Hire Purchase Contracts* (August 1984).

Leverage ◊ Capital Structure

Liability ◊ Claims

Library (Computer) ◊ Hardware/Liveware/Software

Lighting ◊ Illumination

Line and Staff (1) Line functions are those that are specifically charged with the responsibility for directly achieving the objectives of the organization. Staff functions are those responsible for assisting the line. This classification by function seems gradually to be losing favour as the closely interdependent nature of the various functions in the organization is increasingly recognized. Given such interdependence, it seems neither logical nor useful to attempt to classify departments according to their implied contribution to the attainment of organizational objectives. Accordingly many writers now regard the description of some functions as primary, with the relegation of others to secondary status, as more likely to lead to confusion than to clarity in the analysis of organizational relationships. I.C.McG.

Line and Staff (2) A line relationship is the authority relationship between superior and subordinate in the chain of command. A staff relationship is a service or advisory relationship. These usages derive from a (mistaken) analogy with military organization. The concept of a line relationship is reasonably unambiguous, but in military as well as in industrial organization non-line relationships are too complex to permit the use of a single classificatory term. A production department, for example, is likely to interact with the maintenance department, production scheduling, progress department, budget control, personnel department and so on. It would seem very probable that each relationship so established would differ significantly from each of the others. Organization theory, however, has not yet developed a terminology that gives recognition to these differences. The existence of staff relationships violates the principle of unity of command although this violation has been obscured by the insistence that, in theory, such relationships are advisory. Recently, however, there has been a greater willingness to recognize that many 'advisory' relationships involve functional authority and that organizational difficulties frequently result from the failure to make this explicit. ⟨⟩ Authority; Chain of Command; Functional (1). I.C.MCG.

W. Brown, *Exploration in Management* (Heinemann, 1960); J. Child, *Organization: A Guide to Problems and Practice* (Harper & Row, 1984), ch. 3.

Linear Programming ⟨⟩ Mathematical Programming

Liquidity ⟨⟩ Ratios, Financial

Liveware ⟨⟩ Hardware/Liveware/Software

Location of Industry and Regional Problems The depressed economic conditions of the 1930s in the UK drew attention to the plight of several areas dependent upon old-established industries such as coal, iron and steel, textiles and shipbuilding. The problem of these areas was that their basic industries were depressed and alternative employment opportunities rare. The table below illustrates that in the 1980s the problem has recurred and there is a continuing disparity in regional unemployment.

The location of an industrial enterprise depends upon two sets of costs: transport costs and processing costs. Transport costs cover the cost of transporting materials and fuel to the point of manufacture and transporting the finished product to the market. Processing costs depend upon the cost of raw materials, labour, capital equipment and managerial expertise. On the whole there is little evidence of regional variation in processing costs and thus location has been determined in the past by the incidence of transport costs. The majority of our old-established industries are materials-dominated and hence were located close to coal, iron ore and adequate water supplies. On the other hand the new and growing

Percentage unemployed (including school-leavers) by region, May 9 1985

United Kingdom	13.4
South-east	9·8
East Anglia	10·6
South-west	11·8
East Midlands	12·7
West Midlands	15·4
Yorkshire and Humberside	14·9
North-west	16·2
North	18·8
Wales	16·8
Scotland	15·4
Northern Ireland	20·8

Source: Employment Gazette (June 1985).

industries have been freed from the coalfields by the development of new fuels and since, on the whole, transport costs to the market have dominated, they have settled close to the large centres of population in the Midlands and the South-east. Thus, we have the present situation of areas of high unemployment with too little diversification, too much labour and too few jobs. This has meant that when the rest of the economy is booming, Development Areas, as they are sometimes called, are just beginning to grow and hence they suffer when brakes to the economy are imposed.

Since the 1930s government policy has varied both in the amount and type of aid and the areas to which it has been applied. Following the White Paper *Regional Industrial Development* (Cmnd. 9111) and the submissions received in response to it, a 'new' approach to regional problems was launched in November 1984 under the 1982 Industrial Development Act. This takes account of the criticisms of previous policy, which included the extravagance of the existing system, the lack of emphasis on job creation and a dislike of the primacy given to automatic grants. The new policy, according to the Industry Minister, aims to be more cost-effective, putting more emphasis on job creation and reducing the current bias towards capital-intensive investment.

The new policy creates two categories of assisted area, replacing the previous three-tier system, and extends the coverage to 35 per cent of the working population. Intermediate Areas will be eligible for selective regional assistance, whilst Development Areas will be eligible for the new regional development grants as well. Thus automatic grants are being concentrated on the areas of greatest need (15 per cent of the working population). The new rate of capital grant is set at 15 per cent but there is to be a ceiling of £10,000 for each new job created. Alternatively, labour-intensive projects will receive a grant as a fixed sum for each job created, currently set at £3,000. In addition certain service activities will now be eligible for regional development grants. The effect of the new policy is that in 1987/88 it is expected that expenditure on regional industrial incentives will total nearly £400m, some £300m less than if present policies had continued. L.T.S.

> G. Gudgin *et al.*, 'Urban and Regional Policy', *Cambridge Economic Policy Review* (December 1982).

Lock-out Defined by the ◇ Industrial Relations Act 1971, repealed 1974, as 'action which, in contemplation of furtherance of an ◇ Industrial Dispute, is taken by one or more employers, whether parties to the dispute or not, and which consists of the exclusion of workers from one or more factories, offices or other places of work in one or more such places or of the collective, simultaneous or otherwise connected termination or suspension of employment of a group of workers'.

The Act laid down that dismissal by way of a lock-out was a fair, not an unfair, industrial practice (◇ Unfair Dismissal) as long as the person concerned was offered re-engagement. The ◇ Trade Union and Labour Relations Act 1974 contains a provision similar in principle.

In practice it may be difficult to distinguish a lock-out from a strike when trade unionists claim that they are locked out of work and employers claim that their employees are not entitled to be on the work premises since they have taken strike or other action in an attempt to settle an ◇ Industrial Dispute.

The incidence of lock-outs varies by industry, country and time. Britain experienced a high incidence in the nineteenth century, especially in those industries with a tough industrial-relations environment, like coal-mining. ◇ Strike – Causes, Forms, Remedies, Statistics. N.H.C.

Lot Sizes ◇ Batch Sizes

Loudness ◇ Hearing; Noise

M

Machine Assignment and Interference When several machines are assigned to the care of one operator, if two or more of the machines require the operator's attention at the same time, machine interference occurs and waiting time results. This can be expressed as follows:

a = Combined work-time per cycle for operator and machine
    (e.g. working together, setting, loading, etc.)
b = Operator independent work-time per cycle
t = Machine independent work-time per cycle
n = Number of machines
n^1 = Ideal n

If a, b and t are constant then ideally

$$n^1 = \frac{a + t}{a + b}$$

machines must be assigned to the operator. However, where any or all of these values are not stable and/or where n^1 is not an integer, interference is usually unavoidable.

The effect of such interferences, as with any other delay, is to reduce or limit output. Consequently some measure of interference must be available for (1) inclusion as an allowance in the calculation of standard times in ⟡ Work Measurement (⟡ Allowances); (2) use in production planning.

Given certain assumptions about the nature of variables a, b and t, analytical methods may be used to determine working time, least-cost assignment, etc. Alternatively direct-time studies and/or work sampling can be used to determine machine interference, which often accounts for from 10 to 35 per cent of the total time required. R.W.

H. B. Maynard, (ed.), *Handbook of Industrial Engineering* (McGraw-Hill, 3rd ed., 1971).

Machine Controls Devices for providing information or energy for a machine. Typical controls include pedals, joysticks, switches, hand-wheels and knobs.

The ideal control for any specific application is a function of its purpose and conditions of use. The relevant variables to be considered include the speed, range, direction, frequency, duration, precision and force for which control movements are called. Thus cranks are suitable for high rates of rotation and where a wide range of adjustment is required with a fairly heavy load. If, however, the load is light, the extent of the range is fairly small and accurate adjustment is called for, then a knob is probably more suitable. The relative merits of various control devices, together with detailed design recommendations, are well documented.

The correct grouping of machine controls in a cab is of utmost importance in order to ensure that an operator is able to use the controls either simultaneously or in swift succession as required. In such a situation a proper system of coding, based upon position, size, colour or shape, will assist in the avoidance of mistaken operation. In certain cases, a device to avoid inadvertent operation of certain controls is desirable.

Certain associations are generally expected between directions of control movement and the corresponding machine response. An upwards control movement, for example, is usually associated with an upward, forward or increasing response. These expected relationships should, as far as possible, be maintained.

Similarly, there are expected relationships between control movements and resulting display changes. Both qualitative and quantitative aspects require careful attention (⟡ Machine Dynamics; Stereotypes).

Frequently the same physical component serves as both display and control. In this case, special problems arise from competing requirements of the two uses. Design decisions should only be made with full knowledge of the limitations imposed by a compromise solution. E.E.

E. J. McCormick and M. S. Sanders, *Human Factors in Engineering and Design* (McGraw-Hill, 5th ed., 1983).

Machine Dynamics Effective ergonomic design of an operator–machine system must concentrate on three areas of the system: the interface that serves as an input to the human operator (⟡ Displays); the interface at the machine input (⟡ Machine Controls); the properties of the hardware system that determine the relationship between its inputs and displayed outputs. To facilitate operator–machine effectiveness, both

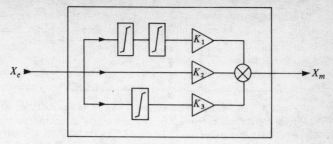

Figure 1. The dynamics of an acceleration-aided system. The relation between the control output, X_c, and the machine output, X_m, is given by the equation

$$X_m = k_2 X_c + k_3 \int X_c \, dt + k_1 \int\!\int X_c \, dt$$

the qualitative and the quantitative aspects of machine dynamics (◊ Stereotypes) should be engineered to suit the relevant characteristics of the human controller.

In the case of a simple linear relationship between control and display movements, the critical design factor is the ratio between control displacement and corresponding display movement. Optimization of this ratio may reduce positioning time by several seconds.

The introduction of more sophisticated control mechanisms brings about the need to satisfy numerous design criteria dictated by the characteristics of human performance. Time-lags in human response of the order of half a second or so are typical, and are dependent upon the sensory modality of the signal input, its intensity, its uncertainty (◊ Information Theory), its duration, its complexity and several other factors.

The functional relationship between machine input and display output requires careful design attention. In many tracking tasks, such as those associated with vehicle guidance or process control, the relation between control movement and corresponding display movement may be nonlinear. An example of one such system is illustrated in figure 1. Here the machine output comprises a summation of three functions that are related to the input signals by amplification factors (K_1, K_2, K_3) and/or time integrals. The ratio of the amplication factors in such a system (in this case it is an acceleration-aided control system) must be established empirically, being dependent upon the type of signal input, the properties of the control elements, etc.

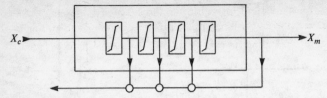

Figure 2. A fourth-order control system in which four signals are mixed to provide the feedback to the display. This 'quickening' makes the operator's control task much easier

Should there of necessity be three or more stages of integration relating the movement of a control element and the consequent system response, control performance is greatly enhanced by the application of quickening, i.e. the production of a contrived display fed from a number of sources within the system, suitably combined. A quickened fourth-order system is illustrated in figure 2. E.E.

Macro-economic Models Macro-economic models, as their name implies, are the formal representation of economists' notions about the determination of such macro variables as consumption expenditures, investment expenditures and total employment. As such they are relevant to government policy-making, quite apart from their role in economics. Whilst a considerable number of models have now been built for various countries, only one country, Holland, has incorporated a full model into its planning procedure. In other countries part of a model is sometimes in use, although this does not always imply the existence of a full model.

The purpose of such models is twofold. On the one hand they tell us about the behaviour of groups in the economy such as consumers and producers who are simultaneously acting together. On the other hand they can tell us something about the likely path of certain key variables in the future.

The simplest type of model that will serve for illustrative purposes is given below. It consists of a consumption function, equation (1), and the national income identity, equation (2), there being no government or foreign-trade sector.

$$C_t = a + B Y_t \tag{1}$$
$$Y_t = C_t + I_t \tag{2}$$

where C_t = purchases of consumption goods
I_t = purchases of investment goods
Y_t = aggregate output (= income), all at time t

These two equations are called the structural equations of the model because they explain the structure of all or part of the economy. As it stands, however, knowledge of a and B will not enable us to determine C_t, I_t and Y_t because we have too many variables and too few equations. Suppose, however, we assume that investment decisions are given by some process unrelated to economic conditions. Then we say that investment is an exogenous variable, because it is determined outside our model. Now we are left with two variables to be determined by the model, C_t and Y_t, and we term these variables endogenous variables. Solution of (1) and (2) will yield values for C_t, and Y_t, determined by a, B and I_t.

$$C_t = \frac{a}{1 - B} + \frac{B}{1 - B} T_t \tag{3}$$

$$Y_t = \frac{a}{1 - B} + \frac{1}{1 - B} I_t \tag{4}$$

For obvious reasons these two equations are called the *reduced-form* equations.

This model has only been used for illustrative purposes. If we are interested in the behaviour of consumers then we need the structural version of the model. If, however, we are interested in tracing the impact of a change in I_t, then we must use the reduced-form version.

Realistic models of advanced economies may require many hundreds of equations, depending upon the degree of disaggregation. In addition, many endogenous variables in equations such as (1) will be found to depend upon lagged variables as well as current variables. In all cases, however, their purpose is to show the structural and reduced-form relationships. Problems of data collection and estimation abound but this is no argument against the models themselves, but rather a stimulus to improvement, for the government and other users of these models will thereby see more clearly the implications of alternative policies. ⟡ Model (in Economic Analysis); Economics. L.T.S.

R. L. Thomas, *Introductory Econometrics* (Longman, 1985), Ch. 11.

Mail Order The process by which manufacturers or wholesalers sell to their customers, using postal or delivery services to effect distribution (⟡ Distribution Mix). In Britain this business is most commonly conducted through female, part-time agents, who pass catalogues amongst potential customers and act as a distribution point. The method more common in North America, and which is growing in Britain, involves the use of small key advertisements in newspapers, etc. The telephone is also increasingly being used in addition to letter post for the placing of orders. ⬙ Retailing. G.S.C.W.

Maintenance The various activities involved in keeping equipment or a system in working order, or in returning equipment or a system to working order.

In practice equipment is expected to break down and/or require attention; consequently an operational definition of maintenance must involve the concept of reliability, that is, it must ensure at minimum cost that equipment operates at a certain level of reliability or increase the reliability of equipment.

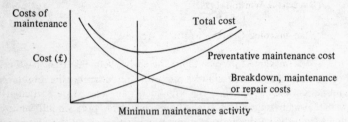

Reliability of equipment can be retained or improved by:
(1)   Improvements in equipment design.
(2)   Use of a sufficiently large repair department to minimize breakdown time.
(3)   The use of preventive maintenance to minimize breakdowns.
   In addition reliability of a production system can be improved by:
(4)   Sufficient work in progress between production stages to minimize the probability that the breakdown of equipment at one stage will affect production at successive stages.
(5)   Provision of duplicate equipment or excess capacity.

Only (2) and (3) above are direct approaches to ensuring or improving reliability. There will always be a need for a repair or breakdown function since, even with ⬙ Preventive Maintenance, breakdowns will still occur. The object is to minimize total maintenance cost by:
(1)   Determining, often for each piece of equipment, the optimum relationship between breakdown and preventive maintenance, from (a) a distribution of breakdowns obtained either from records, other users or manufacturers, and (b) the relative total costs of preventive and breakdown maintenance for the equipment or system.
(2)   Determining the optimum amount of replacement or repair work

to undertake as a result of, or to prevent, a breakdown. When failure occurs or is expected in a component the following alternatives are available: (a) replacement of that component only; (b) replacement of that and all similar components; (c) replacement of that component and selected others (e.g. those exceeding mean life). Optimum policy may be determined by means of simulation or from cost and life data.

(3)   Determining optimum staff requirements, i.e. balancing the cost of staff with the cost of waiting for maintenance, either from records or perhaps by using simulation or queuing theory. R.W.

R. Wild, *Techniques of Production Management* (Holt, Rinehart & Winston, 1971); R. Wild, *Production and Operations Management* (Holt, Rinehart & Winston, 1984).

Man–machine Chart ◊ Multiple Activity Chart

Man–machine Interface Since the early 1960s this term has been widely used in the ergonomics literature to describe the points of contact between people and the equipment they use. More particularly writers have in mind two types of boundary: those at which information flows from the hardware to the operator (displays); and those at which the operator provides the information to the machine (controls). Much of ergonomics has consisted of efforts to avoid procrustean approaches to the design of interfaces and to introduce ways in which the characteristics of human performance are systematically taken into account.

In the 1980s the term has acquired a particular connotation due to its use within the government-sponsored research effort in ◊ Information Technology (the Alvey Programme). In this context there has been a shift of emphasis towards the engineering development of such specific devices as pattern recognizers, and of speech recognizers to allow direct voice input. ◊ Information System. E.E.

Man–machine System ◊ Ergonomics

Management Accounting The provision of information required by management in the formulation of policies, the planning and control of business activities, and the selection of appropriate courses of action from available opportunities (◊ Accounting).

The accounting system consists of the store of information derived from the application of *accounting method* (◊ Accounting System) to the analysis of financial data from past *transactions and events* relating to that organization and its exchange and production activities.

A more comprehensive definition of the nature of management accounting, which will serve also as a foundation for developing an efficient accounting function within enterprises, may be based upon the following five complementary aspects:

(1)   Regarded as a method of processing financial information to satisfy the needs of the decision-maker who is concerned with the achievement of organizational objectives, in the context of an uncertain situation.

(2)   Regarded as a kind of statistical technique in which data relating to transactions and events is observed, tabulated, analysed and presented for purposes of decision and control.

(3)   Considered in its relationship to other disciplines and techniques required for the construction of effective accounting systems and functions.

(4)   Considered in relation to the practices and conventions of the accountancy profession, at any given time, and their relevance to organizational purposes.

(5)   Considered as an application of the 'duality principle' to the construction of accounting systems and statements.

In a historical context the term management accounting has originated from the need to distinguish its requirements from those of traditional financial accounting with its emphasis upon reporting parties external to enterprises. This traditional approach, with its preoccupation with 'stewardship' accounting, has resulted in a rather haphazard and partly conflicting collection of conventions, definitions and principles, which often have little relevance to the needs of enterprise management (⟡ Accountancy Conventions).

In contrast, the motivating ideas of management accounting are (1) that accounting measurements only make sense in the light of the objectives and purposes stated for that particular calculation; (2) that accounting figures can only be justified in terms of the insight that they give to the present situation and to future action; (3) that accounting analyses must serve principally for decision and control purposes.

For decision purposes, flexibility is an essential requirement of accounting analyses, since the concept of costs and revenues required varies with the kind of decision – whether it is for make or buy, pricing, advertising programmes, capital additions, methods of financing, etc. (⟡ Costs; Costing Systems). Generally the concept required depends upon the economic analysis relevant for each alternative under consideration. Also the estimates must be in terms of forecasts and expectations of the future, supported by historical accounting data rather than wholly determined by it. ⟡ Cost (in Accounting Systems).

For control purposes, in contrast, it can be argued that the emphasis should be on uniformity of standards, especially where the accounting information is required for more routine business operations. But perhaps more notably the information for control should be relevant to the control *of people by people* rather than of (impersonal) 'factors of production'. Therefore the accounting control data should be seen as communications intended to influence the behaviour of people. Put in this way, behavioural considerations tending to modify technologically derived standards and budgets become of primary importance (⟡ Control). The behavioural sciences have a direct relevance to accounting, particularly in the areas of motivation and control. The term behavioural accounting reflects the recognition of the importance of the human dimension in accounting.

With regard to the development of management accounting, it may well be necessary to reconsider the structuring and breadth of its content. In principle accounting should be seen as a scarcely separable part of a management science, and the quantitative, behavioural and economic aspects of that science which relate to an effective accounting function should be considered as part of the body of accounting as a discipline, in addition to much of its present substances. E.A.L.

> J. Arnold and A. Hope, *Accounting for Management Decisions* (Prentice-Hall, 1983); M. W. E. Glautier and B. Underdown, *Accounting Theory and Practice* (Pitman, 2nd ed., 1982).

Management Audit ⟡ Auditing

Management by Exception ⟡ Standard Costing; Budgeting, Short-term

Management by Objectives The systematic setting of targets for each employee.

There is little difficulty in setting a target for most machine operators or salesmen, judging their performance by this criterion and arranging some form of payment by their results. It is much more difficult to do this for managerial tasks, however, and a great deal of study has lately been given to procedures for applying a similar system to this type of work.

A job description can readily be drawn up for any job, including those that consist entirely of managing, but these descriptions merely indicate the general area in which employees are to work and what their duties and responsibilities are. They do not set out what results are required over the following weeks, months or years. Management by objectives is concerned with results.

The procedure consists of identifying the key areas of each job and then deciding what level of achievement in each of these areas would represent a satisfactory result. This decision is often made during a discussion between the employee who is being set the target and his superior. The question, 'What are the conditions we would expect to see if this job were being done well?' is often used during these discussions to help identify what key results the employee should be aiming to achieve.

At first widely applied in industry, the technique and the thinking behind it have been extended to organizations in the public sector, more types of jobs being analysed in order to identify the key results required. Experts in this field emphasize the need to dovetail the objectives set for each manager with those set for the department in which the manager works, these in turn dovetailing with the overall objectives of the organization. They also emphasize that it is desirable for the manager to participate in the setting of these objectives with his or her superior.

Considerable skill is often required, however, not only to identify the key results for some managerial jobs, but also to select a challenging but attainable level of achievement. In some organizations the technique has fallen into disrepute as a result of ambitious targets having been imposed, rather than jointly agreed between manager and superior, and their performance linked to promotion, dismissal and remuneration. ⟡ Objectives. E.L.

J. W. Humble, *Management by Objectives* (Management Publications, 1972).

Management Development Finding, training and developing men and women for positions of responsibility in an enterprise, sometimes described as management succession. Management in this context usually excludes supervisors and charge-hands, but includes those in staff positions with important advisory or 'decision-making' duties as well as 'line' managers who have considerable responsibility for the work of others. Management development is a systematic and continuous process, which starts with an analysis of present managerial resources, estimates future needs, and operates policies of recruitment, training, transfer and promotion, to secure and to make the most of these resources. There are three main aspects of management development: (1) the role of senior managers in developing those under them, possibly through a system of ⟡ Management by Objectives; (2) giving potential managers experience of jobs of different kinds and different levels of responsibility; (3) increasing their knowledge of different aspects of business by attending training courses, either inside or outside the particular enterprise. L.S.

T. J. Roberts, *Developing Effective Managers* (IPM, 1974); J. Morris and J. G. Burgoyne, *Developing Resourceful Managers* (IPM, 1973); R. Holdsworth, *Identifying Managerial Potential* (BIM, 1975); B. Taylor and G. L. Lippitt (eds.), *Management Development and Training Handbook* (McGraw-Hill, 1983).

Management Information System ◊ Information System

Management Sciences In the singular, management science is used as a synonym for the application of ◊ Quantitative Methods in management or for ◊ Operational Research.

In the plural, management sciences is used as a synonym for the application of quantitative methods and the social sciences (economics, psychology and sociology) in management. M.J.C.M.

Managerial Economics With the growth of management education in the UK the basic social sciences of economics, psychology and sociology have appeared in another guise – as core subjects in the budding business manager's curriculum. Whilst for undergraduates, and possibly post-graduates, a traditional course in economics is reasonably satisfactory, this has not proved true when the students are middle and senior managers. If this is coupled with the complaint of many industrial economists that much of their previous education had proved irrelevant to their work in industry, then it is not surprising that a new course has emerged. There is, of course, ample precedent for this in the USA, but one may still ask in what sense managerial economics differs from traditional economics.

A cynic may reply that there is no difference and a glance at the contents of any managerial-economics textbook will soon show why. The mixture – demand, costs, profits, investment, etc. – is as before, only the name and order vary. A more positive attitude can be taken, however, when the contents are examined more closely. The various sections are geared more closely to the individual firm; moreover it is the firm of reality and not of arid theory. In addition there is a willingness to use the work of operations researchers, marketing people, management accountants and econometricians. Thus D. C. Hague [1] has sub-titled his book *Analysis for Business Decisions* and a glance at the contents page reveals a considerable reliance upon the methods of operations research and accounting. The sub-title reminds

1. D. C. Hague, *Managerial Economics: Analysis for Business Decisions* (Longman, 1971).

us that this is what managers are paid for and that the stress must be upon theory that is operational; in this way managers can be aided to take better decisions.

It is a point of some debate whether one can make a case for a separate discipline known as 'managerial economics'. Wouldn't it be better to admit that it is just the relevant parts of economics, accounting, marketing and operations research? This argument can be countered in two ways. On the one hand it is possible to argue that the separate areas are welded together by the common use of mathematical and statistical techniques. On the other hand it is also possible to argue that they are welded together by having their roots in economics. Economics is concerned with the optimum use of resources and this is exactly what accountants are trying to do in their analysis of capital projects and operations researchers, in their use of programming methods and analysis of inventory systems. Perhaps the best solution is to incorporate both ideas into the subject matter and we then have a discipline that is rooted in economics and takes its methods from mathematics and statistics. The cynic may feel that this is another example of economists, rather late in the day, attempting to recapture ground previously developed by specialists. In this they may well be correct, but one can only wish that the pace was quicker. ⟡ Economics. L.T.S.

J. L. Pappas, E. F. Brigham, B. Shipley, *Managerial Economics* (Holt, Rinehart & Winston, UK ed., 1983).

Managerial Grid, The The focus of much current training activity is the actual process of managing. This kind of training aims to give managers greater insight into the methods used for getting results through people and how people react to different management methods. The managerial grid, which has been developed by Drs Blake and Mouton, concentrates specifically on managerial behaviour. The managerial grid seminar is the first step of grid organization development, which is a systems approach to increasing managerial and organizational effectiveness.

Prework for a Managerial Grid Seminar

Those attending a managerial grid seminar are required to do some thirty hours prework, during which they learn the grid as a framework for thinking about management. At this stage seminar participants answer a series of questions concerning their own managerial behaviour and the climate or culture of their organization.

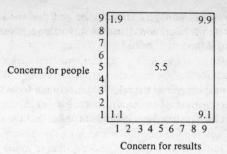

Concern for results

The Managerial Grid

The grid is based on the traditional dichotomy of concern for people and concern for production or results. The horizontal scale from 1 to 9 depicts degrees of concern for results, whilst the vertical scale, also from 1 to 9 depicts degrees of concern for people. Since concern is neither all present nor all absent 1 denotes low and 9 high concern. Five basic styles of management, which are amplified in *The Managerial Grid* by Blake and Mouton, can now be identified on the grid:

9.1 *Management* (*scientific management*). Efficiency in operations results from arranging conditions of work in such a way that human elements interfere to a minimum degree.

1.9 Management (*country-club management*). Thoughtful attention to people's need for satisfying relationships leads to a comfortable, friendly organization atmosphere and work tempo.

1.1 Management (*impoverished*). Exertion of minimum effort to get required work done is appropriate to sustain organization membership.

5.5 *Management* (*middle of the road*). Adequate organization performance is possible through balancing the necessity to get work done with maintaining people's morale at a satisfactory level.

9.9 *Management* (*team management*). Work accomplishment is from committed people. Interdependence through a 'common stake' in organization purpose leads to relationships of trust and respect.

This framework can be used as a framework for thinking and talking about individual and company management practices.

The Managerial Grid Seminar

The one-week seminar, which has been developed over a period of ten years, is run by Scientific Methods Inc. (Blake and Mouton's organization) as a public seminar, with representatives from different companies, or by line managers as an in-company programme. The objectives of the seminar are:

(1) *Personal learning.* Learning the grid as a framework for thinking and talking about management, learning about one's own managerial style and the managerial values on which this style is based.

(2) *Developing effective team work.* A series of team tasks provide an opportunity to learn how candid communication, commitment to objectives and the constructive handling of conflict contribute to effective team work.

(3) *Group dynamics.* When representatives from different teams meet to resolve issues of mutual interest, objectivity can be impaired by personal managerial styles and team loyalties. These issues are closely examined in a problem-solving situation.

(4) *Organization.* Established practices and traditions constitute the culture of an organization. Through team discussion based on a multiple-choice questionnaire an 'ideal culture' is described. The ways in which this ideal differs from existing practice represent the objectives of a grid organization development programme.

During the seminar teams of six to nine people work on complex problems, with each team determining its own method of working. At the conclusion of each task team effectiveness is compared and is followed by a critique session during which the quality of team work is assessed by team members and specific plans prepared to improve performance.

In tackling these tasks grid participants develop understanding of each other's approach to problems and decision-making. This experience forms the basis for aiding each person to recognize their own managerial style and how others react to it. This proves to be a most stimulating task during which individuals gain considerable insight into their own strengths and weaknesses as managers.

Grid Organization Development

Improved performance at work is often difficult to accomplish and part of the problem lies in transferring newly gained knowledge to sound application at work. This is true of almost any training course, including the grid seminar. Effective follow-up is needed in order to derive maximum benefit and this is the aim of grid organization development.

Phase one. The managerial grid seminar, with emphasis on personal learning, constitutes the first phase.

Phase two. Work-team development is a self-administering phase, where people who are jointly responsible for specific tasks or work areas define the action needed to improve their own and their unit's effectiveness.

Phase three. Where intergroup co-ordination is ineffective or inadequate, progress towards organizational goals is impaired. The problems that may exist in the relationships between departments, headquarters and branch offices, or management and union are examined during this phase, to develop improved co-ordination.

Phase four. Phases one, two and three concentrate on creating the conditions needed for effective development of long-range plans. During phase four corporate objectives are established and an organization blueprint is drawn up.

Phases five and six. These phases are concerned with implementing the plans, and with consolidation and review.

These six phases should be used as a guide for grid organization development rather than as a fixed programme. Successful implementation is more adequately assured when top management is directly involved and line managers undertake full responsibility for each phase.

Conclusion

The managerial grid approach to management training has been built upon a foundation of earlier research by behavioural scientists like Argyris and Likert, which established the importance of paying equal attention to people and to task requirements in achieving enterprise objectives. It also integrates attention to individual behaviour and a concern for effective team work, so that it can be developed into a form of organization development. W. J. Reddin, following a similar approach, introduced the extra dimension of managerial effectiveness, whilst Blake and Mouton subsequently added personal motivation as a third dimension to their grid framework.

The key ingredients of the grid approach may be summarized as: participation; candour; trust and respect; involvement and commitment; the resolution of conflicts through open confrontation; the value of mutual agreement; the synergy generated by effective interaction between boss and subordinate; the mutual setting of objectives by boss and subordinates as a basis for organization and direction of work; the use of critique and feedback as a basis for learning from work experience. ⟨⟩ Group Methods of Training; Teams. C.M.H.H., amended by E.L.

R. R. Blake and J. S. Mouton, *The Managerial Grid* (Gulf Publishing Co.,

1964); W. J. Reddin, *Managerial Effectiveness* (McGraw-Hill, 1970); R. R. Blake and J. S. Mouton, *The New Managerial Grid* (Gulf Publishing Co., 1978); R. R. Blake and J. S. Mouton, 'The New Managerial Grid in Action', in B. Taylor and G. Lippitt (eds.), *Management Development and Training Handbook* (McGraw-Hill, 2nd ed., 1983).

Managerial Unionism This phenomenon increased rapidly in Western Europe in the 1970s. Four separate types of management unions co-exist in Britain: largely separate managerial unions (e.g. the British Association of Colliery Management); unions for both managers and professionals (e.g. the Association of Management and Professional Staffs); vertically expansionist white-collar unions (e.g. the Association of Professional, Executive, Clerical and Computer Staff); and vertically expansionist blue-collar unions (e.g. the Technical, Administrative and Supervisory Section of the Amalgamated Union of Engineering Workers). Managerial Unionism is particularly likely to occur amongst managers in the public sector. Survey evidence suggests that nearly a quarter of British managers are in trade unions; membership is particularly likely if a union is present at the managers' level and is recognized for negotiating purposes. ⟡ Trade Union Types – White-collar Union. M.J.F.P.

M. Poole *et al.*, *Managers in Focus* (Gower, 1981); M. Poole 'Why Managers Join Unions: Evidence from Britain', *Industrial Relations*, 22 (1985), pp. 426–44.

Manpower Planning The drawing up of a schedule showing the number of employees of different types that the company will require over a period of years.

Once a company has developed a long-range strategy (⟡ Corporate Planning) it becomes possible to estimate the number of people of all types and categories that may be required over the following years. At the time that these estimates are made, some companies take the opportunity to review their staffing criteria as well as the mere numbers required in each category. Thus it may be desirable to evaluate the performance of employees with different qualifications who have been doing the same job – for example, a company with a large sales force may discover as a result of analysing the records that the sales representatives with the best records are those with a third-class science degree, while those with the worst record have first-class arts degrees. Any such conclusion would, of course, be taken into account when preparing a long-term manpower plan.

The function of the manpower plan is to indicate how many employees will need to be selected, trained, promoted, retired, dismissed and so on over the following years and hence an estimate of the personnel facilities that will be required can also be made. The factors that are usually taken into account in making a manpower plan include (a) the changing nature of the business, (b) the rate of retirement and other causes of staff losses, (c) changes in social and employment conditions, (d) changes in education, (e) changes in job content, (f) changes in the company's organization structure and promotion pattern. A.J.A.A.

Malcolm Bennison and Jonathan Casson, *The Manpower Planning Handbook* (McGraw-Hill, 1984).

Manpower Services Commission Under the Employment and Training Act 1973 the Manpower Services Commission (MSC) was set up to run the public employment and training services. The MSC is separate from the Government but accountable to the Secretary of State for Employment. The Secretary of State for Education and Science is also fully involved in the consideration and approval of the MSC's plans and proposals affecting non-advanced further education in England. In respect of its operations in Scotland and Wales the MSC reports to the Secretaries of State for those countries and a Committee for each country advises the Commission on manpower, training and the implementation of its plans and programmes nationally.

The first objective of the MSC is to safeguard the provision of skilled manpower for the present and future needs of industry. This involves the Commission in the promotion of occupational training in a form that enables entrants of different ages and educational backgrounds to acquire agreed standards of skill appropriate to the jobs available, and that opens up opportunities for adults steadily to increase their skills and knowledge during their working lives. The second major objective – one of those contained in the *New Training Initiative* (Cmnd. 8455) of 1981 – is to move to a position where all those under the age of 18 can continue in full-time education, or have planned work experience. Other objectives of the MSC include the provision of an efficient, accessible and cost-effective employment service, and the provision of a range of services to help job-seekers who have particular difficulty in obtaining suitable work or training.

The MSC has ten members who serve for a term of three years. They comprise a chairman, three members appointed after consultation with the Confederation of British Industry, three appointed after consultation with the Trades Union Congress, two after consultation with local education authorities and one with professional education interests. In pursuit of its objectives, the MSC is organized into three operating divisions (Employment, Training and a Skillcentre Training Agency) and two support divisions (Resources and Planning, and Personnel and Central Services).

MSC programmes are paid for mainly by grants-in-aid, which cover about 70 per cent of the total outlay. The rest, including activities such as the Community Programme, Community Industry and Sheltered Employment, is paid for directly by the Department of Employment or from receipts for services provided. In 1983/4 the Youth Training Schemes provided training and work experience for 354,000 young people, of whom 80 per cent were school-leavers, whilst the Training Opportunities Scheme for unemployed adults enabled 66,200 people to complete training courses. Another 113,000 long-term unemployed were provided with temporary full-time or part-time work on projects under the Community Programme, provision for which is to be doubled in 1986/7. Plans were also announced in 1985 to expand the Youth Training Scheme, so that in 1986 16-year-olds could receive two years of job-related training, and 17-year-olds one year, leading to a recognized vocational qualification.

In 1983 the MSC promoted a Technical and Vocational Education Initiative to establish projects run by local education authorities for 14–18-year-olds, which incorporated work experience as an integral part of the programme. In 1984 the Government gave the MSC new responsibilities by enabling it to purchase a more significant proportion of work-related, non-advanced further education provided by local education authorities, thereby discharging the function of a national training authority. E.L.

> *MSC Annual Report 83/84; MSC Corporate Plan 1984–8: Employment –the Challenge for the Nation* (HMSO, 1985).

Manufacturing Policy The establishment of objectives for the manufacturing function, the determination of procedures to achieve these objectives, and their implementation. Manufacturing objectives must reflect the business or corporate objectives, but the manufacturing function should influence and contribute to the formulation of business policy, particularly in respect of the determination of the products and the markets for them. These decisions can influence the nature of the manufacturing system and the demands placed on it. In general the achievement of manufacturing objectives will include the establishment of an appropriate manufacturing system, its capacity, the

scheduling of work and appropriate inventory management procedures.
R.W.

> T. Hill, *Production/Operations Management* (Prentice-Hall, 1983), ch. 14.

Mareva Injunction An injunction issued by the English courts to
prevent a defendant from removing certain specified assets from the
jurisdiction, and thereby nullifying the benefit, of a future judgment in
the plaintiff's favour. It is named after the first case in which such an
injunction was granted in 1975 and has only temporary effect. The plaintiff may be asked to provide an indemnity should it be decided in the
subsequent hearing that the granting of the injunction was unjustified.
J.C.E.M.

> Schmitthoff and Sarre, *Charlesworth's Mercantile Law* (Stevens & Sons,
> 14th ed., 1984).

Marginal Costing ◊ Break-even Analysis; Overheads; Cost (in
Accounting Systems)

Marginal Efficiency of Capital ◊ Internal Rate of Return

Market Models and Competition Whilst the models of markets
used by economists often seem to have little value as direct aids to
decision-making, nevertheless they provide a useful way of classifying
actual firms and suggest the types of competition that may occur. The
table below shows the major models, classified according to number of
producers, type of product and ease of entry.

Market model	Number of producers	Product	Entry
Pure (perfect) competition	Many	Homogeneous	Unrestricted
Monopolistic competition	Many	Differentiated	Unrestricted
Pure oligopoly	Few	Homogeneous	Restricted
Differentiated oligopoly	Few	Differentiated	Restricted
Monopoly	One	—	Restricted

The firm in pure competition must accept the price that is set by the
market. Easy conditions of entry reduce the opportunity for large profits
and the number of firms rules out concerted action. Such industries are
usually producing raw materials or agricultural produce. They often
tend towards chronic overcapacity and wide swings in prices, production

and incomes. Hence one often sees governments intervening to introduce orderly marketing and raise productivity.

The situation in monopolistic competition is identical apart from the fact of differentiated products. Thus producers have some slight control over price, and competition can be undertaken through advertising, packaging and service, as well as price. The retail trade exhibits many of these characteristics.

Pure oligopoly often develops from pure competition as the benefits of economies of scale are realized. Producers can exercise price control, although this is limited by the homogeneity of products. Since prices are interdependent, price leadership and price agreements are often found in such industries. The production of raw materials is again a source for this type of market model.

Differentiated oligopoly is a model in which price and non-price competition flourish, although experience suggests that price wars are purely destructive. Producers have control over price but usually the main competition comes from brand advertising, product improvements and innovations. Price wars cannot be ruled out, however, particularly if competitors threaten the market leader. Industries such as cars, cigarettes, soap and detergents conform closely to this model.

Monopoly is now closely associated with the nationalized industries such as coal, gas, electricity and railways. Producers, in theory, have complete control over price or output and hence over profit levels. This is one reason for the government control. Competition can still occur, however, as has happened in domestic fuel supply for central heating. ⇨ Competition. L.T.S.

R. G. Lipsey, *An Introduction to Positive Economics* (Weidenfeld & Nicolson, 6th ed., 1983).

Market Segmentation Seeks to differentiate between buyers and users of an identical product or service in terms of relevant marketing characteristics. Until the recent development of attitude analysis in marketing (⇨ Motivation Research), it was common to segment markets in terms of age, socio-economic groupings based on occupation and gross income, ethnic groups or geographical location. There have been numerous instances where these are not prime determinants of purchase, nor relevant dimensions for different marketing strategies. Two new categories have been added: personality, e.g. gregariousness, conservatism, ambitiousness; and buyer behaviour, e.g. usage rate, end use, brand or channel loyalty (⇨ Branding) and price sensitivity. With segmentation analysis marketing management can develop its total sales more effectively by the use of different approaches to each segment. The cold-remedy market has been shown to be segmented in terms of: users who believe that the remedy will be effective; users who do not believe it will help but wish to feel that they are doing something; non-users who feel that the remedies are useless and do not wish to do anything. To consolidate or develop marketing to each segment calls for a different approach. A wide range of research techniques can be employed both to analyse a market for relevant segments, and to measure the effectiveness of marketing approaches to them (▷ Marketing Research). G.S.C.W.

P. Kotler, *Marketing Management: Analysis, Planning and Control* (Prentice-Hall, 1984) ch. 3.

Market Survey An overall appraisal for a product or service that an organization offers or proposes to offer to a market. It will normally indicate not only the market situation for the commissioning organization but also the position of competitive forces and future trends. The investigation will frequently be made by the collection of previously unknown data, but may be made by the collation of existing information (▷ Desk Research). The former pattern is most common in consumer markets where few official or trade statistics are available; the latter is more common in industrial and agricultural markets. The original investigation may occasionally be conducted via a census of a total relevant population, but will generally involve the selection of representative respondents (▷ Sampling) by either quota or random sampling procedures. A uniform, structured questionnaire may be used to gather the relevant information and the findings published as a report. Where the survey examines a market of considerable complexity, or involves interviewing a well-informed population concerning the product or service – e.g. architects, computer technologists – a less structured approach may be used in the questioning. A wide variety of other research methods are available and are sometimes used, either in conjunction with or in place of the questionnaire survey or desk-research investigation (▷ Marketing Research).

Some controversy centres around the method of report presentation that allows the findings of such a survey to be most effectively communicated. The Market Research Society lays down a code for its members, insisting that they provide sample, time and methodological details, etc. G.S.C.W.

Standards in Market Research (1954, revised 1965 and 1973).

Marketing Marketing can usefully be defined as 'the process in a society by which the demand for economic goods and services is anticipated or enlarged, and is satisfied through the conception, physical distribution and exchange of such goods and services'. Hence any individual company satisfying demands of this nature must always be involved in a marketing process. The success of an enterprise, however, will depend on the skill with which its management is able to give satisfaction and obtain the appropriate net profit. Two of the most significant factors affecting how easy it is to achieve this are the nature of demand in a market, and the nature of the forces competing for the incomes that can be allocated to any particular product or service. The ever-increasing consciousness in companies of the need to look closely at the marketing process has largely come about as a result of dramatic shifts in these factors in recent decades.

Three key ideas dominate the pattern of marketing in all advanced market economies: marketing orientation, marketing research and marketing management.

Marketing orientation is the philosophy of business management derived from the acceptance of the need to plan and control the marketing process consciously within a company. It can only affect the character of policy decisions if it is effectively embraced by top management. Once paramount, however, its ramifications for the development of new products and services and for diversification programmes are extremely important. It involves a definition of a company's purpose beyond the offering of particular products or services; the company exists to satisfy a need, e.g. that of travelling from Glasgow to London. Whether this is most effectively accomplished by stagecoach, canal barge, train, aeroplane or hovercraft is a subsidiary consideration.

Once a company has consciously embraced this concept, two functions must be established to facilitate its implementation: (1) contact must be made with the customers who have the needs to be satisfied; (2) the customers must effectively receive what the company seeks to offer. These are the roles of marketing research and marketing management respectively.

Marketing research is charged with the continuous task of monitoring the marketing itself and any extra-market factors liable to influence customer behaviour in the given market, e.g. economic trends, the political situation (especially in export markets). The data that is collected will be in the form of regular surveys and analyses of economic goods and services currently available (those of the company itself and of its competitors), and *ad hoc* studies from time to time.

The launch of a new product illustrates well the nature of such *ad hoc* work. It could involve the testing of the concept of the product by describing it to potential users before a prototype was prepared. The next stage would be to build a few prototypes for testing by customers. Finally, if all has gone favourably, a limited launch on to the market will often be made. The optimum combination of promotional activity, distribution and price elements will be sought and customers' purchases and reactions measured.

A second major field of marketing research is measuring the effectiveness of the activities of marketing management.

Marketing management is the engineering function in the marketing process. The marketing manager is responsible for the totality of a company's market offering – the range of products and their packaging, the prices charged, the discount structures offered, the communications media employed (television, press, outdoor hoardings, cinema, personal salesmen, direct-mail circulars, etc.), and the channels through which the product or service is made available (retailers, mail order, automatic vending, door-to-door selling, etc.) The marketing manager's activity determines whether or not the company meets its financial objectives. The sale of products and services is normally the sole revenue generator in a company; most of the remaining personnel are engaged solely in incurring costs. Hence marketing management must maintain continuous contact with those colleagues in the company responsible for manufacturing the products or providing the service for sale, and with those financial colleagues responsible for controlling budgets, raising capital and distributing profits. Marketing managers are concerned with market opportunities based on their interpretation of the continuous monitoring implicit in marketing research; their colleagues are concerned with technical and financial possibilities.

Professional marketing education developed in Britain in the early 1960s, through the large professional organization, the Institute of Marketing (18,500 members in 1985). It offers a three-year diploma course on a part-time basis, taught in many polytechnics and colleges of technology. In the mid-1960s the universities began to develop marketing as a subject for study either for higher degrees alone, or as a major part of an advanced education for management.

Teachers of marketing at an advanced level established an annual conference in 1965, and in 1967 the *European Journal of Marketing*, reporting current research, theory and development, was founded. In 1966 the British Productivity Council established a National Marketing Council to promote the subject and to develop research and teaching in Britain. The Economic Development Committee for the Distributive Trades also implicitly assumed a general responsibility for marketing in Britain at the time of Harold Wilson's second Productivity

Conference in 1967, which was devoted to marketing and distribution.

By the 1980s it is fair to say that a very widespread understanding and acceptance of marketing dominates in most organizations. In particular, the world recession of the late 1970s and early 1980s focused attention on the need to adopt creative approaches towards the marketplace if business is to be built on sure foundations. G.S.C.W.

G. Wills *et al.*, *Introducing Marketing* (Pan, 1984).

Marketing Audit The process by which a marketing organization attempts to develop an independent judgement of the quality and direction of its effort. It examines the entire marketing effort of a company (◊ Marketing Mix), or a specific aspect of it, covering its objectives, programme, implementation, and organization, for the triple purpose of determining what is being done, appraising what is being done, and recommending what ought to be done in the future. Such audits are most effective if conducted on a periodic basis rather than *ad hoc* in the face of a crisis. They may be conducted either internally – through the cross-transfer of company personnel, by the individuals involved, by superiors, through a formalized audit office or task force – or by external consultants. The important criteria in the choice of auditors are objectivity, breadth of experience and familiarity with company operations. G.S.C.W.

Marketing Channel ◊ Distribution Mix

Marketing Communications Mix The combination of methods chosen from time to time by a marketing organization to communicate about, and thereby promote, goods or services that are offered. It is seen as an integral part of the total ◊ Marketing Mix, and consequently communications-mix management, whilst aiming to optimize resource allocation, avoids doing so at the expense of the total activity. The principal media of communication available are ◊ Advertising in the general and trade press (◊ Audience Measurement), commercial TV, direct mailings, outdoor sites and posters, cinemas, ◊ Packaging, point-of-sale promotion, ◊ Merchandising, ◊ Public Relations and personal salesmanship (◊ Selling). The marketing communications mix within any particular industry often tends to inertia and a breakaway – both within distribution channels and in relation to end-users – becomes psychologically difficult for any individual organization. For example, a particular industry may devote a very high proportion of its expenditure to TV advertising and to point-of-sale display materials, with a relatively passive role for personal salemanship. Another may use keyed press advertising and mail-order catalogues (⟡ Mail Order). To change from one style of mix to another has implications for the total employment status of the marketing activity in an organization, and for its structure, as well as the financial investment of goodwill implicit in an extant mix. G.S.C.W.

E. Crane, *Marketing Communications* (J. Wiley, 1965).

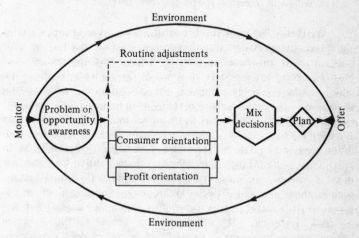

The marketing concept

Marketing Concept The philosophy of management that postulates that in all consideration given to the marketing of a product or service the needs of the customer must be paramount, subject to the governing factor of an organization's profit objective (see Figure above). Although widely accepted as common sense, only since the Second World War have mass-market demand conditions (⟡ Discretionary Income) and organization structures within companies (⟡ Marketing) made its effective implementation possible. The main difficulty in implementing the marketing concept lies in the distortion that occurs in securing details of customer needs and/or reactions to any market offering. Mass markets have presented the major problems. The development of marketing research methods (⟡ Marketing Research) largely based on modern sampling methods (⟡ Sampling) has overcome this in many ways. The philosophy has always been implicit in jobbing or custom-built production, with their direct channels of communication. Prior to the present substantial growth of discretionary incomes, management philosophies tended to be dominated by production objectives, followed by sales objectives, as ends in themselves (✧ Selling). The phrase is thought to have been first adopted in the General Electric Company (USA) *c*. 1952 to mean that marketing established for the engineer, the designer and the production controller what customers wanted, what price they were willing to pay, and where and when the product would be wanted (✧ Marketing Mix). G.S.C.W.

G. Schwartz, *Science in Marketing* (J. Wiley, 1965), chs. 4 and 5.

Marketing Environment The amalgam of those factors affecting the market that are external to the company's sphere of direct influence but that act as constraints on company behaviour (✧ Marketing). The most significant are generally identified as (1) the legal system within which marketing takes place; (2) the ethical/moral values institutionalized in any particular society at any point in time; (3) the economic system and level of individual and national income (✧ Discretionary Income); (4) the psychological mechanisms of the individual that condition behaviour and the interpretation of messages (✧ Branding; Motivation Research); (5) the group influences that condition the behaviour of the individual, especially as described in sociology; (6) cultural factors, such as those analysed in social anthropology and linguistics, of importance particularly in cross-cultural or export marketing (✧ International Marketing); (7) spatial aspects of human settlement, which influence, for example, the location of trading centres, depots and gravitation of custom, as studied in economic geography, human ecology and social physics (✧ Retail Gravitation); (8) institutionalized channels for the distribution of goods and services (✧ Distribution Mix) and organization structures within companies and market agencies. The relative importance of any of these factors will vary according to the product or service under offer the time and place. The development of study in this field as an integrated approach in marketing is of recent origin, and in many areas involves the development of new theoretical bases for understanding customer behaviour, such as psychological and sociological economics. G.S.C.W.

S. H. Britt, *Consumer Behaviour and the Behavioral Sciences* (J. Wiley, 1966).

Marketing Experimentation The use of experimental design to analyse individual elements in marketing activity. It involves balancing unwanted variables in a situation, by such means as control or randomization, in order to ensure that any variations are the result of the test stimulus rather than some spurious effect. In addition the statistical significance of a result should be assessable. The most common form of experimental design in marketing research is the split or matched sample. At its simplest level, say in the test of two new products, one matched half of a sample will try product A first and the other product B first. The method of experimentation is also used in test marketing (◊ New Product) where a product is launched in two or more areas, with different total marketing mixes; in advertising; price; distribution. The use of experimentation as a research technique in marketing is still rare compared with the observational methods, such as questionnaire surveys, retail audits and panels (◊ Marketing Research). It faces major problems in certain areas, such as test marketing, where to match samples initially and to sustain the match over time is still not completely feasible. However, its use is greatly increasing in those areas where matching is practicable, and where the time for the conduct of an experiment can be kept relatively short, e.g. product placement, pre-testing of advertisements. G.S.C.W.

Marketing Logistics ◊ Physical Distribution Management

Marketing Mix The combination of procedures and policies adopted from time to time by an organization in its marketing programme. The various elements may be combined in a wide variety of ways in order to achieve marketing objectives, and management normally seeks to minimize the cost overall. This approach to marketing management was first formulated by Neil Borden at Harvard University in 1948. The twelve variables he lists in his model are: product planning, branding, channels of distribution, personal selling, advertising, promotion, mix, packaging, display, servicing, physical handling, and fact finding and analysis. The formulation of an optimum mix (◊ Marketing Experimentation) has to be undertaken in the framework of market forces beyond the short-term direct control of the marketing manager. These include buyer behaviour, trade behaviour, competitors' behaviour and position, and government restraint (◊ Marketing Environment). Finally, in the short term, mix alternatives can only be effectively selected in the context of a company's existing resources. The model emphasizes not only the interdependence of the action variables, the market forces and company resources, but also the interaction of each constituent variable on one another (◊ Operational Research). ◊ New Product, Product Mix; Pricing (Market Pricing); Prices (Theory of); Branding; Distribution Mix; Selling; Advertising; Marketing Communications Mix; Packaging; Merchandising; Physical Distribution Management; Marketing Research. G.S.C.W.

Marketing Plan ⟡ Sales Forecast

Marketing Research That function in a business which is specifically charged with providing information to facilitate the making of
marketing decisions. These decisions can be classified as either operational, i.e. relating to problems encountered in the continuous process of
marketing a range of products or services; or *ad hoc*, i.e. arising out of
particular problems or developments. The stages of the problem-solving
process are matched with a variety of techniques, of which the most
popular are shown in the following table (⟡ Market Survey; Retail Audit;
Consumer Panel).

The sequential process of research

Stage	*Techniques*
1. Problem-awareness and conceptualization	Monitor trade press
	Appraise current practice
	Marketing feedback
	'Related-area' reading
2. Hypothesizing and problem-refinement (qualitative stage)	Group discussions
	Motivational research
	Unstructured interviews
	Memomotion cameras and photographic observation
	Laboratory experimentation
	Consumer 'clinics'
3. Validation and quantification	Surveys
	Retail audits
	Panels
	Mass-observation
	Marketing experimentation

The first marketing-research department is thought to have been established in the United States by Charles Parlin in 1923 and the first formal
commercial investigation was his classification of department-store
shopping habits. The massive growth of marketing research began in
Britain after the Second World War as many markets became more
competitive and in the face of rising consumer discretionary incomes.
The Market Research Society, the largest professional association, was
established in 1947 and now has some 5,000 members. The Industrial
Market Research Association is a somewhat smaller organization.

Over 600 companies in the UK are estimated to have marketing-
research departments of their own, with an annual expenditure in

the region of £100,000,000. Most market research, however, is sub-contracted to consultancy agencies; there are currently more than 200 in Britain. G.S.C.W.

Organizations Providing Market-Research Services in Great Britain (Market Research Society, published annually).

Mass Production Mass production has been adopted as a generic rather than specific term. Although the term was first used around fifty years ago, the type of systems that it now describes are considerably older. Large-quantity production is as old as large-quantity demand. Only the manner in which the concept is translated into practice has any claim to be of recent origin. Historically the stimulus for mass production derived largely from the invention and increasing availability of mechanized methods of production. Tools such as lathes, drilling machines, forges, etc., were important in that their development gave rise to perhaps the simplest aspect of mass production: the quantity production of single-piece items from single machines.

A second aspect of mass production deals with the manufacture of more complex items, such as domestic appliances, motor vehicles, etc., which depend on a different type of mass-production technology, the central feature of which is product flow; it is therefore usually referred to as flow production. Because of their complexity or composite nature, such items cannot usually be manufactured by one tool or piece of equipment. They normally require the services of several facilities. The mass production of such items, a more recent development than quantity production, is dependent on the continuous flow of the products through or past a series of production facilities.

Flow production is most easily achieved for liquid products. For example in petroleum refining, the product and the raw material have a propensity to flow, which facilitates the design of the flow process. Similarly many foodstuffs, drinks and other fluid products lend themselves to this type of production. In contrast, 'hard' discrete items such as engine cylinder blocks, motor vehicles and domestic appliances do not possess this characteristic. Hence considerable effort must be made to design flow systems for their manufacture. The mass production of complex discrete items using the flow principle is one of the most important achievements in manufacturing technology and one of the most important aspects of mass production. Indeed the importance of this method of manufacture is such that, for many people, the term mass production is synonymous with flow or assembly-line production (⟨◊⟩ Assembly Lines).

Thus flow production may be divided into flow processes, designed

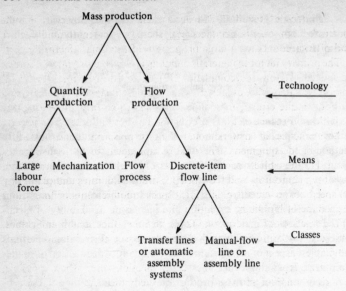

for the manufacture of large quantities of bulk, fluid or semi-fluid products, and flow lines, which use the same principle of efficient material and product flow in the manufacture of large quantities of complex, discrete items. Flow lines in which manual labour is used, essentially for product assembly, are often referred to as manual flow or assembly lines, whilst those using automatic material transfer between automatic machining 'stations' are normally referred to as transfer lines or machines, or, in the case of assembly work, automatic assembly systems.

Recently, prompted largely by behavioural problems such as high labour turnover, absenteeism, etc., some companies have in part replaced manual flow-line work by systems of individual or group manual working (✧ Group Working). In such cases, work – normally assembly work – which would normally have been undertaken on an assembly line is executed by people working individually or in groups. In such cases, the work-flow characteristic does not predominate and individual tasks are usually enlarged or enriched in comparison with the tasks of workers at stations on flow lines (✧ Job Restructuring).
R.W.

R. Wild, *Mass Production Management* (J. Wiley, 1972).

Materials Administration ✧ Materials Management

Materials Handling The need to move and otherwise handle materials, components, products, etc., is a basic process in manufacture and often accounts for a large proportion of total manufacturing cost.

The primary factor in materials handling is movement. Material should be moved (1) towards completion; (2) on or by the same device; (3) smoothly, safely and quickly; (4) the shortest distance; (5) easily and without undue effort; (6) economically; (7) to co-ordinate with other activities, processes, etc.

The practice of materials handling is primarily concerned with methods and equipment. The type of equipment to be used depends upon: (1) the objects to be moved (size, weight, quantity, condition, mobility); (2) routing and sequence; (3) production rates and quantities; (4) speed of movement required; (5) special requirements or limitations (e.g. shape of buildings, etc.).

The relation of materials handling to other functions is important. Efficient ⟷ Plant Layout may eliminate, reduce or facilitate materials handling.

Storage is an important associate function and, where possible, materials handling and storage should be combined.

The recording and analytical techniques of ⟷ Method Study are particularly useful in the study and design of materials-handling systems, memomotion photography and flow-process charts being frequently used.

The need for effective materials handling is self-evident. Handling can account for up to 40 per cent of total manufacturing costs. Approximately 25 per cent of all industrial accidents are associated with faulty handling and inadequate materials handling may result in high work-in-progress, deterioration and damage, an increase in labour costs, underutilization of space, etc. R.W.

H. K. Compton, *Supplies and Materials Handling* (Business Books, 1968); R. Wild, *Production and Operations Management* (Holt, Rinehart & Winston, 1984).

Materials Management A concept that covers materials organization as a whole rather than as a series of elements. It involves effective collaboration between the various elements in the materials system to achieve commonly agreed objectives. Many management problems occur between departments (elements) rather than in them. Materials management tries to reduce the problems caused by sub-optimization at the 'element' level to benefit the system as a whole.

The scope of materials management concerns the flow of materials from the supply market into an organization to the point where those materials are converted into the firm's end product(s). Responsibilities include collaboration with designers on material component specifications, purchasing – which includes finding suitable economic sources of supply – incoming traffic, goods receiving and inspection, supplier quality control, inventory control (raw materials, components, and possibly work-in-progress) and production material control. In some cases internal transportation and ⇨ Materials Handling would be included, as would the disposal of surplus materials and scrap.

A materials-management organization provides delegation of responsibility and authority with regard to materials. It reduces the possibility that departments may have overlapping responsibilities (which is not uncommon with regard to materials in conventional manufacturing company structures). The concept recognizes the importance of the management principle of accountability by providing a manager who is responsible for all materials decisions – a condition lacking in conventional organization. ⇨ Purchasing. D.H.F.

> P. Baily and D. Farmer, *Materials Management Handbook* (Gower, 1982).

Materials Requirements Planning (MRP) A procedure used in production and inventory planning, by means of which known customer-demand requirements are 'exploded' to produce 'gross' parts, components or activity requirements. These 'gross' requirements are then compared with available inventories to produce 'net' requirements, which are scheduled within available capacity limitations. M R P procedures usually require the use of extensive data processing by computers. ⇨ Production Planning and Control. R.W.

> J. Orlicky, *Materials Requirements Planning* (McGraw-Hill, 1974).

Maternity Rights. Employees who become pregnant have four basic statutory rights. Because the detail of these rights is extremely complex only a bare outline can be provided here.

First, a woman is entitled to maternity pay from her employer where she remains in employment (though not necessarily working) up to the eleventh week before her child is due, at which time she must have been continuously employed by the organization for two years. The payment equals 9/10ths of gross basic pay for the first six weeks' absence. A central Maternity Pay Fund reimburses employers for this expenditure.

Second, any woman who qualifies for maternity pay is also entitled to return to her former job (as defined by her contract of employment) on no less favourable terms. In effect the legislation provides a period of 'maternity leave' of some forty weeks since the employee will normally stop work eleven weeks before the expected date of confinement and must return within twenty-nine weeks of the birth. There is some flexibility about the exact date of return, which can be delayed by the employee by up to four weeks on certified medical grounds and similarly by the employer for any reason. An employer who refuses to allow a woman to return to her old job or to re-employ her where some suitable vacancy exists may be guilty of unfair dismissal. If her post has been lost through redundancy during her absence and no other suitable work is available she will then be entitled to a redundancy payment.

The exercise of either of these rights is conditional upon the woman giving advance notice in writing of her intentions, in accordance with a set of deadlines laid down in the legislation. In practice many women do not have the minimum service necessary to qualify initially, decide against returning to work, or simply fail to meet the strict notification procedures.

Third, dismissals due to pregnancy or for a related reason are presumed to be unfair, though this presumption can be rebutted where, for example, the employee is incapable of doing her ordinary work and there is no other work that she can suitably be offered. Because claims of unfair dismissal ordinarily require the employee to have had two years' continuous service prior to dismissal, a woman dismissed for pregnancy may be better advised to formulate her claim under the Sex Discrimination Act 1975, where there is no requirement for any minimum period of service.

Finally, all pregnant employees are entitled to a reasonable amount of time off with pay to enable them to keep medically approved, ante-natal-care appointments. Unlike the other maternity provisions, there is no qualifying period of service here, nor need a woman be employed full-time before she can take time off work for this purpose. ⟡ Discrimination. K.W.

T. Gill and L. Whitty, *Women's Rights in the Workplace* (Penguin, 1983).

Mathematical Programming This is a generic term used to describe a set of related mathematical techniques used in operational research to solve resource scheduling problems (⟡ Allocation Problems; Optimization).

The most commonly used member of the family is known as linear programming (LP), so-called because there is a straight-line relationship between the variables in the problem. An example would be if the total cost of producing a batch of an item is directly proportional to the batch size. That is, if it costs £10 to produce 100 items, it costs £20 to produce 200, £30 to produce 300, etc. If all the variables present in an allocation problem are related in this simple way, it may well be appropriate to use LP. Surprisingly, many problems have been found to fulfil these requirements, and the technique is used extensively. There are a number of sub-techniques of LP that are each appropriate for particular problems. The most generally applicable is the simplex method, whilst others are the transportation method (so called because, among other applications, it can be used to find the cheapest way of transporting goods from factories to warehouses) and the assignment method (useful for finding the best way of assigning workers to jobs).

In some problems all the variables do not have linear relationships and non-linear programming techniques have been developed. Among these are quadratic programming (where there is a 'squared' relationship between some of the variables), and stochastic programming (where the exact relationships between some variables are uncertain). M.J.C.M.

Harvey M. Wagner, *Principles of Operational Research* (Prentice-Hall, 1975).

Mayo, Elton ◊ Hawthorne Investigations

Mean ◊ Measures of Location

Mean Absolute Deviation ◊ Measures of Dispersion; Inventory or Stock-control problems

Means In a business context means are often confused with ends or objectives partly because the means of a senior executive can also be one of the objectives of their junior. For example the objective of a sales director may be to increase sales and to achieve this end one of the means chosen might be to take on more sales people. The task of taking on these representatives might fall to a junior manager and this becomes their objective. The junior manager decides in turn that one means by which this can be achieved is to advertise these vacancies and this may become the objective of an assistant. There may thus be a hierarchy of means and objectives.

The only criterion by which the efficacy of a means may be judged is whether it results in the objective being achieved without running counter to any moral code in force within the company. ◊ Constraints; Objectives (in Planning); Business Policy. A.J.A.A.

Measures of Dispersion The variability of a given measure, or statistic (e.g. heights of Englishmen or diameters of ball bearings) can be represented visually by a histogram or frequency distribution (✧ Statistics). This visual representation is not suitable for the algebraic manipulations used by statisticians, which require a quantitative representation. This is achieved by using one or more measures of location and dispersion of the distribution. The two most commonly used measures of dispersion are as follows:

(1) *Range.* The difference in value between the items of lowest and highest value. For example if a manager's suits (✧ Measures of Location) cost £230, £340, £160, £520, £250, the range of the cost of his suits is £520 − £160 = £360.

Although this provides the easiest and most obvious measurement of dispersion, because it gives equal attention to all the items it may give a misleading impression of the pattern of the dispersion. If the salaries of nine managers in an organization are £12,500, £13,000, £14,000, £17,000, £20,000, £23,000, £25,000, £30,000, £300,000, the range of salaries is £300,000 − £12,500 = £287,500, although the salary range of the first eight managers is only £30,000 − £12,5000 = £17,500. Thus when all nine are included the range of £287,500 gives an inaccurate picture of the pattern of remuneration of the managers. Furthermore if the dispersion of a distribution is obtained from taking a sample (✧ Sampling), the range of the sample is likely to increase progressively as the sample-size increases. This follows because any increase in the number of items in the sample cannot possibly decrease the range of the sample already obtained but can only maintain or increase it.

(2) *Standard deviation and variance.* The extent of the dispersion of a given value is reflected in the extent of its deviation from the mean value of all the items. Thus the mean cost of the suits in the first example above is £300, so the first deviates by −£70, the second by +£40, etc. (see table on p. 320). By virtue of the definition of the mean, the sum of these deviations from it will be zero, but if we square the terms, because all the squared terms will be positive, the sum will not be zero. If this sum is divided by one less than the number of items,[1] a representative measure of dispersion is obtained. This measure is known as the variance and its square root is known as the standard deviation. The detailed calculation for the above example is given below the table.

1. For technical reasons that cannot be discussed here, the sum of the squares of the deviations is divided by one less than the number of items rather than the number of items (that is four rather than five in the example).

	Value	Deviation from mean	Squared deviation
	230	− 70	4,900
	340	+ 40	1,600
	160	−140	19,600
	520	+220	48,400
	250	− 50	2,500
Total	1,500	0	77,000

$$\text{Mean} = \frac{1,500}{5} = 300$$

$$\text{Variance} = \frac{77,000}{4} = 19,250$$

$$\text{Standard deviation} = \sqrt{19,250} = 139$$

To summarize, the variance and standard deviation are calculated as follows:

(1) Calculate the mean value of group of items.

(2) Calculate the deviation of each value from the mean.

(3) Square each deviation and calculate the sum of these 'squared deviations'.

(4) Divide by one less than the number of items in the group to obtain the variance.

(5) Calculate the square root of the variance to obtain the standard deviation.

Another measure of dispersion that is worthy of mention is the *Mean absolute deviation* (MAD). This measure has little mathematical justification, but is more convenient to calculate for practical application (◇ Inventory or Stock-control Problems) than the standard deviation. It is arrived at by subtracting each observation from the mean, ignoring the sign, summing, and then dividing by the number of observations. In the above example it would mean summing the deviations 70, 40, 140, 220, 50, to give 520 then averaging to 104. There is an approximate relationship between MAD and standard deviation: standard deviation ≃ 1·25 × MAD. M.J.C.M. and R.S.S.

P. G. Moore, *Statistics and the Manager* (Macdonald, 1966) pp. 27–31.

Measures of Location A quantitative representation of the variability of a given measure or statistic (e.g. heights of Englishmen or diameters of ball bearings) is achieved by using one or more measures of location and dispersion of the distribution (⇔ Measures of Dispersion; Statistics). The three most commonly used measures of location are as follows:

(1) *Arithmetic mean*. More usually called mean or expected value, this is the sum of the total value of all the items (e.g. the sum total of heights of all Englishmen) divided by the total number of items (e.g. the total population of Englishmen). For example a manager might buy five suits in two years, paying the following prices for each of them: £230, £340, £160, £520, £250. His total expenditure on suits is: 230 + 340 + 160 + 520 + 250 = £1,500. The mean price he pays is 1,500 ÷ 5 = £300. Hence the mean is what the layperson calls the average. Statisticians prefer to use the term 'mean' since 'average' is sometimes confused with the median.

(2) *Median*. If we arrange all the items in order of value (which is usually done in a histogram), the middle item (of an odd number of items) is the median item and its value is the median. If there is an even number of items, the median value is taken as the arithmetic mean of the two middle items. Thus the median has as many items below it as above it. When plotting a histogram each class interval has a height proportional to the number of items in it. It follows geometrically that the area below the median class interval equals the area above it. Similarly, in a frequency distribution a vertical line drawn through the median value divides the distribution into two halves of equal area.

The mean is much more suitable for algebraic manipulation but the median represents the location of the centre of the distribution. If a distribution has a small number of items with very low or very high values, these values will deflate or inflate the mean considerably. They will not unduly affect the median, however, since this identifies the middle item, not the middle value. For example suppose the salaries of nine managers are £12,500, £13,000, £14,000, £17,000, £20,000, £23,000, £25,000, £30,000, £300,000. Eight are 'middle managers', whilst the ninth is the chief executive of a large company. The median salary is the fifth (£20,000), which is fairly representative of eight of the managers' pay. In contrast the mean is 468,300 ÷ 9 = £52,033, which represents no one's pay.

Because a small group earning relatively high pay compared direct with the rest can inflate the mean figure, median salaries are invariably quoted in executive salary surveys.

(3) *Mode*. Many distributions occurring in real life are roughly bell shaped, with the frequency of items of a given value rising to a maximum and falling off again. The mode, or modal value, is the value of the most frequently occurring item and therefore corresponds to the maximum height in a histogram. The term is derived from the French 'à la mode' – the most fashionable item. The advantage of the mode is that it can often be located quickly visually; however, as two grossly dissimilar distributions can have the same mode, it is only of value as a quick comparison between two distributions that are likely to be of similar shape. M.J.C.M.

M. J. Moroney, *Facts from Figures* (Penguin, 1951), p. 34 ff.

Mechanistic and Organic Management Terms used by T. Burns and G. M. Stalker to differentiate two contrasting systems of management. The mechanistic system is characterized by a precise subdivision of the total organization into sections, each with its own semi-discrete objectives. Co-ordination is achieved by superiors in the hierarchy and by formal procedures. Individual tasks and responsibilities are precisely specified and the majority of interactions are between superior and subordinate. There is, in other words, a heavy emphasis on formal organization. In contrast an organic system places considerable reliance on the members of management forsaking their specialist preoccupations and adapting their behaviour in voluntary and spontaneous co-operation with colleagues in pursuit of common objectives as the situation may require. Rights and responsibilities are assumed or conceded with changing circumstances. Very little use is made of formal authority; most interactions, even those between supervisor and subordinate, are, or resemble, consultations between colleagues.

Burns and Stalker do not suggest that either system of management exists in its pure form to the total exclusion of any elements of the other, but their research indicated a clear division between those managements that emphasized the mechanistic system and those that emphasized the organic. The mechanistic seemed to work when the organization was operating in comparatively stable conditions, so that events could be foreseen and anticipated by the devising of appropriate procedures. The organic was most suited to situations of rapid change and uncertainty, when fluid organizational practices were necessary to achieve the swift responses required. ⟡ Bureaucracy; Formal Organization. I.C.McG.

T. Burns and G. M. Stalker, *The Management of Innovation* (Tavistock, 1966); C. B. Handy, *Understanding Organizations* (Penguin, 1985).

Media ⟡ Marketing Communications Mix

Median ⟡ Measures of Location

Medical Services Arrangements made for the supervision of the health of employees and for their treatment at the place of employment. Under the ⟡ Factories Act 1961 minimum standards are laid down for the provision of first aid, and for the medical examination of young people under sixteen and of employees working in certain processes that are dangerous to health (⟡ Industrial Disease). A comprehensive concept of a firm's industrial medical service includes measures taken to prevent illness, such as the provision of good lighting, heating and ventilation, washing facilities and canteens at the workplace, as well as arrangements for medical supervision and for quick and competent first-aid treatment. Some larger establishments provide services for the care of the teeth, the feet, for regular medical checks, including X-ray examinations and even, in a few cases, for the care of mental health. It is sometimes maintained that an industrial medical service should be established as part of the National Health Service, with increased responsibilities for appointed factory doctors and with industrial medical officers as agents of the health service rather than as employees of companies. Defenders of the present system point to improvements in the health of industrial workers in the last fifty years, including the almost complete elimination of the more serious industrial diseases. L.S.

Health and Safety Executive, *Guidelines for Occupational Health Services*, HSE. 20 (HMSO, 1980).

Medium-term Financial Strategy ⟡ Monetary Policy

Memomotion Record A method of recording activities using a cine- or video-camera designed to take pictures at longer intervals than normal. The time interval available normally ranges from one frame/sec. to one frame/30 seconds.

This method of recording is particularly suitable for: (1) studies of work involving a group of workers; (2) long-cycle and irregular-cycle work (⟡ Method Study).

Memomotion photography is a method of activity sampling and should be treated as such. Since the sampling interval is fixed and regular it is less suitable for recording repetitive, constant-cycle work than either continuous recording or random sampling (⟡ Work Sampling).

As well as being a useful means of recording activities during a method study investigation, memomotion photography is often used to record movement patterns for ⟡⟩ Plant Layout purposes. R.W.

Mental Age ⟡ Intelligence

Merchandising The use of display and promotional devices, specifically at the point of sale, for goods and services (⟡⟩ Marketing Communications Mix). The term sometimes includes ⟡⟩ Packaging, and in North America was formerly used as a synonym for ⟡⟩ Marketing. Point-of-sale promotion and display are most common in consumer markets, particularly for products sold through self-service/supermarket outlets (⟡⟩ Supermarket). The growth of such retailing activity has led to an increased use of such promotion and display. The most frequently used devices are free samples and gifts, self-liquidators (cost covering), premium promotions, cut-price offers, and the use of window and interior display, special dump bins and racks. The specific marketing objectives of the dominant incentive schemes are as follows: (1) sample give aways/free send-ins – to secure customer trial; (2) self-liquidators – to gain display in a store and catch the eye; (3) consumer clubs and voucher schemes – to develop brand loyalty (⟡⟩ Branding). Such incentive ideas are also used in relation to retailers and wholesalers in order to secure distribution. Variations of discount structures, etc., are termed 'dealer loaders' and have become increasingly frequent as competition for shelf-space in self-service stores has increased. This type of merchandising can also be found in industrial markets. The Institute of Point-of-Sale Advertising was established in 1967. G.S.C.W.

Mergers A merger by acquisition occurs when one firm absorbs another so that the latter ceases to exist. A merger by combination generally occurs when two or more firms join together to form a new firm. Examples of the general objectives of mergers are: quick growth; reduction of overall risk by diversifying products; control of markets; access to finance or cheaper finance; large-scale research (important in industries subject to rapid technological change); pooling of managerial talent; economies of scale in production, etc.

In arriving at the terms of a merger a number of factors are important, for example: earnings, dividends, market values, going-concern values (or book values), sufficiency of working capital. Additional factors that are likely to influence the valuations of merging firms include the bargaining powers of the parties to the merger and the generally recognized weaknesses and strengths of the companies concerned, e.g. their relative images as regards technology, management calibre, business leadership, product image, etc. E.A.L., amended by P.J.A.H.

Merit Rating A method of rewarding workers according to their merit or worth to the enterprise over and above the normal or acceptable performance of a job. It may be described as a form of ⟨⟩ Performance Appraisal, which is used for the purpose of pay. Whereas ⟨⟩ Job Analysis is used as a method of arriving at fair comparative rates for different jobs, merit rating is used as a method of ranking workers. Different workers doing the same jobs will perform differently; they will vary in co-operativeness, time-keeping, quality of workmanship and length of service. Even if pay is related to individual output, these other factors also have their importance. Merit rating starts by listing the factors to be taken into account and then rates workers under the different heads. There are a number of ways of making these comparisons, from simple rankings and 'paired comparisons' to more sophisticated methods such as the 'forced-choice' method and the 'critical-incident' approach. The aim is to reduce the subjective element in the judgement of the merit of an employee, and to arrive at standards that are consistent and that can be explained and justified to those to whom they are applied. L.S.

British Institute of Management, *Merit Rating* (BIM, 1954).

Method Study The systematic recording and critical examination of existing and proposed ways of doing work, as a means of developing and applying easier and more effective methods and reducing costs (British Standard 3138).

Method study is the creative aspect of ⟨⟩ Work Study. By means of a defined procedure either improved methods of doing existing jobs or efficient methods of doing new jobs are developed in order to achieve near optimum use of staff, materials and machines. Frequently work measurement may be necessary in order to compare alternative work methods.

The basic method-study procedure consists of the following steps:

(1) *Select the job to be studied.* Work study and hence method study should be applied where maximum or useful economic returns will be obtained. The following factors should be considered: (a) anticipated life of job; (b) labour content – cost of labour, ratio of man-hours to machine-time; (c) extent of job – output, man-hours involved; (d) investment in equipment, tools, etc.

(2) *Record job method.* Possible methods: memomotion

photography, multiple-activity chart, outline process chart, flow process chart ⇄ Simo Chart, ⇄ Cyclegraph/Chronocyclegrath.

(3) *Examine critically*. First, establish the purpose of the activities, the place at which they are done, the sequence, the person performing the activity and the means. Second, establish alternative place, sequence, person and means and suggest improvements.

(4) *Develop improved method*. Attempt to: eliminate activities, combine activities, change sequence, simplify remaining activities.

Utilize principles of motion economy, i.e. minimum movements, simultaneous movements, symmetrical movements, natural movements, rhythmical movements, habitual movements, continuous movement.

Consider the working environment, workplace layout and design of tools and machinery.

(5) *Define method*. Use written standard practice, job descriptions, operating instructions, as applicable.

(6) *Install and maintain*. Prepare layouts; demonstrate method; train workers; modify records, payment systems, etc.; rehearse; review progress; modify, if necessary. R.W.

R. M. Barnes, *Motion and Time Study* (J. Wiley, 5th ed., 1963); R. Wild, *Production and Operations Management* (Holt, Rinehart & Winston, 1984).

Micro-processors The advance of technology has dramatically reduced space requirements and the cost of computing. It is now possible to contain the computing power of the ⇄ Computer of twenty years ago in a desk-top box, at a cost of a few pounds, compared with many thousands of pounds. Managers in the 1980s will take for granted their own powerful desk computers, known as micro-processors, with access to large company data banks, which will provide all the information necessary for running a business. R.S.S.

Mode ◇ Measures of Location

Model ◇ Operational Research; Model (in Economic Analysis)

Model (in Economic Analysis) A model has been defined as 'the formal representation of the notions that we have about a phenomenon'.

Thus whilst the notions may be familiar ones about the workings of a market or an economy, the formal representation of this in an abstract model is relatively new. The 'formal representation' is a simplified version of reality, containing only those aspects of reality the model-builder considers important (the model-builder is free to change the model if omitted factors are later found to be important). This has at least two advantages. First, the assumptions and implications of the model can be seen more clearly in the language of mathematics than in that of everyday speech. Second, the model becomes more amenable to statistical estimation.

A useful distinction is drawn between *exact* and *stochastic* models, the former belonging to the province of economic theory, the latter to that of econometrics. Below we present the same basic model in an exact and a stochastic form. In both cases the purpose is to explain economists' notions about the determination of equilibrium price and quantity in a market.

Exact	*Stochastic*	
$q_t^d = f(p_t)$	$q_t^d = f(p_t, u_t)$	(1)
$q_t^s = g(p_t)$	$q_t^s = g(p_t, v_t)$	(2)
$q_t^s = q_t^d$	$q_t^s = q^d + w_t$	(3)

where q_t^d = quantity demanded at time t

q_t^s = quantity supplied at time t

p_t = price at time t

u_t, v_t, w_t = random normal disturbance terms at time t

Both models contain a demand function, supply function and an equilibrium condition. Consider, however, the two demand functions, equation (1). Knowledge of p_t and the functional form will be sufficient to determine q_t^d in the exact model. The corresponding equation in the stochastic model tells us that even if we know the functional form and p_t, other influences are at work on q_t^d, some of them known, others unknown. All we can assume is that the combined influences follow the normal law, are random and have a zero mean.

Does this mean that the exact model is to be preferred? The answer to this is no, since the two models serve different purposes. Whereas a knowledge of f and g will enable one to calculate the equilibrium price and quantity for the exact model, if we have price/quantity data obtained from a market in the real world, the sketching out of the stochastic model is an essential prelude to obtaining estimates of the demand and supply functions, f and g.

Although our example has been taken from a particular market, the concept of a model obviously has applications in macro-economics, in addition to its use in other subjects such as operations research and marketing. Even though one may not wish to (or cannot) obtain knowledge of the functions because of the lack of data, the concept is still useful as an aid to understanding the causal mechanism at work. ⟨⟩ Economics; Econometrics. L.T.S.

J. Stewart, *Understanding Econometrics* (Hutchinson, 2nd ed., 1984).

Monetarism Popularly the main idea of monetarism is that inflation is caused by too rapid a rise in the supply of money; to reduce inflation, the growth of the money supply should be progressively reduced until it is growing in line with the growth of productive potential. However, underpinning this idea is a sophisticated framework of thought, which owes its origin to the work of Professor Milton Friedman, beginning with his restatement of the quantity theory of money in 1956.

The work of Friedman and his associates re-emphasized the relevance of money in the modern economy in contrast to the versions of Keynesianism that had tended to limit money and monetary policy to a subsidiary role in favour of the budget and fiscal policy. Friedman argued that in the long run changes in the money supply influenced the value of nominal (i.e. current-price) variables but had minimal effect on the quantity of output and employment. This rested upon two key propositions of monetarism: (1) that the demand-for-money function is stable, and in particular is more stable than the consumption function or investment function of Keynesian economics; (2) that money is a commodity that may be substituted for a wide range of other commodities and financial assets. Hence monetarists have emphasized that monetary policy would have a direct impact upon aggregate demand whereas Keynesians argued that the initial impact would be restricted to the financial sector, which is linked to the real-goods sector by interest rates and their effect on investment. Moreover, they argued this link was weak because investment-demand was relatively interest inelastic (⟨⟩ Investment in the Economy), hence the primacy they assigned to fiscal policy.

The direct impact of monetary policy can be crudely seen by using Fisher's equation of exchange:

$$MV \equiv PT$$

where M = quantity of money supply
V = velocity of circulation
P = price level
T = volume of transactions

If we assume that *T* equals the full-employment level of transactions and V is constant at its equilibrium value, then the equilibrium price level is determined by the quantity of money (assuming real money demand equals real money supply). If the money supply is increased above the level of the demand for money, then people will spend their excess money balances on goods; since the output of goods cannot change then prices must rise, thereby helping to restore the equality of real money demand and supply.

The theoretical framework used by modern monetarists is much more complicated than that outlined above and in addition it is now accepted that changes in the money supply can affect both output and employment in the short-run, if the economy is not at the full-employment level. In this case, the effect of spending the excess money balances will initially lead to a rise in output and prices will only rise as the full-employment level is approached. It has been suggested that the time-lags between money-supply increases and an effect on output could be nine months to a year, with a further nine months to a year before there is an effect on prices. However, this does enable us to understand the stance on monetary policy of governments that have espoused monetarism: declining target growth rates for the money supply should yield declining rates of inflation, with a time-lag of eighteen months to two years. For zero inflation the money-supply growth rate should equal the growth of productive potential (i.e. the natural growth of full-employment output over time).

One final point often associated with the monetarist position, again initially made by Friedman, is that there is no long-term trade-off between inflation and unemployment. This implies that the long-term ⟫ Phillips Curve is vertical at the natural rate of unemployment, i.e. the rate that is determined in the long-run by the interaction of real forces in the labour market. ⟫ Monetary Policy. L.T.S..

D. J. Morris (ed., *The Economic System in the UK* (Oxford, 3rd ed., 1985).

Monetary Policy Monetary and fiscal policy are used by the UK Government to try to achieve such macro-objectives as a high level of employment, strong economic growth, stable prices and a satisfactory balance of payments. All governments have similar objectives, but so far no government has managed to attain all these objectives simultaneously. Throughout the post-war period up to 1971, the emphasis of monetary policy was on influencing the cost and availability of credit to the various sectors of the economy. This was achieved through the structure and level of interest rates but in addition much reliance came to be placed upon hire-purchase controls and the control of bank lending through quantitative and qualitative restraints, including ceilings on advances, liquid-asset ratios and special deposits. In this respect the monetary authorities were clearly influenced by the Radcliffe Committee Report of 1959, which emphasized the importance of the whole liquidity position of financial institutions and individuals to their spending decisions and willingness to borrow and lend. Both the authorities and the Radcliffe Committee were sceptical about the value of controlling monetary aggregates (⟷ Money Supply).

In 1971 the Bank of England issued a consultative document, 'Competition and Credit Control', which made new proposals for regulating the extension of credit by the banks and deposit-taking finance houses, the aim of the proposals being to make for a more competitive banking system and more flexible methods of influencing monetary conditions.

The main weapons of monetary policy were now to consist of: changing the minimum lending rate offered by the Bank of England to the discount market, and hence the other short-term rates linked to it; open-market operations to affect all banks' policies through their reserve-asset ratio; and requests for special deposits to be lodged by all the banks with the Bank of England. All banks and finance houses were covered by the new policies, not just the clearing banks. In addition the banks' interest-rate cartel was terminated and quantitative restrictions on bank lending were abolished, although the banks were still given general guidance on the areas to which they should direct their lending.

However, with the much greater inflation of the 1970s and the rise of ⟷ Monetarism, increasing attention has been paid to the growth of the money supply itself, culminating in the introduction by the Conservative Government in 1980 of its medium-term financial strategy (MTFS). This involved the setting of targets and projections for the main monetary aggregates and the public sector borrowing requirement (PSBR) for a number of years ahead, the aim being to influence expectations and hence lower inflation. At the same time a Green Paper on Monetary Control (Cmnd. 7858, 1980) was published by the Treasury and the Bank of England, which examined alternative techniques of monetary control and opened the area for discussion with interested parties. The money supply can theoretically be controlled by an appropriate combination of fiscal policy, which affects the PSBR, and interest rates. This therefore leads to the question, 'What determines interest rates?'

Until 1981 the key interest rate was known as the minimum lending rate (MLR), originally introduced in 1971. The MLR is the rate at which the Bank of England will give assistance – by loans or rediscounting bills – to discount houses that are forced by shortage of funds to go to the Bank of England as lender of last resort. Originally linked to short-term interest rates so that it moved with them, the link system finished in 1978 when the MLR was fixed by policy decision. However, following the discussions above, the MLR was discontinued in 1981 (although it could be introduced if necessary) and the Bank of England now influences interest rates through open-market sales and purchases of bills at rates selected with reference to bands of bills, in terms of maturity, embracing one or more very short-term rates. This, it was thought, would allow money-market conditions to determine interest rates, but events in 1984/5 have shown that this is not always the case. For example, in December 1984 the Chancellor of the Exchequer reimposed MLR for a few hours to protect the pound when it almost fell to dollar parity, and in July 1985 the Bank of England adjusted its minimum dealing rates in the market to help bring down the clearing banks' base rates. Some commentators have therefore suggested that we now have a minimum bill rate replacing the minimum lending rate.

Besides influencing the money supply, it is impossible to ignore the fact that our interest rates are an important determinant of sterling's exchange rate with other currencies and this therefore restricts the freedom of the monetary authorities to allow interest rates to settle at levels appropriate to the domestic economy. Thus, in July 1985, despite high unemployment of 3·2 million and a sterling–dollar exchange rate of 1·3–1·4, UK interest rates were considerably higher than those in Germany, Japan and the USA, with consequent effects upon industry's costs and ability to expand and export. The authorities, however, appear unwilling to allow interest rates to fall, because of the adverse effect on the pound, which in turn affects import prices and inflation. This has therefore led some commentators to suggest that the real target of monetary policy is the exchange rate rather than the growth of the money supply, particularly as controlling the monetary aggregates has not been easy and they may give ambiguous readings. According to the Bank of England, £M3 (✧ Money Supply) expanded by 2 per cent in June 1985, which brought the increase over twelve months to 12 per cent, well outside the 1985 MTFS target of 5–9 per cent and even above the ceiling of 11 per cent laid down for 1980/1 when the MTFS was introduced. On the other hand M0 rose by 5·25 per cent in the year to June 1985, well within its target range of 3–7 per cent. Clearly the debate on the most appropriate instruments and measures of monetary policy is by no means over. ✧ Monetarism. L.T.S.

A. R. Prest and D. J. Coppock, *The UK Economy: A Manual of Applied Economics* (Weidenfeld & Nicolson, 10th ed., 1984).

Money Supply It is generally accepted that money has three functions in an economy: to act as a medium of exchange, as a store of value and as a unit of account.

As a medium of exchange money enables us to avoid the cumbersome process of barter, whereby products are exchanged against each other. Without money the modern economy as we know it would cease to function, such is the degree of specialization in goods and services.

Money is also useful as a store of wealth since it represents a claim on goods that can be exercised in the future. However, to be a satisfactory store of wealth prices should be stable.

Finally, the units in which money is measured (pounds and pence, dollars and cents) are generally used as the units in which values are expressed and assets and debts defined and measured.

In modern monetary systems the money supply consists of coins, bank notes and bank deposits. With the rise of ⟫ Monetarism in recent years several measures of money supply have attracted attention in the U K because of their supposed relationship with future ⟫ Inflation. Currently two measures are given targets as part of the Government's ⟫ Monetary Policy, namely M0 and £M3, but other measures are monitored as well, particularly private sector liquidity (P S L2).

M0 consists of notes and coins in circulation with the public, money in banks' tills and bankers' operational balances with the Bank of England. £M3 consists of notes and coins in circulation, private-sector sterling, sight-and-time deposits in banks and private-sector holdings of sterling certificates of deposit. Thus M0 is a measure incorporating the medium of exchange function, whilst £M3 includes the store-of-value function as well since people may hold some of their wealth in time deposits whilst using their sight deposits by issuing cheques to purchase goods and settle debts. With the increasing sophistication of the monetary system £M3 is very sensitive to switches of funds between banks and building societies. To many people a deposit in the building society is exactly the same as a deposit in the bank. Hence for some time a measure has been used of private-sector liquidity (P S L2). This differs from £M3 by including building-society deposits, private-sector holdings of money-market instruments (treasury bills etc.), national-savings deposits and eliminating long-term (maturity over two years) private-sector sterling time deposits.

In May 1985 the following values obtained (all seasonally adjusted): M0, £14,020 m; £M3, £114,780 m; P S L2, £200,448 m. L.T.S.

Monopolistic Competition ⟫ Market Models and Competition

Monopoly ⟫ Market Models and Competition; Monopoly Policy

Monopoly Policy The British approach to monopoly power is to examine cases individually and judge each on its own merits. This reflects the fact that few, if any, conclusive statements can be made about the effects of monopoly power, either from theoretical reasoning or empirical research.

A monopoly was defined by the Monopolies and Restrictive Practices Act, 1948 as existing where at least one third of the supply of a good came from a single firm or group of firms. If such a situation were thought to exist, the President of the Board of Trade could request the Monopolies Commission to verify its existence and pronounce upon its effects on the public interest. This latter phrase is open to considerable interpretation: where does the public interest lie if large profits are ploughed back to finance new capital expenditure or research and development? The framers of the Act were concerned that consumer preferences for goods should be met and that efficient methods of production and distribution should obtain, and these objectives occur in various guises through subsequent reports of the Commission.

The Monopolies Commission has been reorganized several times in order to carry out its duties of reporting and recommending on a given situation. Until 1953 the Commission of ten members considered each case together, but from then until 1956 the size of the Commission was increased to twenty-five and several cases could be considered simultaneously by smaller groups. The passing of the Restrictive Practices Act, 1956 took away from the Commission what at the time was considered to be a significant part of its work, i.e. its work on restrictive trade practices. Thus the Commission was returned to its pre-1953 size and mode of operation. In 1965, however, with the passing of the Monopolies and Mergers Act its size was increased again but, in addition, its sphere of interest was widened to cover investigations of the possible effects of proposed mergers. The latest change occurred with the passing of the Fair Trading Act 1973, for under this legislation the post of Director General of Fair Trading was established with the power to gather detailed preliminary information before deciding whether to refer a monopoly situation to the Monopolies and Mergers Commission. Amongst other important developments introduced by this Act was the lowering of the monopoly criterion from one third to one quarter and the widening of the area of application to take in local as well as national monopolies.

Amongst the results of monopoly power that have caused concern are the failure to develop research and development expertise (Supply of Industrial Gases), the restriction of competition (Supply of Wallpaper), the use of price, advertising and promotion policies specifically designed to support monopoly power (Supply of Household Detergents), and the earning of abnormally high profits (Supply of Contraceptive Sheaths, Supply of Chlordiazepoxide and Diazepam). The 1973 Act gave the Director General power to negotiate with companies in the light of the Commission's proposals as an alternative to the imposition of statutory orders, and in some cases the Office of Fair Trading has been given the task of monitoring future pricing policy. (Supply of Contraceptive Sheaths, Supply of Breakfast Cereals, Supply of Household Detergents). On the other hand, the general feeling is that evidence is more favourable to single-firm monopolies than the original drafters of the 1948 Act anticipated (Supply of Primary Batteries, Supply of Building Bricks, Supply of Flat Glass).

The function of looking into proposed mergers was introduced in 1965 as a way of curbing the growth of future monopolies. Under the 1973 Act the Director General keeps mergers under review, but the final decision to make a reference lies with the Secretary of State for Trade and Industry. As before, a merger may be referred if a monopoly situation would result, or if it would involve the taking over of gross assets exceeding £30 m (raised from £15 m in July 1984).

Most mergers are cleared without a reference to the Commission. For example in 1984 the Office of Fair Trading considered 259 mergers that came within the scope of the Fair Trading Act (other than newspaper mergers), but only four references were made by the Secretary of State to the Commission, the Director General's advice being not accepted in one further case. Usually these reports have to be completed within six months, and amongst the factors taken into account by the Commission are the present and future state of competition in the industry, the regional distribution of employment, the efficient use of resources, and industrial innovation. Representations can be made by all interested parties but there is no requirement that a merger should be shown to be positively 'in the public interest', only that it is either 'against the public interest' or 'not against the public interest'.

There is no doubt that this aspect of monopoly policy is controversial, being bound up with government policy towards business. For example, during the merger mania of 1965–70 a number of very large mergers were sponsored by the Government and not referred to the Commission. Nowadays greater stress seems to be laid on the potential loss of competition as a criterion for referral to the Commission and the climate has become somewhat less favourable to mergers, with the publication of several reports[1] on the disappointing results of previous mergers. However, the statistics quoted above show that the majority are still not

1. See, for example, G. Meeks, *Disappointing Marriage, a Study of the Gains from Merger* (DAE Occasional Paper No. 51, CUP, 1977).

referred. Undoubtedly this has meant an increase in the importance of the merger policy of the Mergers Panel (a committee of Civil Servants and Office of Fair Trading staff), which recommends whether a bid should be referred. Lobbying against a potential reference has become the most important stage in justifying a merger, and lobbying for a reference the central weapon in resisting an unwelcome takeover bid. This is illustrated by the recent decision (July 1985) to allow Guinness to proceed with their bid for Arthur Bell without reference to the Commission.

Of the cases that have been referred to the Commission, about half have been found to be against the public interest. Recent cases of interest are GKN's bid for AE (rejected 1984), Trafalgar House's bid for P & O (accepted 1984) and BET's bid for Initial (accepted 1985). Usually the Secretary of State accepts the verdict of the Commission but an exception occurred in 1982 when the proposed takeover of Anderson Strathclyde by Charter Consolidated was allowed, even though the Commission had recommended by a four to two majority that it might be expected to operate against the public interest. This caused much controversy and led to the resignation of a member of the Commission, Professor Andrew Bain. The fact that the Chairman of the Commission was in the minority does raise the question whether all members' views are to be given equal weight.

One disadvantage of the approach used to police monopolies was remedied with the passing of the Competition Act 1980. Previously the whole of an industry needed to be studied, even though the main target for investigation was a single firm, but this Act empowered the Director General to carry out a preliminary investigation to establish whether a particular course of conduct carried out by a person in the course of business amounted to an anti-competitive practice. If it was found to be so, a reference to the Commission could be made, the task then being to establish, usually within six months, whether an anti-competitive practice is, or was, being operated and whether it is against the public interest. Clearly this time-period is much shorter than the time taken for full-scale monopolies reports. Possible examples of such practices are price discrimination, predatory pricing and the use of selective distribution channels. An early case involved the Raleigh bicycle company, which was refusing to supply bicycles to discount stores and favouring specialist cycle shops. Following a report by the Commission in late 1981, the Director General accepted undertakings from the company that it would not refuse to supply bicycles, other than those with the Raleigh brand name, to such stores. L.T.S.

P. J. Devine *et al.*, *An Introduction to Industrial Economics* (Allen & Unwin, 3rd ed., 1985); *Annual Report of the Director General of Fair Trading 1984* (HMSO, 1985).

Monte Carlo Techniques ⟡ Simulation

Morale The extent to which the members of a group identify with the aims and activities of the group. Earlier usage of the term included its application to the emotional state of individual persons divorced from a group context but current usage is in accordance with the definition given.

If the interests of different groups are occasionally, or in some respects, conflicting – and this is certainly the case in an industrial organization – it is quite possible for morale in each of the conflicting groups to be high whilst that in the total organization would be comparatively low. Indeed, the ability of a group to engage successfully in conflict from time to time may be a condition of high morale. There is evidence to support that this is in fact the case and that an inability to exert a positive influence over a situation is likely to lead to low morale in a group. It follows that low morale cannot be inferred from the existence of occasional disputes, even if some of these result in strike action. The degree of interest and involvement in group activities and the levels of absenteeism and labour turnover are more valid indications of the state of morale, although absence and turnover are both affected by other variables.

High morale is not necessarily related to high productivity, although the failure of research to identify any consistent correlation between the two may be due to the adoption of too narrow a definition of productivity. It is difficult to resist the common-sense conclusion that high morale must be reflected in productivity *at least in the long run*. ⟡ Alienation; Conflict. I.C.MCG.

W. H. Scott *et al.*, *Coal and Conflict* (Liverpool University Press, 1963) ch. 2; V. H. Vroom and E. L. Deci (eds.), *Management and Motivation* (Penguin, 1970); P. Brannen, *Authority and Participation in Industry* (Batsford, 1983), ch. 4.

Motion Study First used by Frank and Lillian Gilbreth to describe their contribution to what was afterwards called 'scientific management'. They described motion study as consisting of 'dividing the work into fundamental elements; analysing these elements separately and in relation to one another; and from these studied elements, when timed, building methods of least waste'.[1] ⟡ Gilbreth.

In the UK motion study is often considered synonymous with ⟡ Method Study. However, motion study is only a part of method study, i.e. it is the study of the various *movements* that together constitute the work *method*.

1. R. M. Currie, *Work Study* (BIM, 2nd ed., 1963), p. 6.

Because of the wider implications, the term method study is recommended by British Standard 3138 in preference to motion study.

In the USA motion study and method study (as well as methods research, methods analysis and methods engineering) are often used interchangeably, although the American Society of Mechanical Engineers' definitions distinguish between motion study – a study of movements – and method study – a study of the sequence of motions.

Motion study utilizing ⟡ Simo Charts or ⟡ Cyclegraphs, i.e. the most detailed type of motion study, is usually referred to as micromotion study. ⟡ Predetermined Motion Time Study. R.W.

Motivation (of Individuals and Groups) The process of initiating and directing behaviour. Individuals produce and sustain behaviour when they find it rewarding to do so; that is, when the behaviour accomplishes an objective that satisfies a need. As far as industrial organizations are concerned, employees will be motivated to carry out the duties assigned to them to the extent that to do so satisfies their personal needs. Whilst it has long been recognized that individual needs are complex and unstable, considerable reliance has been placed on financial incentives as a motivating device. Undoubtedly financial rewards are extremely important not only for the material needs they indirectly satisfy but also for their symbolic significance as indicators of social and personal worth and status. In recent years, however, there has been an increasing disillusionment with the effectiveness of financial incentives and, following the theoretical assumptions of A. H. Maslow, attention has been directed to the need to place greater emphasis on rewards intrinsic to the work itself as a necessary supplement to the traditional extrinsic rewards. Accordingly, once provision has been made for adequate earnings and satisfactory general working conditions, attempts are made to structure the work situation so as to provide opportunities for increased independence and personal accomplishment. On the whole, research data appear to support the general validity of this approach but it must be borne in mind that motivation is highly complex and that personal needs differ greatly from one person to another and within the same person over time. ⟡ Alienation; Job Enlargement; Morale. I.C.McG.

V. Vroom, *Work and Motivation* (J. Wiley, 1964); D. McGregor, *The Human Side of Enterprise* (McGraw-Hill, 1960); C. B. Handy, *Understanding Organizations* (Penguin, 1981).

Motivation Research (in Marketing) The process of seeking to identify the attitudes, habits and motives that trigger behaviour, most particularly in the purchase of goods. Findings are used to make more effective promotional appeals and product formulations. The techniques involved, of which the most common are the small group discussion/ interview (perhaps six to eight respondents) and the depth/unstructured interview, cannot always solicit a direct revelation of motives but rather comments that, with interpretation, indicate the factors determining behaviour. Such interpretation relies heavily on the insights developed through psychoanalysis, and many of the leading practitioners are psychologists and sociologists. The most famous pioneer of the technique was Ernest Dichter, who still practises in North America, although the standard work on the subject was written in Britain: H. Henry, *Motivation Research* (Crosby-Lockwood, 1957). The technique caused a controversy when first introduced into ⟨⟩ Marketing Research since it was considered by many to be unethical, but was defended on the grounds that participants were volunteers in any event. Large samples are not normally taken with depth/unstructured interviews since it is contended that the relatively small variety of attitudes in a population will normally be present in a small group. However, the extent to which any particular attitude, habit or motive is held in any population must be quantified in a structured interview (⟨⟩ Market Survey). An extensive group of tools has been developed to facilitate this (⟨⟩ Attitude Scales). G.S.C.W.

Multiple-activity Chart Also known as a man–machine chart or work-planning chart, it records the activities of two or more subjects (people or machines) on a common time-scale.

The activities and their duration are represented by blocks drawn against a time-scale. Since it is difficult to include much detail on such diagrams, multiple-activity charts constitute a less detailed method of recording work methods than proven charts (⟨⟩ Gantt Chart; Method Study; Process Charts).

Although there are many different conventions, depending on the purpose of the chart, the following is usual.

Independent work. Operator working independently of machine, e.g. preparing material, reading drawings; machine working independently of operator, i.e. operation requiring neither physical nor mental attention of operator.

Combined work. Operator working with machine or vice versa, hand operation, e.g. hand feed.

Waiting. Either operator or machine waiting for the other, or both for something else. R.W.

Multiple Criteria Decision-making Despite the everyday need for management to take decisions in an environment of conflicting choices, it is only recently that much attention has been paid to the issue of multiple criteria. It has normally been assumed that some form of hierarchy of decision or preference rating could be devised, with each decision consequence weighted on a common scale, the most attractive being given a greater weight than those of less appeal. If such a weighting could be agreed, then the multiple criteria could be readily reduced to one. In practice, this is not common and other approaches have been adopted, such as goal programming and trade-off analysis. Much of the work is carried out in the field of ⟨⟩ Mathematical Programming. ⟨⟩ Optimization. R.S.S.

R. L. Keeney and H. Raiffa, *Decisions with Multiple Objectives* (J. Wiley, 1976).

Multiplier, The During the depression of the 1930s the theoretical approach of economists to the problems of the economy was changed by the publication of *The General Theory of Employment, Interest and Money* by J. M. Keynes. One important development was the idea of the multiplier, developed by Lord Keynes from earlier ideas of R. F. Khan. In essence the multiplier process shows how sustained changes in the level of components of final expenditure in the economy (⟨⟩ National Income Accounts) can produce multiplied effects on the level of gross national product. The importance of this development of thought for an economy in the grips of a depression is hard to exaggerate, because it showed, for example, that increases in investment demand, if sustained, would lead to increased levels of GNP and hence of employment. However, the idea is also useful for the full utilization of resources, and in conjunction with the acceleration principle (⟨⟩ Investment in the Economy) it offers some insights into the fluctuations in GNP that occur in most economies from time to time.

The multiplier, in its simplest form, shows the effect on a simple economy of a change in investment demand. Such a simple economy is usually postulated to have no foreign-trade sector or government sector, but the multiplier can be modified to take account of these moves to reality. Traditionally macro-economists have been as much interested in the equilibrium of the whole economy as micro-economists have been in the equilibrium of particular markets. Thus the multiplier was originally developed as a static concept from a comparison of two equilibrium positions, but later work has focused attention upon its essentially dynamic character.

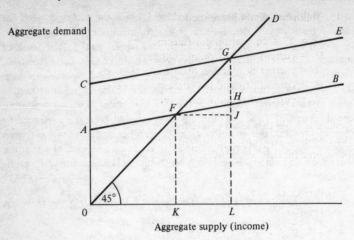

The figure above shows the static multiplier as the simple economy moves from one equilibrium position to the next. Equilibrium here means that aggregate demand – the total demands upon the system – balances aggregate supply – the total output of the system.

In this case we imagine an economy with only two sectors, a consumer sector and a business sector. The demands that they make upon the system at any given level of income (= output) are shown by the schedule AB. The economy will be in equilibrium at output level OK because at this level of output aggregate demand is also equal to OK (since $FK = OK$). Suppose now that investment demands increase, causing the aggregate-demand schedule to rise vertically by amount GH. We then have a new aggregate-demand schedule CE and hence a new equilibrium level of output OL. A comparison of these two equilibrium positions using simple geometry shows that whilst investment demand has increased by GH, the equilibrium level of output (= income) has increased by GJ ($= FJ = KL$), which is greater than GH. The multiplying factor is referred to as the multiplier.

The following numerical example conveys exactly the same principle as before but the actual process of change from one equilibrium position to the other is made clear. The following assumptions are made:

(1)   The consumption function is of the form $C_t = 0.6\ Y_t + 150$.
(2)   Investment demand is 50 initially and then rises in period 2 to 100. It does not vary with income levels.
(3)   Output in the current period is equal to the period's aggregate demand.

The following symbols are used:

$O_t = Y_t$ = current output (income)
O_c = current production of consumer goods
O_i = current production of investment goods
C_t = current demand for consumption goods
I_t = current demand for investment goods

Starting from the initial equilibrium position in period 1, with investment demand equal to 50, the example shows what happens in subsequent time periods when investment rises to 100.

Period	$O_t = Y_t$	O_c	O_i	C_t	I_t	Aggregate demand $(C_t + I_t)$
1	500	450	50	450	50	500
2	500	450	50	450	100	550
3	550	450	100	480	100	580
4	580	480	100	498	100	598
5	598	498	100	508·8	100	608·8
625		525	100	525	100	625

In period 2 the demand for investment goods increases by 50 but output cannot adjust until the next period. In period 3 output and income increase to 550 because the new investment demand is satisfied. However, because consumption demand is dependent upon income it now increases to 480 ($C_t = 0.6 \times 550 + 150 = 480$). This consumption demand cannot be met until period 4, when output of consumer goods rises to 480. However, this means that income is now 580 and thus again consumption demand exceeds the available supply of consumption goods and aggregate demand exceeds aggregate supply. However, we notice that the increments to aggregate demand in each period are diminishing: each is 0·6 of the previous increment. In fact the progression of the aggregate-demand column follows that of a geometric progression, ultimately reaching 625. Thus the final increase in output (= income) is 2·5 times the initial increase in investment demand. At this point the system is in equilibrium again because aggregate demand and aggregate supply are in balance.

Whilst this is only true for a simple economy, the principle is widely applicable. Thus the introduction of a government sector and a foreign-trade sector means that increases in government spending and export demand set off multiplier processes of their own. Against this, however, not all the additional income reaches the final consumer because some

$$125 = 2 \cdot 5 \times 50 = \frac{1}{1 - 0 \cdot 6} \times 50$$

In general, then, one can say that

$$\Delta Y = k\Delta I = \frac{1}{1 - c} \Delta I$$

where ΔY = increment to total income (output)
   ΔI = increment to investment
   k = multiplier
   c = marginal propensity to consume

disappears into undistributed profits, taxes or into the purchase of imports. Such 'leakages', as they are termed, act to reduce the value of the multiplier, which for this country has been put at around 1 to 1·5. This compares with estimated marginal propensities of 0·5 to 0·7, which would give multipliers ranging from 2 to 3·3. ⟨⟩ Comsumption Function; Growth in the Economy; Employment. L.T.S.

E. Shapiro, *Macroeconomic Theory* (Harcourt Brace Jovanovich, 5th rev. ed., 1982).

Muscular Work Movement is achieved by muscular contraction. The energy required for contraction is stored in the muscles within the large glycogen molecules. These disintegrate to produce glucose, the breakdown of which liberates energy and produces lactic acid as a waste product. No immediate supply of oxygen is required for this series of reactions, but an 'oxygen debt' is created, in that oxygen is required for the further breakdown and removal of the lactic acid. Thus, in the long term, the amount of oxygen consumed is proportional to the amount of physiological work performed. It must be noted that a certain expenditure of energy takes place without obvious movement, since work is done by such muscles as the heart, in addition to those involved in the maintenance of posture.

Numerous equipments and techniques are available to measure the rate of oxygen consumption and hence the physiological energy-cost of any activity of human performance. This energy-cost provides one index for evaluating different methods of performing a particular task. E.E.

Myers, Charles Samuel It is probably to C. S. Myers (1873–1946) that the greatest debt is owed for the establishment of industrial psychology in the UK.

Following a distinguished undergraduate career in the natural sciences, Myers later qualified in medicine and achieved eminence as an experimental psychologist in the first British laboratory at Cambridge. His interests were directed largely towards the application of psychological principles in the fields of medicine, education and industry. In 1922, being disillusioned by the lack of support at Cambridge, Myers resigned his readership to devote full-time attention to the National Institute of Industrial Psychology, which he had founded two years previously with H. J. Welch. Myers was elected the first president of the British Pschological Society in 1920 and served as editor of the *British Journal of Psychology* from 1913 to 1924. E.E.

N

National Income Accounts Fundamentally the national income accounts (or social accounts) show the results and interconnections of economic activity in the country during a particular calendar year. The economic activity of the country is viewed in three logically distinct ways: (1) as the result of expenditure decisions; (2) as the result of production decisions, and (3) since production necessitates factors of production, as giving rise to factor payments.

In August of each year the Central Statistical Office produces the *National Income Blue Book*, which provides full statistical detail on the three ways of measuring economic activity. It is now an international convention that the aggregate measure of economic activity for a country is its gross national product, but the term national income also has a special meaning besides being the general term used for such studies. Another widely used term is gross domestic product (GDP), which is equal to the gross national product minus net property income from abroad. This is a measure of the goods and services produced as a result of economic activity in the UK. In addition, the *Blue Book* contains a wealth of subsidiary material, known as the social accounts, which is useful in examining the progress and interconnections of different sectors of the economy such as the personal sector and the government sector.

Although the August publication refers to the previous calendar year, quarterly estimates of the national income are also produced in *Economic Trends*. Of necessity they lack the detail of the *Blue Book*, but nevertheless they are important for forecasting purposes.

The table opposite illustrates the three methods of measuring the economic activity of the country.

On the expenditure side we see that the decision-makers are consumers, firms, government bodies and overseas consumers. Their demands are satisfied by the industries and services that make up the 'value-added' section of the table. Lastly, we note that the proceeds of economic activity go to wage and salary earners, self-employed people, firms in the form of profits, and the holders of overseas property (net).

The initial impetus to the development of systems of national accounts came from the publication in 1936 of Lord Keynes's book *The General*

Gross national product (UK) 1983

Expenditure	£m	Income	£m	Production (value-added)[4]	£m
Consumers' expenditure	182,427	Income from employment	170,072	Agriculture, forestry and fishing	5,535
General government final consumption	65,859	Income from self-employment[1]	23,123	Energy and water supply	29,645
Gross domestic fixed-capital formation	49,559	Gross trading profit of companies[1,2]	41,530	Manufacturing	62,258
Value of physical increase in stocks and work-in-progress	267	Gross trading surplus of public corporations[1]	9,661	Construction	15,319
Exports of goods and services	79,768	Gross trading surplus of general government enterprises[1]	−109	Distribution, hotels and catering, repairs	35,002
Less imports of goods and services	−76,582	Rent[3]	17,424	Transport	11,543
Less taxes on expenditure	−49,865	Imputed charge for consumption of non-trading capital	2,456	Communication	7,092
Subsidies	6,056	Less stock appreciation	−4,326	Banking, finance, insurance, business services and leasing	31,067
		Residual error	−2,342	Ownership of dwellings	15,761
Gross domestic product at factor cost	257,489	Gross domestic product at factor cost	257,489	Public administration, national defence and compulsory social security	18,027
		Net property income from abroad	1,948	Education and health services	24,021
		Gross national product at factor cost	259,437	Other services	16,415
		Less capital consumption	−36,490	Adjustment for financial services	−11,854
		National income (i.e. net national product)	222,947	Residual error	−2,342
				Gross domestic product at factor cost	257,489

Source: United Kingdom National Accounts (1984).

1. Before providing for depreciation and stock appreciation
2. Including financial institutions
3. Before providing for depreciation
4. The contribution of each industry to the gross domestic product before providing for depreciation but after providing for stock appreciation

Theory of Employment, Interest and Money. This was reinforced by the Second World War, during which use was made of national income accounts for the overall control of the economic system. Today, in many developed and developing countries the basic structure of the national accounts lies at the heart of government economic planning and fore-casting. This is because the accounts provide the size of the key variables that influence the level of gross national product and from them one can work out rates of growth in these variables and their interconnections. For example consumer expenditure is a key variable and one can work out the relationship between growth of consumer expenditure and growth of personal disposable income. ◇ Forecasting for the Economy, Short-term. L.T.S.

National Insurance ◇ Industrial Injuries

Negotiable Instruments A negotiable instrument is a document embodying a debt of a sum of money, where the document enjoys the quality of negotiability. Normally a debt of money may be transferred (assigned) by the creditor to a third party, but this assignment must be made in writing, written notice of it must be given to the debtor and the third-party assignee acquires no better title to the debt than was pos-sessed by the assignor. With a negotiable instrument, however, the transfer may be effected by mere delivery of the instrument without the necessity of either a written assignment or written notice to the debtor, and the third party who receives such an instrument in good faith acquires a good title to it, irrespective of the title of the transferor. The only exception to the rules about transfer apply to bills of exchange and promissory notes, which require a written endorsement for purposes of transfer.

Whether or not an instrument enjoys the quality of negotiability de-pends largely upon commercial custom. Negotiable instruments include bank notes, bills of exchange, cheques, promissory notes, treasury bills and dividend warrants. It is unlikely that further instruments will be added to this list by commercial custom, but statute law could be used to create further negotiable instruments. W.F.F.

D. Richardson, *Guide to Negotiable Instruments* (Butterworth, 7th ed., 1983).

Net Present Value The net present value (NPV) of an investment project is the difference between the present value of revenues (or bene-fits) and the present value of costs (or sacrifices) when all revenues and costs are discounted back to the present time by reference to the cost of capital (◇ Capital, Cost of).

Assuming that the whole of the investment outlay is made immediately then the NPV is usually defined as follows:

$$NPV = P - I$$

where P = present value of periodic future flows of revenues and costs, as defined below

I = investment outlay, assumed to be paid out entirely at the commencement of the project's life

$$P = \frac{Y^1}{(1 + i)} + \frac{Y^2}{(1 + i)^2} + \ldots + \frac{Y_n + S_n}{(1 + i)^n}$$

where Y = net cash flow, i.e. revenues less costs, in time period 1, 2, 3 ... n

S_n = scrap or realizable value from the project, received in year n

n = life of the project in number of time periods, e.g. one year.

i = cost of capital to the firm

If the NPV is positive then the project in question is acceptable, according to present-value theory, since in present-value terms a profit after earning a sufficient rate of return is shown. A negative value for NPV indicates that the project is expected to earn less than a sufficient rate of return and is therefore unacceptable.

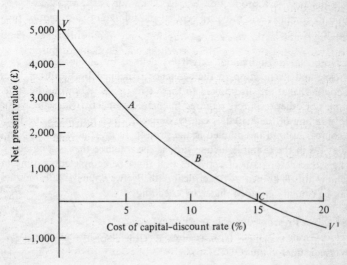

It can be shown that the present value and the ⟨⟩ Internal Rate of Return are generally equivalent criteria (although in some specific situations the latter may be misleading).

For example, consider a project that has an initial investment of £5,000 and a net cash flow for the following ten years of £1,000. The NPV of such a project will vary with the firm's cost of capital. As this increases so will the rate at which the future receipts are discounted, and the NPV will fall. The relationship can be shown by the figure on p. 347, in which the curve VV' shows the NPV of this project as the cost of capital increases. As the cost of capital increases the present value falls indefinitely, eventually becoming negative. For example, the NPV is given by point A on VV' (approximately £2,700) when the cost of capital is 5 per cent. When the cost of capital is 10 per cent, the NPV is approximately £1,100. At C, where VV' and the cost-of-capital axis intercept, the NPV is zero, at a discount rate of 15 per cent. Since the internal rate of return is defined as that rate of interest (or discount) at which the NPV equals zero, the cost of capital at this point defines the internal rate of return. ⟨⟩ Discounted Cash Flow. E.A.L., amended by P.J.A.H.

Network Analysis A generic term that describes a number of techniques used to plan and control complex projects consisting of a set of interrelated activities. The essence is to represent the sequential relationships between the activities by a network of lines and circles.

For example, the pattern of activities required to complete the move of a machine in a production line to a new site is shown below.[1] The time to complete the move is kept to the minimum to minimize production losses.

Note that an individual activity is defined by a line between two circles, and its position in the sequence is defined by the other lines (activities) that are also linked to these two circles. Knowing the time, money or other resources required to complete an activity, a schedule or dove-tailing of the activities can be derived, which minimizes the total resources utilized in completing the project. In most common applications (as in the example below) time is the resource that is minimized. The sequence or path of activities that must be completed on time to achieve this is known as the critical path. Network-analysis techniques can be roughly grouped under two headings:

1. This example is taken from G. R. Gedye, *Scientific Method in Production in Management* (OUP, 1965).

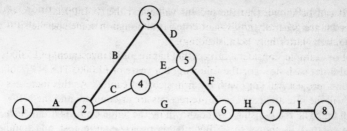

		Must be preceded by	Can be followed by	Estimated time (days)
A	Prepare plans	—	B, C, G	4
B	Clear site	A	D	3
C	Dismantle machine	A	E	2
D	Prepare foundations	B	F	4
E	Move machine to new site	C	F	1
F	Install machine	D, E	H	4
G	Run services (electricity, etc.)	A	H	6
H	Connect up services	F, G	I	1
I	Test and check machine on new site	H	—	1
—	Critical path (17 days)			

1. *Critical Path Method* (*C P M*) assumes that the time required to complete an activity can be predicted exactly, identifies the critical path and calculates the total time along it.

2. *Program Evaluation Review Technique* (*P E R T*) recognizes that the time required to complete an activity cannot usually be predicted exactly and allows for this in evaluating the critical path.

Both methods may be extended to evaluate the utilization of costs and other resources.

Typical applications of network-analysis techniques are: construction

Markets	Technology		
	No change	*Improved*	*New*
No change	—	Reformulation	Replacement
Strengthened market share	Re-merchandising	Improved	Product-line extension
New	New uses	Market extension	Diversification

projects; R and D projects; maintenance projects; promotion and launching of new products; Line of Balance (LoB) problems in production scheduling. M.J.C.M.

K. G. Lockyer, *An Introduction to Critical Path Analysis* (Pitman, 1964).

New Issue Market ◇ Capital Market

New Product The product offered to a market when either the technology involved in its manufacture or the market to which it is offered is new to the company (the area enclosed by heavy lines in the figure on p. 349).

It can take any of the forms indicated but should be distinguished from the variety of modifications to existing products shown outside the heavy lines. New products constitute product innovation and marketing

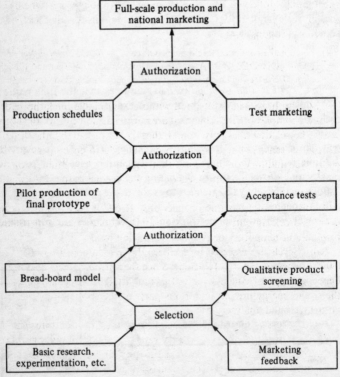

A sequence of new product development

management normally subjects such innovation to a rigorous series of tests as indicated in the figure on p. 350 (⟡ Marketing Experimentation.) G.S.C.W.

G. Wills, D. Midgley and R. Hayhurst, *Creating and Marketing New Products* (Staples, 1973).

New-technology Agreements The so-called micro-electronic revolution has had important repercussions for industrial relations in recent years. Almost invariably the introduction of new technologies is accompanied by extensive consultation (⟡ Joint Consultation), but in some companies new-technology agreements have been signed, which involve extensive trade-union involvement in the implementation (and, sometimes, the planning) process. There have been at least eighteen new-technology agreements in the electronics industry. A typical finding from research, too, is that ⟡ Disclosure of Information to employees increases substantially following the signing of new-technology agreements, although the overall impact on employees and unions is rather less than is sometimes supposed. M.J.F.P.

National Economic Development Office, *The Introduction of New Technology* (NEDO, 1983); A. Sorge, G. Hartmann, M. Warner and I. Nicholas, *Microelectronics and Manpower in Manufacturing* (Gower, 1983).

Noise In the sense of sound without identifiable pitch, noise consists of a complex of vibrations that are not in harmonic ratio. In another sense 'noise' describes any sound that is unwanted by the listener. This latter sense of the word has been enlarged to encompass any signal, either auditory or otherwise, that occurs in a communication system but contains no intelligence for the recipient (⟡ Information Theory).

Acoustical noise has three deleterious effects: it may produce reductions in work output; it is annoying and produces discomfort; it may bring about temporary or permanent hearing loss.

Noise levels are assessed in decibels above a standard basal level of 0·0002 dynes/sq. cm. (⟡ Hearing). Since the various effects of noise are dependent upon frequency as well as amplitude, it is usual to measure the sound energy present in various parts of the spectrum by means of an octave band analyser.

Hearing loss is measured by establishing the absolute threshold for pure tones over the whole frequency range. The typical audiogram (i.e. the plot showing hearing loss as a function of frequency) of persons suffering from damage as the result of exposure to noise displays a marked dip in the region of 4 kHz.

Control of noise may be facilitated in numerous ways: at the source by attention to design and maintenance of machinery; by the introduction of screens and enclosures and the proper use of sound-absorbing materials. Should work be necessary in noise that cannot be adequately attenuated, the use of ear defenders is advisable. E.E.

C. M. Harris (ed.), *Handbook of Noise Control* (McGraw-Hill, 2nd ed., 1979).

Non-parametric Statistics Parametric statistics (seldom referred to as such) is the branch of statistics that employs continuous ⟨⟩ Frequency Distributions. Not all data conform to these distributions and, more important, the precise nature of the population from which a set of data has come may not be known. In such circumstances, non-parametric statistics may be used. The tests (⟨⟩ Hypothesis Testing) reply on comparative data (e.g. whether vehicles perform better with one grade of petrol than with another) and these results are tested against known distributions, such as the binomial. In the petrol example, the expectation is that the number of cars performing well on one grade of petrol will be the same as those performing well on the other. The non-parametric test seeks to determine if the difference in these proportions is significant, such that one could conclude that one petrol is better than the other. Non-parametric tests are less powerful than parametric ones, i.e. the case for rejecting a hypothesis must be stronger in non-parametric statistics. Nevertheless, it is an important and growing branch of statistics and many sophisticated and valuable techniques have been developed. R.S.S.

Richard P. Runyon, *Non-parametric Statistics: A Contemporary Approach* (Addison-Wesley, 1977).

Norm A standard of specific behaviour expected of and by the members of a social group. The term refers to the actual behaviour expected and not to some theoretical ideal. The existence of agreed standards of behaviour greatly facilitates group action and enhances group solidarity. Some norms (e.g. those concerning social manners) may simply serve the purpose of making group life more pleasant, some (e.g. those concerning dress) may serve to increase the group's sense of identity and others (e.g. those concerning output standards, loyalty to other members) may serve to protect the group from other competing or hostile groups. Some norms may be so loosely or erratically enforced that they may barely be said to exist at all, whereas others may be strictly enforced. Enforcement of norms is likely to be most rigorous when the group feels itself under threat from either internal or external forces. Violation of group norms by a new member will probably be treated charitably and the newcomer may receive gentle correction. However, deliberate violation, particularly if ostentatious, is likely to be interpreted as an act of hostility and the group members will react accordingly, perhaps by withdrawing from the violator the privileges of group membership or, in extreme cases, by acts of physical violence. ⟡ Informal Organization; Social Control; Values. I.C.McG.

> J. A. Litterer, *The Analysis of Organizations*, (J. Wiley, 1965), ch. 6; T. Lupton, *Management and the Social Sciences* (Penguin, new ed., 1983), pp. 71–5.

Normal Distribution ⟡ Frequency Distributions

Numerical Control The effective control of machines and equipment (e.g. machine tools) directly from numerical information – usually directly, or indirectly, using computers. This technique was first demonstrated in about 1952. NC has developed from simple sequence control, using computer-prepared punched tapes, to include permanently connected control – computer numerical control (CNC) and the direct numerical control (DNC) of several machines by one minicomputer, working on a time-sharing basis. DNC is now an essential aspect of any computer-aided manufacturing system or of ⟡ Computer-integrated Manufacturing. ⟡ Computer-aided Design; Computer-aided Manufacture. R.W.

O

Objectives (in Planning) An objective may be defined as any aim or goal. This definition, which is by far the most common in use, causes some confusion, partly because it can be confused with ⟡⟩ Means and partly because an aim or goal can be any result that anyone wishes to achieve over any period of time, however trivial.

For example, 'Complete this report by lunch-time today' is a valid objective in this sense. It causes confusion to have to distinguish between such ephemeral, short-term objectives and what are sometimes known as long-term objectives, especially since agreement is seldom obtainable on what is long-term and what is short-term.

Much of this confusion disappears if an objective is defined as the *raison d'être* of an organization, that is to say, its purpose, the reason for its existence. An objective thus becomes fundamental to the very existence of the organization, such that if it fails to achieve it, it can be said to have failed as an organization. It is thus possible to judge whether an organization is succeeding or not by observing the extent to which it is achieving its stated objective. For example, if it is decided that a company exists in order to make a satisfactory profit, then it can clearly be seen whether or not the company is succeeding or failing *as a company* by observing whether its profits are satisfactory or not.

In the same way it is possible to state the objective of a department by referring to its fundamental purpose within the organization: thus a research department may have the objective of 'preparing the products and processes that the company will need in the next few years'. Its success can be judged by the extent to which these products and processes have been prepared when they are required. Similarly, the objective of any manager may be determined by reference to the fundamental purpose of the job they are doing.

On this second definition an objective is the answer to the question, 'What is it for?' The more clearly and unequivocally the answer is stated the more readily can it be seen how the organization, department or person is progressing towards the objective. In the case of an organization invariably the answer will be that the organization exists to bring some benefit to a person or group of persons: all organizations exist to benefit someone and if they fail to produce that benefit they fail as an organization. However, it should be noted that to define an objective completely it is necessary to state both the intended benefit and the beneficiaries. Thus merely to state that an organization exists 'to make a profit' or 'to give aid' is only a partial answer. One needs to know also for whom the profit is to be made and to whom the aid is intended to be given. ⟡ Business Policy. A.J.A.A.

Objectives, Financial ⟡ Financial Management; Capital, Cost of

Obstacles and Opportunities An obstacle is any event that might make the achievement of an objective more difficult. An opportunity is any such event that might make it less difficult. In addition to obstacles and opportunities a company's ⟡ Strength and Weakness also affect its ability to achieve its objective.

In general the larger the company the more obstacles it can overcome: for example a large company might be able to bring such pressure to bear upon a government as to force it to remove a tariff or quota that was restricting its overseas market, or to overcome the objections of a Preservation Society to a proposed factory extension – a small company might have less success against such obstacles. Obstacles to profit are usually fairly readily identified. Opportunities, however, usually need to be sought out with diligence before they can be identified and exploited: companies need to study changes in their markets closely before being able to discern a new area to exploit and to study their competitors' weaknesses with some care before turning these to their own advantage.

The point has been made that overcoming an obstacle cannot increase profits, it can only prevent them falling. Increased profits can only come from exploiting new opportunities. A.J.A.A.

Occupational Training ⟡ Industrial Training

Off-line/On-line The term 'on-line' describes computer installations that control industrial or commercial operations while they are occurring. Data on the operations are observed, calculations performed and results obtained quickly enough to enable the outcome of operations to be controlled. For this reason a computer can be said to be working in 'real time'. Examples of on-line installations are process-control applications in the chemicals, oil and steel industries and ticket reservation systems in commercial airlines.

The term 'off-line' describes computer installations that control a process but are not directly linked to the process and are only required to produce the results of calculations at relatively infrequent intervals. Examples of off-line installations are gas or electricity billing and customer accounting in banks. A customer's gas or electricity bill is computed on a monthly or quarterly basis whilst individual customers' bank accounts are usually checked at the end of each day. M.J.C.M.

Office Employment Working conditions in offices are governed by the Offices, Shops and Railway Premises Act 1963. The Act defines an office as a building, or part of a building, used solely or mainly for office purposes, i.e. one of the following: administration, handling money, telephone or telegraph operating and clerical work in general, including writing, bookkeeping, sorting papers, filing, typing, duplicating, machine calculating, drawing and the editorial preparation of matter for publication.

The provisions of the Act dealing with health, safety and welfare largely repeat the corresponding provisions of the Factories Act, adapted to meet the special needs of office employment. The provisions of the Act are enforced by the inspectors of the ⬦ Health and Safety Executive as far as offices situated in factory buildings are concerned, while other offices are supervised by district and borough councils. Like the Factories Act, the 1963 Act will be replaced eventually by the new machinery set up under the Health and Safety at Work Act 1974. ⬦ Health and Safety Legislation. W.F.F.

I. Fife and E. A. Machin, *The Offices, Shops and Railway Premises Act, 1963* (Butterworths, 1963).

Oligopoly ⬦ Market Models and Competition

Operating Lease ⬦ Leasing

Operational Analysis ⬦ Operational Research

Operational Planning ⬦ Tactics

Operational Research (OR) Known in the USA as operations research or operational analysis, OR is defined by the UKOR Society as '... the application of the methods of science to complex problems arising in the direction and management of large systems of men, machines, materials and money in industry, business, government and defence. The distinctive approach is to develop a scientific model of the system, incorporating measurements of factors, such as chance and risk, with which to predict and compare the outcomes of alternative decisions, strategies or controls. The purpose is to help management determine its policy and action scientifically.'

O R specialists will be trained to take a broader view of any problem than managers themselves. Ideally, operational research sees the problem in the context of the overall company system of interacting parts, aware that actions taken in one part of the organization are likely to produce effects elsewhere. In practice, since any business situation is necessarily dynamic by nature, it is not always possible to consider concurrently all aspects of a management problem and only those immediately and directly relevant may be treated in the scientific way.

Once a problem has been identified, it must be formulated as precisely as possible. The next stage is to devise a model of the system or sub-system. The operational-research model is not a physical one, as when designing ships, buildings, domestic appliances or product packaging, but mathematical. Just as the wing and fuselage stressing of an aircraft may be examined by mathematical equations as well as by testing a miniature version in a wind tunnel, so can a business problem often be represented by quantitative relationships.

In using the word 'model', operational research conforms to the terminology used by other scientists. Nowadays, most scientists use the term model rather than law or theory to describe the conceptual framework they have erected to describe a particular aspect of reality. Thus Newton's so-called law of gravitation is a mathematical model that describes the gravitational interactions of bodies.

A model is a representation of reality; it attempts to condense many variables into one (known as a homomorphism). Its purpose is to identify the alternative decisions available to management, compare the outcomes of these alternatives and so discover which decision is best. For example it is possible to model the process of production planning and to determine thereby the effects on the profitability of different production plans. If management is convinced that the best policy has been identified, it may be implemented.

The scientific approach of O R manifests itself in three ways:

(1) Emphasis is placed on objective observation and recording of data during the model-building period. Realistic model-building in O R requires similar skills to those required in the traditional sciences.

(2) Scientific method identifies through observation a hypothesis that is said to hold if subsequent evidence cannot be found to refute it. Similarly an O R model will be useful only if it stands up to practical use.

(3) A great deal of the work in O R is of a quantitative kind. Often the

emphasis is upon finding an optimum solution within the limitations and constraints of the model (⟡ Optimization). In practice, it may not be possible to achieve the optimum but the model will have pointed the way for management to proceed.

Despite the similarities there are significant differences between O R and traditional science. Traditional science, for example physics, is made up of two parts: (1) the activities of physicists engaged in investigating various phenomena of the physical universe, establishing theories and building models of the phenomena under study, and the experimental and analytical techniques they use; (2) the body of knowledge known as physics, which is, at least in principle, a synthesis of the individual models for the various phenomena, forming a conceptual unity that embraces the whole physical universe.

At present O R is not attempting to build a unified body of knowledge like physics. O R scientists are concerned with solving immediate problems and employing the techniques, mainly mathematical, at their disposal. Work on new techniques and the improvement of the existing ones is continuous and constitutes an important area of development of the discipline. In fact, however varied their business or industrial content, operational problems can often be reduced to a single problem of simple conceptual structure, or a combination of a few. It has been suggested that at present only eight types of problem structure have been discovered and these are described elsewhere (⟡ Allocation, Competitive, Queueing, Replacement, Routeing, Search, Sequencing, Inventory or Stock-control Problems).

The techniques employed depend on the nature of the problem, for example on whether it is static and deterministic (i.e. independent of time with quantities that are fixed) or dynamic and probabilistic (i.e. varies in time with quantities that are subject to variability or uncertainty). Some of the more useful techniques are discussed under ⟡ Decision Theory; Decision Trees; Heuristic Programming; Mathematical Programming; Network Analysis; Risk Analysis; Simulation (Computer). M.J.C.M. and R.S.S.

B. H. P. Rivett, *Model Building for Decision Analysis* (J. Wiley, 1980).

Operations Management Systems for the provision of goods or services are often referred to as operating systems, hence operations management concerns the management of both manufacturing systems (provision of goods) and service systems. Operations management is not only related to but includes ⟡ Production Management, and whilst in many cases reference to operations management is synonymous with manufacture, sufficient similarity exists between goods-producing and service systems to justify a common approach to their study and management. R.W.

T. E. Vollmann, *Operations Management* (Addison-Wesley, 1973); R. Wild, *Production and Operations Management* (Holt, Rinehart & Winston, 1984).

Operator Training ⟡ Industrial Training

Opportunities ⟡ Obstacles and Opportunities

Opportunity Cost Costs are defined by economists in terms of forgone opportunities or alternatives. The cost of a given factor of production is the maximum value that the factor could earn in an alternative use. Similarly, the cost of using a particular factor input to produce a given product is the value of the best opportunity that is forgone in not using the factor input in an alternative way.

Confusion sometimes arises between the way in which economists and accountants view costs and profits. Accounting or explicit costs are those outlays of a firm that we usually think of as expenses. Expenses include such payments as wages and salaries, raw-material expenditures and explicit payments for rent and interest. However, it is quite likely that some factors of production will be already owned by the firm, in the sense that the owners will have put their capital and skill into the firm. The cost of using these particular factors should not be neglected in any true consideration of costs and they are called implicit or opportunity costs. Thus the true cost of using the owners' capital is the next-best return they could earn on it elsewhere, an opportunity they forgo by investing in this particular firm. Similarly, the true cost of using the owners' time and talents is the next-best return they could earn from them, an opportunity they forgo by working with this particular firm. These opportunity costs must also be included if we are to move from the accountant's view of profit to the economist's view of profit.

The use of opportunity costs by accountants as part of the routine system of control is not possible. However, opportunity costs are often used when non-routine issues are under consideration, for example in pricing, investment and divestment. ⟡ Costs. L.T.S. and J.V.P.

R. G. Lipsey, *Introduction to Positive Economics* (Weidenfeld & Nicolson, 6th ed., 1983).

Optimization The process by which the best solution or result may be obtained. In mathematical terms, optimization is a rigorous concept: it is necessary to define a precise, objective function that is to be optimized (maximized or minimized) within a number of constraints placed upon the variables. An example would be the production of a given recipe at minimum cost from a variety of ingredients, each of which may be purchased at different prices and each of which offers different combinations of nutritional value to satisfy the nutritional needs of the recipe.

In practice an exact mathematical description may be hard to derive and often the concept of optimization is used without defining its context, for example in the expressions 'maximizing profits' or 'minimizing competitive price advantage'. In such cases it may be more appropriate to think in terms of achieving results within acceptable boundaries. The word 'satisficing' has been used to express the attainment of a satisfactory and sufficient solution.

However, it may be that managers see problems not in terms of optimizing or satisficing, but that they adapt to circumstances. Special offers and discounts are offered on products that are selling badly and production lines may be changed to accommodate the latest fashion: the word 'adaptivizing' has been used to describe this attitude. ⟨⟩ Mathematical Programming. R.S.S.

R. L. Ackoff, *A Concept of Corporate Planning* (J. Wiley, 1970), pp. 6–22.

Options The development of options theory and the erection of traded-options markets are, arguably, the most significant occurrences in the recent history of financial management. 1973 saw the publication of a now famous paper by Black and Scholes entitled 'The Pricing of Options and Corporate Liabilities' as well as the formation of the Chicago Board Options Exchange to deal in traded options. Rarely do theory and practice coincide with such elegance.

Options theory. Many financial decisions may be thought of as choices between alternative courses of action, which include the opportunity to accept or reject the option to pursue a future course of action. Thus a ⟨⟩ Capital Budgeting decision may require assessment of the relative benefits of investing now or acquiring the option to invest in the future. Similarly the value of a commitment fee paid to a banker to secure a pre-arranged credit facility lies in the worth of the option to exercise that facility given that credit and/or interest-rate conditions, for example, may have changed in the meantime.

Option-valuation models tend to be mathematically complex but the underlying logic is that the value of an option subsists in the combined worth of (1) the time span remaining to maturity/expiry of the option and (2) the scope for variation between the market price and the exercise price (i.e. the price specified in the option contract) attaching to the underlying commodity or security.

Traded options. A traded option is a marketable right either to buy (a *call option*) or to sell (a *put option*) a security at a prescribed price on a prescribed date. Originating in Chicago, traded-options markets have since been founded in other financial centres with well-established secondary stock markets, including New York, Singapore and London.

The following illustration show the principal elements of a call option. Suppose that an investor believes that the shares of A BC plc, which are quoted on the Stock Exchange and stand at a price of 250p each, are attractive and that the price is likely to rise in the near future. Clearly, if the investor has sufficient money available, they can buy, say, 1,000 shares at a cost of £2,500. If A BC shares rise to 300p, as they hope, they will make a profit of £500. Of course, if the share price should fall by a similar amount, they would show a loss of £500 but they could decide to continue holding the shares in the hope of a recovery. By the use of options, the investor can approach this decision in a different manner. Suppose they buy a three months call option on 2,000 shares at a premium of 25p per share, costing £500, and that they keep the remainder of their money invested securely elsewhere. If, in the course of the next three months, the share price rises to 300p, they will show a profit of £500 (£1,000 − £500, the cost of the option). If, on the other hand, their judgement is wrong and the share price falls, then at the end of three months when the expiry date of the option is reached they will have lost £500. Thus the buyer of an option stands to lose the whole of the premium if their judgement is wrong, but can never lose more than the premium. The buyer of shares however, can, lose their entire investment, if, in the worst case, the company goes into liquidation. P.J.A.H.

Organization A social group deliberately created and maintained for the purpose of achieving specific objectives. This definition distinguishes organizations of the formal or bureaucratic type from other forms of social system.

The objectives of the organization are usually made explicit and their achievement involves the division of labour, often to a considerable degree, procedures for the co-ordination of effort, a hierarchical authority structure and, particularly in business organizations, economic measures of performance. The basic units of an organization are roles, not persons, so that, at least in theory, the organization may continue unchanged despite frequent changes in personnel. The importance of organizations in modern society has been increasing at an accelerating pace but they have become the subject of systematic study only during the last two or three decades.

The process of determining the activities necessary to achieve the objectives most economically, structuring the relationships among the roles thus created and ensuring the effective operation of the total system is also termed 'organization'. ⬦ Authority; Bureaucracy; Formal Organization; Organizational Theory; Role; Specialization. I.C.McG.

> J. E. T. Eldridge and A. D. Crombie, *A Sociology of Organizations* (Allen & Unwin, 1974), ch 2; G. Mouzelis, *Organization and Bureaucracy* (Routledge & Kegan Paul, 1967); C. B. Handy, *Understanding Organizations* (Penguin, 1982).

Organization Development Planned and integrated effort to improve the effectiveness of an organization through the restructuring of its processes on the basis of behavioural science.

The application of an organization-development programme involves a careful diagnosis of the organization's shortcomings, the preparation of a strategy for change and the marshalling of the physical and intellectual resources that the programme is seen to require. Typically organization development, as the term implies, seeks improvement in the total organization, or in a quasi-autonomous sub-organization, recognizing that to be effective change in any one part of the system requires supportive change in other parts.

Organization development conceives the ideal organization as being characterized by comparative clarity in the objectives established at all levels, a high degree of commitment to those objectives, open and honest communications throughout the system, open expression of disagreements, a constructive approach to conflict resolution and a culture that supports personal integrity and growth. I.C.McG.

> R. Beckhard, *Organization Development: Strategies and Models* (Addison-Wesley, 1969); K. Legge, *Evaluating Planned Organizational Change* (Academic Press, 1984).

Organization and Methods (O and M) The application of ⬦ Work Study to the detailed administrative, clerical and office operations of an organization in order to improve the methods and procedures in use. It is therefore a study of the problems affecting the development, management and operations of offices. Other names given to this kind of activity are systems and procedures, clerical work study and systems analysis, although the scope of the latter term has considerably widened in recent years to cover activities outside offices.

Generally the methods of O and M consist (1) of questioning the need for the procedures relating to a given area of activity and (2) if the activity can be justified, of examining the effectiveness of the individual operations involved.

The scope of O and M, like work study, is perhaps limited mainly by the lack of a general and well-developed conceptual framework for criteria of efficiency and the methodology of working. E.A.L

HM Treasury, *The Practice of O & M* (HMSO, 2nd ed., 1965).

Organization Theory 'The study of the structure and functioning of organizations and the behaviour of groups and individuals within them' (D. S. Pugh).

Despite the importance of formal organizations to modern societies, they have been objects of systematic study for little more than one generation. During the nineteenth century various industrialists published their own personal philosophies of management, either describing the organization of their own factories or explaining the enlightened nature of their treatment of their labour force. However, it was not until the early days of the present century that attempts were made to formulate general propositions concerning organizational structure and processes. Early contributions to an understanding of organizations came from three main sources: the scientific-management movement, industrial psychologists and the classical theorists. The primary concern of all three was to increase managerial efficiency.

The scientific-management approach, pioneered by F. W. Taylor, concentrated on shop-floor organization and developed techniques for studying, analysing and measuring the work of the operative, and for scheduling and recording work-in-progress. It may be argued that the 'scientific managers' were more concerned with the problems of analysing and improving performance at shop-floor level than with the creation of general theories of administration, although Taylor's determination to maximize managerial expertise led him to advocate the use of functional authority and to suggest an appropriate structure. Their work also did much to stimulate interest in management as a rewarding subject for intellectual application.

The First World War further focused attention on industrial problems and academic behavioural scientists became increasingly involved. Psychologists, both in Britain and in the USA, studied the problems of personal adjustment experienced by the newcomer to factory work and sought to systematize the hitherto haphazard process of selection, placement and training. Research was conducted to ascertain the effect on the operative of various elements in the organizational environment such as heat, light, ventilation, hours of work and the number and distribution of rest pauses.

Between the two world wars, classical organization theorists sought to develop principles of management that would guide general managers in their task of structuring and administering business organizations. The contributions came almost entirely from practising managers and reflected their concern with practical problems such as departmentalization, co-ordination, control and the distribution of authority.

The shop-floor approach of the scientific-management school and the industrial psychologists and the general-management approach of the classical theorists were complementary yet they remain distinct. It may even be suggested that the development of general theory was retarded by the activities of the scientific managers, whose methods promised quick and dramatic improvements in efficiency and so possessed a greater appeal than the more abstract general principles of the classicists. The two approaches were linked by the report on the ⟨⟩ Hawthorne Investigations, when attention was drawn to the contrast between actual employee behaviour and the expectations of management. The Hawthorne studies emphasized the importance of studying industrial workers, not in isolation, but in relation to the wider organizational context in which they were located. This context, it was suggested, should be viewed as a social system.

Since the Second World War behavioural scientists – psychologists, social psychologists and sociologists – have been increasingly attracted by the organization as a field of study and, being mainly academic in orientation, they have been concerned primarily to develop theory rather than to seek specific solutions to *ad hoc* problems. Accordingly a coherent body of knowledge is gradually emerging, to which the name organization theory has been given. However, organization theory is not yet as coherent as it needs to be if it is to reach a mature development. The representatives of many academic disciplines have turned their attention to the study of organizations and have contributed to the growing understanding of their functioning. Mathematicians, economists, biologists, engineers and others have all examined organizational behaviour from the standpoint of their respective disciplines. It is therefore not surprising that an all-embracing theory has not emerged. Instead, a number of organizational theories grounded in different disciplines are being developed and this process will presumably continue. Common to nearly all the approaches, however, is the concept of an open system: a theoretical construct representing the interdependence of a number of variables interacting with each other and with the environment. The range of relevant variables is extremely large, perhaps infinite, so each discipline has to select those variables most relevant to its own considerations, recognizing that by so doing, it inevitably presents a very incomplete view of reality. The least esoteric of these developments and therefore, perhaps, the most likely to be of use to the industrial manager is the *social-system model* of the behavioural scientist. As psychologists and sociologists begin to abandon their interdisciplinary demarcation lines, the prospects for the advancement of organization theory seem bright. ⇨ Classical Organization Theory; Human Relations; Scientific Management. J.C.McG.

D. S. Pugh, 'Modern Organization Theory', *Psychological Bulletin,* vol. 66, no. 4 (Oct. 1966), pp. 235–51; M. Albrow, 'The Study of Organizations – Objectivity or Bias', in *Penguin Social Sciences Survey, 1968* (Penguin, 1968); M. Rose, *Industrial Behaviour* (Penguin, 1978).

Overheads Overhead, as an accounting term, is generally defined as the cost of indirect materials, indirect labour and indirect expenses. Overheads may also be defined as the sum of all business costs that cannot be traced to specific units of output or are not traced because it is inconvenient or too costly to do so. Traceability in this context refers to identification with the unit of output in the physical sense of being 'embodied' in that output. Two essential characteristics of the accountant's overhead cost classification are, firstly, that such costs are common costs with respect to specific individual units or batches of output and, secondly, that they contain both fixed and variable cost elements. Alternatively overheads are sometimes defined as being synonymous with indirect costs, to distinguish them from the three categories of direct costs: direct raw materials, direct wages and direct expenses. Overhead costs are usually classified for purposes of accountability into a number of categories reflecting the organization of the business. For example they may be classified into factory, warehouse, packing and distribution, selling, research and development, general administration, financial, non-operating, etc.

The most important aspect of overhead cost accounting is the question of an allocation or attribution of overheads to the costs of units of output and to the costs of alternative courses of action when making business decisions. Advocates of absorption costing procedures emphasize the need to allocate all costs (whether fixed or variable) to outputs and decision alternatives because 'one must allocate all costs on some convenient basis in order to recover them'. In contrast, marginal (or direct) costing advocates suggest that attempts to allocate the unallocable, namely fixed and common overhead costs, merely misinform the decision-maker and that only costs that vary with the volume of output or the implementation of a particular decision alternative can be (and should be) attributed to that output or alternative. Nevertheless, there is a real danger in marginal costing if decision-makers fail to recover enough 'contribution' to meet fixed costs.

It is important to distinguish the traditional accountant's use of the term overhead, as defined above, from that of the economist; the economist generally defines overhead costs as fixed costs and would tend to be in sympathy with marginal costing procedures. ⟐ Costs. E.A.L., amended by J.V.P.

J. C. Drury, *Management and Cost Accounting*, (Van Nostrand Reinhold (UK), 1985).

Overtime A variable amount of time, usually measured weekly, worked by individuals over and above the agreed minimum of standard hours for their industry and for which they are paid at a rate in excess of the agreed basic wage.

There has been an increasing amount of criticism of the level of overtime worked in British industry in recent years but this has not prevented it from rising to an average of about seven hours a week for adult males. Virtually every industry has some overtime and over a third of industries work an average in excess of five hours a week. The week ending 15 October 1977 provides a typical example of overtime spread.

Industry	Operatives working over as a percentage of all operatives	Average hours worked over in the week
Food, drink, tobacco	36·9	10·1
Chemicals and allied industries	33·1	9·8
Metal manufacture	40·3	9·7
Engineering and electrical	39·6	8·5
Vehicles	41·2	7·5
Textiles	24·7	8·2
Clothing/footwear	8·0	5·3
Paper/printing	38·5	9·0

Source: Department of Employment Gazette (December 1977).

Overtime patterns tend to be regular and permanent: the same industries, firms and individuals work high overtime. This regularity in itself casts doubt on the validity of the argument that overtime, the level and

Business expansion by extending credit

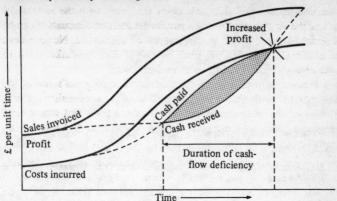

distribution of which is determined almost entirely by ⟡ Workplace Bargaining, is a necessary auxiliary in the struggle to meet production deadlines and heavy short-term work loads. In no other country, with the exception of France, is so much overtime worked, and yet the indices of overall production and productivity have risen more slowly here than elsewhere over the past two decades. The highest levels of overtime tend to occur in those industries with the lowest basic rates. This suggests that overtime, far from being at the discretion of management, is in fact an indispensable component of many weekly wage packets – indispensable because the low basic rates paid in many industries are insufficient to meet the needs of those workers with only average financial commitments. Far from facilitating essential additional output, much of the overtime worked seems to arise out of a desire to waste time at work in order to obtain an adequate wage. There are some conspicuous examples of firms that have managed to effect drastic cuts in overtime through the implementation of productivity agreements without any loss of output, e.g. Esso, Fawley. ⟡ Productivity Bargaining. N.H.C.

> E. G. Whybrew, *Overtime Working in Britain*, Royal Commission on Trade Unions and Employers' Associations, research paper No. 9, (HMSO, 1968).

Overtrading Generally regarded as one of the most common causes of business failure, overtrading is characterized by a firm expanding more rapidly than the available sources of finance (particularly profits) will reasonably allow. The diagram above illustrates one cause of overtrading – rapid expansion by a business that stimulates sales activity through increasing the period of credit given to its customers.

The key to avoiding collapse is to ensure that the business has sufficient funds available to it to finance the cash-flow deficit during the period over which it accumulates. P.J.A.H.

P

Pacing Two forms of work pacing are evident on assembly or flow lines. Mechanical work pacing occurs on moving-belt type lines, whilst operator pacing predominates on non-mechanical lines (◇ Assembly Lines). Mechanical pacing exists when workers are constrained to complete their operations with a certain allowed time. Rigid pacing occurs when workers are given an absolute time, neither more nor less, to complete their operation. Pacing with margin exists where there is a tolerance about the allowed time.

Rigid pacing rarely occurs, but pacing with margin is normal in this type of work, e.g. workers on an automobile assembly line give themselves margin by riding along the line whilst completing their operations.

Too little margin can lead to ◇ System Loss, i.e. in the diagram below the curve represents the time required by the worker to complete the operation (between 20 and 140 seconds but usually about 60 seconds). If the allowed time is 50–70 seconds, there will be frequent occasions on which the worker will not be able to complete the operation and similarly occasions on which too much time is allowed. A similar effect may occur on non-mechanical lines, since although short-term variation in operation times is generally accommodated by the existence of ◇ Buffer Stocks between stations, longer-term balance must be maintained and hence workers are to some degree constrained by their colleagues.

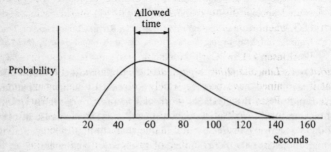

To reduce or eliminate these losses, the pacing effect must be reduced by one of the following methods, each allowing the worker to offset unusually long cycle times with unusually short ones. (1) The job is made available to the worker for as long as possible, e.g. where workers on an assembly line are fed with jobs placed on a moving belt, closer spacing increases the time available. For example, for a worker who can reach 2 feet up and 2 feet down the belt, job spacing of 4 feet on a 4 feet/min. belt makes the job available for 1 minute; 2 feet spacing on a 2 feet/min. belt, whilst providing for the same line output, makes the job available for 2 minutes. (2) Larger buffer stocks are provided between the stations on non-mechanical lines, thus effectively 'disconnecting' workers at adjacent stations on the assembly line. R.W.

Packaging (in Marketing) The wrapper or container in which a product is enclosed to facilitate distribution and use. The marketing approach towards the design of packaging has undergone substantial change in recent decades. Protection of the contents, the original purpose, is now deemed only one of many functions performed by the packaging; it is seen as a vitally important part of communications in consumer markets (◊ Marketing Communications Mix). In industrial markets particular attention is paid to the problems of handling, storage and shipment, especially through the use of bulk packaging which breaks out into smaller packs (◊ Design). This latter pattern is familiar also in consumer markets. Eight general principles have been evinced for good packaging: (1) it should be integrated in design, particularly in terms of colour and typography, with the other communications media of the organization; (2) it should be designed to be eye-catching; (3) it should establish its own identity; (4) it should be appropriate to the product in terms of users' subjective expectations; (5) it should be aesthetically pleasing; (6) it should invite handling; (7) it should be well constructed, as durable as necessary for its purpose and convenient in use, paying particular attention to pack size for, e.g. storing, table use; (8) it should be designed specifically to communicate with its market segment (◊ Market Segmentation). G.S.C.W.

Parkinson's Law Cyril Northcote Parkinson wrote his classic *Parkinson's Law and Other Studies in Administration* in 1958. The ideas that it contained have become widely known in management circles. Like the ◊ Peter Principle, the work of Laurence J. Peter, Parkinson's ideas were introduced satirically but came to be treated as matters of serious concern by academics and management practitioners.

The book consists of a number of propositions, all relating to the main theme that in organizations there appears to be only a limited relationship between the size of the organization's task and the numbers of people recruited to perform it, so that the growth of administration inevitably becomes separated from the work itself. Hence the law that 'work expands to fill the time available for its completion'.

The process by which administrations proliferate depends, according to Parkinson, on the way in which officials choose to organize their work. Typically they multiply subordinates, not rivals. This is because there exists an almost universal desire to protect their positions and their control over particular functions, rather than to share their responsibilities for these functions with colleagues. Moreover, officials make work for each other, so that Parkinson portrays administrations as closed systems in which routes are devised regardless of their relevance to the real purposes of the organization.

Parkinson also introduces the 'law of triviality'. This relates to the performance of committees concerned with policy-making decisions, and applies to the incompetence of committee decision-making. Items requiring detailed technical explanations, especially where high capital costs are involved, are passed without demur, since some officials will not wish to reveal their ignorance. But when more mundane items come up and quite trivial costs are involved, a far greater amount of time and energy will be consumed as each committee member endeavours to assert his personal competence.

Finally, Parkinson introduces a law that states that 'expenditure rises to meet income'. Again this is linked to the competence of the administration. Given a particular level of income, means will always be found to increase expenditure to meet it, irrespective of whether such expenditure can be completely justified. P.B.

C. N. Parkinson, *Parkinson's Law* (Penguin, 1986).

Participation The act of taking part. A major problem confronting the leaders of large-scale organizations is that of how best to maximize the commitment of the rank and file to their own specific tasks and to the goals of the organization as a whole. The problem has been particularly acute in large industrial organizations and since the advent of a widespread factory system of production various remedies have been tried or advocated. There were some who believed, like Marx, that the ⇩ Alienation of the worker was due principally, if not entirely, to the pattern of ownership of the means of production. Accordingly it was urged that the system of ownership be radically changed – guild socialism, syndicalism or state ('public') ownership have been proposed as alternatives. Others considered that it would be sufficient if the pattern of ownership were modified through the use of profit-sharing, employee shareholding or co-partnership schemes. More recently attention has concentrated less on the question of the ownership of the organization than on the administrative processes that characterize it, and formal systems of joint consultation or, in some cases, joint decision-making have been advocated. The success of any of these measures is difficult to gauge with any accuracy but it seems safe to observe that none seems to have led to a very marked increase in commitment.

There is, however, a gradual accumulation of research data that appears to support the contention that commitment is likely to be enhanced if the persons concerned participate in the making of decisions that affect them personally, particularly those that affect them directly. It may be, of course, that in some cases a change of ownership pattern may be a necessary preliminary to the requisite change in administrative structure and practice but in general a solution is increasingly being sought in a modification of the day-to-day practices of managers and supervisors. The formal machinery of joint consultation enables the participation of only a small minority of the labour force and the involvement of the majority requires that a participative style of supervision and management be adopted throughout the organization. Additionally provision is made for increased participation by the restructuring of tasks so as to permit a much greater degree of individual initiative and judgement in their performance. ⟡ Alienation; Authority; Job Enlargement; Joint Consultation; Motivation; Specialization. I.C.McG.

P. Brannen, *Authority and Participation in Industry* (Batsford, 1983).

Partnership A partnership is defined by the Partnership Act, 1890 as 'the relation which subsists between persons carrying on a business in common with a view of profit'. The relationship that gives rise to a partnership may be based on an express agreement (generally embodied in a partnership deed) but it may also be implied from the conduct of the parties. Thus whenever a person shares in the profits of a business conducted by another, he will be deemed to be his partner. The partners in a partnership are jointly liable for all contractual commitments entered into on behalf of the partnership and are jointly and severally liable for all wrongs (torts) committed by or on behalf of the partnership.

In England and Wales the firm, unlike a company, is not a separate legal entity and legal actions will have to be brought against the partners and not against the firm. The partners may select the firm's name and have a free choice in doing so, except that they may not select one that is similar to that of another firm so as to be likely to mislead the general public. Unless the firm name includes the full names of all the partners, the name and address of each partner must be stated legibly on all business letters and other documents, and the full names of the partners must be displayed on the firm's business premises to which the public have access. The requirement to register the name of the firm was abolished along with the Registry of Business Names by the Companies Act 1981. ⟡ Company Law. w.f.f., amended by j.e.c.m.

C. D. Drake, *The Law of Partnership* (Sweet & Maxwell, 3rd ed., 1983).

Patents A patent is a monopoly right granted by the Crown to the inventor of an invention. The Patents Act 1977 radically altered the previous law relating to patents, bringing UK law into line with the European patent system. The Act provides that a patent may only be granted for an invention that (1) is new, (2) involves an inventive step and (3) is capable of industrial or agricultural application. An application for the grant of a patent is made to the Patent Office and, if granted, lasts for twenty years from the date of application. The Act established a Patents Court with High Court status to hear appeals from the Comptroller General of Patents, Designs and Trade Marks.

An invention made by an employee is deemed by the Act to belong to his employer if made in the course of his normal duties, though the employee can be awarded compensation, if such is just. d.v.e.r., amended by j.c.e.m.

T. Blanco White, *Patents for Inventions* (Sweet & Maxwell, 5th ed., 1983).

Patterns of Growth Firms may grow either by internal expansion or by mergers and takeovers; the patterns of growth are frequently referred to as horizontal and vertical integration. In recent years many firms have diversified their activities and are frequently described as conglomerates.

Horizontal integration refers to a situation in which a firm grows by extending the production of its existing products or services. This may be because the firm has unexploited technical and marketing economies of scale and thus grows from within. An example of this would be the expansion of Asda into the South of England and Sainsbury's into the North of England. However, a firm may recognize deficiencies in its own organization and see in a rival a way of remedying them: such motives appeared in the inquiry into the proposed merger of Montague Burton and United Drapery Stores in 1966. Alternatively a firm may try to buy market share and expertise, as became apparent in the inquiry into the proposed merger of GKN and AE in 1984.

Vertical integration refers to a firm growing either into retailing and additional production processes or into the ownership and manufacture of raw materials and components. Clearly a frequent way of accomplishing this end is to acquire other firms, but it need not necessarily be so. The motives for vertical integration are usually fear of supplies or outlets being curtailed and the desire, with modern manufacturing methods, to maintain even flows of production. A desire to safeguard their supply of good-quality tube steel was one reason why Tube Investments purchased the Round Oak Steel Works in 1953. Similar fears prompted the purchases in the 1950s of Briggs Motor Bodies and Fisher & Ludlow by Ford and BMC respectively. The development of Courtaulds, in the textile industry, is an example of vertical integration by internal growth and by mergers and takeovers, as is the development of Bass in the brewing industry.

Diversification, leading to possible designation as a conglomerate, refers to growth in the direction of different products, which may have a common technical base, use existing marketing facilities or have no relationship at all. The uncertainties of economic life are one reason for this pattern for it ensures that all one's resources are not tied to one product or market segment. Another reason may be that although technical economies in the existing product range have been exhausted there are still marketing and managerial economies unexploited. Yet another reason may be the existence of surplus funds available for investment. A good example of this type of development is ICI, with its diverse interests in agricultural chemicals, drugs, petrochemicals and fibres. The term conglomerate generally refers to the particular nature of the business organization, generally consisting of a holding company and a group of subsidiary companies engaged in dissimilar activities. In recent years the two most successful conglomerates have been the Hanson Trust and BTR. The Hanson Trust has taken over such dissimilar companies as London Brick and Everready Batteries. In 1983 BTR took over Thomas Tilling, itself a conglomerate, in the largest UK conglomerate merger so far. At the time the Director General of Fair Trading argued that the bid had no industrial logic behind it and since there was little or no industrial overlap between the but companies it was allowed to go ahead without reference to the Monopolies Commission. L.T.S.

J. Bates and J. R. Parkinson, *Business Economics* (Blackwell, 3rd rev. ed., 1982).

Payback Period This is a measure of the attractiveness of an investment project widely used in practice ($\diamondsuit$ Capital Budgeting). However, since payback defines a period of time it is not as such a measure of return. It measures the time-period by the end of which the initial investment outlay is expected to be returned by the funds flow resulting from the initial outlay. For example, if investment projects *A* and *B* both require an initial outlay of £1,000 and *A* returns £250 per annum and *B* £200 per annum in additional net cash flows (◊ Funds-flow Analysis) and the number of years over which the flows are expected to continue are 4 and 8 respectively, then the payback measures are:

Payback period for *A* = 1000/250 = 4 years
Payback period for B = 1000/200 = 5 years

Since *A* returns the investment outlay more quickly it is, according to the payback criterion, a more desirable project. Yet 'common sense' tells us that *B* must be more worth while. In fact, if the interest costs of financing the investments are recognized then *A* will achieve a loss, since it recovers no more than the initial outlay, whereas *B* returns considerably more. It is therefore clear that where payback is used in practice, it should not be relied upon without taking other aspects of the investments into account.

The principal defects of this method are therefore that: (1) no account is taken of what happens after the end of the payback period; (2) the timing and, therefore, value of cash flows within and beyond the payback period are ignored (◊ Discounted Cash Flow).

Justifications made for the use of the payback criterion relate to the ease of its measurement and, in so far as the uncertainty of cash flows increases with distance in time, its ability crudely to quantify project risk. E.A.L., amended by P.J.A.H.

Payroll Deductions ◊ Check-off

Pedal ◊ Machine Controls

Percentiles It is often convenient to express a frequency distribution of values in terms of the percentage of the whole population of values that occurs at or below a particular value. Such a method of expression is in general use, for example, to describe the range of anthropometric dimensions in a given group of people. Thus the fiftieth percentile (or median) is the value below which half the population appears and the tenth percentile is that below which 0·1 of the populations appears.

A typical extract from an anthropometric table appears below.

From such a table it can be concluded that, for example, the stature of

Measurement	Percentiles (inches)				
	1st	5th	50th	95th	99th
Male stature	62·7	64·6	69·0	73·4	75·2
Female stature	56·5	58·4	62·8	67·3	69·2

99 per cent of the whole population falls within the range 56·5″–75·2″. ◊ Measures of Dispersion; Measures of Location. E.E.

Perfect Competition ◊ Market Models and Competition

Performance Appraisal A systematic method of assessing the performance of employees in their jobs with a view to helping management decisions on promotions, transfers, training or changes in pay (◊ Merit Rating). This is a process that is undertaken, more or less informally, whenever an employee's future is being considered. Modern methods involve a regular and systematic procedure whereby employees' immediate superiors are required to assess the subordinates' performance over a period of time and under given heads. Present practice sometimes includes an initial self-appraisal by individual employees, followed by an interview with their manager, at which an agreed appraisal may be reached. This process may result in an agreement on targets relative both to individual performance and work to be done for the period ahead. Appraisals of this kind are one aspect of a system of ◊ Management by Objectives, which is operated at all levels of an enterprise. The purpose of this approach is to reduce the 'sitting in judgement' aspect of superior/subordinate relationships and to increase the sense of shared responsibility and involvement among employees, in the lower as well as the higher ranks of management. L.S., amended by E.L.

G. A. Randell, P. M. A. Packard, R. L. Shaw and A. J. Slater, *Staff Appraisal* (Institute of Personnel Management, 1974); D. Gill, B. Ungerson and M. Thakur, *Performance Appraisal in Perspective: A Survey of Current Practice* (Institute of Personnel Management, 1973); D. Gill, *Appraising Performance: Present Trends and the Next Decade* (Institute of Personnel Management, 1977); R. Bennett, *Managing Personnel and Performance: An Alternative Approach* (Business Books, 1981).

Performance Rating The comparison of an actual rate of working against a defined concept of a standard rate of working.

The standard rating is defined as 'corresponding to the average rate at which qualified workers will naturally work at a job, provided they know and adhere to the specified method and provided they are motivated to apply themselves to their work' (BS 3138).

During a ⟨⟩ Time Study a worker's observed performance is 'rated' in order to convert observed times to basic times:

$$\text{Basic time} = \frac{\text{Observed time} \times \text{Observed rating}}{\text{Standard rating}}$$

On the British Standard performance scale, standard rating is equal to 100, i.e. an observed rating of 50 is equal to half the standard rate of working.

British Standard scales and terminology are by no means exclusively adopted. Several other performance scales are in use, and often two points are defined, a higher one equivalent to 100 on the BS scale, corresponding to the rating and performance of piece-workers (but not always called standard rate or performance), and a lower one corresponding to the rating and performance of time-workers, i.e.

British Standard scale	60/80 scale	75/100 scale	100/133 scale
100	80	100	133
	60	75	100
0	0	0	0

Methods of Rating

Although standard rating is defined (above), in practice the concept of a standard rate of working is a function of the situation, depending, for example, on physical conditions, company policy, etc. The time-study observer is trained by the use of training films and exercises to recognize a standard rate for different jobs and in different conditions, based on, for example, effort required, skill used, pace of work, physical conditions, difficulty of job, etc.

Various methods of performance rating have been devised, ranging from entirely subjective procedures to more quantitative approaches in which numerical values are allocated to certain different aspects of the work, e.g. the physical or mental effort involved. Nevertheless it is impossible, using direct time study, to guarantee absolute uniformity of rating within a company and even less between companies. R.W.

R. M. Currie, *The Measurement of Work* (BIM, 1965).

Peripheral Equipment ⟡ Computer

Personality In common usage the meaning of 'personality' can vary between eccentricity and sex appeal. To the psychologist the term signifies the integrated organization that determines each individual's pattern of behavioural responses to the environment. Thus the study of personality is essentially the study of differences between people. The fact that particular human responses are seldom completely predictable is an indication of the complexity of the organization involved; the study of psychology is possible because human behaviour is not completely random.

There have been numerous theories of personality structure, each of which tends to be associated with a set of techniques for measuring differences between individuals. Questionnaires and inventories, for example, are used to assess attitudes and interests. The projective techniques rely upon an interpretation of a person's response to a minimal stimulus, such as an incomplete sentence. Psychoanalytic techniques involve the interpretation of data from free association, the analysis of dreams and perhaps responses evoked under hypnosis.

During the last twenty years or so, the introduction of powerful statistical methods has made possible the handling of large amounts of data on human responses and has facilitated the classification of some of the most important dimensions of human personality (⟡ Factor Analysis). E.E.

C. S. Hall and G. Lindzey, *Theories of Personality* (J. Wiley, 3rd ed., 1978).

Personnel Management The part of the process of managing that is concerned with the policies, procedures and practices governing the recruitment, selection, training, promotion, remuneration and working conditions of the people employed by an enterprise. Personnel management is thus part of the job of anyone who manages other people, as well as the description given to the function of specialists called personnel managers or personnel officers.

As enterprises have grown in size, the tendency has been for the work of management to be subdivided, initially into such primary functions as manufacturing, selling and purchasing, and later into functional areas like accounting and personnel management, concerned with the resources of money and people. Since work generally has become more specialized, greater knowledge is now required by those choosing employees for jobs. In addition, scarcities of certain types of human resource in countries using complex technologies, allied to the growth in membership and bargaining power of ⟪⟫ Trade Unions, have further encouraged the development of personnel management as a separate function staffed by specialists knowledgeable in such areas as industrial psychology, industrial sociology and ⟪⟫ Organization Theory (⟪⟫ Psychology; Social Sciences).

Social scientists in these fields have extended the knowledge of human behaviour within organizations and have helped to devise more reliable techniques and procedures for the ⟪⟫ Selection and ⟪⟫ Motivation of individuals and for influencing performance in working ⟪⟫ Groups. Personnel management today therefore goes far beyond a concern for the ⟪⟫ Welfare of employees, which characterized the policies and practices of some employers in the nineteenth and early twentieth centuries, who felt that they had a responsibility to ensure good working conditions for women and young employees considered unable to protect themselves from exploitation by the employer. Today, in the face of strong trade unions and a greater understanding of motivation, employers not only aim to provide fair conditions of employment, but also seek to make work more satisfying for employees. To this end, employees are being enabled to make fuller use of their abilities and interests at work by the redesign of jobs and a recognition of the satisfactions to be derived from membership of a working group.

In implementing the policies of an enterprise that concern employees and their relationships with each other, personnel management thus becomes involved with employment, remuneration, training, working conditions, employee services and industrial relations, as well as questions of organization development and ⟪⟫ Communication.

Employment includes all those tasks that are performed in order to secure the efficient and flexible staffing for an undertaking; that is to say, recruitment, selection, placement, appraisal, transfers, promotion and dismissals. Hours of work, holidays, overtime, rest pauses are also included under this heading. As a means to this, personnel records have to be kept and be kept up to date, giving the necessary information about all employees, including relevant facts in their personal histories. Remuneration is concerned with the rates of pay and earnings of wage- and salary-earners and may be based on trade union agreements and on job evaluation, which form the basis for a wage and salary structure for the whole enterprise. It also covers the actual payment of ⟪⟫ Wages and salaries, whether weekly or monthly, and whether in cash or by cheque (⟪⟫ Salary Structure). ⟪⟫ Industrial Training is undertaken to equip employees to carry out efficiently the tasks they have to do. It is the employer's responsibility to provide a safe and healthy working environment. Certain standards, in most cases minima, are prescribed by the

Factories Act, Health and Safety at Work Act, and the Offices, Shops and Railway Premises Act (⟡ Welfare and ⟡ Accident Prevention). Employee services cover pensions, sick pay, holiday fund and similar schemes, to many of which employees make a financial contribution; other services are the provision of canteens and rest-rooms.

⟡ Industrial Relations is the whole field of relationships between employer and employees, although it is sometimes used in a restricted sense to apply to those between trade unions and employers. In the context of personnel management it includes arrangements for ⟡ Joint Consultation through works committees or councils, face-to-face dealings between foreman and shop steward or between works manager and trade union official. It is concerned with the agreements between the two sides of industry and the disputes and conflicts that arise both before and after such agreements are made (⟡ Advisory, Conciliation and Arbitration Service; Collective Bargaining; Dispute; Productivity Bargaining; Shop Steward; Strike).

The growing body of research in ⟡ Cybernetics and ⟡ Organization Theory is demonstrating the relation of the structure of organizations and of systems of communication to behaviour and performance at work. The relevance of this knowledge to effective management makes it an integral part of the personnel function. What responsibilities and authority are given to specialists working in the personnel function will depend upon the nature of the enterprise and the context within which it operates, and what is considered to be the most effective way of organizing its resources to achieve its objectives. L.S., amended by E.L.

A. Fowler, *Personnel Management in Local Government* (Institute of Personnel Management, 1980); D. Torrington and J. Chapman, *Personnel Management* (Prentice-Hall, 1983); D. Guest and T. Kenny (eds.), *A Textbook of Techniques and Strategies in Personnel Management* (Institute of Personnel Management, 1983).

Personnel Management Adviser ⟡ Industrial Relations Officer

Personnel Manager ⟡ Personnel Management

Personnel Officer ⟡ Personnel Management

Personnel Policy ⟡ Personnel Management

PERT ⟡ Network Analysis

Peter Principle, The An idea introduced in 1969 by Laurence J. Peter and Raymond Hull in a light-hearted study of occupational incompetence, which subsequently became the subject of more serious debate and controversy. Its continuing appeal suggests that the Peter Principle concurs disturbingly with the beliefs and perhaps the experience of many people who work in organizations.

The premises of the principle can be stated quite briefly. Incompetence in organizations is universal. In every kind of organization people are to be found who are incapable of performing their jobs, and the causes of this phenomenon are not random. They derive from certain characteristics of the rules governing the placement and promotion of employees. One of these is that employees are frequently promoted from positions of competence to positions in which they act incompetently. This type of promotion is so common that it has come to be embodied in a dictum that states that 'In a hierarchy every employee tends to rise to his level of incompetence', or, 'The cream rises until it sours'. Thus the final promotion is typically from a level of competence to a level of incompetence, and upward mobility will end in an unsuccessful promotion as regards performance.

From this principle is derived Peter's Corollary, which states that 'In time, every post tends to be occupied by an employee who is incompetent to carry out its duties'. Organizational collapse is only avoided because the work that has to be done is performed by those who have yet to reach their personal level of incompetence.

The validity of the principle and its corollary are stoutly defended by Laurence Peter. He claims that their existence can be seen in many case studies, some of which he quotes to very good effect. There is the case, for example, of R. Driver, the autocratic teacher, ascending the educational hierarchy to become Assistant Superintendent. At this level he is expected to participate in school-board policy discussions, using democratic procedures that are completely alien to his previous experience. He seeks to dominate the board by an autocratic style that leads its members to regard him as incompetent. He receives no further promotion. Citing these case histories is as near as Peter wishes to come to objectivity.

There is, however, a further defence. This is an hilarious treatment of apparent exceptions to the principle, exotically categorized as the percussive sublimation, the lateral arabesque, Peter's inversion, hierarchical exfoliation, and the paternal in-step. These are organizational manoeuvres or devices to maintain the consistency of the hierarchy and to deceive people outside it by pseudo-promotions, obscurantism and the rejection of super-competence. The purpose of these subterfuges is to preserve the principle that nothing fails as well as success.

As a self-described hierarchiologist, Peter is careful to point out that what the ordinary sociologist or psychologist calls 'success' is really the achievement of the 'final placement'. The pathology of the final placement, or 'final placement syndrome', receives much attention. At the level of incompetence people eventually become aware of their unproductivity, and they display various medical and non-medical reactive symptoms. These include the rationalization of incompetence by galloping phonophilia – the simultaneous use of two or more telephones to keep in touch with subordinates; papyrophobia – keeping a clean desk; fileophilia and the teeter-totter syndrome – inability to make decisions appropriate to the employee's rank. The 'buckpass' is one technique used by teeter-totter victims to ensure that decisions are promptly passed to others.

It follows that those who seek the key to health and happiness at work must avoid the disorders associated with final promotion at all costs. To do so, Peter suggests his survival strategy. This is to create the impression that they have already achieved their level of incompetence by displaying one or more of the non-medical symptoms of final placement. This is called the condition of creative incompetence. Practised successfully in any ways that do not directly hinder the performance of the main duties of a position, and always carefully concealing the fact that one is actually trying to avoid promotion, this should be sufficient to fend off the terminal promotion. One example of creative incompetence given by Peter is that of the highly successful departmental manager who avoided promotion by occasionally parking his car in the space reserved for the company president. P.B.

Phillips Curve The Phillips curve takes its name from Professor A. W. Phillips, who, in 1958, produced the results of a statistical analysis into the relationship between the level of unemployment and the rate of

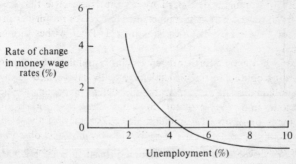

change in money wage rates over the period 1861–1957 in the UK. The relationship is illustrated in the diagram on p. 381.

If unemployment is taken as a proxy measure of pressure on resources, then the relationship indicates demand-pull inflation: low unemployment (high pressure of demand) leads to high rates of change in money wage rate (inflation) and vice versa. In functional terms the relationship is illustrated as follows:

$$\Delta W_t = f(U_t)$$

where ΔW_t is the rate of change in money wage rates and U_t is the unemployment rate, both at time period t.

Phillips's calculations suggested that, as far as policy-making was concerned, it might be possible to achieve stable prices with an unemployment percentage of around 2·5 per cent since this would then yield wage-rate inflation of 2·5–3 per cent which would be just about offset by the rate of growth in productivity, thus leading to a zero change in retail prices.

Over the period 1958 to approximately 1966 the Phillips curve seemed remarkably stable and a useful theoretical underpinning for those economists who believed that by manipulating aggregate demand the economy could be finely tuned to run at a given level of unemployment (pressure of demand) and therefore inflation. However, since that time the original formulation has gone adrift, as levels of unemployment became associated with higher and higher levels of inflation. Only in the 1980s, with the 'monetarist' experiment, has there been some sign of a restoration of the Phillips curve in its original formulation.[1] In what

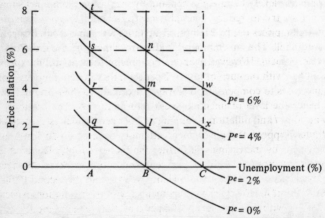

1. M. Lewis, 'Money and the Control of Inflation in the UK', *Midland Bank Review* (Summer 1985).

ways, therefore, has the original formulation been modified to take account of the experience of the seventies?

Critics of the Phillips curve argued that it failed to take account of realities in the labour market. In particular it was real wages that were determined by the wage bargain and hence any change in the level of retail prices would be taken into account by workers who would seek compensation in the form of higher money wages to restore their real wages. This approach was used by Professor Friedman (⟨⟩ Monetarism; Money Policy) in 1968 and he also fitted this revised Phillips curve into a monetarist framework, claiming that whilst there might be a short-term trade-off between unemployment and inflation there was no long-term trade-off.

The expectations augmented Phillips curve, as it became known, is illustrated below. Following convention, price inflation is measured on the vertical axis. The labour-market mechanism is as follows:

$$\Delta W_t = f(U_t, \Delta P_t^e)$$

This states that the change in money wage rates is a function not only of the level of employment (U_t), but also of the expected rate of inflation (ΔP_t^e is the expected change in retail prices), all at time period t.

In the diagram OB is the natural rate of unemployment, where the rate of inflation is fully anticipated and thus real wage levels are entirely determined by the real conditions of the labour and product markets. Initially the economy is at point B, experiencing zero inflation, which is expected to continue, and no productivity growth. The government now increases the level of aggregate demand by increasing the money supply in order to try to reduce unemployment. Demand for products and labour rises, prices rise by 2 per cent, and more workers are hired because real wages fall. Thus unemployment falls as we move up the first Phillips curve to point q. However, workers now revise their inflation expectations in line with the current rate of 2 per cent, they demand money wage rate increases to compensate, real wages rise again to their original level and hence the level of unemployment returns to OB. The economy is now at point l and inflation is running at 2 per cent, which is expected to continue. Suppose the government attempts once again to lower unemployment by increasing still further the money supply. Demand for labour rises, prices rise by 4 per cent and more workers are again employed because real wages fall. Hence we move up the second Phillips curve to point r. However, workers again revise their inflation expectations in line with the current rate of 4 per cent, they demand money wage rate increases to compensate, real wages rise again to their original level and hence the level of unemployment returns to OB. The economy is now at point *m*, but with inflation running at 4 per cent, which is expected to continue.

From this simple explanation various conclusions follow that may throw light on the inflationary experience of the 1970s. Policy-makers may be able to lower unemployment in the short-run at the expense of an increase in inflation, but in the long-run no such trade-off is possible. Any attempts to do so will lead to steadily accelerating levels of inflation at the natural rate of unemployment, as workers' inflation expectations are revised. Thus the Phillips curve becomes vertical in the long-run. The only way of keeping unemployment below the natural rate would be by consistently 'fooling' workers' inflation expectations, moving steadily through *q*, *r*, *s* and *t*. The price of this is an acceleration of inflation from 2 per cent to 6 per cent and even this may not work if workers begin to anticipate the accelerating rate of inflation, for this would simply drive unemployment back to the natural rate, but at even higher levels of inflation. Finally policy-makers would find that any attempt to reduce the rate of inflation will almost inevitably lead to a level of unemployment above the natural rate, as workers' inflation expectations again take time to adjust, this time in a downwards direction.

The inflation/unemployment experience of the UK in the 1970s and 1980s is illuminated by this analysis: the rapidly rising prices of the early and mid-seventies coupled with slowly rising unemployment, followed by the steady fall in inflation in the eighties coupled with rapidly rising unemployment.

This analysis of the inflationary mechanism has found much favour with the Conservative Government of Mrs Thatcher, which has argued strongly that it can do nothing by conventional macro-economic means to lower the natural rate of unemployment and that short-term measures will only trigger off new inflationary pressures. Instead it has concentrated on lowering inflationary expectations by means of the medium-term financial strategy (⟡ Monetary Policy) and lowering the natural rate of unemployment by improving job information and retraining opportunities and by attacking restrictive labour practices.

Theoretical analysis abounds where the Phillips curve is concerned and further suggestions have been made that, in the face of rational expectations on the part of individuals in the economic system, even the short-run trade-off between inflation and unemployment may not exist.

A final point to note is that the natural rate of unemployment should not be confused with the idea of full employment (or the level of unemployment consistent with it). It has recently been estimated at 11 per cent for males in the UK in the period 1980–83, having risen from around 2 per cent in 1955–66.[1] The authors of this study make the following points with regard to recent inflation experience: the reduction of inflation in recent years can be explained by the fact that actual unemployment has been higher than the natural rate. Similarly the increase in inflation between 1967 and 1974 can be explained by the fact that actual unemployment was somewhat below the natural rate, which is estimated to be 4 per cent for the period. Between 1975 and 1979 wage inflation came down, even though unemployment was below the esti-mated natural rate for the period (8 per cent). The authors suggest that this may have been the result of incomes policies in force at the time. ⟡ Inflation, Monetarism, Monetary Policy, Supply-side Economics. L.T.S.

D. Morris ed., *The Economic System in the UK* (OUP, 3rd ed., 1985).

Physical Distribution Management The treatment of all decisions relating to the physical movement of output as a unified total system. The system consists of eleven cogs, which centre on inventory manage-ment as illustrated in the figure on p. 386. The system objective is to maximize the total profit potential. This concept is of recent origin and many organizations do not yet embrace it. They treat the cogs separately and a substantial degree of suboptimization is encountered in terms of, e.g. stock levels, warehouse location, channel selection (⟡ Distribution Mix). It does, however, provide the managerial framework for optimiza-tion and offers an opportunity for employment of more capable ex-ecutives than hitherto in this sector of business. The concept is attributed to Wendell Stewart, as recounted in 'Physical Distribution: Key to Improved Volume and Profits', *Journal of Marketing*, vol. 29, January 1965. In the late 1970s the Centre for Physical Distribution Management established in London evolved into an Institute for Physical Distribution Management with a rapidly growing membership as more and more organizations recognized that physical distribution was an area where enhanced professionalism could bring about not only reduced costs but additional profitability through improved customer services. G.S.C.W.

M. Christopher *et al.*, *Effective Distribution Management* (Pan, 1981); *International Journal of Physical Distribution and Materials Management* (MCB University Press).

Picketing consists of the posting of persons outside premises, usually in furtherance of a strike or other industrial action. It has

1. R. Layard and S. Nickell, 'The Causes of British Unemployment', *National Institute Economic Review*, no. 111 (February 1985).

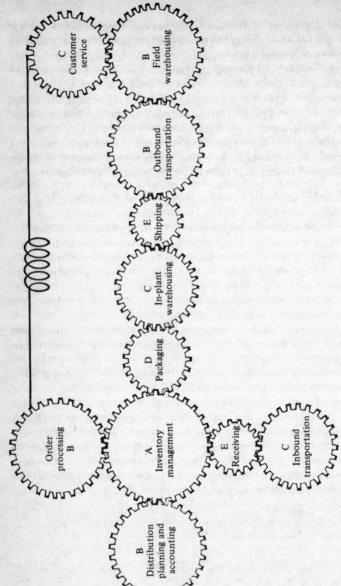

Activity cogs in a distribution system

Source: redrawn from Wendell M. Stewart, 'Physical Distribution: Key to Improved Volume and Profits', *Journal of Marketing*, vol. 29 (January 1965), p. 66.

attracted considerable attention in recent years, principally as a result of the increased use of 'flying pickets' and dramatic, if somewhat untypical, instances of 'mass' picketing.

The police have wide powers available to them under the criminal law to control picketing. Section 7 of the Conspiracy and Protection of Property Act, 1875 first sought to regulate the practice by creating a series of offences punishable by fine or imprisonment. Thus it continues to be an offence for any person to try to compel another to do or abstain from doing anything (such as going in to work) which that other has a legal right to do. The section makes it unlawful to use violence or intimidate another person or to damage his property; persistently follow him about; hide his tools or other property; or watch and beset his home, work or any other place where he happens to be. The conduct of pickets may easily result in other criminal liabilities, including obstruction of the highway or of a police officer in the execution of his duty. The police have a duty to prevent reasonably apprehended breaches of the peace, and anyone who wilfully hinders them in this duty – for example by refusing to move on when asked – risks arrest and conviction for this offence. Serious disorder may result in charges ranging from the use of threatening or abusive words or behaviour, assault, criminal damage, to unlawful – or even riotous – assembly.

During the 1984–5 miners' strike over 10,000 prosecutions were brought for a variety of offences alleged to have been committed on picket lines.

Various statutory provisions over the years have afforded *peaceful* picketing some protection. Currently section 15 of the Trade Union and Labour Relations Act 1974 provides that: it shall be lawful for a person in contemplation or furtherance of a trade dispute to attend – (1) at or near his own place of work or (2) if he is a trade union official, at or near the place of work of a member of his union whom he is accompanying and whom he represents, for the purpose only of peacefully obtaining or communicating information or peacefully persuading any person to work or to abstain from working.

This protection is narrower than it might appear at first sight. It confers no right on pickets to detain a person, whether on foot or in a vehicle, in order to put across the strikers' case, nor to enter onto the property picketed since this would amount to a civil trespass.

So far as the civil law is concerned, effective picketing commonly involves persuading other workers to break their contracts of employment by not going in to work, as well as interfering with the employer's commercial relations with customers and suppliers. The 1974 Act protects the pickets against these torts (i.e. civil wrongs) so long as the pickets comply with the terms of section 15. They must act peacefully, attend for the permitted purposes pursuant to a genuine trade dispute and, most importantly, only picket their *own* place of work. 'Flying' or 'secondary' pickets are thus ordinarily acting unlawfully, and in consequence an employer may be able to obtain an injunction and/or damages from a civil court.

A code of practice on picketing issued by the Secretary of State for Employment contains additional advice and recommendations, e.g. that there should normally be no more than six pickets at any entrance to a workplace. The code may be expected to influence the way the police in practice exercise their discretionary powers to control the size and positioning of picket lines, as well as litigation in the civil courts. In 1985, in an action brought by working miners against their own union and various of its lodges and officials, a High Court judge granted an injunction to prevent more than six strikers peacefully picketing outside their own pit. ⬦ Strike – and the Law; Trade Dispute. K.W.

R. Kidner, *Trade Union Law* (Stevens & Sons, 2nd ed., 1983) ch. 11; P. Kahn, *et al.*, *Picketing: Industrial Disputes, Tactics and the Law* (Routledge & Kegan Paul, 1983).

Piece-rates ⬦ Wage Drift; Wage; Wage Systems

Planned Maintenance ⬦ Preventive Maintenance

Planning (in the Economy) The idea of planning arouses strong feelings in people – to some it is a dirty word, whilst to others it conjures up visions of the promised land. This dichotomy of attitude stems in part from the different meanings of the word. A clear difference between a planned system and a non-planned system is provided by Sir Robert Shone in an article in the *Economic Journal*, March 1965. He says that planning 'contrasts directly with the classical approach summed up in the phrase of Adam Smith that the individual "is brought as by an invisible hand by seeking his own advantage to secure that of the community at large"'. Thus planning indicates for each individual 'what is the expected contribution of his own work and that of his fellows to the life of the community'.

Starting from this viewpoint the old idea of planning conjures up visions of central direction of the economy such as the country became accustomed to during the period 1939–45. Resource allocation was accomplished by the physical requirements needed to produce the final goods for the war effort, rather than by the interplay of market forces. The Government decided upon the structure of final demand and resources of land, labour and capital were allocated accordingly. Such an exercise would appear to be dependent for its success largely upon the degree to which all members of the community believe in the major national objective. Obviously in wartime planning of this variety has a good chance of success. The keynote of this overall planning is physical control backed up by authority to discipline if targets and schedules are not met. Clearly to maintain such control would be difficult in peacetime because national objectives are then by no means so clearly defined. This explains to some extent the growing dissatisfaction with the controls that were carried on by the Labour Government after the war.

The formation of the National Economic Development Council (NEDC) in 1962 marks the beginning of a new type of planning in the UK. The initial desire for it stemmed from a belief that short-term considerations were weakening the basic economic strength of the country and that benefits would flow from the setting of a new national objective: economic growth. Thus the Labour Government of that time created a new Department of State in 1964, the Department of Economic Affairs (DEA), specifically charged with responsibility for improving the medium-term prospects of the economy, whilst the Treasury retained control of short-term demand management. The basic standpoint from which the NEDC and later the Department of Economic Affairs worked was that it would be a useful exercise to indicate where the economy was going over the next five years. Hence this type of planning became known as 'indicative planning'. The plan for the five years ahead was based partly upon industrialists' expectations and partly upon the Government's desires (expressed in the National Plan of 1965). The publication of a target rate of growth would at least make industry, trade unions and the Government be aware of the implications for each of them if the target rate was to be achieved. Unfortunately this new attempt at national planning failed shortly after its inception when in 1966 the Government introduced deflationary measures to protect the pound and strengthen the balance of payments, making the growth targets of the plan unattainable.

The failure of the National Plan and the subsequent demise of the DEA resulted in the discrediting of national planning, largely because it seemed difficult to ensure that the tools of economic policy at the micro- and macro-level were available to enable the growth rate to be fulfilled. Thus the Conservative Government of 1970–74 and the current one moved steadily towards a market-orientated economic philosophy, laying particular stress in recent times on supply-side policies (⟨⟩ Supply-side Economics). In contrast the Labour Government of 1974–9, whilst not reviving medium-term national planning, did continue in its belief that government leadership and extensive intervention in industry were necessary to overcome the fundamental problems of the economy. Thus in *An Approach to Industrial Strategy* (1975) no growth-rate targets appeared and little co-ordinated planning at a national level was envisaged. Instead the task of revitalizing manufacturing industry was passed to sector working parties (SWPs), whose job was to formulate action programmes in order to improve the performance of their industries. These bodies work closely with the NEDC and report to it.

Both the NEDC and the SWPs remain and have produced many useful reports. Since they include employers, trade unions and the Government they are a particularly useful forum for the analysis of problems, even if they lack the power to implement solutions. However, under a Conservative Government they occupy a much less prominent position in government policy. L.T.S.

P. Hare and M. Kirby, *An Introduction to British Economic Policy* (Wheatsheaf Books, 1984).

Plans Although some plans by their nature are clearly long-term and some are clearly short-term there is no hard and fast rule to distinguish between them, nor does there appear to be any difference in kind, only in degree. Two features that are common to both are the number of variables and the extent of uncertainty.

Short-term plans are, by their nature, more concerned with the efficient use of existing resources while long-term plans may embrace the provision of new physical resources as well as the efficient use of existing ones. Since it usually takes time to provide new physical resources they cannot be considered in short-term planning. So long as the plan is limited to manipulating existing resources the number of variables to be considered is limited; as soon as the time horizon of the plan is extended to include the possibility of altering the existing resources or adding to them, the number of variables to be considered in the plan increases. The longer the range of the plan the greater is the number of variables that may have to be taken into account.

The second feature that increases as the range of planning extends is uncertainty. All forecasts are inaccurate. Since plans are based on forecasts and since plans must be prepared with these possible errors in mind, the greater the range of the plan the more seriously will these errors have to be considered by the planner.

These two features are present in all plans, but they become of overwhelming importance in long-range planning. ⟡ Forecasting; Strategy; Tactics. A.J.A.A.

Plans, Contingency Prepared responses to events that may occur.

Normally such plans are not prepared in great detail and they are often not prepared at all unless the event is likely to be of such importance as severely to affect the company's ability to achieve its objectives.

A typical example of contingency planning occurs when a company recognizes that sooner or later its plant may be put out of action by some catastrophe and that no insurance can cover it for loss of customer goodwill. Accordingly it may make arrangements with its competitors, its suppliers, its transport contractors and so on to maintain deliveries on its behalf in that event. The thoroughness with which contingency plans are prepared will depend upon the probability of the event occurring, in the opinion of the management, and the likely severity of its effects. A.J.A.A.

Plant Bargaining ◊ Workplace Bargaining

Plant Layout Layout problems occur at four levels in an industrial context: (1) factory location ⟹ Location of Industry; (2) layout of departments within the plant; (3) layout of facilities within departments; (4) workplace layout ⟹ Work Study; Ergonomics.

Items (2) and (3) can be considered the macro and micro versions of the same problem, which is to obtain a relative location of departments and facilities to achieve most efficient operation.

The arrangement of production facilities is determined in the main by the type of production. There are three types of facilities layout.

(1) *Layout by process* (*layout by function*). All facilities for performing the same or similar functions are grouped together, i.e. lathes, milling machines, etc., are found in separate areas. Layout by process is associated with jobbing in small-batch production and has the following characteristics: (a) it allows specialized supervision; (b) facilitates the provision of service; (c) failure of machines or absence of workers does not disrupt production excessively; (d) good machine utilization; (e) operations may be missed and 'bad' jobs delayed because of the necessary flexibility of control; (f) high work-in-progress.

It is appropriate where there is a variety of products; small batch sizes; intermittent demand for products.

(2) *Layout by product* (*flow or line production*). One product or component is produced in one area with the necessary facilities. Layout by product is associated with mass and large batch production and has the following characteristics: (a) little material handling is necessary; (b) good machine utilization; (c) low work-in-progress; (d) production control is facilitated; (e) minimum floor space is required; (f) machine breakdown disrupts production; (g) production is geared to fastest

machine; (h) effective use of labour, i.e. minimum training, job specialization, etc. ⟡ Job Analysis.

It is appropriate where there are large batch sizes or continuous production; standardized design; stable demand; a continuous supply of
material.

(3) *Layout by fixed position*. Used where the material or principal
component is fixed or must remain in one position, e.g. the building of
aircraft, shipbuilding, civil engineering. Unlike in the previous layouts
the facilities move to and from the product. It is characterized by: (a)
poor facility utilization (particularly on remote work, e.g. civil engineering); (b) the ability to accommodate variety in product, changes in
design, etc.; (c) satisfaction for intermittent demand.

The product, and hence parts to be manufactured, and the method of
manufacture will determine machinery requirements. Storage, inspection, etc., will be required, and total space requirements for each area or
department can be calculated, making allowance for movement, development, etc.

The criterion used for layout planning is normally materials handling or transport cost, so an investigation of the pattern of inter-
department or interfacility movement is required before a layout may be
developed using one of the many techniques. ⟡ Plant Layout Techniques.
R.W.

J. M. Moore, *Plant Layout and Design* (Macmillan, 1962); R. Muther,
Systematic Layout Planning (Cahners, 2nd ed., 1973).

Plant Layout Techniques Irrespective of the technique adopted,
the criterion normally used in developing plant layouts is the minimization of the total material handling or transport cost. Two approaches
exist; (1) the consideration of dominant parts only, i.e. to simplify the
problem consider only the products or parts that constitute the majority
of production in terms of quantity or value; (2) methods considering the
complete range of products.

Cross charts and relationship charts may be used to record the pattern
of material handling or transport and indicate the desirable relative
location of departments (see pp. 393 and 394).

Given the size of departments and the desirable relative locations, two
methods exist for developing a layout: (1) graphic methods, using tem-
plates, diagrams, etc., to develop a layout that meets the above requirements and fills the requirements of existing buildings, etc.; (2) analytical methods, using heuristic algorithms to minimize total material
handling cost.

To Dept. From Dept.	1	2	3	4	5	
1	14	13				
2			29	18		
3	4		7			Loads/week
4		8		1		
5	5			9		
6		26				

Cross chart

Several computer programs exist. These fall into two categories: (1) non-interactive programs such as C R A F T (Computerized Relative Allocation of Facilities Technique); (2) interactive and graphics based procedures – the latter include the use of C A D procedures. ⟡ Computer-aided Design. R.W.

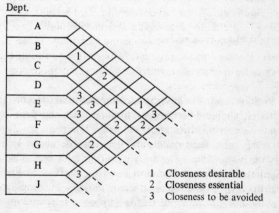

Relationship chart

1 Closeness desirable
2 Closeness essential
3 Closeness to be avoided

E. S. Buffa, *Modern Production Management* (J. Wiley, 4th ed., 1973); J. A. Tomkins and J. M. Moore, *Computer Aided Layout – A Users Guide* (American Institute of Industrial Engineers, 1977).

Point-of-sale Promotion ◊ Merchandising

Poisson Distribution ◊ Frequency Distributions

Political Levy ◊ Trade Union – Politics

Population ◊ Statistics

Portfolio Selection The objective of portfolio selection is to base the choice of an investment opportunity upon the aggregate characteristics of a collection, or portfolio, of investments. The term can be applied to the selection procedures of either an investor on the Stock Exchange or a company engaged in ◊ Capital Budgeting.

Traditional approaches to investment selection were concerned simply to maximize the overall rate of return from a portfolio. However, influential work by Markowitz recognized that the investor will typically require either the maximum return consistent with a prescribed measure of portfolio risk, or its corollary, namely the minimum exposure to risk consistent with a specified rate of return. Portfolio risk was shown to comprise both the possible variation in expected returns of individual securities and the degree of association (or lack of it) between the return of one investment and that of another.

Although the Markowitz model and later variations have been applied to selecting portfolios of securities quoted on the Stock Exchange, little progress has been achieved in improving, in general, the methodology of capital budgeting. P.J.A.H.

H. Markowitz, *Portfolio Selection: Efficient Diversification of Investments* (Yale University Press, 1971).

Position Audit The study of a company's position in relation to its environment. Before determining a long-term strategy for a company a corporate planner needs to know where the company stands today and what factors have shaped its past. The planner needs to be able to identify the reason why the company's profits have moved as they have, whether it has gained or lost a share of the market, how effective its research department has been and so on, thus gaining an insight into the company's current strengths and weaknesses. It is also necessary to know what lies ahead in the environment so as to identify any obstacles and opportunities. The position audit is the summary of these four main factors that the corporate planner needs before a strategy can be devised for the company. ⟢ Corporate Planner; Obstacles and Opportunites; Strategy; Strengths and Weaknesses. A.J.A.A.

Posters ⟡ Advertising

Post Processor A program written to enable the data and information prepared for the numerical control of a machine to be translated from the numerically controlled (NC) computer to a particular machine. Whilst a standard NC programming procedure can be used, the manner in which it is implemented is dependent on the characteristics of the machine. Hence each type of machine will require its own NC post processor. ⟢ Numerical Control. R.W.

Posture Correct posture is essential in order that maximum working efficiency may be attained and if discomfort and the risk of injury are to be minimized. Two complementary programmes are necessary to achieve these goals: equipment of all types must be properly designed for the people using it and training schemes are necessary in order to teach safe and efficient ways of deploying the body. The latter programme is usually confined to the lifting and handling of heavy articles, but might well be extended to include such simple postures as those of standing and sitting.

Occupational studies of the design of equipment in relation to posture have included examinations of motor-vehicle cabs, aircraft and space-vehicle cockpits, computer consoles and crane cabs.

Fairly extensive studies have been carried out into the nature of seated posture and the design of chairs. The main weight of the body, when seated, should be upon the bony ischial tuberosities and very little pressure should be exerted on the underside of the thighs. Nothing should press behind the knees, and it should be possible for both feet to be placed upon the floor or upon a foot-rest. Backrests should provide proper support in the small of the back and should be shaped to accommodate the natural curvature of the spine. ⟢ Ergonomics. E.E.

Power The ability to exert a positive influence over objects, persons or situations. This ability may derive from many sources: for example it may be based on superior physical strength, superior or specialized knowledge, an ability to inspire by personal example, charisma, the use of material rewards or punishments, the creation of social obligations through demonstrations of affection or friendship, skilled oratory, influence or control over resources. It is unfortunate that the concept of power has pejorative connotations, for this has limited not only the rational discussion of the concept but also the recognition of its importance.

Every organization attempts to define the powers of its various members. The right to exercise such power is called authority and tends to be limited to the minimum considered necessary for the efficient discharge of the member's duties and responsibilities. Not all power, however, is legitimate and in any organization there are members who are generally perceived to possess power that the organization does not formally recognize: for example persons who have privileged access to information, who are in close social contact with those who possess legitimate power, or who are believed to be able to influence decisions, particularly decisions affecting rewards. There tends to be competition among the members of an organization for power and for those roles that are associated with power, not only for the sake of the power itself but also for the higher rewards and status that such roles usually carry. An understanding of the distribution of power in an organization is essential for an understanding of the social relationships among the members. ⬦ Authority; Charisma; Status. I.C.MCG.

Alan Fox, *Beyond Contract: Work, Power and Trust Relations* (Faber & Faber, 1974); A. Pettigrew, *The Politics of Organizational Decision Making* (Tavistock, 1973); I. Mangham, *Politics of Organizational Change* (Greenwood Press, 1979).

Predetermined Motion Time Study (PMTS) 'A work measurement technique whereby times established for basic human motions (classified according to the nature of the motion and the conditions under which it is made) are used to build up the time for a job at a defined level of performance' (British Standard 3138). PMTS differs from ⬦ Time Study because it is an indirect method of obtaining basic times for jobs (⬦ Work Measurement).

PMTS systems at least originally relate to fundamental motions, and consequently it is possible to obtain basic times for all jobs (fundamental motions being by definition the lowest common denominators of human work). In this respect PMTS differs from ⬦ Synthetic Timing, which is concerned with job elements. Many systems are available, e.g. work factor; master standard data; basic motion time study; methods time measurement (MTM).

MTM is perhaps the best known and is the only non-proprietary PMTS system. Because the PMTS data is derived from an extensive analysis of man jobs (usually from motion films) greater

Distance moved inches	Time TMU*				Weight allowance			Case and description
	A	B	C	Hand in motion B	Weight (lb) up to	Factor	Constant T	
¾ or less	2.0	2.0	2.0	1.7	2.5	1.00	0.0	
1	2.5	2.9	3.4	2.3				
2	3.6	4.6	5.2	2.9	7.5	1.06	2.2	A Move object to other hand or against stop
3	4.9	5.7	6.7	3.6				
4	6.1	6.9	8.0	4.3	12.5	1.11	3.9	
5	7.3	8.0	9.2	5.0				
6	8.1	8.9	10.3	5.7	17.5	1.17	5.6	
7	8.9	9.7	11.1	6.5				
8	9.7	10.6	11.6	7.2				B Move object to approximate or indefinite location
9	10.5	11.5	12.7	7.9	22.5	1.22	7.4	
10	11.3	12.2	13.5	8.6				
12	12.9	13.4	15.2	10.0	27.5	1.28	9.1	
14	14.4	14.6	16.9	11.4				
16	16.0	15.8	18.7	12.8	32.5	1.33	10.8	
18	17.6	17.0	20.4	14.2				
20	19.2	18.2	22.1	15.6	37.5	1.39	12.5	
22	20.8	19.4	23.8	17.0				C Move object to exact location
24	22.4	20.6	25.5	18.4	42.5	1.44	14.3	
26	24.0	21.8	27.3	19.8				
28	25.5	23.1	29.0	21.2	47.5	1.50	16.0	
30	27.1	24.3	30.7	22.7				

*1 TMU = ·00001 hour

Source: H. B. Maynard, G. J. Stegemarten and J. L. Schwab, *Methods Time Measurement* (McGraw-Hill, 1948).

accuracy and consistency result. There has been a tendency recently to develop systems concerned with larger units of work (e.g. MTM 2). This has resulted because the systems based on fundamental motions (e.g. MTM 1) were often time-consuming and expensive to apply.

Computer-based PMTS is now common, and several PMTS have been developed specifically for computer usage (e.g. MOST, 4M, DATA). This approach is of value in manual and 'clerical' work study.
R.W.

R. Wild, *Production and Operations Management* (Holt, Rinehart & Winston, 1984).

Preference Shareholder ◊ Claims

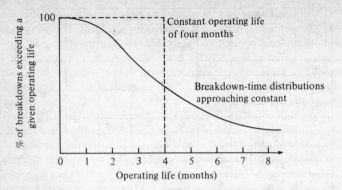

Present Value ⟡ Discounted Cash Flow (DCF)

Press Relations ⟡ Public Relations

Prestige The degree of esteem in which a person is popularly held. This definition, which seeks to maintain a careful distinction between 'prestige' and ⟡ Status, is regarded by many to be rather pedantic. The distinction is frequently not made, so the terms may be regarded as interchangeable. I.C.MCG.

Preventive Maintenance Two direct methods are used to ensure or increase the reliability of equipment or production processes: preventive maintenance and breakdown maintenance or repair (⟡ Maintenance).

There are two facets of preventive maintenance: (1) regular inspection to detect the need for repairs or replacement to prevent breakdown; (2) a regular maintenance routine, determined by experience or manufacturers' recommendations to avoid or reduce wear, etc.

Preventive maintenance is more suitable and particularly beneficial where: (1) breakdown-time distributions are known and accurate and have low variability, i.e. if the operating life is known and constant, preventive maintenance can be arranged just prior to 'breakdown' (see figure above; (2) the cost of preventive maintenance is less than that of breakdown maintenance. This is often the case even when the down time is greater for preventive maintenance. For example in an automated process, preventive maintenance can be scheduled to take place during inoperative periods, whereas breakdown even for short periods will stop the whole plant. The cost of preventive maintenance is often offset by providing operating stability. R.W.

Price Commission ⟡ Prices and Incomes Policy.

Prices, Theory of A firm's pricing policy is an important element of its competitive strategy but it must be considered in relation to product and promotional policies. As far as traditional micro-economics is concerned, interest in prices stems from their role in allocating scarce resources rather than their determination within the firm. This partly explains the many disagreements over methods of pricing among economists and businessmen.

If the firm is selling in a perfectly competitive market (⟡ Market Models), then it has no pricing because price is determined by the market. The forces of demand and supply interact to determine the price that will clear the market and the individual firm strives to sell as much as it can at this price. In practice the system does not work perfectly, shortages and excess supplies occurring because of imperfect foresight or poor weather conditions. This means that either the Government enters the market, or producers attempt to organize themselves, in order to stabilize prices and incomes. Such a pattern applies to many agricultural commodities and industrial raw materials.

For the firm selling in other than a perfect market (⟡ Market Models), the appropriate price to set is that which satisfies its objectives. If profit maximization is the objective, the profit-maximizing output occurs where marginal receipts and marginal costs are equal (this is the first-order condition). The price of this output can then be read off the demand curve.

The figure on p. 400 illustrates the point, using demand and cost curves. Output OP is the profit-maximizing output, because at this output marginal receipts and marginal costs are equal. The price at which this output can be sold is PR.

From this basic model several variants have been developed to explain the observed behaviour of firms in different structures. Thus the existence of price discrimination leads to a price-discrimination model, whilst the suggested stability of prices in oligopolies has given rise to the kinked demand curve, which enables stability and profit maximization to be preserved in the model.

For a variety of reasons the general approach outlined above has been criticized. The following are among the most important points: (1) firms do not have a sufficiently detailed knowledge of demand and cost data; (2) firms do not seek to maximize profits.

Empirical research into pricing policies has tended to reveal the prevalence of full-cost pricing or some variant of it. In its simplest form this involves the estimation of unit variable costs at some standard level of output and then the addition of percentages to cover overheads and selling expenses with a final, say 10 per cent, profit margin. However, this basic approach appears subject to considerable variation depending upon

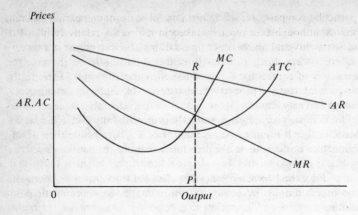

A R   = Average receipts (price) for different levels of output
A T C = Average total cost for different levels of output
M R = The change in total receipts caused by changing output by one unit
M C = The change in total costs caused by changing output by one unit

market conditions, whilst there are still problems involved in the correct measurement of costs. If mark-ups are rigid then prices are entirely cost-determined but evidence does suggest that considerable variation in mark-up occurs in response to various competitive pressures. One of the reasons most often given for adhering to full-cost procedures is that such prices are thought to be 'fair' and consistent with objectives such as earning a 'reasonable' rate of return on capital. Perhaps this indicates that they may serve as bench-mark figures.

Finally mention should be made of what has been termed going-rate pricing. In this case the price of the product is taken from those of its near competitors and the product is then produced in such a way as to match the price with a 'reasonable' profit rate. There is evidence that such a procedure is followed in oligopolies such as the car industry. ⟡ Business Motivation; Costs; Demand Functions; Economics; Market Models; Pricing (Market Pricing); Transfer Pricing. L.T.S.

P. J. Devine *et al.*, *An Introduction to Industrial Economics* (Allen & Unwin, 3rd ed., 1985).

Price–earnings Ratio Measured by market price per share divided by earnings per share, the price–earnings ratio is often referred to as the P/E ratio. It may be said to represent the price that an investor is willing to pay for each pound of current earnings generated by investment in a particular company. It is therefore a useful basis for comparing different shares, although care must be taken in its use. A relatively high P/E ratio (twenty and above is not unusual) may be interpreted in two very different ways. First, it may represent a commentary on the expected longevity of earnings at more or less their current level. Shares in the investment trust and property sectors are notable examples. Alternatively a high P/E may imply the stock market's expectation that future earnings of the company (or sector) concerned will grow rapidly from their current level, i.e. the P/E ratio assumes the role of a *growth* rather than *quality* quotient – not that these are necessarily mutually exclusive. P.J.A.H.

Prices and Incomes Policy A policy for the control of prices and incomes laid down by government in its role as manager of the economy.

No government can avoid having a prices and incomes policy. It may be a policy that involves no direct interference with market forces, including those involved in ⟡ Collective Bargaining over wages and salaries, but even *laissez faire* is a policy. Governments are concerned about the general level of economic activity, and therefore about the general level of incomes. They seek to exercise influence over incomes by means of ⟡ Monetary and ⟡ Fiscal policies. Additionally they may employ administrative controls: to a greater or lesser degree the governments of Britain, the USA, Australia, Sweden, Holland and other countries have interfered with the freedom of collective bargaining in this fashion.

Since the end of the Second World War successive British governments have been concerned with attempts to control ⟡ Inflation and to deal with successive ⟡ Balance of Payments crises, those in 1949 and in 1967 leading to a devaluation of the pound. Governments have sought to contain the level of domestic expenditure, thereby stabilizing domestic and export prices, and to divert more resources to export production. They have often relied mainly on a policy of wage stabilization to hold back domestic consumption, although the changing terminology of administrative control reflects some change in attitude: 'wage restraint' has given way in turn to 'wages policy', 'incomes policy' and 'prices and incomes policy'.

The beginning of the Labour Government's prices and incomes policy of the 1960s was marked by the Joint Statement of Intent on Productivity, Prices and Incomes, signed in 1964 by representatives of the Government, ⟡ TUC and those employers' associations that were forerunners of the ⟡ Confederation of British Industry. The purpose was to raise productivity, keep increases in money incomes in line with real national output, and maintain a stable price level.

In 1965 the National Board for Prices and Incomes was set up to examine cases of price and income behaviour referred to it by the Government and to advise whether or not they were in the national interest. A White Paper set out the criteria for determining prices and incomes, indicating that the average rate of annual increase in money incomes per head should be kept in line with an underlying productivity rise of 3–3½ per cent. Faced with the threat of further government intervention and a compulsory 'early-warning system', the T U C set up its own wage-vetting committee to deal with the flood of claims from its affiliated members.

The next step was taken in 1966, when the Government called for a breathing space of twelve months in which productivity could catch up with the excessive increases in incomes that had taken place. This took the form of six months' voluntary standstill on price and incomes increases, followed by a further six months of severe restraint. Since special treatment was allowable in the case of increased efficiency, of the lowest paid and of acute labour shortage, a tremendous stimulus was given to ⟨⟩ Productivity Bargaining. The criteria for employment incomes were also made applicable to all other forms of personal income, for example there were to be no dividend increases. Most trade unions remained ambivalent in their attitude towards the prices and incomes policy, however, and the Draughtsmen's and Supervisors' Unions fought the freeze in the courts.

The Prices and Incomes Act 1966 established the National Board for Prices and Incomes as a statutory body, rather than a royal commission, its original status. In 1967 its scope was widened, for example price increases in nationalized industries could in future be referred to it. In 1968 responsibility for incomes policy was transferred from the Department of Economic Affairs to the ⟨⟩ Department of Employment.

A further Prices and Incomes Act in 1968 endorsed the Government's power to require notification of proposed increases in prices, incomes and dividends; restricted increases in rents and dividends, allowing standstills to be imposed for up to twelve months and ⟨⟩ Wages Councils orders to be postponed; and introduced the power to impose price reductions. Wage and salary increases below the ceiling of 3·5 per cent per annum now needed the justification of productivity, comparability, low pay or manpower shortage, although such evidence did not inevitably justify increases. Increases above the ceiling could be achieved only by genuine productivity agreements.

The Conservative Government from 1970 disbanded the Prices and Incomes Board and revived the concept of a voluntary incomes policy operated jointly by the Government, the T U C and the C B I. When talks broke down, however, it imposed a standstill on incomes through the Counter-inflation (Temporary Provisions) Act 1972. The second stage in a programme for controlling inflation, intended to last from March to Autumn 1973, provided for the most comprehensive set of economic controls used since the Second World War years. Pay increases for any group of employees were limited to £1 plus 4 per cent of the total wage bill (excluding overtime) in the previous year, with an upper limit of £250 per annum.

Further legislation, the Counter-inflation Act 1973, established a Pay Board and a Price Commission to operate for three years with the power to restrict pay and prices in accordance with a Prices and Pay Code. Stage three of the counter-inflation programme came into operation in the late Autumn of 1973, against a background of rapidly rising world and import prices. It aimed to restrain domestic prices and secure price reductions where possible by strict controls and, on the remuneration side, to limit pay increases to 7 per cent with a flexibility margin of 1 per cent and additions for genuine efficiency schemes, together with provisions for 'unsocial' hours, anomalies and threshold safeguards.

The Labour Government of late 1974 abolished this statutory policy, substituting a reliance on the voluntary measures involved in the Social Contract with the TUC. This ran for two one-year phases, terminating at the end of July 1977 when the trade union movement insisted on returning to 'free' collective bargaining. The ceilings agreed in the Social Contract did appear, however, to have helped reduce inflation from the high level (of the order of 25 per cent) obtaining in mid 1975. In August 1977 the Labour Government resorted to exhortation in order to gain acceptance of its declared ceiling for wages and salary increases of 10 per cent, but was unable to reach agreement with the TUC on phase three. In July 1978, after a formal failure to agree phase four the Government unilaterally declared a 5 per cent maximum, with exceptions for self-financing productivity schemes and rigidly defined special cases. Later, in December 1978, it withdrew sanctions against private companies that breached the policy. Finally in March 1979, following the 'winter of discontent', the Standing Commission on Pay Comparability was set up to examine the terms and conditions of referred public-service workers.

The Conservative Government disbanded the Standing Commission in 1979 and set itself against statutory control of prices and incomes. Nevertheless a pay policy was enforced in the public sector, with cash limits being used to control wage increases. In essence, the Government sought strict monetary control to reduce wage settlements although, arguably, it was high unemployment that was ultimately responsible for lowering inflation levels. Moreover a return to economic growth (particularly in 1984 and 1985) was associated with a rise in pay settlements, particularly in the private sector. Hence, while interest in prices and incomes policies receded in the changed economic and political circumstances of the early 1980s, the problems that they are designed to resolve remain a vital concern. N.H.C., amended by M.J.F.P.

John Corina, *The Development of Incomes Policy* (Institute of Personnel Management, 1965); Reports of the National Board for Prices and Incomes; H. A. Clegg, *How to Run an Incomes Policy* (Heinemann, 1971); A. J. Davies, 'Incomes and Anti-inflation Policy', in G. S. Bain (ed.), *Industrial Relations in Britain* (Blackwell, 1983).

Pricing (Accounting Information for) There has been considerable controversy concerning the appropriate accounting data for the making of pricing decisions. In particular some accountants contend that fully allocated unit costs are appropriate, whilst others have suggested marginal or variable unit costs. The argument between the two schools suggests that some contenders do not always appreciate that a realistic pricing policy requires attention to both demand and competitive factors. The marginalists suggest that if price is above the marginal or variable cost of the product, the firm will be better off, whereas the fully allocated costs school contends that all costs must be covered if the firm is to make a profit in the long run. A proper perspective is perhaps that marginal cost sets a *lower limit* on price, although demand and competitive factors should be paramount in arriving at a price that is likely to be in accord with the achievement of a long-run profit objective. Moreover an unimaginative application of fully allocated unit cost to pricing could result in economic disaster for a firm. If, for instance, the sales volume is falling, then the addition of a share of fixed overhead costs to each unit for pricing purposes will increase price further, causing the sales volume to fall even more. E.A.L.

J. Sizer, *Perspectives in Management Accounting* (Heinemann/ICMA, 1981).

Pricing (Market Pricing) The setting of prices at a level that the market expects or countenances, ignoring company cost considerations. This approach is most closely associated with work carried out since the Second World War at the Sorbonne, Nottingham University and the Glacier Metal Company, and has led to two specific techniques: market-price profile and product-analysis pricing. The first offers the opportunity for price levels to be set in the context of the total marketing strategy the

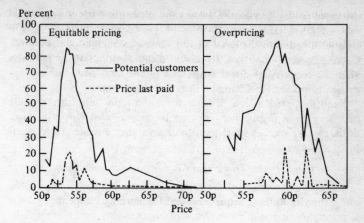

Figure 1. Market-price profile

company wishes to employ and is based on marketing-research interviews. The interviews elicit customers' price expectations for any given
product grouping, and these are plotted as a curve of price willingness
(see figure 1). When this data is available to marketing management and
is compared with the extant structure of brand pricing, a specific price
strategy and the role of price in the total marketing strategy can be
formulated. Product-analysis pricing (see figure 2) makes possible

Figure 2. Product-analysis pricing

delegated pricing decisions in a company where hundreds of price decisions are taken each week (◇ Prices). This approach must be held in contradistinction to the development of new techniques of costing (◇ Costing System) that seek to compute the contribution of products after the recovery of direct costs, and to the total cost recovery approach to pricing (◇ Changing Price Levels, Accounting for).

Neither approach can provide for short-term adjustments made necessary by a competitor's pricing behaviour. Discount structures, deals, etc. are used as short-term tools since they provide greater flexibility. G.S.C.W.

A. Gabor, *Pricing Principles and Practices* (Heinemann, 1980).

Priority Rules ◇ Sequencing and Dispatching Problems

Privatization In common usage, a transfer of ownership of assets from the public to the private sector, as has occurred with Cable & Wireless, Britoil, Amersham International, British Telecom, British Gas and British Airways. This is achieved by setting up public limited companies and the Government then selling 51 per cent or more of the shares in these companies to private investors. The programme was introduced by the Conservative Government that came to power in 1979.

The motives for privatization include the following: a preference for private ownership *per se*; a desire to improve the efficiency of the companies concerned; a wish to raise extra revenue, which may be used to support increased public spending or lower taxes, whilst still apparently meeting targets.

Various questions regarding privatization can be raised, particularly why should a private monopoly be any more efficient, or less likely to use its monopoly power, than a public monopoly? One safeguard developed for British Telecom in this area is OFTEL, the Office of Telecommunications, which is responsible for regulation and consumer representation. Another is the price-increase formula to which the company must adhere. Presumably the arrival of competitors will provide a third safeguard.

Another issue is raised by the analogy likening the privatization programme to an individual pawning the family silver, since assets sold today mean less public revenue in the future. Perhaps the critical questions are what the proceeds are used for – to cut taxes or to increase public expenditure – and which is the most efficient method of stimulating the economy. L.T.S.

M. Beesley and S. Littlechild, 'Privatization: Principles, Problems and Priorities', *Lloyds Bank Review* (July 1983).

Probability The theories of probability and ⟨⟩ Statistics have been developed since the seventeenth century, when mathematicians like Fermat and Pascal were invited by gambler friends to determine the odds in various games of chance. Probability theory is concerned with events in which the outcome is determined by chance, or when enormous numbers of causes combine to produce the final outcome, such that it cannot be predicted with certainty. A simple example is the outcome of tossing a coin. If a coin is unweighted, the outcome of the toss (that is, whether it lands 'heads' or 'tails') will depend on a number of factors such as the degree of force and spin imparted to the toss, air movement, position of the hand when the coin is caught, etc. However, if we toss the coin many times we find that an approximately equal number of 'heads' and 'tails' appear. Because in the long-run heads occur in half the tosses, we can say that the probability of a head occurring is a half. We measure the probability of an event on a scale ranging from 0 to 1, where a probability of 0 means that an outcome is certain not to occur and a probability of 1 that it is absolutely certain to occur. For example if we tossed a double-headed penny, the probability of a tail occurring would be 0, since the coin can never land tails; that of a head occurring would be 1, since the coin must always land heads.

Obviously in many situations there are more than two possible outcomes for an event. For example if we throw an unweighted dice, there are six possible outcomes, but we can say that the probability of a particular number (say 4) being thrown is one sixth.

Using the example of the dice we can also show how the probability of combinations of events can be evaluated. Suppose we wish to know the probability of observing a 3 or a 4 with a single throw of a dice:

Probability of obtaining a 3 $= \frac{1}{6}$
Probability of obtaining a 4 $= \frac{1}{6}$
Probability of obtaining either a 3 or a 4 is the
sum of the constituent probabilities $= \frac{1}{6} + \frac{1}{6} = \frac{1}{3}$

Similarly suppose we wish to know the probability of obtaining a 4 with two successive throws:

Probability of obtaining a 4 on the first throw $= \frac{1}{6}$
Probability of obtaining a 4 on the second throw $= \frac{1}{6}$
Probability of obtaining a 4 on both throws $= \frac{1}{6} \times \frac{1}{6} = \frac{1}{36}$

These addition and multiplication theorems of probability are two of the basic bricks on which the theories of probability and of statistics are built. M.J.C.M.

Stephen P. Shao, *Statistics for Business and Economics* (Merrill, 1976).

Procedural Agreement An agreement that sets up a procedure to regulate conflict between the parties concerned.

The procedural agreement has always existed in the British system of industrial relations but the ◊ Industrial Relations Act 1971, repealed 1974, defined the term as including that collective agreement, or part of it, that relates to consultation, negotiation or arbitration machinery for dealing with terms and conditions of employment or other questions arising between employer(s) and worker(s) or their organizations; negotiating rights; facilities for officials of trade unions or other workers' organizations; and grievance, discipline and dismissal procedures.

The ◊ Industrial Relations Code of Practice stresses the need for clarity in procedural agreements and lists their desirable contents. Procedural agreements can theoretically be distinguished from 'substantive agreements', which concern the substance of agreements on remuneration, conditions of work, fringe benefits, etc. In practice, however, the two often overlap. ◊ Collective Bargaining; Shop Stewards. N.H.C.

H. A. Clegg, *The Changing System of Industrial Relations in Great Britain* (Blackwell, 1979).

Process Charts A graphical method of recording the sequence of activities that occur during a work process, along with any other information necessary for analysis. Process charts are the main method of recording existing work procedures and describing proposed procedures during a ◊ Method Study investigation. The following types of chart are frequently used.

(1) *Outline process chart.* A record of the main parts of a process only (i.e. the operations and inspections). Normally used as a preliminary step prior to a more detailed investigation.

(2) *Material flow process chart.* A detailed record of the sequence of operations, transportations, inspections, delays and storages, which occur to the material during a work process.

(3) *Man flow process chart.* A detailed record of what the worker does during a process, in terms of operations, transportations, inspections and delays.

Example of a two-handed process chart

		Summary per 1 pieces	Present		Proposed	
Date:			L.H.	R.H.	L.H.	R.H.
Charted by:		O	2	5		
Proposed ⎤		⇨	2	4		
Present ⎦ method		▽	2	0		
Operation		D	2	0		
Assemble bolt and nut		Total	8			
		Distance	36″	56″		

Layout

30″
20″ B   N
10″
0″   O   A
10″
20″
   20″10″ 0″ 10″20″

B – Bolts
N – Nuts
O – Operator
A – Assembly

Parts

◄——— 2½″ ———►

Nut   Bolt

Left hand		Right hand
Reach for bolt 18″	O ⇨ ▽ D O ⇨ ▽ D	Reach for nut 18″
Grasp bolt head	O ⇨ ▽ D O ⇨ ▽ D	Grasp nut
Carry to central position 18″	O ⇨ ▽ D O ⇨ ▽ D	Carry to central position 18″
Hold bolt	O ⇨ ▽ D O ⇨ ▽ D	Place nut on bolt
Hold bolt	O ⇨ ▽ D O ⇨ ▽ D	Screw nut on to bolt
Release assembly to right hand	O ⇨ ▽ D O ⇨ ▽ D	Grasp assembly
Idle	O ⇨ ▽ D O ⇨ ▽ D	Carry to box 10″
Idle	O ⇨ ▽ D O ⇨ ▽ D	Release
Idle	O ⇨ ▽ D O ⇨ ▽ D	Return hand to central position 10″

Symbols	Outline	Man	Material	Two-handed
O	Operation	Operation	Operation	Operation
⇨	Transportation	Transportation	Transportation	Transportation
☐	–	Inspection	Inspection	–
▽	–	–	Storage	Hold
D	–	Delay	Delay	Delay

(4) *Two-handed flow process chart* (or *operator process chart*). A graphical record of the co-ordinated activities of an operator's hands, in terms of operations, transportations, holds, and delays (see Figure on p. 409). R.W.

R. M. Barnes, *Motion and Time Study* (J. Wiley, 6th ed., 1968); BS 3138, *Glossary of Terms in Work Study* (British Standards Institution, 1979).

Product Innovation ⬦ New Product

Product Liability The determination of which party in the supply chain, if any, is liable if defective products cause injury to persons or property. There is no specific branch of English law covering this topic, as there is in the USA and certain European countries. The claimant's rights therefore depend on general principles of contract law, specifically the implied terms of the contract of sale (⬦ Sale of Goods) if he or she is the purchaser of the product and thus has privity of contract, or the tort of negligence, which depends on a fault being found by way of an absence of reasonable care by the manufacturer, supplier or distributor. In 1985 the EEC adopted a directive on product liability, which involved making the producers of articles strictly liable for their defective products, i.e. without proof of fault. This will have to be implemented in the UK in due course (⬦ EEC Law), but the exact form of the legislation is not yet clear. J.C.E.M.

M. Whincup, *Product Liability Law: A Guide for Managers* (Gower, 1985).

Product Mix The range of products offered by an organization. Income from the sale of products is normally a company's major, if not sole, revenue-earning activity, hence the combination of products on offer is subject to continuous examination entailing new introductions (⬦ New Product) and deletions. The demand for any one product in a range may sometimes be a function of others in the range but, in general, managements treat each product separately for taxonomic and life-cycle analysis. Substantial economies are available in marketing a wide range of products, provided they are compatible in terms of promotion and distributive channels (⬦ Branding). The figure illustrates the different phases in the market life of a product: the time-scale differs between product groups. Different styles of marketing activity will be associated with each phase in order most effectively to meet the objectives set.

A taxonomy of products within a range has been suggested as follows: (1) today's breadwinners, (2) tomorrow's breadwinners, (3) productive specials, (4) development products, (5) failures, (6) yesterday's bread-

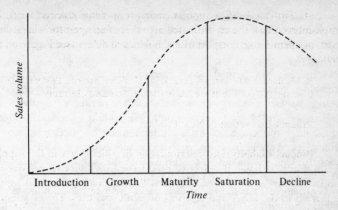

Introduction Growth Maturity Saturation Decline
Time

(Sales volume on vertical axis)

winners, (7) repair jobs, (8) unnecessary specialities, (9) investment in managerial ego, (10) cinderellas. Effective product management is dependent on identifying such categories and ensuring that managerial and financial resources are optimally allocated. Product-cost data is fundamental to such control, and marginal analysis of profit contribution will indicate the time at which resources should be switched. The time-scale over which returns are calculated is of great significance in governing allocation. Increasing attention has been paid in recent years to the cash-flow implications of products at the various stages of their life cycle as well as to the overall profitability of a portfolio. G.S.C.W.

Production Lines ⟡ Assembly Lines

Production Management According to economists, the purpose of production is the satisfaction of 'wants'. Of course human 'wants' are not restricted to the acquisition and use of goods, but also extend to the use of certain services, for example the services of professionals such as lawyers, architects, entertainers, or the use of libraries, transport or retailing systems. Production, according to the economists' definition, is concerned with the provision of both goods and services, but in practice production is usually identified with goods and not services. Production is associated with the creation or manufacture of goods; in fact an adequate definition of the production function is: 'The fabrication or assembly of a physical object by means of equipment, "men" and materials.'

Production is one of the two principal functions of business. The other – marketing – is concerned with the *demand* side of business, whilst production is concerned with the *supply* side. Production management is concerned with the organization and control of the production function or, more specifically, with the decision-making necessary to ensure that goods are made in accordance with the requisite quality standards in the requisite quantities, at the requisite time and at minimum cost.

Production management is concerned with the design and operation of production systems, so the scope and nature of the production manager's job is influenced primarily by the nature of the production system.

There are three basic types of production: jobbing or unique production, batch production and mass production. Each system has its own principles and applications and each makes specific demands on management. Jobbing production is concerned with the manufacture of small, often single, quantities of a large range of different products. The products are normally made to the customer's order rather than for stock, and general-purpose machinery and equipment are used. Because of the difficulty of accurate production planning (often an impossibility) in this type of manufacture, the principal management problem is one of control. Mass production is, basically, the opposite of jobbing production, in that a small range of products is manufactured in very large quantities. The products are manufactured on special-purpose equipment, for stock rather than to customer order. Because this type of production is comparatively inflexible, and because a very large capital investment is involved, it is essential to ensure that an adequate and stable demand for the products exists and that equipment is fully utilized; hence the principal management problem is one of planning. Process production is similar to mass production, involving the same management problems, but production is normally in bulk, rather than in discrete items, and chemical rather than mechanical processes are usually involved. Batch production falls between mass and jobbing production, in that products are manufactured neither singly nor continually, nor are products usually manufactured entirely for stock or entirely to customer orders. Many firms in the engineering industries are involved in this type of production, and the principal problem areas for management concern the size of production batches, the timing of production and the requisite stock levels. Rarely do these types of production exist in isolation, indeed many companies are involved in several types of production and consequently the task of production management is often complex and varied.

Because production is one of the central aspects of business, it has many frontiers with other functions, particularly marketing, personnel and product research and development. Many of the techniques used in production, such as the techniques used in production planning, stock control, quality control, etc., were amongst the first analytical management techniques to be developed, for example statistical methods of stock and quality control were first developed almost forty years ago. As a result a large number of these techniques have subsequently been absorbed into such disciplines as operational research. Because of this overlapping of both responsibility and technique, categorical definition of the scope of production management is hazardous. Consequently the following should be considered only as an outline of the principal areas of responsibility of production management:

(1) *Responsibilities during the* pre-production *stage*. (a) Production engineering (i.e. the design of tools and jigs, the selection of plant, the design, development and installation of equipment) is often within the field of responsibility of the production manager. (b) Plant layout and materials handling, i.e. the design and layout of factories and departments and the design of materials handling systems. (c) Production planning, i.e. demand forecasting, material ordering, production scheduling, workforce balancing and machine loading. (d) Work study (also conducted during production), i.e. the design of work methods and workplaces, the establishment of time standards and the measurement of production.

(2) *Responsibilities during production*. (a) Production control, i.e. the sequencing of jobs, processing of jobs and the updating and correction of production schedules. (b) Stock control, i.e. stock ordering, stock keeping and stock handling. (c) Quality, i.e. inspection, acceptance testing and the control of quality. (d) Maintenance and replacement, i.e. the repair, preventive maintenance and replacement of items of production equipment.

In addition to the areas outlined above, production management is also concerned with the following functions: (1) product design – the design of products to facilitate production; (2) payment systems – the design and administration of incentive payment systems based on work measurement; (3) purchasing – the acquisition of raw materials, parts, sub-assemblies, indirect materials and equipment.

Although production engineering is shown above to be part of the production manager's field of responsibility, this branch of engineering is a well-established profession, taught separately or as part of mechanical engineering, and is not therefore covered by the entries of this book. With this exception, all of the above subjects are covered by separate entries. R.W.

R. Wild, *Techniques of Production Management* (Holt, Rinehart & Winston, 1971); R. Wild, *Production and Operations Management* (Holt, Rinehart & Winston, 1984).

Production Planning and Control Production planning is concerned with the determination, acquisition and arrangement of all facilities necessary for the future production of products, to satisfy either expected or expressed demand. It is concerned with the design of the framework within which functions such as production control, inventory control, etc. will eventually operate.

The extent and details of this function depend largely upon the type and nature of production. In ⟨⟩ Jobbing Production, production planning is a continuous function, mainly involving the scheduling of customer orders against the capacity of existing equipment to satisfy required delivery dates. Because the nature and extent of production facilities are fixed, except for replacement, improvement and expansion, production planning in jobbing production is primarily a routine resource-allocation problem.

In mass or large-scale production, production planning is principally concerned with the future provision of all facilities necessary for the manufacture of a standard product. This is the most comprehensive and complex application, and necessarily involves not only forecasting, design of production layouts and procedures, acquisition of equipment, etc., but also manpower planning and the provision of services, stores, dispatching, etc. (⟨⟩ Assembly Lines).

Production control is concerned with the implementation of a predetermined production plan or policy and the control of all aspects of production according to such a plan or policy. Like production planning, the extent and the details of the production-control function depend mainly upon the type of production system. In mass production on flow lines, the production-control problem is trivial, since the production system, once designed for a given performance, is self-operating; all that remains is to provide the necessary materials and components and remove the finished product. In jobbing production the emphasis is reversed. Here production planning is a routine operation; however, because precise scheduling is impossible, work-in-progress levels are normally high, throughput time is high and a considerable amount of expediting and 'progressing' of production is necessary. Here the production control may involve 'breaking down' a general production plan into individual operations, allocating operations to machines, acquiring raw materials, progressing jobs through the operations, storage, rectification, transport dispatching, etc.

The terms production planning and control are often used interchangeably. Production control is often considered to include the planning function, particularly in small-scale production, and is frequently considered to incorporate responsibility for stock control, quality control, purchasing, etc.

The two functions are complementary and consecutive, their relative importance and complexity depending primarily on the type of production involved. Mass production necessitates complex and comprehensive production planning followed by routine simple production control. Small-scale production results in a routine planning function and a complex control function. R.W.

S. Eilon, *Elements of Production Planning and Control* (Macmillan, 1962); J. L. Colley *et al.*, *Production Operation Planning and Control* (Holden Day, 1977).

Production Theory Economists have devoted a considerable amount of effort to the problem of what determines the allocation of resources in a country. They have also been interested in resource allocation within the individual firm. For a manufacturer just about to set up or extend a plant there may be a variety of ways of producing the product. Likewise a firm with a plant already in existence may still be able to exercise some control over the factor combinations used in production. What advice can be offered to aid these decisions?

The starting-point for such decisions is the concept of a process, which may be defined as the way of performing a task. Thus wheat can be produced from a given amount of land with varying combinations of labour and fertilizer. Many industrial goods can be produced with varying quantities of labour and raw materials. If we are not tied to a particular type of machinery then the same product may be produced using different machines that demand different quantities of labour. In all these cases the ways of producing things are referred to as processes. At one extreme there may be many processes to choose from, at the other extreme very few.

The simplest assumption that can be made about a process is that the inputs must always be used in fixed proportions and output varies directly with inputs. Hence, if for a particular process 4 units of factor Y and 2 units of factor X produce 16 units of output, then 8 units of Y and 8 units of X will produce 32 units of output.

Suppose that two processes are available for producing a given product. The process vectors are shown below:

$$P_A = \begin{pmatrix} 1 \\ 0.5 \end{pmatrix} \qquad P_B = \begin{pmatrix} 0.5 \\ 1 \end{pmatrix}$$

Thus process A requires one unit of factor Y and half a unit of factor X to produce one unit of output, whereas the converse applies for process B. If one unit of Y can be purchased for £2 and one unit of X for £4, which process should be employed in order to maximize production for a given expenditure of £32? Although this example seems, and is, trivial, nevertheless the general formulation of the problem is akin to that facing manufacturers with given resources wishing to maximize production, or alternatively minimize costs of production of a given output. The major difference is that the number of factor inputs and processes will be considerably larger.

The problem can be put formally as follows:

$$\text{maximize} \qquad P = A + B$$
$$\text{subject to} \quad 4A + 5B \leqslant 32$$

$$\text{where } A = \text{level of output from process } A$$
$$B = \text{level of output from process } B$$
$$£4 = \text{cost of producing one unit from process } A$$
$$£5 = \text{cost of producing one unit from process } B$$

The problem can easily be solved by trial and error. For example, if B is zero then A is 8 units. If A is zero then B is 6·4 units. Finally it is easily verified that intermediate positions using both A and B and costing £32 will yield less than 8 units of output. Thus process A should be chosen and operated at 8 units of output.

The fact that this choice of process is determined by the relative prices of factors Y and X is more clearly shown in the graphical solution to this problem on p. 417. The process ray OP_A shows combinations of Y and X that yield given levels of output. The same applies to the ray OP_B, hence we can obtain lines such as EF, GH and CD, which indicate positions of equal output. The line AB is a budget line, the slope of which is given by the price of X divided by the price of Y and whose location is determined by the budget limit £32.

Clearly maximum output of 8 units can only be produced by process A. The total cost at point F is too great, reaching £40. As we can see, however, the choice of process would be reversed if the prices of the inputs were interchanged, thus illustrating the point that it is relative costs that are important in determining which productive methods to employ. This proposition is applicable to both the short- and long-run situation, irrespective of the number of processes and inputs available.
L.T.S.

W. Baumol, *Economic Theory and Operations Analysis* (Prentice-Hall, 4th rev. ed., 1977).

Productivity Bargaining A process enabling employers to reduce or at least stabilize unit labour costs by getting more effective work done and enabling employees to obtain greater rewards for doing it.

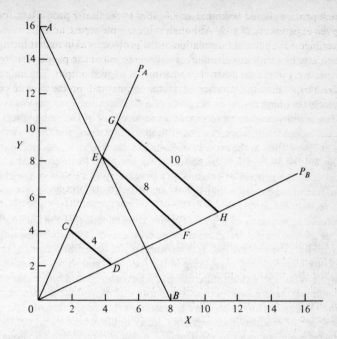

Productivity bargaining usually takes place at the level of the work-place or plant but it may be extended to encompass the company, the group, or the industry. The benefits to management can include the removal of excessive overtime; the relaxation of demarcation and the cutting-down of time-wasting practices; the abandonment of workmen's 'mates' and reductions in manning generally; greater flexibility in the use of labour and in hours of work; the reduction of limitations on output imposed by workers; the introduction of ⟡ Work Measurement, of ⟡ Job Evaluation and of new equipment; and the increase of apprenticeship ratios. Gains to be made by workers can include higher and more stable earnings; increases in holiday and sick pay; shorter hours of work and security against ⟡ Redundancy; better ⟡ Fringe Benefits and promotion prospects; and other less tangible benefits, particularly increased job interest.

A type of 'effort bargaining', productivity bargaining is the result of evolution over many years. In an unsophisticated form it is almost a continuous process under many factory piece-work systems. British productivity bargaining in the 1960s, however, had two new character-istics. It was concerned with controlled achievements and not past performance or vague promises; and, following the Esso Fawley Refinery prototype, it involved highly complex package deals.

Management has always been seeking ways to improve efficiency and in some instances these changes have been executed through collective bargaining, but the stimuli to the development of productivity bargaining in the 1960s were the increasing pressures of competition, the balance of payments problem and the emergence of a ⟨⟩ Prices and Incomes Policy.

Productivity bargaining was made more necessary by full employment, the development by workers of workshop organization, and the growth of joint regulation at the expense of managerial prerogative. Accelerating technological change has enhanced the problem of ⟨⟩ Restrictive Labour Practices. The process of productivity bargaining can result in the elimination of the old distinction between ⟨⟩ Joint Consultation and ⟨⟩ Collective Bargaining.

Practical problems of implementation are a function of the activities of the specific employers' organization and the level at which bargaining can usefully be carried on, and whether plant bargaining can be reconciled with national bargaining in the industry concerned. It was envisaged in the 1960s that future national agreements could be permissive or enabling agreements, setting standards and providing a frame for plant agreements; and in certain circumstances they might embody specific 'pieces' of productivity bargaining, for example, where aspects of the industry were common to most plants, or where the existing national agreements contained restrictive practices on manning, loading and the like.

Possible dangers in productivity bargaining include attitudinal limitations on the part of management and the workforce; the saving up by the workforce of inefficiencies in order to raise the price of jobs; and the disruption of differentials within firms and between firms.

The National Board for Prices and Incomes (⟨⟩ Prices and Incomes Policy) laid down rules for model productivity agreements and new schemes of payment by results in its Report 23. In the late 1960s and early 1970s, however, managements became disillusioned with productivity bargaining, while trade unions lost interest during the wage–price explosion. By the summer of 1977, however, with the demise of the Social Contract and its constraints, managements and unions began to interest themselves in productivity bargaining afresh.

By no means a panacea for all labour–management ills, productivity bargaining does provide an opportunity for management to take the initiative in ⟨⟩ Industrial Relations, to reduce unit labour costs, to reform the social structure of the plant, and to set the scene for future changes.

Accompanying higher levels of unemployment and the decline in official support for a formal prices and incomes policy in the 1980s, interest in productivity bargaining has receded in recent years. However, with the advent of new technologies, there has been concern to establish ⟡ New-technology Agreements and the issue of ensuring appropriate rewards for appreciable gains in productivity has stimulated a series of ⟡ Profit-sharing initiatives. N.H.C., amended by M.J.F.P.

A. Flanders, *The Fawley Productivity Agreements* (Faber & Faber, 1964); H. A. Clegg, *The Changing System of Industrial Relations in Great Britain* (Blackwell, 1979); E. Batstone, *Working Order* (Blackwell, 1984).

Profession An occupation possessing high social status and characterized by considerable skill and knowledge, much of which is theoretical and intellectual in nature. The possession of such skill and knowledge is usually tested by formal examination approved by an authoritative body. The members of a profession subscribe to a code of ethics governing their professional behaviour and define the area of their professional competence, preserving their status by confining the right to practise within the area so defined to those who possess the appropriate formal qualifications. Many occupations are nowadays described as professions although they may not meet all the criteria enumerated above. Traditionally professionals worked independently, placing their skills at the disposal of clients, who were not competent to evaluate the services for which they were paying. In these circumstances professionals claimed to be accountable for their performance only to the judgement of their fellow professionals. With the growth of large-scale organizations many professionals have surrendered their independence and have become employees, a development that has served to blur the distinction between professions and non-professions. As employees, 'professionals' are accountable to their superiors in the organizational hierarchy and, as such, are unlikely to be held legally liable for their own negligence. Further, as employees, 'professionals' will often need to make a choice between pursuing their career within the organization or within the profession. If the former, they may need to acquire skills and knowledge outside their professional specialism so as to fit themselves for promotion into administrative duties and, if the latter, they may wish to move from one organization to another in order to broaden their professional experience. In the former they will seek to impress their employers with their competence as employees and in the latter they will seek to impress their fellow professionals with their competence as professionals. They will be described as professionals to the extent that they identify with their profession rather than with their employing organization. Particularly in recent years, some professional associations have become considerably involved in the negotiation of conditions of employment for their members and in the determination of scale of fees. In this respect many are virtually indistinguishable from trade unions. The most prominent example, despite its indignant disclaimers, is the British Medical Association. ✧ Norm; Role; Values. I.C.McG.

P. M. Blau and W. R. Scott, *Formal Organisations* (Routledge & Kegan Paul, 1963), ch. 3; T. Caplow, *The Sociology of Work* (McGraw-Hill, 1964); T. Lupton, *Management and the Social Sciences* (Penguin, new ed., 1983).

Profit (in Accounting) An accounting profit (or loss) is conventionally defined in terms of the increase (or decrease) in a firm's net assets resulting from its ordinary business activities. Thus items such as profits from the sale of assets other than output of products and capital contributions from investors are excluded from the calculation of the change in the value of net assets. An alternative but equivalent definition of accounting profit, for any given time period, is in terms of the difference between the total amount of revenue from sales of products (or services) for that time period and the amount of assets and resources consumed in earning those revenues (✧ Profits).

The principal defects of the traditional method of business-profits measurement may be said to be the accounting conventions relating to the ✧ Valuation of Assets used in arriving at the change in the value of net assets. In particular the use of historic cost as the valuation base may result in estimates of profit that do not accurately reflect 'reality', particularly in periods of inflation (✧ Changing Price Levels, Accounting for). The measurement of profit (income) is interconnected with the problem of the measurement and valuation of capital. The adoption of alternative concepts of capital valuation would in turn result in different profit measurements. The accounting concept of profit merely represents one of a number of alternative concepts (✧ Valuation of Assets). E.A.L. and C.J.J.

T. A. Lee, *Income and Value Measurement: Theory and Practice* (Nelson, 2nd ed., 1980); E. S. Hendricksen, *Accounting Theory* (Irwin, 4th ed., 1982).

Profit-sharing An arrangement by which employees receive, in addition to their wages or salaries, a share in the profits of an under-taking. It usually takes the form of an agreement to pay annually (or in instalments) a fixed proportion of the profits made by the firm during the preceding year. The case for profit-sharing is based on three points:

(1) *Equity*. Employees have contributed to the profits by their labour (just as investors have contributed their capital) and are therefore entitled to a share of the profits.

(2) *Involvement*. If employees benefit directly from the success of the enterprise, measured by its profitability, they can be expected to be concerned for its success.

(3) *Incentive*. Employees will be likely to work harder for the profitability of a firm if they are to have a share of the profits.

Another approach to profit-sharing encourages employees to become shareholders, and was a feature of the 1978 and 1980 Finance Acts (as amended). The 1978 Act provided for the establishment of Approved Deferred Share Trusts, approved by the Inland Revenue. Under this scheme the company allocates a proportion of its profits before tax to trustees, who purchase ordinary shares on behalf of the employees. Shares normally have to be left with the trustees for two years, no tax having to be paid by beneficiaries until the shares are sold, and none at all if sold after seven years.

The 1980 Finance Act permits Savings-related Share Option Schemes, if approved by the Inland Revenue. Employees contribute an agreed amount for a specified period, at the end of which the savings can be used to purchase shares. The purchase price of shares is based on an option granted at the commencement of the scheme to pay the pre-vailing market price, sometimes at a discount. Such schemes stimulate interest by employees in the profitability of the business. A survey by Income Data Services referred in outline to more than eighty schemes.
E.L.

I. D. S. Study No. 306 *Profit-sharing and Share Options* (Income Data Services, 1984); R. Greenhill, *Employee Remuneration and Profit-sharing* (Woodhead-Faulkner, 1980).

Profits Profit is a term capable of several definitions according to the purpose in hand. As seen by the economist profits are a reward earned by that factor of production known as enterprise. However, in the modern corporation, whilst most people are clear about the traditional factors of production – land, labour and capital – what is enterprise?

As a starting-point we take the term as used by earlier economists in considering the typical business unit of developing economies – the one-man business – where the owner provided at least several of the following services: organization and control, risk-bearing, provision of capital, introduction of product and manufacturing innovations, land and buildings.

However, whilst the return to enterprise was called 'profit', it is quite clear from the above list of services rendered that part of what has been called 'profit' could be more properly ascribed to labour, capital and land. Thus in the modern corporation we find that salaries are paid to managers, rent to the owners of land and buildings and interest to the owners of capital. These payments cease, therefore, to be counted as profit and even if payments are not made to third parties for services because the firm owns its own buildings and land, for example, an imputed payment ought properly to be deducted in order to arrive at profit.

At this point one is left with a residual figure for profit that is the payment for risk-bearing and introducing innovations and that may also reflect the market position of the firm. The shareholders of a corporation clearly bear some risk, but it could hardly be claimed that they act as innovators. Therefore one can argue that some salaried managers receive extra payments for their services as innovators, or that the rewards to this service pass to the shareholders by default, or finally one may believe that both events take place.

One final point should be noted that is important in determining profits as defined above. This is the problem of setting a figure for imputed costs. The economist would say that the opportunity-cost figure is the relevant one, i.e. the return available for the service in the next-best alternative employment. However, it should be clearly recognized that the calculation of such payments is difficult in the absence of market-transactions data and this is why recourse is usually made to historic-cost data, or alternatively, why no deduction is made at all.

As defined above there are three replies to the question, 'Why do profits arise?'

(1) *Uncertainty.* The human environment is always uncertain, in spite of modern aids to managerial decision-making. Profits are therefore seen as a reward to those who take non-insurable risks.

(2) *Innovation*. This approach is closely aligned with the first. The role of the entrepreneur or manager in successfully exploiting inventions is stressed. The introduction of a new product or production process is fraught with uncertainty as to success or failure, but successful innovators steal a march on their competitors and for some time earn extra profits. Ultimately these may be eroded by imitators and hence the innovator must always be on the look-out for new inventions to exploit.

(3) *Monopoly power*. In the event of successful innovators protecting their position in the market by trademarks, advertising, low production costs, brand names, etc., they acquire monopoly power. As this power is maintained, so the profits obtained may be ascribed to monopoly power or 'imperfections and rigidities in the system'.

In economics textbooks the term profits is frequently qualified as 'normal' profits or 'supernormal' profits. 'Normal' profits are usually defined as the amount of profit (minimum rate of return) that a firm must earn in order to stay in the industry and maintain its capital intact. Failure to do so must ultimately mean a decision to leave the industry because better use can be made of the assets in other avenues. 'Supernormal' profits are, then, any profits (rate of return) above 'normal' profits and can be ascribed to short-run market situations due to successful product (or process) innovations or sudden increases in demand, etc., or to monopoly power. In time such profits may be eroded because of the entry of new firms into the industry, although this depends upon the size of the barriers to entry they face. Thus with all costs defined on an opportunity-cost basis, the economist's definition of profits and 'supernormal' profits are the same.

In making judgements about the use of monopoly power the Monopolies Commission frequently makes reference to rates of return on capital employed by the firms concerned (⇨ Monopoly Policy). These are often compared to the average for manufacturing industry and if they are significantly higher, then the Commission may conclude that monopoly power has been abused. As an approximation one could argue that the average rate of return for manufacturing industry is a measure of 'normal' profits and any excess sustained for a long period corresponds to 'supernormal' profits resulting from monopoly power. Steps may then be taken to limit this power.
L.T.S.

A. J. Culyer, *Economics* (Blackwell, 1985).

Programmed Instruction During the 1960s automated methods of training were introduced using a variety of devices generically referred to as 'teaching machines', which incorporated certain principles of learning. The characteristics of these techniques are that material is presented to learners systematically, progressively and in chunks of manageable size, and that their progress is regularly checked. Three basic types of program can be distinguished.

(1) *Linear program*. First advocated and developed by Professor B. F. Skinner, this emphasizes the need to break down a subject-matter into units that can be presented one by one to a student, who proceeds methodically through the whole program.

(2) *Branching program*. This is designed to cope with individual differences in the rate of learning. At the end of each presentation students are obliged to select one of a number of offered solutions to a set problem. The subsequent presentation is a function of the students' selections. A correct answer will lead them progressively on; a faulty answer leads to recapitulation or further explanation. The method of progression through the program is facilitated by the use of a teaching machine or a 'scrambled' textbook.

(3) *Adaptive Program*. This alters its own level of difficulty according to the student's level of performance. Such programs are normally incorporated into the control mechanisms of machines that teach manual or other skills. The learner's speed or error-rate is detected by the machine, the parameters of which are altered as appropriate.

More recently the digital computer has been employed in place of the dedicated teaching machine. Programs may be implemented either on microcomputers or through terminals linked to larger machines. Text, graphics and sound may be employed as input to the learner, whose responses may take the form of keyboard selections or any other computer-interpretable form.

Suites of programs are available to assist in the preparation of the training material as well as to control its presentation and to record students' progress. Applications range from primary schools to the training of airline pilots. E.E.

Programmers ⟫ Computer Program

Promotion (in Marketing) ⟫ Marketing Communications Mix

Psychiatry ⬦ Psychology

Psychology The term was used early in the nineteenth century to mean, literally, 'the science of mind'. Naturally enough, attitudes and philosophies have changed a good deal during 150 years and most psychologists today would prefer to describe their subject as 'the science of behaviour'. Both the nouns are important. 'Science' emphasizes the systematic empirical studies of psychologists that distinguish their approach from the intuitive methods of novelists or political leaders. 'Behaviour' implies an observable event involving the complete, intact organism and distinguishes psychologists from anatomists or physiologists who are concerned with the structure and functions of the individual parts of the body.

Experiments and methodical observations of real-life behaviour have yielded a considerable body of knowledge concerning human nature. Early studies were centred largely around the problems of sensation (⬦ Hearing; Threshold; Vision) and attempts were made to establish quantitative relationships between the properties of subjective sensations and the physical characteristics of the signals (⬦ Brightness; Colour; Noise). Much of the information so obtained is of practical as well as theoretical significance (⬦ Colour Blindness; Displays; Illumination). Other lines of investigation have been directed at the clarification of the abilities of people to process information (⬦ Intelligence) and to perform skilled tasks (⬦ Reaction Time; Skill; Tracking).

Man is essentially a dynamic, changing being and part of psychology is concerned with the developmental processes from infancy through adolescence to adulthood and decline (⬦ Ageing). On a shorter time-scale, people also alter their states either spontaneously or in response to environmental influences (⬦ Adaptation; Fatigue; Learning and Training).

It is convenient to classify the influences of the outside world upon the individual as aspects of the physical environment (⬦ Environment; Heat; Glare; Vibration) or of the social environment (⬦ Attitude Scales; Incentives; Stereotypes). As a consequence of environmental influences overlaid upon an individual's hereditary background, all human beings are unique in their patterns of adjustment. This uniqueness of individual ⬦ Personality forms an important area of research in psychology, which is complementary to the study of typical or universal features of human nature.

Applied psychology falls into three main categories. Each of these has become something of a professional specialization its own right.

(1) *Clinical psychology*. The study of abnormalities in behaviour has always commanded a good deal of human interest. The removal of superstitious elements from the description of such behaviour paved the way towards a rational study and classification of disorders. The clinical psychologist is concerned firstly with diagnosis, using a variety of testing techniques, and subsequently with therapeutic treatment in an attempt to bring about an improved adjustment between the patient and his environment. Psychiatry, which is a branch of medicine, shares this goal of the removal of behaviour disorders, but unfortunately it usually lacks a sound scientific basis.

(2) *Educational psychology*. The study of the development processes together with the general psychology of teaching and learning provide the background material for educational psychology. Specialists in this area are concerned to make recommendations concerning normal teaching techniques (⟡ Programmed Instruction; Learning and Training) to diagnose the sources of backwardness or other individual difficulty, and to provide special remedial facilities.

(3) *Occupational (or industrial) psychology*. Psychological methods and data have been applied to such problems as vocational guidance, personnel selection, training, equipment design, motivation, accidents and job analysis. The industrial psychologist is concerned with all the aspects of contact between people and their occupational environment. In view of the enormous breadth of coverage in this area, there is a tendency towards further specialization. Consequently engineering psychology, which is concerned particularly with the design of equipment and man–machine systems, has emerged as a relatively independent discipline. This subject is sometimes labelled 'human engineering' or 'human factors'. It also forms a substantial part of ⟡ Ergonomics. E.E.

P. Herriot, (ed.), *Essential Psychology* (Methuen, 1975).

Public Relations The conscious effort on the part of an organization to communicate relevant information to its publics that will be to its advantage. An organization's publics may be existing or potential customers, shareholders and other sources of capital, employees, or possibly legislators, if decisions affecting an industry, etc., are imminent. Public relations is a grouping of media used as part of an organization's total communications process, and is often used in a complementary manner to advertising (⟡ Media; Marketing Communications Mix; Advertising). Perhaps the most common form of external public-relations activity is the continuing effort to secure editorial coverage and favourable comment in the main news media, i.e. the press and television. The main methods of securing such coverage are press releases and personal briefings of leading journalists and TV editors. Internally good relations with the organization's workforce are often maintained by house journals, which can range from lavish colour magazines to mimeographed news-sheets. Their purpose is to foster identification with the organization and to ensure that relevant information is effectively disseminated. The Institute of Public Relations is the official pro-fessional body and publishes a quarterly journal, *Public Relations*. G.S.C.W.

Pulse Rate The measurement of pulse rate, usually expressed in beats per minute, has long been used in clinical diagnosis. It has value too in the assessment of work loads, since both physical work and mental stress produce increases in pulse rate. A similar effect is also brought about by increases in ambient temperature.

Considerable variation exists between the resting pulse rates of differ-ent individuals, and it is consequently necessary to use an index of work based upon proportional increase in pulse rate above the basal value for any particular individual. Heavy muscular work (such as running or cycling) will produce maximal values in the region of 200 beats per minute.

Studies on motor-vehicle drivers and aircraft pilots have suggested a close relation between variations in pulse rate and the stress brought about by the performance of certain critical manoeuvres. ⟡ Ergonomics; Muscular Work. E.E.

Purchasing The acquisition of raw materials, components, goods and services for conversion, consumption or resale. The term is more specifically used within business to describe the work of the indus-trial buyer, who purchases primarily for conversion and consumption in the manufacturing process, or that of the retail buyer, who resells to the consumer. The objective of the function can be usefully defined as 'to purchase the right quality of material, at the right time, in the right quantity, from the right source, at the right price'. This definition illustrates the complexity of the role, particularly when long- and short-term considerations are noted. Just as in ⟡ Marketing, it is a matter of judgement as to how the purchasing mix is brought into balance.

The role of the purchasing manager involves careful liaison with production, marketing and engineering colleagues on, for example, product design, and with production and finance on inventory levels. The purchasing manager should be closely involved in 'make or buy' decisions and with ⟡ Value Analysis, value engineering and cost-reduction schemes. In retailing the purchasing manager will need to be closely involved in marketing and distribution. The average manufacturing company spends more than half the money it receives on goods and services, so the impact on the concern of the efficiency and effectiveness of its purchasing management can be substantial. For example it can be shown that a 5 per cent saving in purchasing costs can be equated with an increase in sales revenue of 25 per cent. The converse is also true, where a loss of 5 per cent can erode profit to a similar extent. In retailing the proportion will be even greater; 80 per cent is not uncommon.

A major part of the operational aspect of the role involves the appraisal and selection of suppliers. With the increasing internationalization of business this implies a wide knowledge of potential sources and, among other things, alternative transportation methods, and the ability to appraise potential comparative currency movements. In making source decisions managers should aim to obtain the materials/services they require at the lowest cost to their companies rather than at the lowest price.

In many manufacturing concerns the purchasing manager will be responsible for receiving and storing purchased items, scheduling their receipt with suppliers, keeping company production schedules and disposing of scrap and surplus materials and equipment. A further responsibility will often be the management of the raw material and component inventory.

From the strategic point of view the purchasing manager should exercise perception in understanding the company's supply market environment and be able to project its trends. Among the aspects that need to be considered in this respect are potential competition for available resources; vulnerability in respect of supplies (e.g. single sources, political risks); anticipated supply-cost trends; the impact of technological, legal, political or social factors on the company's supply market in the future; changes in the structure of specific supply markets (e.g. concentration) and their effect on the company.

The professional organization is the Institute of Purchasing and Supply. ⟡ Materials Management. D.H.F.

P. Baily and D. Farmer, *Purchasing Principles and Management* (Pitman,

5th ed., 1985); D. Farmer (ed.), *Purchasing Management Handbook* (Gower, 1985).

Put Option ⟡ Options

Q

Quality Circle Quality circles (QC), or quality control circles, comprise groups of workers and supervisors in a single area or department in an organization, which meet regularly to study ways of improving production quality, and to monitor progress towards such goals. Developed originally in Japan, QC are now widespread in most industries in the West. They provide, in effect, an organizational device depending upon participation and motivation to help achieve quality during manufacture. ⟡ Quality Control. R.W.

M. Robson, *Quality Circles – A Practical Guide* (Gower, 1982).

Quality Control Most present-day goods are manufactured by mass-production methods on machines that repetitively produce *almost* identical units. However, owing to uncontrollable variations in the quality of the processed material and in the settings of the processing machines, no two units are exactly identical. A customer accepts this as the price to be paid for the economies of mass production, but usually there are limits within which the dimensions of a unit must lie (e.g. engineers' 'tolerances'). Manufacturers, if they wish to stay in business, must ensure that most of the units lie within these limits.

Although any units that do not fulfil the specification will usually be scrapped and will therefore incur a loss to the producer, in general it is usually cheaper to design a production system that tolerates the production of a proportion of 'defective' items, rather than to design one that produces 100 per cent 'good' units. Since the properties of successively produced units are subject to variability that can be expressed using statistics, procedures for monitoring and controlling the variability of these properties are termed statistical quality control. These procedures can be roughly grouped under two headings:

(1) *Process control.* This evaluates the properties of the units in an 'on-going' process to ensure that they are keeping within the specified limits. This is usually achieved by means of control charts, in which measures of the required property or properties of successive units are plotted in a form that reveals quickly the random fluc-

tuations and trends present in the measure. If the measures display excessive fluctuations or trends away from the required limits, corrective action can be taken before a large number of 'rejects' have been produced.

(2) *Acceptance sampling*. Unlike process control, which must be performed by the manufacturer, this is usually performed by the customer, who evaluates a number of units by choosing an appropriately designed sample of the units in the lot (⟡ Sampling) and determining the number of 'defects'. If this number exceeds a given value, the lot is rejected; if not, it is accepted. M.J.C.M.

P. D. T. O'Connor, *Practical Reliability Engineering* (Heyden, 1981).

Quantitative Methods It can be argued that there are four academic disciplines underlying management – the social sciences (economics, psychology, sociology) and mathematics – and that other disciplines relevant to management are derived from a combination of two or more of these. The term quantitative methods is often used to describe those branches of mathematics that are relevant to management. These are: (1) certain branches of ⟡ Probability and ⟡ Statistics; (2) ⟡ Operational Research; (3) the branches of mathematics that have been employed in the development of the social sciences.

Because mathematics now plays an important role in management, courses on quantitative methods are often included in management education programmes. M.J.C.M.

Queueing Problems When more customers require a service than there are service facilities to serve them, a queue of customers waiting for service forms. Such situations are common in ordinary life (e.g. queues at bus stops, supermarkets, doctors' waiting rooms etc.) but also occur very frequently in industry. For example partially processed parts may queue before the machine that will process them further, lorries may queue to be loaded at a dispatch bay or aeroplanes may queue to land or take off at an airport.

In these situations conflicting sets of costs have to be balanced. If 'customers' are made to wait a long time in the queue increased direct or indirect costs will be incurred (for example, stockholding costs of work-in-progress stock, slower turnround of delivery lorries and slower delivery service to customers, slower turnround of aircraft and increased fuel costs). The queue lengths and hence the waiting costs can be reduced by providing increased service facilities (more machines, dispatch bays and runways) but introducing these will incur increased capital and running costs. A careful analysis needs to be made to balance the costs associated in generating a queue and those associated with increasing the service facilities. Because the patterns of arrival of customers for service and the service times are subject to variability due to a number of causes, such an analysis is performed using mathematical techniques based on probability theory and statistics, which have become known as 'queueing theory'.

Quite often analysis of queueing problems using queueing theory produces answers that are unexpected from a common-sense viewpoint. For example it may be cheaper to provide an extra service facility which is only used for 50 per cent of the time in order to ensure that very 'expensive' customers are not kept waiting too long. M.J.C.M.

Patrick Rivett and Russell L. Ackoff, *A Manager's Guide to Operational Research* (J. Wiley, 1963), pp. 41–3.

Quickening ◊ Machine Dynamics

R

Range ◇ Measures of Dispersion

Rate of Return The accounting rate of return is generally measured by reference to the net income accruing to shareholders, divided by shareholders' capital invested. This percentage will give a measure of the overall effectiveness of management from an ex-post viewpoint and also of the return to ordinary shareholders.

An alternative calculation relates the net income to the net assets (total assets less current liabilities) of the business. This measure is used with a view to eliminating considerations concerning ◇ Capital Structure (◇ Risk and Uncertainty in Financial Management).

A further variation is to relate operating profits (usually before tax) to an average of total assets, since it can be argued that the efficiency of management is more properly measured by its use of all assets under its control.

Clearly in making comparisons through time a consistent basis for measurement must be maintained. P.J.A.H.

Rate-fixing The establishing of piecework rates by ◇ Time Study; Synthetic Timing; Estimating, etc. It is an infrequently used term that covers precisely the same area as ◇ Work Measurement. R.W.

Ratio Delay Study ◇ Work Sampling

Ratios, Financial Relationships, usually measured in percentages, between accounting figures. Their usefulness lies in the fact that they add to the information content and meaning of single, absolute figures. However, ratios themselves require standards of comparison and without these it is almost impossible to conclude exactly how good or bad a given ratio figure is for a particular business. Such standards still have to be developed. It is reasonable to say that financial ratios give a helpful point of departure for financial analysis but that they tend to raise diagnostic questions rather than provide definitive answers.

Financial ratios may be grouped into the following categories:

(1)   Tests of profitability, for example rate of return, i.e. net profits to capital employed; net profit to sales (or gross income); gross profit to sales (or gross income).

(2)   Tests of liquidity, for example current ratio, i.e. current assets to current liabilities; acid test, i.e. quick assets (cash and easily realized investments) to current liabilities; average debtors to credit sales; average period of collection of trade debts.

(3)   Investment tests, for example earnings per share; price–earnings ratio; capitalization rate or earnings yield; dividend yield. E.A.L. and P.J.A.H.

Reaction Time The interval between the arrival of a stimulus and the initiation of the appropriate response is one of the fundamental lags in human control mechanisms and has formed the subject of many psychological experiments over the last hundred years.

With practice, subjects are able to reduce this lag to less than 0·2 second. Accurate measurement reveals that the reaction time is a function of numerous variables. The sensory modality, for example, is one such variable; reactions to sounds are swifter than those to lights. Again, faster reactions will follow from intense signals than from weak ones.

There is considerable variation between different individuals in their speed of reaction, and in any one individual such factors as the level of motivation play an important part. Reaction times increase when a subject is faced with choice; this increase is logarithmic. The practical significance of this result is that operators' decision times must be allowed for, and that the amount of variety of both input and response should be kept as low as possible in order to achieve fast reactions. E.E.

A. T. Welford (ed.), *Reaction Times* (Academic Press, 1980).

Readership ⟡ Audience Measurement

Real Time ⟡ Off-line/On-line

Receipts and Payments Accounting ⟡ Cash Flow; ⟡⟡ Accrual Accounting

Recruitment Securing a supply of possible candidates for jobs in an enterprise. It is the first stage in the ⟡⟡ Selection process that ends with the placement of an individual in a job. Recruitment begins with information about and contact with the sources of supply of the different kinds of recruit required to fill vacancies in a company. In the case of young recruits these will be schools, colleges, universities and the Careers Service. For older people it will be job centres, trade unions, private employment agencies and a variety of local groups with whom the management and the personnel department have contact. In practice existing employees may be the most useful 'recruiting officers', telling the people they know and meet of possible vacancies in their own firms. Effective recruitment is not just a question of a requisition from a manager or foreman followed by the advertisement of a vacancy or an application to a job centre. It should be related to forward estimates of requirements as part of a policy of ⟪⟫ Manpower Planning, to careful ⟪⟫ Job Analysis and to a consideration of the ethos and organizational health of a particular business. It is in relation to all these factors that the sources of supply will be selected and cultivated, but success in securing the right quality and kind of recruits, though conditioned by the state of the labour market, depends a great deal on the reputation of a firm as an employer and the outside assessment of its standards of ⟪⟫ Personnel Management. This is particularly evident in the recruitment of university graduates and of qualified professional staff. L.S.

B. Ungerson (ed.), *Recruitment Handbook* (Gower, 1983).

Redundancy Dismissal of an employee or group of employees as a result of a readjustment of the operational manpower requirements of an undertaking. This may arise from the closure of all or part of the business, or from a reorganization of work so that a particular job is no longer required. Before the ⟪⟫ Redundancy Payments Act of 1965 there was no effective legal limitation on the right of employers to give notice as and when they wished. The Act requires them either to show that a dismissal is not due to redundancy or to pay compensation to the employee if it is. Under the Act a Redundancy Fund was established, financed by flat-rate contributions from employers, from which not less than two thirds of each redundancy payment made was drawn. In 1984, for example, a total of £645·4 million in redundancy payments was made under the Act, of which £300·1 million was borne by the Fund and £345·3 million paid directly by employers. During the year the total number of payments made was 425,142, of which 36,900 were in the mechanical engineering industry, 43,900 in construction and 42,800 in the distributive trades. In 1977 the Redundancy Rebates Act was introduced, permitting the rate of rebate payable to employers from the Redundancy Fund to vary up or down within the range 35–80 per cent, and an order was made reducing the amount reclaimable by employers from 50 to 41 per cent.

Though many employers were hostile to these payments when the system was introduced in 1965, both the ⟨⟩ Confederation of British Industries and the Government appear to agree now that they have significantly reduced shop-floor opposition to redundancy and have contributed to easier redeployment of labour. In any case only a fraction of the workers made redundant each year qualify for compensation, mainly because of the high proportion with less than the statutory minimum of service.

Many companies, however, in conjunction with the trade unions, seek to work out a redundancy policy for themselves over and above the minimum provisions made by the Act. Once trade unionists have agreed in principle to a measure of redundancy their bargaining position is that the claims of seniority, the 'last in, first out' principle, must be given priority, though in practice these may be modified by the company's manpower requirements and particular individual circumstances. Disputes (⟨⟩Trade Dispute) over redundancy may arise as a result of opposition by employees or trade unions to all or part of a firm's redundancy policy, or in the case of individuals who may disagree with the reason given by the employer for their dismissal and claim entitlement to redundancy pay when they were allegedly dismissed for misconduct. In this way the Act constitutes a deterrent to victimization by the employer and all disputes over payment are heard by ⟨⟩ Industrial Tribunals, which operate under the Act. Appeals to these tribunals by workers to establish entitlement to redundancy payments or the correct amount payable numbered just over 4,400 in 1976. An appeal against unfair dismissal may be made by a former employee to an industrial tribunal alleging wrongful selection for redundancy. L.S., N.H.C. and E.L.

Hilda R. Kahn, *Repercussions of Redundancy* (Allen & Unwin, 1962); D. W. Crump, (ed.), *Dix on Contracts of Employment* (Butterworths, 5th ed., 1976); P. Mumford, *Redundancy and Security of Employment* (Gower, n.d.); C. M. Smith, *Redundancy Policies* (BIM, 1974).

Redundancy (of Information) A sequence of signals may contain more information than the minimum required to convey a given amount of meaning. The excess information within the message is called redundancy. Simple repetition serves as an example. In a system that is free from sources of information loss or error, redundancy might be regarded as completely wasteful and undesirable. In less perfect systems, however, redundancy facilitates the detection and correction of errors.

If there were no redundancy in our normal use of a twenty-six-letter alphabet, then at each point in a printed English text, any one of the twenty-six letters would be equally likely to appear next in sequence. Clearly such is not the case: Q must be followed by U, J cannot follow Z, a J is almost certain to be followed by a vowel. Because of such redundancy, it is possible to tolerate a certain amount of error without losing any part of the intended message. In certain artificial coding systems redundancy is intentionally incorporated in the structure of the symbols as a means of detecting errors (⟡ Information Theory). E.E.

Redundancy Consultation In an attempt to promote greater workplace consultation and to prevent redundancies from being declared without warning, Part IV of the Employment Protection Act 1975 requires employers who propose to dismiss employees as redundant to first consult any *recognized* trade union in advance. Recognition can be formal or informal and may be implied, for example from an employer's practice of negotiating terms and conditions of employment with the shop stewards of a particular union. The duty to consult arises whether or not the particular employees likely to be dismissed are themselves members of the union or qualified to receive a redundancy payment. It is sufficient that the individuals affected belong to a class or grade of workers that the recognized union ordinarily represents in the bargaining process when negotiating with the employer.

Essentially the duty to consult means that employers must provide recognized unions with advance information about proposed job losses. The reasons for the redundancies must be given in writing, together with details of the numbers and descriptions of employees likely to be affected, as well as the proposed method of selecting those to be dismissed. Where a recognized union puts forwards counter-proposals, an employer must 'consider' them. He need not agree to them however, although he must give his reasons if he rejects any such representations. The 1975 Act lays down a timetable for consultations. It must begin 'at the earliest opportunity' and in any event not later than ninety days before the first dismissal takes effect where one hundred or more employees are to be dismissed at any one establishment within a period of ninety days. If between ten and ninety-nine employees are likely to be affected within a period of thirty days, then consultation must begin at least thirty days in advance. Where fewer than ten employees are concerned there is no specified minimum period and consultation must begin 'at the earliest opportunity'.

A recognized union may complain to an industrial tribunal that the employer's duty has not been discharged. If the complaint is upheld the tribunal may make a 'protective award' in favour of the affected employees. Depending on the seriousness of the employer's default the award may be up to ninety days' pay for each employee where one hundred or more are redundant, thirty days' pay where there are fewer than one hundred, and up to twenty-eight days' pay where no more than nine workers are affected. There is a defence where special circumstances (such as a sudden and unexpected loss of business) make full compliance 'not reasonably practicable'.

Regardless of any obligation to consult a recognized union, an employer has the further, and quite separate, duty to warn the Department of Employment of impending redundancies. The DE must be given at least ninety days' advance notice in writing where one hundred or more redundancies within ninety days are contemplated, and thirty days' warning where between ten and ninety-nine such dismissals are expected within thirty days. Failure here is penalized either by a prosecution and fine or, more commonly, by the DE withholding up to 10 per cent of any redundancy rebate due to the employer. ⟡ Redundancy; Dismissal of Employees (Law).ᴋ.ᴡ.

C. Bourn, *Redundancy Law and Practice* (Butterworths, 1983); C. Grunfeld, *The Law of Redundancy* (Sweet & Maxwell, 2nd ed., 1980).

Redundancy Payments Act ⟡ Redundancy

Regional Problems ⟡ Location of Industry and Regional Problems

Regression ⟡ Correlation and Regression

Replacement Cost Accounting ⟡ Changing Price Levels, Accounting for

Replacement Problems Many firms have planned maintenance schemes for machinery on the floor, but only some know when is the right time to replace it. Basically it is the same problem as deciding when to buy new cars. A machine deteriorates and its second-hand value depreciates with the passing of time. As it deteriorates, it falls off in efficiency and requires increased expenditure on repairs and maintenance. The time comes, before the machine is worn out, when the increased capital investment required to buy a new one less the secondhand value of the old one is more than offset by the savings in maintenance and repair costs.

An alternative replacement problem arises with a part such as an electric light bulb, the efficiency of which remains constant throughout its life, but which fails unpredictably. Again, analysis may show a pattern of group replacement that is cheaper than replacing each item as it fails.

Replacement problems can be examined using probability theory and statistical analysis and have led to the development of a branch of statistics known as renewal theory.

An interesting replacement problem occurs with the planning of labour recruitment to balance wastage. One of the UK's largest industrial operational research groups has developed a replacement model to determine the pattern of recruitment of new graduates into the group to offset the loss of trained operational research scientists to other firms. M.J.C.M.

Harvey M. Wagner, *Principles of Operational Research* (Prentice-Hall, 1975).

Resale Price Maintenance Law Resale price maintenance implies that manufacturers of goods try to ensure that their goods are retailed at a price laid down by them. At common law the position depended on whether or not retailers had obtained the goods directly from the manufacturer. If they had done so and had agreed to observe the manufacturer's price, the manufacturer was able to enforce this promise, but if the retailer had obtained the goods from a third party (e.g. a wholesaler) the manufacturer was unable to force the retailer to observe price conditions since in this case there did not exist a direct contractual link between manufacturer and retailer.

However, as a result of the Resale Prices Act 1964 and the decisions of the Restrictive Practices Court, any action taken to maintain minimum resale prices in respect of any goods, except books and medicaments, is illegal. The legislation has now been consolidated in the Resale Prices Act 1976. ⟡ Restrictive Practices. W.F.F., amended by J.C.E.M.

Chitty on Contracts (Stevens & Sons, 25th ed., 1983), ch. 10, part 5.

Reserves ⟡ Claims

Responsibility The obligation to use delegated powers for the purposes for which they were delegated. In this usage, the term is virtually synonymous with *accountability*. The term is also used, however, to mean a duty or activity assigned to a given position or (in the plural) the aggregate of such duties.

It is axiomatic in organizational processes that responsibility should be equal to authority, for power without corresponding responsibility is likely to lead to behaviour uncontrolled by the organization and hence to unintended and probably undesirable consequences. Also such power is particularly resented by those subjected to it. Conversely it is considered unreasonable to hold people responsible for events caused by factors that they are powerless to control: the delegated powers must be adequate for the purpose for which they were delegated.

Although it is possible to delegate both duties and the necessary authority, it is not possible to delegate responsibility. That is to say, superiors are always responsible for the actions of their subordinates and cannot escape this responsibility by delegation. In practice, however, a strict and literal adherence to this precept is liable to lead to inadequate delegation and too close supervision, with a consequent stifling of initiative. ⟨⟩ Authority; Delegation; Power. I.C.McG.

Elliot Jaques, *Measurement of Responsibility* (Heinemann, 1972); C. B. Handy, *Understanding Organizations* (Penguin, 1981).

Responsibility Accounting A system of cost reporting by which costs are accumulated and analysed according to the departmental or divisional responsibilities of individual managers. These costs are then compared with the budgeted or standard costs over which the manager can be said to have effective control.

The basic principles of responsibility accounting require an ordered and logical approach to the formal organization of the business. (1) Each departmental head or cost-centre manager should be assigned the general responsibility, as well as given the necessary authority, for the carrying out of clearly specified tasks or activities (⟨⟩ Management by Objectives). They in turn must be accountable to a superior and their subordinates accountable to them in clear authority lines. (2) A proper understanding must be developed of the factors affecting the area of activity over which managers can be fairly said to have control. (3) The quality of their administration and management must be periodically reviewed.

Once these organizational aspects of responsibility have been settled, it is then essential to consider the cost-accounting implications, in particular the question of which costs, of those attributable or allocable to a department or cost centre, it can fairly be said to have control over. As responsibility reports reflect only those costs over which managers have control, they are useful to superiors for evaluating their past performance and to the managers themselves for improving their future performance. E.A.L.

D. Solomons, *Divisional Performance: Measurement and Control* (Financial Executives Research Foundation, New York, 1965).

Rest Pauses ⇧ Fatigue

Restraint of Trade An agreement in restraint of trade is one whereby a person's freedom of action regarding his or her employment, trade or business is being curtailed. This agreement generally forms part of a bigger contract, traditionally either one of employment or one for the sale of a business. However, the restraint of trade doctrine is not exclusive to these two categories and it is for the court to determine which types of contract fall within it. Thus in recent years the courts have decided that the doctrine applies to 'solus' agreements, i.e. agreements whereby, for example, garages become tied to a particular supplier of petrol. Originally all contracts in restraint of trade were treated as illegal by the courts, but over the years it became accepted that certain restraints might be enforced in the courts. These enforceable restraints are those that are deemed by the court to be reasonable both from the point of view of the parties directly affected and also from the wider point of view of the general public interest. The courts are generally less ready to treat a restraint attached to a contract of employment as reasonable than they are in respect of restraints in contracts where the bargaining power of the parties is rather more equal. In deciding whether a restraint of trade is reasonable, the court will wish to be satisfied that the restraint is reasonable in the interests of both parties: e.g. if, in the case of the sale of a business, the seller undertakes not to compete with the buyer in return for the buyer paying for the 'goodwill' of the business. Further, the court will wish to be satisfied that the person who seeks to impose the restraint has a legitimate interest to protect. Thus a restraint in a contract of employment will be deemed reasonable if its purpose is to protect the employer's proprietary interest in trade secrets or trade connections. It would not be reasonable, however, to prevent an employee from engaging in competition with his former employer where no such proprietary considerations are involved. If a restraint is bad in part the court will treat it as totally void, except in rare cases where, without having to redraft the contract, it is possible to separate the good parts from the bad ones, in which case the good parts will be enforced.

Before 1871 trade unions were regarded as illegal organizations because their deployment of the strike weapon was held to unreasonably restrain trade. Since then, however, statute has freed them from the taint of illegality based solely on this doctrine. W.F.F. and D.V.E.R., amended by K.W.

G. Treitel, *The Law of Contract* (Stevens & Sons, 6th ed., 1983), ch. 11; *Chitty on Contracts* (Stevens & Sons, 25th ed., 1983), ch. 16, part 2(f).

Restrictive Labour Practices Arrangements imposed by employees by which labour is not used efficiently, there being no social or economic justification as far as society as a whole is concerned.

Many restrictions on the use of labour are now generally regarded as desirable. On economic grounds it may, for example, be more efficient to prevent excessive hours of work, since people when tired tend to produce poorer performances. A normal working week of sixty hours might not in some cases be excessive in terms of efficiency but would now be unacceptable on social grounds. Many such restrictions are incorporated in the safety, health and welfare provisions of the Factories Acts.

Some restrictive labour practices that are the product of management decisions may or may not be justified, according to circumstances. Overmanning seems indefensible at times of high employment, but the retention of labour during a temporary recession may make both economic and social sense if it prevents the dispersal of a trained and experienced workforce.

Restrictive practices may be formal and agreed, as between trade unions and management, and even subject to a written agreement after collective bargaining, as in various types of apprenticeship regulations. They may be informal and by no means 'agreed', for example where work groups set their own standards of performance. Trade unions may or may not be involved. In any event, management acquiesces to them and shares the responsibility for their existence.

Restrictive labour practices may occur through ⟨⟩ Demarcation, low effective performance resulting from employment of craftsmen's mates, overmanning, restrictions on output, unnecessary overtime, excessive tea breaks and bad timekeeping practices.

Restrictive labour practices are most marked in industries where there is little security of employment, e.g. shipbuilding, docks. They are also marked where trade unions have considerable bargaining strength, e.g. in the printing industry, where unions have extensive control over entry to employment as well as over jobs. Management weakness is another facilitating factor, e.g. in the newspaper industry, where the product is perishable, where there is considerable competition between employers, and where there is no external pressure such as foreign competition. Tradition and convention, e.g. among crafts, can be significant, although many restrictive labour practices are new, having sprung up with new work situations.

It is primarily management's job to eliminate or reduce restrictive labour practices by improving its handling of industrial relations generally. Unions can help by improving their structure and education programmes. Governments can assist in the last resort, e.g. the Devlin Inquiry into the docks.

In recent years the issue has become less contentious as unemployment and productivity have both risen sharply. Indeed, the focus of attention has shifted to the acceptance or otherwise of new technologies by the workforce and trade unions. N.H.C., amended by M.J.F.P.

Royal Commission on Trade Unions and Employers' Associations, Research Paper No. 4, *Productivity Bargaining and Restrictive Labour Practices* (HMSO, 1967), G. S. Bain (ed.), *Industrial Relations in Britain* (Blackwell, 1983).

Restrictive Practices Restrictive-practices legislation developed from the early reports of the Monopolies Commission published between 1948 and 1955. Many of these reports contained strong criticisms of trade associations rather than the single-firm monopoly and these criticisms were drawn together in the *Report on Collective Discrimination*, 1955, which formed the evidence for the Restrictive Trade Practices Act, 1956. Amongst the practices criticized were price rings, cartels, market sharing agreements, resale price maintenance and collective discrimination against outsiders. Fundamentally they were criticized because they encouraged inefficiency and a quiet life rather than efficiency and innovations.

The 1956 Act outlawed collective resale price maintenance and made it clear that trade agreements were prima facie against the public interest. The onus of proof to the contrary was to rest with the parties to an agreement, who would have an opportunity to prove their case before the Restrictive Practices Court. The case against an agreement was to be presented by the Registrar of Restrictive Trade Practices, with whom all such agreements should first be registered. The composition of the Restrictive Practices Court is such that it marries legal experts and industrial and commercial experts. The procedure is similar to that in any court of law, in that expert witnesses can be called for prosecution and defence.

The types of agreements to be registered were those between at least two persons whereby restrictions were accepted in respect of prices to be charged, conditions of sale, quantities and types to be produced, persons or areas to be supplied and persons or areas from whom supplies might be obtained. Even though such restrictions were deemed to be against the public interest, nevertheless the Court could uphold any restriction that satisfied certain conditions, provided that the Court was also satisfied that the advantages to the public outweighed the disadvantages. These conditions were all designed to encourage serious discussion about the agreement; the one that has been pleaded most often is section 21(1)b: that the agreement confers specific and substantial benefits upon the consuming public.

Application of the Act seems to have changed over time. In the period up to 1960 eleven cases were considered and three agreements had been upheld, but since then the number of cases upheld has increased considerably as defence experts have worked away at the interpretation of section 21(1)b. However, it is undoubtedly the case that many agreements were abandoned without ever being registered.

In 1964 the Registrar was given the further task of presenting for judgement individual resale-price maintenance agreements. Again the presumption was that such practices were against the public interest, but five conditions were provided for possible escape, with an overall survey of benefits and disadvantages if one of the conditions were thought to be fulfilled. The general effect appears to be that many agreements have been abandoned without going to court, but the case fought by the chocolate manufacturers was particularly long and drawn out; the judgement went against the manufacturers.

As one restrictive practice is abandoned so manufacturers find other loopholes in the legislation and in 1968 the Registrar was given further powers to deal with 'information' agreements. Such agreements may provide for the parties to exchange information about prices, costs and allocation of contracts, etc., and in this way the same results as before can be achieved. The 1968 Act, however, weakened restrictive-practices legislation in two important ways. Probably concerned with information agreements, an additional gateway was introduced so that a restriction could be defended on the grounds that 'it does not directly or indirectly restrict or discourage competition to any material degree in any relevant trade or industry and is not likely to do so'. The second way in which legislation was weakened arose out of an attempt to clarify certain apparent conflicts on policy between various government bodies. For example the Economic Development Committee (EDC) for an industry might encourage agreements that were registrable under the Act. Thus the 1968 Act also provides exemption from registration of certain agreements of importance to the national economy, where the object is to promote efficiency or to create or improve productive capacity, and where that object cannot be achieved within a reasonable time except by means of an agreement.

The Fair Trading Act 1973 abolished the office of Registrar of Restrictive Trade Practices and transferred its powers and functions to the Director General of Fair Trading. Further legislation followed in 1976 with the Restrictive Trade Practices Act, which extended coverage to agreements concerning services. This has meant some renewal of activity on the part of the Court, which had almost appeared to have worked itself out of a job, so effective had it been in dealing with traditional cartels. Thus in 1983 three goods agreements and one service agreement were referred to the Court whilst none were referred in 1982 and 1981.

The control of restrictive practices has undoubtedly done away with a vast amount of overt price fixing and other harmful practices instituted by cartels. Between 1956 and 1984 the total number of restrictive agreements registered was 4,215 for goods and 984 for services. The great majority of these have been abandoned and only thirty were subjected to a full court hearing. Of these, only eleven agreements have been approved and two further cases were approved under the resale-prices legislation. Whether such abandonment leads to a more efficient economic system depends very much, however, upon what follows. In some cases an increase in competitive behaviour has followed via prices and discounts, but in others competition has been restricted by information agreements (now to be registered), new but unregistered agreements, price leadership and outright takeover.

Work in this area still continues, however, if not in the public glare of the court-room, and the Director General noted in his 1984 report that an important part of the Office of Fair Trading's work is the investigation of evidence of unregistered but registrable agreements. Also a considerable amount of work goes on behind the scenes persuading the parties to an agreement to remove or modify offending restrictions contained within it. ⟡ EEC Law. L.T.S.

> *Annual Report of the Director General of Fair Trading 1984* (HMSO, 1985); D. Morris (ed.), *The Economic System in the UK* (OUP, 3rd ed., 1985).

Retail Audit The regular measurement of retail trading activity in a sample of retail outlets for purposes of marketing research. The technique involves the selection of a representative sample of outlets, to which visits are made, normally on a monthly basis, to count current stock levels in selected product categories, and to examine deliveries of goods to the outlet and inter-branch transfers. This data provides sales per outlet by the following calculation:

Stock at start + Net deliveries inwards − Stock at close = Sales

In addition to providing total sales, stock-cover in terms of 'week's supply' at the current rate of sale can be computed. The percentage of

outlets that have any particular product and/or brand in stock provides
a measure of distribution, and when the total sales values of a product
through outlets stocking it are expressed as a percentage of the total
sales value of the product, the sterling distribution is obtained. This
latter measure of distribution provides a measure of the quality of distribution as well as the quantity, a matter of importance when the size of
the outlets stocking a product varies widely. The technique was pioneered
in North America in the 1920s by A. C. Nielsen, and this company is the
largest retail audit organization in Britain. G.S.C.W.

Retail Gravitation The movement of customers to retail outlets (⟡
Retailing). The problem has attracted considerable attention in order
both to assess the potential for the development of existing trade and to
facilitate the effective location of new shopping centres. The earliest
attempts to establish relationships between retail trading centres and
their hinterland were made by William Reilly (*Methods for Study of
Retail Relationships*, University of Texas, 1929) and took account of
population mass (P) and distance (D):

$$\frac{Ba}{Bb} = \left(\frac{Pa}{Pb}\right)\left(\frac{Db}{Da}\right)^2$$

where Ba and Bb represent the proportion of trade going to towns a and
b. This gives a breaking point (Db) in miles from town b, for trade
between the two towns of:

$$Db = \frac{Dab}{1 + \sqrt{\frac{Pa}{Pb}}}$$

Where the population of town a is 200,000 and that of town b 50,000,
and the two towns are ten miles apart, this gives a breaking point for
trade $6\frac{2}{3}$ miles from town a and $3\frac{1}{3}$ miles from town b. A number of
more recent models of a deterministic nature have been developed, incorporating modifications for the attractiveness of a shopping centre.
Huff has recently developed a probabilistic model, which can be based
on either empirical ascription of probabilities by interview or deductive
procedures. Deductive methods are still the most common in use. The
contribution of economic geographers through central place theory, and
of social physics in developing an explanation of patterns of gravitation
is increasingly apparent. G.S.C.W.

Retailing The ultimate sale of any goods in small quantities.

Normally it will be the final stage in the distribution of a product or service, which transfers ownership to the person who will control where it will be used (◊ Distribution Mix). It is now commonplace to find retailing as a separate institution in the marketing process, but it is not so long since the producer/retailer existed, and there are signs that many multiple retailers, e.g. Marks and Spencer and Sainsbury, are seeking to influence and control their suppliers. The retailer offers ready access to a wide range of related goods purchased from a larger supply at a discount known as the retail margin. ◊ Mail Order is a special case where the goods offered are seen in a catalogue and requested by post; this sector of retailing is the fastest growth area in Britain today, probably due to the congestion encountered in many shopping centres and the increasing importance of time in a society with many working wives. The abolition of resale price maintenance (◊ Resale Price Maintenance Law) in 1964 has led to an undermining of retail margins. When added to the trends to self-service (◊ Supermarket), larger units and multiple chains with volume advantages in buying from suppliers, this has meant swift changes in the structure of British retailing. Smaller units, particularly in the food trade, have formed voluntary groups with wholesalers in order to secure buying economies; the most important are Wavy Line and Mace. Co-operative retail outlets already had this opportunity through the Co-operative Wholesale Society (◊ Co-operative Movement) but have been unable to maintain their share of the market. The loss of personal influence over customers implicit in the change-over to self-service has been coupled with an increasing tendency for manufacturers to appeal over the retailer's head direct to the customer, using mass advertising and ◊ Branding to create insistence for a product or service and therefore ensure distribution. The pattern and value of distribution in Britain is given in the Census of Distribution, conducted by the Department of Trade on a regular basis. G.S.C.W.

International Journal of Retailing (MCB University Press).

Retirement Policy The arrangements made by an undertaking in connection with the cessation of work by its older employees. These may include courses in preparation for retirement, changes in work and holidays as retirement approaches (gradual retirement), provisions for contributory or non-contributory pensions, special medical, welfare and social facilities both for those nearing retirement and for those who have retired. Any policy must include a decision about the age of retirement, whether this shall be fixed to avoid charges of discrimination and for the sake of administrative convenience, or flexible to allow for the differences between psychological and chronological age, i.e. the wide variation in individual capabilities of people of the same age, which has been studied scientifically by research into the process of ⟨⟩ Ageing. From the point of view of national manpower policy and of making the best use of human resources, more attention is likely to be paid in the future to flexible retirement policies, with associated changes in work load, and to provisions for the health and welfare of older workers. L.S.

M. P. Fogarty (ed.), *Retirement Policy: The Next Fifty Years* (Heinemann, 1982); M. P. Fogarty, *Retirement Age and Retirement Costs* (Policy Studies Institute, 1980).

Reward The total return, tangible and intangible that accrues to individuals as a consequence of their behaviour. A reward may be negative, in the sense that it may consist of the avoidance of an unpleasant consequence, but more usually is positive, in that it wholly or partially satisfies a need. The extent to which individuals will be motivated by a potential reward will be greatly influenced by their need for the reward, by their assessment of the likelihood that they will receive it, and by what they have to do to get it. In an industrial organization the most obvious rewards are monetary and take the form of wages or salaries with or without additional bonuses. Yet other rewards are common: sick pay, pension rights, holiday pay; perquisites ('perks') such as subsidized canteens, company cars, expense accounts, assistance with school fees, privileged access to company products; security of pay and employment; desirable hours and working conditions; social satisfactions including satisfactions intrinsic in the job; the approval of those whose opinions are valued; the prospects of better rewards in the future; status.

These various elements are not always consistent and to some extent more of one may compensate for less of another; security may make up for low job satisfaction, or prospects may compensate for immediate income. The different elements cannot validly be quantified and totalled, yet it seems clear that in practice some such crude summation does take place and a given pay differential may be considered justified because of awkward hours of work, dirty conditions, etc.

Rewards are not distributed randomly throughout an organization but are arranged in an orderly relationship, known as the reward system. Generally the reward system correlates fairly closely with the status system. It is widely considered to be morally right that this should be so, and where, for whatever reasons, there develops a disjunction between the two systems, there will be dissatisfaction, particularly on the part of the individual or group whose rewards are below those implied by their status. If the rewards are not adjusted, the status of the group will decline until the two systems are again in conjunction. ⟡ Motivation; Status. I.C.MCG.

W. Baldamus, *Efficiency and Effort* (Tavistock, 1961); A. M. Bowey (ed.) *Handbook of Salary and Wage Systems* (Gower, 1975).

Right to Work The term may be used in a number of senses. The written constitutions of some countries include this 'right' among the constitutional rights of their citizens. In this context it merely implies that the government of the country should follow an economic policy that will achieve a state of full employment. In the USA and in some other countries the term 'right to work legislation' has been used to describe measures intended to prevent trade unions from insisting on a ⟡ Closed Shop, thus debarring non-unionists from securing employment. Similarly in Britain some judges have used the phrase to justify controlling the way in which trade unions admit and expel members, particularly where the union operates a closed-shop policy. A third meaning that has been given to this term is the implication that employees have a kind of property right to their jobs so that in the event of their dismissal for some reason other than misconduct, their employer should have to compensate them for the loss of their 'property'. The Redundancy Payments Act 1965 introduced this principle, though in a somewhat limited form, into British law. In some continental countries dismissed employees have a right to appeal to an independent tribunal, which may order their reinstatement. In Britain this principle operated only in respect of employees who had to leave their jobs because of call-up for the armed forces. Under the provisions of the Trade Union and Labour Relations Act 1974, in connection with the ⟡ Unfair Dismissal of Employees an ⟡ Industrial Tribunal may order the reinstatement or re-engagement of an unfairly dismissed employee.

A final meaning of the right to work is the right of all citizens to follow their chosen calling or profession without being denied entry by unreasonable restrictions, such as those based on considerations of colour, creed or sex. ⟡ Discrimination. W.E.F., amended by K.W.

F. Meyers, *Ownership of Jobs* (Berkeley, 1964); B. Hepple, 'A Right to Work?', *Industrial Law Journal*, vol. 10, no. 2, pp. 65–83.

Risk Analysis This approach has been developed in ⟡Operational Research to evaluate, in particular, capital investment opportunities. The actual future cash flows and/or other benefits generated by a given investment opportunity are likely to be dependent on the combination of

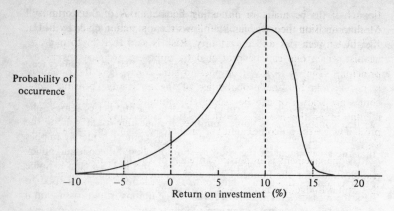

at least a number of factors, each of which is subject to variability and uncertainty. Conventional methods of evaluation assume fixed values for cash flows in each year and calculate the return on investment using a standard technique such as discounted cash flow. Where factors that are each subject to variability and uncertainty will combine according to the laws of probability, it is more meaningful to express the return as a frequency distribution (◊ Statistics) of possible returns, as shown in the figure above.

This shows that the probability of obtaining a return of 0 per cent is small, but that a loss at the rate of 5 per cent is not impossible. The most likely return is estimated at 10 per cent; little chance exists for a return in excess of 15 per cent. This approach improves the basis on which investment opportunities can be evaluated and compared with each other. However, the success of the technique depends, crucially, upon both the quality of the forecast data being used and the ability of the decision-maker to form an 'attitude to risk' that will distinguish between acceptable and intolerable outcomes.

Because the mathematical analysis of the interactions of the factors involved is complex, the yield curve shown in the figure should be obtained by computer simulation of these interactions. This procedure is well illustrated by D. B. Hertz in the *Harvard Business Review* (see below). ◊ Capital Budgeting; Risk and Uncertainty; Simulation. M.J.C.M. and P.J.A.H.

D. B. Hertz: 'Risk Analysis in Capital Investment', *Harvard Business Review*, January/February 1964.

Risk and Uncertainty (in Financial Management) Several distinctions have to be made in discussing financial risk and uncertainty. Modern decision theory generally follows the distinction made by F. H. Knight between risk and uncertainty. Risk is said to refer to matters against which one can be protected by applying ordinary insurance principles. That is to say, it applies to situations where the outcome is not certain but the probabilities of the alternative possible outcomes are known or can be accurately estimated by practical experimentation or the use of statistical data. Uncertainty is said to be present where the outcome cannot be predicted even in some probabilistic sense.

Risk management is important in each of the three major areas of responsibility for the financial manager, namely ⟡ Capital Structure, ⟡ Capital Budgeting and ⟡ Working Capital.

(1) *Capital structure*. Risk here derives from the relationship between equity capital and debt finance and is usually called financial risk. It can be viewed in terms of (a) the respective volumes and (b) the income-distribution effect of the two types of funds. Borrowing (which for some purposes includes preference-share issues also) increases the shareholder's risk and uncertainty. It does so by imposing a charge on profits and cash flow that must be met *before* shareholders become entitled to the residue either in the form of payment of dividends or reimbursement of capital in the event of liquidation. To the extent that borrowing is used to finance investment, so the variability of profits accruing to ordinary (equity) shareholders is increased by the incursion of interest commitments. Since the average return to all investors in the company is generally expected to exceed the rate of interest payable on the debentures and loans, the expected return to ordinary shareholders must increase to the extent that the firm is debt financed. However, when the rate of profit falls below that of the rate of debt capital, the return to equity holders falls further because of the existence of debt. Thus equity holders gain the possibility of higher incomes but at the cost of greater expected variability of income. Since investors are generally assumed to be averse to risk, the question for financial management is what is the rate of compensation, in terms of increased expected rate of income (or dividends), for given additional amounts of financial risk; much of the discussion of 'gearing' revolves around this question. For both the valuation of investment and the cost of capital issues this is a central question.

(2) *Capital budgeting*. Risk that is inherent in the cost and revenue structures, and therefore in the profit structure, of a firm is generally

referred to as business risk. The task facing the investment analyst is to assess the likelihood of variation in the expected return from a proposed investment and the effect that this may have for the enterprise as a whole. This process can be undertaken by employing ⟡ Risk Analysis and the principles of ⟡ Portfolio Selection. Whilst the measurement of risk is reasonably straightforward, it is a much greater problem to specify an 'attitude to risk', i.e. to develop standards by which the acceptability or otherwise of different combinations of expected value and variability of return may be judged.

(3) *Working capital.* The primary consequence of accepting financial and/or business risk is that the flow of cash (⟡ Cash Flow) in and out of the business may differ from the expected pattern. In the worst eventuality this may result in ⟡ Insolvency. Efficient cash management therefore aims simultaneously to achieve two competing objectives. First, by holding a sufficiently large cash balance, to ensure survival of the business through minimizing the risk of insolvency. Second, by holding a sufficiently small cash balance, to maximize shareholder wealth through ensuring that surplus funds, which would otherwise be idle, are profitably invested. E.A.L. and P.J.A.H.

R. A. Brealey and S. C. Myers, *Principles of Corporate Finance* (MGraw-Hill, 1981).

Risk Premium The rate of additional compensation over and above the risk-free rate of return that an investor requires of a risky investment. In the theory of stock-market analysis this premium is widely regarded as comprising two components, which cover, respectively, the systematic and unsystematic risks of a particular security.

Systematic (or market) risk is an expression (formally, the beta) of the sensitivity of an investment's return to changes in the average return of the stock market as a whole. Unsystematic (or unique) risk refers to the potential volatility of return resident in and characteristic of a particular security or class of securities.

In ⟡ Portfolio Selection, whereas systematic risk is not capable of being diversified away, aggregate unsystematic risk may be substantially reduced by selecting approximately ten investments whose returns are imperfectly correlated.

In ⟡ Capital Budgeting the importance of the risk premium is manifested in the specification of a hurdle rate of return, which investment opportunities must meet if shareholders' risk/return preferences are to be satisfied. P.J.A.H.

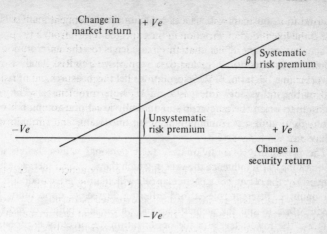

R. A. Brealey and S. C. Myers, *Principles of Corporate Finance* (McGraw-Hill, 1981).

Robot An industrial robot is a programmable manipulative device, used typically in 'pick/move/place', load/unload, locate, and similar operations. As distinct from mechanical, electro-mechanical or hydraulic devices, etc., designed for one specific operation, industrial robots can be reprogrammed to perform different tasks – and indeed to recognize the need to perform different tasks, e.g. through the use of visual facilities and other sensors. Thus in manufacture the use of industrial robots is a form of flexible automation. Hence they are found in situations where some variation of tasks is necessary in the short term (e.g. in welding different versions of the same basic vehicle body shell on a motor-vehicle assembly line) or where equipment must be re-used later for a different type of application. Their principal applications are in machine load/unload operations, welding, paint-spraying, assembly and inspection work, and in situations where it is dangerous to use people. R.W.

H. J. Warnecke and R. D. Schraft, *Industrial Robots* (IFS Publications. 1982).

Role The behaviour expected of the occupant of a given position in a social system. In an industrial organization an attempt is usually made to define such expected behaviour in considerable detail in formal statements, such as job descriptions. Role, however, refers to more than duties and responsibilities. It refers also to the relationships that are to be established with other individuals, to the style and manner of performance, and to the wider social behaviour that the performance of the role involves.

The development of the concept of role leads to the interpretation of behaviour in situational, rather than in personal, terms. Behaviour is thus explained in terms of the expectations held by others in the situation and of the individual's interpretation of those expectations. The role exists apart from the personality of the individual performing the role although of course personality is itself an important factor in personal behaviour.

The personality of individuals – their personal values, beliefs and inclinations – will influence the way in which they perform their role and conversely, the playing of a particular role will, in time, affect individuals' personality. Different roles afford differing degrees of opportunity for modification to suit the inclinations and particular abilities of individuals. At the lowest levels in the organization opportunity is probably minimal and, for example, assembly-line operators will have their role closely prescribed. At the higher levels, executives are able to modify their role substantially in order to make the greatest use of their particular abilities and interests. This partially explains why executives tend to achieve a greater degree of job satisfaction than do manual workers and why it is more difficult for the organization to accommodate a change in executive personnel. ⟡ Social System; Status. I.C.MCG.

J. A. Litterer, *The Analysis of Organizations* (J. Wiley, 1965); T. Lupton, *Management and the Social Sciences* (Penguin, new ed., 1983), p. 82 ff.

Role Conflict Situations in which individuals are subjected to stress due to the fact that the performance of their role or roles seems to require incompatible or impossible behaviour.

Role conflict can arise from several sources. It may be due to a lack of compatibility between role and personality: individuals are unable or unwilling to perform the role, although wishing to do so, or, at least, to avoid the consequence of *not* doing so. It may be caused by lack of clarity in the role so that individuals are unable to perform because they do not know what behaviour is expected of them. Or the expectations may themselves be conflicting, as in the case of industrial foremen, whose subordinates expect behaviour from them which is incompatible with that expected by their superiors. Again, the demands of different roles may conflict. For example, a young executive seeking to establish himself in his career may be required to work long hours and to travel frequently on company business, activities which conflict with the behavioural requirements of his roles of husband and father.

Reactions to role conflict will vary with the individual and the situation but may include the rejection of one of the conflicting roles, deception of one of the groups or persons to lead them to believe that their expectations are being fulfilled when in fact they are not, escape from the situation by resignation, transfer or illness, or increasing anxiety and emotional tension. ⟴ Role. I.C.McG.

Robert L. Kahn, *et al.*, *Organizational Stress* (J. Wiley, 1964); T. Lupton, *Management and the Social Sciences* (Penguin, new ed., 1983), p. 82 ff.

Romalpa Clauses Retention of title clauses used in contracts as an attempt by the seller of goods to retain ownership of the goods until they are paid for, so that in the event of the liquidation of the buyer the goods may be recovered. They owe their name to the case in which this device was first successfully used in 1976. However, in more recent cases such clauses on their own have not been sufficient to retain ownership in goods that have been incorporated into finished articles, nor the proceeds of the sale of such goods, when this has been challenged. Much will depend on the exact wording of the clause, which needs to be carefully drafted to fit the circumstances of the sale. J.C.E.M.

J. Parris, *Retention of Title on Sale of Goods* (Granada, 1982).

Routeing Problems Large sums of money are spent on the physical distribution of goods from producers to customers and on the routeing of collection and inspection services (for example postmen, meter readers, refuse collectors and school bus drivers). If delivery, collection and inspection routes can be designed at minimum mileage or cost, large sums of money will be saved nationally, and routeing problems have received considerable attention. Although such problems can quite often be formulated using ⟴ Linear Programming, it is often very difficult to obtain a rigorous mathematical solution that minimizes costs. However, substantial reductions, as compared with commonsense methods of routeing vehicles, etc., may be obtained by using ⟴ Operational Research techniques and most computer manufacturers have standard programs available for tackling this type of problem. ⟴ Hardware/Liveware/Software M.J.C.M.

Patrick Rivett and Russell L. Ackoff, *A Manager's Guide to Operational Research* (J. Wiley, 1963), pp. 46–7.

Royal Commission on Trade Unions and Employers' Associations ⟡ Industrial Relations – Reform in Great Britain.

S

Safety The safety of personnel and equipment is a problem that has a bearing upon many aspects of industrial management, including design engineering, production engineering, medical services, factory supervision, maintenance services and training.

The well-being of personnel is achieved not only by the avoidance of specific incidents causing injury or death, but by protecting people from the damage that can result from long-term exposure to hazards such as noise, vibration, certain dusts and even poor posture.

Palliative measures to avoid accidents can be taken by establishing a safety-information system, which will identify the causal background of traumatic incidents and hence lead to appropriate changes in equipment design, workplace layout, operating procedures or training schedules (▷ Accident Prevention). A more fundamental approach to the achievement of human well-being demands a more comprehensive programme of system design and management to take due account of the capabilities and limitations of human performance (▷ Ergonomics). E.E.

Safety Stock ▷ Inventory or Stock-control Problems; Buffer Stocks

Salary Structure The organization of salaries according to a systematic comparison of the similarities and differences in occupations. These comparisons can be made by job evaluation (▷ Job Analysis), which normally takes into account skills, qualifications, experience, responsibilities and seniority. A salary structure will be divided into a number of grades and will include scales, usually in the form of annual increases up to a maximum for each grade. These increments may be related to seniority, or length of service in the grade, or to merit (▷ Merit Rating) or to both. In practice there is often a large element of tradition in the actual grading of jobs, if only because of the impossibility of grading jobs in terms of money with scientific accuracy. Actual salaries paid are also influenced by the state of the labour market, so that when there is a shortage of people qualified for particular jobs these salaries will be higher than a job evaluation would suggest they should be. Some grading of salaries exists in any enterprise; the concept of a salary structure leads to a rational approach to the decision about grading and about the relationship between grades, and to the removal, where possible, of inconsistencies and inequities. L.S., amended by E.L.

> M. Armstrong and H. Murlis, *Salary Administration: A Practical Guide for the Small and Medium-sized Organization* (British Institute of Management, 1977).

Sale of Goods A contract for the sale of goods is a contract whereby the property in goods is transferred by the seller to the buyer for a money consideration, called the price. These contracts are governed in the UK by the Sale of Goods Act 1979.

It is important to ascertain when the property in goods passes from the seller to the buyer, since the risk of loss or damage passes with the property. The Act states that the property passes at such time as the parties want it to pass and certain rules are laid down to indicate the position where the parties have not clearly expressed their intention (◊ Romalpa Clauses).

The parties may attach certain terms to the contract; if these terms are vital to the very existence of the contract they are known as conditions, while if they are merely subordinate terms they are called warranties. Both conditions and warranties may be either expressly stated in the contract or may be implied into the contract by law. A breach of a condition entitles the buyer to treat the contract as discharged and to claim damages, while a breach of warranty entitles the buyer to damages only.

Where goods are sold by description there exists an implied condition that the goods supplied will correspond to the description and that they will be of merchantable quality. Where the buyer has indicated to a seller, who is selling goods in the course of a business, the particular purpose for which the goods are being bought, there is an implied condition that the goods supplied will be reasonably fit for this purpose, except where it can be shown that the buyer did not rely on the seller's skill and judgement in advising him. Two further implied terms in the Act state that the seller shall transfer a good title to the goods, and that the bulk of goods sold by sample will match that sample. Breach of these terms entitles the buyer to the return of any money paid and a release from their own obligations under the contract, plus a claim for damages if appropriate.

The protection granted to the buyer has been substantially increased by the Unfair Contract Terms Act 1977. This Act restricts the ability of a seller to exclude or limit their liability under a contract for the sale of goods for breach of implied conditions and warranties. In the case of a consumer sale any clause in a contract for the sale of goods exempting the seller from liability for breach of the above conditions and warranties is to be treated as void and any attempt at exemption is a criminal offence. Where the sale is between two businesses the exclusion of the implied terms is possible if the exclusion clause in the contract is deemed to be a reasonable one in the circumstances (⟡ Exclusion Clauses). W.F.F., amended by J.C.E.M.

R. Lowe, *Commercial Law* (Sweet & Maxwell, 6th ed., 1983).

Sales Forecast The estimate of the sales that an organization will achieve during a future period. There are several ways of calculating this, and a working forecast may be based upon one or more methods. For products that have a stable sales history a good forecast can normally be obtained by statistical methods that project past trends and seasonal patterns into the future. For new or short-life products the estimate is more likely to be compiled from field reports by sales personnel or based upon market models. For products closely allied to other industries it may be calculated from economic indicators.

Sales forecasts may cover a period of up to twelve months or even longer in total, but individual months would normally be calculated separately. They may be broken down further into weeks, individual products or sales areas.

The sales forecast is central to company planning, forming part of the marketing plan, the production and inventory plans, and the financial and cash-flow plans. Careful monitoring of actual sales against forecasts provides an effective control whereby management can be alerted to unexpected change. G.S.C.W.

S. C. Wheelwright and S. Makridakis, *Forecasting Methods for Management* (J. Wiley, 3rd ed., 1980).

Sampling Since it is often impossible or prohibitively expensive to measure given characteristics of each member of a statistical population, a statistician examines a sub-group or sample from it (⟡ Statistics). The accuracy with which the properties of the sample represent the properties of the population from which it is drawn is primarily dependent on the care taken in sampling.

Samples are taken by attribute or variable. If the former is the criterion used, an individual selected by sampling has a specified attribute or characteristic. For example in sampling births we may only wish to know if a baby is male or female. The latter concerns the measure or quantity of a particular characteristic or variable. For example in sampling births we may wish to know the baby's birth weight or height, that is, we are sampling the variable weight or height.

Although each sample must be designed with its specific purpose in mind, there are a number of general approaches:

(1) *Random sampling*. When each member of the population has an equal chance of being selected. Thus if a sample size of 1,000 is chosen for a survey of the heights of Englishmen over twenty years and if eighteen million is the total number of Englishmen over twenty years, each has a 1 in 18,000 chance of being selected.

(2) *Systematic sampling*. When a sample of fraction $1/n$ of the population is required. If every nth member of the population is selected, the required fraction is obtained. This may work well when no cyclical patterns are expected to occur in a population, such as in an alphabetical list of electors or a file of stock cards. However, if cycle patterns are present, it can introduce a bias. For example an electoral roll is normally listed by streets; if a sample is chosen by selecting every fifth household and if the houses are built in groups of five, either an end house or a mid-terrace house will be selected every time, depending on which was chosen initially. Since it is likely that the occupants of end houses will be more prosperous than those in mid-terrace ones (as the former normally cost more money), bias will have been introduced.

(3) *Stratified sampling*. It may be known that there are, or may be, differences between different parts or 'strata' of a population. For example annual income groups or geographical areas can form strata for a national population of industrial workers. If the percentage of the total population in each stratum is known, then the sample may be designed, or stratified, to consist of similar percentages from each stratum. Within a given stratum, the required selections may be made by (1) or (2) above. Quota sampling is a technique commonly used by market researchers, which is really a form of stratified sampling. A market-research interviewer is given a quota or number to interview from each stratum and can stop sampling once he or she has obtained the required quota in every stratum.

(4) *Cluster sampling*. Used particularly in market research, this is best illustrated by an example. To obtain a sample of approximately 200 housewives in England, a county may be chosen, then a town or village within it, and finally a street, all by successive random selections. Once the street has been chosen, all housewives in it may be interviewed. Thus

a sample consists of a cluster of individuals. This method is popular because it is relatively cheap. M.J.C.M.

P. G. Moore, *Statistics and the Manager* (Macdonald, 1966).

Satisficing A term first used by economists to identify the process by which a company strives to reach targets that satisfy sufficiently well the objectives of the company. Once achieved, there is little incentive to do better and exceed them. Satisficing purports to represent the behaviour of a company more closely than the more theoretical concept of profit maximization (⟡ Optimization). The term has become more widely used and is recognized as a more realistic approach to tackling business problems of all kinds. R.S.S.

H. A. Simon, 'Theories of Decision-making in Economics' *American Economic Review* (June 1959); R. L. Ackoff, *A Concept of Corporate Planning* (J. Wiley, 1970).

Scanlon Plan A method, American in origin, of sharing with employees the monetary gains derived from increased productivity.

The object is to concentrate attention on the productivity of a company, factory or department by giving to the employees on a monthly basis a proportion (usually 50–75 per cent) of the savings from the reductions in labour costs made in the unit concerned. Labour costs are to be reduced and productivity increased by suffusing the whole establishment with a realization that workers and management have a common interest in greater efficiency and a more co-operative atmosphere. Thus the Scanlon plan is not so much a formula for sharing productivity bonuses as a whole concept of union–management co-operation, of which increased monetary rewards for the workers are just one side-effect.

Found mainly in small and medium-sized companies in the USA, the plan is normally implemented through a system of committees, on which representatives of every work-group and managerial function serve, and which operate at all levels of the organization. The plan combines the practices of profit-sharing, ⟡ Joint Consultation and suggestion schemes, though its exponents claim that *in toto* it represents something of greater significance than the mere sum of its component parts. The plan is supposed to implicate employees in the success of an enterprise by giving everyone an opportunity to use their own intelligence and ideas to increase productivity. Clearly schemes of this kind are likely to be effective only when the business itself is expanding, when the technology is new and transitory enough to permit useful suggestions from the shop floor, and when worker and management attitudes are dynamic enough to permit new departures in this direction. For these reasons the plan has made few appearances in Britain. The Rootes group, for example, employed a variation of the plan at its Linwood 'Imp' factory, in the form of a factory bonus geared to the level of car sales. But when Imp sales began to fall, the bonus pool began to shrink, with predictably adverse effects on industrial relations within the factory, and eventually the whole scheme had to be abandoned. L.S. and N.H.C.

F. G. Lesieur (ed.), *The Scanlon Plan* (MIT Press and J. Wiley, 1958); Douglas McGregor, *The Human Side of Enterprise* (McGraw-Hill, 1960).

Scenarios Rather than base a major strategic decision upon a 'single-outcome' forecast, which may well turn out to be extremely inaccurate, it may prove more prudent to consider several possible alternative outcomes. Instead of banking on the election of a particular government at the next election, for example, it might be more realistic to devise a strategy that is robust enough to cope with all the probable outcomes of an election – a right-wing government, a left-wing one, a hung parliament, and so on. Another example would be to assume different economic growth rates and to devise strategies for the possible scenarios. The technique of tailoring strategies to meet such 'multiple scenarios' has become the subject of much interest in recent years. A.J.A.A.

J. Chandler and P. Cockle, *Techniques of Scenario Planning* (McGraw-Hill, 1983).

Scheduling Problems ◇ Sequencing Problems

Scientific Management An approach to problems of organization based on, and following the same basic premises as, the work of Frederick Winslow Taylor. Taylor was deeply concerned about the quality of the relationships that existed between management and workers in the factories around him and about the inefficiency and work-dodging that were a feature of the industrial life he experienced. He came quickly to the belief that these troubles were due to managerial laxity. There was a universal tendency to leave the details of work performance to the discretion of the workers and work was therefore performed inefficiently; there was only the crudest understanding of how much work could reasonably be expected of a worker and this led to constant disagreements and bitterness between management and staff; and workers were inadequately motivated to give of their best. Taylor accordingly devoted his life to the development of techniques for the study of work and the determination of the most efficient way for each task to be performed. By careful observation and timing by stopwatch, 'objective' standards of performance could be determined and an incentive system devised that would reward above-standard and penalize sub-standard performance.

Taylor thus believed that managers must accept full responsibility for planning, organizing and supervising work. The skill and experience of the better workers and craftsmen were to be analysed and classified so that they might be reduced to rules, laws and formulae. Thus once the best way to do a job had been ascertained by trained observation, the worker should be scientifically selected and instructed in the proper method. In this way managers would assume the duties for which they were better fitted than the workers and the latter would be free from responsibilities they were not fit to discharge. Taylor was of the opinion that every employee had two needs: high wages and the opportunity for personal advancement. The worker was thus viewed, and treated, as an individual 'work-horse' in social isolation. It was a fundamental tenet that managers should never deal with workers in groups.

The Taylor approach attracted many disciples, most notably F. B. Gilbreth, and exerted considerable influence on management thought and behaviour. Despite the naïvety of the assumptions concerning motivation and the patent exaggeration of the claim to scientific objectivity, scientific management spread rapidly to virtually all industrial countries, including the Soviet Union. It is manifest not only in the growth of departments of work study, production engineering, production scheduling, etc., but also in the attitude that takes the collection and analysis of data as the basis for decision-making, and the increasing rationalization of production processes. ◊ Classical Organization Theory. I.C.MCG.

F. W. Taylor, *Scientific Management* (Harper & Brothers, 1947); M. Rose, *Industrial Behaviour: Theoretical Development since Taylor* (Allen Lane, 1975); T. Kempner, 'Frederick Taylor and Scientific Management', in Tillet, Kempner and Wills (eds.), *Management Thinkers* (Penguin, 2nd ed., 1978); M. Warner, *Organizations and Experiments* (J. Wiley, 1984), ch. 3.

Search Problems These problems were first identified during the war when tactics for searching the oceans for hostile submarines were developed. An oil company faces similar problems in searching an area of desert for oil deposits. In both cases with the resources available (aircraft or money) a decision must be made on what search tactics to use. A large area can be searched quickly, thereby increasing the chances of passing over a submarine, say, but reducing the chances of spotting it should the searcher pass over it. Alternatively a smaller area can be searched slowly, thereby reducing the chances of passing over a submarine. but increasing the chances of spotting it should the searcher pass over it. Probability theory and statistical analysis have been applied to this problem to determine the optimum search policy.

Account auditing is a similar type of search problem and these techniques have been applied to a very limited extent to auditing in large organizations. M.J.C.M.

Patrick Rivett and Russell L. Ackoff, *A Manager's Guide to Operational Research* (J. Wiley, 1963), pp. 53–5.

Seating ⟡ Posture

Selection Choosing from a number of candidates the one most likely to be suited to a particular job. The process of selection starts with ⟡ Recruitment on the one hand and, on the other, with a ⟡ Job Analysis that enables the selectors to identify the qualities, qualifications and experience required in the post to be filled and to list these in a job specification. In practice, particularly for management positions, the selectors are also interested in the overall potential of future employees and with the way in which they will contribute to and develop in the organization. In these cases the specification will be wider than that derived from the job analysis of one occupation. The task of selection is to assess candidates against the job specification, however widely conceived. In doing this, information is required about the candidate's physique and health, general ⟡ Intelligence, special aptitudes, achievements, temperament and personality. Some of these qualities can be measured by tests, e.g. ⟡ Aptitude Tests for specific skills, or by medical examination; others, such as academic or professional qualifications, can be given on application forms. But others are left to a personal ⟡ Interview, which is both an element in the selection procedure and an opportunity for candidates to learn about the job they may be offered and the firm for which they may be working. Some employers supplement interviews with group selection procedures, especially in the recruitment of university graduates. By putting a small number of candidates together and giving them a problem to solve or a subject to discuss, it is possible to compare the performance of the candidates in relation to each other and to discover qualities, intelligence and ⟡ Personality in action, which a face-to-face interview may not reveal. Interviews are often the most decisive part of selection, but research findings have exposed their fallibility. Appropriate training can increase the skills of interviewers and the subsequent reliability of their interviewing. L.S.

E. Anstey, *An Introduction to Selection Interviewing* (HMSO, 1977); B. Ungerson (ed.), *Recruitment Handbook* (Gower, 1983).

Selection Tests ◊ Selection; Aptitude Tests

Selling Exchanging the right to goods or a service with another in return for an agreed sum of money. The function within a company of organizing the distribution and sale of its products or services was formerly described as selling, but this usage is much less common (◊ Marketing). Selling is currently associated predominantly with the act of personal communication, which is an important part of the total concept of marketing communications (◊ Marketing Communications Mix). Controversy exists over precisely which aspects of selling are an art and which subject to scientific treatment. The social sciences, particularly psychology, have been applied extensively to achieve effective and persuasive communication. Rigid analysis of potential sales in geographical areas and the optimization of representatives' journeys are also employed. The most significant use of sales representatives, in terms of securing orders from retail traders throughout the country, has undergone change since the development of mass advertising. Increasingly, such representatives have taken on the additional role of merchandisers (◊ Merchandising), and the soliciting of orders has frequently been made much simpler by brand insistence by customers (◊ Branding). In industrial and technical markets, however, the role of the sales representative has traditionally incorporated that of technical adviser. As technical complexity increases this is increasingly so. The representative's task here has been encompassed by the development of mathematical methods of control for stocks, etc., and an increasing degree of critical assessment in ◊ Purchasing. The field of services selling grows rapidly in most highly developed economies today and this has given rise to new concepts of relationship-management, both before, during and, most particularly, after the sale has taken place, to ensure that a continuous relationship is built up with customers and that there is immediate and continuing contact for repeat orders. G.S.C.W.

Journal of Sales Management (MCB University Press).

Sensitivity Analysis A systematic approach to ◊ Risk Analysis, by which variation in the expected profitability of an investment opportunity is associated with the possible behaviour of individual project variables. Although this process can be undertaken manually, the technique becomes much more powerful when applied to the computer simulation of investment projects. A large number of trials can be readily undertaken to show management which project variables have the most significant impact on project profitability. P.J.A.H.

Sensitivity Training ◊ Group Methods of Training

Sequencing and Dispatching Problems Both sequencing and dispatching are terms describing the process by which the order in which items are to be passed through one or more locations is determined. Within the context of production, the problem is concerned with the ordering of jobs through one or more machines. The term sequencing is normally used when the problem concerns the order of jobs on *several* machines, i.e. determining the sequence of jobs on the machines. The term dispatching is normally used to describe the process by which jobs are placed in order for *one* machine.

Sequencing and dispatching problems, particularly the latter, occur to a large extent and are particularly important in jobbing production. In mass production where a homogeneous set of jobs are to be manufactured by passage through a set of machines in a given order, precise scheduling is possible, i.e. it is possible to predict with some accuracy the time at which any job will arrive at any machine. Quite the opposite situation exists in jobbing production where, because many different products are to be manufactured and manufacturing information is imprecise, accurate scheduling is impossible. As a result, a large amount of work-in-progress stock usually exists and queues of jobs form at departments and machines (◊ Production Planning and Control).

Sequencing. Even in comparatively simple situations involving few jobs and machines, the number of possible sequences of jobs through the machines is so large that rigorous solution of the problem is often impractical. Simple algorithms have been produced for solving highly abstract and simple sequencing problems. Techniques such as linear programming, the branch-and-bound method and simulation have been used, but frequently the amount of computation or the simplifying assumptions made discounts their use in practical situations. ◊ Mathematical Programming; Branch-and-Bound Technique; Simulation (Computer).

One method of overcoming this situation is to consider the problem in terms of single machines only, i.e. to determine in which order available jobs will be processed on one machine at a time, rather than attempt to determine the sequence of jobs for several machines. This is the dispatching problem.

Dispatching. An essential part of production control. In practice both manual and computer-based production control procedures normally rely upon priority-rule dispatching. The use of priority rules enables decisions to be made as and when required, i.e. when machines become vacant; examples of priority rules are as follows.

(1) *Job slack* (*S*). This is the amount of contingency or free time, over and above the expected processing time, available before the job is completed at a predetermined date (t_0), i.e.

$$S = t_0 - t_1 - \Sigma a_i$$

where t_1 = present date
Σa_i = sum of remaining processing times.

Where delays are associated with each operation, e.g. delays caused by inter-machine transport, this rule is not suitable, but the following rule may be used.

(2) *Job slack per operation.* S/N, where N = number of remaining operations. Thus where S is the same for two or more jobs, the job with the most remaining operations is processed first.

(3) *Job slack ratio.* The ratio of the total remaining time to the remaining slack time, i.e.

$$\frac{S}{t_0 - t_1}$$

In all the above cases, where the priority index is negative, the job cannot be completed by the requisite date. The rule will therefore be to process first those jobs with negative indices.

(4) *Shortest imminent operation* (*SIO*). Process first the job with the shortest processing time.

(5) *Longest imminent operation* (*LIO*). This is the converse of (4).

(6) *Scheduled start date.* This is perhaps the most frequently used rule. The date at which operations must be started in order that a job will meet a required completion date is calculated, usually by employing reverse scheduling from the completion date, e.g.

$$x_i = t_0 - \Sigma a_i$$
or $\quad x_i = t_0 - \Sigma(a_i + f_i)$

where x_i = scheduled start date for an operation

$\quad\quad f_i$ = delay or contingency allowance

Usually some other rule is also used, e.g. first come, first served, to decide priorities between jobs with equal x_i values.

(7) *Earliest due date*. Process first the job required first.

(8) *Subsequent processing times*. Process first the job that has the longest remaining process times, i.e. Σa_i, or in modified form $\Sigma(a_i + f_i)$.

(9) *Value*. To reduce work-in-progress inventory cost, process first the job that has the highest value.

(10) *Minimum total float*. This rule is the one usually adopted when scheduling by network techniques.

(11) *Subsequent operation*. Look ahead to see where the job will go after this operation has been completed and process first the job that goes to a 'critical' queue, that is a machine with a small queue of available work, thus minimizing the possibility of machine idle time.

(12) *First come, first served* $(FCFS)$.

(13) *Random*. E.g. in order of job no., etc. Rules (12) and (13) are random, since unlike the others neither depends directly on job characteristics such as length of operation, value, etc. R.W.

S. Eilon, *'Production Scheduling'*, in K. Harley (ed.), *Operational Research 1978 (Proceedings)* (Elsevier, 1979).

Service Level ◊ Inventory or Stock-control Problems

Severance Pay ◊ Redundancy

Severity Rate ◊ Accident Prevention

Share Capital ◊ Claims.

Shares ◊ Claims

Shift Work An arrangement whereby different groups of workers are employed for periods of work during different times during any twenty-four hours.

There are five main types of shift system: (1) fixed or alternating double-day shifts, usually two eight-hour periods between 6 a.m. and 10 p.m., when it is legal under certain conditions to employ women and young people aged sixteen or over; (2) double-day shifts combined with a permanent night shift; (3) three-shift, non-continuous working with breaks at weekends; (4) continuous three- or four-shift systems in which the plant is manned for the full 168 hours in each week; (5) evening shifts for part-time employees and staggered daywork, used in industries such as food preserving which, with different starting and finishing times for different groups of workers, make possible a longer working day without employing individual workers for excessive hours.

With advancing technology, especially in the field of data processing by computers, and the ever-present need to raise productivity, British industry turned increasingly to the use of shift work up until the late 1960s.

In a survey (December 1967) by the Ministry of Labour of nineteen firms in various industries, the following salient points about shift working emerged. (1) In every firm the system had brought about a reduction in hours worked through either the elimination of overtime or a reduction in the length of basic time worked. (2) Shift work can provide a means of making the best use of machinery, attracting extra labour, reducing overtime or meeting peaks in demand. In two out of three firms it had been introduced as a result of the installation of expensive new machinery, thus enabling management to obtain much higher production and hence a higher rate of return on capital invested. This is of particular importance where a particular technology is subject to rapid change. (3) In two thirds of these firms extra labour was required, so the state of the local labour market is a very important factor in the introduction of a shift system. Most firms had difficulty recruiting for the afternoon and night shifts. In some cases part-time and double-day shifts had been introduced to attract women not available for normal day working. (4) Shift work does, however, increase the work-load on management and supervisors, demands prior consultation (◊ Joint Consultation) in detail not only with full-time trade union officials (◊ Trade Union Officers) but also with ◊ Shop Stewards and workers, and entails higher machinery maintenance costs. The need for comprehensive forward planning can hardly be overstressed. (5) It is frequently argued that shift work tends to be inflexible and makes it difficult to cope with production peaks, but all the firms in the survey stressed that it had increased their capacity to spread additional work-loads and made it easier to deal with urgent orders.

Workers appear to prefer permanent shift systems to shift rotation systems, although even shift workers prefer day to night shifts. Shift workers generally experience their working schedule and the living situation associated with it as unpleasant, since many of them have sleeping problems and view shift work as detrimental to their health (although the medical evidence on the state of health of shift workers is conflicting). Shift workers see the compensating advantages in terms of the financial rewards of a shift bonus, the closer relationships they have with other employees on shift work, and a sense of greater responsibility. Management, on the other hand, prefers a rotating shift system because it is less expensive and requires fewer workers to man the same number of work stations. L.S. and N.H.C., amended by E.L.

P. E. Mott, F. C. Mann, Q. McLoughlin and D. P. Warwick, *Shift Work* (University of Michigan Press, 1965); R. Sergean, *Managing Shift Work* (Gower, 1971); P. J. D. Drenth, G. Hoolwerf and H. Thierry, 'Psychological Aspects of Shift Work', in P. Warr (ed.), *Personal Goals and Work Design* (J. Wiley, 1976); J. M. Harrington, *Shift Work and Health* (HMSO, 1978); F. Fishwick, *The Introduction and Extension of Shiftworking* (NEDO, 1980).

Shop Steward A trade union representative in the (work)shop or other workplace. Normally lay, rather than full-time officials, shop stewards have other names in some industries, e.g. 'fathers of chapel' in printing, 'works representatives' in iron and steel, 'staff representatives' in some white-collar unions, but the term shop steward is the one most commonly employed.

To be classified as a shop steward the worker concerned will have to be recognized by their union as having some representative function at the place of work, i.e. it must be part of their job to raise grievances and make claims arising out of the system of wage payment on behalf of a group of members. Traditionally shop stewards were most powerful in firms where some form of piecework as an incentive bonus system existed.

In a few industries, such as mining, where union branch organization is based on the place of work, workplace representation is the formal responsibility of branch officials, e.g. the branch secretary, but this is unusual. In other cases, stewards are mere collectors of union dues and not shop stewards proper, with rights of representation and negotiation.

Shop stewards are mostly to be found in the larger work units and in the largest of all there are often formally recognized leaders of the shop stewards' group, known as 'convenors' or 'chief', 'leading' or 'senior' stewards. Most stewards' work is voluntary, part-time and unpaid.

There was a substantial growth in the number of shop stewards in the 1970s. Indeed by the end of the decade there were probably about 250,000 shop stewards in Britain and they were found well beyond the metal-handling industries. In manufacturing they are all but universal in plants with more than 100 workers, and both private-sector and public-sector services witnessed a significant increase in their numbers in the 1970s. Terry has reported the following further indicators of shop-steward organization.

Shop-steward Organization in Britain (percentage of establishments where a steward is present)

	Private manufacturing industry	Local government
Manual		
Recognized senior steward	74·0	70·0
Full-time steward	11·7	33·0
Regular steward meetings	36·8	50·0
Non-manual		
Recognized senior steward	61·4	73·0
Full-time steward	2·3	17·0
Regular steward meetings	30·0	83·0

Source: M. Terry, 'Shop Steward Development' in G. S. Bain (ed.), *Industrial Relations in Britain* (Blackwell, 1983), p. 69.

Although there has been a decline in shop-steward activity in the 1980s, this is far less than is sometimes supposed.

The methods employed by shop stewards in shopfloor bargaining include comparisons with other individuals or groups, pressure for informal arrangements and unwritten agreements, and various types of sanctions, including the withdrawal of co-operation, insistence on formal rights and customs, limitations on output and restrictions on overtime, and withdrawals of labour. The ⟨⟩ Strike is only the most extreme form of sanction and many are mainly 'demonstrative', to indicate to management that something should be done quickly. Many bring to light genuine misunderstandings and muddles. Most are neither started nor led by politically motivated shop stewards.

A 69 per cent sample of personnel managers has been discovered by Clegg *et al.* to prefer dealing with shop stewards than with local full-time trade union officials, most of all because of their intimate knowledge of the circumstances of the case. Other reasons included a preference for keeping issues within the factory and the need for speedy decisions. This and other evidence suggests that the power of shop stewards has been fostered by management. When the growth of the labour force in a plant makes it difficult for managers to retain individual and personal relations with groups of workers, some form of internal representation is required and the shop-steward system provides it.

Four fifths of stewards are subject to regular re-election and the turnover of stewards' jobs is high. Almost half leave the job because of promotion by management, most no doubt on merit, but some in order to render them innocuous.

Although shop stewards are often linked in the popular press with unofficial strikes and ⟨⟩ Wage Drift (⟨⟩ Wage), there is no doubt that the great majority of them perform an arduous and thankless task responsibly and well. As part of this they occupy a considerable 'helper role' to personnel and to line management. In the extreme case a shop stewards' committee can become a 'union within a union'. Shop stewards' committees, whether company or industry-wide, can provide platforms for militant criticism of official union policy, as do ⟨⟩ Trade Councils. From such platforms would-be rivals to established leaders can advertise themselves.

The ⟨⟩ Industrial Relations Act 1971, repealed 1974, imposed legal duties on unions for the conduct of their shop stewards. The ⟨⟩ Industrial Relations Code of Practice, 1972, provides guidelines on the functions, appointment, status, co-ordination, facilities and training of shop stewards. N.H.C., amended by M.J.F.P.

H. A. Clegg, A. J. Killick and R. Adams, *Trade Union Officers* (Blackwell, 1961); W. E. J. McCarthy and S. R. Parker, Research Paper 10, *Shop Stewards and Workshop Relations* (HMSO, 1968); J. F. B. Goodman and T. G. Whittingham, *Shop Stewards* (Pan, 1973); M. J. F. Poole, 'Towards a Sociology of Shop Stewards', *Sociological Review*, vol. 22 (1974), pp. 57–82; E. Batstone, I. Boraston and S. Frenkel, *Shop Stewards in Action* (Blackwell, 1977); M. Terry, 'Shop Steward Development' in G. S. Bain (ed.) *Industrial Relations in Britain* (Blackwell, 1983); E. Batstone, *Working Order* (Blackwell, 1984).

Sick Pay Employees who are away from work through injury or ill health may be entitled to be paid under the terms of their contract of employment. About 80 per cent of employees have some contractual entitlement by virtue of occupational sick-pay schemes, though provision made by them varies widely.

Regardless of any contractual scheme, since 1983 statute has imposed on all employers an obligation to pay 'statutory sick pay'. This is payable for up to eight weeks' absence in any tax year and is payable at one of three rates, depending upon the level of gross earnings. The first three days of incapacity are disregarded and payment is only due in respect of those days on which the employee would have been working had they not been ill. Like wages, the payments are taxable and subject to national insurance. Any payments made by an employer under an occupational sick-pay scheme can be set off against the sum due as statutory sick pay and vice versa. Employers can recover this expenditure by making appropriate deductions from their national-insurance contributions bill.

Statutory sick pay is not due in certain circumstances, for example where the employee: is employed on a fixed-term contract of not more than three months; becomes pregnant; earns less than the lower earnings figure at which national-insurance contributions begin; or is over state pensionable age, etc.

Once entitlement to statutory sick pay is exhausted after eight weeks' absence, an employee who meets the minimum national-insurance contribution requirements, or whose continuing absence from work is due to ⟡ Industrial Injury, then becomes entitled to *sickness benefit*. This is paid by the DHSS for a further twenty weeks, if necessary, and is currently not taxable. Where absence from work continues beyond twenty-eight weeks, the unfortunate individual is then paid *invalidity benefit* for as long as incapacity lasts, until retiring age if necessary. This DHSS payment is at a higher level than sickness benefit and is neither taxable nor means tested.

The self-employed cannot claim statutory sick pay but are eligible for state sickness benefit for up to twenty-eight weeks provided they meet the Class 2 national-insurance contribution requirements. ⟡ Industrial Injury. K.W.

G. Howard, *Statutory Sick Pay – A Practical Guide* (Oyez Longman 1983); S. Ward, *Social Security at Work* (Pluto Press, 1982).

Signal Detection Theory ⟡ Statistical Decision Theory

Simo Chart (Simultaneous Motion Cycle Chart) A simo chart is used to record the co-ordinated movements of the limbs of one or more workers, the movements being described in terms of fundamental motions on a common time-scale.

The simo chart is used under similar conditions as the two-handed process chart (⟡ Process Charts), but normally results from the analysis of a motion film, and utilizes ⟡ Therbligs to describe the movements taking place. Because of the detailed analysis possible from frame-by-frame examination of a film and the detailed description of the therbligs, simo charts are associated with micromotion study and represent one of the most detailed recording techniques available in ⟡ Method Study. R.W.

Simplex Method ⟡ Mathematical Programming

Simulation (Computer) Operational research scientists often use very sophisticated mathematical analysis to obtain solutions to management problems. However, although the logical structure of, and the numbers involved in, the problems or situations studied are known in many cases, because of the complexity of the problem it is impossible to develop a mathematical analysis and solution. In such circumstances an approach known as computer simulation may be adopted.

A computer program is written that simulates the logical structure of the situation studied. When this program is fed into the computer with the numbers involved, the behaviour of the 'real life' situation can be imitated or simulated by the computer and represented by the computer output. Because computers operate very quickly, many 'years' of simulated behaviour or 'history' may be generated within an hour of computing time.

If, in a given situation, management has three alternative decisions to make or policies to pursue, the outcome of each can be determined quickly by performing three simulations assuming each policy in turn. The policy that gives the best outcome, in terms of maximum profit, minimum cost or whatever measure is chosen, can then be identified. Thus simulation is essentially a 'trial and error' or 'suck it and see' approach, where the experience is generated synthetically by computer. In many situations the numbers involved vary in a random manner and this randomness must also be simulated. Random numbers are generated in simulations by 'Monte Carlo methods', so called because they were first used in the examination of gambling problems.

Simulation has been applied extensively to problems at all levels in business and industry. Indeed attempts are being made to simulate the behaviour of a firm as a whole in its environment through the medium of systems dynamics, which was first developed by J. Forrester and named industrial dynamics.

Although simulation provides a trial and error approach that is cheaper than applying it to the real life situation, it is important to note that large sums can be spent in this way. The cost of performing a simulation often limits the extent to which the technique is applied.
M.J.C.M.

M. J. Sargeaunt, *Operational Research for Management* (Heinemann, 1965), pp. 125–39.

Sinking Fund A means of gradually accumulating a relatively large amount of funds for a specific purpose. The fund is usually invested outside the organization in interest- (or dividend-) bearing investments. Although the creation of such a fund might be termed 'prudent accounting', from the viewpoint of 'good' business economics it may be questioned when such a procedure involves outside investment in a 'safe security'. Clearly there may be a good case for having a certain amount of money fairly readily available for business emergencies, but the investment of large amounts of funds at possibly low rates of return is highly questionable in terms of the opportunity costs of inside investment in a profitable business.

In the case of sinking funds for the replacement of assets, a distinction should be made between such a fund and the annuity method of depreciation. The annuity method is based upon the notion that any asset represents a store of future earning power and should therefore be valued at the present value of the expected future net fund flows attributable to that asset. The annuity method does not imply outside investment for replacement purposes, and the rate of interest used is the estimated rate at which that asset is expected to earn revenue.

In business practice sinking funds are in fact rarely used. Instead firms prefer to budget for investment in fixed assets globally rather than for particular assets in isolation and to provide for the necessary funds by incorporating their requirements into two- or three-year 'cash forecast and requirements budgets' prepared for the business as a whole. E.A.L.

Skill Much of human behaviour comprises learned responses that enable a person to achieve a particular goal. The speed, accuracy and economy with which a goal is approached are measures of skill acquisition.

Skills vary a good deal in their complexity, from walking or running to flying an aircraft or directing a large commercial enterprise. They vary, too, in their demands upon different parts of the organism. At one end of this continuum are 'knacks', i.e. those skills in which the muscular movements are of paramount importance (as, for example, in the golf swing), and at the other end those skills that demand integration of information and the making of decisions.

The rate of skill development depends upon the nature of the skill itself, and also upon the individual, their age, level of motivation, state of fatigue, etc. Most skills require regular repetition if they are to be maintained at their optimal level, although few skills, once acquired, are ever completely lost. E.E.

W. T. Singleton (ed.), *The Study of Real Skills, The Analysis of Practical*

Skills (vol. 1); *Compliance and Excellence* (vol. 2); *Management Skills* (vol. 3); *Social Skills* (vol. 4); (MTP Press, 1978–83).

Skills Analysis ◊ Job Analysis

Social Accounting Concern with the relationship between business and society has resulted in suggestions that more information should be available on the social costs and benefits of business enterprises. A business may provide benefits, such as products and services, employment, etc., whilst at the same time having undesirable side effects, e.g. atmospheric pollution. Social accounting is concerned with the reporting of such social costs and benefits as a means of increasing business accountability. Difficulties in measuring many social costs and benefits constitute a major problem. This practical problem is so great that *The Corporate Report*, whilst seeing merit in social accounting, recommended that 'no obligation to report on social and environmental issues be imposed until acceptable objective and verifiable measurement techniques have been developed which will reveal an unbiased view of both the positive and negative impact of economic activities'.[1] C.J.J.

M. W. E. Glautier and B. Underdown, *Accounting Theory and Practice* (Pitman, 2nd ed., 1982).

Social Audit ◊ Auditing; Social Accounting

Social Control The processes by which a group influences the behaviour of its members in the direction of conformity to the group's standards. The most obvious example of such a process is the legal system, which involves the publication of precise codes of conduct, the establishment of a system of checks to detect violation of the codes and a scale of formalized punishments. In the industrial organization appropriate behaviour may be defined in statements of duties and responsibilities, job descriptions, rule books, etc., and emphasized by formal training: conformity is rewarded by financial bonuses, increments or promotion, or the increased expectations of such rewards; nonconformity is punished by the withholding of rewards or by reprimand, suspension or dismissal. In general it would seem that the more coercion is practised and the more emphasis placed on punishments, the more hostility and resentment are generated and the greater the social tensions in the organization.

The more common forms of social control, however, are continuous

1. The Accounting Standards Steering Committee, *The Corporate Report* (The Institute of Chartered Accountants in England and Wales, 1975).

and are more subtle than the use of formal rewards and punishments. The appropriate behaviour and concomitant attitudes are acquired mainly by imitation, often unconsciously, of the behaviour and attitudes of the members of that social group with which the individual is in most close social contact and whose approval he or she most values. Indeed the strength of the primary-group identification may be considerably more important as a determinant of behaviour than are the rewards and punishments of the formal organization. The problem of how best to achieve compliant behaviour on the part of organizational members is one that currently exercises industrial managers. ⟫ Authority; Discipline; Group; Norm; Role; Role Conflict. I.C.McG.

P. Bowen, *Social Control in Industrial Organizations* (Routledge & Kegan Paul, 1976).

Social Distance The degree of stiffness or formality in a social relationship. Such formality is a recognition of a difference in status between the persons concerned as, for example, between members of different social classes or between superior and subordinate in formal organizations. Social distance in superior/subordinate relationships is associated with the use of authority. It is, therefore, particularly a feature of authoritarian organizations, and is commonly manifest in formal rules constraining social interaction: army officers may be forbidden to fraternize with 'other ranks', the captain of a civil aircraft may be required to stay overnight at a different hotel from that used by crew members. Social distance does not necessarily imply any hostility in the relationship; on the contrary, where the status difference is fully accepted by both persons, the maintenance of social distance will be regarded with mutual satisfaction. However, the existence of social distance militates against the development of free communication between the persons concerned. ⟫ Authority; Communication; Status. I.C.McG.

P. M. Blau and W. R. Scott, *Formal Organizations* (Routledge & Kegan Paul, 1964); C. B. Handy, *Understanding Organizations* (Penguin, 1982).

Social Institution ◊ Institution

Social Sciences Those branches of learning concerned with the study of man and society. The precise delineation of the boundaries of academic disciplines is not possible but by convention the social sciences are held to include economics, political science, psychology, social psychology, social anthropology and sociology. The claim to scientific status, less disputed now than formerly, rests on the fact that each discipline involves the collation and analysis of data derived from a systematic observation of phenomena or controlled experimentation, and the formulation and constant refinement of general principles.

The subject matter of the different disciplines overlaps and each is distinguished mainly by the nature of the concepts it employs and only partly by the range of phenomena studied. The nature of ⟨⟩ Economics and ⟨⟩ Psychology, including social psychology, is discussed in separate entries. Political science is concerned with the forms of power in society, the various bases of power, the manner in which power is exercised institutionally and the ordering of power relationships. The study has increasingly developed an empirical basis and as such has virtually become a branch of sociology (political sociology). Social anthropology, as distinct from physical anthropology, studies approximately the same range of phenomena as sociology but has tended to concentrate on small tribal or village communities in pre-industrial societies and to make almost exclusive use of direct observation and questioning as research techniques.

Sociology seeks to study all those aspects of human behaviour that are socially determined. Including within its focus society as a whole, it necessarily embraces the subject matter of each of the other disciplines discussed above, as well as those features of society that have not yet become the subject of specialist concern. Central to the sociological approach is the concept of the ⟨⟩ Social System: a complex of interrelated parts. At the societal level the most basic of these parts are social ⟨⟩ Institutions, which arise in response to the need to regulate the means to satisfy fundamental human requirements. Thus sociologists study the culture and institutions of specific societies, the structure and processes of the organizations to which the institutions give rise and the nature of the relationships between institutions. Such a study encompasses an enormous range of phenomena and it is not surprising that, in common with other sciences, sociology has been subject to a considerable degree of division into specialisms. Such subdivisions tend to follow, in the first place, the main social institutions; there are thus sociologists specializing in the study of the family, education, work and industry, government, science, religion, etc. All these areas, and many more, have received attention from social scientists other than sociologists. What characterizes the sociological approach is that each area is studied in terms of its relationship to other areas in the total system. For example the industrial sociologist will study not only the structure and functioning of specific industrial organizations with a view to formulating and testing of general principles, but also the relationship between various features of industrial organizations and relevant aspects of the wider society, such as the educational system, social class and social status, and societal values.

However, the term industrial sociology is used by some writers more narrowly to refer to organizational studies at the factory or plant level in the study of particular groups such as managers, various categories of professional employee and white-collar workers. Empirical studies of organizational behaviour date from the ⟡ Hawthorne Investigations and continued with a strong emphasis on factory organization. More recently, however, the sociological analysis of organizations has been advanced by a broadening of research interest to embrace a wide variety of organizations with greatly differing structures and functions. Hospitals, schools, universities, prisons, government departments, trade unions, collieries, docks, churches and many others have been studied and the resulting accumulation of case material has considerably aided the development of organization theory. Such comparative studies are likely to continue and already there are signs that a new academic specialism is emerging – organizational sociology. Such a title, however, gives scant recognition to the work of the social psychologists who have contributed substantially to the development of organization theory. Conversely the use of the term organizational psychology fails to indicate the essential social-systems approach of the developing theory. Perhaps suitable recognition of the interdisciplinary nature of organizational studies will be given by the adoption of the compromise title, organizational behaviour. ⟡ Organization Theory. I.C.MCG.

T. Lupton, *Management and the Social Sciences* (Penguin, new ed., 1983); S. R. Parker *et al.*, *The Sociology of Industry* (Allen & Unwin, 1977).

Social System A network of interrelated roles. There is no limit to the size of a social system; two persons may constitute one (e.g. husband and wife) or, at the other extreme, the entire population of the earth is a social system. All social systems are open, that is to say, every social system interacts with other social systems and every social system is a part of some larger social system. An industrial organization such as a factory may be regarded as a social system. From this point of view the sociologist will endeavour to identify the various constituent elements in the system and to ascertain their relationships to each other and to the organization as a whole, their interaction with the wider society and their functions and dysfunctions. Every social system has certain needs: (1) each person playing a ⟡ Role must understand the behaviour expected of them and must be motivated to produce that behaviour (⟡ Reward System); conversely undesirable behaviour must be discouraged (⟡ Social

Control); (2) there must be some provision for communication amongst the various parts of the system; (3) the system must develop means of protecting itself from, or adapting to, other external systems so as to ensure its own continuity; (4) there must be sufficient consensus on attitudes, values and interests among the members of the system to form a basis for their continued interaction. The business organization is distinguished from other types of social system mainly by its highly differentiated role structure, in which the roles and their interrelationships are rigorously defined, by its elaborate control systems and its preoccupation with the economic attainment of precise objectives. ⟪⟫ Culture; Institution; Organization Theory; Social Control; Status. I.C.McG.

E. J. Miller and A. K. Rice, *Systems of Organizations* (Tavistock, 1967); F. Emery (ed.), *Systems Thinking*, (Penguin, 2 vols., 1981).

Sociology ⟫ Social Sciences

Socio-technical System A conceptual recognition of the interdependence of technical and social factors in organization. A socio-technical system is considered to comprise three elements: (1) *technical factors* – mechanical equipment, technical processes and the physical environment; (2) *social factors* – the relationships amongst the people required to carry out the work, their individual and collective attitudes to it and to each other; (3) *economic factors* – the measures by which the efficiency of the technical and social 'mix' is evaluated.

The concept has been developed mainly by members of the Tavistock Institute of Human Relations and originated from their work in the coal industry. Attention was focused on the organizational problems apparently inherent in the longwall method of coal-mining. Analysis of the situation revealed that the essential co-operation required amongst the three groups performing the main tasks in the work cycle – cutting, filling and conveyor moving – was considerably hampered by the mode of organization conventionally adopted. Despite the interdependent nature of the main tasks, each of the three groups was organized as a discrete unit, occupationally homogeneous, on its own group bonus for payment purposes and separated from the other two groups by the shift system. Thus there were three groups, each intensely aware of its own identity and of its own socio-economic interests. The resultant rivalry and inter-group hostility destroyed any hope of co-operation and productivity was generally low. When the interdependent nature of the tasks was recognized, an alternative form of social organization was seen to be necessary. The occupational differentiation of the three shift groups was abandoned in favour of a total task force of all-round faceworkers, each of whom was capable of cutting, filling or conveyor moving, as the situation required. Bonus payment was earned by the entire face group and shared equally amongst them. The effect of the changed social organization was to break down the inter-group, inter-shift hostility in favour of a group consciousness extending to all who worked on the face, and the co-operation required by the technical factors now became possible. The socio-technical systems approach to organizational design has led to many improvements in productivity. The approach is based on an awareness that productive efficiency requires the optimization of the technical and social mix and not simply the maximization of the technical factors. (The foregoing discussion of the longwall method has been grossly simplified so as to improve the clarity of the discussion of the organizational principle concerned. For a full account of the Tavistock research into coal-mining methods, see E. L. Trist *et al.*) ▷▷ Conflict; Co-ordination; Formal Organization; Group. I.C.McG.

E. L. Trist *et al., Organizational Choice* (Tavistock, 1963); P. G. Herbst, *Socio-technical Design* (Tavistock, 1974); D. S. Pugh *et al., Writers on Organization* (Penguin, 1983), pp. 84–91.

Software ▷ Hardware/Liveware/Software

Somatotype Observations upon the relationship between personality characteristics and physique have been made over many centuries. Numerous classifications of types of physique have resulted from attempts to systematize this relationship. The most comprehensive study in this field is that of W. H. Sheldon and his co-workers, who developed techniques of assessing the physique either from standardized photographs or from a series of anthropometric measurements. An individual's somatotype is expressed by three numerals, which represent a rating on a seven-point scale for each of the primary components: endomorphy, mesomorphy and ectomorphy. Thus, for example, an individual of somatotype 4–7–1 is about average in endomorphy, high in mesomorphy and low in ectomorphy. Endomorphy is characterized by a soft and rounded surface, indicating deficient development of bone and muscle. The mesomorph shows high bone and muscle development and is hard and rectangular in appearance. Linearity, fragility and delicacy are the characteristics of the ectomorph. Of the 343 possible somatotypes less than 100 appear to exist in the human population.

By means of the statistical analysis of data describing individual differences in temperament, Sheldon isolated three primary components of personality, which he named viscerotonia, somatotonia and cerebrotonia. An individual with a high score in viscerotonia is characterized by a love of comfort, of food and of people, and is generally easy-going. High somatotonia scores resulted from a love of adventure and of exercise and from aggressiveness. A high score on the third component implies a lack of sociability, fast reactions and a love of privacy and secrecy.

High correlations have been demonstrated to exist between individuals' personality ratings and somatotypes, relating the components in the following way: endomorphy/viscerotonia; mesomorphy/somatotonia; ectomorphy/cerebrotonia. E.E.

W. H. Sheldon, *The Varieties of Human Physique* (Harper, 1940).

Sound ◊ Hearing; Noise

Span of Control The number of subordinates over whom a given superior exercises direct authority. A management consultant, V. A. Graicunas, first formulated the concept in a paper published in 1933 and appeared to demonstrate mathematically the impossibility of maintaining efficient control if the number of such subordinates exceeded six. Other writers in the classical tradition have broadly concurred. Empirical studies, however, have shown that the span of control of chief executives varies widely and spans as large as twenty have been recorded. It would seem that, in practice, many factors may influence the span of control and inefficiency should not be inferred solely from the shape of the organization chart. The personality of the chief executive, the competence of the subordinates, the use of co-ordinating committees, the desired location of decision-making and the technical complexity of the production processes are all among the influences that affect the determination of a given span of control. Attempts to define an optimum span regardless of the specific circumstances in which it is to be located would seem to be inappropriate. ◊ Authority; Classical Organization Theory. I.C.MCG.

J. A. Litterer, *The Analysis of Organizations* (J. Wiley, 1965); H. D. Koontz and C. J. O'Donnell, *Principles of Management* (McGraw-Hill, 1964); J. Child, *Organization: A Guide to Problems and Practice* (Harper & Row, 1984), ch. 2.

Specialization The fine division of a total task into its component sub-tasks, each of which is then performed by a separate individual.

Adam Smith was one of the earliest writers to draw attention to the economic advantages of specialization in his celebrated account of pin-making in the eighteenth century. Subsequently the division of labour and specialization have been carried to an advanced stage in most industries. The process is apparent not only in the minute subdivision of tasks in mass-production industries but also in the increasing differentiation of managerial functions. However, specialization introduces the concomitant problem of co-ordination. Each sub-unit is highly dependent on the correct functioning of other sub-units and much organizational energy must be devoted to the standardization of operations, the precise planning of production sequences and the development and maintenance of production and quality-control systems. In the resulting administrative complex it becomes difficult for individuals, particularly at the lowest levels in the organization, to understand the importance of their own minimal contribution. Furthermore, the careful and systematic removal from jobs of any opportunity for human error removes, at the same time, opportunity for the exercise of judgement and any element of intrinsic job interest. This process has heightened problems of employee motivation and introduced a tendency towards inflexibility. As a result there is a gradual realization that the benefits of specialization are subject to the law of diminishing returns and a number of managements are considering the possibilities of job enlargement. ⟴ Alienation; Co-ordination; Function (1); Job Enlargement; Profession; Socio-technical System. I.C.MCG.

J. A. Litterer, *The Analysis of Organizations* (J. Wiley, 1965), chs. 9 and 10.

Speech Speech sounds are produced by the expulsion of air from the lungs past the larynx, which provides the basic sound-producing process, phonation. This primary sound tone is then modulated by means of the vocal organs in the throat, mouth and nose to produce a wide range of possible speech sounds. The comparatively small number of different symbols used in the written form of a language gives a misleading impression of simplicity compared with the rich variety of the spoken word.

Individual speakers exhibit different characteristics in their speech habits. Some of the most important of these characteristics are intensity, pitch, speed and the frequency and duration of pauses. Intensities of speech vary not only between different speakers, but between different elements of the language. The amount of sound energy in certain vowel sounds, for example, may be 700 times greater than the energy in a soft 'th' sound in the same word. Different pitches are attained by the utilization of frequencies ranging between about 300 and 6,000 Hz. Speeds much below 100 words/minute are slow; fast talkers can more than double this speed.

The proportion of spoken language that can be understood by a listener depends upon the type of material and upon its context, as well as upon the quality of the received signal. This is usually measured in terms of the articulation index, which is derived from measurements of both speech and noise levels in each of a number of frequency bands. The extent to which noise will affect reliable speech communication may be expressed in terms of the speech interference level, an index that provides a measure of the required intensity level of speech to overcome noise of a given intensity.

Many communication systems, such as the telephone, bring about selective filtering of speech, such that the very high and very low frequency elements are severely attentuated. Intelligibility of speech can survive a good deal of such distortion, particularly if noise is absent.

Experiments upon the characteristics of good talkers indicate that the most intelligible speech results from long average syllable duration, high syllable intensity, the absence of pauses and some variation in pitch. E.E.

G. A. Miller, *Language and Communication* (McGraw-Hill, 1951).

Stability ◇ Feedback

Stabilized Accounting ◇ Changing Price Levels (Accounting for)

Staff (1) ◇ Line and Staff

Staff (2) The collectivity of clerical, secretarial, technical and, perhaps, managerial personnel in an organization, as distinct from the wage-earning, manual workers. Traditionally staff have enjoyed working conditions and benefits superior to those of manual workers. Amongst these benefits have been longer holiday entitlements, greater security of employment, a more pleasant working environment, higher pay and better prospects of promotion. In recent years, a number of factors, principally associated with technology and changes in the social class structure, have caused a critical examination of the privileged position of the 'white-collar' group and many firms have adopted the policy of eliminating or reducing the differences between the two groups. I.C.McG.

P. Bowen, M. Shaw and V. Elsy, 'The Attachment of White-collar Workers to Trade Unions', *Personnel Review*, vol. 3, no. 3 (1974).

Staff Appraisal ◇ Performance Appraisal

Staff Assessment ◇ Performance Appraisal

Staff Association ◇ Company Union

Staff Management That part of ◇ Personnel Management concerned with 'staff' rather than 'labour', i.e. with those whose work is primarily mental or social rather than manual. Shop, office and laboratory workers are normally included in this category, as well as managers, technicians, salesmen and supervisors. In retail stores and large offices, e.g. in banks and insurance companies, the personnel manager is often called the staff manager. In industrial undertakings the personnel department, headed by a personnel director, may include a specialist staff manager and a labour manager, who deals with manual workers. Although the tasks of staff and labour managers are similar, staff work tends to involve more contact with individuals than with groups, for example in selection procedures (◇ Selection), especially for managerial and specialist posts, in fixing salaries and in career development. Staff managers are less likely than labour managers to be concerned with ◇ Trade Union negotiations, except in the Civil Service, local government and nationalized industries; they will be more concerned with ◇ Fringe Benefits and with other questions relating to ◇ Status, security and amenities. With the growth of trade unionism among office workers and improvements in the conditions and status of manual workers there is a tendency for these two sides of personnel management to be assimilated. ◇ Trade Union Types – White-collar Union. L.S.

Staff Status Indicated by advantageous conditions of employment given to the members of the 'staff' in a firm as compared to 'hourly paid workers', e.g. the staff usually work shorter hours, have longer periods of notice, better pension and sick-pay benefits and separate canteens; they may have longer holidays and be paid monthly by cheque instead of weekly in cash. All these things combine to give staff employees a higher standing, or ◇ Status. Changes in social outlook and in technology have led to questions about the validity of these distinctions in status and some firms have removed or reduced them by giving staff status to all or some of those employed in a factory. L.S., amended by E.L.

Institute of Manpower Studies, *Staff Status for Manual Workers* (IMS, 1981); *Developments in Harmonisation* (ACAS, 1982).

Standard Costing Standard costs may be defined as 'predetermined costs related to carefully planned methods of making and selling a product or, in the case of services, rendering a service. In principle there is no difference between standard costs and budgeted costs: both are based on the principle of predetermination of cost. But there is a difference in scope between a budget system and a system of standard costs. Budgeting includes objectives for all activities of a business during a certain period, whereas standard costs relate to detailed costs of operation' (*Cost Accounting and Productivity*, OEEC Report, 1952).

A standard-costing system serves as a method of feedback whereby deviations between actual and predetermined costs for a given period are isolated and reported. Costs are accumulated by departments and cost centres covering the direct and overhead costs allocated to them, which are considered to be the direct responsibility of the individual managers (◇ Responsibility Accounting). Each managerial unit is charged with actual costs and credited with output measured in standard-cost terms. The difference between actual and standard cost is known as variance and represents the discrepancy between actual and standard performance. This total variance is generally broken down into component parts: variances for materials and wages are analysed as price (wage rate) and usage variances; overheads as volume, budget and efficiency variances. A cross-classification in terms of controllability and non-controllability is also attempted. The analysis of standard-costing variances gives a point of departure for the investigation of costs, but since the analysis is not in terms of causation, it cannot settle all issues about control and efficiency.

In so far as standard costs are target costs they implicitly contain assumptions about how people are motivated. It is therefore important that the basis for the setting of standards be investigated from a behavioural viewpoint and to ask whether the particular standards set motivate people in the way that best helps the achievement of a firm's objectives regarding production efficiency and cost minimization. However, from a human-relations viewpoint such economic ends are by no means the only 'values' present when considering a control system such as a standard-costing system. E.A.L.

Management Accounting – Official Terminology (ICMA, 1982).

Standard Deviation ◇ Measures of Dispersion

Statistical Decision Theory The simplest case of decision-making involves the choice between two alternative theoretical models on the basis of a sample of one or more observations. For example it may be necessary to show whether a coin is unbiased or biased on the basis of it falling to show a head eight times from ten tosses. A special case of this general problem forms the basis of the theory of signal detection, where the problem is to distinguish between the presence or absence of a signal in a noise. Two primary indices developed within this theory, namely the detectability of the signal and the criterion employed by the observer, have provided useful ways of describing human behaviour in decision-making situations. E.E.

W. Edwards and A. Tversky, *Decision-making* (Penguin, 1967).

Statistical Tests It is often necessary to compare sets of data to determine if they have certain statistical properties in common. Statisticians have a number of tests that perform these tasks. The most commonly used ones are as follows:

(1) *Student's 't' test.* This test may be used when we wish to compare the means of sets of data. For example, it may be used to determine: (a) whether the mean of a sample of observation differs significantly from the mean of the normal population from which it is drawn; (b) given two independent samples with different means, whether their means differ significantly or whether the two samples may be regarded as drawn from the same normal population.

(2) *'F' test.* This may be used when we wish to compare the variability or variance of sets of data. For example, given two independent samples of different variances, it may be used to determine whether their variances differ significantly or whether the two samples may be regarded as drawn from the same normal population.

(3) x^2 (*chi-squared*) *test.* This may be used when we wish to establish whether an observed frequency distribution conforms to or fits a particular theoretical distribution. When used in this way it is known as the chi-squared test of 'goodness of fit'. For example a personnel director may possess records of the industrial accidents occurring in all the factories in the organization over three years. These records may be expressed in the form of a histogram or frequency distribution showing the number of shifts that occurred in the three years. The frequency of industrial accidents often follows a well-known theoretical distribution known as a ⬦ Poisson Distribution. Using the chi-squared test, the personnel director will be able to establish the measure of the probability

that the observed frequency distribution of accidents is significantly different from a Poisson distribution, or whether the latter provides a 'good fit' to the data. M.J.C.M.

Stephen P. Shao, *Statistics for Business and Economics* (Merrill, 1976).

Statistics Much of the data that managers use is subject to a variability that prevents it being estimated with certainty. For example the dimensions of successive units of a product, the weekly running costs of a particular stage of a production process or the monthly sales of a product may vary due to a number of factors that are individually unpredictable. However, managers may have to make decisions based on the pattern of variation of these quantities. In fact they are in a similar position to actuaries, who must use their knowledge of the pattern of life spans of individuals to fix life-insurance premiums. Both the life spans of individuals and the dimensions, costs, sales figures, etc., arising in industry are subject to variability through a large number of causes. Fortunately for actuaries and managers, the science of probability and statistics has been developed specifically to handle such problems.

Statistics can be defined as the science of collecting and analysing data. To be analysed, data must be presented in a convenient form such as a histogram. This can be illustrated by means of an example. Suppose that a personnel manager wishes to represent the weekly overtime hours worked in a department of sixty operatives, whose individual overtime hours are given below:

3·75	1·50	1·00	5·00	1·38	6·00	4·50	6·00	7·00	6·00
5·50	6·00	3·00	2·63	4·37	1·75	9·25	7·25	6·60	2·75
3·13	5·87	4·87	8·25	2·13	6·13	9·75	6·87	9·63	6·25
6·00	5·50	6·00	3·25	9·00	7·87	5·13	8·13	5·63	7·50
4·50	6·00	5·87	6·00	4·50	5·50	3·75	4·50	7·00	6·00
2·75	7·25	7·63	6·63	8·75	5·83	6·00	4·87	8·00	8·25

The lowest is 1·00 hours and the highest is 9·75 hours. The variations in hours can be divided into nine class intervals: 1·00–1·99, 2·00–2·99, etc. If this is done, the number of operatives in each class can be obtained and a diagram constructed as shown in figure 1.

In this diagram the class intervals are represented on a horizontal scale whilst the vertical height of the columns corresponds to the number of operatives in that class interval. Since each class interval is of equal width, it follows that the area in each class interval also corresponds to the number of operatives. This histogram provides a very convenient

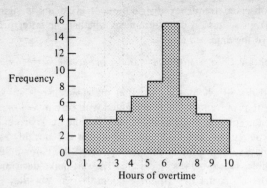

Frequency

Hours of overtime

Figure 1

visual representation of the spread of operatives' earnings and the concentration of earnings in each class.

We can extend the idea of plotting a histogram to introduce another important concept in statistics – the distribution curve. Suppose that instead of the earnings of sixty operatives, we wish to represent the variability of the heights of 100,000 adult Englishmen attending a Cup Final at Wembley, and suppose that each spectator's height had been measured automatically very accurately as he passed through the turnstiles. We could then plot a histogram as shown in figure 2, with 1-inch class intervals and many individuals in each class.

However, since we have 100,000 individuals, we could choose much narrower class intervals, which would each contain a fair number of individuals. In fact we could go on making our intervals finer and finer until the steps in the histogram virtually disappear and a continuous curve is produced, as shown in figure 3. This is known as a distribution curve since it describes the extent of the distribution of the heights of the Cup Final spectators. The area of the curve lying between two points, say A and B, still represents the proportion of the total number of spectators whose heights lie between H_1 and H_2 along the horizontal scale. The concept of this distribution curve (also known as a frequency distribution, since the vertical measure of each point represents the frequency with which the corresponding horizontal measure occurs) is fundamental to statistics and underlies much of the mathematical theory.

In the two examples illustrated, the sixty operatives and the 100,000 Cup Final spectators were the entities under examination. Collectively the aggregate of entities, that is, the sixty operators or 100,000 spectators,

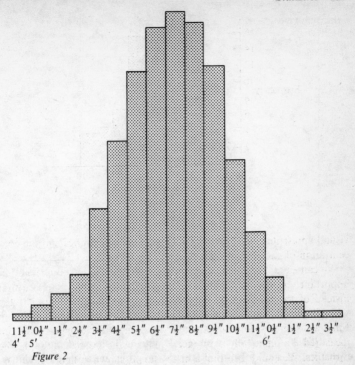

$11\frac{1}{2}''$ $0\frac{1}{2}''$ $1\frac{1}{2}''$ $2\frac{1}{2}''$ $3\frac{1}{2}''$ $4\frac{1}{2}''$ $5\frac{1}{2}''$ $6\frac{1}{2}''$ $7\frac{1}{2}''$ $8\frac{1}{2}''$ $9\frac{1}{2}''$ $10\frac{1}{2}''$ $11\frac{1}{2}''$ $0\frac{1}{2}''$ $1\frac{1}{2}''$ $2\frac{1}{2}''$ $3\frac{1}{2}''$
$4'$ $5'$ $6'$

Figure 2

are known as a population, although often the term is applied to the aggregate of measures rather than entities, that is, we may refer to the population of wages of sixty operatives or of heights of 100,000 spectators.

Often the statistician wishes to analyse characteristics of very large populations. For example, to establish the viewing figures for particular national TV programmes, the population consists of all the people in the UK who watch television. In cases such as this it is either impossible or prohibitively expensive to measure the characteristic of each member of the population so the statistician examines a chosen group, or a sample, of the population (◊ Sampling).

The histogram and frequency distribution discussed above, although useful visual representations of the variability of a measure, are unsuited to algebraic manipulation, so statisticians use other algebraic measures to represent the extent of the variability of the population. Collectively these are known as ◊ Measures of Location and of Dispersion.

M.J.C.M.

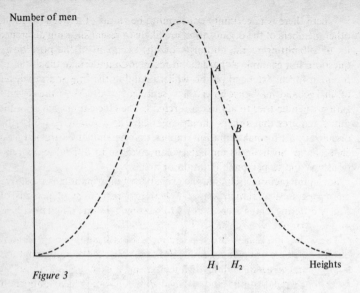

Figure 3

Stephen P. Shao, *Statistics for Business and Economics* (Merrill, 1976).

Status A position in a social system, or more commonly the evaluation of such a position, person or group on a scale of relative esteem.

Technically a distinction is sometimes made between status (the degree of esteem in which a *position* is held) and prestige (the degree of esteem in which a *person* is held). In practice, however, the distinction is often extremely difficult to maintain and even in academic sociological writing the term 'status' commonly refers to the evaluation of a person.

Status is based on many factors. It is closely associated with authority and the reward system: those positions with most authority receive the highest rewards and are accorded the highest status. Status is enhanced by the maintenance of ⟡⟩ Social Distance and the more status-conscious organizations are characterized by a high degree of formality in social relationships, with people addressing each other by status (Matron, Sergeant, etc.) rather than by name. Status may also be based on the skill or educational level that the role requires. It may be influenced, too, by the status system of the wider society: if persons of low status are consistently recruited to certain positions in the organization, those positions will be accorded low status.

Where there is uncertainty concerning the status of a given position, other members of the organization are likely to resent showing deference to, or submitting to the authority of, the occupant of the position in question. For example a chargehand required to undertake the duties of foreman for an extended period whilst retaining the title and privileges of chargehand may encounter the resentment of others in the organization when he tries to act like a foreman. The efficient discharge of his duties requires that others should treat him as a foreman, whilst the organization's formal definition implies that he should be treated as a chargehand. Such status ambiguity can give rise to difficulties in relationships and to personal irritation or anxiety.

Social interaction, including the exchange of information, is most free among persons of similar status. Where groups consist of persons of widely differing status there is likely to be some tension and guardedness in interpersonal relationships.

The wider differences in status are recognized formally in the organization but there are many ramifications and nuances of status that are less well recognized. Subtle distinctions may exist among those of ostensibly similar status and these distinctions may have important behavioural consequences. A high proportion of pay disputes are concerned with differentials rather than absolute payment. Many seemingly lateral transfers are resisted because to the employees concerned the move is to a lower status group and is thus viewed as a demotion, despite managerial assurance to the contrary. ⟡ Authority; Role; Status Symbol. I.C.MCG.

J. A. Litterer, *The Analysis of Organizations* (J. Wiley, 1965), ch. 4; G. Bain *et al.*, *Social Stratification and Trade Unionism* (Heinemann, 1973); P. B. Horton and C. L. Hunt, *Sociology* (McGraw-Hill, 6th ed., 1984).

Status Symbol Anything from which a person's ⟡ Status may be inferred. In organizations in which status is particularly important (e.g. authoritarian organizations such as the armed forces; hospitals) badges of rank may be worn expressly for that purpose. In the industrial organization status differences are not usually proclaimed by badges, although different styles of dress, such as the wearing of white coats or different-coloured overalls, are commonly associated with different occupational grades. Most status symbols arise because of their incidental association with status and not because they are intended to signify status. The range of possible symbols is almost infinite and the identification of a new and unusual symbol is always a source of joy to the industrial sociologist. Office furnishings constitute an almost universal category; in the larger organizations entitlement to office furniture is likely to be formally prescribed in meticulous detail and promotion to a higher status grade may be heralded by the arrival of furniture removers. Size and location of office, title of the position, frequency of pay (by the hour, weekly, monthly) and rights and privileges appropriate to the position all help to signify status and to confirm that status in the eyes of the other members of the organization. Conversely the absence of appropriate symbols can create uncertainty concerning status and give rise to status ambiguity. I.C.McG.

J. A. Litterer, *The Analysis of Organizations* (J. Wiley, 1965, pp. 73–7); J. H. Turner, *Social Stratification* (Columbia University Press, 1983).

Stereotypes Although the processes of classification and generalization are fundamental operations in any system of logical development, without proper control these processes can easily lead to unwarranted judgements based upon inadequate information and insufficient differentiation. Thus we may develop coarse representations of concepts such as 'big business' in such a way that the stereotype is a completely inadequate representation of the real world. Not only concepts themselves, but also the thought processes by which they are manipulated can become stereotyped and hence lead to indefensible conclusions.

In the context of human engineering the term 'population stereotypes' refers to expectations that are found to exist between the relative directions of movement of controls and displays. Violation of these stereotypes in machine design leads to errors in the use of equipment. Some well-known examples are illustrated below. ⟡⟩ Machine Controls. E.E.

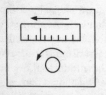  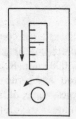

Population stereotype

Stewardship Accounting ⟡ Accountancy Conventions

Stock Control ⟡ Inventory or Stock-control Problems

Storage Media (Computer) One of the principal distinctions between an electronic digital computer and a conventional calculating machine is that the former can store large quantities of data. This storage, or memory, can be used to hold the data and instructions required to perform a calculation and the intermediate and cumulative data that may be produced and required later in the processing before the final output data are generated.

The two interrelated criteria that determine the utility of a storage medium are access time and size. Firstly, in performing a calculation, data are continuously being recalled from storage, operated on and returned to storage. Therefore the time taken for the whole calculation will depend markedly on the access time to data in store. Secondly, since many commercial and scientific applications of computers require the manipulation of large quantities of data and hence require large quantities of storage, it is important that a storage medium be as compact as possible. Since, at a naïve level, it can be argued that the speed of operation of an electronic circuit is ultimately limited by the speed of light, reductions in the physical dimensions of a circuit should increase the speed of response.

In many calculations data can be divided into two groups. Firstly, data that are being manipulated at the current state of the calculations and need to be readily available in storage. Secondly, data that are not currently required but will be wanted later and can be held until required in less accessible storage. Most computer installations reflect these needs by having two levels of storage: (1) internal storage – where data are readily accessible; (2) external or backing storage – where data can be held when not in immediate use. Data are transferred between the two levels as and when appropriate.

(1) *Internal storage.* The first computers used magnetic drums. One of these consists of a non-magnetic metal cylinder with a magnetic coating on its curved outer surface. It rotates about its axis at 3,000–17,000 rpm. Read/write heads are placed over the drum so they can read and write data at specific locations as the drum rotates. The access time of an item of data depends upon whether, when it is wanted, its location is just above or has just passed the head. If the latter is the case then the drum must complete a full revolution before the data become accessible, which may take up to twenty milliseconds. The speed of operation of computers is usually quoted in units that are small fractions of a second (cf. engineers' use of thousandths of an inch). Thus:

$$1 \text{ millisecond } (1\text{m sec}) = \frac{1}{1,000} \text{ second}$$

$$1 \text{ microsecond } (1\mu \text{ sec}) = \frac{1}{1,000,000} \text{ second}$$

$$1 \text{ nanosecond } (1\mu\text{n sec or } 1\text{n sec}) = \frac{1}{1,000,000,000} \text{ second}$$

Later computers used core-storage, consisting of a network or matrix in one plane of two parallel sets of wires, each set at right angles to the other. These wires are threaded through small rings of about 0·1 in. diameter or cores of magnetic material such that a core is placed at the intersection between two wires. One of two magnetic states (representing '1' or '0') of a core is both imposed and measured by the voltage present on the pair of wires defining its location, which together act as read/write heads. Access time to each core is the same and varies between a fraction of a microsecond and two hundred microseconds. Because access time is independent of location, core stores can be described as random access stores.

(2) *External or backing storage*. Magnetic tape is used to store intermittently required data not currently in use. When required it can be fed into the internal store of the computer (⟡ Input/Output).

Magnetic discs are in common use. They have a short access time compared to tape and have a large storage capacity. They consist of a stack of circular metal discs coated on both sides with magnetic material. Data is represented by alternative magnetic configurations. The discs rotate at about 1,200 rpm. The data is written on or read off by a read/write head for each disc face. The read/write heads move in unison and interleave between the discs. A typical six-disc pack can store twenty-two million characters. Access times are in the range 20–200 milliseconds, depending on how far the head has to move. M.J.C.M.

Strategy A proposed action or sequence of actions intended to have a far-reaching effect on the company's ability to achieve its objective.

Strategy is often confused with policy and with tactics. Policy decisions are wider than strategic decisions, which in turn are wider than tactical decisions. Policy decisions often remain valid for a decade or more. Strategic decisions may remain valid for a period of several months to several years. Tactical decisions usually refer to a period of less than one year. These time-spans can only be an approximate guide. While policy decisions can include the setting of overall company objectives and constraints as well as means, strategic decisions usually refer only to means.

Once a policy decision has determined the long-term objectives for the company as a whole, it is the task of the senior managers to decide how best to achieve them over the following years. Unless a policy decision has been made that severely limits the field of study for the strategists, their task will be complex, for the time-span they will be considering may be long enough to allow the complete reorientation of the entire company and its physical resources. They will certainly need to consider the desirability of some of the types of diversification, the changes required in the organizational structure of the company (⟡ Manpower Planning), the need to introduce new product lines (⟡ Marketing), the research effort and facilities required, the building of new, or rebuilding of existing, factories, the location of warehouses and sales offices, and many other complex and far-reaching factors. The range of choice facing strategists is always wide and the element of uncertainty associated with the long-range forecasts upon which they must rely is also large (⟡ Forecasting).

It is usual, once the final choices between these many alternatives have been made, for a long-range plan, or strategy, to be submitted in writing to the board. Once approved, each part of the plan becomes the responsibility of an executive, who may then take a series of tactical decisions in order to implement or, within the limits of their authority, modify the strategy. ⟡ Business Policy; Tactics. A.J.A.A.

Strengths and Weaknesses A strength is any activity at which a company is unusually efficient. A weakness is any activity that it carries out with less than normal efficiency. The definition is often extended to include the physical reason for such efficiency or inefficiency.

Thus a company may be one of the acknowledged leaders in the field of welding titanium – this activity would be one of its strengths. The definition can be extended to include the physical reason for this supremacy and it may therefore be said that among its strengths are its 'special welding equipment' or the 'long experience and knowledge of its technical director'.

Strengths and weaknesses may be present in a firm as a result of historical accident or years of careful cultivation but, whatever the reason, they are crucial to the continued health of the company. In order to be successful or even to remain in business at all, every company has to be good at a certain minimum number of activities; precisely what these must be is a subject of continuing controversy. Some experts believe that all companies must be strong in marketing if nothing else, others believe that management research or finance are the prime requirements of any firm. It seems probable that no hard and fast rule exists and that a more satisfactory answer can be obtained by each individual firm asking itself what it has to be good at in order to be successful in its current line of business and checking these desiderata against its own strengths and weaknesses as the executives see them. Such an inquiry can highlight areas where improvement is essential.

It is essential to make an inquiry such as this before any diversification is undertaken. Many firms have launched out into new fields of business only to find that they do not have the strengths necessary to succeed in this new area or that it calls for efficiency in some activity in which they are weak. ⟡ Synergy. A.J.A.A.

Stress Stress arises from a mismatch between the demands made upon individuals and their capacity to cope with such demands. Small discrepancies may lead to occasional errors or other symptoms of sub-optimal performance, accompanied by feelings of anxiety or tiredness. More severe and prolonged exposure to stressful situations may lead to complete failure of the coping mechanisms, resulting in a breakdown of normal performance accompanied by deterioration in the person's health.

The alleviation of stress can be achieved either by a reduction in the demands made or by an improvement of the coping mechanisms. The former approach might involve a change of job or a redistribution of workload within a team. Many techniques are available to improve the ability to cope (⟡ Counselling). Some of these are cognitive, i.e. they involve the adoption of new strategies of performance; others are affective, i.e. they involve changes in emotional responses to certain types of stimuli. Stress-management techniques also include methods of achieving proper sleep and relaxation during wakefulness. In general, drug solutions are unsatisfactory for long-term demands. E.E.

T. Cox, *Stress* (Macmillan, 1978).

Strike – and Other Industrial Action A strike is an extreme form of industrial conflict. ⟡ Conflict is inherent in any society with different interest groups, each with its own attitudes, expectations and objectives. It is thus inherent in an industrial society between employees and managers.

Conflict at the workplace may also be evidenced by an abnormally high sickness or accident rate (⟡ Accident Prevention); or by abnormally high voluntary ⟡ Absenteeism or ⟡ Labour Turnover; or by other forms of industrial action, such as 'go-slows', overtime bans, 'working-to-rule', or 'blacking' of goods. Industrial discord manifests itself in overt action on the shopfloor more frequently than the official ⟨⟩ Strike Statistics imply. The strike, however, is regarded as the ultimate sanction, which gives reality to ⟨⟩ Collective Bargaining in a free society, the right to strike being one of the basic freedoms enjoyed by employees in a democratic country. Occasionally non-unionists have resorted to strike action.

Historically the strike has been the weapon of manual workers in attempts to maintain and raise the standard of their conditions of employment. Some professions exercise an effective pressure to maintain members' standards by defining minimal terms on which they should accept employment. Some groups have control over entry to their occupations, which is almost sufficient by itself to ensure relatively high rewards to those admitted (⟨⟩ Profession). Strikes are not commonly resorted to by those who have a substantial prospect of individual advancement through competition, rather than advancement by identification with a group, and this is why salaried employees have been comparatively exempt from strike action. Many white-collar employees, however, are now suffering a crisis of ⟨⟩ Status, e.g. bank clerks, teachers. They wish to retain or recover their social status while accepting the fact that they now have much the same economic status as manual workers. They have, therefore, come to accept the institutions and methods of manual workers – trade unions and strikes (⟨⟩ Trade Union Types – White-collar Union).

The effects of strike action are difficult to measure in economic terms. A strike by a key group in a long chain of production and distribution can put many people out of work in the same firm, in other firms and even in other industries. Cost may be indicated by lost output, lost customers and lost management confidence. There may be offsetting factors. Lost output resulting from strikes by dockers and engineering pieceworkers is often quickly made up by extra effort and overtime. The size and duration of car-industry strikes tend to rise in recessions, when some of the output lost would not be readily saleable. In coal-mining an occasional strike appears to increase productivity, although a large strike like the 1984–5 miners' stoppage caused a loss of at least 1 per cent in growth in GNP.

Industrial action such as the 'go-slow' and 'work to rule' can in some cases be economically more damaging than strike action. ⟨⟩ Strike – Causes; Forms; Remedies; Statistics. N.H.C., amended by M.J.F.P.

K. G. J. C. Knowles, *Strikes* (Blackwell, 1952); R. Hyman, *Strikes* (Fontana, rev. ed., 1984).

Strike – and the Law Modern strike law is extremely complex and

politically controversial. The boundaries of legality have been redrawn
several times in the recent past and cannot now be regarded as permanently settled. Curiously there is no general statutory definition of a
'strike', although it has been judicially defined as a 'simultaneous cessation of work on the part of workmen'.

The withdrawal of labour does not normally amount to a criminal
offence, except where any ensuing breach of the strikers' contracts is
likely to endanger human life, cause serious personal injury, or expose
valuable property to destruction. In the twentieth century such prosecutions are virtually unheard of and criminal liabilities have largely
ceased to impede peaceful strikes, although they play an important part
in controlling the conduct of ⟡ Picketing.

Strikes (and certain other forms of industrial action such as blacking)
generally, but by no means always, represent a breach of contract, since
strikers are withholding their labour while their contracts of employment
are still in existence. Their contractual obligation to be available for
work is no longer regarded as suspended merely because any industrial
action is preceded by a strike notice the length of which is equal to that
necessary to terminate the strikers' contracts. Irrespective of whether
industrial action amounts to a breach of contract – and a ban on voluntary overtime may well not be – those dismissed during its currency
cannot complain of unfair dismissal unless only some strikers have been
sacked or, where all have been dismissed, some have been offered re-
employment within three months.

For obvious reasons, individual strikers are rarely sued by their employer for damages for breach of contract. Moreover no court can, by
way of injunction or other order, purport to compel strikers to return to
work. However, court action has increasingly been taken in recent times
against those who *organize* unlawful strikes. What is unlawful in this
context is a complicated question, which cannot be fully answered here.
Broadly, it can be said that those who call, organize or finance industrial
action thereby commit certain torts (i.e. civil wrongs) to the extent that
the strike interferes with an employer's business or contractual arrangements with the workforce and others. Since 1906 the so-called 'right to
strike' has rested on a limited immunity from this tortious liability.
Currently the immunity is contained in section 13 of the Trade Union
and Labour Relations Act 1974, and is valid so long as the organizers
act in contemplation or furtherance of a ⟡ Trade Dispute. If there is no
trade dispute, or if the conduct of the dispute entails unlawful picketing,
or unlawful secondary action, the immunity will be lost. Secondary
action is unlawful where the strike is aimed at third-party employers
unconnected with the dispute, who are not first line suppliers or

customers of the primary employer, nor associated employers; nor companies taking on strike-bound work normally done by the primary employer. Mere sympathetic strikes are also unlawful, as is industrial action designed to force a third-party employer to recognize or negotiate with a trade union or to use union labour only. Furthermore official strikes must be preceded by a secret ballot of the membership likely to be involved.

As a result of the Employment Act 1982 trade unions themselves (as well as individual union officers and officials) are capable of being sued for unlawful strikes that they have authorized or endorsed (◊ Vicarious Liability). Union funds, up to specified maxima depending on the size of the membership, are thus at risk of being seized to satisfy any judgment in damages. A court can also order that unlawful strike or picketing instructions be withdrawn. Wilful failure to comply amounts to contempt of court, for which the union can be fined. There have been several instances of heavy fines and of unions having their funds seized by sequestrators appointed by the courts, and even of funds being temporarily placed in the hands of a receiver. ◊ Strike – Forms; Trade Dispute; Trade Union Act; Trade Union – at Law; Employment Act 1980; Employment Act 1982; Picketing. K.W.

R. Kidner, *Trade Union Law* (Stevens & Sons, 2nd ed., 1983), chs. 8–10.

Strike – Causes Strikes are not the outcome of a single cause. Immediate reasons may be 'basic', i.e. about ◊ Wages and hours; 'frictional', i.e. about working arrangements, rules and discipline; or 'solidarity', as in the case of sympathetic strikes. Underlying these, however, are more fundamental causes to do with the economic situation, e.g. changes in money or real wages, differentials, the position in the business cycle and the level of employment; governmental policy on such matters as prices and incomes and intervention in disputes; management action in such areas as discipline, redundancy, technological and organizational change; and union activity in the areas of demarcation, jurisdiction, the demand for recognition and for the ◊ Closed Shop (◊ Trade Union – Demarcation; Jurisdiction).

This list is not exhaustive. On the union side alone strikes may also be due to ignorance of the employers' bargaining strength, the feeling that it is necessary to keep the union in training, lack of confidence in the official union leadership, failure of communications, specific personalities. In very few cases are strikes engineered by communist or other agitators (◊ Trade Union – Communism). It is competition for leadership that produces militancy in union leaders rather than their political views.

As for ⟪⟫ Shop Stewards, most managements prefer to deal with them rather than with full-time union officials (⟪⟫ Trade Union – Officials), and the most common reason for their surrendering office is promotion by management.

On the management side the tools of management action like ⟪⟫ Work Study and automation produce strikes less frequently than autocratic decision-making and inflexible attitudes. However, 'management prerogatives' are now being matched by the notion of workers' 'rights' in their jobs. Analysis by Turner of workplace demands other than those concerning wage matters has revealed three basic types: demands for an effort bargain (⟪⟫ Collective Bargaining); for changes in working arrangements, methods and the use of labour to be subject to agreement; and for fair treatment of individuals or groups by managers and supervisors. These demands all involve attempts to limit the 'managerial prerogative' or to submit it to agreed rules. Alternatively they reflect an implicit pressure for more democracy and individual rights in the work situation (⟪⟫ Industrial Democracy).

It is certainly clear that both economic and institutional factors are important causes of shifts in the pattern of strike activity over time (⟪⟫ Strike – Statistics). In terms of actual issues, wages have typically accounted for at least half of the strikes that have occurred in post-war Britain (see Table 1).

Table 1. Causes of strikes 1946–73

Cause	Number of strikes	Percentage share of total
Wage increase	904	40·3
Other wage increase	381	17·0
Discipline	134	6·0
Redundancy	136	6·1
Sympathy	63	2·8
Demarcation	60	2·7
Trade union principle	247	11·0
Other	318	14·2
Total	2,243	100·0

Source: J. Duncan, W. E. J. McCarthy and G. P. Redman, *Strikes in Post-war Britain* (Allen & Unwin, 1983), p. 203.

There are important variations in the incidence of strike activity amongst Britain's industries and services. The most strike-prone industries are coal-mining, docks, iron and steel, motor vehicles and ship-

building (see Table 2). Explanations for this diversity include the characteristics of the communities in which strike-prone industries are located,
plant size and technology. However, given the concentration on wage
issues and the characteristics of these particular industries (as Clegg, pp.
244–7, notes), fragmented bargaining and fluctuating earnings are
probably critical.

Table 2. Strike indices, selected industries 1970–80 (annual averages)

	Number of strikes per 100,000 employees		Number of days lost per 100,000 employees	
	1970–75	1976–80	1970–75	1976–80
Coal-mining	63·2	100·2	9,199	421
Docks	168·4	115·9	4,187	1,065
Iron and steel	41·1	28·4	1,117	6,938
Motor vehicles	49·2	37·4	3,422	4,494
Shipbuilding	43·3	22·1	2,867	1,023
Footwear	6·2	14·1	69	146
Furniture	10·3	8·4	70	68
Printing and publishing	6·3	9·3	178	757
Gas, electricity, water	4·2	5·7	202	130
Railways	5·0	4·4	130	267
Distribution	2·2	1·9	17	20
All industries	12·4	9·4	569	567

Source: P. K. Edwards, 'The Patterns of Collective Action', in G. S. Bain
(ed.), *Industrial Relations in Britain* (Blackwell, 1983), p. 222.

Very large disputes in particular industries (such as the miners' strike
in 1984–5) almost invariably have links with wider political issues and
involve the Government as well as unions and management. However,
most major strikes are official and result from a breakdown of negotiations at industry level about a claim by the union(s) concerned for
improved rates of pay and conditions of employment. Official strikes
accounted for approximately 5 per cent of all strikes in 1968 at the time
the Royal Commission reported, but this proportion has tended to increase in the 1970s and 1980s. ⟨⟩ Industrial Relations – Reform in Great
Britain; Strike – Forms, Remedies, Statistics; Wage Systems; Workplace
Bargaining. N.H.C., amended by M.J.F.P.

K. G. J. C. Knowles, *Strikes: A Study of Industrial Conflict* (Blackwell,
1952); Royal Commission on Trade Unions and Employers' Associations,

Report (HMSO, 1968); H. A. Clegg, *The Changing System of Industrial Relations in Great Britain* (Blackwell, 1979); J. Duncan, W. E. J. McCarthy and G. P. Redman, *Strikes in Post-war Britain* (Allen & Unwin, 1983); P. K. Edwards, 'The Pattern of Collective Action', in G. S. Bain (ed.), *Industrial Relations in Britain* (Blackwell, 1983); R. Hyman, *Strikes* (Fontana, rev. ed., 1984).

Strike – Forms

(1) *Constitutional*. A strike called only after the procedure for dealing with ⟨⟩ Industrial Disputes agreed by the union(s) and the employer or the ⟨⟩ Employers' Association has been exhausted (⟨⟩ Grievance Procedure).

(2) *General*. A strike supported by all or most of the trade union movement of a country. The only British case is that of the 1926 General Strike in support of the miners. There is some doubt about its legality. In many countries general strikes for political purposes may be a feature of emergent nationhood or opposition to single-party government.

(3) *Lightning*. A sudden stoppage of work at the workplace, which may be spontaneous, as when tempers flare (known as a 'wildcat' strike in the USA), or planned, as part of a strategy to harass a specific employer or employers in an industry.

(4) *Local*. A strike involving union members in a small geographical area, usually a workplace, plant or company, but occasionally a town or district. Most workplace and plant strikes are short, unofficial and unconstitutional.

(5) *National*. A strike involving the whole of a union's membership wherever it may be found, *or* involving a whole industry and thus all the unions with members employed in it, e.g. a 'national engineering strike'.

(6) *Official*. A strike sanctioned or ratified by the union(s) whose members are on strike in accordance with the appropriate union rules. National strikes are official, but most local strikes are not. There is no legal distinction between official and unofficial strikes (⟨⟩ Trade Union Act 1984).

(7) *Sit-down*. A strike where the employees in question do not walk off the premises but stop work and remain at their workplace. Such strikes are unofficial, unconstitutional and illegal.

(8) *Sympathetic*. A strike by a group of trade unionists not in dispute with their employer(s) in support of and in sympathy with strikers in a trade dispute.

(9) *Token*. A short stoppage, e.g. a one-day strike, which may be official or unofficial, national or local, to indicate the attitude and strength of trade union members in an industrial dispute. If official, this is an economical form of action, making only a limited call on union funds.

(10) *Unconstitutional*. A strike called without using or exhausting the disputes procedure.

(11) *Unofficial*. A strike not sanctioned or ratified by the union(s) concerned. ⟨⟩ Strike – and the Law. N.H.C.

Strike – Remedies Some strikes may be justified. Some, indeed, may be useful to senior management in pointing up weaknesses in the social structure of the firm or inadequacies in junior management or supervision. But many strikes are avoidable, and the problem is one of matching treatment to diagnosis, of providing an 'early warning' system of conflict, and then channelling, reducing and resolving it.

In democratic countries the right to strike is one of the basic freedoms. The extent to which the exercise of this right is legally regulated varies from country to country, but evidence from countries like the USA and Australia, which impose fairly severe legal restrictions on strike action, as well as from Britain itself, does not suggest that such regulation reduces, much less controls, the incidence of strikes.

The Royal Commission report (1968) and subsequent White Paper (1969) suggested that the contribution by government should include speedier and less formal investigation and ⟨⟩ Conciliation; the possibility of strike ballots and a cooling-off period or 'conciliation pause'; investigations by a Commission on Industrial Relations; and the facilitating of trade union recognition and negotiation rights, of speedier resolution of inter-union disputes, and of protection by government agency against unfair dismissal. The now defunct Industrial Relations Act 1971 contained some of these concepts in its 'legal framework' for industrial relations.

On the union side structural rationalization would be of great help, particularly in respect of demarcation and jurisdiction issues, as would training and the development of research facilities. This is true also for employers' associations if they are to improve their services to member firms.

The system of ⟡ Collective Bargaining in Britain requires restructuring where it is disordered and defective, but since most strikes are at the level of the workplace, plant or company, management has a key role in improving the situation. Boards of directors would benefit from positive industrial-relations policies and comprehensive plant and company agreements. Rational company pay structures are needed, together with speedy disputes procedures and company negotiation systems that regularize the role of the ⟡ Shop Steward (⟡ Industrial Relations Code of Practice). Not least, and without the implication of 'kid-glove management', many organizations need to think less in terms of unilateral action and more in terms of participative management, recognizing that the organization is a plural society rather than a unitary one, where every member has common interests on all occasions. ⟡ Employers' Association; Industrial Relations – Reform in Great Britain; Strike – Forms, Statistics; Trade Union – Demarcation, Jurisdiction, Officers, Structure. N.H.C.

B. C. Roberts, *Trade Unions in a Free Society* (Hutchinson, 1962); Royal Commission on Trade Unions and Employers' Associations, *Report* (HMSO, 1968); A. Fox, *Industrial Sociology and Industrial Relations*, Research Papers 3 (HMSO, 1966); H. A. Clegg, *The Changing System of Industrial Relations in Great Britain* (Blackwell, 1979).

Strike – Statistics The pattern of strike activity has varied appreciably over time (see Table below). Distinct periods include: the post-war 'peace', 1946–52; the return of the strike, 1953–9; the shop-floor movement, 1960–8; the formal challenge, 1969–74; the social contract, 1975–9; and legal restraint and unemployment, 1980–86. A rough-and-ready distinction may also be made between the 1960s, 1970s and the early 1980s. During the 1960s the rise of shop-floor bargaining power was associated with an increase in the number of strikes. The main constraint was an incomes policy, but the breakdown of the various phases of ⟡ Prices and Incomes Policy gave a powerful push to the upward trend in strikes. During the 1970s reforms stemming from the recommendations of the Royal Commission on Trade Unions and Employers' Asssocia-tions (and especially the improved procedures for resolving disputes) may have helped to reduce the number of strikes. Moreover although inflationary pressures increased, their effects on strikes were largely

Stoppages 1970–84

Year	Number of stoppages	Number of workers involved (thousands)	Number of working days lost (thousands)
1970	3,906	1,801	10,980
1971	2,228	1,178	13,551
1972	2,497	1,734	23,909
1973	2,873	1,528	7,197
1974	2,922	1,626	14,750
1975	2,282	809	6,012
1976	2,016	668	3,284
1977	2,703	1,166	10,142
1978	2,471	1,042	9,405
1979	2,080	4,608	29,474
1980	1,330	834	11,964
1981	1,338	1,513	4,266
1982	1,528	2,103	5,313
1983	1,352	574	3,574
1984	1,154	1,405	26,564

Source: Employment Gazette, vol. 93, no. 1 (January 1985), table 4.2.

counterbalanced by rising unemployment and a succession of incomes policies. At the end of the 1970s and in the 1980s the total number of stoppages appreciably declined as a consequence of rising unemployment. However there were still periods when long strikes or significant worker involvement led to a substantial number of working days being lost. This was the case during the 'winter of discontent' (1978–9) and the miners' strike (1984–5). N.H.C., amended by M.J.F.P.

J. Duncan, W. E. F. McCarthy and J. P. Redman, *Strikes in Post-war Britain* (Allen & Unwin, 1983); P. K. Edwards, 'The Pattern of Collective Action', in G. S. Bain (ed.), *Industrial Relations in Britain* (Blackwell, 1983); R. Hyman, *Strikes* (Fontana, rev. ed., 1984).

Subjective Probability Management decisions are frequently taken in conditions of uncertainty. The branch of mathematics that deals with uncertainty is ⟨⟩ Statistics, which includes the treatment of ⟨⟩ Probability. Mathematical deduction using the rules of probability is founded upon the principle of frequency of trials, but in management the problems are often unique, with little opportunity for repeated experimentation. In using probability then, managers must make an assessment of their chance of success in a future venture, and make it on a subjective basis.

As more evidence is obtained, the probability estimate may be reviewed and improved. For example a drug company may believe that it has produced a new and effective medicine, but it must conduct clinical trials to be more sure (note that we cannot say 'certain'). A formula that takes account of the new evidence and that calculates the latest probability based on that evidence, as well as the initial probability estimate, was developed by Thomas Bayes 200 years ago, and found to be most useful in recent years. R.S.S.

P. G. Moore, *Basic Operational Research* (Pitman, 1976).

Suggestion Schemes Organized arrangements to encourage employees to put forward their ideas for improving the efficiency, safety or working conditions in a firm. The idea behind these schemes is that all employees, given their technical knowledge and experience, may have ideas about reducing costs or changing methods of work, guarding machines etc., which will be of advantage to the business but which may remain undisclosed if no special encouragement is given. The encouragement usually takes the form of a cash payment related to the value of the suggestion. L.S.

Successful Suggestion Schemes (Industrial Society, 1958).

Supermarket Officially defined in Britain as a retail establishment of not less than 2,000 square feet of sales area, operated on a self-service basis with three or more check-outs. In common parlance the term tends to embrace any type of self-service store using the check-out method of payment for goods selected. Self-service initially appeared in Britain in 1942 as a war-time expedient in the face of staff shortages. It leads to increased flexibility for display and in-store promotion of products (⟨⟩ Merchandising). The Co-operative Wholesale Society (⟨⟩ Co-operative Movement) led in introducing self-service into food trading, but not in broadening of their stocking policies. The conversion by many multiple chains of traditional food stores into supermarkets carrying a wide selection of dry goods led to a major managerial crisis. The much larger units involved in the trend towards one-stop shopping were unable to find capable managers from the conventional source of recruits. Discount houses are a special case of predominantly non-food supermarketing where the overhead costs and service offered to customers are kept to an absolute minimum. The first store of this kind was opened in Southend-on-Sea in 1962. Their growth has been slow compared to that of the conventional supermarket, which offers a congenial shopping environment and customer service, whilst obtaining major economies from saved labour costs and high stock turn-round. In the early 1980s, however, super-stores and shopping malls have taken a firm hold on retailing, with many retailers taking the initiative to establish the centres, thereby catching up with a pattern that had emerged in the USA some ten or fifteen years earlier. G.S.C.W.

Supervisory Training ◊ Industrial Training.

Supply of Goods and Services The Supply of Goods and Services Act 1982 was passed to clarify the law regarding the supply of goods other than by way of a contract covered by previous legislation, such as sale or hire purchase, and contracts for services.

Part I of the Act concerns contracts for work and materials (e.g. repairs and servicing), exchange, barter, leasing, hire, or so-called 'free' gifts. It provides that contracts for goods supplied in these circumstances will contain broadly the same implied conditions as contracts for the ◊ Sale of Goods, i.e. that the goods will be as described and reasonably fit for their purpose, etc.

Part II of the Act requires that all contracts for the supply of a service, with limited exceptions, should be performed within a reasonable time, with reasonable care and skill and, if no price has been agreed, for a reasonable price.

Exclusion of these terms is subject to the Unfair Contract Terms Act 1977 (◊ Exclusion Clauses). J.C.E.M.

G. Woodroffe, *Goods and Services: The New Law* (Sweet & Maxwell, 1982).

Supply-side Economics The phrase came to prominence in the early 1980s with the election of President Reagan in the United States. Hence the ideas behind it are sometimes popularly known as 'Reaganomics', although the term was first used by Professor Herbert Stein of the University of Virginia in 1976 to describe a new way of looking at fiscal policy. The ideas were also embraced in the UK by the Conservative Government of Mrs Thatcher. Instead of stressing demand-management policies as the major determinant of output, much more attention is paid to the allocation and efficient use of labour and capital in the economy.

Particular stress is therefore laid on cutting taxes to increase incentives, breaking up restrictive practices by business and organized labour, making training and education more responsive to industrial needs and cutting the size and role of the public sector of the economy. L.T.S.

B. Bartlett, 'Supply-side Economics: Theory and Evidence', *National Westminster Bank Quarterly Review* (February 1985).

Synergy Synergy is said to have taken place when the combined return on a firm's resources is greater than the sum of its parts. It is sometimes known as the 'two-plus-two-equals-five effect'.

When a company adds to its existing activities the new activity will make use of the company's existing resources to a greater or lesser extent: the extent to which it does so is the extent of the synergy arising from this new activity. Where there is no relation at all between the new and existing activities there will be no synergy, i.e. the return on investment of the company as a whole will simply be the return on the existing activities plus that of the new activity. But where the new activity makes use of existing resources, the return for the company as a whole will be greater than the simple weighted average of the new and existing activities (two plus two equals five).

Synergy can arise from the commonality of resources required by the new and existing activities including not only such physical resources as factories, transport facilities, etc., but also management competence, know-how, research, marketing, operations and starting up economies. In estimating the extent of synergy likely to be obtained from a project, it is possible to prepare a 'capability profile' for the company to determine how far the new activity might mesh with the existing activities. This profile is similar to a list of ⟨⟩ Strengths and Weaknesses. A.J.A.A.

H. Igor Ansoff, *Corporate Strategy* (McGraw-Hill, 1965).

Synthetic Timing An alternative to direct ⟨⟩ Time Study, i.e. a technique for indirectly obtaining basic times for jobs by using: (1) element times from previous time studies; (2) element times from previous studies of other jobs containing the same elements; (3) data derived from an analysis of suitable accumulated data.

Synthetic timing is of particular value where direct time study would be uneconomical or impractical, e.g. on a new job, on short-run jobs, etc. Furthermore it is a more reliable and consistent method, since data from several studies are normally used and the use of a stop-watch on the shop-floor is avoided.

Synthetic timing normally produces basic times, to which appropriate allowances must be added. The procedure normally involves analysing data accumulated from previous time studies and data obtained specifically for the purpose of developing synthetic data.

Three types of job element exist: (1) machine elements, controlled entirely by the machine, e.g. speed, feed, etc.; (2) constant elements; (3) variable elements, which, whilst of a similar motion pattern, vary with changes in, say, weight, distance, etc.

Machine and constant elements usually present no problems. Variable elements are examined to determine the influence of the various factors and possible basic times under varying conditions are expressed as equations, tables or curves. R.W.

System Loss Although a fixed standard time is allowed for a job operation, usually as a result of ⟫ Work Measurement, the worker does not complete every cycle in the same time. An individual's operation cycle time varies, usually forming a positively skewed unimodal dis-

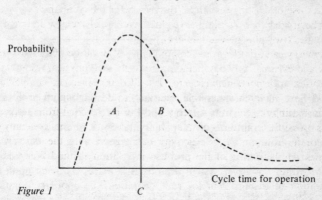

Figure 1

tribution (see figure above).

If a fixed time is allowed for the operation, say *C*, then on some occasions the worker will be able to complete the operation in less than the allowed time (area *A*) and on other occasions will be unable to complete the operation (area *B*). This results in system loss, which has two components corresponding to the two areas.

(1) The worker will be able to complete the operation in less than the allowed time, and hence either waiting time will result or the worker will work more slowly. In either case an underutilization of labour results.

(2)   The worker will be unable to complete the operation, the job will
       pass on to the next operation incomplete and defectives will be
       produced.

Increasing the allowed time for the operation does not reduce total
system loss (it merely reduces area *B* and increases area *A*). Only one
satisfactory solution exists, i.e. to provide a tolerance about the allowed
time as, for example, in figure 2. ⟡ Pacing R.W.

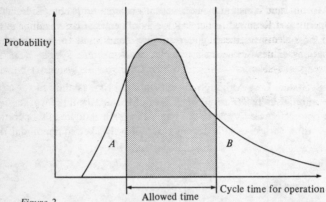

Figure 2

Systemicity A systematic approach to dealing with a problem is
exemplified by ⟡ Systems Analysis and Design. It requires the setting of
objectives, the collection of data, examination of alternatives and the
choice of a solution. A systemic approach takes a much broader view. It
recognizes the nature of the problem in relation to the whole and its
place within the larger system. Emphasis is placed as much upon the
definition of the problem (or root definition), as upon the solution.
Much attention is paid to the *Weltanschauung* (literally the 'world view',
or current attitudes) and to environmental conditions. R.S.S.

    P. C. Checkland, *Systems Thinking, System Practice* (J. Wiley, 1981).

Systems Analysis and Design Before a computer can be installed in
a business application a number of investigations must be performed.
These can usefully be grouped into three stages: (1) *feasibility study*,
which determines whether it is feasible on economic and/or technological
grounds for a computer to perform the desired task. If it is feasible, this
is followed by (2) the *system analysis* stage, which determines the
structure of the existing system into which the proposed computer in-

stallation will be introduced, and (3) the *system design* stage, which is the complete design of the new computer-based system.

The individuals who perform the systems investigations, as distinct from the detailed computer programming, are known as systems analysts. However, in some companies the distinction between the two roles is not clear-cut and one individual may perform both tasks in a given project.

The term systems analysis is also used to a limited extent as a synonym for two other activities not necessarily associated with computers: (1) ◊ Operational Research, since O R workers analyse man–machine systems; (2) systems engineering, a term sometimes used to describe the engineering of new large-scale complex man–machine systems (e.g. a new weapons system, or an intercontinental microwave system). M.J.C.M.

Systems Dynamics ◊ Simulation

T

Tactics Short-term decisions made in response to changing circumstances so as to make the best use of existing resources. Tactical decisions are also those taken to put into effect the details of a strategic decision. These two types of tactical planning result from the fact that strategic plans are usually broad statements concerning the continued use of existing resources or the introduction of new ones. The cardinal feature of the first type, also known as operational planning, is that it consists more of re-planning or revision of plans than of original planning. Circumstances change so rapidly – there may be a surge in demand, a breakdown, a strike at a supplier's premises, a snowstorm – that an operational planner's function must be mainly to revise previously laid plans in response to these events. The sequence of such planning is as follows: (1) a plan for the best use of resources is made for a week, a month or sometimes a year ahead, based upon a forecast of demand, stocks, production capacities, and so on; (2) actual results are monitored; (3) a divergence from the original plan is observed; (4) a new plan is devised, monitored, revised again, and so on, often with a very short time-cycle.

In the sense of the detailed implementation of a strategy, tactics often involve the introduction of new resources. Thus a strategic plan may call for 'the opening of ten new branches in important city centres'. It is then left to the discretion of an executive to decide when and where such branches are to be opened. Precisely which street should be chosen in which city, the best shopping day on which the opening ceremony should be held, and so on, are tactical considerations. ⬦ Strategy. A.J.A.A.

Takeover ⬦ Mergers

Target The precise restatement of an objective, often in figures. Objectives are often stated in rather general, broad terms. Targets are usually precise and unequivocal translations of these. Thus it may be a company's objective 'to improve its return on capital'. Restated as a target this might be 'to raise return on capital to 15 per cent in five years' time' – an aim that is so precise that there can be little doubt whether the company has actually achieved it or not. In the same way an executive may be given the objective of improving labour efficiency; the target may be 'to improve output per head by 4 per cent every year until further notice'.

As a general rule a target set for a company or an individual should be pitched at a level that is challenging but attainable, and it is advisable to discuss the appropriateness of any target with individuals before they are officially expected to achieve it as part of their duties. It is important that the target figure should be verifiable – i.e. that it is possible to determine unequivocally that the target figure has or has not been achieved by the target date. ⟨⟩ Management by Objectives. A.J.A.A.

Taxation (Accounting Treatment) Profits chargeable to taxation for a period often bear little relationship to the profits stated in the accounts for the same period. There are two main reasons for this. First, profits for tax purposes may exclude some income included for accounting purposes, or may be struck after disallowing certain expenses included in the profit-and-loss account; these are 'permanent differences' between taxable and accounting profits. Second, there are 'timing differences' when the accounting period for tax purposes differs from that for accounting purposes. Examples of timing differences are the disallowance for tax purposes of certain provisions; the use of a receipts or payments basis in certain cases for tax purposes whilst an accruals basis is used for accounting purposes; the writing-off of certain capital expenditures more quickly for tax purposes than for accounting purposes. It is clear that the impact of 'timing' and 'permanent' differences between accounting and taxable profits depends, respectively, upon the changing objectives and effects of fiscal legislation over time. 'Stock relief', introduced as a timing difference in the Finance Act 1975, was designed to defer the payment of tax arising on those unrealized profits that were simply the result of inflation and its effect on the valuation of stocks. Because continuing stock relief has resulted in an accumulation of untaxed accounting profit for many companies, it is widely assumed to have acquired the status of a 'permanent' difference; this is despite the strict interpretation that the relief was intended as a deferral, not a cancellation, of legitimate tax liabilities.

Accounting follows the accruals concept and requires that revenues and costs are accrued, matched and dealt with in the profit-and-loss account of the period to which they relate. For accounting purposes, taxation should follow the same rule and the taxation expense shown in the profit-and-loss account should be based on the profits stated in the accounts rather than on the profits chargeable to taxation. Where taxation is deferred (e.g. because tax allowances for capital expenditure exceed the depreciation charged in the accounts), it is generally considered that the benefit of the deferment should be disregarded and the full amount of taxation ultimately due on the accounting profits should be charged as an expense of the period to which the accounting profits relate. The deferred taxation is then recorded separately on the balance sheet. Although this treatment took effect as 'preferred practice' from 1 January 1974, the Accounting Standards Steering Committee is currently continuing to seek a long-standing solution to what has become a protracted debate on the subject.

A different problem concerns the treatment of taxation on dividends and certain other distributions. Since 1 April 1973, when a company pays a dividend it is required to account to the tax authorities for advanced corporation tax (ACT) within fourteen days of the end of the quarter in which the dividend was paid. The ACT is subsequently allowable as a credit (subject to certain restrictions) against the 'mainstream' corporation tax liability of the company. For accounting purposes dividends paid should be shown net and the related ACT should be included in the charge for taxation. In the presentation of the profit-and-loss account, written off ACT should be treated as a charge in arriving at profits after tax (and should therefore be separately disclosed) and not shown as an appropriation of profit. P.J.A.H.

Taylor, Frederick Winslow (1856–1915) His contribution towards the establishment of the very notion of ⬦ Scientific Management is but one of the achievements for which F. W. Taylor is remembered.

Taylor was born in Philadelphia. Medical problems and the prevailing American labour situation forced him to accept employment as a labourer with the Midvale Steel Company but, following a phenomenal series of promotions, he became Chief Engineer at the age of thirty-one. His later studies of work rationalization at the Bethlehem Steel Company are probably the most frequently cited examples in the area of management. Taylor developed a comprehensive policy for the study of human work, stressing the importance of such aspects as the need to analyse and investigate each separate element of a task; the importance of selection and training procedures; the role of proper communication and co-operation between the two sides of industry and the need for equality in the divisions of labour and responsibility.

Four years before his death in 1915, Taylor founded the Society to Promote the Science of Management, later renamed in his honour the Taylor Society. E.E.

T. Kempner, 'Frederick Taylor and Scientific Management' in Tillet,

Kempner and Wills (eds.), *Management Thinkers* (Penguin, 2nd ed., 1978); M. Warner, *Organizations and Experiments* (J. Wiley, 1984), ch. 3.

Taylorism ◊ Scientific Management

Teams Attention to teams in an organizational context is a relatively recent phenomenon. From the 1950s onwards, the complexity of the products and processes typical of the aerospace, chemical and electronic industries necessitated the employment of scientists and technologists from many different disciplines. A high proportion of them worked on research and development, frequently at the boundaries of existing knowledge, where the lines of distinction between disciplines were blurred. To ensure that the available resources were combined efficiently to meet the needs of research and development, many enterprises began to organize work in these fields on the basis of multidisciplinary project teams. Complex tasks like developing a new product were categorized as projects, each of these being assigned to a project leader.

Also in the 1950s the social scientist Rensis Likert presented a view of organization structure as a system of interlocking groups. Within this system each manager in the chain of command functions as a member of his or her superior's managerial team, and in turn as the leader of a team of subordinates. Subsequently consultants like Richard Beckhard concerned with developing organizations into effective systems assumed that teams were the basic units to be changed or modified.

Beckhard has observed that although work teams are interdependent, they are prone to inappropriate competition with each other, which can reduce the overall effectiveness of the enterprise. Team members can be similarly competitive, making it ineffective. For these reasons, consultants often aim to increase organizational effectiveness by improving the relationship between teams or their members, or their methods of working together, as exemplified in the ◊ Managerial Grid approach to change.

In another study of management teams, R. M. Belbin found that effectiveness depended upon having the right combination of individuals in the team, with complementary personalities and abilities. Under normal circumstances, the leader of the team should attend to the setting of its overall objectives and progress towards them, whilst encouraging all team members to contribute to the group effort, treating all contributors on their merits and without prejudice. If, however, a team appears inactive and complacent, a new and different kind of leader may be required to galvanize it into action by an exhibition of drive, a readiness to challenge inertia and ineffectiveness, impatience, opportunism and tough-mindedness.

Effective teams of managers also include someone creative, intellectually able with high critical thinking ability, and imaginative, who can come up with original solutions to problems facing the team. Where the problem relates to the provision of resources or the satisfaction of customer needs, a more extrovert member with a wide range of personal contacts and the ability to respond to a challenge is more likely to offer a solution. In addition. to get the desired results the team needs at least one member who is a good organizer, conscientious and practical and who is committed to implementing the policies and plans agreed by the team; one who is something of a perfectionist to set high standards and attend to detail, and another who possesses the qualities of detachment, hard-headedness and sound judgement to readily assess the value of the ideas and proposals put before the team. Finally an effective team usually has one member who is good at smoothing out disagreements and building up cohesion. In practice an adaptable person may be able to perform well in several roles, so that a highly effective team of managers may be formed of just three or four individuals, although five or six is more usual. E.L.

R. Beckhard, *Organization Development: Strategies and Models* (Addison-Wesley, 1969); R. M. Belbin, *Management Teams: Why They Succeed or Fail* (Heinemann, 1981); M. Woodcock, *Team Development Manual* (Gower, 1979).

Technological Forecasting The process of identifying and assessing future threats and opportunities arising from the development of relevant technology. As such it is a positive rather than a passive process, which can lead to management action designed to change any forecast probabilities. It is a new technique that has emerged with the accelerating rate of change in technology, and is an important tool in effective long-range planning (⟡ Corporate Planning). It will not necessarily predict the precise form in which a technology will evolve, nor the exact timing. As in any forecast, however, it must evaluate the probabilities of future technological changes and their concomitant significance. The rate at which any innovation is diffused through the economy is an important element in the forecast, as is the development within companies of pressures for innovation as existing products reach a mature stage in their life cycle (⟡ New Product). Certain aspects of technological development appear to be beyond the scope of such forecasting, e.g. unpredictable interactions, termed 'spin-offs', unprecedented demand, major new discoveries. The task of integrating forecasts into current decisions is a major problem for management. An American journal deals exclusively with the subject, *Technological Forecasting* (Elsevier). G.S.C.W.

G. S. C. Wills, *Technological Forecasting* (Penguin, 1971).

Technology and Organization The system of machines, equipment and technical methods fundamental to economic performance, together with their associated knowledge, beliefs and values.

Technology, surprisingly neglected for so long by students of organizational behaviour, has been recognized in the last decade or so as an extremely important variable. Joan Woodward showed a relationship between technology (in terms of unit, batch, mass or process production) and organizational structure. By so doing, she demonstrated that many of the principles of management formulated by the classical theorists were specific and not universal application.

It is now known, therefore, that a relationship exists between technology and organizational (and hence social) structure and process. However, this is not to say that organizational structure is determined solely by technology: the work of the Tavistock Institute drew attention to the possibility of basing different organizational arrangements on the same technology. Nevertheless, similar technologies are likely to give rise to *broadly* similar organizational structures and behaviour by limiting the range of structural and behavioural alternatives from which a choice can be made. ⟨⟩ Socio-technical System. I.C.MCG.

J. Woodward, *Industrial Organization: Theory and Practice* (OUP, 1965); M. R. Haug and J. Dofny, *Work and Technology* (Sage Publications, 1977); J. J. J. van Dijk, 'The Socio-technical Approach to Organizations', in P. J. D. Drenth *et al.*, (eds.) *Handbook of Work and Organizational Psychology*, vol. 2 (J. Wiley, 1984).

Telecommunications Communications is the oldest constituent technology of ⟨⟩ Information Technology (IT). The electric telegraph was deployed in the 1840s and was followed by the telephone in the 1880s. Despite the appearance of some text-mode services such as telex, voice has always been the main requirement for public communication services. Telephone technology was based upon analogue techniques and resulted in a huge investment in equipment, all of which was designed to handle voice signals and was quite unsuited for handling digital data. The world-wide telephone system is said to be the largest and most complex man-made device on earth; there are 600 million telephones, all of which can be interconnected. The number of telephones per 100 head of population is a good measure of a country's state of development. The distribution is very uneven at present: there are more telephones in the city of Tokyo than in the whole of Africa.

Microelectronics technology is gradually converting the world's telephone systems to digital operation. This is a complex job. It is relatively straightforward to convert the transmission and switching elements of the inner part of the network to digital operation, but it is a much slower job to convert the edges of the network – the underground copper wires and the telephone instrument in homes or business premises. Some 70 per cent of the capital investment is represented by these mundane peripheral parts of the network.

When the need arose for computers to inter-communicate digital data it was therefore necessary to make special arrangements. Devices called 'modems' can be used to exploit an ordinary telephone connection, but the speed and reliability are limited. Separate networks specially for data can be set up, and a technique called 'packet switching' has proved particularly useful for this. The ultimate solution, though, is to recognize that the world is becoming digital, and that once signals are in digital form it is immaterial to the communication system whether they represent speech, data, text or image. The current thrust is towards the 'integrated services digital network' (ISDN). The ISDN will (and in some countries already can) carry all types of communication traffic, or services, on a single digital network. It is the communication system of the future.

Communication technology has made immense progress, with developments such as satellite communications, high-capacity fibre-optic cable systems for terrestrial and submarine use, computer-controlled switching systems and mobile radio systems. Nevertheless the cost of communications is relatively higher than that of computing. Both are falling, but the cost of computing is falling more quickly. Communication costs are therefore one of the major factors affecting the designs of a computing or information system serving many dispersed sites.

Another is the compatibility of the different pieces of equipment involved in a communication system. Historically the communications community has worked by establishing standards and then building equipment that complies with those standards; communications will not work unless this is done. In contrast the computing community has not been motivated in the same way. Different equipment manufacturers have developed their own sets of standards and some see it in their commercial interest to continue to do so. However, the International Organization for Standardization (ISO), in concert with the Telegraph and Telephone Consultative Committee (CCITT), the equivalent body for telecommunications, has taken the initiative to establish a set of standards that will deal not only with communications but also the interworking of computers. The initiative is called the Open Systems Interconnection (OSI) and the standards are progressively being defined. A major consideration in procuring a computer system that can evolve in the future is the question of which standards to adopt. In several countries there is considerable government and other support for the OSI work.

The communications scene has been transformed not only by the advances in technology but also by radical change in the legal framework regulating it. The traditional view in most countries has been that communications is a natural monopoly of the state, like the postal service. In the UK telecommunications was a state monopoly from 1863 until 1981. The British Telecommunications Act of 1981 and the Telecommunications Act of 1984 have changed the situation completely. There is now competition between two national providers of basic communications (British Telecom and Mercury) and the provision of more complex services (so-called value-added network services, or VANS) is open to almost unlimited competition. Services such as electronic mail, financial systems, ticket reservation, viewdata and others now operate in a fully competitive market. This has transformed traditional attitudes and brought a much wider range of choice to the user. The competitive environment has also meant changes in the tariff structure, which have undermined traditional assumptions about the cost-effectiveness of large organizations running their own private communication networks. Continual reassessment is now essential. Similar 'liberalization' of telecommunications has taken place in the USA and Japan, and is likely to pervade much of Europe.

In summary the world's communication systems are changing from analogue to digital operation. The new digital systems such as the ISDN are being designed to handle all forms of traffic. Technical advances together with a radical change of legal framework have made communications a fast-moving and highly competitive field. Examples of communication systems are given in the entry for ⟡ Information System. D.J.S.

Peter Zorkoczy, *Information Technology – An Introduction* (Pitman, 2nd ed., 1985).

Temperature ⟡ Heat

Test Marketing ⟡ Marketing Experimentation

T-group ◊ Group Methods of Training

Therbligs The activities of a worker can be described in terms of eighteen fundamental elements. Each of these elements is called a therblig, after Frank B. Gilbreth, who was initially responsible for defining fundamental work elements.

The classification is based on an analysis of the purpose for which a movement is made, rather than on physiological definitions. Because of the precise nature of therblig descriptions, their use facilitates very detailed method study. Therbligs are normally used in conjunction with ◊ Simo Charts and involve the use of motion photography to record the movement. These two elements constitute the basic technique of micromotion study (◊ Method Study).

Each therblig is identified by a symbol and colour, see chart on p. 521.

N.B. The therblig 'Find' is sometimes omitted since it is considered as equivalent to select. R.W.

J. Barnes, *Motion and Time Study* (J. Wiley, 6th ed., 1968).

Threshold One of the most intensively investigated of human functions is that of sensitivity to incoming sensory stimulation. Two types of threshold may be described for each sensory modality. The absolute threshold defines the minimum strength of signal that is detectable. The differential threshold defines the minimum change in the signal that gives rise to a detectable subjective difference.

No single threshold value can be quoted for any sensory channel, since the detectability of signals depends upon a large number of factors. In the case of light, for example, the absolute threshold is dependent upon such factors as wavelength, duration of signal, state of adaptation of the eye, and part of the retina receiving the signal (◊ Adaptation; Colour). There is a further complication in that an individual's threshold will fluctuate from moment to moment. The convention is to define the threshold as the amplitude of the signal perceived 50 per cent of the time.

Differential thresholds are governed largely by Weber's Law, which states that subjective differences in signal amplitudes depend upon *proportional* increases in signal strength. ◊ Ergonomics. E.E.

Time-sharing (Computers) Since a ◊ Computer consists of a number of specialist units that can work partially independently of each other, it is desirable to co-ordinate their operations so as to obtain the most efficient overall working.

Symbol	Name	Colour
⊃	Search	Black
⊂⊃	Find	Grey
→	Select	Light grey
∩	Grasp	Red
⊓	Hold	Gold ochre
⌣	Transport load	Green
9	Position	Blue
#	Assemble	Violet
∪	Use	Purple
⧣	Disassemble	Light violet
◯	Inspect	Burnt ochre
⚇	Pre-position	Pale blue
⌢	Release load	Carmine red
⌣	Transport empty	Olive green
⌐	Rest for overcoming fatigue	Orange
⌃	Unavoidable delay	Yellow
⌣ₒ	Avoidable delay	Lemon yellow
ℓ	Plan	Brown

When a computer performs a calculation the program and data pass in sequence through the input unit, processor and output unit. For most of the duration of the calculation two of the three units will be idle and clearly such an arrangement is inefficient. If a way can be found for the computer to handle several calculations simultaneously by performing the different stages of the calculations on the different units simultaneously (e.g. if the input for one calculation is fed in simultaneously with the output from another being fed out), higher equipment utilization will be obtained. Such an arrangement is known as time-sharing.

Time-sharing may be achieved by having special electronic equipment (hardware) or special programs (software) providing control routines that enable peripheral units to work simultaneously (in parallel). Arrangements can also be made for a number of programs to be processed simultaneously on the computer as a whole. Interchange of the programs between individual units is arranged according to a set of priority rules so as to make maximal use of facilities. The manipulations of the programs are under the control of a master, or executive, program. This facility is also known as parallel or multi-programming.

A development of growing importance is the provision of units that give remote access to a computer operating on a time-sharing basis. A teletypewriter unit in, say, Yorkshire can be linked directly by telephone line to a computer in London. Users in Yorkshire dial a telephone number and their unit is immediately connected to the computer, which they may then use, just as if it were in the same room. A number of companies in the UK and USA offer such computing facilities and it is a mode of operation that will grow rapidly. Details of two current uses of remote-access terminals are described under ⟡ Computer. M.J.C.M.

Time-span of Discretion 'The longest period which can elapse in a role before the manager can be sure that his subordinate has not been exercising marginally sub-standard discretion continuously in balancing the pace and the quality of his work' (Elliot Jaques, *Time-span Handbook*). The concept was developed by Jaques in the course of his work with the Glacier Metal Company and arose out of an attempt to establish salary levels and differentials that would be regarded universally as equitable. Although it was appreciated that length of service might be accorded some recognition through a system of increments, it was considered that basic salary should be closely related to the level of work performed. Existing systems of job evaluation seemed to be inadequate in that they included elements not directly related to work content and failed to identify the factor or factors in the work itself which might meaningfully be measured for payment purposes. There was, Jaques claimed, a discernible consensus as to the appropriate payment, whether expressed in hourly, weekly, monthly or annual rates, for a given level of work. Analysis of the nature of work suggested the existence of two elements: a prescribed content and a discretionary content. The prescribed content consists of that aspect of the task that is subject to detailed instructions so that the performer has simply to obey: there is no feeling of responsibility. The discretionary content consists of the aspect of the task in which the performer must exercise personal judgement: here a weight of responsibility is felt. The notion of equitable pay was considered to be related to the discretionary content and the attempt to measure this element led to the development of the time-span of discretion. Time-span theory is a useful addition to the growing body of knowledge of ⟨⟩ Work Measurement, yet it has been strongly criticized from several quarters. Economists complain that the theory ignores both the effect and the legitimacy of economic forces influencing payment structures, and sociologists reject the basic thesis that time-span is the only factor influencing subjective judgements about the fairness of pay.

Like Frederick W. Taylor half a century before him, Jaques believed that the universal application of his system would eliminate the chief cause of conflict between management and employee, in that objective measurement would replace collective bargaining. However, as might be expected, few trade unionists have been prepared to concede to management control of wage differentials based on time-span analysis and its main application has been in salary, as distinct from wage, administration. I.C.McG.

Elliot Jaques, *Time-span Handbook* (Heinemann, 1964); Elliot Jaques, *Equitable Payment* (Heinemann, 1961); Alan Fox, *The Time-span of Discretion Theory: An Appraisal* (IPM 1966); D. S. Pugh *et al.*, *Writers on Organizations* (Penguin, new ed., 1984), pp. 193–8.

Time Study 'A work measurement technique for recording the times and rates of working for the elements of a specified job carried out under specified conditions and for analysing the data so as to obtain the time necessary for carrying out the job at a defined level of performance' (British Standard 3138).

Time study is now normally considered that part of ⟨⟩ Work Measurement concerned with the direct timing of job elements by means of a suitable time device (e.g. a stop-watch). This distinguishes it from indirect time-study methods such as ⟨⟩ Synthetic Timing, ⟨⟩ Predetermined Motion Time Study and analytical ⟨⟩ Estimating.

The object of time study is to establish the time that should be required by a worker to do a job in a prescribed manner, under standard conditions and at a defined level of performance. Such data are of value (1) to calculate work schedules; (2) to assist in ⟨⟩ Method Study; (3) for incentive schemes; (4) to determine standard costs; (5) to determine labour requirements; (6) to measure operating efficiency; (7) for machine allocation, etc.

Direct time study normally involves the following steps. (1) Divide the job into elements for convenience of study. (2) Time a sufficient number of elements to obtain the observed time. (3) Rate the worker's performance for each of the timed elements in order to convert the observed time to the basic time.

$$\text{Basic time} = \frac{\text{Observed time} \times \text{Observed rating}}{\text{Standard rating}}$$

Standard rating = 100 on the British Standard scale. Standard rating corresponds to the 'average rate at which qualified workers will naturally work at a job, provided they know and adhere to the specified method and provided they are motivated to apply themselves to their work' (British Standard 3138). ⟡ Performance Rating. (4) Add ⟡ Allowances to the basic time to obtain the standard time. R.W.

R. M. Currie, *The Measurement of Work* (BIM, 1963); R. G. Seabourne, *Introduction to Work Study and Statistics* (Longman, 1971).

Tracking Much of the study of human control performance has taken the form of experiments on tracking: the subject is faced with a moving display and is required to carry out appropriate movements in an attempt to minimize an error function.

There are two basic designs of tracking task. In pursuit tracking subjects see both a target, over which they have no control, and a follower, whose position is determined by them. Their task is to keep the follower upon the target. Such a task might be performed by an anti-aircraft gunner. In compensatory tracking there is only one moving part on the display, the position of which is determined partly by the tracker's control movements and partly by external circumstances. An example of a compensatory task is a motorist attempting to drive at constant speed over undulating country.

Tracking accuracy is a function of such variables as the shape and speed of the independent track, the type of display and control used, in addition to the skill of the individual tracker. ⟡ Ergonomics. E.E.

M. Hammerton, 'Tracking', in D. H. Holding (ed.), *Human Skills* (J. Wiley, 1981).

Trade Association ⟡ Employers' Association

Trade Dispute The organizing of strikes is not legally actionable by those who suffer financial loss in consequence so long as the immunity contained in the Trade Union and Labour Relations Act 1979 operates (⟡ Strikes – and the Law). That immunity is only available, however, where the organizers have acted 'in contemplation of furtherance of a trade dispute'. This formula requires there to be a dispute that is imminent or already in existence between workers and their own employer and that 'relates wholly or mainly to' one or more specified matters, including terms and conditions of employment, hiring and firing, discipline, the allocation of work, etc. Some disputes between the Government and certain workers (such as teachers) are treated as trade disputes even though technically the Government is not their immediate employer. This will be so where a government minister can effectively veto any negotiations or settlement through a statutory power or through representation on some statutory joint body.

Strikes that are not predominantly concerned with matters of economic self-interest to the immediate parties involved do not qualify as trade disputes and so do not attract the statutory immunity in the 1974 Act. Such disputes are sometimes described as 'political strikes' although this phrase should be used cautiously, since a strike may still be a trade dispute, despite some extraneous motive, so long as it is mainly about terms and conditions, etc. On the other hand there would be no trade dispute where a strike was called merely to protest about the passage of legislation, for example, or to object to the privatization of a nationalized industry in circumstances where there was no genuine fear of consequent job losses. Where there is no trade dispute, those employers directly affected by the industrial action may sue in the courts.

Regardless of whether a particular strike does constitute a trade dispute, government has a number of options that may help resolve matters. ACAS may be asked to make its services available; a court of inquiry into the circumstances of the dispute could be convened; or, where essential services are threatened, troops can be called on by virtue of the emergency powers legislation. ⬧ Strikes – and the Law. K.W.

O. Kahn-Freund, *Labour and the Law* (Stevens & Sons, 3rd ed. by P. Davies and M. Freedland, 1983), ch. 8.

Trade Mark Some distinguishing mark that is used on or in connection with goods with a view to indicating that these goods are those of the owner of the trade mark. The owner of the trade mark may be a manufacturer or a retailer.

In order to acquire property rights to a trade mark it is necessary to register it with the Registrar of Trade Marks. The registration is valid for seven years but may be renewed for up to another fourteen years. A trade mark may be assigned by its owner, generally in connection with the sale of a business. W.F.E., amended by J.C.E.M.

A. Michaels, *A Practical Guide to Trade Marks* (ESC Publishing, 1982).

Trade Union – Amalgamations There has been a marked tendency for the number of trade unions to decline over time. In 1965 there were

172 trade unions affiliated to the ⟨⟩ T U C, a figure which had declined to 93 in 1984. The spur to this development is considerable merger activity encouraged by the Trade Union (Amalgamation) Act 1964. Moreover industrial unions are vulnerable to changes in the fortunes of particular industries and craft unions to the exigencies of technological change (⟨⟩ Trade Union – Types). These pressures tend to produce amalgamations, usually with large general unions. The consequence, too, is that membership of British unions has become increasingly concentrated into the largest associations (80 per cent of union members are in associations with over 100,000 members). M.J.F.P.

R. Undy, V. Ellis, W. E. J. McCarthy and A. M. Halmos, *Change in Trade Unions* (Hutchinson, 1981); *Annual Report of the Certification Officer* (1984); *Trade-Union Congress Directory* (1985).

Trade Union – at Law The Trade Union and Labour Relations Act 1974 defines a trade union as an organization of workers whose principal purposes include the regulation of relations with employers, or a federation of such organizations. The organization may be permanent or temporary. 'Worker' is defined to include employees, independent contractors and Crown servants. A trade union is an 'independent' trade union if it is not employer dominated, nor employer controlled, nor subject to interference by an employer tending towards such control. It is important to know whether a trade union is 'independent' since, while it would be an unfair dismissal if an employee were dismissed for refusing to join or to remain in a non-independent union, it would not be unfair if the union in question were an independent one.

The legal status of trade unions since 1974 is that the union is treated as an unincorporated association but it still enjoys some of the privileges of an incorporated body, e.g. it may sue or be sued in its registered name and it may enter into contracts in that name. This means for example that a member can sue to prevent officials acting contrary to the union's rule book, which constitutes a contractually binding constitution defining the rights of the union and its members. Consequently no member can be expelled or otherwise disciplined except in accordance with the terms of the rule book. Since 1980 members and would-be members have had an additional statutory right to complain of 'unreasonable' exclusion or expulsion by a union operating a closed shop at their place of work. Here reasonableness is not defined exclusively by what the rule book contains.

The registration of trade unions is voluntary. The Certification Officer maintains a register of listed trade unions. Listed trade unions enjoy certain advantages compared with unregistered ones, i.e. tax relief on provident income and easier transfer of property standing in their name.

The legal position of unions has varied widely over the years. For much of the nineteenth century they were regarded as illegal organizations because they unreasonably restrained trade. After 1871, when voluntary registration was first introduced, unions were by statute also freed of the effects of the restraint of trade doctrine. In 1906, following judgment in the *Taff Vale* case, a Liberal government, fearful that court actions by employers seeking compensation for strike losses would bankrupt the trade union movement, gave unions what amounted to an absolute immunity in tort (though not in contract). In recent years the desirability of so wide an immunity was called in question and in 1982 it was repealed. Now a union is only protected where an individual strike organizer would be (⟡ Strikes – and the Law). The Employment Act 1982 also makes unions vicariously liable for all unlawful industrial action that designated categories of officials have authorized or endorsed. ⟡ Freedom of Association; Closed Shop. W.F.F., amended by K.W.

R. Kidner, *Trade Union Law* (Stevens & Sons, 2nd ed., 1983), ch. 1.

Trade Union – Ballots The term ballot covers all circumstances in which an individual union member records his or her vote on a specific issue or policy in an election. It may be more or less secret and the votes may be counted at workplace, branch, union office or outside the premises (the ballot paper itself being returned via shop steward, branch officer or postal services). A *secret ballot* covers circumstances where a ballot is obviously held in secret and a *postal ballot* refers to arrangements involving the dispatch and return of ballots through the post.

Many unions have used ballots for both the election of officers and for strikes or other industrial action but the issue has assumed a particular prominence as a result of the ⟡ Trade Union Act 1984. The provisions of the Act stipulate that members of trade union governing bodies should be directly elected by individual secret ballot of the union's members. Its purpose is also to make trade unions' immunity for organizing industrial action conditional on the holding of secretly and properly conducted strike ballots and to enable members of trade unions with political funds to vote at regular intervals on whether trade unions should continue to spend money on purely political matters. The effect on actual union behaviour remains to be seen. But it is clear that ballots do not necessarily increase union democracy (active participation by the ordinary member in policy and oppositional checks may be far more important), nor do they guarantee the election of moderate leaders. M.J.F.P.

R. Undy and R. Martin, *Ballots and Trade Union Democracy* (Blackwell,

1984); Department of Employment, *Employment Gazette* (August 1984).

Trade Union – Communism Most British trade unions have rules that forbid party political activity within the union of the kind that is normal in national and local authority elections. Yet union elections in practice are often conducted on political lines. At times the Communist Party, too, has been prepared to violate democratic practices. This was demonstrated in the Electrical Trades Union ballot-rigging case heard in the High Court in 1961, as a result of which Frank Foulkes, President of the Union, and Frank Haxell, General Secretary, were removed from office. It was successfully claimed that elections for the Union's chief posts had for three years been fraudulently conducted by means of unlawful conspiracies to substitute, miscount, destroy or invalidate ballot papers. The influence of the Communist Party on British unions has probably declined over time but there remains a range of militant groupings that seek to shape trade union objectives and, if anything, the role of ⟡ Ideology in union politics is greater now than in the 1950s and early 1960s. N.H.C., amended by M.J.F.P.

Trade Union – Demarcation Demarcation is the marking out of a given job or set of jobs as appropriate to be carried out by the members of a given trade union. Demarcation disputes between unions are disputes about which union should have what job (⟡ Trade Dispute). Demarcation disputes should be distinguished from jurisdiction disputes about which unions should have what members.

The demarcation dispute is typical of unions of the closed, craft type. When confronted by changes in technology, they wish to extend or prevent a decline in their membership and so claim exclusive rights to a new job that has a fringe relationship to a job previously done solely by their members. Demarcation problems are most common in situations involving unions facing a long-term decline in membership.

Demarcation disputes can be and are prevented by resolute and efficient trade union leadership, together with resolute and efficient management. Foresight and early consultation are important. Where disputes of this type develop, management prefer to leave them to be settled by the unions concerned, who work through them without the aid of the TUC Disputes Committee, which has only an advisory role. However in a few industries (e.g. shipbuilding, building, civil engineering) employers have been parties to demarcation agreements, as their interests are clearly affected when a conflict over the allocation of work leads to a ⟡ Strike.

Demarcation disputes can be reduced by the amalgamation of rival craft or ex-craft unions, for example that of the shipwrights and the boilermakers in the shipbuilding industry. They may be prevented by productivity bargaining, not so much by the agreed introduction of multi-craftsmen as by the agreement that work on fringe jobs, usually done by one craft, may be carried out by members of another craft if they could do them equally well. Even where historical justifications for present-day demarcation practices no longer apply, they are so bound up with concepts of job security that productivity bargains aimed, *inter alia*, at their elimination may need to include guarantees by management against redundancy.

The fact that, historically, women were employed generally at lower rates of pay than men has resulted in a fairly clear and well-established demarcation between men's work and women's work throughout the greater part of manufacturing industry. N.H.C.

H. A. Clegg, *The System of Industrial Relations in Great Britain* (Blackwell, 1979).

Trade Union – Government and Administration Trade unions each have their individual character. A union's internal organization is a function of the aims, size and diversity of its membership, but a general picture can be drawn that does not do too much injustice to the realities of each separate situation. Typically the union has a pyramidal structure and the main lines of formal communication are expected to extend from the individual member through the branch, possibly via a district committee, to a national executive committee and, periodically, to a national delegate conference.

The branch (known in some unions by other names, e.g. lodge, club, chapel) is the basic organizational unit. Branches in their size, form and content of meetings should encourage the active co-operation of the membership, but their policy-making power varies from union to union. The branch is usually based on a geographical area and varies greatly in size; the Amalgamated Union of Engineering Workers has set a maximum of 300 members, while the Transport and General Workers' Union has had a branch of 9,000 members. The branch deals with applications for membership and provides for the collection of contributions and distribution of benefits. In a study of a branch in 1952 Joseph Goldstein emphasized membership apathy and showed that attendance at branch meetings could often be as low as 3 per cent. Clearly resolutions in the branch meetings need not necessarily represent the views of branch membership. It is often suggested that where numbers permit, unions should base their branches on the workplace, rather than on some wider geographical area, in order to stimulate greater interest and attendance and to tighten the link between the ⟨⟩ Shop Steward, the local leader at the workplace, and branch officials, who are responsible for formal two-way communication between the branch and the main body of the union. This can work well, as in the Steelworkers' Union, but in other cases, e.g. the National Union of Mineworkers, it has made no apparent contribution towards reducing independent, unofficial action.

District organizations are concerned with the proper functioning of branches in the district and with local negotiations. They are composed of delegates from branches and the secretary may be a lay member or a full-time official. Some have a wide measure of autonomy. The Transport and General Workers' Union also has regional committees, regional trade group (or 'industrial') committees, and national trade group committees.

The national executive committee is the governing body or top leadership of the union, responsible for its day-to-day operation and subject only to the national delegate conference. It can influence the conference, containing as it does the principal national officers, of whom the general secretary (⟨⟩ Trade Union–Officers) is normally the most important and who, except in the very small unions, is always a full-time official.

The national delegate conference, which meets annually or at longer intervals, is the supreme authority of the union and is usually composed of delegates from branches or larger units, together with the national executive committee. The committee normally presents to the conference a report on its work over the previous period and this is discussed. Motions and amendments are submitted by branches or district organizations. The conference is sometimes responsible for electing the principal lay officers, the full-time officials, the executive committee or part of it.

It is apparent that the study of a trade union as an organization cannot be effected solely by examination of its rule book. Both its formal and informal organization structures are products of more than its legal rules. Nevertheless rule books could often be clearer, and many might be redrafted with advantage, for example with regard to the rights of members. N.H.C.

J. Goldstein, *Government of British Trade Unions* (Allen & Unwin, 1952); J. D. Edelstein and M. Warner, *Comparative Union Democracy* (Allen & Unwin, 1975); R. Undy and R. Martin, *Ballots and Trade Union Democracy* (Blackwell, 1984).

Trade Union – Jurisdiction The jurisdiction of a trade union is, in effect, its sphere of influence in terms of membership and potential membership. Jurisdiction disputes between unions are about which unions should have what members (◇▷ Trade Dispute). Jurisdiction disputes should be distinguished from demarcation disputes (◇▷ Trade Union – Demarcation) about which union's members should have what jobs.

The strategy of a trade union determines the nature of its membership, i.e. the kinds of workers it will organize. Thus in Britain the recruitment area of the original, closed craft unions (◇▷ Trade Union Types – Craft Union) was clearly marked. This was not so for the newer, open unions, operating over a broad front (◇▷ Trade Union – Structure). Jurisdiction disputes, involving rivalry for the same potential membership, could thus arise. Rivalry can also clearly occur between two open unions.

Many British unions have developed agreements with rival organizations establishing methods of resolving jurisdictional conflict, but the key code of behaviour for settling such disputes has been laid down by the ◇▷ TUC. This is based on the recognition of established 'organizing rights' and was developed by the TUC Disputes Committee, set up specifically to summon unions in conflict, to hear evidence and to issue an award in each case. Sanction for disobeying the Committee's award is expulsion from the TUC, but this has only occurred in the case of two small unions.

'Procedures for the Avoidance of Disputes', known as the Bridlington Rules laid down at the 1939 TUC Congress, were developed from the Hull Rules of 1924. The Bridlington Rules require that no one who is, or who has recently been, a member of any trade union should be accepted into membership by another union without inquiry; that no union should accept a member of another union where inquiry shows that the member is under discipline, engaged in an ◇▷ Industrial Dispute, or in arrears with contributions; and that no union should start organizing activities at any establishment in respect of any grade of worker in which another union 'has the majority of workers employed and negotiates wages and conditions', unless by arrangement with that other union.

The Bridlington Rules comprise an injunction to cease poaching another union's (potential) members and do not provide a positive inducement to the rationalization of union jurisdiction. Further, the rules involve some restriction on the freedom of members to belong to particular unions.

In the USA jurisdictional conflict is bitter and ruthless; in Germany the problem is solved by industrial unionism (◇▷ Trade Union Types – Industrial Union). British unions prefer to tackle the problem by willingness to compromise on claims. A few unions steer a course between

Scylla and Charybdis: the National Union of Public Employees has built itself up partly by a skilful exploitation of the gaps between other unions' spheres of influence. N.H.C.

S. W. Lerner, *Breakaway Unions and the Small Trade Union* (Allen & Unwin, 1961); John Hughes, Royal Commission on Trade Unions and Employers' Associations, Research Papers 5 (Part 1): *Trade Union Structure and Government* (HMSO, 1967).

Trade Union – Membership Trade union membership can be measured by total count or by 'density'. The density of membership is an index given by: actual union membership/potential union membership (number of civil employees) × 100. Both figures have altered appreciably over time. In general the 1970s saw an upsurge in trade union membership. For example, TUC affiliated membership was 9,402,170 in 1970 and grew to 12,172,808 in 1980. Accompanying the return of mass unemployment and the recession in the 1980s, membership then fell sharply to 10,082,128 in 1984. So far as density is concerned the peak year was 1979, when nearly 56 per cent of Britain's workforce belonged to trade unions (this fell to under 50 per cent in 1984). More generally, too, the Certification Officer reported a total membership in trade unions of about 11,300,000 in 1983 and a peak year of 13,200,000 in 1979.

	Membership	
Union (in order of size)	1980	1984
Transport and General Workers' Union	2,086,281	1,547,559
Amalgamated Union of Engineering Workers	1,378,580	1,005,087
General, Municipal, Boilermakers and Allied Trades	967,153	875,187
National and Local Government Officers' Association	753,226	780,037
National Union of Public Employees	691,770	689,046
Union of Shop, Distributive and Allied Workers	470,017	403,446
Association of Scientific, Technical and Managerial Staffs	491,000	390,000
Electrical, Electronic, Telecommunications and Plumbing Union	420,000	365,000
Union of Construction, Allied Trades and Technicians	347,777	260,000
National Union of Teachers	248,896	210,499

Source: Trades Union Congress Annual Reports, 1980, pp. 615–25, and 1984, pp. 665–75.

Women and white-collar workers have been increasingly likely to join unions, but the 1980s witnessed sharp declines in the fortunes of unions reliant for membership on manufacturing and construction industries. This is shown in the table on p. 532, which records the changes in membership in Britain's ten largest unions between 1980 and 1984. N.H.C., amended by M.J.F.P.

G. S. Bain and F. Elsheikh, *Union Growth and the Business Cycle* (Blackwell, 1976); *Annual Report of the Certification Officer* (1984); *Trades Union Congress Directory* (1985).

Trade Union – Officers Trade unions depend heavily on their active members and from these are chosen both lay and full-time officials. The great majority are lay officials, who include ⟨⟩ Shop Stewards, workplace committee members, branch officers, district committee delegates, executive committee workers, national conference delegates and a number of national presidents and treasurers. Most full-time officials are employed chiefly as negotiators, although they may carry the title of area, district, regional, divisional or national organizer. Another group of full-time officials are employed as branch, area, district, regional or divisional secretaries, and usually have both negotiating and administrative duties. The chief full-time official is the General Secretary. The post of General Secretary is an organizational post but it is also a symbol of a union's status, both in the trade union world and in the world at large. It is the key union office.

With the growth in size, complexity and geographical coverage of unions, they have found it increasingly necessary to delegate to full-time officials many of the functions originally exercised by rank-and-file members. Many decision-making functions have moved upwards from the branch into the hands of the General Secretary, who controls the union's administration and normally the journal. The General Secretary is often the only person with considerable knowledge of the separate specialist sections of the union and thus carries considerable weight with the executive committee and may effectively determine the strategy of national collective bargaining and joint operations with other unions. The post is often held for life; most of those General Secretaries who do have to face periodic elections are returned to office.

It is apparent that the central problem of union management is how to obtain administrative efficiency within the realities of democratic control. Unions attempt to achieve this in many different ways, setting up constitutional checks on the powers of leaders who, in the last analysis, must heed the pressure from the rank and file or face the consequences. While unions have not grown undemocratic, they have developed centralized democratic bureaucracies. Vocal shop stewards and unofficial strikes are all indicative of countervailing forces to the centralizing trend. The internal structure of the union of the future will need to permit both strong central leadership and a greater degree of local autonomy than at present. Paradoxically this is likely to call for an increase in the size of union staff, both of full-time officials and specialist support; an improvement in the quality of union officers; and better research and administrative departments. N.H.C.

H. A. Clegg, A. J. Killick and R. Adams, *Trade Union Officers* (Blackwell, 1961); G. S. Bain (ed.), *Industrial Relations in Britain* (Blackwell, 1983).

Trade Union – Organization Rights ⇨ Freedom of Association

Trade Union – Politics Political action as practised by British trade unions is concentrated largely on Parliament, although union branches also take action on local government questions. The national political work of unions is carried on partly by the General Council of the ⇨ T U C and partly by individual unions, which vary widely in their interest in parliamentary affairs. Some unions brief M Ps concerning embryo or actual legislation; some support candidates at elections by contributing towards election expenses. If a union's nominee is elected, the union may also contribute towards the candidate's expenses as an M P. The miners, who once had over thirty sponsored M Ps, form the largest group in Parliament, and a number of other unions are responsible for the candidatures of several members. The National Union of Teachers at one time promoted candidates in all three parties. Most unions, however, have no members of their own in Parliament and rely for assistance on trade union M Ps or other members of the Labour Party.

Many unions also make contributions to the funds of the Labour Party and support it in publications, meetings and conferences. These political activities are subject to conditions prescribed by legislation, in particular the Trade Union Act, 1913, following the Osborne Judgment. This allows a union to spend funds for specified political purposes provided the majority of the members have balloted in favour of such political action and that the expenditure is made out of a separate fund. Members may contract out of payments into the political fund by formally indicating objection. This allows for Conservative and Liberal trade unionists, together with other objectors for whatever reason. It was noted in a Political and Economic Planning study in 1963 that 57 per cent of the members of the Draughtsmen and Allied Technicians Association contracted out of the union's political levy on behalf of the

Labour Party, although this union was known as a militant and somewhat left-wing organization. At the end of 1983 fifty-eight unions maintained political funds, valued at £6·6 million.

The ⟨⟩ Trade Union Act 1984 requires a trade union that already has a political resolution in force and that wishes to continue to spend money on political objects to pass a political resolution again on a further ballot of members at least once every ten years. N.H.C., amended by M.J.F.P.

Trade Union – Structure British trade unions, like those of Scandinavia, conform to a unitary system of industrial relations, so that there are no internal divisions on religious or political grounds as in many industrial relations systems elsewhere in continental Europe; nor is there the 'economic pluralism' typical of the American scene, where unions raid each other for members, although some 'poaching' can occur (⟨⟩ Trade Union – Jurisidiction).

The familiar classification of British unions by structural type (⟨⟩ Trade Union Types – Craft, General, Industrial, White-collar Unions) is inadequate to explain the nature of many of them. So are the terms 'vertical', e.g. industrial unions, and 'horizontal', e.g. craft unions, as general unions appear in both roles in different sectors of the economy. Since distinctions between such union types are increasingly blurred, it is now more useful to think in terms of new categories according to the strategy and tactics of unions. In the terminology of Professor Turner of Cambridge the distinction is between 'closed' (military analogy, 'strongpoint') unions, and 'open' (military analogy, 'broad-front') unions. A closed union will delineate sharply its area of recruitment to a specific grade of worker, and sometimes to a specific industry and therefore region; an open union will recruit all types of worker. In practice many unions are now intermediate types, open in certain directions of recruitment interest but closed in others. For example the Amalgamated Union of Engineering Workers is descended from a craft union with a closed skilled nucleus, but is now open to the recruitment of supervisory grades and semi-skilled engineering workers. The degree of openness of a union is a function of the attitudes of its membership and officers to recruitment.

Initiative in recruitment and amalgamation of unions since 1945 has increasingly altered the balance of the trade union movement as a whole. Continuing change in the structure of the movement by natural growth reveals little sign of evolution towards industrial unionism, but large, open unions have continued to flourish. Industrial-type union organization appears more often as an aspect of internal union arangements, or in the form of a very broad interest in one section of the economy. A number of unions organized on more strictly defined industrial lines are in numerical decline as regards membership.

Union development also shows a shift in the size-structure of the movement. This is a continuing shift towards large-scale relatively open unions, which allows more economies of scale but appears unlikely to resolve the central structural problem of British unionism, namely the multiplicity of unions and overlapping in particular sectors or occupations.

Between the Bridlington Rules (✧ Trade Union–Jurisdiction), set up to limit inter-union competition in overlap areas, and the activities of federations of unions operating in the same industry, there is a large and important hinterland of multilateral and bilateral union agreements on matters such as 'spheres of influence' and joint operation, for example in Joint Industrial Councils with multiple representation on the employees' side. Rationalization could better be accomplished by a more permanent and positive ✧ TUC initiative such as a co-ordination and development committee set up on the lines of the present Disputes Committee. N.H.C.

John Hughes, Royal Commission on Trade Unions and Employers' Associations, Research Papers 5 (Part 1): *Trade Union Structure and Government* (HMSO, 1967); H. A. Clegg, *The Changing System of Industrial Relations in Great Britain* (Blackwell, 1979).

Trade Union Act 1984 This made provisions for secret ballots to be used in trade union elections and for industrial action. It also made provision for regular votes of the membership on whether money should be spent on political party matters.

Part I of the Act covers *secret ballots and trade union elections* (✧ Trade Union – Ballots). Section 1 of the Act requires the principal executive committee of a trade union to be elected by secret ballot of the union's members. Section 2 lays down that all elections to the principal executive committee of a trade union must comply with the following requirements: (1) entitlement to vote at the election must be accorded equally to all members of the union unless they are in certain listed groups, such as newly joined or student members, which are also excluded from voting under union rules; (the Act also allows unions under their rules to restrict the electorate for particular seats on the executive to members in particular occupations, geographical areas and/or constituent sections within the union); (2) voting in the election must be by the marking of a ballot paper and without interference from, or constraint imposed by, the union or any of its members, officials or employees; (3) so far as is reasonably practicable, every person entitled to vote must: be enabled to do so in secret; be sent a voting paper by post; be given a convenient opportunity to return it by post; and be enabled to vote without incurring any direct cost; (4) votes cast in the election must be fairly and accurately counted (although accidental inaccuracies not affecting the outcome are to be disregarded); (5) no member of the union is to be unreasonably prevented from standing for election nor required to belong to a particular political party in order to do so; (however, the Act allows unions to exclude particular classes of members from standing for election through their rules).

The requirements of the section do not apply to overseas members of a union nor in relation to uncontested elections.

Section 3 of the Act allows a union to hold a workplace or semi-postal ballot rather than a full postal ballot where it is satisfied that there are no reasonable grounds for believing that a workplace or semi-postal ballot would not meet the requirements of section 2 (other than those relating to voting by post).

Section 4 places a duty on trade unions to compile and thereafter maintain, by means of a computer or otherwise, a register of the names and addresses of their members, and section 5 provides that a member of a union can apply to the Certification Officer or to the High Court (or, in Scotland, to the Court of Session) for a declaration that the union has failed to comply with one or more of the provisions of Part I of the Act.

Part II of the Act covers *secret ballots before industrial action*. Section 10 removes immunity from legal action in cases where trade unions do not hold a ballot before authorizing or endorsing a call for a strike or any other form of industrial action that breaks or interferes with the contracts of employment of those called upon to take part in it. It also makes it a condition of immunity that a majority of those voting vote in favour of the action, that the ballot is held no more than four weeks before the industrial action begins and that the ballot satisfies the requirements of section 11.

Section 11 sets out the conditions strike ballots must satisfy. Entitlement to vote must be given to those, and only those, who the union reasonably believes will be called upon to take or to continue to take strike or other industrial action. Immunity will be lost if any member is called on to strike after being denied entitlement to vote. The question on the ballot paper must invite a 'Yes' or 'No' answer and specify whether the action involves a strike or other type of industrial action involving voters in a breach of their contracts of employment. So far as is reasonably practicable, every person entitled to vote:

(1)   must be supplied with a ballot paper, or have one made available

during working hours (or immediately before or after working hours) either at the employees' workplace or at a place more convenient to them;

(2)   must be given a convenient opportunity to vote by post *or* an opportunity to vote during working hours (or immediately before or after working hours) at the employees' workplace or at a place more convenient to them *or* a choice between these two methods of voting.

The detailed results of the ballot must also be made known to those entitled to vote.

Meanwhile, Part III embraces *political funds and objects*. Section 12 provides that trade unions that have in the past balloted their members under the provisions of the Trade Union Act, 1913 to enable them to spend money on 'political objects' must in future ballot their members at least every ten years if they wish to continue to do so. It means in particular that any of these trade unions that did not hold a ballot in the nine years before 31 March 1985 needed to do so before 31 March 1986. Section 13 updates the existing provisions in the 1913 Act that require the approval of the Certification Officer for political fund ballot rules. It provides in particular that the Certification Officer must be satisfied that the rules provide for ballots either by post or at the workplace. The section also makes it clear that ballot rules must be approved by the Certification Officer before each ballot, and enables trade unions to adopt ballot rules by a decision of their principal executive committee in the case of the first review ballots held under the provisions of the Act (before 31 March 1986). Section 14 deals with the assets and liabilities of the separate political funds that, under the 1913 Act, trade unions must have if they wish to spend money on political objects. In cases where a union has lost its authority to spend money on political objects, the section provides that only contributions to the political fund received before the loss of the authority may be added to the political fund; it prevents union members from being required to contribute to the fund; and it enables unions to transfer assets of their fund to another fund of the union without being in breach of trust or of their rules. The section also provides explicit statutory clarification that no political fund deficits may be paid off from union funds other than the political fund, and that unions must not at any time transfer into their political funds money not appropriate to those funds. M.J.F.P.

Department of Employment, *Employment Gazette* (August 1984), pp. 378–80.

Trade Union and Labour Relations Act The main purpose of the Trade Union and Labour Relations Act 1974 was to repeal the Industrial Relations Act 1971. It did this but re-enacted, with some changes, the part of that Act dealing with unfair dismissal. It also filled in some gaps left by the repeal. In particular it provided legal immunities for those carrying out certain actions in contemplation or furtherance of a trade dispute. The Industrial Relations Code of Practice orginally introduced under the Industrial Relations Act was retained. As before, the Code is not legally enforceable but continues as a set of guidelines. For example it may be used as a yardstick in industrial tribunal cases. N.H.C., amended by M.J.F.P.

Trade Union Types – Craft Union A union where the basis for organization is the possession of certain trade skills. Craft unions are typically associated with apprentice training, which the union may control. Demarcation (⟡ Trade Union – Demarcation) of specific jobs, that is, the claiming of such jobs only for workers with particular trade skills, is characteristic of craft unions and is a device used by them for holding and strengthening the labour-market position of workers with such skills. They control entry to these jobs completely in the ⟡ Closed Shop. New materials and methods may result in demarcation disputes between different types of skilled workmen and hence different craft unions, each concerned to minimize actual or imagined employment insecurity.

In their pure form craft unions are thus horizontal in character, seeking to unite all workers of a particular craft or trade irrespective of the industry in which they happen to be engaged. They were the earliest British unions, appearing as small, local, ephemeral societies in the eighteenth century: a number have continuous histories from the mid-nineteenth century, for example the engineers' union. They have a higher membership density and a higher membership participation in union affairs than is the case in other unions and, by virtue of their higher earnings originally, they tend to provide more and higher benefits from higher subscriptions.

A small number of unions of the pure craft type still exist but for many years the share of craft unionism among British workers has declined. This has resulted from the decline in craftsmanship, so that a number of unions containing members doing skilled work would be better called skilled unions. It has resulted also because, in order to arrest their actual or relative decline in membership or influence, some former craft unions have enlarged their recruitment to embrace semi-skilled and unskilled workers, although the original craft core has continued as an aristocracy and still provides the leadership, as, for example, in the Amalgamated Union of Engineering Workers. ⟡ Trade Union – Structure. N.H.C.

Trade Union Types – General Union A union with no limitation of recruitment interest, either occupationally or industrially.

General unions originated in the last two decades of the nineteenth century for labourers who had previously not been organized. Eventually they came to recruit workers in virtually unorganized, established industries like road passenger services; semi-skilled and unskilled workers in industries where craft unions were established, like engineering; workers of all grades of skill in new industries; and small groups of workers for whom craft or industrial unions were unable or unwilling to cater. Thus for workers who are industrially and occupationally mobile, general unionism offers continuity of membership. Because of their size, general unions have the advantage of economies of scale and provide efficient services to members, for instance legal, research and educational facilities.

Each of the general unions has its industrial strongholds. The Transport and General Workers' Union has its main strength in transport; the General and Municipal Workers' Union in public services, especially the gas industry and the manual work of local authorities; while most of the members of the Union of Shop, Distributive and Allied Workers are co-operative society employees. Even so, general unions have widespread membership, with the advantages of spread of interests and risks, and the concomitant managerial problems that go with considerable diversification. This means that they find it difficult to maintain effective democracy, the more so since they experience a high membership turnover. For this reason the Transport and General Workers' Union has provided for some autonomy by creating a number of trade groups within the organization, e.g. docks, road passenger transport, road commercial transport, building and construction, engineering, chemicals, municipal, agricultural, etc. Even so, problems remain by virtue of the communication problems between the membership and the upper echelons of the union. ⟡ Trade Union – Structure; Trade Union – Officers; Trade Union – Government and Administration. N.H.C.

Trade Union Types – Industrial Union A union that seeks to organize all workers, of whatever craft, trade, occupation or grade, in a specific industry.

Industrial unionism tends to appeal to workers where there are production skills peculiar to an industry and not transferable to other industries; where there are conditions of work specific to one industry; and where there are promotion possibilities open through various grades of work. It has the advantage for members that it strengthens the unity of workers in the industry concerned and, since industrial unions tend to be large, they can provide efficient services. Further, such a vertically organized union can act decisively and with considerable strength in an industry because of the nature of its coverage. At the same time employers, usually organized on industrial lines, prefer to negotiate with a single union rather than a number who may not be in complete accord with each other.

Industrial unionism has been relatively unsuccessful in establishing itself in Britain due to the persistence of craft interests; the coverage across many industries of general unions; and the difficulties of organizing both manual and non-manual workers. Even the few industrial unions that are established, such as the National Union of Railwaymen and the National Union of Mineworkers, do not cover the whole of their industry. A better term for these, perhaps, would be single-industry unions.

Historically industrial unionism in Britain started as an offshoot of syndicalism in the early years of the twentieth century and did not have much importance until many years after the craft and general workers' unions were established. It was then advocated as an efficient structure for trade union organization and as a method whereby workers could take control of an industry and, ultimately, of society. Since 1945 it has been resuscitated as a device for improving trade union efficiency and for reform of the union structure. Comparisons have been made with the (limited) industrial unionism of Sweden, the more complete example of the post-war German trade union movement and the American examples typified by the United Automobile Workers. The ⟨⟩ T U C reports of 1927 and 1946 accepted industrial unionism as a plausible ideal and an objective for organizational evolution. Even the T U C, however, has now recognized that the complex of interests within the British trade union movement renders the achievement of this ideal impossible in Britain. ⟨⟩ Trade Union – Structure. N.H.C.

Trade Union Types – White-collar Union A union in the 'white-collar' or non-manual area of employment, including government administrators and executive officials; foremen and supervisors; professionals; scientists, technologists and technicians; artists, musicians and entertainers; clerical and administrative workers; salesmen, representatives and shop assistants.

Potential white-collar membership has grown rapidly since the turn of

542   *Traded Options*

the century with the expansion of white-collar occupations. The white-collar share of total union membership increased from about 20 per cent in 1911 to 25 per cent in 1931, 31 per cent in 1948 and 49 per cent in 1979. Although the rate of transfer from manual to white-collar employment began to slow down in the 1970s, the white-collar share of potential union membership is already more than 50 per cent and will continue to grow throughout the 1980s.

Most white-collar unionism is concentrated in the public sector of the economy, the largest union of this type being the National and Local Government Officers' Association. With the possible exception of the distributive trades, manufacturing industry has the lowest density of white-collar unionism. The nature of the bureaucratic structure would appear to assist the growth of white-collar unionism in the public sector, but a major force in both public and private sectors has undoubtedly been government policies. Both world wars resulted in government policies that made it easier for unions in the private sector to exert pressure for recognition and harder for employers to resist it. Although recent growth is impressive, expansion of union membership among white-collar workers in private industry is limited chiefly by the recognition problem still facing the unions catering for these workers. ◇ Trade Union – Structure; Managerial Unionism. N.H.C., amended by M.J.F.P.

G. S. Bain, *The Growth of White-collar Unionism* (Clarendon Press, 1970); G. S. Bain (ed.), *Industrial Relations in Britain* (Blackwell, 1983).

Traded Options ◇ Options

Trades Council A locally based body representing trade union branches in the locality, usually a town or district.

Trades councils are in no sense TUC 'branches', yet they are the counterparts of the ◇ TUC at the local level. Trades councils function as local co-ordinators of trade union activity. They undertake recruiting campaigns; raise funds, undertake propaganda and organize sympathetic action if requested to do so as a result of a dispute; promote educational, social and cultural ventures among local trade union members; and represent trade union interests in relations with local government agencies. In recent years the functions of trades councils have been expanded by the fact that government departments consider them the proper bodies to nominate trade union representatives to local tribunals, advisory bodies, planning bodies, hospital boards, etc.

With the centralization of much ◇ Collective Bargaining and the rise of local Labour Parties in the early twentieth century, their prestige and influence diminished. To prevent them from falling prey to Communists and other minorities (◊ Trade Union – Communism) the TUC attempted to develop the trades councils as its local agents since 1924. From 1934 it instructed them to exclude Communists from office. The TUC has also prescribed model rules for them and 'reorganizes' those that misbehave. In particular, trades councils must regard themselves as policy-executing and not policy-making bodies and must not indulge in political activities. In consequence, most of the mixed 'Trades and Labour Councils', formerly so numerous, have been divided. The TUC has considerable powers over trades councils because the national unions wish them kept in their place.

In England and Wales trades councils are represented at the TUC by a simple fraternal delegate but in Scotland they may, and do, affiliate direct to the Scottish TUC. N.H.C.

H. A. Clegg, *The Changing System of Industrial Relations in Great Britain* (Blackwell, 1979).

Trades Union Congress (TUC) A permanent association of British trade unions founded in 1868 to consider questions of importance to trade unionists and to give publicity to these considerations. Today the functions of the TUC can be said to exercise influence; to defend the name of the unions by developing a public image of a responsible movement; and to provide research, publicity and representative services for the trade union movement as a whole. The TUC does not spend money on political action, nor does it have a political fund, although many of its affiliated unions are also affiliated to the Labour Party.

The TUC is composed solely of affiliated unions of which there were ninety-three in 1984. Affiliated unions range in size from the Transport and General Workers' Union, with over 1·5 million members to the Sheffield Wool Shear Workers' Union with twenty-six members. Affiliated membership in 1984 was 10,082,128 members.

The TUC operates through its Annual Congress, its General Council and its full-time staff of officials led by the General Secretary. Affiliated unions are entitled to send to the Annual Congress one delegate for every 5,000 members or part thereof. Congress has three main functions: to consider the report of work done by the General Council during the previous year; to transact business placed on the agenda by affiliated unions; and to elect certain members of the General Council for the coming year. Decisions may be taken by show of hands or, more rarely, by formal vote. On such occasions voting is by card issued to union delegations according to membership. The business of Congress is conducted in public, in that meetings are televised and reported by the press.

The executive body of the TUC is the General Council. All unions with more than 100,000 members are automatically entitled to a seat, with up to five seats for larger unions. Eleven seats are reserved for smaller unions, with a ballot being held among these unions at Congress. A further six seats are reserved for women trade unionists, with all unions with women members able to nominate and vote for candidates in this section. The General Secretary is elected by Congress, and is ex officio a member of the General Council, but unlike other members is not subject to annual re-election.

The General Council meets at least once a month and is mainly concerned with examining the detailed work carried out by the committees it appoints to deal with a particular range of subjects.

Neither the General Council nor Congress can override the autonomy of affiliated unions, but there is a strong moral obligation to carry out their decisions. Standing orders do give them certain disciplinary sanctions. The rules of Congress, including suspension from membership, are subject to appeal to Congress.

The General Council does not normally intervene during a strike unless so requested by the union(s) involved, but it has the power to call union representatives together when there is a likelihood of negotiations breaking down and causing other affiliated trade unionists not directly involved to suffer by unemployment or otherwise.

At the request of an affiliated union the General Council may investigate a dispute between unions. Disputes Committees of the TUC exercise a triple function: that of a fact-finding commission, a conciliating body and a judicial tribunal. The principles guiding the Disputes Committees in their decisions on inter-union disputes are based on those adopted at the 1939 Congress and are known as the Bridlington Rules (✑ Trade Union – Jurisdiction).

The detailed work of the TUC is carried out by permanent staff employed in departments dealing with, for example, economic policy, employment policy, organization, social insurance, and international affairs. This work is co-ordinated by the General Secretary, whose potential influence as chief spokesman for the TUC is considerable.

TUC representatives sit on many public bodies with government and employers, including the National Economic Development Council, the Manpower Services Commission and the Council of the ✑ Advisory, Conciliation and Arbitration Service. At international level the TUC represents British workers in the International Labour Organization and is affiliated to the International Confederation of Free Trade Unions and the European Trade Union Confederation.

A large part of the TUC's resources is devoted to trade union education and in 1984 a national centre for trade union education was opened in North London.

There are T U C regional councils in the English regions and a Welsh Trades Unions Council. In more than 400 towns and cities there is a ⟨⟩ Trades Council registered with the T U C, where local representatives of union branches meet to discuss common problems. And at county level these form county associations of trades councils.

The T U C is financed by union affiliation fees, each union being required to pay the T U C for each member of the union (60p in 1985).

The organization and methods of the Scottish Trades Union Congress resemble those of the T U C, with which it closely works. It is, however, a distinct and separate institution that performs for trade unionists in Scotland many services that the T U C, by reason of its geographical remoteness, could not render as effectively. N.H.C., amended by M.J.F.P.

Trades Union Congress Directory (1985).

Training ⟨⟩ Industrial Training

Training Officer The member of the staff of a company who has special responsibility for the training and education of employees (⟨⟩ Industrial Training). In a large firm the Training Officer may be head of a department with several assistants and instructors. In small firms they may have other responsibilities as well as training. The duties of a training officer include advising the company on training policy and ensuring its implementation; organizing internal training courses and arranging for attendance at outside courses; and teaching, which may include some instruction in skilled work and the conduct of ⟨⟩ Induction courses for new recruits. The essential function of a training officer is to give a specialist service to production, sales, office and other 'line' managers – to advise and assist with the training of their staff – but this is qualified by overall responsibility to the company for giving all employees equal opportunities for training and development so as to improve their individual contributions to the enterprise. As training is closely related to other aspects of ⟨⟩ Personnel Management such as ⟨⟩ Recruitment, transfer and promotion, the training officer is a member of the personnel department, or works in close liaison with the personnel manager. L.S., amended by E.L.

A. Rodger, T. Morgan and D. Guest, *The Industrial Training Officer – His Background and His Work* (Institute of Personnel Management, 1971).

Transactional Analysis Largely developed by a psychiatrist, Dr

Eric Berne, in California, transactional analysis is concerned with the interactions ('transactions') between people, as expressed in their behaviour. According to Berne, a certain set of behaviour patterns in a given individual corresponds to one state of mind. This gives rise to the idea of an 'ego state', so that if a person's state of mind changes, another set of behaviour patterns may be observable in the individual. In practical terms an ego state is a system of feelings accompanied by a related set of behaviour patterns. Berne argues that each individual has a limited repertoire of ego states, and categorizes them as follows: (1) ego states resembling those of parental figures; (2) ego states that are directed towards the objective appraisal of reality; and (3) ego states that were fixated in early childhood but are still active in the individual. In everyday terms these are described, respectively, as parental, adult or child ego states.

Behavioural transactions between two individuals are likely to be satisfactory if each is behaving in accordance with the same ego state, e.g. adult–adult. Problems arise if transactions are 'crossed', e.g. adult–child, where the person behaving in the adult ego state is responded to by someone behaving in the child ego state. Transactional analysis is primarily concerned with crossed transactions of this nature. Dorothy Jongeward asserts that it can be used in organizations to increase a person's on-the-job effectiveness because of better self-understanding and greater insight into personalities and behaviour. It may also help to solve personal and family problems. E.L.

E. Berne, *Games People Play* (Penguin, 1967); D. Jongeward *et al.*, *Everybody Wins: Transactional Analysis Applied to Organizations* (Addison-Wesley, 1973); R. de Board, *Counselling People at Work* (Gower, 1983), p. 60 ff.

Transfer of Undertakings In 1981 regulations made under the European Communities Act 1972 were introduced in order to safeguard the position of workers when a commercial undertaking is sold as a going concern. Previously dismissal resulted from a sale or merger affecting the identity of the employer. The new owner might agree to keep on some or all of the existing workforce but was not obliged to do so. In contrast the vendor was obliged to make redundancy payments to those employees who were not hired by the purchaser.

As a result of the 1981 regulations the contracts of those employed in the undertaking are now transferred automatically to the new owner along with the business itself. No dismissal results from a 'relevant transfer' and in consequence statutory and contractual employment rights and seniority (excluding pension entitlements) are preserved. The purchaser loses the opportunity to pick and choose whom to keep on, while the workers cannot object to the change in the identity of their employer nor claim to have been dismissed. If the purchaser or the seller does dismiss any employees (whether or not they have been transferred) for a reason 'connected with the transfer', such dismissal is deemed to be unfair unless the employer can show that 'economic, technical or organizational reasons' entailed a change in the workforce. In this event the dismissal *may* be fair if it meets the usual, if rather vague, standard of 'reasonableness in all the circumstances'. Alternatively it may amount to redundancy if the job itself disappears as a consequence of reorganization. In either case an employee will need the usual two years' service in order to lodge a complaint with an industrial tribunal.

As well as automatically transferring employment contracts, the regulations effect two other major changes. First, they provide that any trade union that is recognized by the transferee or transferor shall be consulted and informed in advance by the appropriate employer about the likely impact of the transfer (including its 'legal, economic and social implications') on the group of workers represented by the union. Again, the duty is not confined to the effects of the transfer on those who are being transferred. This obligation resembles the consultation requirement that arises where an employer proposes to make employees redundant (⟨⟩ Redundancy Consultation). Failure to discharge the duty is actionable before an industrial tribunal, which may award each affected employee up to two weeks' pay as compensation.

Second, the regulations go some way to ensuring that any established industrial-relations environment continues to operate, at least where the undertaking transferred maintains an identity that is distinct from the remainder of the purchaser's business. The new owner thus inherits existing collective agreements, including those conferring recognition and negotiating rights on any trade union. However, as a matter of law, once transferred there is little to prevent either side from seeking to re-negotiate or even cancel such collective agreements. Not only are collective agreements not normally binding contracts, but the regulations are expressly made subject to section 18 of the Trade Union and Labour Relations Act 1974, with its presumption against legal enforceability.

Finally it should be said that the effect of the regulations is less extensive than might appear. This is because the commonest method of acquiring a corporate employer is through a takeover bid to obtain a controlling share interest. This leaves the identity of the company untouched, even though the identity of the shareholders who control the company has changed. Because share, as distinct from asset, transfers have no effect on the company's identity nor on its contracts, they are outside the regulations. The regulations deal only with cases where the business itself changes hands. ⟡ Mergers; Collective Agreements in Law. K.W.

P. Davies and M. Freedland, *Transfer of Employment* (Sweet & Maxwell, 1982); K. Williams, 'Business Transfers and "Acquired Rights"', *The Law Teacher*, vol. 16, no. 1 (1982), pp. 29–36.

Transfer Pricing One definition of an economic organization or entity is that it is an area of productive activity (or collection of working people) in which the control exercised by economic markets in the allocation of resources is replaced by control by administrative authority. A transfer-pricing system is an attempt by a firm to decentralize decision-making amongst managers by the use of an internal pricing system, which will also encourage, motivate or 'coerce' the individual manager to make decisions that will achieve the firm's objectives. Thus it is an attempt to secure the advantages of the market-price mechanism in achieving an efficient allocation of resources within the firm without relinquishing the advantages of being one economic unit.

A firm that uses a cost-accounting system to allocate costs to divisions and productive centres of the firm, which in turn are attached as unit costs (or 'price tags') to the goods and services and are transferred from one division or centre to another, implicitly if not explicitly uses a transfer-pricing system. However, in order to be effective a transfer-pricing system should motivate managers to make decisions about buying-in, producing and selling goods and services that take account of the marginal and opportunity costs of resources. For such purposes it is clear that the use of fully allocated average accounting costs, probably the most frequently used transfer-pricing basis, is likely to lead to un-economic decisions. Consequently alternatives such as marginal or variable costs, market prices, market-based negotiated prices, market prices less a sales commission, etc, have been suggested. E.A.L.

D. Solomons, *Divisional Performance: Measurement and Control* (Financial Execution Research Foundation, 1965).

Transportation Method ⟡ Mathematical Programming

Truck Acts The essence of the truck system is that employees, as a condition of their contract of employment, are compelled to accept part of their remuneration in kind, i.e. in goods or services. There is evidence that the system was in existence in England as far back as the fifteenth century, although it was not until the nineteenth century that legislation was passed to deal with the abuses to which it gave rise. The Truck Acts, 1831–1940 prohibit payment of wages otherwise than by legal tender; outlaw the system of 'tommy' shops (i.e. shops owned by employers at which workers were compelled to spend part of their wages, often by exchanging tokens with which they had been paid); and prohibit deductions from wages by way of fines or for bad workmanship, except where provided for expressly by the contract of employment and by notices displayed at the workplace.

The Truck Acts, which only cover 'workmen' employed in 'manual labour', tend to be seen nowadays as an outmoded obstacle to the spread of 'cashless pay'. In 1983 the Government announced its intention to repeal legislation while retaining protection against arbitrary deductions from wages. Currently, because of the Payment of Wages Act, 1960, even 'workmen' can be paid by cheque or direct credit where they request it in writing. W.F.F. amended by K.W.

G. W. Hilton, *The Truck System* (CUP, 1960).

Turnover ⟡ Labour Turnover

U

Unfair Contract Terms ◇ Exclusion Clauses; Sale of Goods

Unfair Dismissal A statutory right not to be unfairly dismissed has been available to most employees, including apprentices and Crown servants, since 1972. The law is contained in Part V of the Employment Protection (Consolidation) Act 1978 as amended. Between 30,000 and 40,000 complaints a year are lodged, the majority being settled or otherwise disposed of without a hearing via ◇ ACAS conciliation officers. Of the cases that are heard by industrial tribunals, less than a third are decided in favour of the complainant employee.

The employee must prove that: they were dismissed from employment that involved at least sixteen hours per week, or eight hours where they had been employed by the organization for five years; had two years' continuous service prior to dismissal, or one year where the number of employees exceeded twenty and the employee was in post prior to June 1985; they were below the usual occupational, or the statutory, retiring age – sixty-five for men and sixty for women; and had filed their complaint within three months of dismissal. Dismissal occurs where the employer terminates the contract with or without notice, fails to renew a fixed-term contract, or where the employee leaves in response to a substantial breach of contract on the part of the employer – the so-called 'constructive dismissal' provision.

The employer must then show that they dismissed the employee for one of the following reasons: capability or qualifications; conduct; redundancy; supervening illegality; or 'some other substantial reason'. It is then for the tribunal to make up its mind in accordance with 'equity and the substantial merits of the case' whether the employer has acted reasonably in all the circumstances, bearing in mind the size and administrative resources of the employer's undertaking. What is fair or unfair is very much a conclusion of fact for the tribunal on the evidence available. Essentially the tribunal must ask itself 'what would the reasonable employer have done?' In making this judgment the tribunal is entitled to take into account the recommendations of the ACAS *Codes of Practice* on discipline and dismissal. Other considerations include whether the employee's behaviour warrants dismissal (rather than some lesser penalty); whether the employer has acted consistently, as well as reasonably and on the basis of adequate evidence; and whether any proper internal disciplinary procedure has been followed. The fact that a party is guilty of a breach of contract is simply one of a number of material factors, none of which is necessarily determinative in every case.

In certain instances the question of fairness is predetermined by the legislation itself. Thus it is automatically unfair to dismiss an employee because of their membership of, or participation in, the activities of an independent trade union. Equally it is unfair to dismiss an employee who refuses to join a union that is not independent, or indeed any union, except where there is an approved ⬦ Closed Shop in operation. In principle, where there is a closed shop non-membership is a sufficient ground for dismissal, although there are a number of exceptions to this. For example dismissal would be unfair if the individual could show a conscientious or other deeply held personal objection to membership, or if they were employed prior to the introduction of the closed shop and were at that time a non-member and had remained so since. It is also automatically unfair to select employees to be made redundant in breach of an agreed or customary procedure or on the basis of their union status. Such union-related dismissals are remedied by more generous compensation and neither the two-year-service rule nor the retiring-age disqualification apply.

On the other hand the dismissal of those who strike or take any other form of industrial action (whether or not in breach of their contract of employment) cannot be challenged before a tribunal, unless only some of the strikers are dismissed or, if all are dismissed, some but not all are re-hired within three months. In effect dismissing strikers is automatically fair so long as they are sacked during the currency of the dispute.

The usual remedy for unfair dismissal has proved in practice to be compensation, although the legislation was drafted in such a way as to give priority to the power of the tribunals to order re-employment. ⬦ Dismissal of Employees (Law); Redundancy. K.W.

S. Anderman, *Law of Unfair Dismissal* (Butterworths, 2nd ed., 1985); K. Williams, 'Unfair Dismissal: Myths and Statistics', *Industrial Law Journal*, vol. 12, no. 3 (1983), pp. 157–65.

Union Shop ⬦ Closed Shop

Unity of Command The principle that each subordinate shall report to, and receive instructions from, only one superior. The principle is dear to the hearts of the classical theorists and has been repeatedly reaffirmed, often with biblical support (Matthew 6:24, Luke 16:13). The problems that could arise if the principle were violated are obvious enough: conflicting instructions and divided responsibilities and loyalties. Undoubtedly many organizations suffer from a lack of clarity in their organizational structures, but research indicates that the successful violation of the principle is extremely common. Good co-ordination between dual heads can considerably reduce the risk of their issuing conflicting instructions to their common subordinate and in the absence of conflicting orders the question of divided responsibilities and loyalties does not arise.

In recent years, however, although many managements have failed to recognize the fact, the principle of unity of command has been steadily eroded by the increasing use of functional authority (◊ Functional 1). The near sacred regard in which unity of command has been held has un-fortunately hampered the re-examination of the questions of personal authority and responsibility that the spread of functional authority has necessitated. ◊ Authority; Functional 2; Responsibility. I.C.McG.

Unofficial Strike ◊ Strike – Causes, Forms, Remedies, Statistics

User-friendly Systems The manufacturers of computer hardware have expertise in electronics; writers of operating systems and applica-tions programs have expertise in software; neither necessarily has any formal understanding of the capabilities and limitations of human performance. As a consequence, accounts of computerized systems that are difficult, or even impossible, to use are by no means rare.

The term 'user-friendly' is applied to those systems in which the needs of the user have, supposedly, been fully taken into account. Ideally the factors involved would include the ergonomics of the hard-ware, the software and the supporting documentation, such that system users are able to perform their tasks with the maximum efficiency and the minimum stress. E.E.

Utility The concept of utility is closely associated with decision analysis (◊ Decision Theory). Ideally when considering a management problem possible courses of action should be compared on a common scale and often money is taken to be the common measure (◊ Cost-benefit Analysis). If such a measure can be found, it is frequently called 'equiv-alent monetary value'. However, it is not always possible to determine a precise cash value, and even if one were found it might not directly influence a decision, as at first appears. For example a course of action that might achieve a gain of £100,000 but a loss of £250,000 if it did not turn out so well might be acceptable to a large thriving company, but far less attractive to one that is small and struggling. The latter might not even be able to survive if the loss were incurred and therefore could not contemplate it. The concept of utility enables such factors to be taken into account and translates the effects of potential outcomes in terms of a common, usually non-monetary, scale where values are known as 'utils'. R.S.S.

P. G. Moore, *Basic Operational Research* (Pitman, 1976); B. H. P. Rivett, *Model Building for Decision Analysis* (J. Wiley, 1980).

V

___

Valuation of Assets The normal basis of the valuation of assets for accounting purposes has been historical cost (♢ Accounting Conventions). Falls in value through business use are recorded by writing off the ♢ Depreciation of fixed assets and by writing down stock-in-trade (which is normally valued at cost or market value, whichever is the lower). Increases in value, on the other hand, are not normally recorded, although some companies periodically revalue certain types of assets (e.g. land and buildings) that appreciate in value. The impact of inflation in the 1970s resulted in public disquiet as to the validity and usefulness of published financial statements based upon historic cost. Recommendations by the accounting profession that published financial statements be adjusted for changes in general purchasing power (♢ Changing Price Levels, Accounting for) were followed by the establishment of a government committee (the Sandilands Committee) to inquire into the problem of inflation accounting.

The Committee, which reported in 1975, recommended that 'value to the business' should be adopted as the valuation concept. This approach can be viewed as a reversal of the opportunity-cost concept and has been defined by Bonbright (1937) as follows. 'The value of a property to its owner is identical in amount with the adverse value of the entire loss, direct and indirect, that the owner might expect to suffer if he were deprived of the property'.[1] This definition of value in relation to loss leads to the use of the term deprival value. Deprival value will be one of the following three values: (1) the current purchase price of the asset, i.e. replacement cost (R C); (2) the net realizable value of the asset (N R V); (3) the net present value of the asset, obtained by discounting all expected future net receipts (N P V).

There are six possible relationships between these values,[2] giving the following values to the business:

1. J. C. Bonbright, *The Valuation of Property* (McGraw-Hill, 1937, reprinted by The Michie Company, Virginia, 1965).
   2. R. H. Parker and G. C. Harcourt, *Readings in the Concept and Measurement of Income* (CUP, 1969).

Value to the business
1. NRV > NPV > RC   RC
2. NRV > RC > NPV   RC
3. NPV > RC > NRV   RC
4. NPV > NRV > RC   RC
5. RC > NPV > NRV   NPV
6. RC > N R V > NPV   NRV

The question of asset valuation is extremely complex and lies at the heart of the problem facing accountants when attempting to measure capital and profit. Historic cost as the value base owes its importance to history and the desire of the accountant for objective verifiable evidence of a transaction. The use of historic cost is closely linked with the traditional stewardship view of accounting (⟡ Accountancy Conventions). There are, however, at least five other main approaches to valuation, namely: (1) historical cost adjusted for changes in general purchasing power; (2) replacement cost; (3) net realizable value; (4) net present value; (5) value to the business.

The abundance of concepts of value raises doubts as to the likelihood of any single concept being capable of satisfying all the information needs of all the users of accounting statements at all points in time. It may be that users require knowledge of different values in relation to their specific needs at particular points of time. If so, financial reports based upon a single value concept will always be subject to criticism. C.J.J.

T. A. Lee, *Income and Value Measurement: Theory and Practice* (Nelson, 2nd ed., 1980).

Value Analysis The application of the techniques of ⟡ Method Study to the product design function.

The basis of the approach is identical to that used for the study and development of work methods, i.e. (1) select the product to be studied; (2) evaluate the purpose, design and cost of the product and its components; (3) develop designs for components and products to perform the function at a lesser cost, i.e. develop designs of greater 'value'; (4) examine the various designs; (5) adopt the design with highest 'value'; (6) implement and review the results.

'Value' in this context is defined as the least cost for reliably providing the correct function, at the correct time and place and at a correct standard of quality. Value analysis, therefore, is a procedure that specifies the function of products or components, establishes the appropriate cost, creates alternatives and evaluates them.

Value analysis is most applicable where very large quantities of an item are being produced, so that fractional amounts saved on the manufacturing cost can result in substantial savings.

It has been criticized as a redundant discipline since analysis of value and comparison of alternative designs is a function carried out by all designers, and hence there is no need for an additional person, team or profession to perform the function. Whilst this may be true it is nevertheless equally true that re-evaluation of designs after a period of time often presents the opportunity for cost reductions, e.g. resulting from the use of newly developed materials, processes, etc.

The main achievement of value analysis has been to attract attention to the cost factor in the design function. A team approach is normally used with, for example, a value analysis 'engineer' acting as chairman of a team drawn from cost accounting, production, design and purchasing. ⟡ Design. R.W.

American Society of Tool and Manufacturing Engineers, *Value Analysis in Manufacturing* (Prentice-Hall, 1967).

Value for Money Value for money (VFM) describes the benefits obtained from expenditure, both in financial and other terms. The phrase is in extensive use in public organizations, where it is difficult to measure value in terms of output.

Value-for-money reviews or audits are often carried out alongside statutory audits of public bodies. These may be regarded as an objective and systematic study of: (1) the nature and functioning of the organization's managerial systems and procedures; (2) the economy and efficiency with which its services are provided; and (3) the effectiveness of its performance in achieving objectives. VFM may, therefore, be identified with the three organizational objectives of economy, efficiency and effectiveness in service provision. J.V.P.

J. Hatch and J. Redwood, *Value for Money Audits* (Centre for Policy Studies, 1981); *Economy, Efficiency and Effectiveness* (HMSO, 1983).

Values Fundamental beliefs, either generally or personally held, that serve as the criteria by which all social alternatives are appraised. Values always involve an emotional commitment, in that people feel strongly that behaviour in accordance with the value is 'good', whilst behaviour in violation of the value is 'bad'. The value may not be something wholly attainable (e.g. absolute honesty) but may be, nevertheless, something towards which one should constantly strive.

Differences in values underline many of the differences in behaviour that occur in industrial organizations. Thus common managerial values include a belief in the sanctity of authority as an organizational principle and in the importance of personal advancement, whilst shop-floor values may include a belief in the importance of shared power leading to negotiated rules of behaviour governing the relationship between management and workers, and in the importance of collective loyalty through which there can be general advancement. These conflicting values may lead managers to become over-concerned with the maintenance of managerial prerogatives whilst trade unionists assume the right to participate in organizational decision-making, to question orders and, where appropriate, to disobey. Similarly managers may elaborate systems of individual incentive bonuses and merit-rating, whilst trade unionists press for equality of treatment.

Values are acquired by the individual, often during childhood as a result of family influences, but also during adulthood as a result of experience and widening social contacts. Values differ from one society or group to another and will change over time. An individual's values do not change easily, although a process of modification usually takes place continuously during a person's lifetime. ⊘ Norm; Role. I.C.McG.

P. M. Blau and W. R. Scott, *Formal Organizations* (Routledge & Kegan Paul, 1963); G. Hofstede, *Culture's Consequences* (Sage, 1980).

Value to the Business ◊ Valuation of Assets

Variable Costing ◊ Cost (in Accounting Systems)

Variance ◊ Measures of Dispersion

Vendor Appraisal ◊ Purchasing

Vertical Integration ◊ Patterns of Growth

Vibration The most common sources of vibration are transport vehicles, such as ships, aircraft, cars and agricultural vehicles. The effects upon the human body may include discomfort, headaches, nausea, pain and permanent internal damage, in addition to severe decrements in working performance.

The type and severity of these effects depend upon the amplitude, frequency and duration of the vibration as well as the physiological and psychological condition of the individual.

Motion sickness results most commonly from very low frequency vibration. At higher frequencies severe discomfort and fatigue may occur. The natural frequencies of different parts of the body lie in the range 3–9 cycles per second. Within this range resonance resulting in anatomical damage may arise from exposure. Experiments upon animals indicate that injury may result from displacement of the abdomen or from mechanical collisions between lungs and the heart.

Numerous damping devices are available to protect human beings from deleterious effects. Correct posture is of the utmost importance, and appropriate training procedures may help people to cope. E.E.

S. Cole, 'Vibration and Linear Acceleration', in W. T. Singleton (ed.), *The Body at Work* (CUP, 1982).

Vicarious Liability A rule of law that makes A liable for the civil wrongs (torts) of B. An injured third party may then sue either A or B or both. Vicarious liability arises most commonly where B is the employee of A and has caused the loss or damage while 'acting in the course of their employment'. This concept has been the subject of considerable litigation. The question appears to be whether the employee was doing what they were employed to do or doing something reasonably incidental to it, albeit doing it badly or even in a way that was illegal. Thus if B injures C, a fellow employee, through negligence, C may sue A, their common employer, even if B was flouting the employer's safety procedures or the provisions of, say, the Health and Safety at Work Act. Employers must be insured against liability for injuries at work (◇ Employers' Liability), and they usually insure themselves against potential liability arising in other circumstances.

In theory, though it rarely happens in practice, an employer who has to pay compensation merely because of the doctrine of vicarious liability can sue the employee whose fault actually caused the harm and recover an indemnity. In contrast an employer is not normally liable for the wrongs of independent contractors engaged to undertake work or to provide services.

Vicarious liability can arise in other circumstances where B can be regarded as the agent of A. If A loans their car to B in order that B may drive it at least partly for A's purposes, A will be vicariously liable alongside B for any injuries caused through B's careless driving. Similarly a trade union is liable for losses caused by unlawful industrial action that has been 'authorized or endorsed' by someone who, according to the Employment Act 1982, is a 'responsible person'. This includes the union's principal executive committee, its president or general secretary, as well as employed officials and others empowered to so act under the

union's rules (a category that does not normally include shop stewards).
K.W.

Winfield and Jolowicz on Tort (Sweet & Maxwell, 12th ed. by W. V. H. Rogers, 1984), ch. 21.

Vision The human eye comprises a roughly spherical case, fitted with a variable-diameter aperture (the pupil) controlled by the iris; a zoom, or variable focal length, lens; and a photo-sensitive layer, the retina, connected to the optic nerve.

A variety of mechanisms is involved in the visual perception of space, including relative size and interposition of objects, perspective and accommodation effects. Binocular cues are derived from convergence and stereoscopy.

Visual acuity is determined by the size of the retinal image, together with such factors as levels of illumination and contrast ($\Diamond$ Brightness; Illumination). Retinal image size is a function of object distance, R, and object size, S, and is usually measured in terms of visual angle. For general purposes this angle, A, is given by

$$A = \frac{S}{R} \text{ radians}$$

Common defects in vision result from the inability of the lens to provide a sufficient range of accommodation. Short sightedness, or myopia, results from excessive convexity of the lens, such that the image falls short of the retina. Distant objects cannot then be focused sharply. The condition may be corrected by the use of a concave lens. Conversely, long sightedness, or hypermetropia, may be corrected by the use of a convex lens. There is a tendency towards long sightedness with increasing age. $\Diamond$ Colour; Colour Blindness. E.E.

R. N. Haber and M. Hershenson, *The Psychology of Visual Perception* (Holt, Rinehart & Winston, 2nd ed., 1980).

Visual Display Terminals The most common VDT comprises a cathode ray tube display together with an alphanumeric keyboard. The terminal may be the interface of an independent computer or may be remotely linked to a distant machine ($\Diamond$ Information System).

Numerous questions have been raised concerning the well-being of VDT users ($\Diamond$ User-friendly Systems). Complaints have included eye-strain, headache and facial rashes. Even epilepsy and cataracts have been under discussion. Whilst not all investigators are in agreement concerning these issues, the use of VDTs is sufficiently widespread for the possible hazards to be kept under close review. E.E.

B. Pearce (ed.), *Health Hazards of VDTs* (J. Wiley, 1984); A. Cakir, D. J. Hart and T. F. M. Stewart, *Visual Display Terminals* (J. Wiley, 1980).

Visualizing ◇ Advertising

Vocational Guidance Many causal factors lead individuals into their occupations, not all of which are rational. The task of the vocational counsellor is to guide the processes of occupational choice to the mutual benefit of individuals and their employer. The counsellor assesses the abilities, interests and aspirations of a client, usually by means of interviews, questionnaires and standardized tests, and is then able to suggest occupations that may be suitable and to provide guidance concerning educational and other requirements for suitable occupational positions. E.E.

J. O. Crites, *Vocational Psychology* (McGraw-Hill, 1969).

W

Wage The payment made to workers for placing their ability and energy at the disposal of an employer.

'Money wages' must be distinguished from 'real wages', which are the goods and services money wages will buy. Real wages thus depend on the movement of prices. Rising prices during ◊ Inflation mean falling real wages if money wages remain unchanged.

Ideally national agreements should set the frame, and the limits, within which ◊ Workplace Bargaining and plant and company bargaining about payment by results and other pay systems should operate (◊ Wage Systems). In practice most national agreements merely set minimal standards for pay, with differentials for skill, sex and possibly other dimensions, e.g. area.

Rates of pay are fixed in relation to a standard working week. Time worked above this is 'overtime', which is paid at premium rates. These may vary according to the time of the week in which overtime occurs and may be calculated on piece-rates, time-rates or flat payments for each hour of overtime. Post-war reductions in the standard working week have had a minimal effect on actual hours worked in Britain and many employees depend on overtime earnings. A higher incidence of overtime in a company may indicate considerable underemployment in normal working hours (◊ Productivity Bargaining). Shift pay is also paid at premium rates.

Holidays with pay are now typical of most British industries, calculations being made in a wide variety of ways, but often on time-rates or average earnings.

It is possible to view a given wage as a function of supply and demand in a number of interrelated markets and indeed theories of wage determination have been developed mostly by economists. There are, however, important social and political determinants, e.g. traditional, legal, ideological and institutional factors have combined historically to keep women's wages at a lower level than those of men. The Equal Pay Act 1970 embodied the principle of 'equal pay for equal work'.

A worker's earnings may be enhanced by various forms of ◊ Profit-sharing and co-partnership but strictly these additions to income are not wages but appropriations from profits. Such schemes are regarded by some as a form of ⟨⟩ Industrial Democracy. ⟨⟩ Collective Bargaining; Fair Wages Clause; Wages Council. N.H.C., amended by M.J.F.P.

> H. Phelps Brown, *The Inequality of Pay* (OUP, 1977); H. A. Clegg, *The Changing System of Industrial Relations in Great Britain* (Blackwell, 1979).

Wage Drift The tendency for paid wages to rise faster than would result from the increases agreed under industry-wide collective bargaining. Alternative names for this phenomenon are 'wages gap', 'earnings gap', 'earnings drift', and 'workplace margin'. N.H.C., amended by M.J.F.P.

Wage Systems The two main forms of wage payment are by time (time-rates) and by piece (piece-rates). Even the simplest, or 'straight', piece-rate systems often embody an element of time-rates. 'Waiting time' pay (i.e. while waiting for work to arrive) is also based on time-rates. Many workplace wage systems now embody 'payment by results' (PBR), which attempts to establish a formal relationship between pay and output or effort. The least sophisticated version employs piece-rates only but most such systems in Britain are more complex and tend to be 're-gressive', i.e. the effective pay per unit declines as output rises. Payment by results schemes are alternatively known as incentive (payment) schemes, as they are intended to provide a financial incentive to greater effort.

In most company wage structures the pay packet is made up of a number of elements, including a fixed 'basic' amount, a variable 'output' element, and a 'fall-back' provision to give a minimum wage irrespective of production. A bonus on output or results may be calculated by the day, week, month or any other period.

Despite a tendency for the coverage of PBR schemes to fluctuate, there has been a steady long-term tendency for PBR earnings to make up a lower proportion of total earnings. Currently the majority of manual workers are paid by results in roughly 32 per cent of establishments, but in 1982 the percentage of total earnings composed of PBR was only 7·6 per cent compared with 11·4 per cent in 1968.

The term 'piece-work' is applied also to incentive or premium bonus systems where effort is measured in time rather than output. A standard time is set for the job and a bonus paid in relation to time saved in performance. Such systems lend themselves to work-study techniques, including the measurement of effort in 'standard minutes'. There are many types, e.g. Taylor Differential Piece-rate, Rowan System, Accelerating System, Bedaux System. 'Synthetic times' may be prepared for standard job elements and from these the time allowed for a job can be quickly determined (✧ Predetermined Motion Time Study; Synthetic Timing).

Under ✧ Rate-fixing (or ✧ Estimating) a time or price is set by a specialist rate-fixer or foreman. This is a subjective process and subject to ✧ Workplace Bargaining. In some industries (e.g. cotton) it is possible for trade unions and employers to agree piece-work price lists, or in the shoe industry standard times, on an industry-wide or district basis, but it is much more usual for these matters to be negotiated on the shop floor.

Where work study is involved in fixing wages, the ideal system is to start with ✧ Method Study and then proceed to ✧ Work Measurement. A common fault is to omit method study or perform it superficially. Timing (✧ Time Study) followed by ✧ Performance Rating, with the addition of ✧ Allowances for rest, contingencies, etc., then give the time for the job. This can be used as a basis for a rate, possibly with the addition of a bonus for performance. There is an element of arbitrariness in the process and bargaining may take place at any stage, but the system does produce work standards.

More recent and less conventional systems of payment by results are 'measured day work', 'high time-rates', 'premium pay plan', and the Rucker and ✧ Scanlon systems. Payment-by-results systems normally apply to the individual worker but may be operated on a collective basis, e.g. for the gang, group, department, works.

Most union leaderships support or accept payment by results but there is less agreement at the workplace and much dissatisfaction with the constant bargaining, the inversion of customary skill differentials (semi-skilled operatives on bonus systems often receive more than skilled workers on time-rates), and the lack of pay-packet stability.

'Direct workers' in production may well be paid by results while 'indirect workers' ancillary to production, e.g. maintenance staff, are paid on time-rates. The most common method of dealing with the resultant problem is to pay indirect workers a 'lieu bonus' calculated on the average bonus of direct workers. This may be illogical, and more indirect workers are now being paid on incentive schemes based on work study, e.g. by using analytical estimating in the case of maintenance workers.

Company wage arrangements should embody a formal structure of occupational rates and 'standard earnings', but in practice they are often irrational, even chaotic. A logical structure can be introduced by employing such devices as ✧ Job Evaluation (✧ Job Analysis) with or without

⟡ Merit Rating. ⟡ Collective Bargaining; Industrial Relations – Reform in Great Britain. N.H.C., amended by M.J.F.P.

> W. W. Daniel and N. Millward, *Workplace Industrial Relations in Britain* (Heinemann, 1983); D. Marsden, 'Wage Structure', in G. S. Bain (ed.), *Industrial Relations in Britain* (Blackwell, 1983).

Wages Councils Wages councils were set up in Britain by the Wages Councils Act, 1945, replacing the earlier trade boards. They provide machinery for an indirect form of statutory wage regulation where no facilities for collective bargaining, or only inadequate ones, exist. Each council has a tripartite membership, consisting of an equal number of persons representing employers' and employees' interests, together with three independent members appointed by the Secretary of State. The function of each council, since 1975, has been to fix not only the remuneration but other terms and conditions of employment of workers in the relevant industry. Before the proposals of the council are implemented in an order they are published in draft form to all affected persons. Employers and employees in the industry are given a fortnight in which to lodge objections with the council.

Once the council has made a wages-regulation order, employers would be guilty of an offence if they paid employees at a rate below that given in the order and employees would also be able to recover by civil action from the employer any difference between the statutory wage and that actually paid to them. Special inspectors are appointed by the Secretary of State to ensure observance of the provisions of the Act.

As a result of the extension of ⟡ Collective Bargaining by 1985 only twenty-six wages councils now survive, covering some 2·5 million workers, most of whom are women employed in retail distribution, hairdressing and catering. In 1985 a Green Paper discussing possible abolition was published, since the Government regards them as constraints on the labour market and on the creation of new jobs. W.E.F., amended by K.W.

> C. Pond, *Who Needs Wages Councils?* (Low Pay Unit, 1983).

Warehouse ⟡ Automated Warehouse

Weber, Max ⟡ Bureaucracy

Welfare That part of ⟡ Personnel Management concerned with the physical and mental well-being of employees. Personnel management as a separate activity started as welfare, and the first personnel managers were welfare officers or welfare superintendents, whose main duties were to look after the well-being of women and young people. This involved concern with the conditions of work as well as with the personal, some-times domestic, problems of employees. It soon led on to questions of ⟡ Recruitment and training and it was only a matter of time before the original concept of welfare was enlarged to include all aspects of the human side of an enterprise and to include all employees. Today the ex-pression 'industrial welfare' is usually restricted to (1) the provision of facilities such as cloakrooms, lavatories, rest rooms, canteens, social and sports clubs; (2) ⟡ Fringe Benefits, many of which are designed to reduce hardship in sickness or old age; (3) personal counselling for those with domestic and other problems. One part of the Factories Act lays down minimum standards of welfare provision and, in addition to the facilities mentioned under (1), it covers such things as drinking water, seats and first aid. Similar arrangements have been made for office workers and others under the Offices, Shops and Railway Premises Act 1963. The law lays down minimum standards; many employers go further, both from a sense of responsibility for the well-being of those who work for them and because good welfare facilities may help with recruitment and pro-vide the right environment for good work. L.S.

A. O. Martin, *Welfare at Work* (Batsford, 1967).

White-collar Union ⟡ Trade Union Types – White-collar Union

Whitley Committee ⟡ Joint Industrial Council

Whitley Council ⟡ Joint Industrial Council

Wholesaling The part of the distribution process of goods that offers the products of many manufacturers, in bulk, to a wide range of users or customers. It involves buying and selling, assembly, sorting and storage of merchandise (⟡ Distribution Mix). Whilst in certain trades it has become traditional to exclude the use of separate institutions for the wholesaling function this is only generally achieved by reallocating it. The sorting function, in particular, carried out through wholesaling is widely thought to improve the efficiency of transactions. Special cases of wholesaling exist where sole agents are used, e.g. the textile trade and brokers. Recent trends in ⟡ Retailing, and the increased size of manu-facturing units have led to pressures on wholesaling from both sides in the distributive process, and substantial changes have taken place in its structure (⟡ Branding). In groceries and other trades multiple retail chains have taken over wholesaling function themselves, thus imitating the co-operative retail societies (⟡ Co-operative Movement). Wholesalers receive their revenue as a percentage mark-up on the value of the goods they handle. The percentage varies according to the speed at which the merchandise can be turned over and its value. Most trades have standard margins, which are generally lower than the margins obtained by re-tailers. One of the major costs incurred is warehousing, and mathematical techniques to minimize the costs both of storage and of delivery to various customers are well developed. ⟡ Routeing Problems. G.S.C.W.

Woodward, Joan ⟡ Technology and Organizing

Work ⟡ Muscular Work

Work Design (in Production) Work design is concerned with work content, methods and procedures, work in this context being defined as those activities essential for production. Work is only one part of the 'job', so job design also concerns social relations, payment, supervision, etc.

There are no proven procedures or general rules for optimum work design, but merely a set of apparently conflicting requirements, resulting from experience, theory and hypothesis.

Work design can be considered in two parts: work content and work method (see figure on p. 567). Work content is influenced by product design, equipment, layout and output. Work method is influenced by work content, technological constraints (e.g. production methods), organization, ergonomics, etc.

The two traditional bases for work design are work simplification to obtain the advantages of division of labour, and Gilbreth's principles of motion economy (⟡ Motion Study). Both these concepts have been, and remain, important, but also there is no question that they are insufficient in themselves.

Whilst ergonomic theory considers the total man–machine rela-tionship, ergonomic practice is often confined to the physical relationship (⟡ Ergonomics). The psychological needs of the worker are of paramount importance and should influence both work content and work method. It is frequently argued that continued work simplification will frustrate the needs of the individual and result in reduced productivity, and that ⟡ Job Enlargement is necessary to increase productivity. Yet many job-enlargement experiments have not resulted in the expected improvement in productivity. Clearly it is unreasonable to expect different individuals to react in the same manner to the same work, or individuals in different

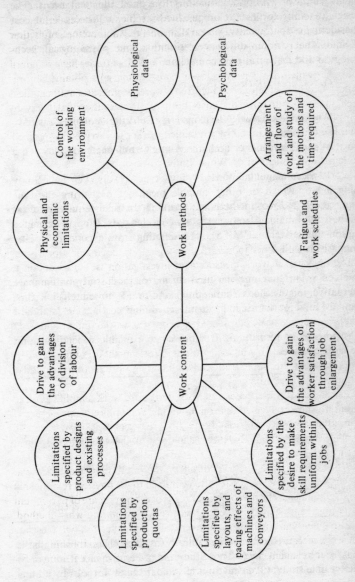

Relationship of factors determining work content and work methods (source: G. Nadler, *Work Design*)

The circles in the diagram contain the following text:

Work methods connects to:
- Physiological data
- Psychological data
- Control of the working environment
- Arrangement and flow of work and study of the motions and time required
- Physical and economic limitations
- Fatigue and work schedules

Work content connects to:
- Drive to gain the advantages of division of labour
- Drive to gain the advantages of worker satisfaction through job enlargement
- Limitations specified by product designs and existing processes
- Limitations specified by production quotas
- Limitations specified by layouts, and pacing effects of machines and conveyors
- Limitations specified by the desire to make skill requirements uniform within jobs

568   *Work Measurement*

geographical or economic situations to exhibit identical needs. The design of work for maximum productivity (i.e. minimum total cost considering output, quality, labour turnover, etc.) is therefore a function of individual worker differences, situation and physiological, technological and organizational constraints. R.W.

G. Nadler, *Work Design* (Irwin, 1963).

Work Measurement A term covering the different methods used to establish the time required by a qualified worker to carry out a specified job at a defined level of performance. Along with ⟡ Method Study, it is a principal component of ⟡ Work Study.

Work measurement methods are of two types: (1) direct ⟡ Time Study using a stop-watch or other suitable means of measuring the time required; (2) indirect methods of obtaining the time required, i.e. (a) synthesizing job times from previously collected data; (b) predetermined motion time systems (PMTS); (c) estimating from experience and by comparison with other jobs.

The object of a work measurement investigation is: (1) to obtain a time for a job that may be used during method study to compare alternative job methods (basic time) and/or (2) to establish a time standard for a job for use in payment, scheduling, costing, etc. (standard time).

Various work measurement methods are available depending upon the circumstances:

Method	Constraints
Direct time study	Existing job
Indirect time study	
Synthetic timing	Non-existing job; data available from previous time studies
PMTS	Non-existing job; synthetic timing impossible or undesirable; accuracy required
Analytical estimating	Non-existing job; incomplete or no data for synthetic timing; approximation acceptable

A work measurement exercise typically involves: (1) establishing basic times for job elements by ⟡ Time Study and ⟡ Performance Rating or by indirect time study; (2) calculation of standard times for jobs by adding ⟡ Allowances to basic times.

Work measurement, particularly performance rating and the determination of allowances, is the most subjective aspect of work study and is often criticized as inaccurate, inconsistent and even inappropriate. Because of the differing skills and methods used by work-study practitioners, inaccuracies and inconsistencies may result in direct time study. Consistency is an advantage of indirect time study, particularly PMTS. The principle of work measurement assumes a single 'best' way of performing work; it is known, however, that operators normally vary their work methods and that work cycle times are not constant. R.W.

R. M. Barnes, *Motion and Time Study* (J. Wiley, 6th ed., 1968); R. G. Seabourne, *Introduction to Work Study and Statistics* (Longman, 1971).

Work Planning Chart ◊ Multiple-activity Chart

Work Sampling Also known as ratio delay study, work sampling is one of the techniques of ◊ Work Study by which information can be obtained about the nature of a particular job or activity. As the name implies, instead of continuous observations, either random or regular sampling is used to provide information about the occurrence of delays, utilization of resources, etc (◊ Sample).

The advantage of work sampling is that in appropriate circumstances adequate information can be obtained at substantially less cost than would be involved in a continuous study. For example after completing a direct time study of an operation, it may be necessary to give an allowance for unavoidable delays and infrequently occurring ancillary duties. The frequency with which such contingencies arise and their nature may be determined by work sampling.

Work sampling using either photography or direct observation is frequently used: (1) to determine the utilization of machines, labour, etc.; (2) as a method of work measurement in clerical or other fairly irregular work activities; (3) to determine or verify work measurement contingency allowances.

Often the main objective is an analysis of an activity as, for example, in ◊ Memomotion Photography. Such studies are frequently undertaken to determine the nature of activity or movement in an area, e.g. an analysis of the nature and quantity of traffic prior to plant layout or re-layout. R.W.

B. L. Hansen, *Work Sampling for Modern Management* (Prentice-Hall, 1960).

Work Study 'A generic term for those techniques, particularly method study and work measurement, which are used in the examination

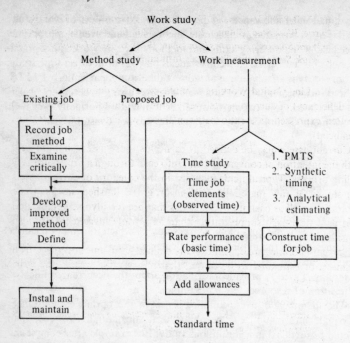

of human work in all its contexts, and which lead systematically to the investigation of all the factors which affect the efficiency and economy of the situation being reviewed in order to effect improvement' (British Standard 3138). ⟡ Method Study; Work Measurement.

The primary objects of work study (known as time and motion study in the USA) are, by analysis of all the factors which affect the performance of a task, (1) to develop and install work methods that make optimum use of the human and material resources available; (2) to establish suitable standards by which the performance of this work can be measured.

Work study is not restricted to particular situations or industries but nevertheless finds its major application in relation to repetitive physical human work situations.

The complementary techniques of method study and work measurement are used: (1) for an existing job (a) record existing work methods; (b) critically examine those methods; (c) develop and define improved methods; (d) establish time standards for job; (e) install and maintain work methods; (2) for a proposed job (a) develop and define work methods; (b) establish time standards for job; (c) install and maintain work methods. R.W.

R. M. Barnes, *Motion and Time Study* (J. Wiley, 6th ed., 1968); R. M. Currie, *Work Study* (Pitman, 2nd ed., 1963); R. G. Seabourne, *Introduction to Work Study and Statistics* (Longman, 1972); BS 3138 *Glossary of Terms in Work Study* (British Standards Institution, 1979).

Working Capital Working capital is generally defined as the excess (or deficiency) of current assets over current liabilities. The relationship is often expressed as a ratio between these two categories (⟡ Ratios, Financial).

Current assets may be defined as cash plus those assets that are held with the intention of converting them into cash through a firm's ordinary selling process. Typical items included in the category of current assets are stocks of raw materials, work-in-progress, finished stocks, trade debtors, as well as cash itself. Securities that are readily marketable and held as a near-cash supply rather than as a trade investment are also considered to be current assets.

Current liabilities are conventionally defined as all amounts owed by a business, or estimated to be owing, that are payable within one year. ⟡ Cash Flow. E.A.L., amended by P.J.A.H.

R. A. Brealey and S. C. Myers, *Principles of Corporate Finance* (McGraw-Hill, 1981); K. V. Smith, *Readings on the Management of Working Capital* (West Publishing Company, 1980).

Workplace Bargaining Negotiation between management and workers' representatives on those procedural and substantive issues that are susceptible to regulation at plant and/or company level. 'Procedural' issues may be defined as anything relating to the resolution of grievances (⟡ Grievance Procedure) and the formal stages or levels of ⟡ Collective Bargaining. 'Substantive' issues are concerned with the terms and conditions of employment, e.g. wages, hours, holidays, overtime, fringe benefits.

In factories where some form of incentive payment system (⟡ Wage Systems) is in use, rate-fixing constitutes the fundamental bargaining practice on which the whole edifice of workplace negotiation is built. Where ⟡ Shop Steward power is generally strong, in engineering and motor vehicles, the source of this strength can usually be traced to the existence of an incentive payment system, the day-to-day operation of which provides ample opportunity for individual argument and collective action. Firms that are not members of ⟡ Employers' Federations and where the employees are organized in large, general unions (⟡ Trade Union – Structure) whose official apparatus is overstretched will be particularly susceptible to workplace bargaining on a wide range of issues between company management and shop stewards. Even many federated firms have long realized that the frequently unsatisfactory calibre of federation and trade union officials alike makes regular negotiation with company shop stewards an unavoidable necessity. It has been the experience of companies that have engaged in ⟡ Productivity Bargaining that detailed negotiation over aspects of job regulation peculiar to one plant or company inevitably concentrates negotiating activity within the confines of the company concerned.

The Royal Commission on Trade Unions and Employers' Associations (⟡ Industrial Relations – Reform in Great Britain) confirmed that, in the conditions existing in the 1960s, national agreements between the officials of employers' associations and trade unions only dealt with basic terms and conditions of employment. These were invariably geared to the needs and liabilities of the smallest, weakest, federated employers and were greatly supplemented by the bigger and more profitable companies, especially those operating in 'tight' regional and local labour markets. The size of the employer, the profitability of the business and the strength of the trade union representation all determined the scope for workplace bargaining about the supplements above and beyond the minima agreed at the national level.

Towards the end of the 1960s firms began to give more formal recognition to their shop stewards and to introduce ⟡ Job Evaluation as a means of rationalizing their payment systems. Firms also negotiated written agreements that acknowledged what had hitherto been custom and practice and clarified responsibilities. This led to a five-fold increase in the number of shop stewards paid for devoting their entire working time to union activities. In the 1970s, however, two factors began to affect the pattern of workplace bargaining. The first was the support of the major unions and the TUC for the multi-phased incomes policy of the Labour Government aimed at restricting wage and salary increases in an attempt to control inflation. The second, which reflected the consequences of company mergers in the 1960s, was the increase in the number of multi-plant firms, often operating in several different industries. The latter development naturally led to strategic decisions being made more frequently away from the workplace, and was countered by some shop stewards, in such industries as clothing and electrical engineering, with the establishment of 'combined committees' of stewards representing a multiplicity of workplaces with a common employer. Some of these committees, as in the electronic and food-manufacturing industries, have been created by managements that prefer to negotiate on a multi-plant basis, even though this may cause problems for local union branch organizations.

At the beginning of the 1980s workplace bargaining had become a major influence on the rates of pay for manual workers in private manufacturing industry, especially in the larger establishments. Influenced by the economic depression, the other issues most frequently negotiated at the workplace were physical working conditions, redeployment of labour, manning levels, redundancy, changes in production methods, and recruitment. L.S., N.H.C. and E.L.

N. Singleton, *Industrial Relations Procedures*, DE Manpower Papers, no. 14 (HMSO, 1975); P. D. Anthony, *The Conduct of Industrial Relations* (IPM, 1977); W. W. Daniel and N. Millward, *Workplace Industrial Relations in Britain* (Heinemann, 1983).

Works Committee ◊ Joint Consultation

Works Council ◊ Joint Consultation

Workstation ◊ Information System

Y

Yield The annualized rate of return earned on an investment. The investment community uses several different definitions of yield, each designed to fulfil a specific purpose.

Flat yield. The nominal return on an investment whose capital value is not expected to change during ownership, e.g. a interest rate quoted by a bank on a fixed-term deposit or the coupon rate attaching to a government security.

Running yield. The yield obtained by dividing the flat yield quoted on an investment by the prevailing market (*not* nominal) value of an investment, e.g. the flat yield on £100 nominal of a government stock is £8.50 or 8·5 per cent. The current market value of the stock is £63.50, so the running yield is

$$\frac{8 \cdot 5 \times 100}{63 \cdot 5} \approxeq 13 \cdot 5 \text{ per cent}$$

Redemption yield. This form of yield is designed to recognize any capital gain or loss to be expected over the ownership lifetime of an investment. Expressed as an annualized rate, the element of capital appreciation (or depreciation) is added to (or deducted from) the running yield to give an aggregate, redemption yield.

Dividend yield. The current annual rate of dividend payable on a share expressed as a percentage of the market price of that share, i.e.

$$\frac{\text{Nominal value of share}}{\text{Market value of share}} \times \text{Dividend (\%)}$$

$$\text{e.g. } \frac{\text{£}1.00}{\text{£}2.50} \times 15 \text{ per cent} = 6 \text{ per cent}$$

The dividend yield is a measure of the *cash* return that shareholders are receiving on the current value of their investment and it is in the nature, therefore, of a running yield.

Earnings yield. Arithmetically earnings per share divided by the market value of the share, i.e. the reciprocal of the ◇ Price–earnings Ratio. Conceptually the earnings yield is designed to recognize that the dividend yield of a share does not incorporate the benefit attributable to the shareholder of earnings retained within a business for future investment (i.e. not paid out as dividend). Since shareholders are unlikely to be able to predict the future value of their holding (and thereby calculate any capital gain/loss and hence a redemption yield), the earnings yield is an approximation of the opportunity cost that shareholders implicitly are attaching to the use of their funds. P.J.A.H.

Z

Zero-base Budgeting In theory zero-base budgeting (ZBB) is a planning, budgeting and operating process that requires all managers in an organization to justify their entire budget each year in detail. Basically all managers have to explain why they should spend any money. In practice ZBB and similar systems are difficult to implement, and many organizations have found that the idea works well when managers are required to prioritize their budget request and justify, say, the lower 20 per cent only. J.V.P.

P. A. Pyhrr, *Zero-base Budgeting* (J. Wiley, 1973); J. V. Pearson and R. Michael, 'Zero-base Budgeting: A Technique for Planned Organizational Decline', *Long-range Planning Journal*, vol. 14, no. 3 (1981), pp. 68–76.

Zipf's Law The 'Principle of least effort', as expounded by G. K. Zipf, states that human behaviour is governed by an attempt to minimize the probable average rate of work required to achieve certain goals. Sometimes conscious efforts are made to minimize effort; the allocation of dots and dashes to serve as Morse symbols on the basis of letter frequencies serves as an example. Other instances of the conservation of effort seem to lack such systematic planning. Zipf produces a considerable volume of evidence in the form of statistical analyses of natural languages to show how his principle operates. He has shown that samples from a wide variety of sources conform to the rule that there is a simple linear relationship between the frequency of occurrence of any particular word, and its place in the rank order of occurrence frequencies. This relationship may be expressed in the form

$$\log p_n = A - B \log_n$$

where n signifies rank order of occurrence, p_n the frequency of occurrence, and A and B are constants. This same law has been derived from purely theoretical assumptions based upon the mathematical theory of communication by B. Mandelbrot. E.E.

G. K. Zipf, *Human Behaviour and the Principle of Least Effort* (Addison-Wesley, 1949).